DATE DUE

			PRINTED IN U.S.A.

）

Children's
Literature
Review

Guide to Gale Literary Criticism Series

For criticism on	Consult these Gale series
Authors now living or who died after December 31, 1959	*CONTEMPORARY LITERARY CRITICISM (CLC)*
Authors who died between 1900 and 1959	*TWENTIETH-CENTURY LITERARY CRITICISM (TCLC)*
Authors who died between 1800 and 1899	*NINETEENTH-CENTURY LITERATURE CRITICISM (NCLC)*
Authors who died between 1400 and 1799	*LITERATURE CRITICISM FROM 1400 TO 1800 (LC)* *SHAKESPEAREAN CRITICISM (SC)*
Authors who died before 1400	*CLASSICAL AND MEDIEVAL LITERATURE CRITICISM (CMLC)*
Black writers of the past two hundred years	*BLACK LITERATURE CRITICISM (BLC)*
Authors of books for children and young adults	*CHILDREN'S LITERATURE REVIEW (CLR)*
Dramatists	*DRAMA CRITICISM (DC)*
Hispanic writers of the late nineteenth and twentieth centuries	*HISPANIC LITERATURE CRITICISM (HLC)*
Native North American writers and orators of the eighteenth, nineteenth, and twentieth centuries	*NATIVE NORTH AMERICAN LITERATURE (NNAL)*
Poets	*POETRY CRITICISM (PC)*
Short story writers	*SHORT STORY CRITICISM (SSC)*
Major authors from the Renaissance to the present	*WORLD LITERATURE CRITICISM, 1500 TO THE PRESENT (WLC)*

ISSN 0362-4145

volume 37

Children's Literature Review

Excerpts from Reviews,
Criticism, and Commentary
on Books for Children
and Young People

Alan Hedblad
Editor

Sharon R. Gunton
Associate Editor

 **Gale Research**

An ITP Information/Reference Group Company

I T P
Changing the Way the World Learns

NEW YORK • LONDON • BONN • BOSTON • DETROIT
MADRID • MELBOURNE • MEXICO CITY • PARIS
SINGAPORE • TOKYO • TORONTO • WASHINGTON
ALBANY NY • BELMONT CA • CINCINNATI OH

STAFF

Alan Hedblad, *Editor*

Sharon R. Gunton, *Associate Editor*

Linda R. Andres, Shelly Andrews, Joanna Brod, Elizabeth A. Des Chenes, Motoko Huthwaite, Julie K. Karmazin, Thomas F. McMahon, Gerard J. Senick, Diane Telgen, *Contributing Editors*

Marilyn Allen, Paul Zyskowski, *Assistant Editors*

Marlene S. Hurst, *Permissions Manager*
Margaret A. Chamberlain, *Permissions Specialist*
Susan Brohman, Diane Cooper, Maria Franklin, Arlene Johnson, Michele Lonoconus, Maureen Puhl, Shalice Shah, Kimberly F. Smilay, Barbara A. Wallace, *Permissions Associates*
Edna M. Hedblad, Margaret McAvoy-Amato, Tyra Y. Phillips, Lori Schoenenberger, *Permissions Assistants*

Victoria B. Cariappa, *Research Manager*
Donna Melnychenko, *Project Coordinator*
Maria E. Bryson, Frank Castronova, *Research Associates*
Alicia Noel Biggers, Julia C. Daniel, *Research Assistants*

Mary Beth Trimper, *Production Director*
Mary Kelley, *Production Associate*

Barbara J. Yarrow, *Graphic Services Manager*
Erin Martin, *Desktop Publisher*
Willie Mathis, *Camera Operator*
Pamela A. Hayes, *Photography Coordinator*

∞™ This book is printed on acid-free paper that meets the minimum requirements of American National Standard for Information Sciences—Permanence Paper for Printed Library Materials, ANSI Z39.48-1984.

Library of Congress Catalog Card Number 76-643301
ISBN 0-8103-8951-7
ISSN 0362-4145
Printed in the United States of America

ITP™   Gale Research Inc., an International Thomson Publishing Company.
ITP logo is a trademark under license.

10 9 8 7 6 5 4 3 2 1

Contents

Preface   vii
Acknowledgments   xi

Preface

L iterature for children and young adults has evolved into both a respected branch of creative writing and a successful industry. Currently, books for young readers are considered among the most popular segments of publishing. Criticism of juvenile literature is instrumental in recording the literary or artistic development of the creators of children's books as well as the trends and controversies that result from changing values or attitudes about young people and their literature. Designed to provide a permanent, accessible record of this ongoing scholarship, *Children's Literature Review (CLR)* presents parents, teachers, and librarians—those responsible for bringing children and books together—with the opportunity to make informed choices when selecting reading materials for the young. In addition, *CLR* provides researchers of children's literature with easy access to a wide variety of critical information from English-language sources in the field. Users will find balanced overviews of the careers of the authors and illustrators of the books that children and young adults are reading; these entries, which contain excerpts from published criticism in books and periodicals, assist users by sparking ideas for papers and assignments and suggesting supplementary and classroom reading. Ann L. Kalkhoff, president and editor of *Children's Book Review Service Inc.,* writes that "*CLR* has filled a gap in the field of children's books, and it is one series that will never lose its validity or importance."

Scope of the Series

Each volume of *CLR* profiles the careers of a selection of authors and illustrators of books for children and young adults from preschool through high school. Author lists in each volume reflect:

- an international scope.

- representation of authors of all eras.

- the variety of genres covered by children's and/or YA literature: picture books, fiction, nonfiction, poetry, folklore, and drama.

Although the focus of the series is on authors new to *CLR*, entries will be updated as the need arises.

Organization of This Book

An entry consists of the following elements: author heading, author portrait, author introduction, excerpts of criticism (each preceded by a bibliographical citation), and illustrations, when available.

- The **Author Heading** consists of the author's name followed by birth and death dates. The portion of the name outside the parentheses denotes the form under which the author is most frequently published. If the majority of the author's works for children were written under a pseudonym, the pseudonym will be listed in the author heading and the real name given on the first line of the author introduction. Also located at the beginning of the introduction are any other pseudonyms used by the author in writing for children and any name variations, including transliterated forms for authors whose languages use nonroman alphabets. Uncertainty as to a birth or death date is indicated by question marks.

- An **Author Portrait** is included when available.

- The **Author Introduction** contains information designed to introduce an author to *CLR* users by presenting an overview of the author's themes and styles, biographical facts that relate to the author's literary career or critical responses to the author's works, and information about major awards and prizes the author has received. The introduction begins by identifying the nationality of the author and by listing the genres in which s/he has written for children and young adults. Introductions also list a group of representative titles for which the author or illustrator being profiled is best known; this section, which begins with the words "major works include," follows the genre line of the introduction. For seminal figures, a listing of major works about the author follows when appropriate, highlighting important biographies about the author or illustrator that are not excerpted in the entry. The centered heading "Introduction" announces the body of the text. Where applicable, introductions conclude with references to additional entries in biographical and critical reference series published by Gale Research Inc.

- **Criticism** is located in three sections: **Author's Commentary** (when available), **General Commentary** (when available), and **Title Commentary** (commentary on specific titles).

  - The **Author's Commentary** presents background material written by the author or by an interviewer. This commentary may cover a specific work or several works. Author's commentary on more than one work appears after the author introduction, while commentary on an individual book follows the title entry heading.

  - The **General Commentary** consists of critical excerpts that consider more than one work by the author or illustrator being profiled. General commentary is preceded by the critic's name in boldface type or, in the case of unsigned criticism, by the title of the journal. *CLR* also features entries that emphasize general criticism on the oeuvre of an author or illustrator. When appropriate, a selection of reviews is included to supplement the general commentary.

  - The **Title Commentary** begins with the title entry headings, which precede the criticism on a title and cite publication information on the work being reviewed. Title headings list the title of the work as it appeared in its first English-language edition. The first English-language publication date of each work (unless otherwise noted) is listed in parentheses following the title. Differing U. S. and British titles follow the publication date within the parentheses. When a work is written by an individual other than the one being profiled, as is the case when illustrators are featured, the parenthetical material following the title cites the author of the work before listing its publication date.

    Entries in each title commentary section consist of critical excerpts on the author's individual works, arranged chronologically by publication date. The entries generally contain two to seven reviews per title, depending on the stature of the book and the amount of criticism it has generated. The editors select titles that reflect the entire scope of the author's literary contribution, covering each genre and subject. An effort is made to reprint criticism that represents the full range of each title's reception, from the year of its initial publication to current assessments. Thus, the reader is provided with a record of the author's critical history. Publication information (such as publisher names and book prices) and parenthetical numerical references (such as footnotes or page and line references to specific editions of works) have been deleted at the discretion of the editors to provide smoother reading of the text.

- Centered headings introduce each section, in which criticism is arranged chronologically; beginning with Volume 35, each excerpt is preceded by a boldface source heading for easier access by readers. Within the text, titles by authors being profiled are also highlighted in boldface type.

- Selected excerpts are preceded by **Explanatory Annotations,** which provide information on the critic or work of criticism to enhance the reader's understanding of the excerpt.

- A complete **Bibliographical Citation** designed to facilitate the location of the original book or article precedes each piece of criticism.

- Numerous **Illustrations** are featured in *CLR*. For entries on illustrators, an effort has been made to include illustrations that reflect the characteristics discussed in the criticism. Entries on authors who do not illustrate their own works may also include photographs and other illustrative material pertinent to their careers.

Special Features: Entries on Illustrators

Entries on authors who are also illustrators will occasionally feature commentary on selected works illustrated but not written by the author being profiled. These works are strongly associated with the illustrator and have received critical acclaim for their art. By including critical comment on works of this type, the editors wish to provide a more complete representation of the author's career. Criticism on these works has been chosen to stress artistic, rather than literary, contributions. Title entry headings for works illustrated by the author being profiled are arranged chronologically within the entry by date of publication and include notes identifying the author of the illustrated work. In order to provide easier access for users, all titles illustrated by the subject of the entry are boldfaced.

CLR also includes entries on prominent illustrators who have contributed to the field of children's literature. These entries are designed to represent the development of the illustrator as an artist rather than as a literary stylist. The illustrator's section is organized like that of an author, with two exceptions: the introduction presents an overview of the illustrator's styles and techniques rather than outlining his or her literary background, and the commentary written by the illustrator on his or her works is called "illustrator's commentary" rather than "author's commentary." All titles of books containing illustrations by the artist being profiled as well as individual illustrations from these books are highlighted in boldface type.

Other Features: Acknowledgments, Indexes

- The **Acknowledgments** section, which immediately follows the preface, lists the sources from which material has been reprinted in the volume. It does not, however, list every book or periodical consulted for the volume.

- The **Cumulative Index to Authors** lists all of the authors who have appeared in *CLR* with cross-references to the biographical, autobiographical, and literary criticism series published by Gale Research Inc. A full listing of the series titles appears before the first page of the indexes of this volume.

- The **Cumulative Index to Nationalities** lists authors alphabetically under their respective nationalities. Author names are followed by the volume number(s) in which they appear.

- The **Cumulative Index to Titles** lists titles covered in *CLR* followed by the volume and page number where criticism begins.

A Note to the Reader

CLR is one of several critical references sources in the Literature Criticism Series published by Gale Research Inc. When writing papers, students who quote directly from any volume in the Literature Criticism Series may use the following general forms to footnote reprinted criticism. The first example pertains to material drawn from periodicals, the second to material reprinted from books.

[1]T. S. Eliot, "John Donne," *The Nation and the Athenaeum,* 33 (9 June 1923), 321-32; excerpted and reprinted in *Literature Criticism from 1400 to 1800,* Vol. 10, ed. James E. Person, Jr. (Detroit: Gale Research, 1989), pp. 28-9.

[1]Henry Brooke, *Leslie Brooke and Johnny Crow* (Frederick Warne, 1982); excerpted and reprinted in *Children's Literature Review,* Vol. 20, ed. Gerard J. Senick (Detroit: Gale Research, 1990), p. 47.

Suggestions Are Welcome

In response to various suggestions, several features have been added to *CLR* since the beginning of the series, including author entries on retellers of traditional literature as well as those who have been the first to record oral tales and other folklore; entries on prominent illustrators featuring commentary on their styles and techniques; entries on authors whose works are considered controversial; occasional entries devoted to criticism on a single work or a series of works; sections in author introductions that list major works by and about the author or illustrator being profiled; explanatory notes that provide information on the critic or work of criticism to enhance the usefulness of the excerpt; more extensive illustrative material, such as holographs of manuscript pages and photographs of people and places pertinent to the careers of the authors and artists; a cumulative nationality index for easy access to authors by nationality; and occasional guest essays written specifically for *CLR* by prominent critics on subjects of their choice.

Readers who wish to suggest authors to appear in future volumes, or who have other suggestions, are cordially invited to write the editor.

Acknowledgments

The editors wish to thank the copyright holders of the excerpted criticism included in this volume and the permissions managers of many book and magazine publishing companies for assisting us in securing reprint rights. We are also grateful to the staffs of the Detroit Public Library, the Library of Congress, the University of Detroit Library, Wayne State University Purdy/Kresge Library Complex, and the University of Michigan Libraries for making their resources available to us. Following is a list of the copyright holders who have granted us permission to reprint material in this volume of *CLR*. Every effort has been made to trace copyright, but if omissions have been made, please let us know.

COPYRIGHTED EXCERPTS IN *CLR*, VOLUME 37, WERE REPRINTED FROM THE FOLLOWING PERIODICALS:

The ALAN Review, v. 9, Spring, 1982. Reprinted by permission of the publisher.—*Appraisal: Children's Science Books*, v. 13, Spring, 1980; v. 14, Fall, 1981; v. 22, Autumn, 1989; v. 23, Winter, 1990; v. 23, Summer, 1990; v. 24, Autumn, 1991; v. 26, Spring-Summer, 1993. Copyright © 1980, 1981, 1989, 1990, 1991, 1993 by the Children's Science Book Review Committee. All reprinted by permission of the publisher.—*Archaeology*, v. 33, September-October, 1980. Copyright the Archaeological Institute of America, 1980. Reprinted with the permission of *Archaeology* Magazine.—*Atlas*, v. 13, February, 1967. © 1967 by Aspen Publishing Company, Inc. Now published as *World Press Review*. Reprinted by permission of the publisher.—*Best Sellers,* v. 29, April 1, 1969; v. 38, March,1979; v. 39, August, 1979. Copyright 1969, 1979 by the University of Scranton. All reprinted by permission of the publisher.—*Booklist,* v. 73, October 1, 1976; v. 73, March 15, 1977; v. 73, March 1, 1978; v. 76, May 1, 1980; v. 77, November 1, 1980; v. 79, June 15, 1983; v. 80, October 1, 1983; v. 80, April 1, 1984; v. 80, April 15, 1984; v. 81, October 15, 1984; v. 81, April 15, 1985; v. 82, November 1, 1985; v. 83, September 15, 1986; v. 83, October 1, 1986; v. 83, May 15, 1987; v. 84, July, 1988; v. 85, October 15, 1988; v. 85, March 15, 1989; v. 85, April 1, 1989; v. 85, June 1, 1989; v. 86, November 1, 1989; v. 86, November 15, 1989; v. 86, December 15, 1989; v. 86, March 1, 1990; v. 86, April 15, 1990; v. 86, May 15, 1990; v. 86, June 15, 1990; v. 86, July, 1990; v. 87, March 1, 1991; v. 87, August, 1991; v. 88, September 15, 1991; v. 88, August, 1992; v. 89, February 15, 1993; v. 89, June 1-15, 1993; v. 90, October 1, 1993; v. 90, October 15, 1993; v. 90, November 1, 1993. Copyright © 1976, 1977, 1978, 1980, 1983, 1984, 1985, 1986, 1987, 1988, 1989, 1990, 1991, 1992, 1993 by the American Library Association. All reprinted by permission of the publisher.—*The Booklist,* v. 66, June 15, 1970; v. 67, January 15, 1971; v. 69, January 1, 1973; v. 70, October 15, 1973; v. 71, September 15, 1974; v. 71, May 15, 1975. Copyright © 1970, 1971, 1973, 1974, 1975 by the American Library Association. All reprinted by permission of the publisher.—*The Booklist and Subscription Books Bulletin,* v. 65, July 1, 1969. Copyright © 1969 by the American Library Association. Reprinted by permission of the publisher.—*The Book Report,* v. 2, March-April, 1984. © copyright 1984 by Linworth Publishing, Inc., Worthington, Ohio. Reprinted with permission of the publisher.—*Books for Keeps,* n. 35, November, 1985; n. 42, January, 1987; n. 44, May, 1987; n. 45, July, 1987; n. 56, May, 1989; n. 64, September, 1990. © School Bookshop Association 1985, 1987, 1989, 1990. Reprinted by permission of the publisher.—*Books for Young People,* v. 1, October, 1987 for "Morgan, May, Melinda: New Heroines Offer Humour and Fantasy" By Bernie Goedhart. All rights reserved. Reprinted by permission of the publisher and the author.—*Books for Your Children,* v. 7, Summer, 1972; v. 18, Autumn-Winter, 1983; v. 22, Summer, 1987; v. 26, Spring, 1991. © *Books for Your Children* 1972, 1983, 1987, 1991. All reprinted by permission of the publisher.—*Books in Canada,* v. 13, December, 1984 for a review of "Chin Chiang and the Dragon's Dance" by Mary Ainslie Smith; v. 15, November, 1986 for a review of "The Sparrows Song" by Mary Ainslie Smith./ v. 17, June-July, 1988 for a review of "Morgan the Magnificent" by Anne Denoon; v. 18, December, 1989 for a review of "The Name of the Tree" by Linda Granfield. Both reprinted by permission of the respective authors.—*Book World—The Washington Post,* November 11, 1984. © 1984, Washington Post Book World Service/Washington Post Writers Group. Reprinted with permission of the publisher.—*British Book News*, Children's Supplement, Autumn, 1981; Spring, 1982. © *British Book News* 1981, 1982. Both courtesy of *British Book News.*—*British Book News Children's Books,* December, 1987. © The British Council, 1987. Reprinted by permission of the publisher.—*Bulletin of the Center for Children's Books,* v. 24, April, 1971; v. 27, November, 1973; v. 29, September, 1975; v. 30, September, 1976; v. 30, January, 1977; v. 32, October, 1978; v. 32, May, 1979; v. 34, October, 1980; v. 35, January, 1982; v. 36, November,

COPYRIGHTED EXCERPTS IN *CLR*, VOLUME 37, WERE REPRINTED FROM THE FOLLOWING BOOKS:

and Robert H. Boyer. *Fantasy Literature: A Core Collection and Reference Guide*. Bowker, 1979. Copyright © 1979 by Reed Publishing. Reprinted with permission from R. R. Bowker, Division of Reed Publishing (USA) Inc.

Children's
Literature
Review

John Bellairs

1938-1991

American author of fiction.

Major works include *The Face in the Frost* (1969), *The House with a Clock in Its Walls* (1973), *The Figure in the Shadows* (1975), *The Treasure of Alpheus Winterborn* (1978), *The Curse of the Blue Figurine* (1983).

INTRODUCTION

A popular writer of swift-paced supernatural mysteries for middle graders, Bellairs is noted for creating Gothic thrillers that feature appealing intergenerational teams of protagonists who struggle and ultimately prevail against various forces of evil. In his approximately eighteen books, Bellairs devised what are considered ingenious plots that draw from the repertoire of elements common to horror stories—ghosts, wizards, haunted houses, unseasonal storms, screaming plants, mummies, tombs—but brightened them with humor, magical tricks, and the certainty of a happy ending. Bellairs has been lauded for his unique blending of bizarre happenings with the mundane, his tight, action-packed writing style, his ability to evoke an eerie, terrifying atmosphere, and his realistic adolescent characters, each of whom grows in self-confidence and courage with the help of a considerably older friend. In his trilogy *The House with a Clock in Its Walls, The Figure in the Shadows,* and *The Letter, the Witch, and the Ring* (1976), for instance, Bellairs features protagonists Lewis Barnavelt and Rose Rita Pottinger—Lewis an overweight and athletically inept youth struggling with feelings of inferiority, Rose Rita a determined tomboy who fears the onset of womanhood. As in most of Bellairs's stories, the two are paired with somewhat eccentric but endearing adults who assist them in their adventurous encounters with the supernatural, and in the process help them to gain self-acceptance and a more healthy understanding of differences among people. Marilyn Stasio notes that "no less than any other good work of escapist fiction," Bellairs's stories "excite readers because they involve believable and likable characters with whom we can empathize in moments of danger." Although sometimes criticized for creating plots with contrived endings and too much reliance upon coincidence, Bellairs is widely acknowledged as unfailingly entertaining and has commanded a special readership among young devotees of the Gothic novel. Stasio adds: "After allowing . . . for the originality of Bellairs' artistry and the ingenuity of his craftsmanship, it does seem that the deeper appeal his stories hold for children is no different from the psychological satisfaction adult readers derive from good genre literature. With the detective-hero as our ego stand-in, we enjoy both the vicarious thrill of looking our secret terrors in the eye and the intense pleasure of punching them in the nose."

Biographical Information

Bellairs was born and raised in Marshall, Michigan, which he described as a "beautiful small town" full of "strange and enormous old houses" that captured his imagination. New Zebedee, the town depicted in his trilogy about Lewis and Rose Rita, is based upon his recollections of this childhood home. Bellairs began his career as a college instructor of English, first in Minnesota, then in Illinois and Massachusetts, until he was able to become self-supporting as a full-time writer of fiction. He admits his children's books are largely autobiographical: "the bullies, the scaredy-cat kid Lewis, the grown-ups, the everyday incidents—all come from my own experience." Besides teaching and writing, Bellairs enjoyed acting in community theater, an experience which many commentators have credited for helping to develop his skill in creating dialogue. At the same time, his avid reading of history, ghost stories, and the works of Charles Dickens all influenced both the style and content of his work. Bellairs died in 1991; his good friend and fellow mystery writer Brad Strickland completed his unfinished manuscripts and posthumously published *The Mansion in the*

Mist (1992), *The Vengeance of the Witch Finder* (1993), and *The Ghost in the Mirror* (1993).

Major Works

Although the author intended *The Face in the Frost* for an adult audience, reviewers have questioned whether the book should be classified for adults or for children. Inspired by Tolkien's *Lord of the Rings,* the fantasy juxtaposes frightening, imaginative incidents and comical interludes as it describes two good magicians, Prospero and Roger Bacon, who travel through enchanted territory and encounter incredible obstacles in their determination to stop an evil sorcerer and his wicked spells. *The House with a Clock in Its Walls,* aptly illustrated by Edward Gorey, was Bellairs's first novel written for young adults. This story features ten-year-old Lewis, recently orphaned, who comes to live with his uncle Jonathan, a wizard. Together with his uncle's next-door neighbor, Mrs. Zimmermann, also a wizard, the three set out to find and destroy the source of a mysterious ticking sound in the walls of the uncle's strange old house. The noise emanates from a clock left there by evil witches who had formerly occupied the home, having programmed the device to destroy the world. *The New York Times Book Review* comments, "The author has dusted off the paraphernalia of ancient magic and made us newly aware of the difference between good and evil." The sequel, *A Figure in the Shadows,* sees a return of Lewis, Uncle Jonathan, and Mrs. Zimmermann. This time a magic coin, ostensibly protecting timid, pudgy Lewis from sixth-grade bullies, unexpectedly brings back the sinister ghost of its original owner. Suspense and surprises—both frightening and funny—constitute what *Kirkus Reviews* describes as a "nice, comfy ghost story." In *The Treasure of Alpheus Winterborn,* fourteen-year-old Anthony Monday teams up with the town librarian, sixty-eight-year-old Miss Myra Eells, to search for a fortune rumored to be buried somewhere within the library by its millionaire founder. A straightforward mystery, humorous and suspenseful, it was later made into a television movie for children. *The Curse of the Blue Figurine* focuses on the last of Bellairs' intergenerational teams of sleuths, Johnny Dixon and his formidable partner Professor Childermass. When Johnny finds a blue Egyptian ushabti and takes it home, despite a warning note that says "Whoever removes these things from the church does so at his own peril," he unleashes diabolic forces, culminating in a mountaintop showdown with the spirit of a mad priest. Dudley Carlson maintains that "the real questions that Bellairs is exploring in these stories [are those involving] a child's concern with comfort and security in his *real* world. The supernatural elements are the shadow representations of that frightening real world. They function as a very convenient mythology that can stand for anything that frightens us. For a kid, this can be anything from nuclear war to losing your mother in the supermarket." For shy Johnny, terrified of strict adults, fast hard balls, high places, and germs, Carlson goes on to say, "Every time [Johnny] zaps a monster or outwits a witch, he also vanquishes a personal demon." Johnny grows in self-esteem and coping skills through each of the succeeding seven books featuring him and his cantankerous companion.

Awards

Bellairs received a *New York Times* outstanding book citation for *The House with a Clock in Its Walls* in 1973, and was honored with a Parents' Choice award for *The Curse of the Blue Figurine* in 1983. In addition, he has won several child-selected awards for his books.

GENERAL COMMENTARY

Craig Shaw Gardner

SOURCE: "Reading on the Edge of Your Seat," in *Book World—The Washington Post,* November 11, 1984, pp. 13-14.

Want a good, creepy read? A children's librarian I know always says she gets as many requests for scary books as any other kind, right up there with horse stories and baseball novels. And she always shows kids books by John Bellairs.

Bellairs has written a few adult books, including the well-received ***The Face in the Frost.*** But he is best known for his children's books, especially ***The House With a Clock in Its Walls,*** which was a "New York Times Outstanding Book" for 1973. Bellairs wrote two sequels to ***House, The Figure in the Shadows,*** and ***The Letter, the Witch, and the Ring,*** and then went on to write five other young adult books, all of them published by Dial, the most recent of which is ***The Spell of the Sorcerer's Skull.***

Excepting ***The Treasure of Alpheus Winterborn*** (a straight mystery adventure), John Bellairs' children's books deal with the supernatural, and ***Skull*** is filled with mysterious jack-o'-lanterns and skeletons appearing out of nowhere, along with the disappearance of the hero's best friend, the elderly Professor Childermass. Twelve-year-old Johnny Dixon sees strange things in the windows of Childermass' house and runs over to investigate. When he gets inside, the house appears to be deserted, but what happens next is Bellairs at his creepy best:

"Halfway to the window Johnny froze. He had seen something out of the corner of his eye, a sudden image in the small rectangular mirror that hung over the bureau. He turned and looked. In the mirror he saw the professor's face, looking haggard and disheveled. His eyes pleaded and, as Johnny watched, his lips formed silent words. *'Help me.'"*

Bellairs, though, is far more than just a creepy storyteller. The best children's authors, from A. A. Milne to Beverly

Cleary to Daniel Manus Pinkwater, all draw on their own experience, as children and parents, to give their characters verisimilitude. Bellairs' stories are often set in the early 1950s when the author was a child, and the books are filled with detailed and often very funny reminiscences of what it felt like to be young then. *Skull* has some wonderful, offhand passages about the main character's everyday life, like the following:

"That evening, after school, Johnny and Fergie went to the movies together. This was a Friday night habit of theirs, and they went in good weather or bad, to lousy movies or to good ones. On this particular Friday, they happened to land a really rousing, slam-bang pirate movie. They always sat way down in front and munched popcorn and made smart remarks, until the usher came down and threatened to throw them out if they didn't shut up."

It's this balance between the supernatural and the everyday, told with Bellairs' humor, that makes his books so special. Because of this, Bellairs' most successful books have been *The House With a Clock in Its Walls* and *The Curse of the Blue Figurine.*

Both these books introduced series, and in each Bellairs spent more time "setting the scene" with his own brand of humorous detail. But luckily, *Skull* doesn't lack in that department, either, with Bellairs taking the time to show scenes of everyday life in between all the spooky doings.

Bellairs' books also nearly always feature a strong friendship between a child and an older adult, usually lovable eccentrics like Professor Childermass. In *Skull,* Bellairs expands this theme in the developing friendship between Johnny Dixon and Father Higgins, a priest Johnny believes to be a stern authority figure, until Johnny visits him about midway through the book:

"Johnny's mouth dropped open. He was completely dumbfounded, and also very amused. So Father Higgins played the guitar! He normally looked so stern and forbidding that . . . well, it was like finding out that the mayor loved to roller skate! As Johnny watched, the priest put the strap of the guitar around his neck, played a few opening chords, and then launched into a loud, lusty chorus."

As in all Bellairs' books, it is through this friendship, and the acts of both Johnny and Father Higgins, that the supernatural forces are conquered. In the end, it's the power of friendship that wins in *Skull,* and, as in the other Bellairs' books before it, the novel is not only very creepy, but very reassuring as well.

Gary D. Schmidt

SOURCE: "See How They Grow: Character Development in Children's Series Books," in *Children's literature in education,* Vol. 18, No. 1, Spring, 1987, pp. 34-44.

[Like Madeleine L'Engle and Susan Cooper,] John Bel-

lairs, an author whose work has received little critical attention, uses [a] form of integrated sequence in his three occult suspense novels: *The House with a Clock in its Walls, The Figure in the Shadows,* and *The Letter, the Witch, and the Ring.* Like many other children's novels of the past twenty years, his blend the real and the supernatural. In them, Lewis Barnavelt struggles to come to terms with his weight and athletic ineptitude, and Rose Rita Pottinger struggles to accept the fact that she is a girl. These conflicts go on while they battle various demons and evil spirits together with Lewis' Uncle Jonathan and their neighbor Mrs. Zimmerman, who are both witches of the good sort.

Bellairs develops both sides of this plot line as the reader moves through the three novels. Lewis begins in *The House With a Clock in its Walls* as an overweight ex-altar boy whose world is unmade when his parents are killed in a car accident and he moves to New Zebedee. Here he faces the humiliation of choosing up team sides, the bullying of Woody Mingo, the isolation imposed by a cold schoolyard, and, later, the ego-stabbing embarrassment of a girl standing up for his honor. He is temporarily befriended by Tarby, the most athletic—hence the most popular—kid in the school, but is abandoned when he struggles to bind himself to Tarby, envisioning him more as an avenue of escape than anything else.

Yet by the end of the first novel, Lewis, thrown together with an uncle and neighbor who are themselves considered somewhat odd by the community, begins to learn that differences are not faults, and that courage is not "riding your bicycle through bonfires and hanging by your knees from the limbs of trees"—two of the things Tarby excelled in. This recognition carries through into the second novel, *The Figure in the Shadows,* so that Lewis is able to befriend Rose Rita with none of the cloying attachment he had wished to impose on Tarby. He still fears his schoolmates, but learns through his friendship with Rose Rita the acceptance of self that leads to growth.

By the beginning of *The Letter, the Witch, and the Ring,* Lewis is ready to face the risks of Scout Camp, leaving the stage clear for Rose Rita to work out her own role difficulties, difficulties which stem from her fears in the second novel of growing up and leaving her tomboy life behind her. Unwittingly she herself begins this process when, in the beginning of the final novel, she hangs up the beret she had worn all through the second novel as a symbol of her rejection of a girl's life.

The structure of this sort of integrated sequence allows for a type of character introduction which traditional trilogies do not permit. A character can be established in an earlier novel and then left for development in future novels, so that the reader watches that character's importance grow. Bellairs uses this technique with Rose Rita. At the end of *The House with a Clock in its Walls* she is introduced as Lewis' new friend in almost the last sentence. She shares the stage with Lewis in the second novel, but then dominates it in the last.

The plot lines also develop subtly as the sequence progresses; most of the sustained development involves the supernatural placements of the plots. In *The House with a Clock in its Walls,* Bellairs builds on the mythic *topos* that the weak and innocent perform the grave and mighty deeds of the world, and this theme emerges more and more strongly through the three novels. In the first, Lewis confronts the evil spirit alone and escapes eternal entombment only by the supernatural might of Mrs. Zimmerman. A similar sequence occurs in *The Figure in the Shadows;* only this time the evil spirit defeats Mrs. Zimmerman, and her powers are destroyed. It is left almost completely to Rose Rita to save the bewitched Lewis. In the third novel Mrs. Zimmerman has become helpless, and, in fact, is transformed into a chicken. Rose Rita must save her now, and she is able to do this in part because of her emerging acceptance of self.

Neither of these patterns is random, nor are they fulfilled in any one novel. Instead, the patterns emerge as the separate narratives are integrated, together forming a history of the self-acceptance of Lewis and Rose Rita and an example of the rise of the innocent over the evil. Each of the earlier experiences of the characters shapes their reactions to later experiences.

In all of these integrated series, those of L'Engle and Cooper and Bellairs, the position of each novel as a part of a longer history emphasizes the cyclical nature of myth, of story, of experience. The barest plot outline of each of these works shows an astonishing similarity to others of the sequence; in their essence, they are variations on a theme. But the nature of experience is that it is cyclical, with the cycles changing subtly with growth and development. It is this type of real growth that is reflected in integrated novels in a way impossible in other forms of fictional series. While Dorothy and Pippi and Dolittle remain static characters, Lewis and Rose Rita and [L'Engle's] Meg and the children of Cooper's series change and develop, reacting to their past. The technique of integrating novels is not necessarily artistically better, but it is more closely a mirror of the reader's experience.

Marilyn Stasio

SOURCE: "Under the Spell of Scary Stuff," in *The New York Times Book Review,* June 9, 1991, p. 53.

I have just spent a long rainy weekend buried under a quilt, devouring salty peanuts and a stack of John Bellairs mysteries. It was heaven. Do I *hafta* get up from the couch and grow up?

The catchy titles of these chiller-dillers—all 12 of them, beginning in 1973 with *The House With a Clock in Its Walls* and including *The Spell of the Sorcerer's Skull* and *The Revenge of the Wizard's Ghost*—sound like something a kid might think up in the dark. The creepy Edward Gorey illustrations—of tumbledown mansions and inclement weather and frightful creatures peering out from thickets of crosshatched pen strokes—look like something

a kid might tape to his walls. The stories themselves, in a sense, are also the work of a child's mind.

"I write scary thrillers for kids because I have the imagination of a 10-year-old," the author, who died earlier this year at the age of 53, once said. "I love haunted houses, ghosts, witches, mummies, incantations, secret rituals performed by the light of the waning moon, coffins, bones, cemeteries and enchanted objects."

Much like other mysteries, these short works of the imagination are designed and constructed with the fine storytelling craft of an adult master. Each plot opens with a strange event that poses a classic puzzle. In *The Chessmen of Doom* for instance, a chessboard provides a clue to a missing corpse. Cryptic notes from beyond the grave hold the solution to *The Secret of the Underground Room.* Elsewhere, youthful detectives must interpret the meaning of ciphers, rebuses, poems, invisible writing and sundry coded messages. With good cause, characters in these stories are forever dashing off to do library research.

Faithful to the energetic traditions of the suspense thriller, Bellairs moves the action at a furious clip. Scenes shift dramatically from underground tombs to storm-swept mountain crags, as the hero races to rescue his friends from the "nefarious and diabolical practices" of evil sorcerers—while evading such horrors as "a figure with hollow mummy eyes and a withered mummy face and claw-like mummy hands."

No less than any other good work of escapist fiction, these hair-raising adventures also excite readers because they involve believable and likable characters with whom we can empathize in moments of danger. "He was brainy and shy and had trouble getting people to like him," Bellairs describes his young hero, Johnny Dixon, whose wonderfully warming friendship with cantankerous old Professor Childermass ("who terrified most people") makes them an endearing detective team.

But, although parents no doubt appreciate the literary merits of these books, I wonder if the good writing alone explains Bellairs's great popularity with readers between the ages of 9 and 13. (His books have sold a quarter-million copies in hard cover and more than a million and a half copies in paperback.)

"It's definitely the scary element that appeals to readers," says Linda Perkins, a librarian with the Berkeley (Calif.) Public Library. "They love getting goose bumps." Ms. Perkins, who has found Bellairs a big hit in classroom book talks, adds that the fright is never traumatizing, because "it's a controlled scare. They always know that the characters are going to get out of danger at the end. It's also reassuring that there are adults in these books who are good adults, in that they listen to the children and take their fears seriously."

This assessment seemed confirmed by a 12-year-old acquaintance who feels that she has personally outgrown Bellairs, but who has passed on her well-thumbed collection to her younger sister. "His stories are pretty spooky," she offers, "but they're too predictable to be *really* scary. There's always a young person and an old person who are friends, and a puzzle or riddle that has to be solved or else something terrible will happen. At first, the kid tries to solve the riddle himself and gets in trouble. But when the young person and the old person help each other, they solve the mystery and there's no more danger. The stories are all different, but the pattern is always the same."

Well, O.K., maybe a 12-year-old girl is too tough a critic to engage in this sort of literary discussion. (She's probably too sophisticated for salty peanuts, too.) According to Dudley Carlson, a librarian with the Princeton (N.J.) Public Library, Gothic mysteries dealing in supernatural elements are best enjoyed by children who are still sorting out fact from fantasy, an intellectual process that generally occurs around fourth or fifth grade. "The fuzzier the mental ground between what's real and what's imaginary, the more appealing the story becomes," she says. "It's not so much ghosts as the *possibility* of ghosts that fascinates kids."

After allowing, then, for the originality of Bellairs's artistry and the ingenuity of his craftsmanship, it does seem that the deeper appeal his stories hold for children is no different from the psychological satisfaction adult readers derive from good genre literature. With the detective-hero as our ego stand-in, we enjoy both the vicarious thrill of looking our secret terrors in the eye and the intense pleasure of punching them in the nose.

"The real questions that Bellairs is exploring in these stories," says Ms. Carlson, are those involving "a child's concern with comfort and security in his *real* world. The supernatural elements are the shadow representations of that frightening real world. They function as a very convenient mythology that can stand for anything that frightens us. For a kid, this can be anything from nuclear war to losing your mother in the supermarket."

By genre conventions, Johnny Dixon, who appears in most of the tales, is a terrific hero for taking on such formidable existential chores. A realistic little boy with recognizable problems—his mother has died, his father is far away fighting a war and he feels alienated in the new town where he has gone to live with his grandparents—Johnny reflects all the exaggerated fears and self-doubts natural to anyone in his position. He is scared of heights, thin ice, damp ground and tetanus. He is also leery of crabby people, stern adults, tossing a baseball and making friends. But every time he zaps a monster or outwits a witch, he also vanquishes a personal demon.

The bad magic unleashed by an Egyptian ushabti in *The Curse of the Blue Figurine* is really Johnny's own anger with a schoolyard bully. In *The Chessmen of Doom,* he learns from a good witch not to judge people on superficial appearances. By solving the tough puzzle in *The Secret of the Underground Room,* he comes to recognize and value his own keen intelligence. In one of his most harrowing adventures, *The Mummy, the Will, and the*

Crypt, he finds the courage to face his grandmother's illness and confront the awful "fear that he would be abandoned." In anybody's book, that's true heroism.

TITLE COMMENTARY

THE FACE IN THE FROST (1969)

Frederick Michael Lauritsen

SOURCE: A review of *The Face in the Frost,* in *Library Journal,* Vol. 94, No. 4, February 15, 1969, pp. 776-77.

Take two wizards named Prospero and Roger Bacon, place in a land that never was, involve several types of men with which wizards would have truck, and set them out to fight Melichus—another wizard who is evil incarnate! These are the ingredients of a fantasy invented by John Bellairs. One of the greatest hinderances in fantasy is that the plot and characters become stock, lacking depth. Mr. Bellairs has not completely surmounted these problems, but he has used imagination and invention to evoke nostalgia, interest, and some comedy. The book is recommended to wizard buffs.

Best Sellers

SOURCE: A review of *The Face in the Frost,* in *Best Sellers,* Vol. 29, No. 1, April 1, 1969, p. 10.

For those who have enjoyed J. R. R. Tolkien's highly imaginative *Lord of the Rings* and similar fantastic tales, **The Face in the Frost** should be quite enjoyable. For John Bellairs has woven a tale of two old wizards, Prospero and Roger Bacon, who are threatened with the ultimate peril at the magic of Melichus, an evil wizard who has mastered the cipher in which an old book of spells is written and is bent on destroying all life in the Northern and Southern Kingdoms (separated one from the other only by the Brown River). There are secret tunnels and trolls and weird happenings enough to impart a chill to the reader. Marvelous is the collection of comets and galaxies and constellations of King Gorm, and marvelous, too, the plants the green-thumb monk has grown. Pursued by the evil genius right up to the end, you know that Prospero (and his friend Roger) will defeat the bad wizard and save the countryside, but it would not be fair to disclose just how that comes about.

The Booklist and Subscription Books Bulletin

SOURCE: A review of *The Face in the Frost,* in *The Booklist and Subscription Books Bulletin,* Vol. 65, No. 21, July 1, 1969, p. 1209.

Flashes of humor and horror are intermingled in an old-fashioned fantasy-adventure in which good is pitted against evil. Reunited after a long separation Prospero and Roger Bacon, two bumbling but adroit wizards, are frightened by a series of strange happenings in and around Prospero's bizarre house. The two journey north pursuing the source of the threatening evil, hearing along the way rumors of widespread eerie dreams, fearful gray shadows, and the inexplicable frost that forms on windows only to melt at dawn after becoming a frightening face that seems to eat itself up. For a special readership.

Lin Carter

SOURCE: "The Young Magicians: Some Modern Masters of Fantasy," in *Imaginary Worlds: The Art of Fantasy,* Ballantine Books, 1973, pp. 159-73.

Where will the fantasy writers of the first rank come from in the years and decades ahead? That's a foolish question to ask, I suppose, but at least it is an easy one to answer: they will come from among the fantasy readers of today.

Some of them may well be onstage already, however many may still be waiting in the wings. . . .

I have read three absolutely first-class fantasy novels published since [J.R.R. Tolkien's] *The Lord of the Rings* first appeared in print in this country during the mid-1950s. And *only* three—for however many decent, good, or even excellent new novels have been printed in the last twenty years or so, there are three that seem to me to tower above all the rest.

The first of these is *The Last Unicorn* by Peter S. Beagle. . . .

[The second] is a remarkable first novel by an Englishwoman named Joy Chant. The book is called *Red Moon and Black Mountain* . . .

The third and last of my choices of the best fantasy novels to appear since *The Lord of the Rings* is a book that has received virtually no recognition as yet, overlooked alike by reviewers and fantasy buffs. The novel is called **The Face in the Frost,** by a writer of amazing brilliance and charm named John Bellairs. Although it was packaged as a children's book, don't let that stop you from hunting it up . . .

The Face in the Frost opens in a mood of wacky hilarity. There is this cranky old magician named Prospero, see— "and not the one you are thinking of, either"—who lives in a wacky country called "the South Kingdom," which is split up into scores of vest-pocket kingdomettes with grandiose names like "The Grand Union of the Five Counties," "The Duchy of Irontree-Dragonrock," and so forth (not unlike the comic-opera hodge-podge of miniature duchies and princedoms in Lloyd Alexander's *Marvelous Misadventures of Sebastian,* or the crazy-quilt landscape of Oz, for that matter).

Prospero lives in "a huge, ridiculous, doodad-covered, trash-filled two-story horror of a house," with gutterspouts carved into "whistling sphinxes and screaming bearded faces" and a front porch decorated with "carved bears, monkeys, toads, and fat women in togas holding sheaves of grain," a house cluttered with Victorian bric-a-brac and thaumaturgical paraphernalia—jars of mandrake roots, alembics, a brass St. Bernard dog with a clock in his tummy, Hands of Glory, grimoires, mahogany chests covered with fat cherubs and tiger mouths "that bit you if you put your finger in the wrong place," a library of books with titles such as *Nameless Horrors and What to Do About Them,* and "of course," the dreaded *Krankenhammer* of Stefan Schimph the Mad Cobbler of Mainz, as well as a magic mirror gone zany from boredom which shows the eighth inning of the 1943 game between the Chicago Cubs and the New York Giants, and sings madly to itself,

> "O-ver-head the moon is SCREEEEEAMING, Whi-i-te as turnips on the Rhine. . . ."

until poor old Prospero feels like blowing out its brains, if it *had* any brains, which, of course, being only a mirror, it hasn't. Along comes an old crony of his called Roger Bacon—"one of Prospero's best friends and a pretty good sorcerer in his own right"—with a tale about a mysterious and long-lost grimoire and a supposedly equally long-dead magician named Melichus Magister. And the plot begins to thicken on the spot . . .

The tale is rich, hilarious, inventive, filled with infectious good-humor, grisly horrors, slithering Evil, bumbling monarchs, and enough Various & Sundry Menaces of the supernatural variety to keep the now-defunct Gothic soap opera *Dark Shadows* running for another decade. Bellairs is a marvelous writer who has obviously read all the right books with enthusiasm, and his own venture into the genre is one of the most exciting debuts in a long time.

Marshall B. Tymn, Kenneth J. Zahorski, and Robert H. Boyer

SOURCE: A review of *The Face in the Frost,* in *Fantasy Literature: A Core Collection and Reference Guide,* R. R. Bowker Company, 1979, pp. 51-2.

The jacket of the 1978 Ace Books paperback edition of this book quotes Ursula K. Le Guin's comment about **The Face in the Frost:** "This is authentic fantasy by a writer who knows what wizardry is all about." The book is, in fact, a compendium of magical properties and events, with the emphasis on the Gothic varieties: books of spells, tarot cards, prophetic globes, wraiths, ancient curses, shape shiftings, magical keys, travel through mirrors, and much more. The plot on which all of these details hang is the conflict between the congenial wizards Prospero and Roger Bacon and the power-mad Melichus. Until near the conclusion, however, the plot is more that of a detective story than of wizardly combat, since Prospero and Roger must race numerous clues to discover who and then where their opponent is and how he is trying to use the most powerful of all the books of wizardry. Melichus, almost distractedly, throws in all varieties of Gothic creatures to scare Prospero and Roger, who are very human and susceptible wizards, somewhat akin to T. H. White's absent-minded Merlin. They are, nonetheless, equal to the challenge and successfully thwart Melichus. The book is genuinely frightening at times and quite serious about its magic, but a playfully humorous tone is rarely absent. Occasionally, in fact, one suspects the author of writing a parody of fantasy. Few fantasy motifs seem to have been omitted. There is even a pumpkin turned into a carriage, since Prospero cannot ride a horse. In the end, however, the reader is satisfied and pleased that Bellairs has been making fun with magic, and not at it. The book is not a theme book but an impressive display of magical fireworks.

📖 THE HOUSE WITH A CLOCK IN ITS WALLS (1973)

Publishers Weekly

SOURCE: A review of *The House With a Clock in Its Walls,* in *Publishers Weekly,* Vol. 203, No. 13, March 26, 1973, p. 70.

For devotees of the genre, here's the genuine article, a ghost story guaranteed to raise hackles. Young Lewis arrives to live with his uncle, Jonathan, when his parents die, and he is delighted with the new house. It has secret passages, stained glass windows and all kinds of surprises. Almost at once, he finds that his uncle and a neighbor, a motherly soul named Mrs. Zimmermann, are witches but dedicated to good works. They are trying to find a clock hidden in the walls of Jonathan's house, left there by the former owners, both bad witches. The clock goes on ticking and the three must find and stop it before it strikes and marks the end of the world. In the chilling finale, good conquers evil, of course. Bellairs's story and Edward Gorey's pictures are satisfyingly frightening.

Kirkus Reviews

SOURCE: A review of *The House With a Clock in Its Walls,* in *Kirkus Reviews,* Vol. XLI, No. 9, May 1, 1973, p. 514.

Gorey's creepy-cozy drawings accurately project the ambience of the big old house in tiny New Zebedee, Michigan, where ten-year-old Lewis, newly orphaned by an auto accident, goes to live with his benign and rather seedy warlock uncle Jonathan. With the help of gray-haired Mrs. Zimmerman, the cookie-baking witch next door, Jonathan amuses his nephew with an eclipse of the moon and other frivolous pastimes—but the uncanny happenings become more sinister when Lewis himself, to impress a friend, manages to summon malignant Mrs. Izard, the house's former occupant, from her tomb. Lewis redeems himself in the end and destroys Mrs. Izard's evil

From The House with a Clock in its Walls, *written by John Bellairs. Illustrated by Edward Gorey.*

power by finding and breaking a clock which the lady's sorcerer husband, now dead, had programmed to destroy the world. Bellairs doesn't bother to supply either motivation or blueprints for the Izards' antisocial scheme, but if the cavalier and capricious handling of the occult by characters and author alike precludes any bone-deep shudders, the house lives up to its promise of a few gratifying Halloween shivers.

School Library Journal

SOURCE: A review of *The House with a Clock in Its Walls,* in *School Library Journal,* Vol. 19, No. 9, May 15, 1973, p. 91.

The House with a Clock in Its Walls is an unsuccessful attempt to produce a seriocomic tale of the supernatural set in a modern small town. Lewis, a 10-year-old orphan, comes to New Zebedee, Michigan, to stay with his Uncle Jonathan who lives in a three-story stone mansion with a tall turret. Uncle Jonathan is an inept wizard, his neighbor and friend, Mrs. Zimmermann, is a witch, and the previous owners of the house (both recently deceased) were

Isaac Izard, an evil warlock, and his wife. Hidden in the walls of the house is Isaac's magic clock, ticking away the minutes until doomsday. Lewis' efforts to find the clock only succeed in bringing Mrs. Izard back from the grave even more determined to destroy the world. In the end, her machinations are foiled by Lewis, who destroys the clock in the nick of time. Lewis' adventures are neither funny nor chilling, merely implausible.

The Booklist

SOURCE: A review of *The House With a Clock In Its Walls,* in *The Booklist,* Vol. 70, No. 4, October 15, 1973, p. 227.

A light occult novel in which orphaned Lewis goes to live with his Uncle Jonathan, a wizard who owns a rambling mansion previously inhabited by the now deceased Izzards, dealers in black magic. A mysterious ticking within the mansion walls bodes ill, Jonathan feels, and his intuition is borne out when Lewis unknowingly resurrects Mrs. Izard on a midnight graveyard Halloween outing. Freed, she resumes her husband's unfinished task of bringing about the end of the world—a task closely linked with the ticking in Jonathan's mansion. Bellair's tale is weakened by the loose juxtaposition of diabolical elements and levity, but nonetheless is palatable fare for younger dabblers in the occult.

Zena Sutherland

SOURCE: A review of *The House with a Clock in Its Walls,* in *Bulletin of the Center for Children's Books,* Vol. 27, No. 3, November, 1973, p. 37.

Newly orphaned, Lewis is a plump ten-year-old who has come to live with his Uncle Jonathan; he finds himself very much at home in the old, odd mansion and he quickly becomes fond of both Uncle Jonathan and his next-door neighbor and boon companion, Mrs. Zimmerman. But there's something odd going on: the ticking noise in the walls of the house, the strange things Uncle Jonathan does; Lewis discovers that his uncle has magic powers, that he himself has acquired some occult ability, and that there is a major power struggle between their well-meant white magic and the dire plans of an extinct (but haunting) former owner. Black magic against white, good against evil; the mood and suspense are artfully created and the illustrations exactly right for the eerie tale. The plot is a bit cumbersome at some points in the story, but it's imaginative, the characters and dialogue are convincing, and the relationship between Lewis and his adult friends is sympathetically drawn.

The Booklist

SOURCE: A review of *The House with a Clock in Its Walls,* in *The Booklist,* Vol. 71, No. 18, May 15, 1975, pp. 961, 963.

Lewis Barnavelt, earlier met in ***The House with a Clock***

in Its Walls contends with the mysterious powers seemingly resurrected by an amulet once belonging to his grandfather. His fantasy of standing up to Woody Mingo, a bully who taunts him, comes true when Lewis beats him in a fight; but the strange dictum, "venio," or "I come," that turns up in unexpected places worries him, and a phantom intruder who waits in the shadows inspires terror. His best friend, Rose Rita, locks the amulet away, but Lewis is driven to find it, finally succumbing to the ghost's increasing powers. It remains for his uncle Jonathan, a wizard, along with a witch friend, Mrs. Zimmermann, to figure out the forces at work and rescue Lewis from the phantom. Crisp prose and well-wrought suspense maintain the story's pace, and the background of Lewis' insecurities and his friendship with Rose Rita add a personable dimension to this entertaining occult novel.

E. Colwell

SOURCE: A review of *The House with a Clock in Its Walls,* in *The Junior Bookshelf,* Vol. 42, No. 5, October, 1978, pp. 253-54.

An entertaining fantasy about not-too-serious supernatural experiences. Lewis, fat and clumsy, lives with his uncle who is a "white" magician. Somewhere in his uncle's odd house is a clock that ticks day and night. It has been placed there by a wizard and his wife and when it stops, the end of the world will come. But how to find it? The search involves a breathless chase by ghosts and the opening of a tomb where the wizard is buried. Most of the mysterious happenings cause only a titillation of the nerves but there is one moment of sheer horror when Lewis (aged 10) opens the door at midnight and sees the "white fungus blotch which was the face" of an old woman he used to know and whom he knows to be dead. Very sensibly he faints.

The characters in the story are very odd indeed—Mrs. Zimmerman who is an educated witch with a degree, the podgy and lonely Lewis with his lively and almost fatal curiosity, and Mrs. Izard who has escaped from her grave and falls to dust in an unpleasant way when Lewis outwits her.

Edward Gorey is a fitting illustrator for such an uncanny tale.

Michele Landsberg

SOURCE: "Adventure, The Great Game: *The House with a Clock in Its Walls,"* in *Reading for the Love of It: Best Books for Young Readers,* Prentice Hall Press, 1986, pp. 145-46.

John Bellairs is an American writer of Gothic mysteries with overtones of the supernatural who is worth noting for the warmth of his characterization. His most popular, and still, I think, his best novel, is ***The House with a Clock in Its Walls,*** which is enlivened by the humorous, affectionate tone of the relationships between pudgy Lewis Barnavelt, his Uncle Jonathan, and Mrs. Florence Zimmerman, the uncle's friend and neighbor.

The orphaned Lewis comes to live in Uncle Jonathan's turreted mansion, which, he discovers, is haunted by a mysterious ticking noise. The particularly engaging tone of the book springs from the comical clash between appearances of cozy normalcy and matter-of-fact revelations of the supernatural: Uncle Jonathan and Mrs. Zimmerman, for example, are sympathetic poker-playing buddies—and nonchalant practitioners of witchcraft.

There are some chilly moments of real fearfulness in the book, and one wonderful scene in which Uncle Jonathan casts a moon-eclipsing spell, which fills the garden with sudden magic. Lewis, putting his ear to the ground, can hear the earthworms and sense the slow collapse of "the delicate ivory skeleton" of a cat. Lewis has coaxed his uncle to this unwonted display of prowess in order to win over a school sports hero as a friend. But the swaggering Tarby sneers at the spell the moment the enchantment is over, and by this token we know he is no true friend. It is indicative of the jaunty humor and offbeat eclecticism of the story that, at the end, Lewis has made a new friend, Rose Rita Pottinger, who knows the names of all the different kinds of cannon: "Saker, mimion, falconet, demiculverin . . ." recites Lewis. "Aah," screams Uncle Jonathan in exaggerated protest, "That's all I need! An expert in Elizabethan ordnance!"

📖 *THE FIGURE IN THE SHADOWS* (1975)

Publishers Weekly

SOURCE: A review of *The Figure in the Shadows*, in *Publishers Weekly*, Vol. 207, No. 4, January 27, 1975, p. 285.

The author published *The House With a Clock in Its Walls* last year, a fine and chilling ghost story which was received enthusiastically. In Bellairs's new book, we find the same unlikely young hero, fat Lewis, the orphan who lives with Uncle Jonathan, a wizard. Once again, the reader is in for special treats as Lewis gets hold of a diabolically magic coin and evokes an evil spirit. The suspense is terrific as the boy is drawn deeper into danger and all the resources of those who love him seem to be used in vain. It's great fun to be back in the company of neighbor Mrs. Zimmerman, a kind witch, and, maybe most of all, of Rose Rita who remains true to Lewis.

Kirkus Reviews

SOURCE: A review of *The Figure in the Shadows*, in *Kirkus Reviews*, Vol. XLIII, No. 9, May 1, 1975, p. 511.

It's the same old lard-ass Lewis of *The House With a Clock in Its Walls*, accustomed to living with a practicing wizard and more worried about getting tough enough to take on class bully Woody Mingo. Lewis is still palling

around with Rose Rita (rather atavistically described as a "tomboy") but he soon picks up a more unsettling companion—a ghost called up by Grandpa Barnavelt's lucky piece. Notes slipped through the mail slot and a sudden rush of power during a scrape with Woody presage Lewis' kidnapping by the vengeful specter. The switch in illustrations from Gorey's brooding interiors to Mayer's rumpled urchins only reinforces our suspicion that a less gullible kid than Lewis wouldn't fall for any of this. Still, a nice comfy ghost story for stay-at-homes who'll be relieved to know that the grownups can yet protect them against the powers of darkness.

Alix Nelson

SOURCE: A review of *The Figure in the Shadows*, in *The New York Times Book Review*, May 4, 1975, p. 26.

Just when you think the art of magical derring-do must be vanishing, along comes John Bellairs's **The Figure in the Shadows**. Fat Lewis Barnavelt, sixth-grade coward, vows to do in the class bully by any means he can muster: diet, push-ups, Charles Atlas—but it takes a magic amulet from his grandfather's trunk to save the day, and it almost costs him his life. He is rescued from his Walter Mitty exploits, and from the wizard who haunts the amulet, in the nick of time by his indomitable girl friend, Rose Rita, by his warlock uncle, Weird Beard, and by a good witch, Mrs. Zimmermann, who did her Ph.D. on magic amulets! Never mind your fayries and amorous corpses; fat heroes and witches with doctorates are what I want my daughters to read.

Zena Sutherland

SOURCE: A review of *A Figure in the Shadows*, in *Bulletin of the Center for Children's Books*, Vol. 29, No. 1, September, 1975, p. 2.

A sequel to **The House with a Clock in its Walls** has the same cast: orphaned Lewis, a timid boy who has found a very happy home with his uncle; Uncle Jonathan and his neighbor Mrs. Zimmerman, both benevolent sorcerers; and Lewis' friend Rose Rita, who has all the nerve Lewis wishes he had. Lewis hopes the old coin he's found in a trunk is an amulet, but it doesn't seem to help him with the class bully. It is magical, however, and it is evil; using it, Lewis evokes the shadowed figure of a ghost and puts himself in great danger. Again here, as in the earlier book, Bellairs combines effectively an aura of brooding suspense and the down-to-earth characters of Mrs. Zimmerman and Jonathan, whose attitude toward magic is practical. Smoothly contrapuntal, often amusing, and adroitly constructed and paced.

📖 *THE LETTER, THE WITCH, AND THE RING* (1976)

Louise Lampman

SOURCE: A review of *The Letter, The Witch, and the*

Ring, in *Children's Book Review Service,* Vol. 5, No. 1, September, 1976, p. 6.

Concluding the trilogy which included **The House with the Clock in Its Walls** and **The Figure in the Shadows,** again there is a contest between black magic and white magic, and once more familiar characters are engaged in a tense struggle for supremacy. Although the title is too similar to another familiar series, the plot is fresh, gripping, and finely drawn. Juvenile readers will find this book good escape reading.

Kirkus Reviews

SOURCE: A review of *The Letter, the Witch and the Ring,* in *Kirkus Reviews,* Vol. XLIV, No. 18, September 15, 1976, p. 1038.

Winding up the hocus-pocus begun in **The House With the Clock in Its Walls** this takes Lewis' friend Rose Rita on a Northern Michigan vacation with Mrs. Zimmerman, the grandmotherly witch who has just inherited a cousin's farm up there. But another old lady, jealous of Mrs. Zimmerman for stealing her beau 45 years earlier, uses witchcraft and a magic ring to turn her rival into a hen, and Rose Rita, snooping about, is almost killed herself before she gets hold of the ring . . . saving her friend Mrs. Z, who must then save her from the ring's compelling power. "I wish I were a boy" is, Bellairs hints, what baseball-playing Rose Rita is about to intone—but despite the satisfying exactness of his time-and-place details, Bellairs' understanding of a 1950 "tomboy" is only skin deep. And of course his sorcery only skims the cauldron.

Denise M. Wilms

SOURCE: A review of *The Letter, the Witch, and the Ring,* in *Booklist,* Vol. 73, No. 3, October 1, 1976, pp. 246-47.

Spunky Rose Rita Pottinger, who figured secondarily as Lewis Barnavelt's best friend in the previous novel of this trilogy, comes to the fore here to rescue their witchy friend Mrs. Zimmermann from a spell cast by evil witch Gert Bigger. Mysterious events befall Rose Rita and Mrs. Zimmermann when they travel to Michigan to look over a farm the good witch has inherited from a cousin. This deceased relative also informed Mrs. Z. in his final letter of a ring which he believed to be magical. It turns out to be the legendary ring of King Solomon, which confers special powers on its wearer. But it's been swiped by Mrs. Bigger, who covets its power; in the mistaken belief that Mrs. Z. is in search of the ring, Mrs. Bigger temporarily does away with her. Rose Rita, now on her own, takes it upon herself to set matters straight, and she does, sort of, although in the end it's the restored Mrs. Zimmermann who saves her from succumbing to the ring's power. The plot is a bit harried, but the writing is brisk and the characters are vigorously drawn.

Sarah Law Kennedy

SOURCE: A review of *The Letter, the Witch, and the Ring,* in *School Library Journal,* Vol. 23, No. 4, December, 1976, p. 67.

The Letter, the Witch, and the Ring stars Rose Rita and Mrs. Zimmerman, the kindly witch, with fat Lewis and his Uncle Jonathan, the inept wizard, relegated to minor roles. Rose Rita is saved from a dull summer when Mrs. Zimmerman inherits a farm and a magic ring from an eccentric uncle and then discovers that the farm-house has been ransacked and the ring stolen. A chillingly evil neighbor uses the power of the ring to turn Mrs. Zimmerman into a chicken, and in a suspenseful climax, almost bewitches Rose Rita. A successful finale that adroitly blends the everyday with the supernatural.

Zena Sutherland

SOURCE: A review of *The Letter, the Witch, and the Ring,* in *Bulletin of the Center for Children's Books,* Vol. 30, No. 5, January, 1977, p. 71.

A sequel to **The House with a Clock in Its Walls** and **The Figure in the Shadows** is not about Lewis and his uncle but about their neighbor Mrs. Zimmermann (who has magical powers) and Lewis's friend Rose Rita. Miffed because Lewis is going off to camp, Rose Rita is delighted when Mrs. Z. invites her along to get a magic ring she has inherited. The ring is in a desk drawer in the now-empty farmhouse where her cousin had lived. But strange things happen. Mrs. Z. finds her face scratched off on an old photograph—Rose Rita hears an intruder in the night—Mrs. Z. disappears. Breaking into the home of a woman she suspects, Rose Rita is caught and held prisoner, then escapes with the ring; the woman turns into a tree. This doesn't have quite the pace and cohesion of earlier books, but it has lots of action, the appeal of magic, and a dauntless heroine.

Ruth Hawthorn

SOURCE: "Suitable for Children," in *The Times Literary Supplement,* No. 4018, March 28, 1980, p. 362.

[**The Letter, the Witch and the Ring**] is written in a marvellously direct, open style, light even when it is serious or when the tension is building up to something really scary which it does frequently as the story progresses. It is a book in the best E. B. White tradition. Adults and children take each other seriously; they either please or menace as equals, and this straightness enables John Bellairs to move easily from everyday to magic without any affectation at all. It has strange and pleasingly realistic pictures by Richard Egielski which capture the atmosphere of the writing perfectly.

This is Bellairs's third book, with some of the characters from **The House with a Clock in its Walls.** The hero is

Rose Rita, a thirteen-year-old resisting the demands of American teenagerhood with a complicated feminism. (Her mother insists on describing her best friend Lewis as her boyfriend, to Rose Rita's rage.) But she has a genuine ally, in her aim to remain a person, in her friend Mrs Zimmerman. Mrs Zimmerman is a witch, but of an unthreatening kind: she drives a 1950 Plymouth and specializes in snapping lighted matches out of the air.

Rose Rita and Mrs Zimmerman go on a touring holiday together, while Lewis spends the summer at boy scout camp, and strange things occur all over northern Michigan. But the background of the main drama is a spooky farmhouse that Mrs Zimmerman has inherited from her eccentric cousin Oley, and the neighbouring properties belonging to a wonderful array of characters from the seedy rural community. It is a book I would have loved at that age; Rose Rita really is someone you could have had as a friend. Bellairs somehow manages to get inside that quality without being too self-consciously sensitive.

Margery Fisher

SOURCE: A review of *The Letter, the Witch and the Ring,* in *Growing Point,* Vol. 19, No. 3, September, 1980, pp. 3744-46.

Finally, a tale of magic adventure which exhibits that particular bite of sardonic humour that is the glory of the best fantasy from America. *The Letter, the Witch and the Ring,* a sequel to *The House with a Clock in its Walls,* continues the story of Mrs. Zimmerman, that notable witch whose terse wisdom and common sense helped bespectacled Lewis to keep his courage up through some dangerous situations. Lewis is now off to Scout camp, and his friend Rose Rita, angry at being left to find her own amusements and at being denied a part in boys' enterprises, is delighted to be invited to join Mrs. Zimmerman on a visit to the country to view a farmhouse left to her by a cousin. A smaller legacy of a magic ring Mrs. Zimmerman dismisses as a mere fancy of her eccentric relative's, but it proves to be real enough, none other than Solomon's ring, which can alter personality disastrously while conferring considerable powers on its owner. The ring disappears and reappears in sinister circumstances and the journey proves perilous indeed, for Mrs. Zimmerman is being persecuted at a distance by uncouth Gertie Biggers, a secret black witch, who keeps the store in Ellis Corners and who has trespassed in Cousin Oley's cottage to some purpose. Rose Rita, who is only thirteen, thinks herself tough enough to match any boy, but Mrs. Zimmerman's sudden illness and her mysterious disappearance call upon every bit of the girl's courage and initiative. The mystery and tension of the story are brilliantly sustained and underneath enchantments and magic accidents runs the theme of a girl looking nervously yet with eagerness into the future; for Rose Rita, an intelligent tomboy, is afraid of the feminine role which she knows she must soon assume, and the psychological aspect of the book gives it a sturdy reality and an emotional depth that frame and illuminate the fantasy.

B. Clark

SOURCE: A review of *The Letter, the Witch and the Ring,* in *The Junior Bookshelf,* Vol. 44, No. 6, December, 1980, p. 300.

In this sequel to *The House with a Clock in its Walls,* Rose Rita Pottinger is taken on a mysterious journey by the witchy Mrs. Zimmermann to a farm left her by an eccentric relative. Odd events occur on their arrival, and Mrs. Zimmermann seems to become strangely unlike herself. Rose Rita proves her worth by driving the car when Mrs. Zimmermann is taken ill very suddenly, although this episode seems as far-fetched as the rest of the book. If you like some peculiar characters in the story you are reading, with a general feeling of sinister threat hanging over all, then you will enjoy reading how Rose Rita pieces together the bits of Mrs. Zimmermann's past from the actions and remarks of other characters, especially Gert Bigger who keeps the local store.

THE TREASURE OF ALPHEUS WINTERBORN (1978)

Publishers Weekly

SOURCE: A review of *The Treasure of Alpheus Winterborn,* in *Publishers Weekly,* Vol. 215, No. 6, February 6, 1978, p. 102.

Every bit as well told, slyly humorous and fascinating as Bellairs's trilogy [that began with *The House with a Clock in Its Walls*] is his fourth thriller. Young Anthony Monday works as a page for his dear friend, Miss Eells, town librarian. They are excited when they find a clue to a secret treasure, left by long-dead Winterborn, eccentric millionaire. Unfortunately, the discovery brings them the dangerous attentions of Philpotts, Winterborn's evil nephew. The villain breaks into Miss Eells's house and bashes her over the head. When she recovers, she finds he has stolen what he believes will bring him the hoard. But the message is a dead end, whereupon Philpotts gets after Anthony and the narrative rushes into a hair-raising encounter. Finding out what the treasure consists of is the final surprise in a story jumping with them.

Barbara Elleman

SOURCE: A review of *The Treasure of Alpheus Winterborn,* in *Booklist,* Vol. 3, No. 1, March 1, 1978, p. 1098.

His parents' continual quarrels and his father's subsequent heart attack trigger Anthony's determination to find the eccentric Alpheus Winterborn's legacy, supposedly hidden within the town. While working with his good friend Miss Eells, the local librarian, he finds clues pointing first to the old Winterborn mansion and then to the library itself. Anthony's attempts to play detective boomerang, however, until the night when he is inadvertently trapped in the library with Hugo Philpotts, the sneaky bank vice-president who thinks himself to be the rightful heir. Anthony proves a plucky hero, eventually solving the mystery and finding the treasure, only to unearth an unusual story as puzzling as the treasure itself. Aside from the weak characterization of Philpotts, this is a brisk, full-bodied mystery filled with tantalizing clues and bits of humor.

Kirkus Reviews

SOURCE: A review of *The Treasure of Alpheus Winterborn,* in *Kirkus Reviews,* Vol. XLVI, No. 8, April 15, 1978, pp. 435-36.

Like [Ellen] Raskin's *Westing [Game]* amateur archaeologist Alpheus Winterborn is one of those millionaires of fiction who delight in mystifying survivors with cryptic treasure hunts. And Anthony, whose father has a heart attack early on and whose mother is obsessively insecure about money, is determined to find the rumored treasure. He comes upon the first clue accidentally while dusting the library which old Winterborn had financed; and from then on Anthony and his librarian friend Miss Eells pursue leads and misleads, hassled all the while by the ruthless competition of a Winterborn nephew, banker Hugo Philpotts. Bellairs ends extravagantly with the rest of downtown evacuated for an expected flood; Philpotts overhearing Anthony's guess as to the treasure's location; an injured Miss Eells out cold in the library; Anthony seeking help but Philpotts instead forcing him up the steeple to fetch the treasure; Anthony banging for the fire department, which arrives with the town in tow; and the treasure, now Anthony's, revealed as an angel from the ark of the covenant. Even though the old statue's identity is never absolutely certified, a more modest find—not to mention a less melodramatic finale—would better suit the story. Nevertheless, Bellairs drops clues and plants obstacles tidily enough to give mystery fans a run for their money.

Irma Pascal Heldman

SOURCE: A review of *The Treasure of Alpheus Winterborn,* in *The New York Times Book Review,* April 30, 1978, p. 44.

Thirteen-year-old Anthony Monday works for his friend Miss Eells, the town librarian. When he died, Alpheus Winterborn, a millionaire with a penchant for archeology, bequeathed the library to the town, and rumor hath it that he buried treasure somewhere within its walls. When Anthony and Miss Eells stumble on a clue to the buried treasure, life gets exciting and dangerous. Enter Philpotts, the villainous nephew of Alpheus, who spares no malevolence in trying to prevent Tony and Miss Eells from finding the treasure. There is a grandstand climax, with not the least of the plot's many surprises being what the treasure turns out to be. Once again, John Bellairs deftly combines tongue-in-cheek humor with good solid suspense.

Drew Stevenson

SOURCE: A review of *The Treasure of Alpheus Winterborn,* in *School Library Journal,* Vol. 24, No. 9, May, 1978, p. 84.

Bellairs has a knack for concocting bizarre plots within the framework of the commonplace. Young Anthony Monday feels his family's only hope of fiscal survival following his father's heart attacks is for him to find *The Treasure of Alpheus Winterborn.* Winterborn was an eccentric millionaire who designed and built the Hoosac, Minnesota Public Library where Anthony works as a page under his spunky librarian friend Miss Eells. When Anthony finds a strange clue hidden by Winterborn above the library's fireplace he knows he is on the right path, but before he can claim the riches, he must face Hugo Philpotts, nasty nephew of Winterborn, alone in the library on a stormy night. Hugo is the perfect villain, from his sinister name to his icy stare, and Miss Eells and Anthony are likable good guys.

Zena Sutherland

SOURCE: A review of *The Treasure of Alpheus Winterborn,* in *Bulletin of the Center for Children's Books,* Vol. 32, No. 2, October, 1978, p. 23.

Hearing his parents worriedly discuss family finances, Anthony decides he will search for the treasure that reportedly has been hidden by the town's late benefactor, Mr. Winterborn. Since one of his best friends is the librarian, Myra Eells, Anthony begins his search in the library, spurred by finding an old coin and a message that ends, "Good hunting." Winterborn, an eccentric, had lived in the library before it was opened to the public. Miss Eells and Anthony are hampered in their efforts by a wily, acquisitive nephew of Winterborn, a man who is a respected local banker but who is unmasked in a dramatic climax, dangling from a rooftop's loosened ladder, as an unscrupulous persecutor who has endangered the lives of the two protagonists. The story is rather overburdened with melodramatic incident toward its end, and the characterization of the banker (and, to a lesser extent, of Miss Eells) seems overdrawn, but the book has pace and suspense, and the ending should satisfy readers, for Anthony does find the treasure and gains a great deal of money.

THE CURSE OF THE BLUE FIGURINE (1983)

Publishers Weekly

SOURCE: A review of *The Curse of the Blue Figurine,* in *Publishers Weekly,* Vol. 223, No. 6, February 11, 1983, p. 70.

Bellairs, author of a prize-winning suspense trilogy . . . [that includes] *The House With a Clock in Its Walls,* tells a fourth spellbinding story here about a nice boy whose one slip puts him in thrall to an evil ghost. Johnny Dixon, an orphan, lives with his grandparents whose friend is irascible but kind Professor Childermass, schooled in folklore. The professor says that the unquiet spirit of a priest, Father Baart, haunts the local church and Johnny, finding a strange blue figurine in the church basement and keeping it, learns that the Baart legend, reeking of horrors, is no rumor. The boy is drawn into a world of madness as the events rush on to a crisis on a mountaintop where the ghost has Johnny at his mercy, and Professor Childermass fights against terrible odds to save him. Bellairs's characters are irresistible and so are the flashes of humor that brighten the macabre doings.

School Library Journal

SOURCE: A review of *The Curse of the Blue Figurine,* in *School Library Journal,* Vol. 29, No. 9, May, 1983, pp. 93-4.

Combine flesh and blood characters with an eerie atmosphere as moody as a cold rainy day in March and the result is a horror story to be savored until the final page. The terror for young Johnny Dixon begins when cranky eccentric Professor Childermass tells him that St. Michael's Church is haunted by Father Baart, an evil sorcerer who mysteriously disappeared years ago. When Johnny finds a blue Egyptian figurine hidden in the church basement, he takes it home in spite of the warning note from Father Baart threatening harm to anyone who removes it from the church. Then, while praying in the church one night, Johnny meets the mysterious Mr. Beard who gives him a ring. Soon after he begins wearing it Johnny realizes that it is the ring which has power and in turn he is now under the control of Mr. Beard. Readers are kept on pins and needles until Johnny's final mountaintop showdown with the terrifying spectre.

Kirkus Reviews

SOURCE: A review of *The Curse of the Blue Figurine,* in *Kirkus Reviews,* Vol. LI, No. 10, May 15, 1983, pp. 578-79.

Another of Bellairs' nicely shivery magic tales, featuring, again, a boy of the Fifties displaced from his home. With his mother dead and his pilot father off to the Korean war, Johnny Dixon is living with his grandparents and spending time with their broadly characterized eccentric neighbor Professor Childermass. The professor tells Johnny a chilling tale about the apparent vengeful magic and mysterious disappearance of Father Remigius Baart, who was rector of the local church back in the 1880s. And so, inevitably, while dodging the class bully, Johnny finds himself in the basement of that very church—and finds there a hollowed-out missal containing a statue shaped like an Egyptian mummy case and a note, signed RB, threatening peril to the soul of "whoever removes these things from the church." But Johnny panics and dashes from the church, clutching the book with its statue . . . and thus begins the unsettling series of events that leave

him pale and plagued with nightmares. On a later visit to the empty church a mysterious Mr. Beard gives Johnny a ring of power and summons him to a midnight meeting in a park. The worried professor trails Johnny to the park, observes him talking to no one (as it seems to him), and recommends a psychiatrist and a weekend outing. Johnny seems to improve . . . until he and the professor, on their outing, confront the spirit of evil sorcerer Baart/Beard in an all-night, mountaintop battle between light and dark. Bellairs handles the snug suspense expertly, never confounding readers' expectations, but fulfilling them with communicable relish.

Zena Sutherland

SOURCE: A review of *The Curse of the Blue Figurine,* in *Bulletin of the Center for Children's Books,* Vol. 36, No. 10, June, 1983, p. 183.

Hiding from a bully in the church basement, Johnny takes what looks like a book and proves to be a box containing a scroll and a small blue figurine that looks like an Egyptian ushabti. These, plus a ring given him by a seemingly kindly man he meets, Mr. Beard, are the magic objects that put him in unhappy thrall to a ghost, for "Mr. Beard" is the ghost of a mad rector of the Catholic church in which the ushabti had been secreted. Johnny's friend the professor takes him to a psychiatrist (a stereotyped character) who tries to help; the professor takes Johnny off on a trip to help him forget his worries, and they are followed by the ghost, who endangers both their lives; they are saved by a rock slide precipitated by an earthquake. Bellairs is not at his best here; the story is concocted, the realism and fantasy don't mesh, the characters are flatly depicted, and the style is intermittently labored. What's left to appeal to the reader are the action, the suspense, and the occult.

Barbara Elleman

SOURCE: A review of *The Curse of the Blue Figurine,* in *Booklist,* Vol. 79, No. 20, June 15, 1983, p. 1335.

Prowling through the church to avoid the neighborhood bully, Johnny accidentally finds a grimy, cobwebbed book that has been carved out to hold an old Egyptian figurine. Disregarding the warning, "whoever removes these things from the church does so at his own peril," he takes the book home, sure that its contents are linked to the curious legend about demented Father Baart, whose ghost supposedly haunts the church. Despite evidence that the artifact is fake, strange things begin happening, and soon Johnny fears that it does indeed hold evil powers. Before long he and his friend, Professor Childermass, are involved in a frightening, intensely dramatic confrontation, concluding in a heart-stopping climax that discloses the mystery surrounding Father Baart. Bellairs intertwines real concerns with sorcery in a seamless fashion, bringing dimension to his characters and events with expert timing and sharply honed atmosphere.

Selma G. Lanes

SOURCE: A review of *The Curse of the Blue Figurine*, in *The New York Times Book Review*, September 25, 1983, p. 29.

In his fourth ghostly thriller, John Bellairs heeds the maxim: "Shoemaker, stick to your last." Though this latest novel introduces a new hero, the 12-year-old Johnny Dixon, and is unrelated to the previous trilogy, the author employs the same disarming devices to win our acceptance of some crucial otherworldly trappings. These include the restless and malign spirit of a long-dead, mad clergyman, Father Remigius Baart; a cursed Egyptian tomb figurine and a magic ring capable of destroying its wearer's enemies.

The year is 1951, the setting a backwater Massachusetts town called Duston Heights. Mr. Bellairs meticulously catalogues the specifics of this time and place: afternoon snacks of "Ritz crackers spread with pink pimento-flavored cream cheese"; an Atwater Kent table-model radio; a black Sessions clock on the sideboard. And so we instinctively grant him credence when he introduces a sepulchral villain and attendant supernatural paraphernalia.

Cannily, the author defuses audience skepticism by providing two adult scoffers within *The Curse of the Blue Figurine:* Professor Roderick Childermass, the young hero's neighbor / confidant; and a know-it-all psychiatrist with the inspired name of Highgaz Melkonian. After they convince both hero and readers that the tale's bizarre happenings are all products of our overworked imaginations, Mr. Bellairs catches us completely off guard with a hair-raising, grand-whammy climax: a fight to the death between evil spirit and flesh-and-blood boy atop a New Hampshire mountain peak. Susceptible young readers should relish this Gothic spine-tingler.

Allene Stuart Phy

SOURCE: A review of *The Curse of the Blue Figurine*, in *Science Fiction and Fantasy Book Review*, No. 19, November, 1983, pp. 46-7.

The jacket and frontispiece, brilliantly designed frontispiece by Edward Gorey, appropriately establish the atmosphere and tone of this juvenile thriller. A solitary child in pajamas is beckoned toward a desolate landscape by a sinister elderly man in a cape. This boy, Johnny Dixon, is an orphan living in an old house with grandparents. He makes friends with a professor known for his chocolate cake and chess game. Because the child starts speaking of night encounters with a demonic priest, the professor sends him to an inept, comic psychiatrist. Though the first half of the narrative lends itself to the plausible psychological explanation Dr. Melkonian suggests, Johnny is not really suffering hallucinations brought on by grief at the loss of his parents. This reader is not to be betrayed, but is treated in the end to a full-scale manifestation of the supernatural. The lore of ancient Egypt, the poetic luminosity of Roman Catholicism, and the jargon of contemporary psy-

cho-therapy blend in this tale set in the 1950s, a decade given such a golden glow that the story becomes a quaint period piece. There is a major earthquake and a scary journey through a dark wilderness, before an unquiet evil spirit is finally put out of business. Though the publishers recommend the book for grades five and above, it may be read, like Bellairs' earlier tales, with equal pleasure by an adult. In fact, it is an excellent volume for a child and adult to share, especially on a grim, stormy evening.

Anne Raymer

SOURCE: A review of *The Curse of the Blue Figurine*, in *Voice of Youth Advocates*, Vol. 7, No. 1, April, 1984, p. 28.

Shortly after his mother dies, Johnny Dixon's father leaves him with his grandparents. Feeling displaced in a new state and town, Johnny is slow to make friends. One stormy night, an eccentric neighbor, Professor Childermass relates a ghost story about evil Father Baart who was rector of the town church in the 1880s. Soon after, Johnny discovers a hollowed out missal in the church basement that contains a miniature Egyptian figurine called a ushabti and a warning note from Father Baart. Assured by Professor Childermass that he has nothing to fear, Johnny almost forgets the warning and the ghost story until on a later visit to the church, he meets the mysterious Mr. Beard who gives him a magic ring and later summons him to a midnight meeting in the park. Johnny's unusual experiences give him nightmares and put him increasingly in the power of an evil ghost. A worried Professor Childermass tracks Johnny and is soon caught up in a world of madness which culminates in a mountaintop battle between the evil priest and enterprising professor. This is a chilling mystery with fascinating characters, riveting suspense, flashes of humor and an original plot. Although the story has a satisfying ending with no loose threads, readers will want to read the sequel that's in the making. The book jacket captures the scary Gothic elements in the story and should attract younger readers.

Bill Boyle

SOURCE: A review of *The Curse of the Blue Figurine*, in *Books for Keeps*, No. 42, January, 1987, p. 9.

John Bellairs successfully creates here the evocative world of Fifties childhood—listening to radio programmes with unprovocative titles like, 'The House of Mystery,' whilst munching a plateful of Ritz crackers and cream cheese. Mind you, wasn't it still called the wireless in the early Fifties? The anachronism can be easily forgiven for so much of the atmosphere and sense of time is perfect. Johnny, living with his grandparents, is involved in a world of 'grown-up' conversation, littered with archaeological phrases and references. From mummies, it's but a short step in a boy's imagination to ghosts and hauntings, and an even shorter step to being embroiled in an adventure that makes 'The House of Mystery' seem as tame as Larry the Lamb.

📖 *THE MUMMY, THE WILL, AND THE CRYPT* (1983)

Barbara Elleman

SOURCE: A review of *The Mummy, the Will, and the Crypt,* in *Booklist,* Vol. 80, No. 3, October 1, 1983, p. 236.

Not long recovered from their chilling confrontation with the supernatural in *The Curse of the Blue Figurine,* Johnny and his friend, Professor Childermass, are again plunged into another extraordinary adventure. Intrigued by the unsolved clues surrounding a will left by H. Bagwell Glomus, Johnny begins slowly to piece together the puzzle. Two visits to a deserted mansion (one at midnight, the second in a raging blizzard) confirm his suspicions, and despite some frightening encounters he is determined to continue. Though Johnny's ability to solve the mystery from the clues provided stretches credibility a bit, as do some contrivances, the pace is fast and the suspense is compelling. Readers will find themselves quickly caught up in Johnny's personal problems (concern over his Gramma's illness, finally making a friend), as well as in the mystery.

Publishers Weekly

SOURCE: A review of *The Mummy, the Will, and the Crypt,* in *Publishers Weekly,* Vol. 224, No. 17, October 21, 1983, p. 67.

Here's another lovely, funny, frightening thriller readers will thank Bellairs for, the sequel to *The Curse of the Blue Figurine.* Orphaned Johnny Dixon, his cranky but fond friend Professor Childermass and Johnny's Gramma and Granpa play decisive roles again in events involving the boy in a search for the missing will of the late, nasty tycoon H. Bagwell Glomus. A misunderstanding convinces Johnny that Gramma needs money for an operation, so he dares malign forces to earn the reward offered for the missing Glomus document. Venturing into the lair of a wicked manipulator, the lad is knocked unconscious and left in the place as it's set afire. Meanwhile, the professor and a new friend of Johnny's search for him, and it's touch and go as the tale races forward, ending in marvelous surprises for everyone except the villains.

Kirkus Reviews

SOURCE: A review of *The Mummy, the Will, and the Crypt,* in *Kirkus Reviews,* Vol. LI, No. 21, November 1, 1983, p. 190.

In vital respects, very like *The Curse of the Blue Figurine,* last season's spooky debut of young Johnny Dixon and his eccentric old neighbor Professor Childermass; but a letdown only on that score. The new old mystery the Professor lays before Johnny concerns the missing will of H. Blagwell Glomus, cereal tycoon and demonology adept—who may have left three odd objects as a clue, or

may have left the objects merely to annoy his relatives. Johnny hasn't time to puzzle it out before he finds his grandmother acting strange, the victim of a brain tumor, and his own worries mount: his mother is dead, his father is a pilot in Korea, and now? To distract him, the Professor arranges a week's stay in the White Mountains with the Boy Scouts; next to the camp, unsuspected, is the derelict Glomus estate; calling to tell the Professor, Johnny is eyed darkly by a young man and hotel-keeper Mrs. Woodley; and when he and Fergie, a fellow odd-fact collector and a welcome friend, sneak out to the estate at night, the young man is waiting for them—with a gun. Faced down, he tells them he's Chad Glomus, grandson of "good old H. Blagwell"; warns of a malevolent Guardian at loose; and, with "long, loud, hideous yells and shrieks," vanishes. A crazy joke? Or for real? Home again, Johnny learns that his father is missing in Korea—and panics: if his grandmother dies, his grandfather will die too, and he'll be all alone. But the $10,000 reward for finding the will would pay for the best brain surgeon; so, aware that he's not rational, he heads back alone to New Hampshire, and into the clutches of Mrs. Woodley, old man Glomus' sister and now the Guardian's keeper . . . where, in a fiery finale, the Professor and Fergie find

From The House with a Clock in its Walls, *written by John Bellairs. Illustrated by Edward Gorey.*

him, and the will is destroyed. Then, tucking in the personal loose ends, Bellairs has Johnny get the reward anyhow—and has his father appear unheralded at the door. The usual taut narrative, intriguing puzzle, interesting types—but risky in that Johnny's psyche comes to seem part of the pattern.

Drew Stevenson

SOURCE: A review of *The Mummy, the Will, and the Crypt,* in *School Library Journal,* Vol. 30, No. 4, December, 1983, p. 84.

Bellairs has written a worthy sequel to the excellent *The Curse of the Blue Figurine.* He has brought back the same marvelous characters (plus added some new ones) and pitted them against a new villain in a melancholy setting perfectly suited for chills and shivers, which come aplenty. When it rains it pours for young Johnny Dixon. It's bad enough when his grandmother, with whom he lives, is operated on for a brain tumor. But hard on the heels of that crisis comes word that Johnny's father's plane has been shot down over Korea. Johnny is afraid his grandparents won't have enough money to get his grandmother the best medical care possible so he undertakes a daring journey to help out. If he can find the hidden will of the wealthy eccentric H. Bagwell Glomus, he will receive a $10,000 reward. Using the strange clues left by Glomus himself, Johnny tracks the will to an eerie abandoned estate in the lonely White Mountains. Everything does work out for Johnny in the end but not before he has to match wits with a powerful witch and an evil force known as the Guardian. Jolly good show!

Zena Sutherland

SOURCE: A review of *The Mummy, the Will, and the Crypt,* in *Bulletin of the Center for Children's Books,* Vol. 37, No. 8, April, 1984, p. 142.

Worried about his grandmother, who has just had a brain tumor removed, worried about the cost of a possible second operation, and worried about his father, shot down (and missing) in Korea, John decides to solve the puzzle of a lost will and win the $10,000 reward. Like *The Curse of the Blue Figurine* to which this is a sequel, the story founders on an unworkable foisting of fantasy on realism, as well as on a string of coincidences and contrivance. The pace is brisk, and there's lots of action to appeal to readers but the strewing of clues in twelve-year-old Johnny's path is unconvincing, as he encounters a murdering witch who controls an evil force, as well as a series of arcane objects and stereotyped characters.

Allene Stuart Phy

SOURCE: A review of *The Mummy, The Will, and the Crypt,* in *Fantasy Review,* Vol. 7, No. 3, April, 1984, p. 40.

Like its predecessor, *Mummy* is enhanced by a splendid jacket illustration and a frontispiece executed by that master of the comic grotesque, Edward Gorey. Two maps of locales where the action takes place, by the same artist, increase the interest of the reader, who may be a fifth grade child or a closet adult reader of quality children's books. Though the decade is still the 1950s, the hero, Johnny Dixon, now has enough troubles to qualify him as a character in a Victorian juvenile novel. He is still a pale blond child wearing glasses and preferring the company of his aging neighbor, the professor, to that of his peers. Already a half-orphan, his remaining parent, an Air Force officer, has disappeared over enemy territory in North Korea. And that isn't all. Though his elderly grandparents continue to care for him, Grandmother has recently had surgery for a malignant brain tumor.

Sensing the household's desperate need of money, Johnny determines to win $10,000 being offered for the recovery of a hidden will belonging to the recently-deceased Oaty Crisps King, an eccentric millionaire obsessed with both demonology and health foods. Running away from home, Johnny makes plans to search the crumbling country estate of the deceased. He registers in a rural inn operated by a wicked woman who controls an evil spirit known as The Guardian and has murderous designs on inquisitive orphans. Suspense builds to moments of genuine terror, with a nocturnal encounter with a real mummy in a crypt.

Bellairs refreshingly avoids the sentimentalities that so perniciously pervade many juvenile books, and though the horrors he promises are always very real and never subject to rational explanation, his reader can yet be sure that this book will honor that inviolable convention of the genre, the happy ending. *Mummy* offers many pleasures, not the least being a gentle spoofing of the juvenile Gothic and a '50s nostalgia manifested in little touches, such as the television programs Grandmother watches: the *Kate Smith Hour, Milton Berle,* and the original *Search for Tomorrow.* For an adult this is an amusing excursion into the recent past, duller but less troubled times; for the fifth grader here is a time trip to a decade which must seem as remote and quaint as the Victorian era. The book is highly recommended for all who enjoy a narrative of humorously macabre adventures.

THE DARK SECRET OF WEATHEREND (1984)

Barbara Elleman

SOURCE: A review of *The Dark Secret of Weatherend,* in *Booklist,* Vol. 80, No. 16, April 15, 1984, p. 1186.

Anthony, 14, and his librarian friend, Miss Eells, are prowling the supposedly abandoned estate of the late J. K. Borkman when, just as they uncover the dead millionaire's diary, they are driven away by a strange-acting man. Shortly after, the weather turns for the worst; Anthony suspects connections between the eccentric storms and weird notations in the diary. No one believes him, however, except Miss Eells, and the two set off to stop the evil force begun by Borkman to devastate the world. Bellairs creates a believable Minnesota winter setting and compels an inventive plot to a suspenseful climax. A recommended popular read for those who like a tale of the supernatural with a touch of mystery.

Drew Stevenson

SOURCE: A review of *The Dark Secret of Weatherend,* in *School Library Journal,* Vol. 30, No. 9, May, 1984, p. 103.

John Bellairs is a name sure to set a gothic horror lover's heart beating in joyful anticipation of marvelous characters in weird wonderous stories thick with atmosphere, thrills and suspense. His latest book will not disappoint. Anthony Monday and his friend Miss Eells, who readers first met in *The Treasure of Alpheus Winterborn,* make a welcome return in *The Dark Secret of Weatherend.* This time the offbeat duo is pitted against the son of the late J. K. Borkman. The younger Borkman is an evil wizard who is trying to destroy humanity by causing savage weather conditions. To stop Borkman, Anthony and Miss Eells must violate the elder Borkman's spooky crypt. The resulting terror is pure Bellairs. Anthony and Miss Eells may not be the memorable characters that John Dixon and Professor Childermass are in *The Mummy, the Will, and the Crypt,* but they're no slouches either. Readers will relish this one and they will be sorry to see it end.

Kirkus Reviews

SOURCE: A review of *The Dark Secret of Weatherend,* in *Kirkus Reviews,* Vol. LII, No. 6, May 1, 1984, p. 36.

Some of Bellairs' recent sorcery/mystery-adventures (e.g., *The Curse of the Blue Figurine*) have made the characters as important as the spookery. Here, however, the accent is on a wild, ghoulish plot, even if the laconic narration and wry dialogue keep things from getting heavy or morbid. As in *The Treasure of Alpheus Winterborn,* Bellairs' hero is 14-year-old Anthony Monday, growing up in mid-1950s rural Minnesota—with lots of moral support from elderly librarian Miss Eells, his best friend. And the trouble begins when Miss Eells, fending off the boredom of a temporary assignment to a dead "hick town" branch, leads Anthony on a hike to the abandoned Weatherend estate of "major fruitcake" J. K. Borkman: Anthony finds the late Mr. Borkman's handwritten memoirs—all about his apocalyptic ideas on weather-control magic—under some rotting boards. Could there be a link, then, between crazy Borkman and the bizarre weather that soon starts afflicting Minnesota? Anthony thinks so; Miss Eells disagrees. ("You're making a big fat hairy mistake.") But what about the sudden arrival of Borkman's creepy, bearded son Anders—who secretly hypnotizes Anthony and Miss Eells into some highly strange behavior? (Miss E. goes berserk at a prim library tea.) Isn't it obvious that Borkman Jr. "is a cold-blooded fanatic who will stop at nothing to carry out the ghastly plans of his maniac father?" It is indeed. So, with help from Miss E.'s lawyer-

brother Emerson, Anthony and Miss E. launch an attack on Weatherend—only to find themselves repelled by homocidal leaves and other occult forces. Then, determined to learn the Borkman family secrets, they set off for a cemetery in Duluth (the resting place of Borkman Sr.). And finally, after contending with Borkmanesque obstacles along the way (blizzards, shape-shifting goblins), they invade the Borkman tomb and have a creepy showdown with Borkman Jr.—a non-human entity who is handily destroyed (by not-very-persuasive forces). Anthony is less three-dimensional here than he was in his debut; the plot gets murky and frenetic at the close. But Miss Eells remains a no-nonsense, imperfect guardian angel-and there's a nice balance most of the way through between folksy charm and gently intense suspense.

Ethel R. Twichell

SOURCE: A review of *The Dark Secret of Weatherend,* in *The Horn Book Magazine,* Vol. LX, No. 3, June, 1984, p. 326.

A weak beginning and a galloping conclusion enclose an entertaining and satisfactorily scary tale. In a sequel to *The Treasure of Alpheus Winterborn* young Anthony Monday and his indomitable librarian friend, Miss Eells, once again tackle the mysteries and the fiendish villains to which the small town of Hoosac, Minnesota, seems unusually prone. The late J. K. Borkman's reasons for wanting to finish off the world—and incidentally his own home in Hoosac—in an apocalyptic storm are barely credible, and the impetus for Miss Eells's involvement is not entirely clear. Yet the lock-picking librarian does break into J. K.'s deserted carriage house, removes a box he has hidden there, and perhaps deserves all the devilish terror that J. K.'s son Anders doles out in the form of ghastly apparitions, a whirlwind of stinging leaves, and an unseasonable blizzard. Only by some good—and some bad—fortune and by their masterly unraveling of clues do Miss Eells and Tony arrive at J. K.'s sinister mausoleum and successfully outwit the evil Anders. The small-town setting is attractive; and if Miss Eells's actions are more spirited than logical, the story still offers engrossing entertainment.

Publishers Weekly

SOURCE: A review of *The Dark Secret of Weatherend,* in *Publishers Weekly,* Vol. 226, No. 2, July 13, 1984, p. 51.

Edward Gorey's "gravely" comic frontispiece and jacket scenes fit the spirit of the lauded tale spinner's latest thriller. Bellairs takes us back to the Midwest in 1954 and the company of best friends who never heard of a generation gap, 14-year-old Anthony Monday and Miss Eells, the unconventional librarian who defies her 68 years with derring-do. Having found *The Treasure of Alpheus Winterborn,* Anthony and Miss Eells now take on a more dangerous task: frustrating Anders Borkman, who intends to carry out his late father's scheme to visit a new ice age on Earth, wiping out erring humans and bringing forth a pure race. Anders casts spells that make Anthony and Miss Eells behave outrageously in public and she loses her job but the dynamic duo persevere, conquering the demon at last. This is a lusty, fast, witty and intricate entertainment.

Carol D. Stevens

SOURCE: A review of *The Dark Secret of Weatherend,* in *Fantasy Review,* Vol. 7, No. 9, October, 1984, p. 41.

The category of fantastic thriller in which supernatural forces intrude into everyday life is perhaps best typified for adult readers by the novels of Charles Williams, for younger audiences by those of Madeleine L'Engle. John Bellairs brings back two characters from an earlier novel in a work reminiscent of Williams and L'Engle which also manages to retain a strong individuality of style.

The hero, Anthony Monday, is a fourteen-year-old with a fondness for red leather caps, mystery novels, and his best friend, Miss Eells, an eccentric librarian who drives an ancient Dodge. They uncover a plot by the evil Anders Borkman to destroy the world by sorcerous manipulation of the weather. The two must, of course, do battle.

Wit, courage, occult knowledge, and Roman Catholic ritual blend pleasingly in a well-plotted juvenile with interesting characters, and if the ending is a bit tidy, it is also satisfying.

Susan Levine

SOURCE: A review of *The Dark Secret of Weatherend,* in *Voice of Youth Advocates,* Vol. 8, No. 1, April, 1985, pp. 46-7.

Fourteen-year-old Anthony Monday and Miss Eells, a librarian, discover the old diary of J. K. Borkman, a dead eccentric millionaire, when they trespass on his estate, Weatherend. Borkman was interested in weather and his diary reveals his goal of using weather to cleanse the world of present life. At first they think it is nonsense. However, after they meet Borkman's sinister son and strange violent weather occurs, they realize that it is up to them to save the world.

Anthony and Miss Eells, previously appearing in *The Treasure of Alpheus Winterborn,* are delightful characters. There is good use of humor, especially Miss Eells' clumsiness. The suspense builds up well to a satisfying ending.

📖 THE SPELL OF THE SORCERER'S SKULL (1984)

Barbara Elleman

SOURCE: A review of *The Spell of the Sorcerer's Skull,* in *Booklist,* Vol. 81, No. 4, October 15, 1984, p. 303.

Johnny's friend, Professor Childermass, who joined the boy in two other Bellairs tales of the supernatural, (*The Curse of the Blue Figurine,* . . . and *The Mummy, the Will, and the Crypt,* . . .) has suddenly disappeared. A haunted dollhouse and a threatening, lighted jack-o'-lantern, seemingly small clues, provide the only leads. Johnny is determined, however, and, marshalling his friends Fergie and Father Higgins, he heads for a deserted island off the coast of Maine. There, after several plot twists and turns, they ferret out the truth about an ancestral curse and rescue the professor from its evil enchantment. Bellairs' supernatural flair grows more effective with each novel, but his plots grow more complex. Readers who enjoy chilling, nonstop tension and are willing to suspend their disbelief until the conclusion will find this offering another macabre delight.

Kirkus Reviews

SOURCE: A review of *The Spell of the Sorcerer's Skull,* in *Kirkus Reviews,* Vol. LII, Nos. 18-21, November 1, 1984, pp. 93-4.

The third, least compelling adventure for Johnny Dixon—the 1950s boy-hero of *The Curse of the Blue Figurine* and *The Mummy, the Will, and the Crypt.* This time Johnny and Professor Childermass take a vacation trip up to a country inn in New Hampshire, where the Prof immediately spots an unusual shelf clock that was stolen from his ancestral home some years ago: the bottom half of the clock contains a dollhouse room, a replica of the Victorian parlor wherein Prof. Childermass' great-uncle died in a bizarre fashion. Furthermore, during the night, Johnny sees the dollhouse room come to life (!); a tiny skull, from a shelf within the mini-room, falls out of the dollhouse; and Johnny, under some of odd compulsion, secretly pockets this creepy talisman. Unsurprisingly, then, strange things start happening once Johnny and the Prof return to Duston Heights, Mass. A jack-o'-lantern mirage keeps appearing at the windows of the Professor's house. Then the Prof vanishes—appearing to Johnny only in a mirror-vision (mouthing *"Help me"*), leaving behind a few tiny clues. So, with pal Fergie and Catholic priest Father Higgins, Johnny starts on a sleuthing trail after the Professor; the clues eventually lead to a clock museum, a cemetery chapel, and a demon-possessed Professor—all on an island off the Maine coast. And the drawn-out, rather murky finale involves a book of black magic and a vengeful spirit (out to destroy the Professor because of a long-ago crime), with the devil-fighting powers of the True Cross and the Latin church Mass finally saving the day. Throughout, in fact, this thick occult stew is dubiously flavored with Catholic rites and totems—including a prayer to St. Anthony that produces a miraculous clue. ("It was possible that St. Anthony or some higher power had spoken.") More important, while Bellairs turns up the supernatural heat here, he leaves the characters almost entirely undeveloped: Johnny's home-life problems (father in Korea, mother dead, grandmother ill) barely get a mention this time, and there's little pizzazz in the supporting cast. A disappointing follow-up, then, but brightly inventive enough (especially in the creepy dollhouse notion) to provide a new chill or twist every few pages.

Drew Stevenson

SOURCE: A review of *The Spell of the Sorcerer's Skull,* in *School Library Journal,* Vol. 31, No. 4, December, 1984, p. 100.

Is there no end to the suspense John Bellairs can create? If *The Spell of the Sorcerer's Skull* is any indication, the answer is a resounding *no!* Young Johnny Dixon, from *The Mummy, the Will, and the Crypt* etc., is back, but this time he is not teamed up with eccentric but lovable Professor Roderick Childermass, Ph.D. That's because the old professor has mysteriously disappeared. Johnny seeks the help of another marvelous character, Father Higgins. The two "ghostbusters" are joined by Johnny's good buddy Fergie for a trip to Cemetery Island off of the barren coast of Maine. It is there that the professor is found and, though he is under a spell, his rescue engineered. Gradually the pieces of the bizarre puzzle are pieced together, and an old vendetta is, if not laid to rest, at least neutralized. Few writers can draw readers into a plot as quickly and smoothly as Bellairs. His stories are imaginative, exciting and literate. His characters are complex and memorable. This is among his best and that's really saying something!

Allene Stuart Phy

SOURCE: A review of *The Spell of the Sorcerer's Skull,* in *Fantasy Review,* Vol. 8, No. 3, March, 1985, p. 20.

Just as adults used to expect their "Christie for Christmas" as one of the special treats of the season, young readers from the fourth grade on, and possibly their parents as well, may come to feel they deserve each year the pleasure of a new Johnny Dixon adventure. Written with warmth and literary flair, this third volume lives up to the expectations created by *The Curse of the Blue Figurine* and *The Mummy, The Will, and The Crypt.* Professor Childermass, young Johnny's delightfully eccentric neighbor and chum, is this time in deep trouble with the forces of darkness. A sinister dollhouse is found, containing a miniature replica of a room where the professor's great-uncle was brutally murdered. Johnny makes the mistake of taking a tiny ivory skull from the dollhouse, not knowing what is clearly evident to the reader, that the skull has evil powers.

Bellairs is a master at creating mood and atmosphere, though this volume has less period flavor, and even less wit, than the first two books in the series. The suspense is sustained by mysterious disappearances and chases through deserted islands in Maine. Evil forces are, as always in Bellairs' books, very real, though they can be contained by benevolent priests and holy relics. No reader is disappointed by thin "rationalistic" explanations in the last chapter. Children and adults who have not lost their youthful zest can share this book, which is highly recommended for personal and public libraries.

David Bennett

SOURCE: A review of *The Spell of the Sorcerer's Skull,* in *Books for Keeps,* No. 44, May, 1987, p. 22.

This piece of gothic bewitchery should leave its readers fairly breathless by the time they get to the end. It has enough *Boy's Own* B-movie awfulness to make it quite appealing if taken with a massive sack of salt—strictly to ward off the evil you understand!

Goings on in Professor Childermass's ancestral past puts the old codger into danger from the revengeful spirit of one Warren Windrow, who'd tried to kill Great Uncle Lucius, with good cause, I might add. It takes young Johnny Dixon, his sceptical friend Fergie and the doughty Father Higgins to save the day . . . just on the stroke of midnight, naturally!

THE REVENGE OF THE WIZARD'S GHOST (1985)

Ruth Reutter

SOURCE: A review of *The Revenge of the Wizard's Ghost,* in *School Library Journal,* Vol. 32, No. 3, November, 1985, p. 80.

Once again, Johnny Dixon is supernaturally possessed and it's up to eccentric Professor Childermass to rescue him from evil forces. The professor enlists the aid of Johnny's friend Fergie in a desperate search which climaxes in a confrontation with an evil wizard's spirit in a spooky churchyard and an exorcism. This story is only mildly scary, and the plot bears an uncomfortably close resemblance to Bellairs' earlier *The Curse of the Blue Figurine.* Many characterizations are not fully developed, with the notable exception of the lovably cantankerous Professor Childermass. Unfortunately, his comic foil, timid Johnny, is in a coma for the better part of the book. Definitely not one of Bellairs' best, but above average entertainment for young readers, and as usual, Bellairs skillfully incorporates educational tidbits into his narrative.

Ilene Cooper

SOURCE: A review of *The Revenge of the Wizard's Ghost,* in *Booklist,* Vol. 82, No. 5, November 1, 1985, pp. 400-01.

The Windrow curse against the Childermass family, introduced in *The Spell of the Sorcerer's Skull,* returns in this fourth adventure about Johnny Dixon, Byron "Fergie" Ferguson, and Professor Childermass. This time Warren Windrow's ghost possesses Johnny's body. It is up to Fergie, Father Higgins, the Professor, and his friend

Professor Coote to pool their resources to save the boy. When Professor Coote develops a theory that the occult power of the Windrows might be associated with the enchanted Urim and Thummim thought to be lost with the Ark of the Covenant, Fergie and Professor Childermass set out to search the deserted Windrow mansion for the objects of power. Once again, Bellairs creates a gothic spine-chiller, filled with suspense, witty dialogue, and unique characters whose otherwise mundane lives become caught up in incredible events. Bellairs' skillful plot weaving transforms the incredulous into intrigue and fun.

THE EYES OF THE KILLER ROBOT (1986)

Kirkus Reviews

SOURCE: A review of *The Eyes of the Killer Robot,* in *Kirkus Reviews,* Vol. LIV, No. 17, September 1, 1986, p. 1368.

"Johnny gasped in terror—the man had no eyes. Streaks of blood ran down from empty black sockets. 'They took my eyes,' the man moaned."

Johnny Dixon and his friends Fergie and Professor Childermass return in a shivery but contrived adventure involving magic, madness, vengeance and sundry felonies. Some 50 years ago, one Evaristus Sloane had built a robot powered by a spell that required human eyes; now he and his evil wife have constructed another, and fixed on Johnny as the intended organ donor. Quick pacing, plus a thick frosting of standard scary ingredients—forebodings, apparitions, anonymous harassment, a supposedly-empty house, secret rooms and secretive villagers, etc.—make this story palatable, but a very heavy dose of coincidence keeps it from being very nourishing.

As usual, Bellairs leads his readers through a twisty plot, but the twists are disappointingly convenient and predictable.

Drew Stevenson

SOURCE: A review of *The Eyes of the Killer Robot,* in *School Library Journal,* Vol. 33, No. 2, October, 1986, p. 169.

Johnny Dixon and Professor Childermass, along with their friend Byron "Fergie" Ferguson, are back in another imaginative chiller. Here the three are pitted against Evaristus Sloane, an insane wizard and inventor. But even more frightening than Sloane is a robot he invented some 50 years before. The robot was built to look like a baseball player and to pitch balls, but the Professor, Johnny, and Fergie discover a much darker side to the mechanism. After finding the dismantled robot in an abandoned house, the Professor reassembles it. But after placing its eyes back in the empty sockets, the Professor realizes too late that he has resurrected a killer machine. Not only must the robot be stopped but also its mad inventor before

Johnny loses his eyes and his life to a terrifying scheme. As always, Bellairs skillfully runs a current of evil just beneath the surface of the commonplace. The supernatural is mixed with the ordinary so effortlessly and so naturally as to make even the most bizarre people and situations seem possible in a very unsettling way. A unique plot, marvelous characters, and non-stop suspense make for deliciously wicked fun.

Denise M. Wilms

SOURCE: A review of *The Eyes of the Killer Robot,* in *Booklist,* Vol. 83, No. 3, October 1, 1986, p. 267.

A fiendish robot that needs human eyes to come alive is the focus of suspense in this farfetched but energetic fourth story about Johnny Dixon and Professor Childermass. The robot is a figure from out of the past who mystified locals of its time—including Johnny's grandfather—with its stunning baseball pitching abilities. But Johnny's ball-playing grandfather nixed his team's acquiring the humanoid and thereby earned the enmity of its creator. Now the aged inventor has targeted young Johnny to supply the eyes of an improved version, and it's up to Professor Childermass and friend Fergie to figure out the devilish scheme and rescue Johnny from certain doom. While earlier Bellairs books displayed an appealing naïveté and straightforwardness to the writing style, here the author occasionally sounds amateurish. Weak writing undermines the plot, and some readers may find themselves wavering in their willing suspension of disbelief. For horror fans and those who enjoyed other books in this series.

Chuck Hodgson

SOURCE: A review of *The Eyes of the Killer Robot,* in *Fantasy Review,* Vol. 10, No. 3, April, 1987, pp. 44-5.

Mix necromancy with antique robotics, salt with ratiocination, sugar with superstition, season with a crusty old caricature, pour into a mystery-thriller mold over one near-sighted adolescent scapegoat, and boil the pot: behold, another tasty entertainment for the YA market!

Formula, yes, but Bellairs, after four other such novels for teenagers, still has a knack with the recipe; at least, he kept me flipping pages contentedly for three hours. The story centers on Johnny Dixon, whose grandfather was once a star pitcher for the Duster Heights Spiders. Through his neighbor Professor Childermass, Johnny learns that a crazy inventor had once vowed revenge against his grandfather for stopping the sale of a robot pitcher to the team. The prospect of humiliating slugger Cliff Bullard, who has offered $10,000 to anyone who can strike him out, sends Johnny, his friend Fergie, and the professor in search of the antique robot, since legend has it that the old contraption could pitch a fastball at 110 mph. Surprisingly, they find the apparently harmless machine but can't figure out how it works. When the professor glues in the robot's glass eyes, it comes to life.

The villain, of course, is a mad scientist, part mechanic and part necromancer. The gothic twists of the quickly thickening plot are engaging enough; the protagonists are all amiable caricatures, while the villains don't quite terrify—but we're not out to generate nightmares. Wild rides, weird apparitions, dark cellars, last-minute rescues, are quite enough excitement, thank you. And there is, finally, a cozy denouement wherein the reader, along with the characters, can sort out unanswered questions.

No covert messages, no progressive subtext, no moralistic reinforcement, just popcorn time. If that's okay, this confection will do.

📖 *THE LAMP FROM THE WARLOCK'S TOMB* (1987)

Kirkus Reviews

SOURCE: A review of *The Lamp From the Warlock's Tomb,* in *Kirkus Reviews,* Vol. LVI, No. 10, May 15, 1988, p. 758.

In a sequel to *The Treasure of Alpheus Winterborn* and *The Dark Secret of Weatherend,* Anthony Monday, his best friend Miss Eells (an elderly librarian), and her brother (described with some truth by the villain as a "rabbity little know-it-all") defeat the powers of evil—as invoked by an antique dealer who has stolen a magic lamp set up as part of the "bell, book, and candle" charm.

Half-mockingly using the colloquial style made familiar in such series books as the Nancy Drew stories, Bellairs keeps the action moving right along; but there are few surprises in the occasional sightings of a hooded figure, the midnight helicopter ride, or the climactic capture, threat, and escape. The wooden characters are right out of stock and gratuitously unlikely—Anthony, alleged to be a high-school student, seems more like a 12-year-old; Miss Eells' chief professional task is "reorganizing" her card catalog, and she casually clips historic newspapers and rips up old books in order to search for clues.

Entertaining, possibly, but too predictable to hold much suspense.

Ruth Sadasivan

SOURCE: A review of *The Lamp From the Warlock's Tomb,* in *School Library Journal,* Vol. 35, No. 9, June-July, 1988, pp. 100-01.

Miss Eells, the spinster librarian from Hoosac, unsuspectingly buys an antique lamp, which, when lit, unleashes mysterious evil forces. With the help of her young friend, schoolboy Anthony Monday, and her scholarly brother Emerson, she discovers a connection between the lamp and the tomb of the eccentric Willis Nightwood, a dabbler in the black arts. Eventually, the three of them realize that the only way to destroy the dangerous evil forces is to confront them at their source: the Nightwood mansion, located outside a small, isolated Wisconsin town. This addition to the series about Anthony Monday and Miss Eells is typical Bellairs, a mildly scary story of the supernatural with a dash of mystery thrown in for good measure. While the beginning is slow, once the action starts, the narrative moves along at a rapid pace. While the story is occasionally predictable, readers, particularly Bellairs' fans, should find it engrossing.

Ilene Cooper

SOURCE: A review of *The Lamp From the Warlock's Tomb,* in *Booklist,* Vol. 84, No. 21, July, 1988, p. 1832.

Another creepy adventure featuring Miss Eells, the town librarian, and her partner in crime, teenager Anthony Monday. When Miss Eells spots an oil lamp in an antique store, she longs to have it, never guessing that the lamp is an important piece in an occult ritual devised by the late Willis Nightwood. Soon, however, both Miss Eells and Anthony realize the lamp may be responsible for a murder. This is only the beginning of the horror that ensues when the lamp falls into the wrong hands—which it promptly does. Bellairs' facility for describing horrific moments is in full flower, but the plotting is convoluted and the characterizations, at times, weak. The Edward Gorey cover will draw readers in, and the odd happenings should keep them going; fans of the series may welcome this, but it is not one of Bellairs' best efforts.

Janet Hickman

SOURCE: A review of *The Lamp From the Warlock's Tomb,* in *Language Arts,* Vol. 66, No. 2, February, 1989, p. 206.

Dedicated adventure buffs will find a fast read in this tale about a haunted lamp, an unusual tomb, and an unlikely trio of sleuths. When young Anthony accompanies his librarian friend Mrs. Eells to an antique shop, he is disturbed by the owner's eagerness to sell the old woman a Dutch lamp. Serious trouble seems to strike wherever the lamp is at rest, including the murder of Anthony's high school custodian.

The plot in this story is loaded with drama and plenty of suspense cliches, along with many fortuituous events which repeatedly save the hides of the participants. Mrs. Eells' brother Emerson, a rich and talented eccentric, involves himself in the effort to rid Dresbach, Wisconsin, of the lamp's evil spirit, and in so doing discovers an even thicker plot. A small hillside mock tomb has been robbed, releasing both the lamp and the spirit. The greedy antique dealer attempts to become the spirit of Ashtaroth when the moon is full, but she must complete a complex ritual involving the lamp, some stolen statues, and many incantations before she can succeed. Emerson, Mrs. Eells, and Anthony study the details of her wicked plot while suffering the frights of crumpling bodies, hallucinations, and anxiety. Ultimately they are successful.

Bellair's story contains light banter between the three main characters, cliff-hanging chapters and small, swift scenes of cinematic horror which will satisfy young genre lovers from grades four through six. Close scrutiny of the plot would not satisfy sophisticated readers, but the entertaining quality of the story offers polish and practice for readers just beginning to immerse themselves in the detective/ fantastic.

THE TROLLEY TO YESTERDAY (1989)

Zena Sutherland

SOURCE: A review of *The Trolley to Yesterday,* in *Bulletin of the Center for Children's Books,* Vol. 42, No. 9, May, 1989, p. 217.

Johnny (nice boy) and his pal Fergie (not-at-all-nice boy) go along with elderly Professor Childermass on a trip to Constantinople. Since their mode of travel is a trolley that functions as a time machine, their visit takes place in 1453. The story, febrile in pace, is fraught with danger and consists of a series of crises-and-escapes. For readers who like action, the concept of time travel, a bit of history larded in, and some suspense, this should appeal. It is not strong in characterization, however, and has a plethora of plot; the writing style is adequate save for overwrought dialogue.

Kirkus Reviews

SOURCE: A review of *The Trolley to Yesterday,* in *Kirkus Reviews,* Vol. LVII, No. 9, May 1, 1989, p. 686.

In his closest approach yet to self-parody, Bellairs sends an assortment of characters back in time for a series of surreal, hair-raising adventures.

Behind a bricked-up door in his old house, Professor Childermass discovers a trolley that's been modified to travel in time. He concocts a harebrained scheme to go back 500 years and save Constantinople from the Turks; his two young friends, Johnny Dixon and Byron ("Fergie") Ferguson, find him out and invite themselves along. Amidst a confusion of Turkish, Greek, and Venetian soldiers, the three meet Aurelian Townsend—the trolley's modifier—and are variously chased, captured, wounded, and miraculously healed, saved by ghosts, and forced to take a pop quiz by a menacing magic Guardian ("Name the seven kings of Rome"); they also wend their way through tunnels and fly through the air. In the climactic scene, they temporarily save a crowd massed in Hagia Sofia when the professor's snide familiar, the Egyptian god Horus (also known as Bradley), frightens the Turks away with the apparition of a huge falcon singing "The Bear Went Over the Mountain." The companions finally return to the trolley and—after a brief side-trip to a spooky future—lurch safely back to their own time.

Brace yourself for a wild, herky-jerky, tongue-in-cheek ride, not as gruesome as *Eyes of the Killer Robot,* but full of danger nonetheless.

Bruce Anne Shook

SOURCE: A review of *The Trolley to Yesterday,* in *School Library Journal,* Vol. 35, No. 10, June, 1989, p. 102.

Johnny Dixon and his old friend Professor Childermass, along with Johnny's pal Fergie, travel back to 1453, when the city of Constantinople is about to be ravaged by the Turkish invasion. The professor dreams of saving the people who have taken refuge from the Turks in the Church of Holy Wisdom (Saint Sophia) but soon finds himself and his young friends enmeshed in a series of hair-raising adventures. What these characters go through rivals the exploits of the Raiders of the Lost Ark. Aided by a talking Egyptian statue named Brewster, a magical device that enables people to fly, and some ghosts from the Crusades, Fergie and the professor bring Johnny back from near death after he is wounded by a poisoned sword. Several wild escapades later, the time travelers return to their own time. Bellairs has given readers another madcap adventure that definitely requires a willing suspension of disbelief. The coincidences alone in this story strain credulity past the breaking point, but it's all in good fun. Character development takes a back seat to the nutty plot, and first-time readers of the series may wish for more background information about Johnny and his friends. The integration of historical information into the plot makes the book more difficult than some of the earlier Johnny Dixon stories, but fans of Bellairs' unique brand of supernatural adventure story will want to read this one.

Ilene Cooper

SOURCE: A review of *The Trolley to Yesterday,* in *Booklist,* Vol. 85, No. 19, June 1, 1989, p. 1719.

In this sixth adventure featuring Johnny Dixon and his friends Fergie and Professor Childermass, the professor discovers that his house harbors a trolley that can go back in time. The three go on an excursion to Constantinople during the Turkish invasion of 1453, where the professor has dreams of reworking history and preventing a massacre, but this turns out to be harder than he thought. The trio are captured, only to run into the annoying, original owner of the trolley. As the group attempts to return home, adventures come fast and furiously. Readers will ingest a great deal of history, although in some instances this abundance overpowers the story. Still, for fans of the series, or for readers with a historical bent, this latest fantasy from Bellairs should prove entertaining.

Lucy Marx

SOURCE: A review of *The Trolley to Yesterday,* in *Voice of Youth Advocates,* Vol. 12, No. 4, October, 1989, p. 219.

Imagine a trolley car in your basement. A trolley car that

travels through time. Well, that's just what Johnny Dixon, and his friend, Fergie Ferguson discover in the basement of Johnny's neighbor, Professor Childermass. They finally persuade him to take them along on his trip 500 years in the past. They arrive in the old city of Constantinople where they are caught in the war between the Turks and the Christians.

Not only do they find the trolley's inventor trapped waiting for the trolley's return, they are chased by vandals, fly over walls, and are saved from death by ghosts. In the culminating adventure, the Professor's familiar, the Egyptian god Horus, a talking falcon head, temporarily saves the Christians at the Church of the Holy Wisdom. In doing so he almost makes the Professor's dream of rewriting history and preventing a massacre of the Christians come true. All of them finally escape and take the trolley back to their own time. This rip-roaring science fantasy adventure will appeal to the less mature young adult male readers as well as Bellairs's many fans.

CHESSMEN OF DOOM (1989)

John Peters

SOURCE: A review of *The Chessmen of Doom*, in *School Library Journal*, Vol. 35, No. 14, October, 1989, pp. 114, 116.

Professor Childermass and his young friends Johnny and Fergie are swept up in a madman's plot to rule the Earth in this latest addition to the series. Childermass stands to inherit his brother Peregrine's multimillion dollar estate, but only if he can stay on the estate all summer, plus interpret a cryptic rhyme. As usual, Bellairs salts the story with apparitions, vague warnings, deep forebodings, magic effects, tombs, corpses, and the like. The Bad Guy, Edmund Stallybrass, outwits Childermass and the boys at every turn, and finally locks them up in a burial vault and leaves them to die. Enter Crazy Annie, a local witch, who opens the vault, then in the climactic scene, confronts and kills Stallybrass in a wild play of spells and counterspells. Johnny, Fergie, and the professor don't have much to do here except rush about and explain to readers what's happening. The elements of plot and character are slapped together in an arbitrary, disjointed way that leaves plenty of unanswered questions and gaps in logic. A perfunctory outing from an author who has done much better in the past.

Denise Wilms

SOURCE: A review of *The Chessmen of Doom*, in *Booklist*, Vol. 86, No. 6, November 15, 1989, p. 657.

Johnny Dixon and his friend, Professor Childermass, are back again. The pair . . . face further occult adventures that begin when the professor receives a letter from Peregrine, his recently deceased brother, promising him a $10 million inheritance if he has the fortitude to spend

the summer at Peregrine's estate and clean it up without paid help. With the note is a cryptic poem that neither the professor nor Johnny can comprehend. Upon arriving at the remote mansion, Johnny, his friend Fergie, and the professor find strange and scary doings that turn out to be the work of a villainous magician who is perfecting a magical scheme to destroy the world. The story unfolds briskly and relatively smoothly—without the rough edges that have marred some of the other Johnny Dixon stories. The few ghoulish touches aren't overdone, and goodness triumphs satisfyingly over evil. Thoughts of a sequel aren't unwarranted, since the conclusion leaves the door open a crack for further adventures. Bellairs fans should welcome this one.

Kirkus Reviews

SOURCE: A review of *The Chessmen of Doom*, in *Kirkus Reviews*, Vol. LVII, No. 3, December 1, 1989, p. 1744.

With the jacket and a frontispiece by Edward Gorey, Bellairs' seventh book—about Johnny Dixon and the ever-cranky Professor Roderick Childermass—features a British villain who conjures up dark forces to advance his plans to take over the world.

Professor Childermass learns that his brother Peregrine is dead, and with this news comes a riddle with a definite doomsday cast. Further, simply by spending the summer at his brother's Maine estate, the professor can inherit ten million dollars. He takes on the task, accompanied by his two young friends Johnny and Fergie—but none of them lasts the summer. An evil visitor to the estate, Mr. Stallybrass, who has in his possession a chess set of dwarflike pieces, uses black magic to foil the inheritance. He nearly succeeds in putting the deep freeze on the professor, Dr. Coote (an expert on magic and the occult), Johnny, and Fergie. Only a serendipitous meeting with an old witch who collects keys saves them—and the world as well.

Only die-hard fans, enchanted by the previous books, will find solace and entertainment here. Incredible lapses of logic (the professor arrives at idea after idea without the least clue for readers as to his motives or his thinking processes) are shortcuts to long-winded passages that rush over crucial details and events. Formerly riveting characterizations have become, in this book, stock types. Thanks to the professor and Johnny, it's not the end of the world—but perhaps it should be the end of this formulaic series.

Barbara Evans

SOURCE: A review of *The Chessmen of Doom*, in *Voice of Youth Advocates*, Vol. 12, No. 6, February, 1990, p. 369.

Bellairs has written another exciting mystery starring Johnny Dixon and Professor Childermass. When his brother Peregrine dies, Professor Childermass receives a strange riddle in the terms of his brother's will. The will states that the professor must spend the summer at Peregrine's

Back cover illustration for The Lamp from the Warlock's Tomb, *written by John Bellairs. Illustrated by Edward Gorey.*

estate or forfeit the inheritance. Knowing that his brother dabbled in sorcery, Professor Childermass invites Johnny and Johnny's friend Fergie to join him in solving the riddle. Arriving at the mansion, the Professor and boys immediately begin to discover odd things taking place. Unusual symbols, missing chessmen, a strange man with stranger powers, and comets flashing through the sky provide the reader with a fast-paced, exciting story. It makes an excellent read-aloud story.

SECRETS OF THE UNDERGROUND ROOM (1990)

Kirkus Reviews

SOURCE: A review of *The Secret of the Underground Room,* in *Kirkus Reviews,* Vol. LVIII, No. 23, December 1, 1990, p. 1668.

A disappointing addition to a popular series: Much-loved Father Higgins falls prey to the evil spirit of a powerful knight, Masterman. Determined to awaken five of his fellow knights, who exchanged their souls for power centuries ago, Masterman uses Higgins's body to steal what he needs. Trying to intervene, the professor, Johnny Dixon, and Fergie follow the helpless priest to England and

then on to one of the Channel Islands where the knights lie hidden underground.

Though this is presumably tongue-in-cheek, like the rest of the series, the style grows wearisome here, burdened by too many hackneyed phrases and too much stilted dialogue and deprived of not only characterization but humor. Additional copies of Bellair's earlier titles would be a better investment.

Elaine Fort Weischedel

SOURCE: A review of *The Secret of the Underground Room,* in *School Library Journal,* Vol. 37, No. 1, January, 1991, p. 88.

Once again Johnny Dixon and Professor Childermass are called upon to battle the forces of evil, this time to rescue their friend Father Higgins, who has somehow fallen into the clutches of the ghost of a medieval English knight. After reporting a series of strange and upsetting events that have happened to him in his new parish, Father Higgins disappears and the trail leads Johnny and the Professor to Glastonbury, England. There they meet the diabolical Rufus Masterman, whom the Professor recognizes as Father Higgins under the control of an evil spirit. Just how evil is soon made clear as Johnny, his friend Fergie, the Professor, and the Professor's brother Humphrey follow the few clues they have to the island of Lundy in the Bristol Channel. There, Masterman intends to locate and reanimate the bodies of five evil brother knights who sold their souls to the devil in ancient times. As usual, Bellairs moves things along briskly, with enough chills to satisfy readers not quite ready for Stephen King. Characters are drawn with broad brush strokes, and new readers will soon know as much as old fans about the irascible but wise Professor Childermass, dependable Fergie, and loyal Johnny, whose sense of duty gives him the courage to face danger.

Deborah Stevenson

SOURCE: A review of *The Secret of the Underground Room*, in *Bulletin of the Center for Children's Books*, Vol. 44, No. 6, February, 1991, p. 137.

In their latest adventure, young Johnny Dixon, Professor Childermass, and Johnny's friend Fergie follow Father Higgins to England when an evil spirit takes over the gentle cleric's body. The spirit is attempting to return to the Isle of Lundy in order to set free five more demonic knights, so Johnny, Fergie, the professor and the professor's long-lost brother (conveniently endowed with ESP and conversant with magic spells) race to save their friend and prevent the demon from completing his nasty task. In the brief and occasional moments when non-corporeal spirits appear or leave messages the writing manages to convey some spooky atmosphere, but otherwise this is a melange of tourist information about the West Country ("They drank tea and munched cream cakes covered with strawberry jam in an old-fashioned tea shop. By the time they got back to Glastonbury, it was five in the evening. As soon as they got off the bus, they went back to the church of St. John to see if Mrs. Higgins's tomb slab had been moved"), condescendingly colloquial dialogue ("Whaddaya think we oughta do?"), and an arbitrary and coincidental plot that doesn't even satisfy the reader by letting the boys be the final heroes. Lacking the zip of Bellairs' other offerings, it makes the old Stratemeyer Syndicate series, invoked by the professor himself ("Have you been reading too many Hardy Boys adventures?") seem comparative—and inexpensive—models of writerly rectitude.

Rachel Gonsenhauser

SOURCE: A review of *The Secret of the Underground Room*, in *Voice of Youth Advocates*, Vol. 13, No. 6, February, 1991, p. 349.

When their beloved friend Father Higgins begins acting strangely, finds cryptic messages, and appears without warning at their doors and windows only to disappear again, Johnny and Professor Childermass become worried. After his disappearance from his country parish, they decide he must have gone to England where his mother's

ashes lie buried, to make long overdue peace with her. It is there that their pursuit of the evil spirit invading the Father's being begins. Dr. Masterman, who is an escaped spirit of a member of the DeMarisco knight family, is apparently haunting Father Higgins. The knights were a ruthless group—a threat to all. They were buried underground but Masterman escaped. The Professor, Johnny, and Johnny's friend Fergie, joined by the Professor's brother Humphrey, attempt to free their friend and unravel the mystery surrounding Dr. Masterman in this exciting mystery. It's filled with magic and supernatural occurrences and holds the interest of the reader from the first page. Highly recommended for younger YAs as well as mystery buffs. It is easily read and concisely written.

THE MANSION IN THE MIST (1992)

Publishers Weekly

SOURCE: A review of *The Mansion in the Mist*, in *Publishers Weekly*, Vol. 239, No. 22, May 11, 1992, p. 73.

Working as a library assistant in a sleepy town, Anthony Monday is having quite a different summer than he expected. While on vacation with his elderly friends Mr. and Miss Eells, the young man has discovered a passage into another dimension; the three are transported to an underworld by way of a magic chest. When they learn of a plot by the evil inhabitants to absorb humanity into their world, Anthony and his friends get a lot more excitement than they bargained for. Hampered by characters that do little but react predictably to their circumstances, the story must rely on its plot and concept for interest. While the notion of passage into another world is not new, the late Bellairs provides unique twists, as the characters must discover the keys to entry after their original passage is destroyed. Some readers will be caught up in the idea of inter-dimensional travel but others will feel, as these characters do, that they're just along for the ride and may not involve themselves along the way.

Bruce Anne Shook

SOURCE: A review of *The Mansion in the Mist*, in *School Library Journal*, Vol. 38, No. 6, June, 1992, p. 112.

Anthony and his klutzy librarian friend, Miss Eells, plan to spend an uneventful summer with her brother Emerson in an isolated old cottage in Canada. Events quickly take a sinister turn when Anthony finds a mysterious old chest that turns out to be a doorway into a parallel world in which a mad group of beings are plotting the destruction of Earth. The key to their success is a magical object, the Logos cube. Unfortunately for the Autarchs, a former member of their society has realized their evil ways and hidden the cube. Anthony, Miss Eells, and Emerson experience a series of harrowing adventures as they explore the strange world of the Autarchs and search for the object so that they can save the Earth. The atmosphere throughout this adventuresome chiller is appropriately scary and the villains are certainly evil personified, but there are several loose ends. Readers never know why the Autarchs have so much interest in the Earth or why they want to destroy it. Their world is certainly a terrifying place, but its origins and purposes are never made clear. This story will attract Bellairs's fans, but it is not likely to win many new ones.

Margaret Mary Ptacek

SOURCE: A review of *The Mansion in the Mist,* in *Voice of Youth Advocates,* Vol. 15, No. 2, June, 1992, p. 106.

Anthony Monday, a 14-year-old library page, is about to face a long and boring summer when his boss/friend Miss Eells invites him to join her on vacation. Miss Eells, close to 70, plans to spend the summer with her brother Emerson at his isolated cottage on an island in northern Canada. The three are having a fine time when Anthony finds a mysterious chest that appears and disappears. He also starts hearing voices and seeing ghostly figures. Is this his imagination? He starts brooding and the Eellses are worried. Anthony discovers that the chest is the doorway to another world where evil beings are plotting Earth's destruction, and soon he and the Eellses are risking their lives.

The late Bellairs did an excellent job with mystery/fantasy for middle schoolers. His characters have a captivating charm that adds to this spellbinding adventure. Both girls and boys will want to read this. A good alternative to the Hardy Boys.

Kirkus Reviews

SOURCE: A review of *The Mansion in the Mist,* in *Kirkus Reviews,* Vol. LX, No. 13, July 1, 1992, p. 846.

"Would you enjoy living in a world lit by misty moonlight, a world where plants scream and vines try to grab you?" That's what Anthony Monday, his elderly friend Myra Eells (town librarian), and her brother Emerson discover is in store if the Autarchs—a group of hideously deformed sorcerers—have their nefarious way. It's up to the three intrepid adventurers to locate and destroy the crystal cube that's the source of the Autarchs' evil power. Throwing in plenty of conventional ingredients (ghosts, illusions, cryptic clues, secret passages, magic amulets, a witches' sabbath, cliffhangers, last-instant rescues, etc.), Bellairs dishes up a broth spiced with action, suspense, and his usual heap of lucky coincidences. More digestible than some of the author's recent offerings, with all three main characters taking active roles.

Kay Weisman

SOURCE: A review of *The Mansion in the Mist,* in *Booklist,* Vol. 88, No. 22, August, 1992, p. 2010.

Bellairs' young hero Anthony Monday joins librarian Ms.

Eells and her brother, Emerson, for a summer vacation on a remote island in northern Canada. The old cottage where the three stay contains a strange chest that can transport them to a parallel world run by a maniacal group of men intent on controlling the universe. The men have misplaced an object called the Logos Cube; whoever finds it will possess the power to destroy the earth. As usual, the scatterbrained Ms. Eells assists with her excellent research skills, and Anthony saves the day with his common sense and intelligence. Unfortunately, the plot unfolds very slowly, over the course of several months and many pages; not until the last three chapters do readers experience the spine-tingling suspense for which Bellairs is noted. Not the author's best effort, although true fans will be forgiving.

THE GHOST IN THE MIRROR (1993)

Kay Weisman

SOURCE: A review of *The Ghost in the Mirror,* in *Booklist,* Vol. 89, No. 12, February 15, 1993, p. 1059.

Bellairs' latest scary thriller features 14-year-old Rose Rita Pottinger and good witch Mrs. Zimmermann, who were last seen in *The Letter, the Witch, and the Ring.* Spurred on by a mirrored vision of her mentor, Mrs. Zimmermann, accompanied by Rose Rita, travels to Pennsylvania in hopes of regaining her lost magical powers. While driving through a tunnel, the two are mysteriously transported back in time to 1828, where they meet the Weiss family. The travelers must stop an evil sorcerer before he destroys the Weisses and steals a treasure buried on their farm. Although completed by Strickland after Bellairs' death, the story has not suffered. Careful plotting, fascinating details about the nineteenth-century Pennsylvania Dutch, and gripping suspense (several scenes, especially one in which Rose Rita appears trapped in a cemetery full of emerging corpses, ought not to be read alone late at night) make this one of Bellairs' best.

Connie Tyrrell Burns

SOURCE: A review of *The Ghost in the Mirror,* in *School Library Journal,* Vol. 39, No. 3, March, 1993, p. 196.

This novel, published posthumously and finished by Brad Strickland, a longtime Bellairs fan, returns readers to New Zebedee, Michigan—but only briefly. Rose Rita Pottinger, 14, and white witch Mrs. Zimmermann, are transported through time from a warm summer day in 1951 to a snowy 1828 while on a trip to the Pennsylvania Dutch country. The purposes of the trip are to set right a great wrong; help the ghost of Mrs. Zimmermann's mentor, Granny Wetherbee; and restore the witch's lost powers. The novel has much that will appeal to pre-Stephen King fans: magic mirrors, spells, erupting graves, crystals, secret writing, buried treasure. The masterful and believable mix of the everyday and the bizarre, of comfort and terror, that is the author's signature, is evident in this newest offering. Bellairs's sense of timing, creation of atmosphere, and development of wonderfully eccentric characters make this story a sure success.

Kirkus Reviews

SOURCE: A review of *The Ghost in the Mirror,* in *Kirkus Reviews,* Vol. LXI, No. 5, March 1, 1993, p. 296.

It seems only appropriate that death has not brought an end to Bellairs's career; and; happily, this posthumous collaboration has less of a thrown-together feel than his last few books. Having lost most of her magic in *The Letter, The Witch and The Ring,* Florence Zimmerman travels back in time to recover it, taking along her friend Rose Rita Pottinger (14). Together, the two rescue a Pennsylvania Dutch family from an evil sorcerer, uncover an old chest of Revolutionary War gold, and activate a crystal ball that restores Mrs. Zimmerman's powers—not, of course, without negotiating plenty of cryptic instructions, apparitions, lurking evils, spells, and narrow escapes, plus a slavering demon or two. Though the deliciously ghastly climax suddenly comes to a halt so that the sorcerer can rehearse his motives and life story, the plot generally develops in a smooth and coherent fashion, driven along by a pair of active female characters.

Jennifer A. Fakolt

SOURCE: A review of *The Ghost in the Mirror,* in *Voice of Youth Advocates,* Vol. 16, No. 4, October, 1993, pp. 222-23.

As a die-hard Bellairs fan since the age of ten, it was with some trepidation that I picked up *The Ghost in the Mirror.* I experienced a mix of sadness at Bellairs's death and hope that this newest would be better than the last few. Good news! Bellairs fans will rejoice in this comfortably creepy new tale. *The Ghost in the Mirror* returns us to some wonderful characters last encountered in *The Letter, the Witch, and the Ring;* young Rose Rita Pottinger and the eccentric good witch, Mrs. Zimmermann. Brad Strickland, who is completing the manuscripts left by Bellairs, is more than faithful to the characters, and the result is a richer, warmer narrative than we have experienced in Bellairs's last several books.

The Ghost in the Mirror opens in the summer of 1951. Old friends Jonathan and Lewis Barnavelt are off vacationing in Europe, leaving Mrs. Zimmermann in a purple funk over the loss of her magic, incurred in the final battle in *The Figure in the Shadows.* She begins to hear voices and see the face of her long-dead mentor, Granny Wetherbee, in an old mirror. Granny gives instructions on how Mrs. Zimmermann can recover her magic powers, and together with Rose Rita, Mrs. Zimmermann travels to Pennsylvania—emerging unexpectedly from a mountain tunnel into the bitter winter of 1828. The pair are taken in by a Pennsylvania Dutch family, the Weisses, who have

troubles of their own. The quite evil and aptly-named Adolphus Stoltzfuss is trying, for greedy and vengeful purposes, to drive the family off their land by spreading rumors that their benevolent Grampa Drexel is not really a kindly healer, but an evil wizard. It is up to Mrs. Zimmermann to "right the great wrong" and save the Weiss family, and regain her powers in the process. When she is attacked by Stoltzfuss's black magic, however, it is Rose Rita alone who must unravel a Revolutionary War riddle, confront horrifying supernatural dangers, and put a stop to Stoltzfuss's truly demonic scheme before time runs out.

The mounting suspense and ghostly effects are nicely offset with attention to the personalities of the characters. We learn of Rose Rita's failed first dance and her anger and confusion about her changing relationship with Lewis—and about the changes in herself. *The Ghost in the Mirror* offers an enjoyable collection of characters in a nicely-realized historical setting along with plenty of classic spookiness. Readers who already enjoy Bellairs will be happily satisfied with this new addition, and excited by the possibility of seeing these well-loved characters again soon, for there is a hint that Jonathan and Lewis had an adventure of their own while away in Europe. But one does not need to have read any of the previous books. *The Ghost in the Mirror* stands alone as a good, cozy Gothic for middle readers.

THE VENGEANCE OF THE WITCH FINDER (1993)

Publishers Weekly

SOURCE: A review of *The Vengeance of the Witch-Finder,* in *Publishers Weekly,* Vol. 240, No. 28, July 12, 1993, p. 81.

Lewis Barnavelt, the plump worrywart and Sherlock Holmes aficionado last seen in *The Letter, the Witch and the Ring* is making a grand tour of Europe with crotchety Uncle Jonathan. The trip culminates with a surprise visit to their "umpteenth cousin, who-knows-how-many times removed," Pelham Barnavelt, who resides in genteel post-WW II poverty in the family seat, Barnavelt Manor. Together with his new-found English friend, Bertie (the blind son of Cousin Pelham's housekeeper), Lewis explores the overgrown maze on the manor's grounds. When they discover an ancient map—hidden, in classic Bellairs style, in the bindings of a crumbling book—the boys wend their way to the secret center of the maze, where a powerful evil force has long been imprisoned. Overweight, bookish and naturally timid, Lewis is nevertheless capable of true bravery; his endearing character, along with the novel's underlying current of melancholy, makes this much more than run-of-the-mill supernatural entertainment. Chock-full of deliciously spooky details and narrated in a voice that is as cozy as it is ornery, this tale is utterly spellbinding. Although Strickland serves him well, the late Bellairs will be greatly missed.

Kirkus Reviews

SOURCE: A review of *The Vengeance of the Witch-Finder,* in *Kirkus Reviews,* Vol. LXI, No. 16, August 15, 1993, p. 1070.

When Lewis Barnevelt and his uncle Jonathan stop over at the family manor in Sussex during a tour of Europe, Lewis accidentally releases a malevolent spirit, imprisoned since the 17th century. Later, the two are seized by the ghost of Malachiah Pruitt, a Puritan "witch-finder" defeated by a Barnevelt ancestor, now back for revenge. The atmosphere and supernatural effects here are particularly eerie, even for Bellairs; beyond the usual nightmares, portents, apparitions, and peculiar old documents, Lewis must contend with being hustled off to a hidden torture chamber and a vicious invisible monster, and barely escapes a maze with twigs that grasp like fingers and bleed when broken. With the help of Bertram, a blind friend, plus a particularly potent amulet (a nail from the True Cross, no less), Lewis banishes Pruitt and his monster and discovers an ancient golden crown. Formulaic, but satisfyingly hair-raising.

Ann W. Moore

SOURCE: A review of *The Vengeance of the Witch-Finder,* in *School Library Journal,* Vol. 39, No. 9, September, 1993, p. 228.

Lewis Barnavelt and his Uncle Jonathan are spending the summer of 1951 vacationing in Europe. A side trip to their ancestral home in the English countryside acquaints the boy with Malachiah Pruitt who, back in the 17th century, accused Martin Barnavelt of witchcraft. In the manor's maze, Lewis and a new friend accidentally release Pruitt's evil ghost, still seeking revenge on Barnavelt, a wizard who brought about his death. After several scary scenes, Lewis saves the day and everyone lives happily ever after. Unfortunately, *Vengeance* isn't nearly as well written as Bellairs's earlier trilogy. While the characters are intriguing, the book is wordy, awkward, and plodding. Lewis has an annoying habit of saying "gimme," "yeah," "gotta," and "oughta." In addition, the story drags: there is a lengthy first-chapter digression on Sherlock Holmes, and nothing frightening happens until chapter five—with a seven-page sightseeing gap before the ghostly doings continue. Bellairs's fans will lap this up, but direct others who enjoy suspense to the earlier Lewis Barnavelt books—*The House with a Clock in Its Walls* and *The Figure in the Shadows.*

Carolyn Phelan

SOURCE: A review of *The Vengeance of the Witch-Finder,* in *Booklist,* Vol. 90, No. 4, October 15, 1993, p. 440.

This ghost story, finished by Brad Strickland after Bellairs' death, is the fourth in the series featuring Lewis Barnavelt and his magician uncle, an appealing duo who first appeared in *The House with a Clock in Its Walls.* When Uncle Jonathan takes his nephew to England to visit a distant cousin at their ancestral home, Lewis unwittingly releases a ghost who cursed his family centuries before and now threatens to destroy them. Summoning his wits and courage, Lewis saves the day. The characters may be two-dimensional, but the well-devised plot and the spooky atmosphere will please the series' many fans as well as new readers who like their mystery stories scary.

Jennifer A. Fakolt

SOURCE: A review of *The Vengeance of the Witch-Finder,* in *Voice of Youth Advocates,* Vol. 16, No. 6, February, 1994, pp. 377-78.

Hooray! Well-loved characters Lewis, and his Uncle Jonathan Barnavelt are back in this newest gem by John Bellairs, finished by Brad Strickland. Fans of Bellairs and all ghost-story lovers are in for an excitingly chilling read.

On vacation in Europe, Lewis and Uncle Jonathan make a stop in Sussex, England, to visit a distant member of the Barnavelt clan. Their Cousin Pelly is a cheerful, stringy Brit who lives alone in ancient Barnavelt Manor with his housekeeper, Mrs. Goodring, and her blind son, Bertie. Lewis and Bertie quickly become fast friends, and with Bertie's help, Lewis discovers more about the checkered history of the Manor—that it once belonged to his ancestor Martin Barnavelt, who, in 1651, was accused of witchcraft by a truly evil government witch-finder, Malachiah Pruitt. Martin discovered Pruitt's demonic plans, and managed to undo them in time to save himself from execution. Hidden in the back of the volume of Martin's history, Lewis finds an old map, and, deciding that no self-respecting protégé of Sherlock Holmes could ignore such a mysterious adventure, he and Bertie—playing Watson to Lewis's Holmes—decide to follow it. The map leads them to the barren heart of the Manor's overgrown hedge maze where they uncover an ominous tomb—and accidentally loose a terrible evil. The maze comes to life and a frantic run saves Lewis and Bertie for the moment, but the damage is done; the ghost of Malachiah Pruitt has returned, and wants his revenge on the Barnavelt family. Eerie things start to happen, portents of the evil swiftly building around the Manor. Cousin Pelly takes a decidedly sinister turn; Mrs. Goodring acts as if hypnotized; Uncle Jonathan disappears, and Lewis finds that it is up to his quick wits alone to save his friends.

The Vengeance of the Witch-Finder supplies a good ghostly dose of Gothic chills that tingle the imagination in a way that the surplus of gore horror that is currently on the market does not. The increasing suspense and the atmospheric creepiness of the traditional dilapidated English mansion are nicely woven together. It is also a treat to see these particular characters again and watch Lewis develop self-confidence as he attempts to adopt the role of his fearless hero Sherlock Holmes, and form a friendship with Bertie. The historical setting is a neat melding of post-WW II England with the era around the English

Civil War and a dash of Victorian times thrown in for spice. *The Vengeance of the Witch-Finder* is an exciting, fast read, and a fine ghost story for young, and middle readers.

Additional coverage of Bellairs's life and career is contained in the following sources published by Gale Research: *Contemporary Authors*, Vols. 21-24, 133; *Contemporary Authors New Revision Series*, Vols. 8, 24; *Major Authors and Illustrators for Children and Young Adults*; and *Something about the Author*, Vols. 2, 68.

Fiona French
1944-

English author and illustrator of picture books; reteller.

Major works include *The Blue Bird* (1972), *King Tree* (1973), *Snow White in New York* (1986), *Rise, Shine* (1989; U.S. edition as *Rise & Shine*), *Anancy and Mr. Dry-Bone* (1991).

INTRODUCTION

A popular creator of picture books for primary graders and retellings for older children, French is widely celebrated for the artistic appeal of her works, stories drawn largely from folk tales, fairy tales, and myth. Drawing from a variety of sources that range from the stories of Cinderella and Snow White to tales from Africa, China, and Egypt, French is credited with taking a distinctive and original approach to her sources. "By steeping herself in the cultures or period content of her picture books," notes Margaret R. Marshall, "Fiona French produces not only authentic detail but an almost tangible atmosphere, a feat perceivable in her gloriously rich illustrative style and in the entirely suitable economy and relevance of the texts. . . . [There are] masterly relationships between the visual and verbal concepts of each book." French generally addresses themes common to those found in myth and classic stories for children: the triumph of good over evil, of truth over falsehood, of the humble over the proud. As an illustrator, she has sought to capture the mood, period, and cultural background of her subjects by manipulating colors, tones, patterns, and a number of artistic styles in harmony with her carefully researched, detailed settings. Her illustrations have been lauded emphatically and enthusiastically by a wealth of commentators who are nearly unanimous in their favorable estimation of her art. She has been commended in particular for employing techniques that heighten the drama and suspense of her books: in some, she uses color sparingly until the climax of the story, which is painted boldly for an effective contrast; in others, she shadows characters or settings just prior to the climatic scene, which is comparatively flooded with vivid, lively detail. Nevertheless, there has been some concern about the effectiveness of her works in reaching their intended audience. Critics state that while young children may be entertained by French's pictures, they will likely miss entirely the subtle, humorous interplay between text and illustration that is often central to the substance of her stories. These commentators further note that the humor characterizing French's contemporized adaptations of traditional fairy tales, as for instance that which informs *Snow White in New York,* can be appreciated only by older readers. It is for this reason that Marcus Crouch, in a review of *Snow White in New York,* referred to French's effort as "pure and delightful self-indulgence." However, Crouch has also described French

as "a picture book artist of the first rank"; Sarah Ellis adds: "In the early '70s I started to look at picture books for the first time since childhood and was smitten with the ebullient colours and bold design of the British picture books of the period—with Brian Wildsmith, Victor Ambrus, Charles Keeping, and above all, Fiona French. French's output has not been prolific, but each book reveals a unique vision, and a new offering from her is a welcome event."

Biographical Information

French was born in Bath, Somerset, England, but grew up mostly in Devon and Surrey. She was sent to an English convent school while her family lived in the Middle East, although she was permitted to visit Lebanon and Iran briefly. French was interested in art, history, geography, and literature, attending Croyden College of Art, Surrey, from 1961 to 1966 and earning a diploma in painting and lithography. She was first employed as a teacher of art therapy for children at Long Grove Psychiatric Hospital in Epsom, England, and then as a design teacher at Wimbledon School of Art. She was later an assistant to the painter Bridget Riley and a design teacher at Leicester and Brighton polytechnics before turning to freelance illustrating. She has provided pictures for books by such authors as Oscar Wilde, Jill Paton Walsh, and Walter Dean Myers; in 1970, she wrote and illustrated her first picture book, *Jack of Hearts,* which revolves around a birthday feast for the playing-card title character.

Major Works

The detail in French's stories reveals her careful research of the settings of her books. "After about three months writing and research, and with a much clearer idea of the story, I start to do the pictures," French has related. *Matteo* (1976) is painted in the rich style of Florentine High Renaissance art; *The Blue Bird* contains the blues and whites of Wedgwood china; *Aio the Rainmaker* (1975) showcases a brightly and authentically costumed Aio performing African narrative dances; and *Snow White in New York* portrays the American jazz-era of the twenties. The text of *The Blue Bird,* set in seventeenth century China, has an oriental tone, elegant and formal, while its blue illustrations are contrasted against the white of the page like the blue and white porcelains of the K'ang-hsi's reign. In this tale, a young scholar and his neighbor, Jade, seek out an enchantress to learn why Jade's blue bird no longer sings. They discover, however, that the enchantress is evil and intends to make all birds stop singing and to turn people to stone. When the enchantress is destroyed, vibrant colors flood the pages, replacing the blue and white motif. French employs a similar manipulation of perspective in *King Tree,* a picture book about a play being held for the guests of King Louis XIV. The cast are various types of trees vying to be King of the Trees, and the ladies of the court are to choose the winner. French draws landscapes, framed in the forefront, with colors and images designed to compel the eye deeper into the pictures. She effectively contrasts this with abrupt closeups, so that the reader gets the impression that he or she is included among the guests watching the play. Both guests and players are magnificently costumed with rich, deep colors. In this and others of French's early works, critics have noted that the text, while not superfluous, does not exude the energy that distinguishes the artwork. With the publication of *Snow White in New York,* however, many commentators agreed that French had achieved a new balance, complementing her bold, creative pictures with a strong, terse text. In this contemporary version of the fairy tale, Snow White's father marries the Queen of the Underworld. Instead of being left to die in the forest, she is left in New York City, where seven jazz performers take her into their club and make her their singer. The queen poisons the cherry in Snow White's drink, but when her coffin is jostled at the funeral the cherry is dislodged from her throat and she awakens. Reviewers enjoyed French's witty storyline and her use of geometric abstractions, silhouettes, and elongated figures in her illustrations. French used similar patterns in *Anancy and Mr. Dry-Bone,* an adaptation of the trickster tale from African and Caribbean sources. She contrasted solid, mostly black and white geometric forms against pastel backgrounds.

The story is told with amusing colloquialisms and rhythms. Rich Mr. Dry-Bone and poor Anancy compete to make Miss Louise laugh; the winner gets to marry her. Anancy asks to borrow his friends' elegant clothes to impress her, but they give him only their most worn ones. French depicts Anancy in shadow at Louise's door on the page before his outfit of brilliant hues is revealed, adding suspense to the story. On the following page, Louise sees Anancy's motley outfit and bursts into laughter.

Awards

Snow White in New York won the Kate Greenaway Medal in 1986, while *King Tree* was named a Kate Greenaway commended book in 1973. *The Blue Bird* won the Children's Book Showcase award in 1973, and *Anancy and Mr. Dry-Bone* won a Parents' Choice Award in the Story Book Category in 1991.

GENERAL COMMENTARY

Books for Your Children

SOURCE: "Cover Book," in *Books for Your Children,* Vol. 7, No. 4, Summer, 1972, p. 1.

Fiona French is one of the most recent distinguished illustrators to add to the list of superbly produced full colour books that began with the work of Brian Wildsmith and Charles Keeping. As with the books of Charles Keeping however, there are those who find Fiona French's illustrations daunting. They are uncompromising in their feeling for strong design which occasionally overpowers the story and the comment, "Children don't like/understand them" arises.

It depends of course, as it always does, on which children. They are not picture books for babies, but very exciting books for seven, eight, nine year olds easily stirred by the excitement of colour and layer of mystery and violence within a formal framework inherent in each book so far. Fiona French's development as an illustrator can be seen if the books are examined in order of publication:

Jack of Hearts

A popular playing card design has been cleverly adapted and playing card people observe the conquest of knight over knight. Children with an eye and feeling for design may be inspired to make all sorts of patterns and games outside the normal use of the card pack.

Huni

Of the three books discussed here, this is the most courageous. Huni, a boy of ancient Egypt, son of the Pharaoh, must make a journey down the river of night to prove he is not afraid and is fit to wear the Crown in his turn. Egyptian colour, mainly the beautiful strident blue but also buff, red and green, seem to bring alive the Ancient Egyptian culture far more vividly than recent preoccupations with Tutankhamun in colour supplement journalism.

The Blue Bird

Here again the emphasis is on blue, but this time the blue of the willow-pattern and, as in Huni, colour seems to emphasise the book's emotional content.

Jade Lotus's beautiful blue bird stops singing so Chang Ti suggests they find the Enchantress. On their journey they help several other creatures who accompany them and when threatened by the evil of the Enchantress transform themselves to overcome it. A very satisfying story on traditional style of the triumph of courage over fear.

Margaret Carter

SOURCE: "Cover Artist—Fiona French," in *Books for Your Children,* Vol. 18, No. 3, Autumn-Winter, 1983, p. 5.

Put just four of her books in a line—*King Tree, Matteo, Hunt the Thimble* and *Future Story.* Turn the pages of each and you will find it difficult to believe they were all illustrated by the same artist. Fiona French brings a chameleon-like quality to her work, seeing through to the core of a subject and then interpreting it through dedicated research, an objective view and a wholly illuminating creative talent.

King Tree for example tells how the trees chose a king. Set in the reign of the Sun King, its colours are livid—swollen purples, sickly greens—there is menace in its extravagance and opulence. *Matteo* is Florentine: flat washed paint echoes the style of Italian tempera painting. "The picture of characters at a supper table took seven weeks to paint. I needed to get a *trompe l'oeil* effect so that the food and the table dressings stood out from their background . . ." *Hunt the Thimble* is Dutch: good-natured composed faces stare out from the deliberately foreshortened figures. French, Italian, Dutch—and there are others too, one at least painted in the hot colours of Islam, one all cool Chinese blues.

And now there is *Future Story*—a kaleidoscope of fragmented lights, prisms, geometric designs and menacing gravity-released figures which float in the colours of space.

The planet Narvis sends out a distress signal and a starship investigates to find all life on the planet already dead. But the starship crew bring back a crystal which, as the ship returns to earth, begins to activate and turn both the ship and crew into crystal. Faces pale, limbs stiffen, hair freezes . . . only a speedy return to the sun of earth can warm them back to life. Turn the page and there is salva-

tion—the burst of life-giving yellows, oranges . . . and the ship is saved. "Welcome Home."

Written like that the story is simple but "it was written—every word of it—between eight and fifteen times" Fiona says. "The story developed as I went along but there was a lot of reading to do. I found I didn't understand phrases like 'the speed of light'.

And what exactly was Einstein's theory of the Universe? Children's books helped me most—they explained everything simply."

She pays warm tribute to the editors at Oxford University Press. "A good editor seems at once to stimulate and release you. They exchange ideas with you. One becomes in a receptive frame of mind—aware of every thing. Of course the temptation to do too much research is great: research means postponing getting down to the actual 'doing'! It was a publisher's editor who taught me that you have to learn what to discard. You can't think of each picture as a thing apart—you have to think of them all as part of a whole."

Once the roughs for *Future Story* were approved, the actual paintings took only from July to December. Was such an undertaking exhausting? "Not in this case. I went straight into another book—black and white illustrations this time."

She constantly experiments with materials. "At the moment I'm working mostly in water colours but sometimes you need about four applications to get the right vibrancy. I studied under Bridget Riley who is undervalued as an artist over here but much appreciated in America. She taught me so much about colour—the juxtaposition and the gradual building up."

Fiona also works in gouache and at one time—for the illustration to the Chinese tale—in blue ink. "Sometimes you can seem to search endlessly for just the right effect. I couldn't get a satisfactory way of showing hills fading into the distance—and then I saw some paintings on china in a sale and I suddenly saw how you can get it. Then the materials one uses are all important. I've used crayons on gouache to show for example movement of crops in a field; in another picture it becomes cobwebs. The falling figures of *Future Story* were drawn separately and then placed experimentally on their background until exactly the right positions were found. And yet I heard the other day that the average life of a children's book is two years: doesn't it seem a pity that they aren't kept alive and re-issued?"

Fiona French is endlessly fascinated by her subject—and as a consequence it is endlessly fascinating to hear her talk.

Future Story is an arresting and quite novel achievement.

TITLE COMMENTARY

📖 *JACK OF HEARTS* (1970)

Margery Fisher

SOURCE: A review of *Jack of Hearts,* in *Growing Point,* Vol. 9, No. 4, October, 1970, p. 1605.

This new young artist has kept so close to the traditional court cards in story and pictures that her book does not altogether escape monotony, although she has extended the card style to jester, horses and the feast of wild boar, peacock and Paradise sauce which is proper to the medieval scene. Deducing character from the cards, she contrasts the kingdom of Hearts, where 'the sun was always shining' with the land of Spades, 'black and empty', where it was always winter; the Jacks of Hearts and Spades play hero and villain respectively in a melodrama of jousting and courtly love. A very original book.

Publishers Weekly

SOURCE: A review of *Jack of Hearts,* in *Publishers Weekly,* Vol. 198, No. 15, October 12, 1970, p. 55.

Here is a superlative imagination at work, only combined with a superlative talent the result doesn't look like work, but a joyful romp, as a fresh English author-illustrator, Fiona French, brings a pack of playing cards to life in an enchanting story of feasts and tournaments, played against the medieval splendor of the cards themselves.

Kirkus Reviews

SOURCE: A review of *Jack of Hearts,* in *Kirkus Reviews,* Vol. XXXVIII, No. 20, October 15, 1970, p. 1139.

Wherein, smartly, the playing cards play their own hands and their relative power determines who carries the day. "Remember," warns the King of Spades on Jack of Hearts' eighteenth birthday, "neither this wonderful horse, nor the strongest armour, nor the sharpest sword (presented respectively by himself, the Kings of Diamonds and Clubs), nor all the knights of Christendom can stand against the Ace of Spades." In the ensuing tourney, Diamonds and Clubs fight to a draw, Spades and Hearts likewise to the last man, the Jacks—whereupon the irate King of Spades throws down the Ace of Spades . . . and the King of Hearts covers it with the Ace of Hearts, delivering the victory to his son, henceforward "Sir Jack the bravest Heart of all." Satisfaction comes from knowing the cards, and so indeed does comprehension—the characters are the cards, for the most part, not figures extracted or abstracted from them, and against the patterned medieval backgrounds they are indistinguishable except for their insignia. Still novel, stylish and good sport: "The Jokers juggled and turned somersaults while the music played."

The Times Literary Supplement

SOURCE: "Pictures with a Purpose: Prisons and Palaces," in *The Times Literary Supplement,* No. 3583, October 30, 1970, p. 1260.

An impressive newcomer to children's books is Fiona French: *Jack of Hearts,* splendidly produced by the Oxford University Press, uses the formal designs of playing cards to stunning effect, repeating the picture cards again and again in different settings. The occasion is the Jack of Hearts's birthday; feasting and dancing are followed by a tournament in which the four suits do battle, the Jacks and their numbered knights taking the lists in turn. The Hearts defeat all comers until the King of Spades meanly intervenes, but the King of Hearts outwits him and Jack, in his new birthday armour, is dubbed "the bravest Heart of all".

The Junior Bookshelf

SOURCE: A review of *Jack of Hearts,* in *The Junior Bookshelf,* Vol. 34, No. 6, December, 1970, pp. 349-50.

Fiona French is a new artist and a very exciting one. In *Jack of Hearts* she makes dramatic use of the conventional designs of playing cards and produces a book full of gorgeous colour and strong, stiffly formal pictures. An interesting experiment and a promise of very much better things to come. Oxford are fortunate to make so unusual a discovery; Miss French is equally lucky to have her designs so supremely well presented.

The Booklist

SOURCE: A review of *Jack of Hearts,* in *The Booklist,* Vol. 67, No. 10, January 15, 1971, p. 420.

A deck of cards supplies the characters and a medieval castle the setting for a picture-book story of the eighteenth birthday of the Jack of Hearts. After the giving of gifts, a feast, entertainment by the jesters, and dancing, a tournament is held among the Jacks. Despite the trickery of the King of Spades, the Jack of Hearts wins and is dubbed, "Sir Jack, the bravest Heart of all." Interest in the book may be limited, but some children will be intrigued by the imaginative use of playing cards as characters and the eye-catching, patterned illustrations.

Patricia Vervoort

SOURCE: A review of *Jack of Hearts,* in *School Library Journal,* Vol. 17, No. 7, March, 1971, p. 119.

A contrived medieval tale based on the royal face cards of a playing deck. Once upon a time the evil King of Spades gave a splendid horse to the Jack of Hearts on his 18th birthday; however, the gift is under the curse of the Ace of Spades. The birthday festivities include a tourna-

He put her gently on the ground and she began to
dance and sing and rejoice at being alive.

From Maid of the Wood, *written and illustrated by Fiona French.*

ment in which Jack must fight the Jack of Spades and
overcome the imprecation. The illustrated royalty are tak-
en directly from playing cards. With the patterned backgrounds of brick walls, rose windows, ornately tiled floors,
and the flowered tournament field, each page becomes a
garish display of intricate designs in bright colors that
assault the eye. All in all, young listeners, who may be
confused by the power of Aces, will find the story pointless, the illustrations disconcerting.

Zena Sutherland

SOURCE: A review of *Jack of Hearts,* in *Bulletin of the
Center for Children's Books,* Vol. 24, No. 8, April, 1971,
p. 123.

A story based on the characters in a deck of cards, the
busy and colorful illustrations using the figures just as
they really appear, so that the author-artist is manipulating flat surfaces. Only when the Jacks are jousting in
armor are they shown in action, and the medieval stiffness is not inappropriate. The story is not very substan-
tial: all of the royal figures give birthday gifts to the Jack
of Hearts, the powerful King of Spades warning that
nothing can stand against the Ace of Spades. But when
the knights are jousting, and the Ace of Spades is thrown

onto the field, it is robbed of its effect (causing the horse
to rear) by being covered with the Ace of Hearts. The
King of Hearts dubs his son, "Sir Jack, the bravest knight
of all." And there the tale abruptly ends.

📖 *HUNI* (1971)

Gabrielle Maunder

SOURCE: A review of *Huni,* in *The School Librarian,*
Vol. 19, 1971, pp. 81-2.

Anyone interested in the development of children's book
illustration keeps a watchful eye on new artists emerging
from the Oxford University Press, for they are likely to
set new standards.

Fiona French has one other picture/story book to her credit,
Jack of Hearts, which used the stylized framework of a
pack of playing cards as its theme. To my taste it was too
heavy to show the artist as anything more than a clever
adaptor, but in her latest offering, Miss French, again
using a stylized form, though this time that of Egyptian
origin, seems to have found an outlet for her exuberant
colour and her bold drawing. She uses the page skilfully,
spreading brilliant peacock colours across it and combin-

ing this with a simple story, involving a small boy, Egyptian gods and goddesses complete with their fascinating animal and bird heads on human bodies. Together the singing colours, formalized drawings, and conventional legendary plot combine to make a thoroughly satisfying and stimulating addition to the picture book shelf of the seven-and-eights.

E. Hudson

SOURCE: A review of *Huni*, in *Children's Book Review,* Vol. I, No. 5, October, 1971, p. 155.

The dust has now settled on the 1970 Library Association Award winners and whether one agreed with the judges' choice or not (and how easy it was to disagree on this occasion) one thing is certain: already those whose task it is to submit their verdicts will have been looking out for those children's books which seem to them outstanding amongst the many already published and the many which will appear in the last quarter of the year. It would be quite an achievement for any illustrater to be successful with only her second picture book for children, but in *Huni* I consider that Fiona French certainly should be recommended. She created a profound impression with *Jack of Hearts* and her strong sense of colour and design shown then is linked in her new title with the inspiration of a story from Egyptian mythology:

Huni must prove himself worthy of succeeding his father as Pharaoh of Egypt and to do so must endure a journey through the Dark Kingdom of Osiris with all its perils. He succeeds in this and emerges into the daylight—the Kingdom of the Sun-god Ra—knowing that he will be fit to be king.

Fiona French's illustrations are based in style and symbolism on original Egyptian wall paintings. It is her use of colour within first class designs which makes this a picture book well above the ordinary.

M. Crouch

SOURCE: A review of *Huni*, in *The Junior Bookshelf,* Vol. 35, No. 5, October, 1971, pp. 296-97.

Fiona French follows her playing-card book with one about ancient Egypt. Huni is the Pharaoh's son, and the King sends him on a journey down the Nile as a test of his fitness to reign. His heart is weighed against a feather by Thoth and Osiris gives him a blessing to help him through the long night. At length dawn comes out of the river in the shape of a lotus flower. The gravely beautiful book is presented in traditional style, in the conventions of Egyptian wall-painting, with highly formalised and effective, even moving, designs. The book is particularly successful in its skilful gradations of colour which take the reader through day into night and out the other side again. Apparently a minority book, it may prove to have a wider following in practice.

THE BLUE BIRD (1972)

Eleanor von Schweinitz

SOURCE: A review of *The Blue Bird*, in *Children's Book Review,* Vol. II, No. 3, June, 1972, p. 73.

Fiona French has rapidly established a reputation for strongly formalised picture-book design. *Jack of Hearts* took as its visual starting point a pack of cards and *Huni* used, perhaps rather more successfully, the tradition of Ancient Egyptian wall painting. Now we have a Willow Pattern pastiche—derivative without being purely imitative.

The story uses traditional elements to tell how a tortoise, a cat and a rain dragon use their magic powers to help Jade Lotus and Chiang Ti overcome the wicked Enchantress and free the birds she has turned to stone.

The pictures have a pleasing coolness and simplicity in their use of blue wash contrasted with the white page. The design is still formal and, despite a greater fluidity in the forms, there is a heaviness and even an occasional stiffness which is characteristic of this artist's earlier work. Unfortunately the visual impact is seriously weakened by the symbolic use of form and colour in the concluding pages which fails to integrate successfully with the preceding visual sequence.

The text is rather colourless and lacks any feeling for the cadences of the story teller's voice. None-the-less this book comes closer to achieving a visual and thematic harmony than many of the more spectacular productions based on traditional sources which are flooding the picture-book market.

Kirkus Reviews

SOURCE: A review of *The Blue Bird*, in *Kirkus Reviews,* Vol. XL, No. 13, July 1, 1972, p. 721.

The journey of Chiang Ti and Jade Lotus—to ask the enchantress why their caged bird no longer sings—begins amid the blue and white serenity of a Ming porcelain landscape. In return for small acts of kindness they are joined by a tortoise, a cat and a rain dragon who help them defeat the magisterial, winged enchantress when, coveting the bird, she threatens to send a storm to destroy them all. The tortoise grows to the size of a sheltering mountain, the cat becomes large enough to devour the enchantress, and the rain dragon sends a magic shower which dissolves the evil spell and causes the landscape to bloom into a shower of neo-impressionistic foliage. The slight story serves mostly to tie together the delicate panoramas—highly stylized but handsomely stylish just the same.

Publishers Weekly

SOURCE: A review of *The Blue Bird*, in *Publishers Weekly*, Vol. 202, No. 2, July 10, 1972, p. 46.

The setting of this unusual and beautiful book is 17th century China. Jade Lotus, unhappy because her blue bird has stopped singing, asks her friend, Chiang Ti, to go with her to the "enchantress," who might solve the problem. The girl and boy set out and meet a tortoise, a cat, and a rain dragon; all the animals are in trouble and are helped by Jade and Chiang. Their friendliness is repaid when the enchantress turns out to be an evil woman, set on stopping all birds from singing and on turning the humans to stone. The full-color illustrations are based upon the porcelains of the K'ang Hsi's reign and they are a treat to the eye.

The Times Literary Supplement

SOURCE: "All the Colours of the Rainbow," in *The Times Literary Supplement,* No. 3672, July 14, 1972, p. 808.

Fiona French's **The Blue Bird,** a story set in seventeenth-century China, has many of the traditional fairy-tale trappings. Jade Lotus's beautiful blue bird refuses to sing, so she and her friend, the scholar Chiang Ti, decide to seek the help of an enchantress who is said to understand the language of birds. As they travel they befriend various animals who accompany them on their journey, and when the enchantress turns out to be a terrifying enemy with a particular hatred of birds the animals are able to help them. The story is satisfying, and the very striking Willow Pattern style of illustration demonstrates once again Fiona French's skill in working with unconstricted imagination with a rigid formal framework.

M. Crouch

SOURCE: A review of *The Blue Bird,* in *The Junior Bookshelf,* Vol. 36, No. 4, August, 1972, pp. 219-20.

Of all modern masters of pastiche Fiona French is most successful in giving the impression that her chosen manner is natural to her. This time the motifs are Chinese. Her story is full of wonders and terrors, but she maintains the gracious civilised tones of oriental scholarship throughout. The same is true of the elegant formality of her designs. Up to the climax of the story the emphasis is on blues, and only the lovely Jade Lotus brings a little delicate colour into the pictures. But when the wicked Enchantress has been destroyed, a spell is broken and colour floods the pages. A most effective device, even though the design of the last happy pages is markedly less distinguished than the earlier ones. Here is a talented artist whose head at present rules her heart. When she achieves a balance between emotion and reason she will give us an even finer book.

Kitty Ingham

SOURCE: A review of *The Blue Bird,* in *The School Librarian,* Vol. 20, No. 3, September, 1972, p. 285.

I have not seen such original use of colour as in this beautifully written and illustrated story of the blue bird, who was taken by her owner Jade Lotus to an enchantress to recover her lost singing voice. Luckily a neighbour, a tortoise, a cat and a rain dragon go too.

The tale then becomes very dramatic indeed, and colour, except for the clothes of Jade Lotus previously all blue, bursts out on all pages to match the mounting excitement of the story. Colour, drawing and story are all strong and subtle; most highly recommended for younger readers onwards.

Sidney D. Long

SOURCE: A review of *The Blue Bird,* in *The Horn Book Magazine,* Vol. XLVIII, No. 5, October, 1972, pp. 456-57.

Inspired by Chinese porcelain designs, the story tells of the journey a young scholar and his beautiful neighbor Jade Lotus make to see an enchantress, hoping to find out why Jade Lotus' bird no longer sings. The enchantress turns out to be evil; but, in true folk-tale tradition, a turtle, a cat, and a dragon, all befriended by the couple, play a part in the enchantress' destruction. The real spell of the book, however, is cast by the illustrations: Predominantly blue against white, the traditional Chinese porcelain patterns create a rarefied atmosphere of dignity and courtly romance that extends the story far beyond the simple plot line. . . .

Joan Reamer

SOURCE: A review of *The Blue Bird,* in *School Library Journal,* Vol. 19, No. 3, November, 1972, p. 58.

Cool, quiet illustrations influenced by the porcelain of K'ang Hsi's reign complement this simple tale set in 17th-Century China. To find out why her blue bird has stopped singing, Jade Lotus and Chiang Ti, a student, set out in search of the Enchantress. On their journey, they encounter and aid an overturned tortoise, a stranded cat, and a lonely rain dragon. At the palace of the Enchantress, they discover that she wickedly turns birds to stone and threatens them as well. Jade Lotus' kindnesses are repaid when her three animal companions overcome the Enchantress through magical transformations. All the birds are set free, even the blue bird who once more sings. The beautifully executed watercolor illustrations are dominated by shades of blue until the birds are freed and full color is introduced.

The Booklist

SOURCE: A review of *The Blue Bird,* in *The Booklist,* Vol. 69, No. 9, January 1, 1973, p. 448.

When Jade Lotus' bird stops singing, Jade Lotus and Chiang Ti, a young scholar, set out to consult with an

Enchantress who can understand bird language. On the way they are joined by a tortoise, a cat, and a rain dragon, all of whom prove helpful when the evil Enchantress threatens to turn the bird to stone. Inspired by seventeenth-century Chinese porcelain, the lovely, serene illustrations are primarily in shades of blue and white until the final pages where the bright, delicate colors of the drawings reflect the story's cheerful ending.

📖 *KING TREE* (1973)

The Times Literary Supplement

SOURCE: A review of *King Tree,* in *The Times Literary Supplement,* No. 3719, June 15, 1973, p. 686.

Fiona French's sumptuous picture book presents a play performed by the courtiers of Louis XIV in the gardens of Versailles. The theme is the struggle for supremacy among the different trees in the garden, from whose midst the court ladies are asked to choose a king. The richly arrayed fairy-tale figures of the actors, convincingly half-tree, half-courtier, are beautifully done, but, oddly, Miss French's hand seems less sure when she is not dealing with setpieces. However, her pictures repay close attention, yielding nice ironic touches as well as great visual pleasure.

Kirkus Reviews

SOURCE: A review of *King Tree,* in *Kirkus Reviews,* Vol. XLI, No. 13, July 1, 1973, p. 681.

French turns from the stately Chinese porcelain design of *The Blue Bird* to the elegant formal gardens of Versailles in this polished fable about the selection of a king of the trees. Though the oak, laurel, pomegranate, olive and vine all vie for the post, the ladies of the court choose the orange tree (not surprisingly, as he is the first tree to be introduced and the one who suggests that the ladies decide), for he gives fruit like the sun, fragrance from his flowers, and shelter with his leaves. If there is less wisdom in the decision than meets the eye, it is surely for the eye that the story was created. With each tree represented as a man dressed in rich and elaborate manner of the Sun King's court (the vine, for example, all in purple, with grapes for hair and a glass of wine in his hand), the result, like the setting, is both strikingly opulent and highly artificial.

From Snow White in New York, *written and illustrated by Fiona French.*

Publishers Weekly

SOURCE: A review of *King Tree,* in *Publishers Weekly,* Vol. 204, No. 5, July 30, 1973, p. 67.

For sheer opulent beauty, this book's closest rival would seem to be **The Blue Bird,** which Ms. French wrote and illustrated last year. The serious dedication to frivolity which was a feature of Versailles is the theme of **King Tree.** The ladies of the court of Louis XIV are asked to choose a ruler from among the oak, olive, laurel and other trees, including the grape vine. Each is represented in a play by a man appropriately costumed. When all have presented their cases, the ladies consider them gravely, then unanimously choose the orange tree. His fruit glows like the sun, his blossoms are fragrant and his leaves offer gentle shade. . . .

Margaret Maxwell

SOURCE: A review of *King Tree,* in *School Library Journal,* Vol. 20, No. 1, September, 1973, p. 57.

Inspired by the elaborate masques and pageants presented at the 17th-century French court of Louis XIV, Fiona French's lush illustrations recreate the splendor and artificiality of that era as courtiers act out a play in which each of them depicts a tree. The almost nonexistent plot of the play revolves around the decision over which tree is worthy of being king of the trees; after each has presented his case, the orange tree is chosen. Although the illustrations are skilfully done, few children will be interested in the extremely slight story.

Eleanor von Schweinitz

SOURCE: A review of *King Tree,* in *Children's Book Review,* Vol. III, No. 5, October, 1973, p. 138.

Fiona French's three previous picture books have each had a considerable pictorial impact but this is by far her most powerful and original work. It overwhelms the spectator with the weight of its images which add a dimension that no reading of the text would have suggested was possible.

Courtiers at the court of Louis the Fourteenth act out a masque, magnificently dressed to represent different trees. The oak, laurel, pomegranate, olive and vine boast in turn of the fabulous kingdom each would establish if chosen King of the Trees. But after all their wrangling it is the handsome young orange tree who is acclaimed by the ladies of the court.

The text is uneven, sonorous passages jostling with less happy snatches of dialogue, but the visual aspects of the book are handled with stunning confidence. Rich greens, reds and deep purples predominate and there is a dramatic use of perspective, with panoramic long shots framed by the elegant formal gardens of Versailles contrasting with sudden, looming close ups.

This sumptuous book may not prove popular with mass audiences but individuals of all ages who respond to it will have their senses stirred in a manner all too rare in the world of children's books.

Margery Fisher

SOURCE: A review of *King Tree,* in *Growing Point,* Vol. 12, No. 4, October, 1973, p. 2244.

In the artificial poses of a masque, richly costumed and firmly differentiated, trees in human form contend for a crown, with the ladies of the court as judges. The oak asserts his strength, the pomegranate his exotic taste, the laurel speaks of glory, the olive of peace, the vine of riches; the ladies choose the orange, who most resembles *Le Roi Soleil* whose court is here in beautiful disguise. Ingenious, sumptuously coloured, full of sunshine and shadow dramatically contrasted, this is visually a most striking book. The text, less striking, is sometimes so trickily inserted into the page design that it is far from easy to piece together.

M. Crouch

SOURCE: A review of *King Tree,* in *The Junior Bookshelf,* Vol. 37, No. 5, October, 1973, pp. 307-08.

Fiona French continues to be one of the most difficult of the front-ranking artists in the world. Her strange themes and her severely stylised drawings alike present obstacles to the young reader; happily they also stimulate curiosity and the determination to crack even the toughest of her nuts. *King Tree* comes straight out of the artifice and formality of the Court of Louis XIV. The trees—courtiers in masque costume—dispute the supremacy of their own world, and their ladies at length choose the orange-tree. It is all rather odd and pointless, but for the power of Miss French's richly textured designs. These straddle the big openings, presenting a picture of the Sun King's Court, its costume and architecture and its rigid conventions. The book should be a smash-hit in colleges of art, and the ultra-sensitive child may find it a moving experience.

Eleanor von Schweinitz

SOURCE: A review of *King Tree,* in *Children's literature in education,* No. 14, May, 1974, pp. 15-17.

In a disappointing year for picture books **King Tree** stands out as a powerful and original work. Cast in the form of a seventeenth century masque, acted out by magnificently costumed courtiers in the formal gardens of Versailles, this simple dramatic allegory tells how five trees compete for the title of king.

As in previous books by Fiona French the sources of inspiration are visual rather than literary—but here the choice of subject, no longer rooted in the stylized outlines of traditional art, gives wider scope to both the decorative and formal design elements that are her particular strength.

The reader's role is that of spectator, with a sequence of dramatic tableaux passing before him—a theatrical use of the page which works well since the text provides the scenario for the drama. But this is a book whose impact is due to far more than the mere excitement and brilliance of its individual illustrations; for here we see the picture book artist in complete control of her material, pacing and shaping it within a tightly-knit structure.

The composition of double-page openings is handled with absolute assurance: looming close-ups, heavily laden with colour, overwhelm the reader with their intensity; an elegant balustrade suggests an upward movement across the page; panoramic long-shots use perspectives to great effect, compelling the eye down green vistas between clipped ornamental hedges. Sumptuous colour beguiles the eye—rich reds, greens and deep purples are used to characterize the main protagonists, and this provides a linking device which reinforces the flow of images as the pages are turned.

As might be expected when author and artist are one, the text and illustrations are closely tailored to each other and there are none of those verbal superfluities or visual mismatchings which sometimes occur when a picture book artist illustrates an alien text. But, despite some sonorous passages and occasional neat balancing of phrases in the dialogue, the text lacks both the tension and confident flow of the illustrations.

Ultimately, this is a book which remains in the memory as a visual tour de force, lacking that complex and subtle interaction between text and illustration which makes the perfect picture book.

📖 *CITY OF GOLD* (1974)

M. Crouch

SOURCE: A review of *City of Gold,* in *The Junior Bookshelf,* Vol. 38, No. 4, August, 1974, pp. 201-02.

Fiona French is unquestionably a formidable artist and one of the best of contemporary writers of texts for picture-books, but she has still not quite solved the problem of communication. Her books—and her latest is a fair example—are impressive but they lack warmth and urgency. *City of Gold* is a variant of a familiar tale, that of the two brothers who make a journey, one by the primrose path, the other by the strait way. The variation comes through the employment of a psychological and ethical device which does not quite match the spirit of the story. The pictures, presented in brilliant colours and in a stained-glass technique compel attention but do not, in one reader at least, inspire affection.

Publishers Weekly

SOURCE: A review of *City of Gold,* in *Publishers Weekly,* Vol. 206, No. 7, August 12, 1974, p. 59.

Fiona French is the distinguished author-illustrator who can be depended upon, each year, to create something special and totally different from her previous offerings. *City of Gold* features richly ornamental, medieval scenes based on stained-glass designs. The great city needs deliverance from a devil who sits at the gates. Thomas and John, two brothers, determine to fight the beast and become king of the fabulous land. Thomas, a hedonist, takes an easy route while John chooses a longer, harder road. On the way, Thomas stops often to join in local revels while John toils on, pausing only to give away his possession to beggars. What happens when the brothers meet at the gate and confront the devil is unexpected and exhilarating.

Kitty Ingham

SOURCE: A review of *City of Gold,* in *The School Librarian,* Vol. 22, No. 3, September, 1974, p. 233.

The author finds old stories from many countries and retells them in good modern prose, easily understood by children from five onwards. She embellishes the story with glowing, beautifully drawn and coloured pictures. Look at each thoroughly; there are small notes in the clover fields and hay stacks: 'hardly used, difficult road, brambles'. A lovely white horse on the smooth road 'willing to go far'. There are two brothers, two roads, a nobleman in his castle and a demon who mercifully falls into a burning fiery cave. Fiona French has now published five books; you should have them all.

Kirkus Reviews

SOURCE: A review of *City of Gold,* in *Kirkus Reviews,* Vol. XLII, No. 17, September 1, 1974, p. 939.

As in her generally praised **Blue Bird** and **King Tree** French borrows her style from the culture she depicts, and certainly these intensely colored "stained glass" representations would seem to suit what starts as a familiar morality tale about two brothers—a kind and humble one who takes a steep, narrow road to the City of Gold in order to free its people from a fierce demon, and a vain luxury-loving one who chooses the smooth road and wayside pleasures and hopes to be made king. In the end French does veer from the expected course of implacable justice, with the wicked brother undergoing a change of heart and saving the other, whom he had been about to sacrifice to the demon. But without ever having vitalized the conventional theme in the first place, the story still comes off as even stiffer and more superficially medieval than the garish pictures.

The Booklist

SOURCE: A review of *City of Gold,* in *The Booklist,* Vol. 71, No. 2, September 15, 1974, p. 99.

A morality tale in allegory form about two brothers who decide to conquer a demon that plagues the gates to the City of Gold. John takes the rough, narrow road to the city while Thomas, who hopes to become King, takes the easy road and accumulates riches on the way. When they reach the end of their journeys, greedy Thomas sacrifices his brother to the demon but has a change of heart and gives up his jewels in return for John, while the Demon plunges to the depths of his cavern weighted down with treasure. Richly colored illustrations simulating stained-glass windows create a medieval atmosphere; the artist is at her best with the lavish border and scenery patterns and a fearsome red demon, but gets overly stiff and affected at times when depicting people. The text is formal, lending an air of importance to the talc, and should make effective story-telling fare.

The Times Literary Supplement

SOURCE: "Enticing Ingredients," in *The Times Literary Supplement,* No. 3785, September 20, 1974, p. 1011.

Another traditional source—the Christian allegory of the broad road to perdition and the difficult path to salvation—is used as the basis of another juvenile cliff-hanger, Fiona French's *The City of Gold.* In this story both roads lead to the same city, but a frightful demon sits at the end of the broad path, seizing all who approach along it and bearing them down into a fiery pit. John, an unselfish and high-minded young man, approaches the golden city along the hard road while his pleasure-loving brother, Thomas, takes the easy one, but Fiona French arbitrates their fates less rigidly than the originators of the allegory would have done: in a hair-raising climax, the demon is conquered by fraternal affection, ingenuity and sacrifice, and both brothers reach the city safely. The author's masterly illustrations are fashioned in the style of medieval stained glass, glowing with colour and displaying unexpected touches of amusing peripheral detail.

Margery Fisher

SOURCE: A review of *City of Gold,* in *Growing Point,* Vol. 13, No. 4, October, 1974, p. 2481.

Fiona French's new milieu, a medieval city, dictates the sumptuous gilt and scarlet of *City of Gold* and the basic motifs and general style of the book derive from the technique of stained glass. The story, in keeping with the illustrative atmosphere (which I suspect provided the initial impulse) is a small morality concerning two brothers who live near a city enthralled by a Demon. John decides to confront the Demon for the sake of his fellow citizens, Thomas in order to win fame: appropriately, John travels by the narrow road of endeavour and Thomas by a wide

road lined with worldly pleasures. The smallest visual detail has been chosen for its symbolic meaning and the book is a superbly consistent piece of planning, as rich in meaning as it is in colour. The medieval way of teaching through the eye is cleverly reflected in a very striking picture-story book, in the repertoire of a consistently original and interesting author-artist.

Brian W. Alderson

SOURCE: A review of *City of Gold,* in *Children's Book Review,* Vol. IV, No. 4, Winter, 1974-75, pp. 143-44.

Every year we are offered a picture book by Fiona French which seeks to exploit as fully as possible a new line in pastiche. From the playing-card simplifications of *Jack of Hearts* (1970) to the truly splendid evocation of French baroque in *King Tree* (1973) we have seen not merely a different graphic style brought into use, but also the construction of a story which the artist believes to be apt for that style (if not actually associated with it). Now, with *City of Gold,* she has turned to stained-glass and to a narrative which draws upon the vestiges of medieval morality. Hard-working John sets off down the narrow, stony road to rid the City of its Demon; his merry and idle brother Thomas rides away down the smooth road ('leads to good company and riches') with much the same purpose, but less out of kindness than in the hope that the citizens will make him king. When finally the two brothers confront the Demon together, Thomas betrays John into its jaws—only to regret his action at once and quick-wittedly to substitute for his brother the riches that he had gained on his journey.

Now if we do not allow ourselves to be blinded by Miss French's panache as a book-artist, we will find that neither the morality nor the illustration of this story is wholly successful. Of the first, one is compelled to say that it is contrived in a fashion inadmissible to even the crudest moral philosophy: a whole sequence of contradictions obscuring the basic intention that strenuous righteousness should be seen to triumph over easygoing pride; and of the second, one must point to a decline from the nicely worked-out details at the start of the book (the mapping of the roads, the incorporated 'asides', like the dedication which is set in the hem of a gown on page seven) to the, admittedly dramatic, but, visually, far less rewarding scenes at the end. (Indeed, as John is being haled off to the Demon's fiery pit, a medieval thinks-bubble makes him say 'Oh Dear!'). On the evidence of Miss French's past responsiveness to her texts, it is perhaps not surprising that this slackening of command over the nuances of the pictures coincides with the story's own decline into the option of an easy way out.

Donald K. Fry

SOURCE: A review of *City of Gold,* in *School Library Journal,* Vol. 21, No. 8, April, 1975, p. 44.

Two brothers, virtuous John and profligate Thomas, set out to free the *City of Gold* from its oppressing Demon. John struggles on the stony road while Thomas takes the easy one. Later they both meet the Demon, and in a series of ruses and reversals, Thomas throws John to the Demon, saves him again, and sinks the monster. Despite a muddled plot, casual characterization, and dubious moral (clever sinner overcomes evil), this has punch. The colorful illustrations, take-offs on medieval stained glass windows, have a fanciful and offbeat humor (little messages and asides are hidden in the pictures) that children should like.

AIO THE RAINMAKER (1975)

Elaine Moss

SOURCE: "The Unclassified Appeal," in *The Times Literary Supplement,* No. 3826, July 11, 1975, p. 771.

Folk tales distil the wisdom of the ages and convey universal truths with effortless ease. The most impressive of the folklore picture books this season is Fiona French's *Aio the Rainmaker,* a visually enthralling interpretation of the African ritual dance which enacts the story of Aio who persuaded the Ancestors to give rain to the earth and bring an end to the dry season. In page after splendid dust-dry page we see the dancer impersonating leopard, antelope, chameleon, parrot, monkey and python—all too thirsty to hunt or fly or obey the laws of Nature for their own survival. But when Aio promises first fruits to the Ancestors if only they will send water, the dark clouds gather and the dancer raises his grateful face to the slanting windblown rain that will bring fresh life to the people and animals of the Earth. Fiona French is a versatile artist who has already made picture books rooted in Chinese, Egyptian and medieval European culture: her African orison, playing on themes as old as time itself, is her best so far.

Gabrielle Maunder

SOURCE: A review of *Aio the Rainmaker,* in *The School Librarian,* Vol. 23, No. 3, September, 1975, p. 219.

'A talent to amaze'—Fiona French, that is. In each of her previous books she has shown a marvellous ability to adapt distinctive artistic styles to her own personal expression. *Huni,* her Egyptian book, was a blend of the tight formal calligraphy and the eye of the contemporary artist, producing a dramatic and remarkable book. *The*

From Snow White in New York, *written and illustrated by Fiona French.*

Tree King resulted in the same sensitive blend between eighteenth-century woodcut and modern technique.

This, her latest, is less restrained by preconceived ideas, since it is an adaptation of African art, and yet it triumphantly produces a book essentially tribal in its appearance. The pages abound with ritual masks and poses, drawn with a superb sense of rhythm and line which uses the pages both as a discipline and a shape to be exploited. The double spread showing the Leopard-man, the Python and the Scorpion is the finest in the book, demonstrating an artist growing in confidence and expertise with each production. Would that Attenborough's *The Tribal Eye* on television could capture half so well the dignity and complexity of tribal custom.

Publishers Weekly

SOURCE: A review of *Aio, the Rainmaker,* in *Publishers Weekly,* Vol. 214, No. 12, September 18, 1978, pp. 166-67.

It has been far too long since the marvelous works of French have been seen in this country. Here is an example of the British artist's best, the story of Aio's struggle to save the people of his African village from the ravages of the drought. The strong movement in the paintings and their fiery colors—in contrast to Aio's masklike, dignified face—are awesome in their beauty. The poetic text tells how Aio implores the spirits of Ancestors to send rain as he dances to imitate the leopard, the python, the antelope and other animals—all dying of thirst. The Ancestors heed the Rainmaker's pleas and promise relief in exchange for his assurance that the people will remember them forever. Few books can offer such lasting rewards as this, for *all ages.*

Patricia Jean Cianciolo

SOURCE: "The Imaginative World: *Aio, the Rainmaker,*" in *Picture Books for Children,* second edition, American Library Association, 1981, p. 171.

Each year, at the end of the dry season, the African people tell in dance and song this story about Aio the Rainmaker, and how, many years ago, he finally persuaded the Ancestors to unloose the rain after a long drought. The oversized paintings in full color depict authentically masked people acting out this legend in dance, as it is traditionally done in Africa and by turning the pages, readers get an impression of their movements. All in all, a rare visual experience is in store for the readers of this fascinating picture book.

📖 *MATTEO* (1976)

Elaine Moss

SOURCE: "A Delicate Balance," in *The Times Literary Supplement,* December 10, 1976, p. 1551.

Fiona French's *Matteo* for instance is probably, from a purely aesthetic standpoint, her most brilliant piece of work so far. The spirit of the Florentine Renaissance, its sculpture, paintings, palaces and mosaic patios, rises from the pages with a more startling impact than is created by many a poor postcard reproduction of an old master. The meagre text, however, is planned to fit in to a patch of sky here, a white oblong on an inlaid marble pillar there. As a piece of writing *Matteo* is flat and uninteresting; yet as an example of ingenious book design it outshines the rest.

Maureen Duffy

SOURCE: A review of *Matteo,* in *The Spectator,* Vol. 237, No. 7746, December 11, 1976, p. 23.

Fiona French's *Matteo* seems more designed for the collective than the individual stocking. The story has a nineteenth-century moral ring to it and the illustrations, which are mainly painted in shades of dried blood, are presumably meant to give children vicarious experience of early Renaissance Florentine art. Matteo, the sculptor, is trying to finish his entry for the grand public competition for a statue to stand in the square when Alessandro, a rich man whose splendid villa has just been built, comes and asks Matteo to carve a statue for him. Matteo says he is too busy on his competition entry—so Alessandro decides to pay him out with a very cruel joke, which he does by attacking Matteo's sense of identity as an artist. Matteo's sanity is saved by winning the competition and he then carves a statue for Alessandro. The morality of children's literature need not be as simple as is sometimes suggested but this story seems very confused. Alessandro's house has been built and decorated for him by 'friends' who, presumably, have not been paid since, as any child knows, you don't pay 'friends' to do things for you. Why then is Matteo so cruelly punished for wanting to finish his competition entry? Presumably because the artist is meant to work for a rich man for nothing, instead of for the public for something. If he doesn't, he is labelled arrogant and made to see his mistake.

M. Crouch

SOURCE: A review of *Matteo,* in *The Junior Bookshelf,* Vol. 41, No. 2, April, 1977, p. 77.

No less than Errol le Cain, Fiona French matches her style to her subject. Eclecticism pays off in *Matteo* which is the story of a successful practical joke played in the high Renaissance. Matteo the sculptor affronts a wealthy patron, and he and his friends pay him back effectively. It is left to the sculptor to make graceful amends in the manner of the time. It is not only the beautifully drawn backgrounds, architecture and delicately framed landscapes, which convey the atmosphere of sixteenth-century Italy. The characters too, in cast of feature as much as dress, are perfectly in tune with their surroundings. The pictures display extreme virtuosity, but here is not just a clever book; it is a genuine recreation of an age and its people. Miss French's best to date.

Tony Dyson

SOURCE: A review of *Matteo,* in *The School Librarian,* Vol. 25, No. 2, June, 1977, pp. 125-26.

To turn the pages of Fiona French's **Matteo** is to embark upon an enthralling ramble through the streets and workshops of Renaissance Florence. One crosses paved, colonnaded piazzas, from time to time catching glimpses of the green and white geometry of the Cathedral's looming walls and Brunelleschi's dome floating above. One almost hears the soft swish of a silken cloak and the stubborn pecking of a sculptor's chisel; and the dry whiff of Carrara marble dust is upon the still air. Merchants and their attendants flit brilliantly garbed in pictorial space borrowed, quite appropriately, from Piero della Francesca and his like. So rich, interesting and apt—except for the sudden stylistic inconsistency of a flirtation with Cubism on a couple of double spreads—are Miss French's visual evocations of Tuscany that one can quite easily ignore the flimsy story and feast exclusively upon the pictures.

Publishers Weekly

SOURCE: A review of *Matteo,* in *Publishers Weekly,* Vol. 214, No. 20, November 13, 1978, p. 63.

Again, French's panoramic treatment and coruscating colors make the reader-viewer feel assimilated into her setting. This time, it's Renaissance Italy, where Matteo, an ambitious sculptor, gets into a spot of trouble. Matteo refuses a commission from Allessandro, a rich man, who devises a scheme to exact gentle revenge. He invites the sculptor to a dinner where he and his friends pretend Matteo is a wool merchant, heavily in debt to his host. Their act is so convincing that Matteo doubts his true identity. Later, the news that he has won the Grand Sculpture Competition relieves his mind and, besides, compels Matteo to realize he has invited the teasing through his temperamental selfishness. In a beau geste, he presents Allessandro with a lovely statue, to discharge the debt of the "wool merchant."

HUNT THE THIMBLE (1978)

Margery Fisher

SOURCE: A review of *Hunt the Thimble,* in *Growing Point,* Vol. 17, No. 2, July, 1978, p. 3370.

In seventeenth century Amsterdam a small boy, playing with brother Pieter and sister Anna, leads the puzzled pair out of the house and through the streets till in his excitement he knocks over a market stall and his clever hiding-place is revealed. For children there is the pleasure of being one step ahead of the seekers (though a sharp eye is needed to find the thimble in each scene); for everyone, there is the pleasure of finely composed scenes, quietly and surely reflecting the atmosphere of the old city and its prosperous folk. Once more Fiona French has created a unity from historical detail and a homely situation brilliantly visualised.

Sarah Hayes

SOURCE: "The Power of Pictures," in *The Times Literary Supplement,* No. 3979, July 7, 1978, p. 763.

Fiona French has a pleasing visual idea in **Hunt the Thimble,** set in the boldly coloured and patterned world of seventeenth-century Amsterdam: a little boy hides a thimble where all can see it but those who are looking for it. Some of the spreads are powerfully composed, but young readers will worry about the changing appearance of the small boy, although his toy horse, on which the thimble is hidden, remains recognizable throughout. The adults, with their large heads and severe features, verge on the grotesque.

M. Crouch

SOURCE: A review of *Hunt the Thimble,* in *The Junior Bookshelf,* Vol. 42, No. 5, October, 1978, p. 250.

Here is evidence, if such were needed, that the Oxford University Press has not lost its cunning in making the fine picture-book. A book with a difference, moreover. Fiona French can switch styles as readily as she can find new topics. Here she turns to seventeenth-century Holland, to the small, neat, tidy world of Vermeer and consequently to an intimate domestic scene. Three children play together. Edo hides the thimble, and the others hunt for it, in vain. Yet it is there all the time, in almost every picture, just where one would not think to look. Edo and his brother and sister have ageless faces to go with their miniature-adult dress. Their small drama is played out against the background of Amsterdam, its busy streets and markets, its neat and elegant houses. Fiona French's drawing is less formal than usual, although it still prefers a series of postures to movement. The use of colour is freer than has been her practice. As always the book has been fully researched, and all the details are precisely rendered and accurate.

Ruth M. McConnell

SOURCE: A review of *Hunt the Thimble,* in *School Library Journal,* Vol. 25, No. 6, February, 1979, p. 40.

Using a more childlike theme than in her **King Tree** (Walck, 1973), this interesting British illustrator designs a colorful picture book around the indoor game of three children in a well-to-do 17th-Century Amsterdam family. A series of poster-like double spreads dominated by glowing oranges, blues, and greens portray the various rooms through which an increasingly irritated older brother and sister search for the thimble that innocent-faced Edo so cleverly hides. The pair chase out after Edo through wintry scenes of the canal and market until the runaway's crash into a stall produces a rain of (unlikely) foodstuffs and the hidden thimble. The simple text, well-spaced and in large type, literally rests on the illustrations, which derive elements from such 17th-century artists as Vermeer but assume a jolly life of their own, with sister's doll, Edo's pull-horse, and older brother's sling shot and pipe adding nice touches throughout.

Zena Sutherland

SOURCE: A review of *Hunt the Thimble,* in *Bulletin of the Center for Children's Books,* Vol. 32, No. 9, May, 1979, p. 153.

The story of a child in Amsterdam is illustrated by busy, rather stiff paintings that fill the oversize pages, with stiff figures in medieval dress and with interesting details of period and locale in both interior and exterior scenes. The story is very weak: Edo hides the thimble, his older siblings can't find it and complain to various adults in the household; Edo runs off into the street, tumbles into a vegetable stall and disrupts it. His sister, who had run after him, sees the thimble. Edo helps pick up the vegetables (and bread, fish, and other things that have spilled from the "vegetable stall") and the children walk home with the maid, who's also chased Edo. Stilted writing, and a plot that seems concocted to afford opportunity for the illustrations.

THE PRINCESS AND THE MUSICIAN (1981)

Margery Fisher

SOURCE: A review of *The Princess and the Musician,* in *Growing Point,* Vol. 20, No. 3, September, 1981, p. 3947.

The Persian richness of Fiona French's latest artistic interpretation depends on colour, treated almost symbolically—blue for a Prince from distant lands, gold for a rich suitor, a deeper blue for the moonlight meeting of the musician and the melancholy princess, a range of green and yellow as he plays away her troubles. Each page is framed with jewelled decorations and the ornateness is firmly controlled by careful selection and further disciplined by a strong dramatic note in the placing of figures and the formalised gestures of the Shah and his daughter and the humble but triumphant musician-suitor.

Margaret A. Banerjee

SOURCE: A review of *The Princess and the Musician,* in *British Book News,* Children's Supplement, Autumn, 1981, p. 11.

The Princess and the Musician lavishly displays the

splendour of the Persian court. Youssef, young and poor, is one of the Shah's musicians and is in love with the Princess Shirin. Many princes come to woo her with costly gifts, but one after the other is rejected by the Shah. Love is triumphant when Youssef offers to sing a song which will take away the cares and sadness of the Shah, and with the same song captures the heart of the Princess. Children from the age of four will enjoy the visual beauty of the book and the story at its most simple level. Older children will find some food for thought and revel in the detail of the pictures.

Naomi Lewis

SOURCE: "With Pictures and Conversation," in *The Times Educational Supplement,* No. 3412, November 20, 1981, p. 36.

Fiona French's approach is less intricate. Her manner alters with each new book's theme. But in each we find the same rich, unhurried style, the trick of catching motion in a pose of elegant stillness: a frozen move in dance. And in each, the artist's brief and simple text holds and advances the story perfectly. Her latest book, *The Princess and the Musician,* has also an eastern-flavoured tale. Youssef, a young musician, has great gifts but no money. How can he win the Shah's daughter? His chance comes when the Shah finds cause to reject each one of the many proud suitors. It could be that the hot oriental red-gold-flame of so many pictures fatigues the reader's attention after a while. Happily they are contrasted by exquisite night scenes in jewelled greens and blues, and by a glorious daylight apple-green (double-page) painting of Youssef winning both Shah and princess by his song.

M. Crouch

SOURCE: A review of *The Princess and the Musician,* in *The Junior Bookshelf,* Vol. 45, No. 6, December, 1981, pp. 242-43.

There is plenty of more-than-oriental splendour in Fiona French's new book. The story, of a humble musician who wins the Shah's beautiful daughter where many princes have failed, is neat and told with most commendable brevity. The big full-page pictures are strongly stylized, with much Persian conventional decoration and strong reds and blues. They are most admirable if one does not mind the wooden attitudes and fixed expressions which are part of the convention.

Frances Ball

SOURCE: A review of *The Princess and the Musician,* in *The School Librarian,* Vol. 30, No. 3, September, 1982, p. 222.

Youssef, a poor musician at the Persian court, loves the Shah's daughter. He waits silently while more favoured

So Noah, he built him, he built him
An arky, arky.
Built it out of hickory barky, barky.
Children of the Lord.

From Rise and Shine, *written and illustrated by Fiona French.*

suitors visit the palace, but none are successful. Eventually the worried Shah needs music, Youssef speaks of his love, and wins the hand of the princess. A simple tale with an exotic setting. The wealth and formality of the court are reflected in the rich colours and intricate patterns of the illustrations. Each page has a predominant colour which also appears beneath the text. Gold and blue occur frequently. As a page turns and the colour changes, it is as if we are following a stately dance through spotlit stage sets. The characters never quite escape from their magnificent surroundings to become people we care about, but their story can be watched with pleasure.

JOHN BARLEYCORN (1982)

Margery Fisher

SOURCE: A review of *John Barleycorn,* in *Growing Point,* Vol. 21, No. 5, January, 1983, p. 4013.

The old rhyme with its sturdy praise of real ale has been magnificently illustrated in scenes of country work and weather in which Fiona French's constantly diversified techniques make for dramatic and exciting viewing. In this book, forceful contrasts of staring white with misty backgrounds, swirling brushwork and plain, unshaded statements of colour, enforce the point of the song. The

atmosphere of the rural past is active rather than quaint, and most memorable in this striking picture-book.

M. Crouch

SOURCE: A review of *John Barleycorn,* in *The Junior Bookshelf,* Vol. 47, No. 1, February, 1983, p. 12.

Fiona French has taken the old rhyme of seedtime and harvest and turned it into a gorgeous celebration of the procession of the seasons. Notice with what fine economy she dispenses colour, giving each opening internal harmony and building up page by page to her big climaxes. She is, I think, at her best when she is least explicit, but it would be mean quibbling to attempt a criticism of the scene of peasant junkettings. One of the memorable picture-books of recent years.

Barbara Sherrard-Smith

SOURCE: "The Arts: *John Barleycorn,*" in *Children's Books of the Year, 1982,* edited by Barbara Sherrard-Smith, Julia MacRae Books, 1983, p. 75.

A strikingly original imaginative interpretation, brilliantly executed, of the traditional folk song. On the very last page, words and music appear together, but first comes a series of evocative double spread paintings, each illustrating one verse—the sense of space, of power, of the changing of the seasons, is tremendous.

FUTURE STORY (1983)

Celia Berridge

SOURCE: A review of *Future Story,* in *The School Librarian,* Vol. 31, No. 4, December, 1983, p. 342.

In a series of gorgeous compositions which swing boldly across the double spreads, Fiona French has created a short space tale with the flavour of the future to it, and yet in a style which quite young children will assimilate. *Future story* breaks new ground in the picture-book format. It is brilliant, breathtakingly simple, a superb use of colour printing, and the story is so embedded within the graphics as to defy description. Stunning—see for yourself.

Zena Sutherland

SOURCE: A review of *Future Story,* in *Bulletin of the Center for Children's Books,* Vol. 38, No. 2, October, 1984, p. 24.

In an oversize book, the highly stylized, brilliantly colored pictures are often crowded and sometimes confusing because of abstraction or the dominance of design over visual narration. The story is told by messages to and from a starship in which a crew of three makes an attempt to rescue the survivors on a dying planet, but finds no signs of life, only a crystal. It appears that crystal has encapsulated and killed all life; only the warmth of the earth's sun can save the last survivor in the specimen crystal. And—not in the text but in the final picture—a fourth silhouetted form follows those of the three astronauts. The pictures display French's technical proficiency, but they as often obtrude on the story as they extend it; the story has conflict/solution but the form (terse messages) gives it a cold quality. The future setting and the space rescue should appeal to readers.

Marge Loch-Wouters

SOURCE: A review of *Future Story,* in *School Library Journal,* Vol. 31, No. 5, January, 1985, p. 74.

This unusual science fiction picture book takes readers on a "You Are There" mission of rescue and space adventure. Three hundred years in the future, a starship and her crew is sent on a rescue mission to a dying planet. Once there, the crew finds no signs of life. On their return journey to Earth, they learn that they are carrying the seed of crystalline destruction from the planet on their ship. The crew themselves begin to turn slowly to crystal until the rays of the Earth's sun revive them and destroy the deadly crystals. French's futuristic illustrations are full of bright primary colors and geometric figures set against the darkness of space. The brief text is presented as radio transmissions and read-outs which lend an air of immediacy to the story. The design of the book is striking; it is composed of double-page spreads, some wordless and others with the text skillfully integrated in the illustrations. French presents a story that is more serious and realistic than is usually found in science fiction for this age group. Children who enjoy space and science fiction will find this to be a book that they can pore over again and again.

Elaine Moss

SOURCE: A review of *Future Story,* in *Picture Books for Young People, 9-13,* edited by Nancy Chambers, second edition, The Thimble Press, 1985, pp. 45-6.

[*Future Story*] . . . must be the first quality word-and-image construct (picture book!) to break through Earth's stratosphere and communicate with readers in a language and pictures that derive almost entirely from the technological revolution in electronics. Fiona French's text, in her story about a space mission that very nearly failed, is composed in the staccato language of the computer. Her pictures of the planets, the dark 'sky', the brightly lit interior of the Photon Starship Spectra 3 (with its crew floating towards death through contact with an irradiating crystal) are inspired by colour transmissions on television of the astronauts' view of Earth. If all this sounds chilling, it isn't—because the rays of the sun bring the dying starship crew back to glowing life on a page that will remain for ever in the memory.

MAID OF THE WOOD (1985)

Books for Keeps

SOURCE: A review of *Maid of the Wood,* in *Books for Keeps,* No. 35, November, 1985, p. 21.

Another tale which means more than it says. Four men create a woman from a piece of wood: the woodcarver makes the shape, the tailor dresses it, the jeweller adorns it, the holy man breathes life into it. As she rejoices at being alive the men start to argue over who owns her; she thanks them for creating her and goes on her way 'to see what the world is like'. Meanwhile the wolves still lurk in the corners of Fiona French's strong and atmospheric pictures.

Naomi Lewis

SOURCE: A review of *Maid of the Wood,* in *The Times Educational Supplement,* No. 3670, November 15, 1985, p. 48.

Fiona French is, at her best, one of the most impressive

picturebook artists of today. In her *Maid of the Wood* she returns, in part (not entirely though) to the manner of her *King Tree,* most striking of all her books. As always, she devises her own text, and does this well. Four men return from market through a thick dark forest. They build a fire for warmth and safety, and take turns to keep it alight. The woodcutter fends off sleep by carving a wooden doll. The tailor makes it a bright peasant dress. The jeweller gives it tiny rings and necklace. The holy man gives it life. Morning comes, and off she dances into the world. But the core of the book is not in the girl; it is in the power and mystery of the dark, the shadowed midnight faces dominating the page; this artist at her best.

G. Bott

SOURCE: A review of *Maid of the Wood,* in *The Junior Bookshelf,* Vol. 49, No. 6, December, 1985, p. 258.

Benighted in a dense forest, four men build a fire to scare off the wolves and each takes a turn to be on watch. To pass the time, the woodcarver shapes a wooden doll; the tailor sews a dress for her; the jeweller decks her in necklace and rings; the holy man breathes life into her. As she dances and sings, the four men quarrel over her but she refuses to belong to any of them and dances away to "see what the world is like".

A minimal text acts as gloss to a splendid set of colour paintings. The human figures and the doll are large size— on occasion a head occupies a full page. Colours range from the sombre greens and blues of the forest and the sinister black wolves to the startling orange of the jeweller's costume and the doll's multi-coloured dress which, through several pages, changes from light to dark blue to yellow to pink and white.

Aidan Warlow

SOURCE: A review of *Maid of the Wood,* in *The School Librarian,* Vol. 34, No. 1, March, 1986, p. 33.

A very simple modern fable by one of our most skilful artist-authors. Four craftsmen, huddled round a fire in a deep wolf-infested forest, create a beautiful girl puppet who mysteriously comes to life. They quarrel about who should possess her—but of course she now has a life of her own and dances off to explore the world. Fiona French's exotic, highly stylised pictures make a powerful impression.

Barbara McGinn

SOURCE: A review of *Maid of the Wood,* in *School Library Journal,* Vol. 33, No. 2, October, 1986, p. 160.

This story has many of the earmarks of a folktale but since no acknowledgement is given, one can only assume that it is an original tale. Four men spend the night in a

forest inhabited by menacing wolves. To keep the wolves at bay, they build a fire and take turns on watch. To stay awake, each man finds something to do to fill the time. The woodcutter carves a piece of wood into a doll; the tailor makes clothing for the figure; the jeweler makes a necklace and rings; the holy man breathes life into the wooden doll. The four men argue about to whom she now belongs, but the now life-like doll leaves them to see the world. The story is an interesting one, but it seems to go nowhere. The sentences are short and almost void of lively verbs and adjectives to brighten the story line. Full-color, whole-page watercolors do little to lift the book above the ordinary. The night trees and the wolves will entice browsers, but the illustrations of the four men and the doll are severe; some seem more designed to frighten youngsters rather than to enhance the text.

📖 *SNOW WHITE IN NEW YORK* (1986)

Publishers Weekly

SOURCE: A review of *Snow White in New York,* in *Publishers Weekly,* Vol. 231, No. 6, February 13, 1987, p. 93.

Astonishing pictures highlight this sophisticated book about a classy New York dame named Snow White. Her troubles come when her father marries the Queen of the Underworld, who resents Snow White's popularity. Snow White is left by one of the Queen's henchmen to die on the streets of New York, but she stumbles into a club where seven jazzmen make her their singer. She's a hit again, so the Queen throws a party for her, doctoring Snow White's drink with a poison cherry. All of New York turns out for the funeral, but when her coffin is jolted, Snow White wakes up; the cherry was merely lodged in her throat. Suave and witty, this story is elevated by its pictures to dizzying, art deco heights. This might be readers' first look at a unique style of art, but they may wish for a change in the ending—Snow White's stepmom should have been given a pair of cement shoes!

Val Bierman

SOURCE: A review of *Snow White in New York,* in *Books for Your Children,* Vol. 22, No. 2, Summer, 1987, p. 15.

Extraordinary picture book with its astonishing Art Deco illustrations and a story with a new twist to the traditional tale. Snow White is a poor little rich girl who falls foul of her father's new wife—the Queen of the New York Underworld! Snow White finds work as a singer with seven jazz men and is spotted by a newspaper reporter who just knows she'll become a star. (I said it was different!) The tale follows the traditional line but the poisoned apple becomes a cocktail cherry but of course all ends well and Snow White and her reporter live happily ever after! Stunning picture—great fun for sevens and over.

Helen Pain

SOURCE: "Carnegie and Greenaway: The 1986 Winners," in *Books for Keeps,* No. 45, July, 1987, p. 11.

The Kate Greenaway Award is presented each year to an artist who has produced the most distinguished work in illustration of children's books. Fiona French is no stranger to the picture world for the older child. In *Snow White in New York* she provides a 1920's setting for a retelling of this well-known tale, with jazz musicians substituting for the seven dwarfs of the original story. This stunning visual presentation, using strong line and colour, marries text and illustration together in total sympathy, and has great appeal for the older reader. A work of high technical excellence.

M. Crouch

SOURCE: A review of *Snow White in New York,* in *The Junior Bookshelf,* Vol. 51, No. 4, August, 1987, pp. 160-61.

Fiona French's new picture-book must be described as pure and delightful self indulgence. She has retold the story of 'Snow White' in the context of 'Twenties New York. The wicked stepmother is a Queen of the Underworld who consults her fortune in the *New York Mirror.* Snow White, abandoned in the jungle of the city, takes up with a jazz septet and becomes lead singer. Her Prince is a journalist who knows star quality when he sees it. And so on. . . . It is all done with tremendous style and with an unfailing sense of period. But a children's picture-book? No. She has done it, as every honest artist must, for herself.

Zena Sutherland

SOURCE: A review of *Snow White in New York,* in *Bulletin of the Center for Children's Books,* Vol. 41, No. 7, March, 1988, p. 135.

Snow White, in this Art Deco spoof of the traditional tale, is a Kewpie-doll blonde, and her newly-acquired stepmother is a slinky brunette Theda Bara. Angry at what she sees in the *Mirror* (the *New York Mirror*) praising Snow White, the villainous stepmother tells a bodyguard to kill Snow White. The rest of the plot is adapted in similar style: S.W. is taken in by 7 jazz musicians when the hit man lets her go; her sleep is caused by a poisoned cherry put into her cocktail, her recovery (cherry dislodged when a coffin-bearer stumbles) leads to marriage when a handsome society reporter smiles at her awakening. This sophisticated picture book may not be appreciated by very young children, but independent readers (who do not need the very large print that's used) should enjoy as much of the joke as they can comprehend. Distributed in 1987 in this country, the book won the 1986 Kate Greenaway Award in Great Britain, and the illustrations are indeed distinctive, with geometric abstractions, handsome use of silhouettes, and intriguing complexities of perspective and color used as backgrounds for the svelte,

elongated figures in John Held style.

Susan Hepler

SOURCE: "Fooling with Folktales: Updates, Spin-offs, and Roundups," in *School Library Journal,* Vol. 36, No. 3, March, 1990, pp. 153-54.

Like [Roberto] Innocenti, Fiona French plays with setting in *Snow White in New York* (Oxford, 1988), but she has also created an entirely new story. Snow White, sent downtown to "get lost" by her society-crazed stepmother, becomes a jazz singer and is courted by a reporter. A poisoned cherry in her cocktail does her in but she is saved at her funeral when one of the seven jazzmen pallbearers lurches while carrying the coffin and the cherry is dislodged. Brightly colored patterned shapes, bold black line, and silhouettes set this sophisticated variation in the art deco era of the 1920s.

CINDERELLA (1987)

Margaret R. Marshall

SOURCE: A review of *Cinderella,* in *British Book News Children's Books,* December, 1987, p. 12.

After Fiona French's award-winning *Snow White in New York,* whose basic story was transposed into contemporary times, her new picture book is a traditional setting of *Cinderella.* As the story depends more on characterization than scenery, the illustrator has given due prominence to the people in terms of clarity of outline, bold colours and sumptuous detailed costumes, though the fairy grandmother is portrayed as a kindly, plump, motherly figure in warm fur-trimmed overcoat. The brief text is set on multi-coloured wash backgrounds and is meant to be read to children aged about five upwards.

M. Crouch

SOURCE: A review of *Cinderella,* in *The Junior Bookshelf,* Vol. 52, No. 1, February, 1988, pp. 18-19.

After her outrageous assault on 'Snow White' Fiona French gives us a sober and unsurprising *Cinderella* in which she keeps to the bare bones of the story and refrains from personal comment. The drawing is as strong as ever, but the interest is all on the surface, as if this has been a task wished upon the artist. Her personality emerges only in the psychedelic tones of the background washes.

Publishers Weekly

SOURCE: A review of *Cinderella,* in *Publishers Weekly,* Vol. 233, No. 7, April 29, 1988, p. 75.

Last year's winner of the Kate Greenaway Medal for *Snow*

White in New York. French turns away from the Jazz Age and goes back to a Regency period of Empire waistlines and ornate coiffures. A straightforward telling with short, caption-like pieces of text keeps track of the action on each page. Cinderella is given a soft, smudgy beauty, as is her fairy godmother, while the gruff stepsisters and stepmother are trifling caricatures. All are set on a vast, illusory space of watercolor clouds, elastic landscapes and elongated tree lines. The approach to this fairy tale isn't nearly as novel and fresh as that found in *Snow White,* but the saucy, irreverent look of the pictures is most welcome.

Zena Sutherland

SOURCE: A review of *Cinderella,* in *Bulletin of the Center for Children's Books,* Vol. 41, No. 11, July-August, 1988, p. 236.

Effective in use of color and equally effective in combining bright-blurred backgrounds and strongly defined forms within the composition of single or double pages, this oversize picturebook version of the familiar tale is a good choice for group use. The retelling is bare-bones simplified, with some stepsisterly rancor and all violence removed; while a few adults will probably feel such treatment makes the version appropriate for the read-aloud audience, few can claim that the pared-down retelling has much suspense or stylistic distinction.

RISE & SHINE (1989; published in England as *Rise, Shine!*)

Publishers Weekly

SOURCE: A review of *Rise and Shine,* in *Publishers Weekly,* Vol. 235, No. 12, March 24, 1989, p. 67.

Many children know the rousing tune that goes with the lyrics that French has adapted from a black spiritual. Readers of this book may well burst into song—but falter, because the words now don't fit. "The Lord said to Noah, / 'There's gonna be a floody, floody. / Get those children out of the muddy, muddy,' / Children of the Lord / . . . So Noah, he built him, he built him / An arky, arky. / Built it out of hickory barky, barky. / Children of the Lord." And at the end, people of all races trail upward toward St. Peter and the gates of heaven. The ark looks like a patchwork quilt supported by sticks; green fields, ready and waiting for the weary voyagers, are pieces of that same quilt. In this highly stylized version of the biblical tale, crayon and watercolor pictures set the stage, with mirage-like drawings of distant cities tucked into the corners. Fetching fare, but for those who don't know the song, the text may seem rather corny and flat-footed.

Kirkus Reviews

SOURCE: A review of *Rise and Shine,* in *Kirkus Reviews,* Vol. LVII, No. 8, April 15, 1989, p. 624.

"Rise and shine,/And give God the glory, glory/Children of the Lord": the "folk adaptation of an American black spiritual" is a cheerful summary of the familiar story of Noah's Ark. Here, Greenaway-winner French illustrates it with skill and some humor, at one point showing the animals' faces green with seasickness. The rich fabric of Noah's robe is echoed in the Ark's brilliant patchwork pattern; the lowering sky and raging sea are rendered with a fine eye for texture; the animals—a child's natural focus—are more precisely drawn, their long procession winding two by two across the desert. These disparate-sounding elements are harmoniously blended for a beautiful addition to the many Noah books.

The music is omitted, unfortunately, but the conclusion—a parade of people from different times and places entering heaven ("If you get to heaven before I doosie . . . Tell St. Peter 'Don't be so choosy'")—is a nice touch.

Chris Powling

SOURCE: A review of *Rise, Shine!* in *Books for Keeps,* No. 56, May, 1989, p. 29.

Taking the words of a traditional spiritual as her text, Fiona French enlarges rather than diminishes. When they approach the Heavenly Gates in the best double-spread in the book, the Children of Her Lord are seen to be representative of humanity at large—Sikhs, Buddhists, Muslims, Christians and all, as well as the Jews of the original story. The *best* double-spread, did I say? Well, maybe the second-best. Just before it comes:

> 'The animals, the animals
> They came out by threesie-threesie
> Seems they'd heard about the birds and beesy-beesy
> Children of the Lord.'

You don't have to be Fiona French to make the most of that. But it helps if you are.

Raymond Briggs

SOURCE: "The Logic of Nonsense," in *The Times Educational Supplement,* No. 3806, June 9, 1989, p. B10.

Rise Shine! is a Noah's Ark story. The blurb says the text is based on a traditional Negro spiritual (perhaps a more up-to-date term might be Gospel Song) but, as with many song lyrics, the words in print are dire. "'There's gonna be a floody, floody / Get those children out of the muddy, muddy.' Children of the Lord."

The ark itself ("Build me an arky arky, / Build it out of hickory barky, barky") seems not to be made of barky at all, but of striped deckchair canvas. The animals are delicately and charmingly drawn and a nice idea is that they come out in threes (seems they'd heard about the birds and beesy, beesy).

The penultimate picture is extraordinary. It shows a gigantic yellow diving board in the sky leading to a pair of flimsy Texas DIY pearly gates which stand open revealing nothing but a 10,000 foot drop. St Peter sits on a kitchen chair with its back legs perilously close to the edge. Along this board walk several pairs of strangely elongated people, all 12-feet tall, including Muslims, Hindus, Buddhist monks, and Hare Krishnas; all strolling along to the Christian gates. "This is the end of my story, story / Hope you found it hunky-dory, dory." I'm afraid I found it baffling-waffling.

Kathy Piehl

SOURCE: A review of *Rise and Shine,* in *School Library Journal,* Vol. 35, No. 11, July, 1989, p. 64.

French's book joins Barbara and Ed Emberley's *One Wide River to Cross* as one of the few based on a musical rendition of the Noah story. The rhythmic language of the black spiritual buoys listeners along, while French's majestic illustrations add visual delight. Rather than retelling the Genesis story, the book expresses the joy of salvation experienced once by Noah and again by those who reach St. Peter at the heavenly gates. Noah, with his unruly beard and dressed in colorful flowing garments, builds a massive ship to house the animals. The vibrant, striped patterns of his robe recur both on the ark itself and on the fruitful hillsides after the flood subsides. The quilt-like effect catches the eye and makes the book a good choice for group sharing. The only oversight is the absence of a musical score so that those unfamiliar with the tune could join in the uplifting melody that demands to be sung.

M. Crouch

SOURCE: A review of *Rise, Shine!,* in *The Junior Bookshelf,* Vol. 53, No. 4, August, 1989, pp. 159-60.

Fiona French's Noah's Ark picture-book uses for its text a splendid negro spiritual, and this has clearly inspired her to some of her most imaginative work. Ark, Noah's gown, sea and fields—all are strongly stylized, and the bold stripey designs give a sense of unity to the whole. Against these the animals, drawn with rather more naturalism than the rest, stand out to powerful effect. There are some memorable pages: the Ark balanced precariously on the very tip of Ararat, the Chosen crossing a bridge suspended on air to Peter's Gate, perhaps best of all the Ark alone and half submerged on a wild blue-green ocean.

Margery Fisher

SOURCE: A review of *Rise, Shine!* in *Growing Point,* Vol. 28, No. 3, September, 1989, p. 5222.

In many years of superb work Fiona French has never repeated herself and the style of her version of the story of Noah is as unusual and striking as ever, with its cheer-

fully striped Ark and swirling waves and with the elongated, formalised figure of Noah presiding over wooden-toy animals; the background suggests first an Arabian town and camel trains, then a jungle scene glimpsed against the astonishing sight of a procession of assorted folk (Arabian, Spanish, American) processing toward the Golden Gates. The text, which takes the form of a negro spiritual, is even more unusual and diverting. 'The animals, the animals. They came in by toosie, toosie' and at the end 'The animals, the animals. They came out by threesie, threesie'; and the final wish 'This is the end of my story, story. Hope you find it hunky dory, dory. Children of the Lord', is one which nobody could deny.

THE MAGIC VASE (1991)

James Riordan

SOURCE: A review of *The Magic Vase,* in *The Times Educational Supplement,* No. 3879, November 2, 1990, p. R4.

Fiona French's ***The Magic Vase*** draws on Pueblo Indian folk patterns and tells of Maria the potter who shows a philistine artdealer the real value of art. The simple story may not thaw the heart of spivs who peddle antiques, but it does draw a simple moral for children (that true art should not be measured in banknotes) and proves the point by its delicate blend of words ("All the greed and anger poured out of his heart like liquid fire") with exquisite folk patterns and vivid colours.

Melanie Guile

SOURCE: A review of *The Magic Vase,* in *Magpies,* Vol. 6, No. 2, May, 1991, p. 28.

Fiona French, a Kate Greenaway Medal winner, is an original and versatile talent. Her latest, ***The Magic Vase,*** is a very unusual picture-story book. French tells the simple tale of a successful, acquisitive collector who returns to the Pueblo Indian village of his birth to buy a valuable vase. Maria, the village potter, sets out to show him the true "value of all things," with the help of the wild animals of the canyons. Realising that only things with monetary value will reach the heart of this man, she blends the animals into a rare "vase" from which they speak out of their own vibrant, living beauty. In the hands of a lesser artist, this is where things could go wrong, veering into platitudes and bathos, but French's animals leap out of the page in huge, dominating shapes and gorgeous colours, attesting to the sheer, unstoppable energy of living things. ***The Magic Vase*** explores the clash of aggressive materialism with cyclical nature and, for once, nature wins, but there is no didacticism here. Indeed, the pictures carry much of the meaning, in rich and telling detail. The man's inharmonious world is hinted at in the eclectic shapes surrounding him in the first opening, and also in the colours of his tie which echo the desert snake's but are all jarringly fragmented in pattern. In contrast,

Miss Louise lived on the other side of the hill.
She wasn't rich and she wasn't poor.
She was very clever and very, very beautiful.
But Miss Louise had never laughed
in her whole life, so the first man
who could make her laugh,
that was the one she'd marry.

From Anancy and Mr. Dry-Bone, *written and illustrated by Fiona French.*

everything about Maria speaks of harmony, from her earth-toned colours to her gesture of greeting to the cliff-top bear. *The Magic Vase* is a subtle, complex work, and it is beautiful to look at. Children from the age of five or so will be enriched by it.

Kirkus Reviews

SOURCE: A review of *The Magic Vase,* in *Kirkus Reviews,* Vol. LIX, No. 20, October 15, 1991, p. 1342.

A Greenaway medalist noted for her dramatic use of design contrives a sophisticated fable. A greedy art dealer pays a Native American potter a few dollars for a beautiful vase he believes will make his collection the best in the world, but she, in turn, has tricked him: the pot is composed of a coiled snake and decorated with other real animals who all come to life and chide the dealer, pointing out that whatever he owns will belong to someone else after his death. Somehow, this reforms the dealer by teaching him the true value of all things. The message demands an audience mature enough to understand that works of art may have fabulous monetary value; the flamboyantly handsome illustrations, with their two adult characters, make it appropriate for older children or even adults.

Roger Sutton

SOURCE: A review of *The Magic Vase,* in *Bulletin of the Center for Children's Books,* Vol. 45, No. 5, January, 1992, pp. 124-25.

Vibrantly patterned, desert-tone pastels illustrate a rather preachy, occasionally confusing tale of a greedy art dealer who is taught "the value of all things" by an Indian potter. When the art dealer comes to her village demanding a valuable vase, Maria the potter enlists the help of the animals to create the fabled vase and teach the dealer a lesson. A snake becomes the coils, and a bear, rabbit, birds, and fishes (in the desert?) become the design. While the man is gloating over the vase, the animals whisper to him and the snake uncoils and delivers the sermon: "Your collection of vases only belongs to you during your lifetime. And when you are dead they will be auctioned away and belong to someone else, and after that to someone else, and someone else." Stricken by the futility of it all ("'I've been tricked,' cried the art dealer") the man repents, and Maria gives him a small pot. Some events are puzzling, as when the snake seems to uncoil a page before it's supposed to; and a reference to the dealer going "back to Maria," is odd, because we haven't been told he's left. It's not a great story, but the gorgeously rendered landscapes and the dramatic transformation of the vase, growing larger and coming to life, steal the show.

Joan McGrath

SOURCE: A review of *The Magic Vase,* in *School Library Journal,* Vol. 38, No. 4, April, 1992, pp. 91-2.

An aquisitive art dealer learns to appreciate the transitory nature of his hoarded wealth, and gains satisfaction from living each day fully rather than wasting it on an endless quest for "more." The man's collection of vases is the second best in the world. According to rumors, one vase, if acquired, will make it the best of all. It is in the hands of a woman from his own village in the Southwest. He goes in search of the treasure, but Maria is too wise for him. With her magical skills and the help of the animals, she teaches the greedy man "the value of all things," and he returns to the city a softened, chastened, happier man. This story of the mutability of values is in itself good but not great. French's illustrations, however, bring an otherwise run-of-the-mill plot to fiery life. Her rich colors and evocation of the desert landscape are of extraordinary strength and beauty.

📖 *ANANCY AND MR. DRY-BONE* (1991)

Sarah Ellis

SOURCE: "A British Invasion," in *Quill and Quire,* Vol. 57, No. 8, August, 1991, p. 22.

In the early '70s I started to look at picture books for the first time since childhood and was smitten with the ebullient colours and bold design of the British picture books of the period—with Brian Wildsmith, Victor Ambrus, Charles Keeping, and above all, Fiona French. French's output has not been prolific, but each book reveals a unique vision, and a new offering from her is a welcome event.

Anancy and Mr. Dry-Bone is "an original story based on traditional characters from Caribbean and African folktales." Mr. Dry-Bone, a skeleton rich man, and Anancy, a cool dude, engage in a competition to see who can make the beautiful Miss Louise laugh, and thus win her affection. With the help of animal friends, Anancy is successful. The words are simple and rhythmical, perfect for reading aloud: "Mr. Dry-Bone turned himself into a bat that flapped and a cat that spat; he turned himself into a pig that honked and a rabbit that did nothing." But it's the pictures, with their printed fabric borders, loose flowing line, and black silhouettes against wild jungle skies, that give the story its dash.

Betsy Hearne

SOURCE: A review of *Anancy and Mr. Dry-Bone,* in *Bulletin of the Center for Children's Books,* Vol. 45, No. 1, September, 1991, p. 10.

Elegance is French's hallmark, whether the style is Art Deco, as in her Greenaway Medal picture book *Snow White in New York,* or in these innovative paintings that combine Caribbean colors with black and white silhouette patterns. The story is a contest between the rich, skeletal Mr. Dry-Bone (Death) and the poor, handsome trickster Anancy. Both are courting clever, beautiful Miss Louise, who will marry the man who can make her laugh. Mr. Dry-Bone conjures to no avail, but Anancy dresses in bits of clothing from all the animals and makes Miss Louise—a seamstress—laugh till the tears roll down her face. The visual balance of flamboyance and restraint is nowhere so evident as in the contrast between Anancy's shadowed appearance at Miss Louise's door, in the next-to-last double spread, and the final surprise of his outfit sunbursting on the viewer in brilliant hues. Even the endpapers harmonize linear intricacy with symmetrical simplicity. Here's a graphic classic for the folklore shelf.

Kirkus Reviews

SOURCE: A review of *Anancy and Mr. Dry-Bone,* in *Kirkus Reviews,* Vol. LIX, No. 17, September 1, 1991, p. 1160.

A Greenaway medalist noted for offbeat stories as well as exciting graphics borrows from African and Caribbean folklore to spin her own tale. Mr. Dry-Bone, turned out fine in top hat and checked trousers, has a flat, white face—not scary but clearly a skull. Black Anancy's warmly rounded face hints of mischief; he's sleek in his close-fitting jeans. Both want to marry Miss Louise, but she'll have only the one who makes her laugh. Mr. Dry-Bone, a conjurer, becomes one beast after another to no avail. Anancy's animal friends loan him their clothes but only their second best, resulting in "the weirdest get-up"—and laughter that wins him his bride. The pointed subtext here is mellowed in an amiable conclusion (even Mr. Dry-Bone laughs); meanwhile, French plays the vibrant black-and-white patterns in her fabrics and architecture against gently glowing sunsets and judicious touches of intense color to stunning visual effect. A thoughtful, entertaining story in a unique, richly imaginative visual setting.

Julie Corsaro

SOURCE: A review of *Anancy and Mr. Dry-Bone,* in *Booklist,* Vol. 88, No. 2, September 15, 1991, pp. 158, 160.

The double-page spreads in this picture-book version of an original trickster tale based on African and Caribbean sources are used with mastery by French, winner of the prestigious Greenaway Medal. Her striking, stylized paintings contrast bold, black silhouettes and solid, mostly black-and-white geometric forms against intense, pastel backgrounds. Simply written with comic colloquialisms and rhythm, the story is spare yet appealing. Pitted against rich Mr. Dry-Bone to make the beautiful Miss Louise laugh, poor Anancy asks to borrow elegant clothes from his animal friends but instead receives only well-worn items. When Anancy finally reveals his weird getup to Miss Louise, laugh she does. The game element, the small yet significant details, and the creative use of color to mirror the story's progression will appeal to the eagle-eyed young.

Publishers Weekly

SOURCE: A review of *Anancy and Mr. Dry-Bone,* in *Publishers Weekly,* Vol. 238, No. 42, September 20, 1991, p. 132.

With eye-catching art and a saucy tone, French (*Rise and Shine; Snow White in New York*) tells an original story based on characters borrowed from Jamaican and African folktales. Both Mr. Dry-Bone and Anancy attempt to win the hand of Miss Louise who is "very clever, and very, very pretty." Determined to marry the first man who makes her laugh, Miss Louise is not impressed with Mr. Dry-Bone, a skeletal scarecrow in black-and-white checkered pants who woos her with his conjuring tricks. Anancy, a handsome black man, borrows clothing from various animals to create a ridiculous outfit and ends up making everyone laugh, even Mr. Dry-Bone. The story is slight, but French's language is street-smart and jazzy. The illustrations—vibrant background colors overlaid with complex black-and-white silhouettes—are singular and striking.

Susan Giffard

SOURCE: A review of *Anancy and Mr. Dry-Bone,* in *School Library Journal,* Vol. 37, No. 10, October, 1991, p. 94.

This original story, based on traditional motifs and characters and set in the Caribbean, shows Anancy as a comic hero rather than in his usual role as trickster. A very hip Anancy, in human form, borrows amusing clothes from various animals. By making Miss Louise laugh for the first time, he wins her hand. His rival, a skeleton conjurer named Mr. Dry-Bone, good-naturedly wishes them well. The illustrations are far more striking than the slight story. French's flattened, near-silhouette figures in black, white, and brilliant color move over warm watercolor washes. The settings are heavily influenced by the ornate wood-carvings and wrought-iron work of Caribbean architecture. Beginning readers will welcome the large print. Direct, vigorous language makes the story a possible choice for group sharing, although the lack of conflict and the anticlimactic ending may disappoint Anancy fans.

Margery Fisher

SOURCE: A review of *Anancy and Mr. Dry-Bone,* in *Growing Point,* Vol. 30, No. 4, November, 1991, p. 5608.

Fiona French creates dramatic scenes by contrasting the severe black and white of rich Mr. Dry-Bone with the animal colours of Anancy, poor co-suitor of pretty Miss Louise, who is shown as flowery, fluttery and perhaps a little spoilt. However, she does make the expected folk-tale reply to the pleas of the rivals when Anancy's costume (borrowed tiger-skin, Dog's top hat, Alligator's 'shiny black evening shoes' and a parrot's discarded feather) actually makes her laugh, where Mr. Dry-Bones' conjuring tricks and antics have made no impression. The generous size of the pages in this latest interpretation of a traditional motif allows for bold dramatic postures and the embellishment of endless small decorative details which invite prolonged scrutiny of the pages.

M. Crouch

SOURCE: A review of *Anancy and Mr. Dry-Bone,* in *The Junior Bookshelf,* Vol. 55, No. 6, December, 1991, p. 240.

Fiona French is the ultimate designer among today's picture-book makers, and the images which burst out from the pages, the more dramatically because splashes of dazzling colour are accentuated by a predominant black-and-white, are stunning in their impact. Some of the forms are most appealing, a splendidly elongated pig, for example, or a frightened cat bristling in silhouette on the roof. But the pseudo-folky story of how Miss Louise is wooed by man-about-town Mr. Dry-Bones and poor-but-honest Anancy, although it has the authentic Caribbean lilt, seems to me to be an essentially adult concept. I hope I am proved wrong, for here is a picture-book artist of the first rank in top form.

Lolly Robinson

SOURCE: A review of *Anancy and Mr. Dry-Bone,* in *The Horn Book Magazine,* Vol. LXVIII, No. 1, January/February, 1992, pp. 57-8.

Fiona French has written an original Anansi story, taking characters and elements from Jamaican and African tales and placing her story in a Caribbean setting. Rich Mr. Dry-Bone, a well-dressed skeleton, and poor Anancy, depicted as a young black man wearing a derby, both want to marry beautiful, clever Miss Louise. "But Miss Louise had never laughed in her whole life, so the first man who could make her laugh, that was the one she'd marry." When she won't laugh at any of Mr. Dry-Bone's acrobatics or conjuring tricks, Anancy prepares for his turn. He tries to borrow finery from his animal friends, but each can only lend his second best. Dressed outlandishly in Tiger's striped jogging suit, Monkey's butterfly bow-tie, and Dog's hunting hat with ears, he looks supremely silly, eliciting laughter at first sight from Miss Louise. The text has an informal folk-tale lilt and is illustrated in French's signature style: strong black-and-white patterns with colorful background washes.

📖 *KING OF ANOTHER COUNTRY* (1992)

The Junior Bookshelf

SOURCE: A review of *King of Another Country,* in *The Junior Bookshelf,* Vol. 57, No. 1, February, 1993, p. 12.

Fiona French's vividly relentless African patterns dominate this large, sumptuous picture book. *King of Another Country* briefly relates Ojo's story, a young man who always wanted to be awkward, who always said 'No'. In the forest he encounters a 'fierce creature' and is taken through a door in a tree into a new world. Ojo returns home a changed person.

Undoubtedly Fiona French's story and her glorious art work make for a consummately executed book. However, there is, I am sure, a strange distancing between the story and the reader. One is entranced, yet unmoved. Young readers will gaze endlessly, but will they really warm to the book and be drawn in? I have my doubts. *King of Another Country* is almost *too* rich for the contemporary child's taste.

Janet Taylor

SOURCE: A review of *King of Another Country,* in *The School Librarian,* Vol. 41, No. 1, February, 1993, p. 15.

Ojo is a disagreeable young man, he always says 'No', and never says 'Yes'. One day he ventures a little too far into the forest and meets a fierce creature. 'I am King of the Forest', says the fierce creature. 'You could be a king, too, if you said "Yes" as well as "No".' Ojo is then given the opportunity to learn how to say 'Yes'.

This simple tale is very well told and has most striking and unusual illustrations. These give the book a wider appeal than its being purely a moral tale for children. The pages are filled with vivid colour, evocative of African weaving and prints.

Publishers Weekly

SOURCE: A review of *King of Another Country,* in *Publishers Weekly,* Vol. 240, No. 7, February 15, 1993, p. 238.

Oversized, uncommonly dynamic illustrations spark an otherwise slight and disjointed story about a selfish young man named Ojo, who refuses anyone who asks for help. When bid to become king of another (magical) country, Ojo finally says "yes"—one too many times, in fact, and so he is returned to his village, a changed man. The straightforward, active text ("Ojo chose a wife. She was as beautiful as the dawn") enhances the book's storytelling quality, but misses out on dramatic opportunities. For example, the use of a familiar fairytale device proves disappointing—when Ojo's wife opens a disallowed door, the consequences are singularly unexciting. French's elaborate art has the stylized, dancing energy of Gerald McDermott's work; the pictures' rich patterns suggest African fabric designs, sometimes utilizing several contrasting motifs and ornate borders. Each successive spread seems increasingly imposing, and even the brilliant endpapers sing with rhythm and color. Characters in statuesque poses and theatrical attitudes glide across these pages with the sureness and grace of a finely rehearsed pageant.

Marilyn Iarusso

SOURCE: A review of *King of Another Country,* in *School Library Journal,* Vol. 39, No. 4, April, 1993, p. 96.

Ojo, who lives in an African village, always says, "No" when his neighbors ask for his help. When a spirit who is King of the Forest offers to make the selfish young man a king if he can learn to say, "Yes," he becomes the ruler of a blessed magical kingdom. His positive approach is all that is required for the realm's prosperity and happiness. He is warned by the village elders that he must never look behind the carved door, but when his beautiful wife suggests they open the door, Ojo agrees. The face of the King of the Forest is revealed and the couple is banished back into the real world. By now, however, Ojo has learned that there are times to say yes and times to say no. He is a more considerate and helpful neighbor and he and his wife live happily. This original moral tale has a short, simple text. French's brilliantly colored and patterned double-page illustrations are enjoyable. Because of its size, the accessibility of the story, and the vivid paintings, the book will be useful for story hour programs.

Kirkus Reviews

SOURCE: A review of *King of Another Country,* in *Kirkus Reviews,* Vol. LXI, No. 7, April 1, 1993, p. 455.

A Greenaway medalist known for her striking graphic effects (*Snow White in New York,* 1986) adopts an African setting and motifs for her latest fable. Preoccupied with his own pursuits—hunting; playing drums while others sleep—Ojo refuses to help anyone until a tree spirit—roused to anger when Ojo takes his fruit—takes him to a kingdom within the tree, where he becomes king on condition that he sometimes says "Yes" instead of "No." Ojo rules well, marries, and in time returns with his wife to his village, more accommodating and also happier because he's learned to say "Yes." The simply told tale offers a vital message to those ready to absorb it, but the vibrant art is of most interest here. Juxtaposing decorative geometric patterns in harmonious arrays of saturated colors with filmy skies of tissue-paper tints, the artist fashions one richly imaginative, beautifully designed spread after another. Unusually handsome.

Janice Del Negro

SOURCE: A review of *King of Another Country,* in

Booklist, Vol. 89, Nos. 19-20, June 1-15, 1993, p. 1856.

Contrary Ojo always says "no," no matter what anyone asks him. The fierce King of the Forest tells Ojo he could be a great king if he would only learn to say "yes," too. Ojo promises to try and eventually becomes a wise king who rules well. He marries, and his new wife loves him because he is generous and always says "yes." But with his wife's encouragement, Ojo says "yes" one time too many. The couple find themselves back in Ojo's old village, where, it turns out, they live happily, with Ojo sometimes saying "yes," and sometimes saying "no." Though cataloged as fiction, this work follows the traditional folktale pattern very closely and has the feel of an orally transmitted story. French's illustrations, which create a fantastic environment for the story, intrigue the eye with hot colors and ornate, textilelike graphics. The story will be especially useful for reading aloud to older picturebook audiences and for readers looking for a visual and verbal stretch.

Additional coverage of French's life and career is contained in the following sources published by Gale Research: *Contemporary Authors New Revision Series,* Vol. 40; *Major Authors and Illustrators for Children and Young Adults*; and *Something about the Author,* Vols. 6, 75.

René Goscinny

1926-1977

Albert Uderzo

1927-

Goscinny: French author of fiction.

Uderzo: French illustrator.

The following entry presents criticism of the *Asterix* series.

Major works in the series include *Asterix the Gaul* (1969), *Asterix in Britain* (1970), *Asterix and the Great Crossing* (1977).

INTRODUCTION

Goscinny and Uderzo are internationally renowned as the creators of the *Asterix* comic strip, which they fashioned into a number of stories that have been acclaimed for their genial humor and verbal and visual wit. In a collaboration in which Goscinny penned the texts and Uderzo crafted the illustrations, the two originated a story, set during the Roman occupation of Gaul in 50 B.C., in which one small fictitious Breton village defends itself valiantly against the Roman soldiers of the surrounding garrisons. This village is the home of Asterix, a short, feisty Gaul who refuses to be subjugated by the "civilizing" influence of the Romans. Roman rule, as depicted in the story, is marked by officialism, regimentation, and—poking fun at modern issues—a lack of regard for nature and the environment in a zealous wave of expansion. The plots of the *Asterix* tales are primarily centered on innocuous situations and predicaments, and the action is of a strictly comic violence where the barbarism of the times is reduced to fights of the "biff-bam-pow" variety in which bodies are tossed about without fatal injury. Although the cast of characters changes with the location, there are four Gauls who appear consistently: Abraracourcix, the chief of the tribe, a formidable warrior and respected leader who believes it is inevitable that the sky will fall on his head; Assurancetourix, the bard, with a voice so inferior he is usually gagged by the others; Obelix, Asterix's constant companion, a tremendously strong, gentle, and often hungry giant; and Asterix, quick-witted and brave, entrusted with the most dangerous of tasks by his tribe. The humor of the series depends, to a great extent, on allusions to the intrinsic variations between the cultures Asterix encounters in his travels. Each nationality bears distinctive behavior, temperament, and speech patterns, all lending themselves to exaggeration and stereotype. The satire extends even to the characters' names: all Gallic appellations end with "ix" in the tradition of the folk-hero

Uderzo (left) and Goscinny with Asterix and Obelix.

Vercingetorix, the leader of a revolt against Caesar; Gothic names end in "ic"; there is a Spanish chief called Huevos y Bacon, a Roman named Osseus Humerus who has two daughters, Tibia and Fibula, and an Egyptian architect called Edifis.

Commentators note that Goscinny's linguistic humor is complemented nicely by Uderzo's art, which is distinguished by the artist's striking manipulation of light, movement, gesture, and perspective. Isabel Quigly writes: "Like Gilbert and Sullivan, Goscinny and Uderzo . . . are clearly indivisible. Which is form and which content? Often you can't tell when a joke is linguistic or visual, or exactly where it began to be funny in the first place." In harmony with Goscinny's spoofs of ethnic diversity, Uderzo employs assorted typeface for the words spoken by various peoples: Gothic print for the Goths, hieroglyphics for the Egyptians, and so on. Uderzo also utilizes numerous sight gags and comic references to the past: for example, oil lamps are used in place of light bulbs when ideas are conceived by a character; Cleopatra is always shown in profile because the artist of her royal court "doesn't like modern art"; and there are exaggerations of gestures and facial expressions, size and motion. Both Goscinny and Uderzo pointedly stated that their works were created solely for entertainment and diversion, and the broad gaiety and gentle mocking tone of the strip are generally credited for its appeal to readers of all ages. By the late 1960s, *Asterix* books had been published in English and several other languages. Asterix had become the most famous comic strip figure in France, and expressions from the strip—like Obelix's "Ils sont fous, ces Romains!" ("These Romans are crazy!") could be heard on streets throughout the country. A number of commercial products and services bear the Asterix name, which was also given to France's first orbiting satellite and one of its theme parks. In 1992, more than three decades after he was introduced, Asterix was cited in a survey as the most popular cartoon character in Europe.

Biographical Information

Born in Paris, France, Goscinny was raised in Argentina before journeying to the United States as an aspiring cartoonist in 1945. He held a number of jobs in New York, including work as a cartoonist for *Mad* magazine, before returning to France in 1954. There he met fellow cartoonist Uderzo, who was born in Italy but moved with his family to France at an early age. The two discovered the makings of a very fruitful collaboration. Goscinny wrote: "I was not a very good illustrator because I was mainly interested in the script . . . So, when I met Albert Uderzo, who was writing his own texts without enjoying it, he immediately suggested a temporary association—I would write the text and he would illustrate it." In 1959 Goscinny co-founded *Pilote*, unusual in its focus as a comic weekly for adults; until this time, the comic strip in France was directed primarily to a child audience. In *Pilote*'s first week of publication, Asterix appeared. Based on the illustrated history books commonly used as texts in French schools, the *Asterix* strip told its own version of the Roman occupation of Gaul. By 1961, the strips were collected and published in book form as *Astérix de Gaulois* (translated in 1969 as *Asterix the Gaul*). In the English-language version of the book, translators tried to capture the same zaniness as the original; the bard Assurancetourix is re-named Cacofonix, the chieftain Abraracourcix becomes Vitalstatistix, the druid Panoramix is dubbed Getafix, and Obelix's dog (named Idéfix in the original series) is called Dogmatix. Despite the difficulty of reconstructing a play on words or reference to French culture or history, the *Asterix* books have been translated successfully into many languages and have proven popular worldwide.

Major Works

Each book of the *Asterix* series follows variations on the same plot: the Gauls grapple with a challenge and overcome it, usually with the help of the village druid's magic potion and Asterix's cunning. Critics agree, however, that the plots of the books are relatively unimportant; the humor

hinges on the sight gags, innuendos, and puns that are generously sprinkled throughout. Both the text and illustrations play on the French national pride which, when exaggerated, is shown in the Gaul's superiority and in the prominence of certain stereotypical characteristics in other ethnic groups. In *Asterix in Britain*, for example, the Britons dress in tweeds, are obsessed with having a well-kept lawn, and drink hot water and milk every afternoon (since tea has yet to be discovered). When Asterix travels to Spain (*Asterix in Spain*, 1971), he invents bullfighting; in Egypt (*Asterix and Cleopatra*, 1969), the rotund Obelix unintentionally breaks off the sphinx's nose. Asterix visits America in *Asterix and the Great Crossing*, and Goscinny and Uderzo make sport of Native Americans and Vikings alike. When Goscinny died suddenly in 1977, Uderzo completed and published some of their final collaborative efforts. Since that time, he has written and illustrated several further *Asterix* books.

Awards

Goscinny was named Chevalier of Arts and Letters by the French Minister of Culture in 1967; he was also named Chevalier de l'Order du Merite.

GENERAL COMMENTARY

Jean-Noël Gurgand

SOURCE: "The Astérix Phenomenon," in *Atlas*, Vol. 13, No. 2, February, 1967, pp. 53-6.

[*The following excerpt is from an essay that was translated from the Paris newsweekly* L'Express.]

On Wednesday, August 31, General de Gaulle at Pnom-Penh let the world know what he thought of America's power. On that very day, the publishing house of Dargaud in Paris released **Astérix chez les Bretons** [*Astérix in Britain*], the eighth volume of a collection about the assistance given by the Gauls to the Britons, namely, the ancestors of the English, in shaking off the invading Roman civilization.

A success for de Gaulle and a triumph for Astérix. Once more it had gotten too hot for the American soldiers and the Roman centurions.

And when, last March, the presidential DC-8 landed at Orly, the first edition of 600,000 copies of **Astérix chez les Bretons** was practically sold out. This was unprecedented: a million Astérix books sold since the beginning of 1966. All titles issued in new editions before the end-of-the-year holidays. Ever since the first French satellite, launched last November 26 from the Hammaguir base, was baptized Astérix by Michel Chevalier, a member of the French space program, the writer René Goscinny has been appearing monthly on television. Astérix as a radio serial is one of the most popular programs on France-Inter. There is no longer a teacher in France able to use the word "astérisque" and keep control of his class.

The thread of Astérix's adventures is uncomplicated. A bellicose and cunning malcontent, Astérix wages merry war against all comers with the aid of Obélix, the village menhir supplier, Panoramix, the village druid, Assurance-tourix, the bard, and Abraracourcix, the valiant chief of the tribe. Astérix's guiding principle is not to let anyone step on his toes, his pride is to have avoided civilization by Caesar's legions, his power is the magic potion made exclusively for him by Panoramix, his weapon is a chestnut, and his goal is a tranquil life, mixed with occasional drinking bouts and boar-hunts, in his village.

In six years and eight episodes, Astérix has swept his way with robust puns and lusty brawls as easily through the heroes of classic comic strips as through cohorts of Roman legionnaires in combat formation. In his victorious course, Jungle Jim, Zorro, Tintin, Buffalo Bill and Mandrake have bitten the dust and the centurions have been flattened.

"We don't quite understand what is happening to Astérix," comment his "parents," René Goscinny, 40, and Albert Udzero, 39. Goscinny (scenarios and texts) had met Udzero (drawings) in a Belgian agency twelve years ago. Both were doing strips, texts and drawings on their own. One wrote better than he drew and the other drew better than he wrote, so they decided to join forces. Their first brain child was Oumpapah, a very unwarlike Indian. It enjoyed a *succès d'estime;* in other words, it was practically a failure.

One day, they decided to take an inventory of all the comic-strip heroes since the very beginning. They noted that the French never inspired anyone. They did research, came up with a formula and employed names easily remembered. Astérix was born.

In their opinion, the success of Astérix is due more to the parents' amusement than the children's: each finds something in it. "It relaxes us," say the grownups who make no secret about their reading the strip. Not only is it "nothing to be ashamed of," but adults are able to come across bits of sly humor that the children miss. "It amuses me," remarked a teacher in the course of a recent interview, "to see the Goths speak in Gothic letters and the Egyptians express themselves in hieroglyphics. Or else that unfortunate legionnaire weighed down under his shield after Obélix's devastating march and groaning: 'To battle! Back to battle! And they told me I would see the world. . . .'"

For the children who like *Astérix* because it is funny, it is also educational. The adventures of Aplusbégalix and Pacotéalargus are in reality illustrated first lessons of Latin and history. Caesar is no longer the remote personage of Plutarch, and the way Uderzo maneuvers the legions, the tactics of the Roman army become understandable.

According to Gilbert Chateau, who is preparing a serious study on comic strips, the success of Astérix is due mainly to its quality: quality of the characters, of the gags, of the drawings. And there is originality of theme and style. "With Astérix, there is no identification with the character. He is not handsome and is of indeterminate age. He is more dirty than intelligent. His only 'heroic' side is his invincibility, but it is almost a ridiculous invincibility. Astérix is a hero of the second rank."

Among the other reasons for its success, Chateau mentions the puns and the anachronisms such as the fool disguised as Napoleon who takes himself for "one doesn't know whom," the motto on the wall reading "Rome Sweet Rome," the centurion Langelus having the bells rung, and the Roman decurion bawling at an underling, "You're going to get eight days."

Neither Gilbert Chateau nor Goscinny looks for deeper reasons or profounder motivations in the enthusiasm for Astérix shown by millions of today's Frenchmen.

And yet . . .

Do not the French of 1966 recognize themselves in these "irreducible, courageous, scabby, obstinate, carousing, squabbling, ridiculous" Gauls? Goscinny's Gauls grouse at rising prices, the boats which disturb the fishing, the polluted air of Lutetia, the traffic bottlenecks during vacations and the bad temper of the hotelkeepers who sneer at the promiscuity of the Romans ("They are crazy, those Romans!"), the curious eating habits of the English ("They are crazy, those Englishmen!"), and the strange customs of the Egyptians ("They are crazy, those Egyptians!"). At the same time, they help the oppressed against the oppressor, the civilian against the military and the individual against society; they render justice by greatness of soul, and their goodness of heart makes the evil and the traitorous look ridiculous.

The mockery spares no one and nothing: "I was in the war, I, monsieur, I was at Gergovia, I, monsieur." "Gauls, Gauls, the hour is grave!"

The Goths with their goose step and spiked helmets yield from time to time to their passion for invasion, the English try to plant their lawns wherever they can, and the Romans make war to keep peace, but Astérix intends to remain master of his domain.

It is not the legionnaires and their decurions who are the threat. They are the goof-offs and loudmouths of all times and countries. Honestly speaking, they are rather likable, and, in any case, they are good businessmen. The fear is of that distant and redoubtable Rome. In the face of that steam-roller civilization, the Gallic national weapon, the chestnut, even loaded, risks not weighing very heavily in the wind of History.

But what does it matter as long as the Gauls are united? Of course, there are some traitors like Quatrédeusix; he admits: "I am a villain, but after all, it is inevitable. But

I don't do what I do without reason. I do it for money." The collaborators are more serious: "During the period of the Roman occupation, there were two kinds of Gauls in Gaul. First of all, there were those who accepted the Pax Romana and attempted to adapt themselves to the powerful civilization of the invaders . . ."

These, like the chief Aplusbégalix, "venal, brutal, ambitious and unscrupulous," dress in togas, divert the river to replace it with an aqueduct, have a bust of Caesar in their homes, swear only by Jupiter, and send their kids to learn Rosa-Rosae-Rosam at Professor Berlix's School of Living Languages.

After the legions, the noun declensions. After the colonization by arms, civilization by culture. Can Caesar maintain the Pax Romana in his empire with pila and sesterces? It is the question de Gaulle asked at Pnom-Penh. For the Gauls, there is no doubt about the answer: it is no, as long as the cock has spurs and the druid can prepare his potion.

The formula for the magic potion is, of course, secret. All that is known is that it contains mistletoe and lobster. "To tell the truth, the lobster is not absolutely necessary, but it does give flavor." For Goscinny, it has just the same significance as Popeye's spinach, but sociologists see in it the symbol of the man with a sense of the future—de Gaulle.

"These exegeses are meaningless," claims Goscinny. "I assure you that I am not a nationalist or a chauvinist or a xenophobe. I love my country in the manner of those who have lived away from it a long time. That is all."

Small, dark-haired, with an expressive face which crinkles when he laughs, Goscinny has lived several years in Argentina and the United States, where he worked in a rubber factory. He returned to France after he had been replaced by a machine. His ambition then was to tell funny stories. "A humorist who makes a few people laugh is an amusing type. A humorist who makes only himself laugh is either an imbecile or an innovator. A humorist who makes a large public laugh is a professional humorist."

He speaks slowly in a low voice. Meticulous in dress and a confirmed bachelor, he has a loathing of the country and of vacations. His last pleasant memory of a holiday: two months on a boat in order to spend three days in Argentina. He has no hobbies or enthusiasms, and now that he is successful, he would like to celebrate in some way, but he does not know how. He envies Uderzo for his Jaguar E, but he does not like automobiles. His only pleasure is work. Although at the present he is one of the most sought-after writers in the world, he has not changed his way of life. Each morning he goes to the newspaper, *Pilote,* of which he is the managing editor, and then, in the afternoon, he returns home to prepare the new adventures of Astérix, Lucky Luke (with the artist Morris), and Petit Nicholas (with Sempé).

The coming episodes, *Astérix et les Normands* [*Asterix*

and the Normans] and *Astérix légionnaire* [*Asterix, the Legionary*], will have Obélix, menhir supplier, playing a more and more important role. Astérix is a symbol while Obélix is a human. Symbols are infallible and Obélix is not that always. Symbols do not have imperfections— Obélix is too fat—or great loves—Obélix is going to fall for Falbala, a cousin of the Gallic beauty, Boufiltre. Because of her, he will even go on a diet to lose weight.

Describing all this, Goscinny is as delighted as Uderzo is when he is drawing. "Our only ambition is to have some fun. Other explanations are just not true." They are indignant at the adaptation of Astérix in Germany where he has become "Seggi, the Little German," a sort of Nazi hero in quest of revenge. Frightened at the possible repercussions, Goscinny filed suit and had Seggi stopped.

The fabulous welcome given to Astérix reveals a deep feeling. There is no doubt that the comic strip, a means of expression simpler and more immediately accessible than any other, is the ideal repository for the myths and symbols of its time.

Researchers of the C.E.L.E.G., The Center of Literary Studies in Graphic Expression, patronized by Raymond Queneau, Alain Robbe-Grillet and Alain Resnais, remind us that in the United States before the Second World War the Americans' desire to participate in the conflict was more clearly shown through comic strip heroes than through governmental declarations.

Superman is the American ideal and Tintin is the standard-bearer of the West facing the Communist world. Identification with Astérix is at once more subtle and more universal. It does not take place on the level of character, but rather in a state of mind, a manner of being. It is in resistance more than in conquest that Gallic virtues are best revealed.

That is why Astérix has conquered the French more easily than Caesar conquered Gaul. And that is why Gauls and Gaullists, united across the centuries, jubilant and smacking themselves on the thighs, point to themselves as the civilizers. Around the roast boar of national euphoria, with a gourd of magic potion within hand's reach, they await the next episode which they hope will be as good as the preceding ones.

The Times Literary Supplement

SOURCE: "Here come the Gauls," in *The Times Literary Supplement,* No. 3501, April 3, 1969, pp. 347-48.

By Toutatis and Belenos, Astérix in English! Astérix, a French comic strip drawn by Albert Uderzo and written by René Goscinny, appears in a format similar to that of the Belgian Tintin. The first volume, *Astérix le Gaulois* [*Asterix the Gaul*], was published in 1961. There are now twelve of them—one every year except 1965 when there were two, and 1966 when there were three. Their sales are enormous: the most recent volume sold 1,300,000 copies in a single month. Some eighty commercial firms use the name of Astérix on their products and there are Astérix films and all the other by-products of a success that, nationally at any rate, is on the scale of James Bond or Charlie Brown or the Beatles.

The stories are set in the year 50 B.C. As every schoolboy reader of *De Bello Gallico* knows, "Gallia est omnis divisa in partes tres". But apparently Caesar misled his readers, preferring to conceal the existence of a fourth part of Gaul which had resisted his all-conquering legions. This was a Breton village, the inhabitants of which made life extremely difficult for the unfortunate Roman garrisons at Petitbonum (*petit bonhomme*), Aquarium, Laudanum and Babaorum (*Baba au rhum*). The village owes its continued-independence to the Druid Panoramix, who has concocted a potion which gives the drinker superhuman strength. The recipe of the potion is, of course, secret; Panoramix will only reveal that it contains mistletoe and lobster (the lobster is not necessary, but it improves the flavour).

For Astérix in a tight corner, quaffing the magic potion has much the same effect as that produced in Captain Marvel by pronouncing the word "Shazam"; or in Popeye by the consumption of spinach (indeed, Astérix bears a marked resemblance to Popeye). Immediately he is capable of Herculean feats. *Paf! Boum! Quille! Aie!* and the

Goscinny as a child.

Roman legion, or whoever the unfortunates may be that are threatening his safety, are left bruised, battered, and broken-speared, hanging from the branches of trees and sprawled about the landscape with stars circling around their heads.

Astérix is a small man, his outstanding attributes being intelligence, quick wits, cunning and resourcefulness. He himself (like Tintin) is rather ordinary: he is the Everyman of the strip. As with Tintin, it is the supporting cast that gives the story interest. Chief of these *dramatis personae* is Obélix, who plays Captain Haddock to Astérix's Tintin. When he was a baby, Obélix fell in a cauldron of the magic potion, as a result of which the effects are permanent. His job in the village is delivering menhirs (megaliths). His passions in life are eating wild boar and beating up Romans. The only time he ever gets really annoyed is when someone calls him fat. He is invaluable in fights but disastrous when it comes to knocking on doors (he always smashes them). His constant companion (in the recent stories at least) is a dog which is as small as Obélix is huge. This dog is nothing like such an interesting character as Tintin's Milou, but he has a better name—Idéfix.

Panoramix, Astérix, Obélix, Idéfix: the names of all the Gauls end in -ix, on the analogy with Vercingetorix, who led a rather less successful revolt against Caesar. This suffix gives room for endless puns on French words and phrases ending in *-isque, -ique* and *-is* (*panoramique, astérisque, obélisque, idée fixe*). The chief of the village is Abraracourcix (*à bras raccourcis*). This impressive ruler has only one fear—that the sky will fall on his head. The cast of main characters is completed by the bard Assurancetourix (*assurance tous risques*) whose singing is so appalling as to constitute at moments of crisis a secret weapon second only to Panoramix's potion. At other times, by any methods necessary, he is made to shut up.

The plots of most of the stories follow a fairly standard pattern. The Romans (or occasionally another enemy) try to subdue the intrepid Gauls and are rebuffed by one or more of the Gauls' retaliatory resources—Panoramix's potion, Obélix's strength, Astérix's guile or Assurancetourix's singing. The formula is enlivened by the comedy which is either verbal (there are excruciating puns) or else consists of *1066 and All That* historical jokes, anachronisms and topical allusions.

But there is a good deal of repetition from one story to the next, and after reading one the interest of the others is in proportion to the extent to which they diverge from the formula. A change of setting gives a refreshing opportunity for a whole range of new jokes, as for example in ***Astérix et Cléopatre*** [***Asterix and Cleopatra***] which appeared in 1965—not long after Elizabeth Taylor's *Cleopatra*. The first frame of the story quotes Pascal's tag about how, if Cleopatra's nose had been shorter, the face of the whole world would have been different. The second frame shows us Cleopatra. She is beautiful, but her nose is undeniably on the long side, and it is a subject about which she is extremely sensitive. (As for the Sphinx's nose, that was lost when Obélix was clambering about on it.) To prove that the Egyptian people have not lost their genius, Cleopatra bets Caesar that they can build a sumptuous palace in Alexandria in three months. With the help of the Gauls and their potion, she just manages to meet the deadline.

For the English reader, however, by far the best story is *Astérix chez les Bretons* [*Asterix in Britain*] a work of friendly retaliation against the Englishman's stereotype of the comical garlic-eating, onion-selling, beret-wearing, ooh-la-la-ing froggy. The British tribes have been beaten by the Romans because of their refusal to fight on the weekends, and because they insist on knocking off in mid-battle for cups of hot water with a dash of milk (the tea habit obviously antedates the discovery of tea). The defeated British are obliged to call on their friends across the channel for help and Astérix and Obélix put things right by bringing over a barrel of the magic potion.

The British are shown as being extremely polite and formal, shaking hands all the time (in fact, surely, we shake hands less often than any other European nationality). British food, of course, is disgusting, and our ancestors apparently lived as we do in rows of tiny identical houses with perfect grass lawns, they drank warm beer, drove on the wrong side of the road, wore tweeds, and so on.

But the best things in this story are the Anglicisms. An Englishman agrees with someone by saying "Il est, n'est-il pas?" Other sayings include "Combien étrange", "Bonne chance, et toute cette sorte de choses", "Bonté gracieuse!", "Je dis. Ca c'est un morceau de chance!" and, when attacked by the unsporting Romans at the weekend, "Aoh! choquant! Ce ne sont pas des gentils hommes."

In all the stories the Gauls are victorious over such lesser breeds as are foolish enough to come into conflict with them—Romans, Goths, Normans, or whoever it may be. The element of crude nationalism here is strong and is not only Gallic but also Gaullist (the first French satellite, after all, was called Astérix). And what is Panoramix's potion but a *force de frappe*?

A cartoon in *L'Express* a couple of years ago showed a group of Frenchmen watching an international football match on television. As goal after goal was scored against them the men became more and more dejected, until the match ended and they were totally downcast at their country's defeat. The last drawing of the cartoon showed them with gleeful smiles on their faces as, having switched off the television, they sat reading Astérix.

This cartoon explains a lot of the commercial success of Astérix in France, just as the success of Astérix goes some way to explain the long reign of General de Gaulle. Like Astérix, the General treats Anglo-Saxons and other foreigners with *hauteur*. Blindly ignoring unacceptable realities, Gauls and Gaullists alike appear happiest when throwing foreigners into confusion. Of course, it's all good clean fun: de Gaulle isn't actually going to go to war against his allies, any more than Obélix ever causes fatal

injuries in the Roman patrols he assaults. A few black eyes and bloody noses perhaps, and a lot of hurt pride and trampled dignity, but nothing more serious.

And when it is French dignity in the real world that is suffering, Astérix is always reassuringly there to restore it in fantasy. The clearest example is in sport. Before the 1964 Olympics the French newspapers were full of boasts about how many medals they were going to win. In the event they did extremely badly (if memory suffices, their only gold medal was won by a horse). In the 1968 Olympics France did less badly, but this time heavy insurance against further humiliation had been taken out well in advance. This insurance was in the form of *Astérix aux jeux Olympiques* [*Asterix at the Olympic Games*]. In a sense, whatever happened in Mexico was irrelevant: Astérix had won his gold already. And because Astérix so closely reflects French self-esteem it seems very unlikely that, whatever topical allusions the strip may have, there will ever be references to anything in the real France of today that shows the serious divisions in the nation. . . .

And now Astérix, which seems so calculated to pamper to the French national psyche, is being sold to the English. The first volume to be translated, *Astérix le Gaulois,* makes an extremely good job of finding English equivalents for the puns and allusions in the original. The names of Astérix and Obélix have, rightly, remained unchanged. Getafix is an excellent substitute for Panoramix, as are Cacofonix for the bard Assurancetourix, and Vitalstatistix for the chief Abraracourcix: perhaps they are even slight improvements. "Bang! Biff! Boom! Kerplonk!", however, does not have quite the force of the original's "Paff! Biff! Boum! Schplokk!" But this is a small point. Clearly the job of Englishing Astérix is in very capable hands. (One wonders how the ingenuity of the translators will cope with *Astérix chez les Bretons*.)

Those who prefer to read Astérix in the original, however, should find helpful the notes for English readers that are being sold with the French editions now also available here. These notes spell out some of the more complicated jokes and explain difficult idioms and recondite allusions. This presentation in both languages does Astérix proud. It will be interesting to see what kind of success the books enjoy here: somehow, perhaps wrongly, one had never imagined Astérix as being for export.

Joel Oppenheimer

SOURCE: "Lots of Gaul," in *The Village Voice,* Vol. XXV, No. 1, January 7, 1980, p. 31.

The *Asterix* series, originally in French (but not suffering in translation), comprises some 20-odd books detailing the doings of the citizens of the only Gaulish village not occupied by the Romans in the year 50 B.C. Asterix is the village's leading warrior—small, feisty, and shrewd. His boon companion is an amiable giant named Obelix. Together they wreak havoc, albeit good-naturedly, among the Roman camps that ring the village: Aquarium, Compendium, Laudanum, and Totorum.

As may be obvious from these names, vocabulary and puns are two of the books' strong points—and part of what makes it possible for a grownup to read them to kids with some interest as well as pleasure. Asterix and Obelix are abetted in their patriotic endeavors by Getafix, the venerable village druid, who mixes the strange herbal potion that gives our hero super-human strength (Obelix needs none, because he fell in a vat of it as a child). Cacofonix, the bard, and Vitalstatistix, the chief, and assorted other Gauls also figure prominently as the adventures take us all over the known pre-Christian world. Ethnic jokes are on full display, merrily. The Britons stop work, play, or war, every afternoon to drink hot water; the Egyptians speak in hieroglyphs, the Goths in blackletter; the Greeks all have straight-line noses and are cousins, from tourist guide to Olympic official.

Uderzo's drawings are bright and clear and complex enough to delight any literal-minded child, while Goscinny's text bubbles along, never missing a chance for a wisecrack, double entendre, or interesting sidetrack. Justice, of course, always triumphs, but in devious enough ways to satisfy the most jaundiced adult.

Russell B. Nye

SOURCE: "Death of a Gaulois: René Goscinny and Astérix," in *Journal of Popular Culture,* Vol. XIV, No. 2, Fall, 1980, pp. 181-95.

The history of the French comic strip begins at the turn of the century, as in Europe generally, under strong American influence. Early French strips reflected American popular patterns—adventure strips such as "Camember the Sapper" (Christophe); "The Pieds-Nickeles" (Forton); family strips "The Fenouillard Family" (Christophe); and the famous "Zig and Puce" (Alain St. Ogan). Comic strips from the United States and Belgium (where much of the European trade was concentrated) were reprinted widely in French newspapers. The "Journal de Mickey" from America and the Belgian "Spirou," along with Hergé's Belgian *Tintin* dominated the children's and adolescent market in the thirties and forties.

In 1949 France, however, began restricting imported comic strips in an attempt to encourage French talent, resulting in the appearance of such comic magazines as *Vaillant* (1950) and *Pilote* (1959), aimed at adult readers. Comic books in hardcover began to appear in the early sixties, usually collections of previously-published strips, later of originals. Relatively expensive, these books soon established comics as serious cultural artifacts. Lycées and universities introduced courses in the study of comics, while reputable journals and newspapers published scholarly analyses and critiques. Interested scholars, in fact, in the sixties formed the Center for the Study of Graphic Literature and Expression, dedicated to the investigation and evaluation of comics as an art form.

"Astérix" appeared at exactly the right time to reinforce the shift in French comics from children's to adult entertainment. René Goscinny's scripts operated, as he explained, on several levels of humor, satire and plain old-fashioned gag-writing. Albert Uderzo's drawings fitted Goscinny's ideas perfectly. After "Astérix," many of the younger cartoonists wrote "serious" strips for mature audiences—*Charlie Monthly,* one of the more popular comic journals, published its hundredth volume in 1977. In "Astérix's" wake came the bright young cartoonists of the sixties and seventies—Fred, Gotlib, Cabu, Reiser, Masse, Claire Bretecher, Giraud, Pichard, and more. It would not be too much to call René Goscinny the father of them all.

René Goscinny was born August 14, 1926 in Paris. When his father, a businessman, was transferred to an overseas post in Argentina in 1928 the family moved to Buenos Aires, where young René went to a French school. In 1938 the family moved back to Paris. René had just passed the "bac" examination for entry into university when his father died in December, 1942. Although France was occupied by the German army, René hoped to escape to London to join de Gaulle's "cadets" but could not. The family returned to Buenos Aires, where he worked for a time in a rubber factory as accountant and complaint clerk. But he liked to draw—he started, he said, when he was four—and he loved cartoons. As a schoolboy he had scribbled on the margins of his notebooks and thought up gags, and like all cartoonists, he wrote later, he "always had a deep desire to tell stories in pictures."

The rubber factory bored him, but to his enjoyment he soon found work as an artist with a public relations firm. Things went well until a client asked him to draw a nude on an olive oil bottle label and in the ensuing argument Goscinny quit. However, the family in 1945 moved to New York at the invitation of an uncle, where he hoped to find a job with the Disney organization. He could not, nor could he enroll in art school, since all the places were taken by veterans on the GI Bill. With his knowledge of English (which he said actually consisted of three verses of Coleridge and some Shakespeare) he got a job as interpreter for a Moroccan import-export firm. He was, curiously, still subject to draft by both French and American armies, and despite the fact, he said, that the American army served eggs for breakfast, he went back to France for military service in the 141st Alpine Infantry. The France he saw—of ruined cities, rationed food, and war-stunned people—was not the France of his imagination. He knew no one, and if he wanted a career as a cartoonist, New York was obviously the place to be. After his discharge he went back in 1947, walking from editor to editor with his portfolio, feeling, he said, "like a *clochard* in a world where I did not belong.'

His luck changed, however, when he caught on with a group soon to found *Mad Magazine,* including Kurtzman, Elder, Swan, Davis, and others, and worked on children's books. Although he did not particularly like New York, he was stimulated by the new wave of comics and met Maurice de Bevre, a Belgian who drew under the name of

"Morris," and several other Europeans (with whom he was to work later) then in the city. Morris encouraged Goscinny to try a strip of his own, which he did, writing and drawing "Dick Dicks," a humorous cop strip. Morris' editor saw it and invited Goscinny to visit him in Brussels if he came back to Europe. The Belgian agency, "World Press," in fact bought nineteen episodes of "Dick Dicks" and ran them later in a journal called *Le Wallonie*.

Encouraged, Goscinny left for France in 1951, to find on arrival that World Press had opened a Paris office. There he met a young French-Italian, Albert Uderzo, who did not like to write just as Goscinny was beginning to tire of drawing. The two men hit it off immediately. Goscinny wrote and Uderzo drew a pirate strip called "Jehan Pistolet" and Goscinny wrote for other artists (eventually at least eighteen) taking whatever jobs he could find to make a living—"Le Capitaine Bibou," "Benjamin et Benjamine," and "Luc Junior," among others.

The problem that Goscinny and other young comic artists and writers faced was simply that the most successful comic journals were aimed at children and adolescents—Hergé's "Tintin" was the standard—and editors were wary of adult-oriented strips. *Pilote,* a journal for adults, was a real breakthrough; Goscinny's scripts and Uderzo's style fitted its sophisticated new format perfectly. *Pilote* published a good deal of their work, but Goscinny's first real success came with "Le Petit Nicolas," drawn by Jean-Jacques Sempe, in 1958, published in *Sud-Ouest*. From then on, Goscinny's career zoomed. That same year he began "Oumpah-Pah, le peau rouge," with Uderzo, and a year later "Strapotin" with Berck.

Astérix, the feisty little Gaul with the drooping mustaches, drawn by Uderzo, appeared first in *Pilote* on October 29, 1959—soon to become (with the possible exception of Charles de Gaulle) the most famous Frenchman of his times. The first album sold 6000 copies, the second 20,000, the third 40,000 and so on. The twelfth, *Asterix and the Normans,* sold over a million, and sales still mounted. A survey in 1969 showed that two of every three Frenchmen knew Astérix. Meanwhile, "Astérix" had been translated into sixteen languages; exhibited in art galleries; quoted in the National Assembly; and had appeared on T-shirts, napkins, watches, clocks, briefcases and elsewhere (about fifty franchises in all) as well as on labels for chickens, cheese, mustard, tomato sauce, mineral water, desserts and laundry detergents.

As if to cap his popularity, officials at the Hammaguir Space Center named the first French satellite Astérix. In 1974 Goscinny and Uderzo, with their editor Georges Dargaud, formed a studio to produce full length animated films—Studio Idéfix, named after Obélix' dog—with a payroll of eighty employees. (Belvision Productions has issued two short Astérix films in 1968 and 1970). *The Twelve Labors of Asterix* appeared from the studio in 1976, when Studio Idéfix also began producing television "vignettes," or short subjects. All these ventures were highly successful. By 1976 Goscinny and Uderzo had published 23 albums, with sales exceeding 55 million.

They had just completed the twenty-fourth, *Astérix chez les Belges* [*Asterix in Belgium*], when Goscinny died suddenly of a heart attack on November 5, 1977. It was, wrote one commentator, "as if the Eiffel Tower had fallen."

More than a little of Astérix' success can be attributed to Albert Uderzo, whose work habits and drawing style fitted the strip to perfection. Goscinny first prepared a complete script for each episode, which he and Uderzo went over at length, discussing character development, background scenery, and twists of plot. Uderzo, therefore, knew the entire plot and could direct his drawings toward the conclusion. After agreeing on the "direct line" (Uderzo's term) of the plot, they emerged with a fairly complete synopsis; each paragraph of script corresponded to a page of drawings, including dialog. His scripts, Goscinny once said, were really movie scenarios; there was "simply a difference in rhythm." In the comic strip,

> it is the reader who chooses the rhythm, but in the cinema, the rhythm is imposed on the viewer. That makes the translation of humor in the comic strip easier than in the cinema, where the unraveling of gags (as in Jacques Tati, for example) is harder to grasp because the rhythm is so rapid. One little subtle gag for which a reader may search in the comic strip cannot be done in the same way in the film. . . . The comic strip, in contrast to the film, requires the art of ellipsis.

If the setting of the episode was unfamiliar, they consulted photographs of the terrain, monuments, ruins, and the like, so that the scenery could be at least minimally authentic. Such "imaginary reconstruction," as Uderzo called it, was perhaps the most enjoyable part of the planning. Unlike some writers, Goscinny welcomed suggestions—Idéfix the dog [later in translation renamed Dogmatix], for example, one of the more popular continuing characters, was Uderzo's idea.

Uderzo began drawing for comic magazines at fourteen, finally breaking into Editions Renan in 1945 with "Flamberge, Gascon Gentleman," a *Three Musketeers*-based parody. His first real success was "Arys Buck," (1946-48) featuring a Li'l Abner type caveman whose sidekick was a small, volatile Gaul with fierce mustaches and a horned helmet. He did "Stem Height, The Cowboy," "Tif," and various short-lived strips, working with the well-known writer J. M. Charlier on two popular series, "Pistolin" and "Belloy," in the fifties. With Goscinny he drew "Luc Junior" (1957) and "Le famille Moutonet" (1959). It was "Oumpah-Pah the Indian," however, done with Goscinny, that first catapulted them into prominence. Conceived in 1955 for American publication but not published until 1958 in the magazine *Tintin,* "Oumpah-Pah" was clearly the forerunner of "Astérix."

In its original conception, "Oumpah-Pah" was built about the adventures of the Flatfoot Indian tribe, bypassed by white settlement, which still existed in a remote corner of the Wild West with its language and customs intact. The central character was Oumpah-Pah, a large, naive, gentle Indian who was the tribe's chief hunter and warrior. The strip was filled with sight-gags, linguistic twists, comic red men, and Disney-type animals. Failing to sell the strip, Goscinny and Uderzo shifted the locale to the French and Indian wars in America, pitting (in James Fenimore Cooper fashion) good Indians and good whites (Flatfeet and French soldiers) against bad Indians and bad whites (Shavashavas and Hessians), focusing the action on Oumpah-Pah—now a scout for the French—and an engaging but utterly incompetent tenderfoot French officer named Hubert Pate Feuilletée (Flaky Pastry). After the appearance of "Astérix" in 1959, the two men concentrated on the new strip and allowed "Oumpah-Pah" to lapse in 1962.

According to Goscinny, neither he nor Uderzo gave much thought to the choice of Roman Gaul as the scene of the new comic strip when they discussed it in 1951. "Astérix" was actually planned in two hours, he said, and they simply thought that putting Romans and Gauls together would create a good many amusing situations. Since there were fewer Gauls than Romans, they gave them a magic potion to even things up. Whatever the reasoning, the choice was an inspired one, for every Frenchman has a soft spot in his heart for the Gauls. To the French, the Gaul is the equivalent of the American frontiersman, whose personal qualities form the basis of the French character and whose deeds provide him with a national folklore. No matter whether he was born in Strasbourg or Paris or Martinique or Algeria, or whether his name is Hennessy or Cohen or Filippini or Dupont, the average Frenchman feels kinship with the Gauls, who absorbed their conquerors and created their own unique, individualistic culture. "I know why I like Astérix," wrote one Frenchman.

> He brings back the memory of those guzzlers and brawlers who rejected the Pax Romana, the baths, the aqueducts, the Roman legions, the Goths and Visigoths and Ostrogoths who parade past in goosestep with their pointed helmets. My chauvinism is quite agreeably stirred by him.

If Astérix is chauvinistic it is because the average Frenchman is. "Most French are chauvinistic," Goscinny told *Ouest-France,* "but they're too modest to say so." They gripe and complain and protest, but "look at them when they get twenty kilometers outside the country. They look for a liter of wine and camembert, or complain about the bread, which isn't like it is at home." Astérix is typically French, as Goscinny sees him—hot-tempered, individualistic, impatient of authority, pomposity, and pretense. "There's a little of me in Astérix," he once said, "and a little of Madame Bovary too," as there is in all Frenchmen.

The pattern of each album remains more or less the same throughout the series. Each opens with a map of Gaul:

> The year is 50 B.C. Gaul is entirely occupied by the Romans. Well, not entirely. . . . One small village of indomitable Gauls still holds out against the invaders. And life is not easy for the Roman legionaires who garrison the fortified camps of Babarum, Aquarium, Laudanum, and Petitbonun. . . .

The plot, too, remains the same. Astérix and his friends embark on a journey, encounter adventures in foreign lands, triumph over obstacles, and return home to a celebratory feast of roast wild boar. The reader's enjoyment derives in large part from his anticipation of the characters' reactions in a given situation, wherever it may be.

It is in the characters, of course, that the strip's great appeal lies. There are four fully developed and imaginatively conceived personalities.

Abraracourcix [later in translation renamed Vitalstatistix], chief of the tribe. A majestic, brave, hot-tempered warrior, respected by his subjects and feared by his enemies. He has but one flaw, a peculiar dread that the sky will fall on his head tomorrow. He is also very French. He complains about his liver, is a bit henpecked by his wife Bonemine, looks for bargains in the shops, and gets his own milk in the morning. On formal outings he is carried on a shield by two muscular Gauls who always forget to stoop when they carry him through a door.

Assurancetourix (later in translation renamed Cacofonix), the tribal bard. He hopes to bring culture to the tribe by his songs; he is also tribal historian and reciter of sagas. Opinion of his talents is divided—he thinks he is an unappreciated artistic genius, the rest of the tribe do not. When he sings dogs faint, plants wither, Goths and Romans flee. The tribe usually gag him lest he sing at feasts.

Obélix, Astérix' constant companion. He is a mountain of a man who thinks constantly of food, often at the most crucial moments. His occupation is delivering menhirs, the huge stones, weighing tons, used in constructing the druidic religious circles which can still be seen in Brittany. He is a kind of human truck, and signs of the menhir factory where he works read "Danger, Menhir Crossing" and "Watch Out for Menhirs." Obélix often gives out extra menhirs as gifts and carries one with him since, he says, you never know when one may come in handy. He draws his great strength from an accident in infancy—he fell into a vat of magic potion, the effects of which must be regularly renewed by new batches brewed by the tribal druid, Panoramix [later in translation renamed Getafix]. Obélix is kind, happy and enjoys a fight. He is not stupid, only naive; his innocence and good humor provide an excellent foil to Astérix and his fiery temper.

Astérix, the tribe's jack-of-all-trades. A shrewd, cocky little man with a quick mind, he too draws strength from the magic brew. The villagers entrust him with the leadership of all perilous missions and battle strategy. Together with Obélix, he can beat almost any odds in a fair fight, but it is his wily brain that brings the final victory. Each episode involves a problem that cannot be solved by simply physical combat—that Astérix wins, Goscinny once said, shows that intelligence always defeats force.

The problems of each episode are not serious, nor are the consequences of failure really dangerous. In *The Mansions of the Gods,* it is Caesar's plan to cut down the woods surrounding the Gallic villages to make room for a suburban development. There are far too many Romans to fight, so Astérix engages Assurancetourix to serenade

From The Mansions of the Gods, *written by René Goscinny and illustrated by Albert Uderzo.*

the prospective tenants, which immediately empties the whole housing project. In *Asterix and the Chieftain's Shield,* the Romans, in order to establish control of the fractious tribe, arrange a battle between Abraracourcix and their own challenger, a compliant turncoat, the winner to be made chief. Ordinarily Panoramix' magic potion would guarantee Abraracourcix' victory, but a chance blow on the head from a falling menhir erases the formula from the druid's mind. Even a session with a fellow druid who specializes in psychiatry, Amnesix, fails to restore his memory until the last moment. When the Romans in desperation build a wall around the villages, Astérix and Obélix, in *Asterix and the Banquet,* simply go over it and make a complete tour of France to show the Romans the folly of their plan.

Asterix and Cleopatra (1965) provides a representative example of Goscinny and Uderzo at work. The adventure stems from Cleopatra's wager with Caesar, who had accused the Egyptians of softness and decadence, that she can have the most magnificent palace built in Alexandria in three months. The Royal Architect, Edifis, is stunned. Accustomed only to building pyramids and obelisks, he needs supernatural assistance—only Getafix (Panoramix' name in English editions), the fabled magical druid in faraway Gaul, can help.

Edifis' long trip to wintry Gaul in the Royal Ship *Nash-upset* is successful; Getafix, Obélix (who wonders if crocodiles are good to eat), Dogmatix his dog, and Astérix agree to journey to Egypt to assist him. Once in Egypt, however, the Gauls immediately run into a plot set in motion by Artifis, a rival architect. The rascally Artifis incites the laborers into a sitdown strike, which Getafix solves by giving each a drink of his magic potion, after which they toss two-ton stones about with great pleasure and abandon. But Artifis is not done. By bribing a guide he traps the Gauls inside a pyramid, but Dogmatix finds a way out. Artifis' last desperate attempt fails—he sends a poisoned cake to Cleopatra, presumably a gift from the Gauls. Getafix prepares an antidote, the Gauls eat the cake, and Artifis is thrown to the sacred crocodiles but rescued by the soft-hearted Gauls.

Meanwhile Caesar, fearing to lose his wager, has sent a Roman spy, Superfluous, to report on the palace's progress. Since it is nearly finished, Caesar sends an entire regiment of legionaires to stop it. The Romans are no match for the Gauls, who have demolished Roman legions before. So Caesar loses his bet, Edifis is rewarded with a pile of gold, and the Gallic trio return home to a welcoming feast of roast boar.

A synopsis of the plot, however, fails to convey the full flavor of an Astérix episode since it does not reveal the slightly manic touches of dialogue, sight gags and inside jokes which characterize Goscinny's and Uderzo's work. There are constant references to Cleopatra's nose that all literate Frenchmen immediately identify with Pascal's famous remark about the relation of its length to the course of history. All Gauls have blue noses in winter; Cleopatra drinks pearls in vinegar like Cokes; the Royal Egyptian Scribe has learned Gallic by a correspondence course; the Sphinx lacks a nose (you can see it still) because Obélix accidentally broke it off. When Obélix wants to take an Egyptian obelisk back to France as a souvenir, Astérix refuses to allow it—"That thing in the middle of our village? It would look ridiculous!" Cleopatra is always shown in profile (looking vaguely like a Picasso) because the Royal Sculptor doesn't like modern art. Instead of light bulbs in balloons to indicate ideas, there are oil lamps. The local newspaper is *Pharaoh-Soir.* The engine room of Cleopatra's barge has signals in signs of the Zodiac. As Goscinny told his *L'Express* interviewer, he and Uderzo aimed at "a perfect synthesis of text and picture. One can read it at several levels—not only levels of age, but of perception."

There is violence in "*Astérix,*" but of the old-fashioned POW, WHAP, BAM variety, never cruel or gratuitous. Though the stories are filled with boings, biffs, schplokks, chiplonks, ouapps, and the rest, it is conventional pratfall violence. The Gauls fight Romans, Greeks, Bretons, Egyptians and each other, with many black eyes, bandages, crutches, and the like, but nobody takes it very seriously. The Gauls, who always win, enjoy it; the Romans never learn. In *Asterix Gladiator,* there is naturally violence on almost every page, and in the grand finale Astérix and Obélix quickly demolish twenty-five armored legionaries in what must have been the greatest fight in the history of the games. But it's good fun. The Romans are dented a bit, but they recover.

Goscinny handles what would be normally unfunny violence by removing its sting. The barbarities, tortures and brutalities of Astérix' era are somehow transformed into innocuous play. Vendors at slave markets cry their wares, with "Fresh Gauls today! Fresh Gauls today!" Panoramix the druid, about to be tortured into revealing the recipe for the magic potion, is tied to a table—and a slave tickles his feet with a feather. An Egyptian, about to be thrown to the sacred crocodile as a sacrifice, worries that he may upset the River God's stomach. The gladiators play Twenty Questions to see who fights next; lions flee in absolute terror when Assurancetourix the bard sings at them. As Goscinny said, "I'm a gentle man. I like the warm side of things."

Much of the effectiveness of Astérix derives from Goscinny's play with language—already fully developed in "Iznogoud" and "Oumpah-Pah." French is marvellously adapted to word-play, and Goscinny makes inspired use of its resources. Foreigners speak strange and wonderful French; Englishmen put the adjective before the noun, Africans cannot master the French "r," Germans speak Teutonic beerhall French. Goths naturally speak in Gothic script and ancient Egyptians in hieroglyphics, which are translated interlinearly into French (crowds cheer Cleopatra, for example, by invoking the Sun God, "Ra! Ra! Ra!") Goscinny's gift for dialect is most evident in the names of cities, countries, Gauls, Romans, Normans, and the rest, which *look* authentic and follow wildly logical rules.

Gaulois names end in *ix;* Norman in *ef;* Viking in *sen;* Gothic in *ic;* Egyptian in *is;* Spanish are in two words, after the Hispanic system; Roman in *os, us,* or *um.* All this is more or less historically accurate, but the actual result is far different. Astérix is of course astérisque (asterisk) and his giant friend Obélix is obelisque (monument). Assurancetourix the tribal poet translates as "complete coverage auto insurance" (assurances tous risques). The full gallery of Gallic names is too long to review, but worth mentioning are Panoramix, Boulmix (Boul' Mich or Boulevard St. Michel), Aventurepix (adventure movie), Cetautomatix ("It's automatic"), a physician named Dr. Orthopedix, Moraleastix (moralistic), and a dog named, of course, Dogmatix. No one should be surprised to find a teacher of modern languages named Professor Berlix.

Roman names are equally inventive. The chief villages of the Gauls are Babaorum (rum cake), Laudanum (an opium-based painkiller), Petitbonum (*petit bonhomme,* or "good little man"), Aquarium, and Compendium. One finds a Roman general named Malsinus (sinus headache), others named Aerobus and Stratocumulus, and a spy named Tullius Detritus (garbage). Romeomontaigus takes a moment to figure out. Pactealargus "pas que t'es a l'*Argus*" means "not listed in *Argus*," the French used-car journal, and another, Plutoqueprevus (*plutot que prévus*), or "sooner than expected." A Norman chief is named Complete-

menpaf ("a completement paf," "utterly crazy") while two Viking warriors are Obsen (obscene) or Kerosen. Håråldwilssen the saga-reciter recalls the British Prime Minister of the same name (the Vikings are of course Anglosaxon) and one cannot help but note the terrifying warchiefs Herendethelessen and Odiuscomparissen. (Viking dogs, incidentally, bark Wøøf! Wøøf!) Soupalognon-Crouton, an aristocratic Spanish double name, is of course "onion soup with croutons." Goths are named Cloridic (hydrochloric acid), Liric, Satiric, Electric, and Teleforic (cogwheeled railway)—nor should one overlook the Gothic fishmonger Unhygienic and his wife Bacteria. Sample Egyptians are named Misenplis (hair wave set), Tournevis (screwdriver), and Napodélis (*n'a pas d'helice*—"he has no propeller"). Possibilities are endless, and Goscinny takes full advantage of the device.

Goscinny always denied, vehemently, that "Astérix" had deeper symbolic, ideological or social meanings. "I am essentially an entertainer," he said. "I am not a moralist. I don't give lessons, I am not to be taken seriously, and I like to make people laugh." His closest approach to a "message" came in *La Zizanie [Asterix and the Roman Agent]* (1970). The only way to gain the secret of the magic potion and to conquer the Gauls, the Romans conclude, is to divide them by inducing discord and disunity in the recalcitrant villages. They find the perfect instrument in a shifty-eyed, despicable little Roman named Tullius Detritus, whose very presence at any gathering causes turmoil and violence. True to predictions, Detritus, posing as a deserter, brings greed, jealousy and distrust into the villages, and only after great psychological resistance do the Gauls succeed in regaining their pride and re-forming their solid anti-Roman front. *La Zizanie* is the most thoughtful of the episodes, evoking discussion of the values of unity, self-respect, cooperation, and mutual trust, and is in this respect unique in the series.

But for the most part, Goscinny's disclaimer applies to all of Astérix, as well as to "Iznogoud," "Lucky Luke," and "Oumpah-Pah." "A joke is by nature a confrontation," he maintained, "and I don't think it should become a moral or political platform." In one of his infrequent longer interviews, in 1976, he was quite clear about his position. "People have accused me," he said,

> of all sorts of intentions, all sorts of sins, especially of being political, but I haven't done that and I don't do it. It is essential to me that I make people laugh. That in my way of thinking is the only work of the humorist. The discussions of savants seem always useless to me. . . . My only purpose is to make something that helps people have fun. Not another thing! All the exegeses that have been written (of Astérix) have no relation to reality—there's nothing to make of it.

Nonetheless, given the discovery of comics in the fifties by the intellectual community in America and Europe, it was inevitable that "Astérix" should soon become fair game for the critics. One could read into the scripts a whole set of references to the German occupation of France; to reaffirmations of French values and traditions after a lost war; to the emergence of de Gaulle; to the

Vietcong and the American army; to the conflict of French socialism (Gaul) and the capitalist state (Roman); and to Breton fairy tales and medieval romances. Goscinny was particularly incensed by a rather pompous, intellectualized analysis by Hervé Bernard and S. de Sede in *La nouvelle critique* which explained that "Astérix" was an "ideological vehicle" for "a treatment of the traditional conflict between jacobins and republicans" and "the search for liberty and order in French life from Vercingetorix to de Gaulle, the providential man." Such critics, he replied,

> have the exegesis sickness. When you laugh they want to know why. When a critic wants Uderzo to explain why he puts that line there and this one here, or me to explain why I write that word rather than another—it's time we protested and said they're there because that's where they ought to go, but it seems we don't know our own minds.

On the contrary, it's all simple—people laugh at Astérix "because he does funny things, and that's all. Our only ambition is to have fun." However, Goscinny's denials rarely registered with the critics, and detailed, complicated explanations continued to appear.

There are two strategies central to "Astérix." The first is adapted from the traditional French literary device of the travelling stranger-commentator, which appeared in its best-known form in Montesquieu's *Persian Letters* (1721) and has been endlessly imitated since. In each case a traveller from a presumably naive, "primitive" country, surveying the "civilized" and sophisticated culture of his hosts, comments on its curious customs, language, ideas, and values. The device thus provides a useful vehicle for double-edged satire by placing both cultures in contrast. Goscinny had of course already used this successfully in both "Oumpah-Pah" and "Iznogoud."

"Astérix" sets Gaul against Romans, Swiss, British, Greeks, Germans, Scandinavians and American Indians, among others. That the Gauls always come out best, naturally, is itself a comment on the Frenchman's inherent assumption of national superiority. To the Gauls, all foreigners are strange, irrational, a bit uncivilized, and often not very bright, with curious foibles and odd customs. Even Parisians, Normans, Auvernais, and Nicois are fair game, and Goscinny spears French provincialities with the same accuracy.

Astérix, in this fashion, draws its humor almost entirely from contrasts of cultural, ethnic and linguistic stereotypes. The Swiss climb mountains (Astérix teaches them how to do it right), eat fondue, and are determinedly neutral; Swiss soldiers carry first-aid kits instead of weapons. Bretons wear plus-fours and say "Bonté gracieuse" ("Good gracious!"), "Je dis!" ("I say!") and "joyeaux bien!" ("Jolly good!"). Breton cottages look like Anne Hathaway's and have neatly clipped green lawns; Bretons will neither fight nor work on long weekends, boil all food, drink warm beer, and ride in doubledecked chariots.

Romans (who are not Italian) represent all that Goscinny and Uderzo dislike in contemporary life—bureaucracy, regimentation, the military mind. They cut down forests, pollute streams, cover Gaul with billboards, pave over the fields, build huge apartments and create instant slums. (Roman cities look suspiciously like modern Paris.) They are vain, pompous, self-indulgent, and most of all can neither understand nor cope with individualism, ingenuity, and disrespect for the rules. The Roman battle phalanx is *always* shattered by the Gauls and Roman commanders *always* order it; Roman spies *never* succeed in infiltrating Gallic villages but *never* stop trying. Yet Romans are neither cruel nor villainous; they display a kind of childish ineptitude that both readers and Gauls find amusing.

The second strategem in "Astérix" lies in the fact that it is an extension of a familiar genre—the school history text. The study of French history begins in the first grade and continues through lycée; its materials are familiar to every man, woman and child. The French attitude toward the past plays a crucial role in the formation of the national and the individual character. Their history is drummed into all French so thoroughly that each person has a powerful sense of continuity with preceding generations.

In the early grades the history manuals are heavily illustrated, so that children learn to see the past as pictures. In one older text, for example, Chapter 2 tells the child that "the Gauls were brave but undisciplined. They worshiped many gods. They liked war. They were good farmers and workmen." Gallic life is illustrated by pictures of menhirs, shoes, lamps, cooking utensils, arms, costumes, a Roman camp, and so on. A later text is equally pictorial, profusely illustrated in color, including a panorama of a Gallic village, the ceremonial cutting of mistletoe by a druid, and Caesar's siege of Alesia. The child, therefore, learns to see the French past in terms of images, drawn from a large common fund of history-book illustrations—which stick in his mind forever—Vercingetorix surrendering to Caesar; Hugh Capet crowned King; Saint Louis dispensing justice beneath an oak tree; Charlemagne visiting the schools; Napoleon surveying the field of Austerlitz. French elementary school texts traditionally begin with the words, "Our ancestors, the Gauls," or a similar phrase, and as Goscinny and Uderzo recognized, stories about them "take us back to our discovery of the French past."

Reading "Astérix," then, is in a real sense a re-view of a cultural experience common to all French, part of each one's childhood and a recollection of his or her first consciousness of their heritage. This device not only allows "Astérix" to ring nostalgic bells in the reader's mind, but permits Goscinny and Uderzo to caricature both past and present by superimposing modern ideas and issues on past persons, places and periods—a traditional maneuver familiar to many humorists. Gauls did wear pants with belts and buckles, striped clothing and horned helmets, as every school child knows. They lived in small villages, placed great trust in bards and druids, set up menhirs and domens, and gathered mistletoe for its magical properties as Panoramix does.

Here history stops and parody begins. It is hard to find parts in Gaul for an imported Italian sports-chariot. Road signs say "Slow—Slippery Tiles" and "Caution, Slaves at Work." Billboards advertise detergents that will "make your toga even more purple" and circuses are interrupted by singing commercials. Caesar quotes his own *Gallic Wars* and Danish chieftains say "To be or not to be," while a Viking leader, setting foot on American soil, says "Un petit pas pour moi, un grand pas pour l'humanite." *Asterix and Cleopatra,* for example, comments on the postal system, modern art, labor unions, four-star restaurants, advertising jingles, professional athletics, building contractors and government red tape, to name a few of its targets.

In retrospect, what made "Astérix" so popular, despite its Frenchness, beyond France? Why was it translated into sixteen languages? What would its linguistic ingenuity, its sight gags, its multileveled humor mean to a Japanese, a Brazilian, or for that matter, to an American? Goscinny himself admitted that he did not know, nor was he particularly anxious to find out—if people laughed, he said, that was enough. Yet one may guess, without doing an injustice to Goscinny's own disclaimers. The targets of "Astérix" are universal—pomposity, bureaucracy, regimentation, pretentiousness. There are Romans everywhere, and everybody enjoys seeing them punctured. The Gauls are fully-developed characters whose qualities everyone may respond to—individualistic, ingenious, unafraid, disrespectful of authority, utterly unconquerable.

What Astérix and his friends represent, in effect, is protest—strongly flavored with nostalgia—for a simpler, less-computerized century than the late twentieth has been and the twenty-first is likely to be. To the French and European reader, "Astérix" may seem to be (as several commentators have assumed) anti-American, a protest against the "New Romans" whose pitiless efficiency, mass production, and cultural sameness appear to threaten him with anonymity. However, the feeling could as easily be anti-Russian, anti-Chinese, anti-Japanese, or anti-German; more accurately, it is anti-"progress," anti-technology, anti-twentieth century. The use of the United States as whipping-boy for the problems of modernity has, of course, a long history in France from André Maurois and Georges Duhamel to the present, despite the obvious fact that so-called "Americanism" is simply a phase in the development of modern society that thrives in Paris and Berlin and Tokyo and Moscow as well as in New York. Thus the Japanese in the auto plant, the clerk in the Paris department store, the Berliner in the mazes of civil service, or for that matter the American on the lower rungs of IBM can respond with alacrity to Astérix, Obélix, and their war against Caesar and his pro-consuls.

Modern life, Goscinny said a year before his death, is beginning to look like a battle of computers, with ordinary people caught in the middle. As the target of "Astérix" was the bureaucrat, so that of the new "Obélix" strip was to be the technocrat. The Gauls are holdovers in the bureaucratized, technocratized world of 50 B.C. which looks suspiciously like our own.

The humor of "Astérix" is humane. It hurts, degrades, humiliates no one; it is the universal, gentle humor of Mickey Mouse and Krazy Kat, where the logical is absurd, violence non-violent, anger ridiculous. To the humorist, Goscinny told an interviewer in 1976,

> Anger and aggression are dangerous things after a while; the reader is no longer aroused to it. If the writer wants the spectator to laugh, he must counter anger with sympathy. Humor comes out of gentleness.

Panoramix and Obélix, at the end of *La Zizanie,* sum up René Goscinny's philosophy of laughter very well. "Oh," says Panoramix, speaking of the Gauls, "they are brawlers, hare-brained, heads stuck up in the air, but you have to love them. . . . They are human." To which Obélix replies, "Yes, they're crazy, but they're human."

Anthea Bell

SOURCE: "Translator's Notebook," in *The Signal Approach to Children's Books,* edited by Nancy Chambers, Scarecrow Press, 1980, pp. 129-39.

"Corsica." We're confronting Goscinny and Uderzo's *Astérix en Corse* [*Asterix in Corsica*], my colleague Derek

René Goscinny.

Hockridge and myself. "What would you say is the sum total of English general knowledge about Corsica?"

"Napoleon."

"And?"

"Napoleon, full stop."

Whereas the French have all sorts of inside knowledge and staple jokes about Corsica: wild pigs and chestnuts and ferociously smelly cheese; proud, aloof women jealously guarded by their menfolk; complicated family relationships and the vendetta. And then there's Tino Rossi, popular Corsican singer, mention of whose works permeates this book.

"What on earth are we going to do about Tino Rossi?"

Shelving Tino Rossi for the moment, we start tentatively playing with words. "We'll have to go nap on Napoleon." "And all things bony."

The differing degree of French and English general knowledge about the island is one reason why this title in the *Astérix* saga, published in 1973 in France, has waited until now for an English version. The translation of something which depends as much as *Astérix* on wordplay and puns has, in any event, to be very free, often more of an adaptation, if anything like the same humorous effect is to be produced in English. And if the material on which the jokes are based is unfamiliar itself to the young English reader, there are extra problems. About half Asterix's fixtures against the Romans are played at home, so to speak, and half away. When it comes to the away matches, the French and English share a number of cherished notions about Daft Foreigners. Spain means bullfighting, flamenco, the tourist trade. Switzerland means numbered bank accounts, yodelling, fondue. But when the people of the little Armorican village which persists in defying Julius Caesar take him on nearer home, in other parts of Gaul—or here, in Corsica—the English reader is less likely to share the stock assumptions of the original.

There's another and related reason why this title has waited some time for a translation: the story features a grand reunion of the Gauls' friends from previous books, both foreigners from Britain, Spain, etc., and allies from other parts of Gaul who speak in French regional accents. Since the saga is firmly set in Gaul, with a map of France at the beginning of every book, we could hardly substitute English regional speech without destroying the precarious illusion upon which all translation is based. Give a man from Marseilles, say, a Mummerset accent, and we'd have readers stopping to wonder why. So some different type of joke must be found, since we're determined not to admit defeat and simply translate straight, losing the verbal byplay which, in every *Astérix* book, reinforces the basic humour of the story line. This has sometimes involved the rewriting of whole frames—in one case, of an entire page where the French jokes depended on an Auvergnat accent. (All done, needless to say, with the author's approval.) It was not until we had translated the

titles where this problem arose, notably *Le Bouclier Arverne* (*Asterix and the Chieftain's Shield*) and *Le Tour de Gaule* (*Asterix and the Banquet*) that we could have characters from these books making a guest appearance in *Asterix in Corsica*. . . .

[We] have our basic principles for translating *Astérix*. If we stop to work them out, they're something like this:

a) The idea is to render, as faithfully as possible, the *feel* of the original.

b) With humour of this intensely verbal nature, the translation must follow the spirit rather than the letter of the original; we must therefore often find jokes which are different, though we hope along the same lines as the French jokes.

c) They must, of course, suit Albert Uderzo's wittily detailed drawings, in particular they must fit the expressions on the speakers' faces.

d) From the purely technical point of view, they must be about the same length as the original wording, or we shall create difficulties for the letterer trying to get the English text into the speech-bubbles.

e) Very important: we will try for the same kind of mixture of jokes as in the French, where Asterix appeals on a number of different levels. There's the story-line itself with its ever-attractive theme of the clever little fellow outwitting the hulking great brute; there is simple knockabout humour, both verbal and visual, which goes down well with quite young children; there are puns and passages of wordplay for older children; and there is some distinctly sophisticated humour, depending on literary or artistic allusion, for the adult or near-adult mind.

f) We will also have the same number of jokes as in the French. If we just can't get one in at the same point as in the original, we'll make up for it somewhere else. And we won't drag English jokes in by the hair of their heads, but if there is an obvious gift we'll use it, even if there was no counterpart in the French. (This, again, was done with the author's approval; up to the last two translations, with his personal go-ahead on the typescript of each English version.) Such a gift has been the fact that while the conventional French means of representing a hiccup is "Hips!" its English equivalent is "Hic!", so that drunken Roman legionaries can be allowed to hiccup in Latin: "Hic, haec, hoc." We are grateful to Gibbon, too, since in appropriate places the Romans may be seen declining and falling all over the place.

We were visited, once, by a young man earnestly studying our translations of *Astérix* for a mini-thesis, as part of his work at Nanterre University. He had assigned our versions of every single frame to one of four categories: *un gain, une perte, une équivalence, une compensation.* "You see," said he, "I am treating this like Shakespeare." He was, too; it was rather unnerving. But he certainly had the general idea.

"A lot of names here in *Corsica*." As with the jokes, the ingeniously spoof Gaulish and Roman names of Goscinny's characters, formed as they are of real French words and phrases, usually need rethinking in English. A few, like Stratocumulus, are all right in both languages, but most of the others have to be replaced. Our folder of oddments contains a list of Names Already Used, which we bring up to date after every title, for fear of repeating ourselves: a necessary precaution, as the list now runs to some two hundred and twenty names. By the time we're through with *Corsica* there will be about another thirty on it. We also have odd lists, made from time to time, of possible names *not* yet used. In the current story, Asterix and Obelix are off to help the Corsicans, whose names also end in -ix. Kind little boys write to us with suggestions for Gaulish names; in fact we're usually searching for more *Roman* names, since the basic Gaulish characters go on from book to book, but require a new set of Roman opponents to be polished off each time.

"Not so many Romans as usual in this book, actually. There's this centurion, Gazpachoandalus, early on." We are pleased when, like Goscinny, we can make a whole phrase into a Roman name (Sendervictorius and Appianglorius, a couple of Roman soldiers), but owing to the difference between the normal word order of noun and adjective in English and French, it is generally much harder to make up such compounds in English. . . .

Here, at last, is the page where the French contains a genuine Napoleonic joke, as the Corsican chieftain musters his clans. *"Regardez là-bas, la colonne qui arrive en retard . . . ah, Osterlix, son chef, a du mal à se lever tôt . . ."* And, in the next frame, with the rising sun behind him, the chief adds, *"C'est qu'il est célèbre chez nous, le sommeil d'Osterlix."*

Now, given that English-speakers do know about Napoleon, and even about Austerlitz, you'd think this would be easy, but it turns out surprisingly hard. How many people will recognize an allusion to Napoleon's *"Voilà le soleil d'Austerlitz"*, especially in the attempt we must make to twist it as the French has done? We think this one over for ages. In the end, we come up with two versions. One sticks fairly close to the French. "See that column over there? Led by the son of one of our most famous names . . . the son of Austerlix." The other, after all the extra Napoleonic references we have worked in earlier to compensate for lost French jokes, breaks away from Napoleon entirely. Where else, we ask ourselves, do you also find clans, and a good bit of feuding? We could extract one of the pasta people from the main body of Corsican clan chiefs and use him here. "Yes, we're full of clan feeling . . . see that column over there? Those are the Corsicans whose chief married into a Caledonian clan . . . the clan of Macaronix."

It is a choice between the more sophisticated Austerlitz reference, for which you really need to be approaching A-level standard in history and/or French, and the simpler joke which we hope may appeal to more of the younger readers, and in the end we opt for the latter alternative.

This isn't the course we would—or indeed could—always adopt. We think of such sustained sophisticated jokes as the superb page in *Le Cadeau de Cesar* [*Asterix and Caesar's Gift*]. In the original, Asterix takes on a belligerent Roman soldier in the village pub, and as he launches into a swordfight simultaneously assumes the mantle of Rostand's Cyrano de Bergerac, composing a *ballade* as he fights. *"Ca, c'est envoyé!"* ("That's the stuff!") cries the innkeeper's daughter, as Asterix, like Cyrano, delivers the winning swordstroke on the last line of the *envoi*. In French, this is obviously not one for the youngest readers: it would, we felt, be wrong to simplify. Necessary, then, to substitute something. Most famous swordfight in English literature? Probably Hamlet and Laertes. Lead into it as the innkeeper's wife tells her husband to take no notice of the soldier—have her add, in English, "Act with disdain." Then the Roman can reply, with perfect truth, "I am more an antique Roman than a Dane," and we proceed to assorted quotations from *Hamlet,* with the girl commenting, "A hit, a very palpable hit!" for the *envoi* reference, and going on over the page, where opportunity offers, "He's made a hit with me all right." Inevitably, our version fell short of the lovely stylishness of the French, but we had to do something along those lines, since the passage cried out for a literary allusion.

Here, however, we did have a choice—so the one genuine Napoleonic joke of the original text of *Astérix en Corse* went by the board. . . . How is it, we wonder in passing, we've never yet been able to work in "go by the board", among all the wild boar jokes? We've tried so hard to find variations on the inevitable line "This is a bit of a bore", our rough equivalent to the recurrent French joke about *sangliers* (wild boars) and *cochonneries* (rubbish). But somehow the occasion for "go by the board" has never come up.

We're approaching the end of *Corsica*. . . . The Governor and the pirates are anxious to put out to sea as fast as possible, so "cast off" seems a possible starting point, and we come up with a string of knitting references, beginning with the pirate captain's well-founded suspicion of the Governor's haste: "A bit of plain dealing first. Where's the loot you've purloined?" The pirates sink for the umpteenth time: "Well, do we cast off?" "No point casting pearls before swine." "Was that meant to have us in stitches?" "Cap'n, with due regard, you're a silly knit." And pretty soon afterwards the Gauls are home, indulging in their usual banquet and giving an account of the beauties of Corsica, which now include "some interesting Roman remains, dating from the time of our visit."

I type THE END. We look at it. Forty-four pages of typescript; we can never say exactly how long it takes to translate an *Astérix* album, since one is mulling over the problems of wordplay at all sorts of odd times before coming up with the final version. But it doesn't look much, for all that work and thought. Is anyone going to laugh at the English version? We're far too close to it to know. And we also feel a personal sadness that this is the second English Astérix translation René Goscinny will not read;

we valued his interest and sympathetic understanding of our problems enormously.

There is still *Astérix chez les Belges* [*Asterix in Belgium*] to come. Goscinny had just finished its text before his death. Needless to say, it is thick with Belgian accents . . . our thoughts are already turning that way.

"What would you say is the sum total of English general knowledge about Belgium?"

"Gallant little."

"Brussels sprouts."

"Maybe the E.E.C., these days."

"Waterloo. Napoleon."

Back to Napoleon. . . .

D. J. Hockridge

SOURCE: "Trix of the Trade," in *The Times Educational Supplement,* No. 3405, October 2, 1981, p. 34.

The English version of Asterix is as much an adaptation as a translation. A French student studying for a higher degree chose as his subject the English version of Asterix. He had taken each frame of the original and each frame of the translations we had then done and was comparing them carefully. He found that there were four possibilities: *équivalence, perte, gain,* or *compensation.* When the story was being told, or when a joke occurred that was the same in English then we could translate straight. However, as most readers of Asterix in the original will know, so many of the jokes or comic situations depend on something French, whether it be the situation or the word play, that there must be an inevitable loss in translation. In fact, Goscinny often deliberately engineered situations to reach a climax which would culminate in an outrageous pun. This was a technique he used more obviously in *The Adventures of Iznogoud* where the stories occasionally lose their logical thread but which allow for all sorts of funny word play.

So we have *équivalence* and *perte* but just occasionally there may be something in a frame which suggests an English pun or opportunity for word play which we then supplied, with Goscinny's approval, to make up for the inevitable *pertes* elsewhere. These were the *gains* and the *compensations.*

For example, the names are mostly untranslatable. The Gauls, Abraracourcix (from *se battre à bras recourcis*), Assurancetourix, the bard (from *assurances tous risques*) would be equally meaningless in English. So we tried to find names in English ending in "ix", by analogy with Vercingétorix, the original Gaulish hero, with the same sort of ring: Cacofonix, the bard, Dogmatix, Obelix's little dog, Prawnsinaspix, Vitalstatistix and so on. Roman names presented the same problem. Pacotéalargus (*pas coté à l'Argus*) usually describing an old banger whose price is not even quoted in the Argus, a parisian paper, would have been meaningless translated. . . .

Series of puns and word play can present more complex difficulties. When a group of Roman soldiers, all camouflaged with twigs and leaves, are apprehensively awaiting a Gaulish attack, it is relatively easy to find equivalent phrases and words connected with trees that can be made to sound funny: "I'm trembling like a leaf!", "I'd as lief not be here", "Shut up you big sap!". But on other occasions, the humour may depend on a more subtle appreciation of French culture. . . .

[In *Astérix Legionnaire!* (*Asterix the Legionary*) there is] perhaps the author's finest visual joke. The pirates have been sunk, yet again, and Uderzo draws a faithful representation of Théodore Géricault's "Le Radeau de la Méduse" inspired by the French frigate that sank off the coast of Africa in 1816 and whose 15 survivors were miraculously picked up 12 days later. The captain is saying "Je suis médusé!", a familiar way of saying "I'm stupefied!" or "dumbstruck". The joke is so neat in French. Here was going to be an obvious *perte.* We came up with "We've been framed, by Jericho!" "The spirit caught, the words flying free" was perhaps the nicest comment on our translation by a Professor of French and it's one we treasure.

Charles Bremner

SOURCE: "Asterix: The Gaul," in *The Times,* London, July 9, 1994, pp. 16-17, 20.

The mourning for Asterix may be premature. When the Paris appeal court ruled last month against Albert Uderzo, in a suit against his first publisher, the creator of the indomitable Gaul announced he was packing up his drawing board. Now, sitting in his elegant office a menhir's throw from the Arc de Triomphe, Uderzo is having second thoughts.

He is bitter about a battle over rights with the Dargaud company that has been as long and vain as his hero's bouts with the Romans are quick and triumphant. "I was really shocked by the court decision that went against me," he says. "I am tired and, for the moment, I've decided to stop, but—who knows—perhaps in a couple of weeks I'll feel like getting back into harness."

Uderzo's announcement of the demise of Asterix after 35 years, 29 adventures and the sale of 250 million albums had been greeted by many as a cause for national sorrow.

For millions, the little warrior of the 1st century B.C. is far more than a beloved character from children's stories. Asterix is a patriotic hero, the incarnation of the Gallic soul—or at least an idealised version of it—and easily the most successful ambassador of France in a world conquered by that new imperial force, the Americans.

Alain Peyrefitte, the former justice minister who is now the head of *Le Figaro,* says Asterix embodies President de Gaulle's philosophy that the Frenchman must remain wholeheartedly French. In the Sixties, de Gaulle used to joke that his only rival in fame was Tintin, the boy reporter created by the Belgian genius Hergé, whose legend is undiminished in modern France. But in the Nineties, no Frenchman comes close to the celebrity of Asterix, a Sixties figure whose pugnacious chauvinism gave him more in common with the general than a big nose. In a 1992 survey, Asterix was voted the most popular cartoon character in Europe, well ahead of Mickey Mouse and Tintin.

In more intellectual circles, and in the world of the *bande dessinée* (BD), as comic-strip art is called in France, Uderzo's decision caused rather less emotion. For the cognoscenti of a genre that is taken very seriously in modern Gaul, Asterix, Obelix and their modern Gaul, Asterix, Obelix and their resistant village had never really recovered from the death in 1977 of René Goscinny, the man who wrote the plots that Uderzo turned into pictures. After Uderzo took up the writing—he has produced five adventures since 1980—the plots lost their zing and the gags their wit, the purists say.

Political correctness is a big factor because Asterix is, of course, deemed, like Tintin before him, to be a reactionary, a racist, a misogynist and a homophobe. The women—such as Bonemine (Impedimenta in the English version) and the wife of Chief Abraracourcix (Vitalstatistix)—were always nagging shrews or pretty dolls. Uderzo compounded the offence in his last work, *La Rose et le glaive* (*Asterix and the Secret Weapon*), by depicting a batallion of female legionnaires as classic bimbos who are terrified of insects and give up the fight when the Gauls sell them Paris fashions.

The public doesn't seem too bothered, though. Sales have roared on, *La Rose et le glaive* has so far sold 7 million copies.

Compounding Uderzo's offence, in the eyes of the purists, is his success in turning his hero into a multinational industry that has made him one of the richest men in France. The artist, who was the son of Italian immigrants and started work at 13, answers the exploitation charge without waiting for the question. "They say I've become just a businessman. That's ridiculous. But I don't find anything pejorative about that word. These days it's surely a good thing to be called a businessman. But if I really was just a businessman, I wouldn't have turned out five albums in 14 years; I would have produced at least 28 because I would have hired a team of artists and scriptwriters. But I am still a little artisan who delights in drawing and writing and I haven't the slightest wish to knock them off in some Asterix factory." . . .

The court battle stemmed from the insistence of both Goscinny and Uderzo that Dargaud had deprived them of the rights to their early albums. The artist-businessman says he is now fighting to preserve the true nature of Asterix in the latest film, a big German-financed production which is being tailored to break into the United States, a market that has largely resisted the gallant Gaul and his boar-guzzling chums. He is upset that, in order to please the Americans, the voices have been changed and Obelisk, Asterix's menhir-toting sidekick, has been made even more stupid than usual. The makers also want Uderzo to remove the black pirate, one of the regular characters.

"They say it's racist, but he is part of the crew. If he goes, all the pirates go. Then they want to call it *Asterix in America* and everyone knows perfectly well that America didn't exist in those days, so it's nonsense. I've asked that they call it *Asterix in the New World.* I understand that one has to make concessions to the market, but if we turn Asterix into a Mickey Mouse then I think people will start reacting badly." The film is based on *La Grande Traversée* (*Asterix and the Great Crossing*), in which the heroes reach the New World, where they are captured by a Viking called Kerosen.

Of course, Goscinny and Uderzo never set out to create a national hero or dreamt that psychiatrists and doctoral students would analyse the Freudian symbolism of the Asterix universe, contrasting such things as the feminine curves of the village with the impotent thrusting of the Roman battering rams. And they never guessed that they would bequeath a whole series of catchphrases to the language. These range from Obelix's leitmotif *"Ils sont fous, ces Romains"* to "The only thing they fear is the sky falling on their heads".

"We had no idea he was destined for such success and it's a good thing too, because we would probably have played around with him and destroyed the spontaneity," Uderzo says. The pair teamed up in 1959 at *Pilote,* a groundbreaking BD magazine riding on the post-war comics boom that came from America. . . .

"Goscinny said: 'Let's look for an idea. What do we learn at school about the history of France?' We started at the Stone Age, but that had already been done. So we came to the Gauls. It was as simple as that. Luckily we didn't know that the idea had already been used with a character called Otorix, or we wouldn't have gone ahead."

All French schoolchildren learn about "our ancestors the Gauls", so the references were already there. Goscinny's genius was to turn the traditional view on its head and make the barbarian Gauls appear the civilised ones and the Romans as bungling and totalitarian. "If we had just told the story of what we knew from history, it wouldn't have been funny at all." Uderzo, who speaks with great fondness for his late partner, came up with Obelix and his dog Idéfix. Together they invented the Magic Potion which makes the Gauls invincible. "We had to have something like Popeye's spinach," he says.

The gags based on anachronism were Goscinny's, as were the linguistic tricks. The writers have always tried hard to keep the punning humour of the names in the translations, which now range from Estonian to Indonesian. The tone-deaf bard Assurancetourix (comprehensive insurance), for example, is called Cacofonix in the English version, which has been translated by Anthea Bell and Derek Hockridge since the Gaul was launched in Britain 25 years ago this autumn. But some of the best plays on words elude translation. Among the funniest to French ears is the reversal of syntax and the Franglais in *Astérix chez les Bretons* (*Asterix in Britain*), which is the best-selling album in the U.K. In this, the tweed-wearing ancient Englishmen say such un-French things as *"Bonne chance et toute cette sorte de chose, quoi"* (Good luck and all that sort of thing, what) and *"Je dis, plutôt!"* (I say, rather!).

In an age of multicultural diversity, many critics have been busy charging Asterix with the sin of "perpetuating national stereotypes". Some Belgians were displeased at being portrayed as beer-swilling and not too bright. Some Spanish accused the pair of depicting them as lazy, flamenco-dancing gypsies. Asterix's Germans are beefy and brutish and speak in Gothic script, while the British are nonchalant, red-haired chaps with moustaches, obsessed with cultivating their lawns and stopping battles at teatime. Uderzo says it is all good fun and the huge sales across Europe prove that the fans understand that. "The British appreciated the caricature, because of course it was more than just that. It was the archetype of how the French see them."

The biggest caricature is of the French themselves, and it took a couple of foreigners, as Uderzo and Goscinny were

From Asterix and Cleopatra, *written by René Goscinny and illustrated by Albert Uderzo.*

by origin, to hold up the flattering mirror to their countrymen. Asterix and the Gaullish villagers, with their love of banquets, beer, wild boar and fighting, stand for the joie de vivre and gallant side of the French character, without the infuriating streak that comes out when they get behind a steering wheel.

"The Gauls had this sense of individual freedom which has stayed on in the French character. The Frenchman has always wanted to be different from his neighbour," Uderzo says. "Look at all our political parties and the great number of cheeses—one for every day of the year, as de Gaulle said." Then there is the invincible resister, an image that played well to the French mythology, especially after the wartime occupation.

If you think about it, which is not necessarily advisable with a cartoon, you can see that Uderzo's Romans also have qualities which entered the French character: respect for order, straight roads and centralised administration. The serious critics of the BD, a genre which was elevated to the status of high culture by the Socialist government of Mitterrand, have never been happy about the Asterix message. *Libération,* the left-wing daily that champions the BD, complained that Asterix's village is afflicted by "social totalitarianism, a Poujadist mentality and clerical obscurantism, represented by the druid Panoramix [Getafix]." The Gaullish-Roman feud is the constant of French life, "modernism against archaic reaction", *Libération* said.

Uderzo does not have much time for the self-appointed guardians of the BD as art-form, a tribe which holds its annual high mass at the BD festival at Angoulême. France has always had an affection for the comic strip. The phenomenon went back to the 19th century, took off in 1905 with the invention of Becassine, the naive Breton maid, and surged from the Thirties with Tintin. . . .

Tintin, like Asterix, was originally meant for children. That other genre, the "adult" BD, took off after the youth revolt of May 1968, when a generation of writers and artists flocked to the tradition of the American comics, with their Batman-style superheroes and Dick Tracy private eyes and Buck Rogers spacemen, and turned them into a more sophisticated vehicle for fantasy erotic play and surrealism. At their height, in the mid-Eighties, they were selling tens of millions of albums a year, and were enshrined as intellectually chic by Jack Lang, Mitterrand's flamboyant culture minister. . . .

The wave has now passed in France, leaving many of the avant-garde artists stranded in their intellectual ghetto, while the old children's classics led by Tintin and Asterix sail on. The post-'68 explosion, which turned the BD into "the ninth art" after film and television, was healthy at first, Uderzo says, "But they went to the extreme and went in for scatology and pornography. It's unreadable stuff and it destroys the image of the French *bande dessinée.* I don't think my adult readers are childish, rather the opposite. . . . "

Uderzo is enjoying the last laugh as the publishing world

suffers the slump of the serious comic-strip industry. Life for the poor immigrant's son is kept comfortable by an income reported to be at least £2 million a year. . . .

Is he going to be doing any more drawing? "We'll see. I get less pleasure out of it now because I have been drawing for half a century and that's a lot of time. But on the other hand, I still get pleasure writing a script, something I have been doing for 14 years now. It's always a new beginning every time, and I always have the same fears, like an actor or a singer before the show."

TITLE COMMENTARY

ASTERIX THE GAUL (1969)

John Coleman

SOURCE: "Gallicomix," in *New Statesman,* Vol. 77, No. 1989, April 25, 1969, pp. 591-92.

The time is 50 B.C. and the place a little village somewhere in Brittany. Here a tribe of indomitable Gauls, under their venerable chief, Vitalstatistix, holds out against the Roman invader. The tribe's hero is one Asterix, a dwarfish prodigy of pugnacity with winged helmet and drooping yellow moustaches. His constant companion, Obelix, is a great pigtailed lump of a man, generally to be found toting a giant menhir or two or consuming a brace of roast wild boar. The two other essential characters are Getafix, the village druid, brewer of a magic potion which endows the drinker with the strength of a hundred, and Cacofonix, their unspeakable bard. They all Have Adventures; and began nearly a decade ago as a strip in a schoolboy comic. Since then, there have been 12 books; the first French satellite was called Astérix; now, with the warranty of Tintin behind them, they are starting to cross the Channel in translation. . . .

Bell and Hockridge have done as fine a job with these immensely genial funnies as the team of Lonsdale-Cooper and Turner has been doing, for years now, with Tintin. Some of their inventions are inspired: Getafix for Panoramix, Cacofonix for Assurancetourix, Dogmatix for the puppy Idéfix—these are less translations than transformations. As much is true of the ballooned words: their puns are every bit as good or dreadful as the French. On the first page of *Asterix the Gaul,* the spunky hero walks away from a quartet of slumped Romans dusting his hands and whistling: 'Accidence will happen', runs the legend; 'We decline!' moans one of his victims. The centurion Crismus Bonus is furious and despatches a wan spy, selected by a round of musical chairs, to learn the secret of the Gauls' strength. Prisoners are taken but somehow the Romans get the wrong potion and sprout intolerable beards, whence a spate of hairy gags ensues. Caesar intervenes in the finale, forced to a momentary truce. The Gauls feast, as they do at the end of all the books.

I am no expert on the costumes, customs and buildings of the time, but one is assured that the authors go to pains to get things right. Certainly such items as the erection of a great palace in Alexandria (Cleopatra's on a bet with Caesar) by the numb-fingered architect Edifis, helped out by Getafix and the rest, carry tremendous conviction. The jokes about national types and manners—see *Astérix chez les Bretons* [*Asterix in Britain*] for some splendid cracks about our domestic cuisine and devotion to games—are all the better for taking place against likely backgrounds. And, for all the Gallic oneupmanship, bodies flying in every direction under invincible fists, no one seems to die. My kids like the books, too, and I like them liking them.

Sally Higginson Begley

SOURCE: "Move over, Mickey Mouse," in *The Christian Science Monitor,* May 28, 1970, p. 13.

Hail to the new comic strip hero! Asterix the Gaul is here to join the pantheon along with Mickey Mouse and Pogo. Though he, too, is a little guy, Asterix can outsmart his big friends and his big, numerous enemies.

Since its first appearance in the early '60s, more than a million and a half copies of this book have been sold; 12 volumes' worth of sequels have come out in France: and the end to the adventures is not in sight. They have been translated into Spanish, Italian, Portuguese, Dutch, German, and now into English. The dialogue is truly witty, aimed at above-adolescent intellectual level, sometimes polysyllabic, rich in puns—Latin-French bilingual puns at that—and difficult to reconstruct in another language. (The two Britishers who have wrestled with these problems have pretty well overcome them, except for a few lapses from good taste in choosing names.)

Two years ago at dinner in Paris I was seated beside a roundish man with sharp-looking eyes who seemed—I did not catch his name—to have been all over the world as a newspaper reporter. At dessert the conversation at the table turned to the rather dated French comic strip about that priggish boy, Tintin. Then some newer, French "Far-West" comic strips were discussed in detail by all present—and these were adults, with diplomas.

There came a pause, and I asked, "What do you think of Asterix?" The roundish man began to laugh. "Isn't it enough that I write Asterix: do I have to *think* about him too?" So I learned that I was talking to René Goscinny, who not only entertains dinner partners, but also millions of Europeans of all ages.

I never found out how he managed to write at least four different continuing comic strips at once: Asterix; the two "Far-West" series, Lucky Luke and Les Daltons; plus another about a boy and his dog, Boule et Bill: and still another in plain prose form, Le Petit Nicolas, a fiendish schoolboy, and a best seller too. A whole Goscinny stable of illustrators keeps busy.

Asterix's basic situation is very simple and eternally dramatic, something like that of David and Goliath. He and his friends, Obelix the menhir delivery man, Chief Vitalstatistix, Cacofonix the unmusical bard, and so forth, are holding out in a small village surrounded by legions of conquering Romans, named Crismus Bonus, etc. (A menhir is a heavy, Stonehengelike Druid object.) The action involves cunning strategy, magic powers, horseplay, a few boffbam fights, but is not seriously violent.

Asterix, in his good-tempered way, just manages to win out. Such a modest, unpretentious, *aimable* French hero is an encouraging change from the haughty de Gaulle stereotype we so love to hate. And it does make a pleasant revenge, after those boring years of reading about Caesar's winning wars, to see the Romans falling flat on their faces.

This book would be appreciated by anyone who is studying, and bored with, Latin, French, Roman Civilization, Modern European Culture, or who is just plain learning to read. Imagine the joy of discovering that Latin tags can be funny, that Romans didn't know it all, and that the French have a sense of humor about themselves!

Helen E. Kinsey

SOURCE: A review of *Asterix the Gaul,* in *The Booklist,* Vol. 66, No. 20, June 15, 1970, pp. 1248-49.

The English translation with the original illustrations of a popular French cartoon strip catches satisfactorily the humor of puns and language idioms of the original. The sequences shown in this volume concern the efforts of Asterix and his fellow Gauls to outwit the Roman legions when they attempt to learn the recipe of a secret potion brewed by the druid Getafix. The Asterix strip contains familiar elements of slapstick and satire beloved by American cartoon devotees and it has the added appeal of a Gallic flavor.

ASTERIX IN BRITAIN (1970)

The Times Literary Supplement

SOURCE: "Phoney War," in *The Times Literary Supplement,* No. 3555, April 16, 1970, p. 417.

In one of the best of the Asterix series, the intrepid Gauls and their magic potion are called upon by the beleaguered British for help in staving off Caesar's invading legionaries. This rare example of the *entente cordiale* in action provides ample opportunity for the author and artist to poke fun at British manners. The British, for example, drink warm beer, live in rows of tiny identical houses, refuse to fight the Romans at the weekends, and knock off in mid-battle for a drink of hot water with a dash of milk in (tea has not yet been discovered).

This volume is the severest test of all for the translators.

The excellence of the original lay in rendering English colloquialisms into French, with such results as *"Combien étrange!" "Bonne chance, et toute cette sorte de choses . . ."* and *"Je dis. Ca c'est un morçeau de chance."* The translators do their best with frequent use of such phrases as "I say, what a bit of luck," and "Jolly good show, what!" but the point of the joke has inevitably, disappeared. Still, they have done better than could have been expected.

ASTERIX AND THE BIG FIGHT (1971)

Isabel Quigly

SOURCE: "Isabel Quigly on Asterix," in *Spectator,* Vol. 226, No. 7458, June 5, 1971, pp. 786-87.

Asterix is a small, bulbous-nosed Gaul with a droopy yellow moustache, hero of a series of what the Americans call comic books and we haven't really got a name for: 'strip cartoons' and 'comic strips' sound equivocal and nothing else has yet turned up to replace them. In France, where he started life ten years ago, he is a national figure: in England, two years and six translations old, he is something of a cult. The editor of *Antiquity* is a fan of his; the first French satellite was named after him; a man at Nanterre University is writing his degree thesis on the translation of the first three Asterix books into English.

If, at opposite ends of the pole in knowledge, sophistication and humour, very small boys and professors of archaeology enjoy Asterix, I think it must be because of the neat way in which highbrow and lowbrow are dovetailed in him. Dovetailed, not mixed or blurred: the two coexist, they don't dilute each other. Tough jolly pictures in the slapstick manner of so many cartoonists who turn out a swift daily joke are informed by what it seems is a highly respectable knowledge of the Gaulish background; energetic action, plenty of biffing of Romans and hurling of menhirs, all the whirling fights, belly-flops and squawks that are the staple diet of *Beano* and *Dandy* and will keep the most unliterary child engrossed, go with talk stuffed so full of puns, quotations and allusions, classical, literary and political, that detailed notes are provided for English users of the French edition to explain the more abstruse. In other words, he appeals on all sorts of levels and for all sorts of reasons, not least, in France, for the encouraging way he gives French dreams of glory the chance of being acted out in fantasy; for Asterix, the tough little Gaul, withstands the might of conquerors and always comes out on top.

The Asterix plots are simple, the central situation one that can be adapted to practically anything. Julius Caesar has conquered Gaul but resistance still flourishes in one small village, where, out of mistletoe and lobsters, a druid brews a secret potion that gives the villagers superhuman strength. Roman patrols that venture into the local forest are swept up like leaves and even whole phalanxes of the Roman army reduced to blubbering wrecks. Asterix has to take regular doses of the potion to keep up his strength but his huge friend Obelix, a menhir delivery-man by trade, was dropped into the mixture as a baby and got enough strength to last a lifetime: one absent-minded kick at an oak tree from him and it's felled. Between boar-hunts in the forest. Asterix and Obelix get about the world—to Egypt to help Cleopatra build a temple in record time, to North Africa to rescue a legionary, to Britain to help the resistance with a magic potion, to Rome as gladiators. In each case all ends well with a sumptuous feast at home in the village, boars roasting on the spit, horns overflowing with wine, and the bard Cacofonix safely gagged in case he should decide to burst into song.

Roughly speaking, actions and expressions are simple-mindedly funny, names and language often subtle, even witty. Like Gilbert and Sullivan, Goscinny and Uderzo (respectively text and pictures) are clearly indivisible. Which is form and which content? Often you can't tell when a joke is linguistic or visual, or exactly where it began to be funny in the first place. Besides, language *becomes* visual when Goths talk in Gothic script and Egyptians in pictures, and Roman numerals are used in those little clouds that mean: *'Thinks'*. All the same, if the text had been crudely translated and the pictures left to make their point alone, English readers without fluent French and the originals might have wondered what the fuss was about. What has really sent Asterix round the English-speaking world (and beyond it: Japanese translations are now in progress—how's that for some future thesis?) is the way the text has been rethought and refashioned in English, every pun turned on its head and every allusion matched by another. . . .

Plenty of philological fun can be had from comparing the two texts, but that may make it seem too much like hard work and literary exertion. The point about the Asterix books is also their lowbrow appeal, their schoolboy exuberance, their 'ugly' drawings, their simple, repetitive action, the jokey possibilities of antiquity and of other people's oddities. At their most sophisticated level they are of course adult books, but I have yet to meet a child over eight who didn't seize on one the moment he saw it. The English versions, of which *Asterix and the Big Fight* is the latest, are models of what translation ought to be: the spirit caught, the words flying free.

📖 ASTERIX IN SPAIN (1971)

The Times Literary Supplement

SOURCE: "Striptease," in *The Times Literary Supplement,* No. 3634, October 22, 1971, p. 1332.

It hardly seems possible but Asterix has his counterpart in Spain, where a village under the command of Chief Huevos y Bacon declines to integrate with the Roman world. Caesar, his laurels a little crumpled after he had rested on them by mistake, takes the chief's son as hostage and sends him under escort to Gaul. Here he is rescued by Asterix and proves as great a nuisance to his rescuers as he had been to his escort. After many vicissitudes he is

returned home, by which time the Roman legions are considerably reduced in strength, Asterix has invented bullfighting, and Obelix has learnt flamenco.

Asterix and his creators are as resourceful as ever. There are outrageous puns of the familiar kind—the landlord of a Basque inn offers Asterix "chicken in the basquet"—and genial fun is poked at present-day follies. At the Spanish frontier the Gauls are held up by a long queue of caravanners, in a rich assortment of mobile homes, who are on their way to Hispania for their holidays. "The exchange rate is very favourable for sestertii, and you're sure to find the sun." As always the fun, at its most hilarious, is relevant and scholarly.

There are a few new characters, notably the fishmonger Unhygienix and his loving spouse Bacteria. Interest stays mainly with the resourceful warriors of the Gaulish village, Chief Vitalstatistix, Asterix and Obelix. The dreadful bard Cacofonix comes briefly into his own when he is commissioned to sing the little hostage to sleep with such Celtic lullabies as "I'm Dreaming of a White Solstice".

📖 ASTERIX AT THE OLYMPIC GAMES (1972)

The Times Literary Supplement

SOURCE: "Greek meets Gaul," in *The Times Literary Supplement,* No. 3672, July 14, 1972, p. 812.

Asterix and the entire male population of a certain Gaulish village go to the Olympic Games. Through a legal quibble they enter as Roman citizens, but the rules against drug-taking are rigid and they cannot take advantage of the famous potion from which they derive their strength. For once Asterix does not come out on top. However, an extra race is instituted for Romans only, as a boost to the tourist trade; the bona fide Romans steal the potion, win and are disqualified for doping, so after all Asterix gains the palm.

The jokes are as outrageous as ever, and as relevant. The Gauls have a balanced training diet—boar—and take their rations with them on the hoof. Obelix of course takes his favourite menhir, gift-wrapped, and is disappointed to find there are no dolmens in the Parthenon. The oldest inhabitant, named Geriatrix, likes the Greek girls and feels ten years younger—that is 83—after a late night in a restaurant called Invinoveritas. Names are suitably Hellenic. A professional guide, Diabetes, takes the Gauls in hand and shows them the sights, helped by his cousins Kudos and the hotelier Phallintodiseus. Even the cocks crow Cockadoodledos!

📖 ASTERIX AND THE GOTHS (1974)

The Times Literary Supplement

SOURCE: A review of *Asterix and the Goths,* in *The Times Literary Supplement,* No. 3774, July 5, 1974, p. 714.

Astérix comes storming back with a tirelessly funny story of the Roman conquest. This is held up not only by the inhabitants of a certain Gaulish village but also by the Gothic menace. The two clash when a Gothic task-force kidnaps Astérix's Druid in order to steal the secret of the magic potion. Caught between upper and lower millstones the Romans' sufferings are dreadful. The incidental humours are as delightful and apt as ever, notably in a one-page summary of the Asterixian Wars, which sorts out a complex power-struggle between competing Goths, such as Rhetoric, Metric, Lyric and General Electric. This war culminates in the famous "Battle of the Two Losers".

Elaine Moss

SOURCE: A review of *Asterix and the Goths,* in *Children's Books of the Year: 1974,* Hamish Hamilton, 1975, p. 51.

The invention of new plots by the ingenious Goscinny and Uderzo never fails—neither does the felicitous translation of the Asterix patter by Anthea Bell and Derek Hockridge. In this new richly humorous cartoon story the Gaulish contingent has awesome adventures over the borders of the Roman Empire ("You are leaving the Roman Empire" says a milestone): Asterix and company follow Getafix and Valueaddetax the Druids to their secret Druid of the Year convention where one Druid remarks "The food's a bit sickle-y" and another replies "Pass the Celt". Irresistible Asterix as always outwits all comers, this time the Goths.

📖 *ASTERIX AND THE LAUREL WREATH* (1974)

Russell Davies

SOURCE: "Battling Asterix," in *The Times Literary Supplement,* No. 3785, September 20, 1974, pp. 1001-02.

Up to now, the great thing about Asterix, the comic-book Gaul, has been that he has remained a creature of the printed page, and of the imagination. In a decade when a Womble can be made as real as an Osmond—or vice versa—and even the Belgian boy-hero Tintin has become a stiffly animated screen-star with a piping Harlywed voice, the obstinate Asterix and his tribe hardly venture, so far as I know, from between the shiny covers provided for them by Dargaud Editeur of France and their associated publishers from Leicester to Brazil. The occasional very high-class comic like *Le Monde* can afford to maintain an Asterix strip, but it is a great coup to secure the rights for such a rare excursion. And appropriately so; Asterix's hard-to-get policy is entirely in accordance with that of his fellow Gaulish villagers under their chief Vitalstatistix, as we know him, whose declared aim is to hold out indefinitely against the Roman invaders, their Empire, and their so-called civilization. The village remaining inviolate, Gaul is divided, as more and more informed children are becoming aware, not into three parts, but four.

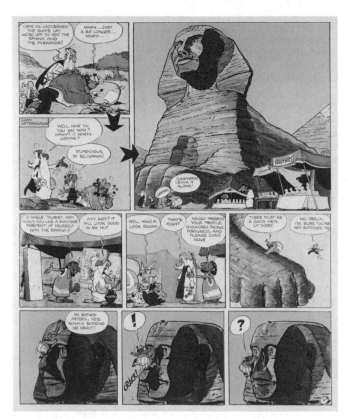

From Asterix and Cleopatra, *written by René Goscinny and illustrated by Albert Uderzo.*

Of Goscinny and Uderzo, creators of this tight little island of enlightened tribalism, I know next to nothing, except that they sound like a pair of cartoon characters themselves; but their working methods have not remained entirely secret. *Asterix and Cleopatra,* a 1965 tale compelled into being by the horrendous spawning of the Elizabeth Taylor epic, announces itself as "The Greatest Story Ever Drawn", in substantiation of which claim the following statistics are revealed: "Fourteen litres of india (sic) ink, thirty brushes, sixty-two soft pencils, one hard pencil, twenty-seven rubbers, 1,984 sheets of paper, sixteen typewriter ribbons, two typewriters, 366 pints of beer went into its creation." The evidence of hard work speaks for itself, but the beer (it may be an equivalent litrage of wine in the French edition, the only Dargaud original I have not been able to turn up in this efficiently distributed series) is the characteristic touch that identifies Goscinny and Uderzo with their creations. Though Asterix is perhaps too dedicatedly alert to be anything more than a social drinker, preferring goat's milk as often as not, and even his near-spherical ally Obelix reaches for the roast boar before the goblet (the convention is that Obelix is seen sinking his teeth into a whole carcass in the one frame, then sitting contentedly behind a fleshless set of white boar-ribs in the next), the two friends do live wholeheartedly in the spirit of the "traditional Gaulish ways" defined at the end of *Asterix and the Big Fight:* "They like their food and drink, a good fight and a bit of fun." If this carries an Andy Cappricious tinge in the English, the French "rigolards, ripailleurs, brailleurs" seems to emphasize the harmless, rustic boisterousness of it all. Yet, lest it should be feared that too much of a virtue is made of riotous living, the latest Asterix adventure to be translated concludes, as we shall see, with a timely warning against the consequences of "orgies of wine".

Asterix and the Laurel Wreath first appeared in France two years ago as *Les Lauriers de César.* The translators, as usual, are Anthea Bell and Derek Hockridge. I suspect Mr Hockridge (having been there myself), of being an Assistant Master at Manchester Grammar School, and also of holding down the curiously mute job of Court Assistant on the television *Crown Court* programme. The variety of ironical perspectives on Western civilization that seems to be gathering must be a great help when a new Asterix comes up for the treatment; certainly the Bell/Hockridge translations have maintained a high success rate, frame for frame. The further conventions of the world they offer will become clear as we go along, but the dominant one is the principle of the magic potion a brew concocted by the village's rather naughtily named druid Getafix. Whoever drinks the potion gains superhuman strength, and is made indomitable but, as Asterix is careful to point out, "not invulnerable". Obelix's personal tragedy is that he fell into the relevant cauldron in infancy; in consequence, he permanently enjoys a limitless muscle-power and, when Getafix's cauldron is on the boil, he is always denied a swig. The situation of Asterix, who has to carry his own supply with him, and has been known to lose it or run out, perhaps borrows a little from Popeye, whose spinach was a similar standby.

This time, we begin not in "the little Gaulish village we know so well", but, as sometimes happens, in enemy territory: Rome. The first frame is a minutely drawn aerial view—the illustrator Uderzo is a virtuoso pilot of the mental helicopter—of the Forum and district. Referring to the French edition, which is equipped with the standard four-page insert of excellent notes by Ronald S. Kirkman, courtesy of Brockhampton Press, we are assured that this bird's-eye view, "though necessarily hypothetical, is based on fact. From our viewpoint above the Colosseum we are looking WNW along the Via Sacra towards the Forum Romanum with its captivating complex of monuments." Mr Kirkman brings to his task exactly the right blend of Norris McWhirter and Mr Chips, and buyers of *Astérix français* in Britain should insist, as firmly as is compatible with Gaulish politesse, on being provided with his vital pamphlet.

Proceeding along one of the Roman streets past a cheerfully gruesome joke a legless beggar on a trolley proclaiming himself "a poor gladiator *in reduced circumstances*", we meet Asterix and Obelix, who are plainly in some sortafix, and conversing, for reasons yet to be explained, in a strange spooneristic fashion. The authors at once intervene, call a halt (a stone Asterix has kicked stops in mid-air) and order a flashback, the beginning of which is signalled by the filmlike "running back" of the frame (stone zips back under Asterix's foot)—a rare hommage to the animated movies from which Uderzo has obviously learnt so much. The real beginning of the story

now follows, prefaced by another aerial view, this time of Lutetia, or Paris. Here again Mr Kirkman's notes salute the accuracy of the plan of the Ile de la Cité settlement, with its temple on the site now occupied by Notre Dame. Asterix and Obelix are rediscovered among the Lutetian traffic, humping along baggage for their chief Vitalstatistix and his wife, Impedimenta, who is determined to visit her metropolitan brother Homeopathix. He and the chief do not get on, as becomes clear in three pages of domestic strife, by the end of which Obelix is emphatically plastered (hence the spoonerisms) and Vitalstatistix has rashly boasted that he will set before the snobby gourmet Homeopathix a stew "caesoned" with Caesar's laurel wreath. The object of the quest for Asterix and Obelisk thus becomes the lifting of the *laureola* from the imperial brow.

We flash forward again to Rome, where the two companions are sold into slavery amid much incidental satire on commerce, Greek statuary and phlegmatic Britons. (The "Oh I say" Briton here does not look much, but his appearance recalls the highly successful *Asterix in Britain, Astérix chez les Bretons,* 1966, which had a whole generation of French students, and English students of French, conversing in literal-English French of the "vraiment, ce n'est pas jouant le jeu" variety.) Our heroes are now apprenticed to the cook Goldendelicius, in the house of Osseus Humerus and his daughters Tibia and Fibula: neater patterns of appropriateness in the names are generally striven for in the English versions, sometimes at the cost of Goscinny's wilder extremes of zaniness.

Asterix's efforts in the kitchen produce a kind of venomous soap curry, which lays out the entire household; the masters remain, however, favourably impressed, especially the dissolute son of the house, Metatarsus, who finds his hangover dispelled by the purgative mess. This success is most unwelcome to the Gauls, who have decided that to be thrown to the lions would be their best chance of getting close to Caesar and his laurels. Having failed yet again to antagonize the family by rousing them in the middle of the night—this is taken as the cue for a "surprise orgy"—they finally achieve their goal in the morning when their master, by now indisposed, dispatches them to the Palace to make apologies for his absence. The jealous cook Goldendelicius has anticipated them. He has told Caesar's guards to expect a Gaullish attack on the Emperor, so Asterix and Obelix, captured, go willingly below to the dungeons. At night they escape with their customary ease, Obelix flicking the lock-casing out of the door with a casual gesture that will recall to many children, and ex-children of a certain age, the demeanour of Desperate Dan, who eats cow-pies (they had horns), shaves with a blowlamp, and punch his assailants through walls leaving an assailant-shaped hole.

A search of the Palace uncovers no laurels, and the Gauls return to their cell. Next morning they are brought before the court. Both prosecuting and defending counsels select the same opening gambit, Cato's "Delenda Carthago", which threatens an embarrassing delay; Asterix resolves the difficulty with an eloquent speech in self-denunciation, and the story seems destined to end with a set-piece in the arena. But, on the day, Caesar is away dealing with pirates (we may safely assume that these are the self-same pirates that Asterix and Obelix unfailingly sink whenever they put to sea), so the thwarted Gaulish pair refuse to appear. While they are haggling in the entrance-tunnel, the head lion eats all his fellow-predators out in the ring, ruining all prospect of sport. The Gauls escape in the confusion that follows, and are recruited by a band of nocturnal muggers. (Uderzo's night-scenes are conspicuously good, and never better than in last year's Asterix, *The Mansions of the Gods,* where the effects of a prematurely activated alarm-clock cockerel on Gaulish village society were beautifully rendered.)

The first victim of the gang, with whom Asterix naturally has no intention of cooperating, proves to be Metatarsus, once more the belated reveller, who leads them to an inn where Goldendelicius is to be found. By a slightly anti-climactic chance, the cook has been rewarded for his services as an informer with the task of holding the laurel wreath over Caesar's head during his processional triumph on the morrow. A crown of parsley (fennel in the French) is substituted, which, though it leaves the triumphant Caesar, according to his thought-bubble, feeling "like a piece of fish", permits our friends to leave for home with their vegetable booty. This is duly served up to the visiting Homeopathix, who ignores the "caesoning", pooh-poohs the grub, and is dispatched vertically out of view by the brawny chieftain. Had Vitalstatistix taken this course of action in the first place, the Roman expedition would not have been necessary, but it is one of the charms of Goscinnian Gauls that they hold their strength in reserve, and try all conventional means first. The final scene is the traditional grand banquet round the bonfire, with the excruciating bard Cacofonix banished, as always, to a corner of the frame, bound hand and foot (but not gagged, for once) to prevent his adding his tuneless contribution to the revels. A parting authorial note tells how the Romans, "having the recipe for a remedy against the excesses of drinking", went into their fatal decline.

Even this severely boiled-down summary of events indicates, I think, that much more is crammed into the forty-eight pages of the average Asterix adventure than one has a right to expect. Swiftness of movement and economy of effect are perhaps not unusual virtues in a comic book, but Goscinny and Uderzo have refined them to a remarkable degree in this series. Much depends on the immediate acceptability of the central figures, and fortunately, one has been able to take them happily for granted from the start. It is not advisable, or even possible to stop and *think* about Asterix (he never does) because he is hardly a character at all, but an all-action principle, for ever on the move. Thus the improbable combination of his tiny stature, his monstrous vigour, his droopy walrus moustache and the demigod-like wings on his helmet nevertheless seem indisputably right. Like Laurel and Hardy, or Morecambe and Wise, these two can share a bed without provoking fruity oohs from the audience; Asterix and Obelix are characters about whose provenance and possible complexity one actively does not want to know more; what is wanted is that they should do what they do. To try

to put an age on them seems almost an impertinent proceeding, and is certainly a foredoomed one. The usual tokens of seniority—the paunch, the whiskers, the bandy legs—just do not add up. Asterix is no more a little old man than he is a baby, though there is a good deal of both in his make-up.

But in any case it is Obelix, the menhir delivery-man, who is liable to capture the children's affection. The outsize, amiable bonehead who does not know his own strength is always a good bet, and Obelix has the additional attractions of being greedy yet perpetually deprived (of his share of potion, at least), incomparably loyal (the nose-to-nose confrontations that sometimes occur between the partners always resolve themselves in tearful embraces), and touchingly devoted to little Dogmatix, alias Idéfix, the Peter Pan of the canine species. He is capable of falling hopelessly in love (see *Asterix the Legionary*) but makes up for such unchildish errors by uttering his all-purpose catch-phrase "These Romans are crazy" on all possible occasions. Ideas above his station have been known to occur to him; he once predicted, for example, that someone, someday might write a book called *The Adventures of Obelix the Gaul.* But this occurred in *Astérix et le Chaudron* [*Asterix and the Cauldron*], a tale that has been passed over by translators, possibly because Asterix permits himself therein to execute a bank-robbery and waylay a Roman tax-collector. No children's hero, after all, looks at his best in pursuit of coin, even when it turns out to be his own.

The position of the Romans is more than incidentally interesting. Though one would not want to push the analogy farther than it seems to want to go, there is a strong flavour of the German occupation about the Pax Romana. The Germans themselves invariably appear as apoplectic Goths in the pre-Hindenburg Prussian mould. They fight among themselves (as they will continue to do for centuries, Getafix accurately predicts), speak in Gothic script, and become disproportionately power-crazy as soon as they get a whiff of the magic potion; but the worst they do in the invading line is to file into Spain in caravans, like the Gauls, en route for the sun. The Romans on the other hand, with their salutes, their barracks, their intensely corrupt regional overlords and their famous discipline, impose themselves in a much more repressive fashion, emerging as a curious combination of military machine and pathetic shambles: historical Romans played by present-day Italians. Where they closely resemble the representatives of the most recent European attempt at Empire—Third the Reich—is in their effect on the Gauls, among whom is produced exactly the same moral dilemma as faced French citizens thirty years ago. It is made almost solemnly clear at the opening of *Asterix and the Big Fight* that there were two sorts of Gauls, the "rigolards" and others we know so well and "ceux qui acceptaient la paix romaine et qui essayaient de s'adapter à la puissante civilisation des envahisseurs". The least comical of all the villains portrayed are the collaborators.

Be all that as it may, I must say I get more pleasure from the Asterix drawings than anything the series has been able to present in the way of plot. No cartoon, except perhaps the jubilantly slapdash "Dennis the Menace", is better than its images, and in this department, Uderzo goes on improving what was always a foolproof technique. His constant changes of viewpoint and focus, the movement he includes in every frame, and his excellent lighting effects are done with a diligence that never looks over-cautious, and his backgrounds are now richer in colour and detail than seemed possible when *Asterix the Gaul* appeared some thirteen years ago. Uderzo has a few highly effective conventions of his own, such as his habit of bordering all wheedling or smarmy speech with a ring of flowers, or the very simple ruse of printing shouts and similar urgent dialogue in fat, black letters, while whispers, mumbles and sulks appear in tiny ones. And he is always willing to try something new.

In the *Laurel Wreath* there is a very daring and delicately stippled pointilliste dawn that is guaranteed to produce in your head the uncomfortable buzzing that ensues when sleep is unnaturally interrupted. Best of all, and this I suppose you would expect from a continental humorist of skill, is Uderzo's mastery of gesture and bodily attitude, whereby so much thought-bubble space is saved. Much of what passes between Asterix and Obelix is unspoken, obscured though so much of their facial area is by moustache and tuberous nose. Even an anonymous background

figure like the Roman sentry guarding Caesar's Palace, in *Laurel Wreath*, can communicate at a glance, through his hunched, quaking back and knees-bend posture, the fact that he is having a fit of the giggles. If Uderzo were not so adept at capturing these little physical clichés, his collaborator's guying of racial and temperamental types might not look so deft, nor so amiable, as it does.

But in the end amiability is all. So insistent are Goscinny and Uderzo on the inoffensiveness of their product that they even prefaced *Asterix in Britain* with a small greeting-cum-manifesto for Anglo-Saxon readers. "Our little strip-cartoon stories", they wrote, "do not make fun of the real thing, but of the ideas of the real thing that people get into their heads, i.e., clichés." I have heard Asterophobes argue that most of these subtleties will be lost on the majority of children, who enjoy the company of Asterix and Obelix, so it is said, for their merry violence, the "unrealistically" innocent hand-to-hand walloping that leaves the enemies of Gaul in untidy, goggle-eyed heaps. But this is what fighting still means, in the practical application of the term, to most children of Asterix age, and we may be thankful for that. Let's not make either a bogy or a fetish (or an American cartoon, or, worse an advertisement) of Asterix, but give him credit for maintaining an international humour based on tolerance. If the ideal sounds pious, the lad himself, at least, is not.

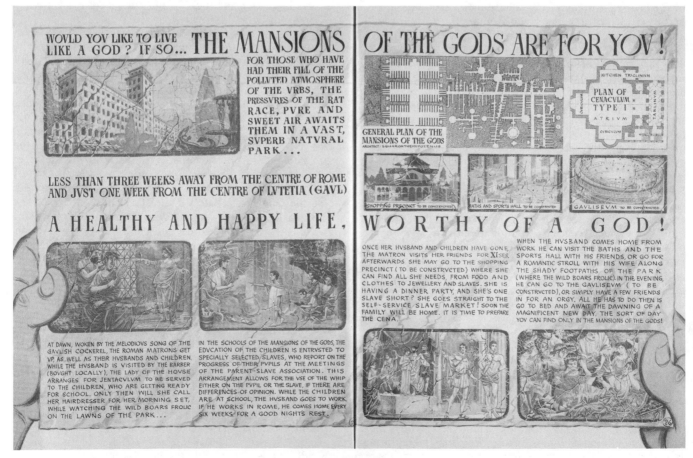

From The Mansions of the Gods, *written by René Goscinny and illustrated by Albert Uderzo.*

ASTERIX AND THE GREAT CROSSING (1976)

Miles Kington

SOURCE: "Stars and Strips," in *Punch,* Vol. 269, No. 7045, September 24, 1975, p. 554.

[*The following excerpt is from a review of the French edition of* Asterix and the Great Crossing *published in 1975.*]

By the 23rd epic Goscinny and Uderzo, author and artist respectively, seem to have run out of steam. Admittedly they have discovered a new country to visit, in America, and there are some good jokes quarried from totem poles, Red Indian customs, rival Vikings and so on, especially as Astérix and Obelix never suspect they have found a new land. But worse even than the fact that much of the humour is repeated from earlier stories is the fact that invincibility becomes boring, and one eventually longs for the two Gaulish heroes to be given a good going over, just as much as one hopes for their stable-mate Lucky Luke to be riddled with bullets sooner or later. Even Muhammad Ali has the sense to lose occasionally.

Margery Fisher

SOURCE: A review of *Asterix and the Great Crossing,* in *Growing Point,* Vol. 14, No. 9, April, 1976, p. 2852.

In **Asterix and the Great Crossing** the two friends [Asterix and Obelix] are once more put in an embarrassing position when they suggest to Unhygienix the fishmonger that it might be possible to sell fresh fish caught in the adjacent ocean rather than the distinctly stale importations from Lutetia. When they set sail they hardly expect to be blown to the New World and with some bewilderment identify the be-feathered inhabitants as Cretans, nor are they at all impressed by the dragon-prowed ship which, its exploratory voyages interrupted by the castaways, carries them back to Gaul. The choice of names for the Vikings is superbly logical, from the chief Herendethelessen to his followers Steptoanssen and Haraldwilssen and their women Gertrude, Intrude, Irmgard and Firegard. Anachronisms are sown unerringly through the narrative and the illustrations bring one up gasping at their effective simplicity—a picture, for example, of Asterix signalling for help on an islet in the attitude of the Statue of Liberty, Obelix joining an Indian war-dance with Spanish variations, and the baffled Viking chief, robbed of his glory as a discoverer of America, asking himself "Tø be ør nøt tø be, that is the questiøn". Wit of this calibre has no frontiers, of generation or of country.

Elaine Moss

SOURCE: A review of *Asterix and the Great Crossing,* in *Picture Books for Young People 9-13,* edited by Nancy Chambers, The Thimble Press, 1985, pp. 35-6.

Just one of the many adventures of Asterix the Gaul—a favourite with me because absolutely every race represented (including the canine) is held up to gentle ridicule. By mistake Asterix and Obelix, when trying to catch fresh fish because Unhygienix the fishmonger only sells imported, sail too far and discover America! The Indians are there, of course—but why do sounds like 'Løøk. Løøk, by Ødin!' echo across the sea? Because the Vikings are discovering America too . . . Perhaps the funniest sequence of cartoons is the one in which the two dogs, Asterix's tiny Dogmatix and the Vikings' huge Huntingsseåssen, try to learn each other's language: 'Woof?' 'Wøøf' 'Høhøhøhø'. A marvellous story, brilliantly told in its own medium with some astonishing night paintings.

Most young readers love Asterix books, but many miss half the fun because adults don't talk to them about the language and the situations. Casual conversations about Asterix enlighten everybody.

ASTERIX AND THE CHIEFTAIN'S SHIELD (1977)

Russell Davies

SOURCE: "Barbarian Invasions," in *The Times Literary Supplement,* No. 3915, March 25, 1977, p. 365.

The empire of Asterix continues to grow. My personal researches into its expansion took a long step forward at the last Cannes Film Festival, where an opulent champagne party was thrown for the two creators, Goscinny and Uderzo, by the distributors of their forthcoming animated feature film—**Les 12 Travaux d'Asterix [The Twelve Tasks of Asterix]**, I believe. The event took place in a balmy hotel garden, among tables laden not with boar, perhaps, but at least with wine; and affixed to the trees round about were original drawings of Uderzo's, showing off that vigour of line which I fear (not having seen the film as yet) may be lost in the animation process, where the energy-charge of single penstrokes is naturally sacrificed to the blur of movement. It was pleasant, anyway, to see at close quarters the two genial maestri, even if they were wearing identical electric-indigo business suits: Goscinny, a roundish, balding, frizzy personage more or less permanently beaming; and Uderzo, a taller, rather more twitchy figure, but quite dashing in a *poete maudit* sort of way. They made a good complementary pair, if a less spectacularly unequal one than Asterix and Obelix themselves. The way they tended to disappear into discreet scrummages of French film executives may, on reflection, have been ominous. But there is nothing about film executives that is not ominous, from the independent artist's point of view.

The present slice of Gaulish history, however, has little bearing on current trends in Asterix's empire-building. It is on old tale, published in France in 1968 under the title **Le Bouclier Arverne;** and it never was one of the best, being a rather bitty item about the recovery of Vercingetorix's lost shield, upon which Caesar, his envoys maltreated (ah, long-lost ablative!) intends to be carried on, in symbolic triumph before the humiliated Gauls. The shield has changed hands several times, unfortunately, and though this enables Goscinny and Uderzo to make some amusing play with the comic-strip equivalent of film-flashbacks, the story does get a bit lost among them. A certain strain shows in the translations of Derek Hockridge and Anthea Bell, too, though the Roman envoy Noxius Vapus will do very well. Fewer and fewer readers, I suppose, faced with a drunken Roman with hiccups in sequence, "Hic! Haec! Hoc!", will know what on earth he is on about.

The drawing is as fine as ever, and in set-pieces like Obelix's emptying a swimming pool by diving into it and the settling of a fallen leaf on the extremely tender stomach of Chief Vitalstatistix ("Oooouuuuch!"), Uderzo displays his usual mastery of time and motion. There is also a demonstration of his psychological grasp of editing—what in film terms would be called "shot-selection". Here Asterix and Obelix, for a rarity have fallen out. We see them from behind, as they walk resolutely down the grass verges on opposite sides of a paved road—down the middle of which the hound Dogmatix is padding in swivel-headed disbelief at this turn of events. There follow two frames in which the two heroes, seen separately, air their sniffish grievances; then one frame in which Asterix, silent and visibly melting, finds his foot straying inward towards the road; then a "single-shot" of Obelix, red-faced, with little puffs of embarrassment-steam issuing from his head, and his toe playing with the outer stone of the pathway.

Then at last, after a tense close-up of the increasingly perplexed dog, where indeterminate decision-making noises burst into the frame from either side, the quarrel is resolved. Asterix bounds across a broad frame into his friend's arms, and our point of view suddenly sweeps up to take in wide and idealistic panorama of distant hills, clouds, etc. A fir tree bows in assent. The whole event could not have been better managed, visually, right down to the fact that the two friends' faces, pressed together in the reconciliatory embrace, are perfectly identical in their bliss, save for a minute distinction made in the thickness of the respective eyebrows.

📖 *THE TWELVE TASKS OF ASTERIX* (1978)

Margery Fisher

SOURCE: A review of *The Twelve Tasks of Asterix,* in *Growing Point,* Vol. 17, No. 2, July, 1978, p. 3349.

The Twelve Tasks of Asterix may be a good film but the book could be a disappointment to anyone addicted to the strip-adventures of the Gallic hero. The plot is clever enough, with nicely chosen tasks (proposed by Caesar as the only possible way to defeat the elusive Gauls). Some are easily performed with the help of the magic potion (a

javelin throw against Veres the Persian, wrestling against Cylindric the German) and in others Obelix's appetite saves the day (he devours the terrible Beast in the Cave soon after finishing off a gargantuan meal produced by Calorifix, "the great chef of the Titans". All very funny. But the text is straight, not strip, and without the speech-balloons, footnotes and terse asides of the other books, the humour begins to look forced and even a little dull. There are good moments—for instance, when the Old Man of the Mountains declaims "O presumptuous mortals . . . one of you, eyes blindfolded, must tell me which of these two piles of laundry was washed in Olympus, the divine detergent"—and the final romp in the arena, like the encounter with the priestesses of the Isle of Pleasure, has a nice touch of parody; but I doubt if any of us will read this book to tatters as we have read the rest.

📖 *ASTERIX AND THE BANQUET* (1979)

Margery Fisher

SOURCE: A review of *Asterix and the Banquet,* in *Growing Point,* Vol. 18, No. 1, May, 1979, p. 3505.

In the Asterix books the historical satire is intellectual in tone and depends as much on nonsensical anachronism and verbal wit as it does on situation. On the run from their enemies, in *Asterix and the Banquet,* the hero and his boon companion Obelix rashly trust to the trade description of a "used chariot", "Nearly new, one matron driver, hardly any mileage"; they are betrayed by the gloomy Gaul Unpatriotix, who explains "I'm a misfit, you see, it's all because of my underprivileged environmental situation"; the road to Nice is blocked by traffic, as "everyone's going south to the seaside for peace and quiet". The verbal inventiveness seems to have run out a little in this book, for there are fewer puns and more of the explosive battle-cries than in some of the earlier adventures. The linear narrative is simple and telling. Julius Caesar, having given up hope of defeating the rebel village, sends Prefect Overanxius to organise a palisade round it to isolate "seditious opinions", whereupon Asterix bets the Prefect that he and Obelix will escape and make a round tour of Gaul, bringing back local specialities for a banquet. Their physical adventures are predictable, so are their escapes, and the humour of the book is at its best in the neat cumulation of comestibles (Lyons ham, sweetmeats from Cambrai, sparkling Rhenish wine [much in demand for launching galleys], Toulouse sausages, Bordeaux oysters). The pictures . . . , rumbustious and knockabout . . . , move the story along briskly, and their active grotesquerie provides a piquant contrast to the wit and drollery of the words.

Additional coverage of Goscinny's life and career is contained in the following sources published by Gale Research: *Contemporary Authors,* Vol. 117; and *Something about the Author,* Vols. 39, 47.

Joanne Ryder

1946-

(Full name Joanne Rose Ryder) American author of picture books, nonfiction, and poetry; reteller.

Major works include *Simon Underground* (1976), *Fog in the Meadow* (1979), *The Snail's Spell* (1982), *Inside Turtle's Shell, and Other Poems of the Field* (1985), *Where Butterflies Grow* (1989).

INTRODUCTION

A prolific and popular writer best known as the creator of nature books for primary graders that effectively blend scientific fact with fantasy, Ryder invites her young audience to pretend becoming butterflies or bears, chipmunks or turtles, as she introduces her readers to the authentic development and life cycles of a variety of creatures. A poet with a love of words and images, she seeks to heighten the child's awareness of the wonders of life by engaging her readers in dreamlike, imaginary travels or transformations that challenge them to view the world as would an insect or animal. Often writing in the second or third person, Ryder is praised for her ability to inspire interest in and reader identification with her subjects through her distinctive approach and inclusion of fascinating, even dramatic, information. Although Ryder has occasionally been cited for excessive sentimentality, commentators have generally concurred in their favorable estimation of the quality of her writing, which is frequently cited as lyrical and poetic, her imaginative presentation of scientific facts, and her ability to address young readers without condescending to them. Christine Doyle Francis writes that "Joanne Ryder's work stands among the finest nature books of the last twenty years."

Biographical Information

Born in Lake Hiawatha, a small town in New Jersey, Ryder grew up with moles and chipmunks outside her house, woods and a waterfall nearby, and parents who shared with her their love of nature. Her mother taught her to appreciate sunsets and other "special moments in nature"; her father imparted his enthusiasm for beetles, caterpillars, and other tiny garden inhabitants. About the time she was five, Ryder moved with her family to Brooklyn, where she enjoyed going to the park and to museums; her parents finally settled on Long Island two years later. An avid reader at an early age, Ryder began writing poetry before the age of ten. She reflects: "By the time I was ten, I suspected I might want to be a writer. I also thought I might like to be a ballet dancer or a veterinarian, too. But I kept on writing, and the writing won out." In high school, Ryder edited the school newspaper; she

subsequently studied journalism and edited the college literary magazine at Marquette University, receiving her degree in 1968. After a period of graduate study in library science at the University of Chicago, Ryder worked as an editor of children's books for Harper & Row. She became a full-time writer in 1980.

Major Works

Ryder's unique way of exercising children's imaginations in teaching them of the natural world was inspired by an exhibit she viewed at the American Museum of Natural History in New York—that of a cutaway of animals in a field through different seasons. This experience led to the first of her nature books for children, *Simon Underground* (1976), which describes a mole who digs tunnels all winter and surfaces in spring. Personalizing the story about a real mole's growth and development with her own reactions to the changing seasons, Ryder hit upon the mixture of fact and fantasy that comprises many of her books. *Fog in the Meadow* relates the plight of a small rabbit lost in the fog and in danger of falling prey to a hungry, opportunistic fox. Described by Ann McKeithen-Boes as "an absorbing natural drama," the story helps the young reader to appreciate how sound and smell help when sight fails. In *The Snail's Spell,* a little boy imagines shrinking to the size of a snail, moving, eating, using his feelers, and sleeping like a snail would, with giant lettuce and mushrooms around him. Critics have commended Ryder's concept and nonanthropomorphic approach. *Where Butterflies Grow,* the story of the metamorphosis of a black swallowtail caterpillar, is told with simple, rhythmic prose, tracing the life of a caterpillar from the time it breaks out of its egg, through the shedding of its skin, its fight to defend itself against enemies, the forming of the pupa, and finally its transformation into a yellow-flecked black butterfly. The title of the book comes from the end page, where suggestions for plantings to attract butterflies to one's own garden make for a unique bonus. *Inside Turtle's Shell, and Other Poems of the Field,* Ryder's sole book of poetry, collectively portrays a meadow and its inhabitants in a one-day sequence from morning to night. Zena Sutherland has written that the poems in this work "have a quiet tenderness and empathy," adding: "Most of the poems are brief, some almost as compressed as haiku; most have delicate imagery; all are evocative." Many of Ryder's nature books for children have been published as part of William Morrow's "Just for a Day" series. In addition to her books that invite children to explore and appreciate the natural world, Ryder is the author of picture book fantasies such as *The Night Flight* (1985), the story of a small girl who has fantastic adventures in her dreams, as well as the "First Grade is the Best" series, a collection of easy readers that highlight the joys of the initial year of primary school. She is also the reteller of Hardie Gramatky's *Little Toot,* Charles Dickens's *A Christmas Carol,* and Walt Disney's film version of *Bambi* for young readers.

Awards

Simon Underground was selected for the Children's Book Showcase in 1977. Ryder received the New Jersey Author's Award from the New Jersey Institute of Technology for *Fireflies* in 1978 and both *Fog in the Meadow* and *Snail in the Woods* in 1980. *Fog in the Meadow* was named Outstanding Science Trade Book of the Year for Children by the National Science Teachers Association in 1979 and a Children's Choice Book by the Children's Book Council and the International Reading Association the following year. *The Snail's Spell* was named a Parents Choice Book by *Parents Magazine* and received the New York Academy of Sciences Children's Science Book Award for younger readers in 1982. *Inside Turtle's Shell, and Other Poems of the Field* was named both Outstanding Book of the Year for Children by the National Council of Teachers of English and Outstanding Science Trade Book of the Year for Children by the National Science Teachers Association in 1985, and was included on the Bluebonnet Award list and the Bank Street Outstanding Book of the Year list. *Step into the Night* was named Outstanding Science Trade Book of the Year for Children by the National Science Teachers Association and received the Commonwealth Club of Northern California Children's

Book Medal in 1988. *Where Butterflies Grow* was named Outstanding Science Trade Book of the Year for Children by the National Science Teachers Association in 1989.

TITLE COMMENTARY

📖 *SIMON UNDERGROUND* (1976)

Zena Sutherland

SOURCE: A review of *Simon Underground,* in *Bulletin of the Center for Children's Books,* Vol. 30, No. 1, September, 1976, p. 16.

Nicely illustrated by [John] Schoenherr's finely detailed pictures of a tunneling mole, this describes at slow pace the instincts that cause a mole to dig a pathway to a deep winter burrow and to emerge again in the springtime. While much of the text gives realistic information, there are anthropomorphic touches that weaken it: Simon the mole whispers "Oooh, it's so empty here," and "thinks proudly 'Nobody knows I'm here.'" The writing style is lyric: "Fragile smells of flowers, the wild smells of the air. Special places to share with others. And tucked away deep down, Simon longed for spring." This may give some concept of seasonal change or animal behavior, but it doesn't serve as a source of information, it has too little action as a narrative, and the text moves slowly. It can serve as a springboard for discussion.

Margery Fisher

SOURCE: A review of *Simon Underground,* in *Growing Point,* Vol. 17, No. 2, July, 1978, p. 3359.

The life-cycle of animals may be demonstrated to children through the medium of a narrative. Though this need not be classed as fiction, there is likely to be a fictional element; some degree of humanisation is inevitable, if only in the use of personal pronouns for clarity. *Simon Underground* ostensibly presents a realistic description of a mole's life round the seasons in terms simple enough for readers as young as eight. In fact, there is a marked degree of anthropomorphism in this impressionistic piece, which takes the form of an extended picture-book. The mole is seen as a "character":

> He yearned for his friends, and he began to remember things he missed. Fragile smells of flowers, the wild smells of the air. Special places to share with others. And tucked away deep down, Simon longed for spring.

When he emerges into the open, Simon does not think of a mate or of food, but sits "facing the sun until it set behind the trees". So far as the text goes, then, this is a type of fiction and children must look to the wash and line pictures [by John Schoenherr] for total accuracy.

A WET AND SANDY DAY (1977)

Kirkus Reviews

SOURCE: A review of *A Wet and Sandy Day,* in *Kirkus Reviews,* Vol. XLV, No. 3, February 1, 1977, p. 92.

A low-keyed evocation of the sensuous receptivity of childhood, via a little girl's report on a solitary jaunt to the beach. The afternoon is a series of sensations and textures, beginning with the "sunny patch" she lands in after jumping off the porch. Then come the bumpy road, the "good dry spot" where she leaves her things while she swims, the sun's slow heat that sticks her to an inner tube, the rain that trickles down and wrinkles her fingers, the squishy walk home through puddles, the chilly house, and at last the warm cocoa she and Mama sip, feeling good. And it does.

Betsy Hearne

SOURCE: A review of *A Wet and Sandy Day,* in *Booklist,* Vol. 73, No. 14, March 15, 1977, pp. 1094-95.

A smooth, summer-rain-on-the-beach mood piece. The young girl who's just at the age of turning from round to long—nicely caught in [Donald] Carrick's blue-and-tan washed drawings—decides to stay on the beach after rain drowns the sun. It's a new experience to get wet from the sky, listen to the splashing sounds, step in all the mud puddles along the road home, brush the wet bushes, and drink hot cocoa in August. There's an extra nice feeling between mother and child, and the first-person narrative will evoke happy times for young East Coast vacationers.

Susan Sprague

SOURCE: A review of *A Wet and Sandy Day,* in *School Library Journal,* Vol. 23, No. 9, May, 1977, pp. 54-5.

Ignoring her mother's warning of "rain later," a little girl runs off to the beach and is the only one left when the rain starts. She snuggles into the wet sand, listens to the sounds of the waves, gets thoroughly wet and "cleaner than if I'd taken a hundred baths" before splashing home. The story is fine for reading aloud. . . . [Ryder] does a nice job of conveying a girl's pleasurable feelings during a summer rain.

FIREFLIES (1977)

Kirkus Reviews

SOURCE: A review of *Fireflies,* in *Kirkus Reviews,* Vol. XLV, No. 20, October 15, 1977, p. 1096.

Though she doesn't mention the chemicals luciferin and luciferase as does Hawkes in her *Let's-Read-and-Find-Out* entry, *Fireflies in the Night* (1966), Ryder includes

more detail that children can grasp. She introduces the glowworm underground, toward the end of his almost two-year larval stage, where he and other glowworms gang up on an earthworm; and later, after the ten-day pupa stage, she has him ignore a similar earthworm: "He will probably not eat anymore." Almost half the book then follows his search for a mate as each kind of firefly flashes its own signal and other males are caught in a spider web or lured by a green-flashing female who mimics their flashes, then eats them when they land. Successful at last, the firefly will only live a few more weeks; by then his offspring will be on their way to hatching. A life cycle smartly observed . . . .

Albert Edward Feldman

SOURCE: A review of *Fireflies,* in *Science Books & Films,* Vol. XIV, No. 3, December, 1978, p. 183.

Fireflies is a pleasant introduction of an insect species. I recommend it for parents who read to their preschoolers and for beginning readers. The illustrations [by Don Bolognese] follow the text and should promote interest. The author traces the life history of the firefly including natural enemies, food and habitat. A serious omission is the control of snails and slugs by larval fireflies. It is unfortunate that the illustrator chose to color fireflies uniformly blue, which is inaccurate. Larval illustrations are more accurate. Overall, the book is worthwhile reading for home and classroom use.

FOG IN THE MEADOW (1979)

Anne McKeithen-Boes

SOURCE: A review of *Fog in the Meadow,* in *School Library Journal,* Vol. 25, No. 9, May, 1979, p. 55.

Fog in the Meadow causes all the small creatures to scutter into their burrows—except rabbit who has lost the way. "Gray in the grayness, the fox paused by the oak tree, waiting patiently for the sound or scent of somebody small lost in the fog." Then the nighthawk overhead begins to scream. Ryder presents an absorbing natural drama that intrigues readers as it builds to a satisfying crescendo. And, it is all accomplished in an easy unassuming style.

Kirkus Reviews

SOURCE: A review of *Fog in the Meadow,* in *Kirkus Reviews,* Vol. XLVII, No. 9, May 1, 1979, p. 515.

How does it feel to be a small animal lost in the fog? Ryder's audience will experience the situation from within, as first the cold wind blows "across the crickets' small black backs" and "past rows of sparrows sleeping in the bare oak tree" and then the fog comes fast, "creeping like moss over the snail's shell." The fox comes quietly too, and a rabbit hides from him in a patch of briars, trying to see or smell her burrow until at last the "familiar sounds" of the other animals help her find her way. Illustrated [by Gail Owens] with a suitable blend of mistiness and precision (though without the text's evocative distinction), this is another empathic brush with nature by the author of *Simon Underground* (1976) and *A Wet and Sandy Day* (1977).

📖 **SNAIL IN THE WOODS (with Harold S. Feinberg, 1979)**

Marion P. Harris

SOURCE: A review of *Snail in the Woods,* in *Appraisal: Children's Science Books,* Vol. 13, No. 2, Spring, 1980, pp. 70-1.

The choice of the Common White-lipped Forest Snail is a wise one. It is of findable size, widely distributed in the East and South and very common. The text simply and effectively follows a complete cycle in the life of this small creature, showing clearly as well its role in the forest food web, and its response to the various natural disasters to which it is prone. The illustrator [Jo Polseno] is to be commended for attempting more species-specific accuracy than I have seen in some recent children's trade books. I am bothered, however, by several aspects of the illustrations. First, the representation of the floor of a deciduous forest seems very misleading. Second, the color of the snail shell in these illustrations does not follow the progression described in the text. Keys call this snail "ivory white to yellowish green," but the illustrations here are usually dark rich brown. Third, I am unhappy about the number of toes on the shrew and the mouse. Last, as, according to text, the shapeblind snail meets its future mate by accidental touch, the illustrator shows them some distance apart in a stance reminiscent of "across the crowded room" without the crowd. In this and the next picture, the illustrator's spatial relations seem to break down in drawing the mate's shell from the left. By showing spiral grooves and no hint of umbilicus, he effectively reverses the impact of the careful use of "it" in the text, raising speculation about which sex is which, or, if the introduction was read, implying that there are great differences of shape and pattern in Common White-lipped Snails. In spite of these limitations, the book is well worth getting. Children get too few chances to view the world through the senses of a non-insect invertebrate, let alone a hermaphroditic one.

Yvonne Heather Burry

SOURCE: A review of *Snail in the Woods,* in *Science Books & Films,* Vol. 16, No. 1, September-October, 1980, p. 33.

Here is a glimpse into the real and silent world of one particular *Snail in the Woods.* This book provides an informative and generally readable approach to an animal

familiar to most children. The scope of the information presented is very complete. The life cycle, predatory relationships and adaptive qualities are adequately discussed. The vocabulary tends to drift to a level a bit beyond the primary reader's capabilities, and one finds sentences that are simply too long. But the large typeface and general format sustain interest. The pleasant illustrations are not totally accurate and tend toward ambiguity at times. A nice line drawing of the snail concludes the text and helps to remedy the situation. This straightforward presentation is ideal for youngsters who are in the process of discovering their natural environment.

📖 **THE SPIDERS DANCE (1981)**

Margaret Bush

SOURCE: A review of *The Spiders Dance,* in *School Library Journal,* Vol. 27, No. 8, April, 1981, p. 117.

The life cycle of a spider from its initial spring flight to establish a home through days and nights of web spinning and waiting for prey to the final chore of spinning protective winter covering for her eggs at her life's end is told in story form and plentifully illustrated [by Robert J. Blake] with pencil drawings and shades of blue, yellow and green. Ryder's text strives for poetic effect and becomes lush with alliteration and adjectives. She creates a good sense of the spider's world, but at times she is evasive, suggesting rather than explicitly stating such events as mating and the spider's loss of a leg to an attacking bird. Augusta Goldin's *Spider Silk* (Crowell, 1964) and Berniece Freschet's *The Web in the Grass* (Scribners, 1972) cover similar material in more informative texts and more attractive formats for the same audience, but this provides good read-aloud material.

Barbara Brenner

SOURCE: A review of *The Spiders Dance,* in *Appraisal: Science Books for Young People,* Vol. 14, No. 3, Fall, 1981, pp. 35-6.

There's some fine writing in this poetic book about spiders. The premise of the book is an excellent one—that scientific facts can be imparted in an original and imaginative way (which we all know but few attempt). Children are sure to enjoy hearing this one read aloud. Phrases like "the spider spins a bridge across an empty space" will linger, tuning up ears as they teach. And author Ryder spins her web just long enough to catch the reader, not so long that he or she will get enmeshed in too much information. A few statements may be a bit gossamer—for instance, one wonders whether kids will be confused by the mention of seven legs on a spider and then, later, eight. Will they realize that Ms. Spider lost a leg and grew a new one? Will they understand "until the sun calls one to lead the others" as an abstract rather than a literal idea? I don't know. But it's all to the good that minds be challenged in such a pleasant way.

I wish the illustrations were better. Seems to me that either they should have been much clearer and more detailed to provide clarity where the text was oblique—or they should have completely matched the mood of the text.

BEACH PARTY (1982)

Kirkus Reviews

SOURCE: A review of *Beach Party*, in *Kirkus Reviews*, Vol. L, No. 8, April 15, 1982, p. 487.

A birthday party on the beach, all family warmth and cosy familiarity. Kate collects shells, as she does each year at Uncle Tony's birthday party. Peter and Rose jump in the waves and go with Mama on the rides. Raymond buries Uncle Tony. Later, Raymond is missing and searched for and turns up deep in a hole he's digging. Everyone eats around the fire, and then "the family drew together and listened to the quiet sound of night." And all the time little Dorothy is trying to remember the "loud, scary, but nice" thing she liked best about last year's beach party. Then come the weekend fireworks and Dorothy remembers, as everyone sighs "oooooooooh!" and "ahhhhhh." [Diane] Stanley pictures the family as white lambs in clothing; she outlines and shades them in dots, which gives them a cuddly, stuffed-toy look; and her clear, deep colors and horizontal scenes, with sun and moon low on the ocean horizon, drive home the mellow mood. The text alone, like others of Ryder's, is nice but a bit limp.

Kathleen Leverich

SOURCE: A review of *Beach Party*, in *The New York Times Book Review*, June 13, 1982, p. 26.

Heart is what **Beach Party** has lots of; it also has sand, gulls, sea breezes, salt—in short, the beach, with all the vast and various wonders it implies to children. Rose, Mama and Papa, Uncle Tony, Kate, Gilbert and most of the other members of the sheep family are veterans of many beach seasons; not so Dorothy. She's smaller and doesn't remember much about the previous year's outing; she slept most of that day. "Ah, but you were very little then," says Mama. "This year will be different."

Each member of this large family has a personality with quirky, idiosyncratic beach habits. Raymond's a fanatic for burying relatives in the sand. Kate collects shells, rocks, driftwood, creeping things. But it's Dorothy whom we follow, with her unfamiliarity and her hazy recollection of something noisy, scary and pretty that surprised her last year and that she hopes to discover again.

It's impossible to say which is the more effective, Joanne Ryder's engaging text or Diane Stanley's expressive illustrations. Both are warm and funny, and in the end, you can't separate the two. They combine to create a classic, authentic beach day, as memorable as any a child ever lived.

THE SNAIL'S SPELL (1982)

Zena Sutherland

SOURCE: A review of *The Snail's Spell*, in *Bulletin of the Center for Children's Books*, Vol. 36, No. 3, November, 1982, p. 53.

There's little story here, just a concept and some very nice drawings [by Lynne Cherry] of plants and animals, a bit repetitive but beautifully detailed, with fine lines and a restrained use of color. A small boy crouches as the text begins, "Imagine you are soft and have no bones inside you. Imagine you are grey, the color of smoke. You are shrinking." The boy's figure shrinks to the size of the tiny snail in the picture, and both are shown in a series of double-page spreads that has the boy feeling and moving and eating as the snail does. At the end, both sleep, and the last picture shows the boy, the snail held gently in his hand; the child is no longer dwarfed by an enormous lettuce and towering mushrooms. Nice to look at, with a concept that may stimulate a child's imagination, this is nevertheless static and slight.

Ellen Fader

SOURCE: A review of *The Snail's Spell*, in *School Library Journal*, Vol. 29, No. 3, November, 1982, p. 73.

Brilliant illustrations and a short nonanthropomorphic text invite an unnamed sleeping, pajama-clad child into a garden teeming with wildlife. The boy gradually shrinks until he is the size of a snail and experiences things as a snail would, including gliding, eating, using feelers, seeing, resting, encountering an enemy and growing a shell. The plot is minimal but the incredibly detailed drawings and the idea of shrinking to enter another world should capture children's imaginations. The major flaw of this fantasy is that the boy inexplicably and suddenly appears full size on the last double-page spread. Likely questions from children: How and why did he get so big?

INSIDE TURTLE'S SHELL, AND OTHER POEMS OF THE FIELD (1985)

Ruth M. McConnell

SOURCE: A review of *Inside Turtle's Shell: and Other Poems of the Field*, in *School Library Journal*, Vol. 31, No. 3, April, 1985, p. 82.

With pithy delicacy touched with humor, the author of picture books and prize nature writing here distills her perceptions of nature into a series of free-verse vignettes with the punch of haiku. She imagines a day in the plant and animal lives of a field in late summer, from foggy dawn to night, when "Turtle / slides his old brown head / under his roof, / turning out the stars." The accompanying softly textured gray sketches [by Susan Bonners] further reveal their lives or their indicated hiding place—as bubbles from pond mud, or the ". . . shadows / seeking shadows" of the night hunters—even past lives, where "under the grass / under the moles / under the rock / dinosaurs sleep." Time and its cycles are caught in the morning glories that "wake up the old stone wall / with blueness, / untwisting and blooming for just one day— / today," but especially in recurrent views of the almost century-old turtle and of a just-born turtle's first day of meadow life. This is a lovely book for third- and fourth-grade readers to explore on their own, but also one to share with all ages.

Carolyn Phelan

SOURCE: A review of *Inside Turtle's Shell, and Other Poems of the Field,* in *Booklist,* Vol. 81, No. 16, April 15, 1985, p. 1200.

Re-creating a field and pond alive with the creatures that inhabit it, Ryder offers a collection of poetry concise, precise, and immediate. The short poems create vignettes of individual animals in turn, focusing our attention on their essential qualities and our perceptions of them. The long-lived turtle dreams of the tall trees that once covered the meadow, "But that was long ago, / nearly a hundred years. / Only turtle / remembers / the cool darkness of trees." The brevity and sensibility of many of Ryder's poems are reminiscent of Japanese poetry, as in "Blackbird's shadow / glides across the pond / chasing / sixty

silver fish." or "The last berries / turn / eat-me-red. / Their bushes / droop / with gray / sparrows." Bonners' soft, exquisite pencil drawings show us the world through a mist, suggesting how a forest appears to a turtle, or tall grass to a leaping mouse, or the dinosaur bones beneath the meadow to the imagination, without defining too much. The book design and illustrations enhance the poems, reflecting their quiet beauty.

Zena Sutherland

SOURCE: A review of *Inside Turtle's Shell and Other Poems of the Field,* in *Bulletin of the Center for Children's Books,* Vol. 38, No. 10, June, 1985, p. 194.

Soft black and white drawings, almost misty yet highly textural, illustrate a book of poetry that speaks of the small creatures of pond and meadow. Like the drawings, the poems have a quiet tenderness and empathy that are reminiscent of the work of Carmen de Gasztold. Most of the poems are brief, some almost as compressed as haiku; most have delicate imagery; all are evocative.

Phyllis G. Sidorsky

SOURCE: A review of *Inside Turtle's Shell and Other Poems of the Field,* in *Childhood Education,* Vol. 62, No. 3, January-February, 1986, pp. 220-21.

The essence of pond and meadow life is evoked in these quiet observations of nature. Each well-chosen word creates lasting images of creatures that inhabit this bucolic

From Catching the Wind, *written by Joanne Ryder. Illustrated by Michael Rothman.*

world. A day passes, night comes. A newly hatched turtle emerges while an old one quietly celebrates his centenary. Soft, gray pencil drawings reflect a knowledge of and a reverence for nature.

THE NIGHT FLIGHT (1985)

Janet Hickman

SOURCE: A review of *The Night Flight,* in *Language Arts,* Vol. 62, No. 7, November, 1985, p. 795.

Anna plays in the park by day and revisits it at night in her dreams, flying out through her window and over city rooftops to the familiar fishpond and the great stone lion, who takes her riding on his back until she wakes "remembering how it felt to fly, / remembering a skyful of pigeons / and a lion roaring by a waterfall." The text is clear in the story it tells and lyrical in its sound, a good choice for reading aloud. The imaginative pictures [by Amy Schwartz], which completely cover every page, are saturated with color. The black of the night sky is a dramatic backdrop for the lush greens of the park, the golden lion, and the simplified shape of Anna floating along in her white nightdress and stiff orange pigtails.

Anne E. Mulherkar

SOURCE: A review of *The Night Flight,* in *School Library Journal,* Vol. 32, No. 3, November, 1985, p. 77.

Anna undertakes a journey to be envied by many a child as well as adults: a fantastic flight through the night sky. As Anna soars and explores her familiar daily haunts, she finds that much is changed in the darkness of night. The city park, usually filled with joggers and bench-sitters, is empty. The goldfish, normally skittish, are tame. Most wondrously, Alexander, the great stone lion, has come alive. Ryder's richly descriptive text often reads as poetry. With flattened perspectives and variegated tones, Schwartz paints, like Rousseau, a primitive world of friendly beasts and tangled vegetation. Page after page she demonstrates her versatility with color, as blues, greens and yellows are brilliantly offset by the night sky. Schwartz and Ryder, each gifted artists in their own right, stretch their capabilities and children's imaginations in *The Night Flight.*

Ilene Cooper

SOURCE: A review of *The Night Flight,* in *Booklist,* Vol. 82, No. 5, November 1, 1985, pp. 413-14.

Anna enjoys playing in the park, where she rides Alexander the stone lion and hopes the goldfish will take bread from her hand. Then, it's time to go home and get ready for bed, but sleep does not come in ordinary ways. A musician in the apartment below sends sweet melodies upstairs, and a dancer above taps on her ceiling. Before long, Anna is floating out her window, flying over rooftops, and landing in the park where goldfish and pigeons become her intimate friends. The next amazement is that Alexander now runs wild and free. Anna climbs on his back and discovers the park's hidden junglelike venues. Too soon, her adventure is over, and Anna drifts back to her room. The next day, remembering it all, she returns to the park, passing the sleeping Alexander. The goldfish evidently remember too, and they eat from her hand as she calls them by name. Ryder's lyrical text, which paints its own word pictures, meets its match with Schwartz' vibrant, brilliantly colored illustrations. Rarely has a night been so black or a jungle so lush and green. Schwartz' rounded shapes work especially well here, giving the pictures the dreamy quality they demand. A perfect pairing of author and artist in this lilting, lovely nighttime adventure.

CHIPMUNK SONG (1987)

Publishers Weekly

SOURCE: A review of *Chipmunk Song,* in *Publishers Weekly,* Vol. 231, No. 18, May 8, 1987, p. 69.

"Imagine / you are someone small / sleeping on a bed of leaves / in a cool, dark room / underground," suggests Ryder in this unusual picture book. [Illustrator Lynne] Cherry's depiction of this scene shows a child curled underground in a chipmunk's den. Throughout the book, her striking illustrations, which are like natural-history museum display cases brought to life, invite the reader into the chipmunk's world. Ryder imaginatively transports readers by using specific concerns: "All day long / you run to the woods, / filling your cheeks / with acorns."

Janet D. French

SOURCE: A review of *Chipmunk Song,* in *School Library Journal,* Vol. 33, No. 10, June, 1987, pp. 88-9.

"Imagine you are someone small sleeping on a bed of leaves in a cool, dark room underground." Taking this opening suggestion literally, just as young listeners might do, Cherry has turned Ryder's simple text about a chipmunk's late summer activities into an extraordinarily attractive picture book. The child that Ryder is addressing is shown on each double-page spread experiencing the same activities as the chipmunk. The miniature child and the animal itself climb into the sunlight, gather berries and nuts, hide from a hawk, prepare their snug burrows, and finally curl up for the long winter sleep. There is no interaction between child and chipmunk, subtly maintaining the distinction between what is real and what is imagined. The fine watercolor and ink illustrations, in cutaways below ground and at chipmunk eye-level above, are full of intriguing, accurate detail in a fresh perspective. Science, art, and imagination are rarely so well served.

Edward Saiff

SOURCE: A review of *Chipmunk Song,* in *Science Books & Films,* Vol. 23, No. 2, November-December, 1987, p. 107.

The excellent text and illustrations of this book will provide a great deal of information on chipmunks to third and fourth graders. The reader is asked to imagine himself as a chipmunk. The story line begins with a description of a burrow. The text and illustrations combine to form a powerful image as the reader feels himself emerging onto the forest floor to look for food while constantly on the alert for danger. After successfully avoiding a foraging hawk, the reader is made to feel that fall has begun, bringing with it the task of collecting and storing food for the winter. Overall, this book is charming and should excite young people to further explore topics such as hibernation, camouflage, predation, and many other of the natural phenomena alluded to in the text and depicted in the figures.

E. Colwell

SOURCE: A review of *Chipmunk Song,* in *The Junior Bookshelf,* Vol. 51, No. 6, December, 1987, p. 272.

A chipmunk is not a familiar animal for English children, but this does not really matter for this is a book which speaks for all wild animals. Both author and artist are deeply concerned for the natural world around them. The author expresses hers in prose that is poetical at times; the artist gives visual expression to the text and extends it as only an artist can. Author and artist are in tune because of a shared interest and feeling.

The author has described imaginatively the life through the seasons of 'small ones who live in darkness', looking for food but with heart beating with fear. The summer passes with all its beauty and plenty, food is stored, a warm bed is made and the 'little ones' sleep in darkness inside the safe earth, awaiting Spring when life will begin again.

The artist has interpreted the text through the life of a chipmunk and a child who shares the life of the woods with wonder and joy. The illustrations in natural colour convey the woodland life evocatively.

📖 *STEP INTO THE NIGHT* (1988)

Publishers Weekly

SOURCE: A review of *Step into the Night,* in *Publishers Weekly,* Vol. 234, No. 11, September 9, 1988, p. 133.

[Ryder] artfully blends poetry and science in this richly illustrated book about a girl who stands "like a shadow / against [a] tall dark tree . . . to see the night begin." As "a chunk of moon / shines above the treetops," one by one, animals appear. Throughout, the narration is second-person, addressing first the girl and then the creatures of the night. "You are a month old," refers to a brown mouse holding "soft berries, eat-me red," while the girl looks on. A skunk, a mole, a firefly, a spider in "a patch of lace / across an empty space," a frog who sings "floating in the darkness"—to each the girl says goodnight and then quietly "leave[s] the night behind." Ryder's lyrical, compelling language and [Dennis] Nolan's extraordinary paintings—full of depth and light, in a photorealistic style—are as breathtaking as the night itself.

Denise M. Wilms

SOURCE: A review of *Step into the Night,* in *Booklist,* Vol. 85, No. 4, October 15, 1988, p. 414.

A young child contemplating the descent of night witnesses the shift in natural activity as daytime creatures settle down to sleep and nocturnal animals begin their movements under the protective cover of darkness. Ryder presents these observations through a direct narrative that spotlights each animal: a mouse foraging for berries, a firefly flashing for a mate, a skunk spraying an incautious intruder. Nolan provides deep, dark atmospheric scenes of the child's world, of moon-drenched greenery, and of the animals at their work. At times the renderings are as subtle as they appear in nature, leaving the reader to look as hard as the young girl for the night life around her. Ryder's information is succinctly presented and smoothly woven into the poetic narrative. A quiet book that might prove especially useful to scouting groups or others wishing to prepare youngsters for nature outings of a similar bent.

Sally R. Dow

SOURCE: A review of *Step into the Night,* in *School Library Journal,* Vol. 35, No. 3, November, 1988, pp. 95-6.

As night begins to fall, a small girl steps outside to observe birds, insects, and animals. She imagines what it would be like to be the different woodland creatures that she sees making their nocturnal preparations. A poetic text creates quiet, dreamy images and helps readers empathize with the natural world. Soft, realistic watercolors in subdued shades of blue, green, and gray suggest the onset of night. Words and pictures combine to create a dreamlike, hushed atmosphere as the spell cast by twilight falls on the outdoors. A thoughtful, lovely picture book, perfect for sharing aloud at bedtime.

📖 *MOCKINGBIRD MORNING* (1989)

Publishers Weekly

SOURCE: A review of *Mockingbird Morning,* in *Publishers Weekly,* Vol. 235, No. 3, January 20, 1989, pp. 147-48.

This companion book to Ryder and [illustrator Dennis]

Nolan's *Step into the Night* is, like its predecessor, a naturalist's delight. A girl is awakened by a mockingbird's song: *"I am here. I am here. Happy day! Happy day!"* As she walks through the woods, and near a pond, she looks and listens, moving in concord with the narrator's directions. "Under the trees / the moss / is like a quiet animal / waiting / for you to come / and touch / its softness. / Feel its fur gently. / Listen . . . / you can almost / hear it purr." She sees a turtle with "bright red eyes," a fish that swirls like "a golden treasure," a dragonfly with "long wings / clear as glass." As she returns, the "summer pictures flicker in [her] mind" and keep her "company / all the way home." Nolan's outstanding illustrations, in his customary photo-realistic style, are drenched with sunlight and shadows—the perfect complement to Ryder's reverent text.

Denise Wilms

SOURCE: A review of *Mockingbird Morning*, in *Booklist*, Vol. 85, No. 15, April 1, 1989, p. 1390.

Ryder's meditative, free-form poetry evokes the quiet somnolence of a summer's day, when observant eyes can find intriguing activity amid the natural stillness. A young girl stands by her window and sees a mockingbird "borrowing his song from a hundred different birds, calling to the empty morning in a hundred different ways." Outside, she notices morning doves searching for food; an animal's burrow; the soft, furry moss of a tree; and a turtle (or is it by rights a tortoise?). A walk takes her to a pond, where a goose preens its feathers and a golden carp flashes in the sun; dragonflies, clouds, and bees are all observed with quiet interest. There is no plot here; rather, Ryder simply catalogs the fullness of nature in a gentle fashion that urges readers to do the same thing. Nolan's illustrations, though they could be more precise, capture the dappled light and quietness of the day. A nice accompaniment to nature-study units, this may speak most clearly to older picture-book readers, who will best sense Ryder's thoughtful mood.

Marcia Hupp

SOURCE: A review of *Mockingbird Morning*, in *School Library Journal*, Vol. 35, No. 11, July, 1989, pp. 75-6.

A young girl explores in the quiet of a summer's morning, observing—passively—all there is to see: a mockingbird in a tree, sunlight on the surface of a pond, clouds chasing across the sky. . . . But despite images of birds and clouds, Ryder's verse never takes flight, perhaps because she falls into the trap of addressing her reader as "you," a choice that burdens her words with an inappropriate pragmatism. Nolan's elegant but lifeless paintings do little more than mirror the words on the page. These full-color illustrations are initially striking and may help to sell this very slight effort, but readers have only to compare the book to Yolen's *Owl Moon* (Philomel, 1987), a similar journey (but on a winter's eve), to know where their time's best spent.

WHITE BEAR, ICE BEAR (1989)

Robert Strang

SOURCE: A review of *White Bear, Ice Bear*, in *Bulletin of the Center for Children's Books*, Vol. 42, No. 6, February, 1989, p. 156.

This is first in a projected series that attempts to show animal behavior from a you-are-it perspective. "Outside your window snow is falling, calling you, changing you . . . ," and "you" become a polar bear (although the term "ice bear" is preferred throughout). While the full-color double-page spreads [by Michael Rothman] successfully evoke the cold drama of the Arctic, the paintings, like the text, rely primarily on a romantic appeal. "The air is cold and good! You feel like running in the cold fresh air." The gimmick encourages an unconscionable degree of anthropomorphism, allowing the bear powers of metaphor ("You . . . see others moving slowly like pale ghosts across the ice") and assigning the power of intent to the moon, which "shines its silver light so you can see the white snow. . . ." The fact that polar bears eat seals is delicately hinted at but ultimately dodged: the seal gets away, and, Max-like, the bear is called to a house by "good supper smells" and turns back into a boy. A sympathetic but sentimental introduction to the polar bear, this needs less whimsy and more facts.

Publishers Weekly

SOURCE: A review of *White Bear, Ice Bear*, in *Publishers Weekly*, Vol. 235, No. 8, February 24, 1989, p. 232.

This first entry in a promising new Just for a Day series delves into the world of the white bear. As with her other books, such as *Step into the Night* and *Mockingbird Morning*, Ryder tells a highly imaginative story that is scientifically accurate. In this story, a boy is transformed into an "Ice Bear" and experiences the beautiful yet brutally cold environment of this creature. Ryder's language is spare and poetic, as she carefully sets out the adaptive characteristics that help the bear in the arctic setting: heavy fur, protective coloration, padded feet, strong claws and a keen sense of smell. Squeamish readers will be relieved to know that the well-paced text stops short of the bear's actually capturing—and devouring—a fur seal for his meal. Rothman's paintings evoke the power of this wild creature, at home in a frosty, blue-green and white arctic landscape, which is only briefly illuminated by a silvery moon and the dancing northern lights.

Carolyn Phelan

SOURCE: A review of *White Bear, Ice Bear*, in *Booklist*, Vol. 85, No. 14, March 15, 1989, p. 1304.

In this picture book, a boy awakens to see snow falling,

beckoning him. Quickly transformed into a polar bear, he runs outside into a North Pole landscape of snowy hills and caves of ice. While he is a bear, his senses and behavior are bearlike. At the end of day, the scent of food draws him back home, where he becomes a boy again, in time for supper. Ryder shifts point of view so smoothly that the boy's transformations seem quite natural. The double-page spreads are dramatic in composition and graceful in their rhythmic repetition of forms. Rothman uses color with subtlety and restraint, creating a dark, ice-blue snowscape where bear and foxes roam the frozen white crust. Below the ice and snow, seals swim, rising occasionally to a breathing hole. Eerily lit by the moon and the northern lights, the setting takes on an otherworldly beauty. Lightly reminiscent of the author's **Snail's Spell** and **Chipmunk's Song,** in which children become tiny enough to accompany small creatures, this takes the premise one step further: a child becomes the animal. The fantasy is immediately both grander and more believable; the identification with the animal, more complete. Through imaginative writing and artwork, the book—the first in Ryder's Just for a Day series—leads readers into deeper sympathy for their fellow creatures.

Kirkus Reviews

SOURCE: A review of *White Bear, Ice Bear,* in *Kirkus Reviews,* Vol. LVII, No. 6, March 15, 1989, p. 469.

A second-person narrative suggests that "you" (a lively boy who looks about eight years old) are inspired by the snow outside your window to become an "ice bear," and are transported to appropriate surroundings where you experience typical polar bear activities (including hunting, but not catching or eating, a seal). The evocative paintings that extend the brief text are attractive, with rich shades of blue predominating, enlivened with dramatic highlights of white and gold. But the whole approach is coy and off-putting, especially in comparison with Matthews' straightforward, more informative, enchantingly photographed *Polar Bear Cubs.*

Patricia Manning

SOURCE: A review of *White Bear, Ice Bear,* in *School Library Journal,* Vol. 35, No. 8, April, 1989, p. 90.

A book that is rich, empathic, imaginative, and eye-pleasing. On a snowy morning, a boy's imagination transforms him into a huge polar bear, who plunges from the warm daylit house into the moonlit Arctic winter. Through a beautiful conjunction of simple, lyrical text and luminous illustrations in blue, white, and green, readers accompany the bear crossing the pack ice, exploring starkly beautiful icescapes, sleeping in the lee of a wind blown drift, patiently waiting at a seal's breathing hole, and wandering solitary beneath a rippling aurora borealis. Returning, the bear/boy bursts through the house door, just boy, exactly in time for supper. The first of a projected series that one hopes will live up to the standards set here.

Anne Rose

SOURCE: A review of *White Bear, Ice Bear,* in *Appraisal: Science Books for Young People,* Vol. 22, No. 4, Autumn, 1989, p. 57.

Inviting both ear and eye into an imaginary exploration of a day at the top of the world, Joanne Ryder, with illustrator Michael Rothman, presents a boy's sensory experiences as they might be if the child were transformed into a great, furry, polar bear.

Effectively using this device in **White Bear, Ice Bear,** the text and illustrations evoke the mystery and vastness of an arctic land using a limited number of elements and a restrained range of colors. Only foxes and seals are seen in the blue-white landscapes that later excitingly expand into the Northern Lights, in several spectacular double spreads near the end of the tale.

Although the initial transition from awakening at home to the transformation into a large beast is somewhat strained, the poetic language and dramatic visuals are expertly blended. Simplicity of presentation reflects a deep sensitivity to nature's intricacies and reveals, in detail, the deceptiveness of a stereotyped perception of a frozen world.

The book is challenging while remaining inviting for younger readers. This is the first of a series in picture book format by the author, under the heading of "Just for a Day", that promises continuing enhancement for early science literature.

📖 *UNDER THE MOON* (1989)

Phillis Wilson

SOURCE: A review of *Under the Moon,* in *Booklist,* Vol. 85, No. 19, June 1, 1989, p. 1727.

The forest floor, a symphony of greens, is dotted with wildflowers and backed by a deep blue-violet evening sky; it is here that Mama Mouse teaches her youngest the essential ways of the world. The wee one learns where the sweet berries hide and where she should go when the owl flies by. When asked where home is, the baby mouse's innocent answer, "we live under the moon," causes Mama to reinforce her lessons. By the process of association—tingly smells, singing and chirping sounds, and warm, soft feelings—Mama helps the young one to identify her nest in the meadow. [Illustrator Cheryl] Harness' moon-drenched meadows, alive with many tiny creatures that young eyes can spy, and twinkling star-studded skies create an engaging atmosphere that complements Ryder's gentle story line; toddlers who are also learning where home is will easily feel empathy with little mouse.

CATCHING THE WIND (1989)

Kirkus Reviews

SOURCE: A review of *Catching the Wind,* in *Kirkus Reviews,* Vol. LVII, No. 13, July 1, 1989, p. 996.

This second "Just for a Day Book" is more successful than its predecessor, **White Bear, Ice Bear,** perhaps because the experiences of the Canada goose here are less prone to false dramatization. This time it's a girl who imagines herself answering the call, becoming a goose and joining a flock as it travels the sky, swims in a pond, and feeds on grass. [Illustrator Michael] Rothman's broad double spreads colorfully evoke the landscape traversed and the many attitudes of the birds in flight and at rest. Readers should enjoy imagining, as the second-person text suggests, what it is like to be one of these beautiful birds.

Robert Strang

SOURCE: A review of *Catching the Wind,* in *Bulletin of the Center for Children's Books,* Vol. 43, No. 1, September, 1989, p. 18.

While the anthropomorphic premise of the series is labored and confusing, this second entry is more successful than the first, **White Bear, Ice Bear.** In **Catching the Wind,** "you" are a little girl who, upon feeling the wind "calling you softly," changes into a Canada goose. You join a flock, "flying and honking across the sky," land and eat at a pond, and resume your flight. While most children will probably understand that the wind doesn't really sing *"Be warm. Come be warm"* to the geese, they will probably not understand that this is a whimsical allusion to migration, and will be confused after a previous reference to the "cold windy sky." However, this book does contain more facts, gracefully presented, than did **White Bear,** and Rothman's paintings have even more drama than the ones he did for that book. Full-color close-ups of the birds in flight and splashing across the pond seem to leap from the page, and the bird's-eyed perspectives of the sky and earth are inviting—but not for "you," who "slide through the open window, where your own warm bed waits to change you again."

Ellen Fader

SOURCE: A review of *Catching the Wind,* in *School Library Journal,* Vol. 35, No. 13, September, 1989, p. 233.

Readers are invited "just for a day" to accompany a young girl on a wildlife adventure as she becomes a Canada goose. Ryder's graceful, quasi-poetic text attempts to capture the physical sensations of flying, swimming, feeding, and preening; to her credit, she does not condescend to children by anthropomorphosis or overwhelm them with too many details, but instead encourages them to create their own images ("You dip your smooth dark bill into the shining water and drink. The cool water slides down your long, long throat"). A surprising amount of natural history is conveyed using this technique but, after all, an average day in the life of a Canada goose is not a terribly exciting one and the lack of any real plot may disappoint some youngsters. Rothman's realistic acrylic paintings offer unusual views and perspectives and add greatly to the book's appeal. The vividness of the illustrations make this a good bet for sharing with groups studying birds and flight; they may just be seduced by the invitation of the geese to "Come along, come along."

Barbara C. Scotto

SOURCE: A review of *Catching the Wind,* in *Appraisal: Science Books for Young People,* Vol. 23, No. 1, Winter, 1990, pp. 49-50.

Looking out her window one fall day, a girl feels the wind. It calls to her, and she finds herself moving through the window, changing into a large bird. She joins a group of migrating geese as they fly over the countryside. They land on a pond, rest, eat grass and take off again. The goose/girl turns in the other direction and flies home. This simple plot is typical of the books in the "Just for a Day" series, where a child becomes an animal for a short time. This kind of scenario has child appeal, and indeed the words and paintings give a sense of immediacy to the reader. The text describes what "you" the goose feel and do. In the paintings, because of the skillful use of scale, the view of the bird being described often seems to be through the eyes of another goose. The artwork has much to recommend it. It is unfortunate that the palette contains so much deep yellow, which adds a drabness to the pictures.

The reader does not learn a great deal of information about Canada geese in this work. In fact, the text simply calls the bird a goose, and even that label is not given until the bird becomes a part of a flock several pages into the story. What is important here is the experience of being a large, wild bird.

Lynne E. Kepler

SOURCE: A review of *Catching the Wind,* in *Appraisal: Science Books for Young People,* Vol. 23, No. 1, Winter, 1990, p. 50.

Have you ever imagined what it would be like to glide through the autumn sky as wild geese do? **Catching The Wind** guides you on an imaginary journey through colorful illustrations and very descriptive text. The portrayal of the Canada (not Canadian as some are likely to say) goose, to which you have been transformed, is precise; waterproof feathers, soft down, webbed feet. The book also takes you through the daily routine of migrating geese.

The book does a wonderful job of giving you the "personality" of the goose without being anthropomorphic.

Edell Marie Peters

SOURCE: A review of *Catching the Wind*, in *Science Books & Films,* Vol. 25, No. 5, May-June, 1990, p. 269.

This book is another winning entry in the *Just for a Day* series. In it, the reader becomes a wild goose and a participant in the story. The text encourages the young reader to feel the lift of the wind against the wings, see the countryside far below, and communicate with the flock. Landings and takeoffs are experienced as the flock searches for food, water, and shelter. Ryder's text is poetic and lends itself very well to a family storytelling experience. While a few basic facts about the life-style of Canada geese emerge in the story, the author's main emphasis is to teach children to respect and appreciate nature. All the author's books are free of scientific terminology, which makes them suitable for beginning readers. The illustrations are stunning and complement the text. It is easy to see why some of Ryder's previous books have won awards from such organizations as the National Science Teachers Association.

WHERE BUTTERFLIES GROW (1989)

Kirkus Reviews

SOURCE: A review of *Where Butterflies Grow*, in *Kirkus Reviews,* Vol. LVII, No. 15, August 15, 1989, p. 1250.

As in her "Just for a Day" books, Ryder's poetic text here suggests that readers take the animal's point of view as she describes its experiences—in this case, a black swallowtail as it develops from egg to butterfly. The focus is on the sensory; fuller, more scientific information appears on a final page. [Lynne] Cherry's precise, delicate, colorful illustrations are the book's outstanding feature, giving the habitat the charm of a close-up view of familiar territory—a lush bed of wildflowers (which fail to change as the season advances), and many other small creatures. An attractive nature book.

Ellen Mandel

SOURCE: A review of *Where Butterflies Grow*, in *Booklist,* Vol. 86, No. 5, November 1, 1989, p. 557.

On the underside of a leaf of resplendently blooming wildflowers nestles the tiny egg of a black swallowtail caterpillar. As it breaks out of its egg, Cherry's meticulously detailed likenesses of its lush garden home follow the creeper's development. Superimposed over this colorful, realistic background are slidelike magnifications depicting the caterpillar shedding its skin, defending itself against a hungry bird, forming a pupa, and emerging as an elegant, yellow-speckled, black butterfly. Gentle and respectful, as if not to disturb nature's order, Ryder's poetic text guides readers through the garden and the metamorphosis taking place there. Suggestions for plantings to

attract the black swallowtail butterfly conclude this rare naturalistic presentation.

Margaret Bush

SOURCE: A review of *Where Butterflies Grow*, in *Appraisal: Science Books for Young People,* Vol. 23, No. 3, Summer, 1990, pp. 47-8.

Ryder's list of science picture books has grown very quickly (polar bear, chipmunk, Canada goose, snail, lizard have all been covered), and all of the books invite the reader to imagine the experience of an animal for a day or through the life cycle. "Imagine / you are a creeper / thin and dark / living on / a long lacy leaf." This rather poetic account follows the hatching of a small egg into a caterpillar which grows, sheds its skin, and eventually becomes a pupa from which a swallowtail butterfly finally emerges. The text doesn't complete the cycle by having the butterfly mate and lay eggs, but a concluding page explains the process in a bit more detail. However, this final explanation is a broad sketch, which provides little scientific terminology and does not tell, for instance, the size of the butterfly, the specific length of life span, or the geographical range where this species is found. The book is pretty, with broad expanses of lush greenery and flowers. Against the larger scenes Lynne Cherry makes effective use of small framed insets, sometimes in a series, to highlight the stages of growth and change. Some of the animals, as well as the boy and girl at the book's beginning, are overly cute in greeting-card style, but she provides pleasing scenes with plenty to see. On some pages the print appears in white space, but usually the text is set onto the painting. Though the tone is a bit precious at times, some teachers will like the fanciful scheme for initiating discussion, and the book is an attractive introduction to the butterfly life cycle.

John R. Pancella

SOURCE: A review of *Where Butterflies Grow*, in *Appraisal: Science Books for Young People,* Vol. 23, No. 3, Summer, 1990, p. 48.

The poet in the author emerges in the text. Words and phrases are much more eloquent than those usually found in childrens' nature books. Add beautifully detailed color drawings, double-paged throughout, and this becomes a delightful read, an informative and entertaining book. The illustrator has obviously studied real life or actual photographs to capture the natural feeling of life forms and their surroundings. This is an in depth presentation of the life cycle of the black swallowtail butterfly. Egg to creeper (caterpillar) to resting (pupa) to adult are described and illustrated. The reader is the subject in the narrative, assuming the role of the insect and how it feels to go through the stages. A technique that works is to include smaller, magnified inserts into the larger drawings to show sequences of growth, molting, forming of the pupa, the emerging as an adult, and feeding. There is no terminol-

You are cool and sleepy
and you creep up,
your long padded toes
clinging to the cool wall.
You leap over the windowsill
into your shadowy room,
where you change again....

From Lizard in the Sun, *written by Joanne Ryder. Illustrated by Michael Rothman.*

ogy to deter interest, yet nothing is lost in the stories of the growth cycle, food selection, and defense mechanisms. An end page summarizes the text into a more technical discussion and describes how to "grow" butterflies in your garden.

A CHRISTMAS CAROL (1989)

Susan Hepler

SOURCE: A review of *A Christmas Carol,* in *School Library Journal,* Vol. 35, No. 14, October, 1989, p. 41.

In pared prose, Ryder retells Dickens classic for young readers, and while the bones of the tale are here, the flesh is missing. Pen-and-ink illustrations [by John O'Brien], washed in watercolor, give the appearance of coarse hand-tinted etchings. Better to acquire another copy of the original, illustrated by Lisbeth Zwerger (1988) or Trina Schart Hyman (1983) than to hurry this one into young readers' hands. Some stories are worth the wait.

UNDER YOUR FEET (1990)

Publishers Weekly

SOURCE: A review of *Under Your Feet,* in *Publishers Weekly,* Vol. 237, No. 6, February 9, 1990, p. 60.

Like their *Step into the Night* and *Mockingbird Morning,* Ryder and [illustrator Dennis] Nolan's quiet picture book portrays a child observing natural wonders. This time Ryder asks readers to be aware of creatures who live

under the earth's surface—moles, worms, salamanders, snakes, otters. The tone is reverent and hushed, the illustrations splendidly vibrant and accurate. A cross-section of earth reveals the boy above tying his hiking boot while below him "Thousands of worms / huddle in balls / deep in the ground, / breathing quietly / through their soft skins." Ryder attempts to unify the book structurally with frequent mention of the seasons and by repeating the refrain "Can you feel them?" but the devices often seem strained. Rather than suggesting that the reader imagine scenes below, the author becomes overly literal when she asks, "Can you feel [jumping mice] dreaming / of warm spring nights?" or "Can you feel [worms] resting / safe and warm / all winter long?" Nevertheless, both language and art offer an intriguing look at the world under children's feet.

Susan Scheps

SOURCE: A review of *Under Your Feet,* in *School Library Journal,* Vol. 36, No. 4, April, 1990, p. 110.

Like its companion books—*Step into the Night* (1988) and *Mockingbird Morning* (1989)—Ryder's latest close-up look at nature urges readers to search carefully for the small hidden creatures around them. They are everywhere in Nolan's now-familiar photorealistic, earth-toned watercolors—in holes and tunnels, under rocks, or protected by the hazy green water of a pond. Unlike the first two volumes, which cover brief periods—the twilight hours and early morning—this one spans the seasons, hinting at warm weather dens and hiding places, as well as subterranean winter burrows. The poetic text pairs the actions of a boy with those of the creatures hiding nearby. The sophisticated poetry and abrupt jumps from season to season will better suit school-age children than preschoolers. Many of Nolan's paintings exhibit a deft use of perspective that gives them a three-dimensional quality. One painting cleverly shows the shadows of Canada geese on the ground, while another features animals hidden murkily in the mud. There is, however, an unevenness to the illustrations. Lifelike creatures and natural objects are sometimes coupled with the flat lines of saplings, lifeless blades of grass, or one-dimensional animals. Despite this, text and illustrations do provide a quietly appealing nature lesson.

Carolyn Phelan

SOURCE: A review of *Under Your Feet,* in *Booklist,* Vol. 86, No. 18, May 15, 1990, pp. 1805-06.

Ryder speaks directly to readers, encouraging them to become aware of the wild animals sharing their world: "Tucked in the earth, or deep in the pond, hidden by leaves or ice, small creatures live nearby. You can listen, but you may not hear their voices. You can look, but you may not see them moving. Yet they are there. Try and see if you can feel them." Following a boy through the seasons, the book shows and tells of the animals beneath his feet: moles race along their tunnels below the ground, fish dart though the lake as he swims, worms huddle together in deep winter burrows, a cricket beneath a stone feels the ground shake as the boy passes. Using occasional cutaways to show scenes above and below the ground, Nolan's expressive watercolor paintings extend horizontally across each double-page spread, their essential realism softened but never sentimentalized. Cataloging-in-publication data classifies the book as poetry, but librarians may prefer to place it with picture books. Although the text has a poetic quality typical of Ryder's style, its unity urges reading the book as a whole rather than regarding each bit of text as a separate poem.

LIZARD IN THE SUN (1990)

Carolyn Phelan

SOURCE: A review of *Lizard in the Sun,* in *Booklist,* Vol. 86, No. 13, March 1, 1990, p. 1348.

As in her other Just for a Day series titles, such as **White Bear, Ice Bear,** Ryder again takes readers imaginations into the body of another species through an unexplained, magical transformation. Here a boy awakens and, touched by the sun, changes into a green *anole* (a chameleonlike lizard). He explores the yard—eating, drinking, running, hiding, and knowing the world in a new way. Ryder's cogent text focuses not on the transformation, but on the experience of being a lizard, perhaps the best way to give children respect for a species sometimes viewed with disgust. [Michael] Rothman's evocative paintings portray a suburban house and yard as a habitat, with birds and bugs living out their days as hunter and hunted, seen from the anole's perspective. Shades of colors change throughout the day as the sun shifts from dawn to daylight to

dusk. With its precise, poetic language and well-composed illustrations, this is another successful picture book in a consciousness-expanding series.

Karen Wehner

SOURCE: A review of *Lizard in the Sun,* in *School Library Journal,* Vol. 36, No. 6, June, 1990, p. 115.

The essence of the anole is caught through a subtle blending of clear, lyrical text and vibrant illustrations. After suggesting that readers undergo an imaginary transformation into a tiny green lizard, the text then describes what it would be like to live as one for an entire day, briefly highlighting the physical sensations readers would experience while engaged in typical activities. Although the text is relatively sparse, much information is imparted about the behavior of the anole. This is due, primarily, to Ryder's grasp of imagery. An "Author's Note" expands somewhat upon the data offered on major physical and behavioral characteristics in the main text and mentions some of the factors involved in the reptile's color-changing mechanisms. Rothman's brightly painted two-page spreads (blues, greens, and browns predominate) convey a real sense of the animal's natural habitat and perfectly match the mood of the text. This third addition to the series will make a fine family read-aloud.

WHEN THE WOODS HUM (1991)

Publishers Weekly

SOURCE: A review of *When the Woods Hum,* in *Publishers Weekly,* Vol. 238, No. 6, February 1, 1991, pp. 79-80.

Author of the Just a Day series, Ryder employs a fictional framework to reveal facts about a little-known insect, the periodical cicada, which appears only every 17 years. One spring, Jenny's father takes her outdoors to show her many "wingless creepers" crawling from tiny holes in the ground. The cicadas shed their outer skins, unfurl their wings and soon make the woods hum with their chirping sound. After the insects mate, new creepers hatch from eggs and crawl into the earth, "hidden for a very long time." Jenny is a grown woman when the cicadas next resurface, and she brings her son back to her father's house to watch the mating process. Offering an unusual amalgam of science and sentiment, this intriguing account will appeal to those readers not ordinarily interested in the former. At times vague and undefined, [Catherine] Stock's illustrations are decidedly uneven; her best work here focuses on the cicadas in their various life stages.

Deborah Abbott

SOURCE: A review of *When the Woods Hum,* in *Booklist,* Vol. 87, No. 13, March 1, 1991, p. 1402.

This volume on the life cycle of periodical cicadas (13- and 17-year life spans) is fiction, but it doubles nicely as a science book. A father takes his young daughter, Jenny, to the woods one spring and summer to observe what he had seen 17 years before—the coming of the cicadas. They watch as the new insects emerge from underground, shed their skins to become adults, and grow. Soon they begin a noisy hum that signals the beginning of the mating season. Afterward, the females lay eggs, die, and the next generation of nymphs returns underground to grow and wait. Jenny's life passes. She marries, then has a child of her own. One spring she, her father, and her son, Raymond, together explore the same woods and again watch the wonder of the cicadas. Ryder writes descriptively, accurately, and warmly as she spins this family yarn, while providing solid science information. Stock's delicate watercolors, which quietly capture the scenes in the woods, reflect the positive parent-child relationships and provide interesting insect close-ups, both above and below ground. The author's note in the front and the detailed cicada sketches at the end are a plus.

Kathleen Odean

SOURCE: A review of *When the Woods Hum,* in *School Library Journal,* Vol. 37, No. 8, August, 1991, p. 154.

An intergenerational family story serves as a vehicle to describe the periodical cicada, an insect that lives underground for 17 years and then emerges to mate. When the cicadas appear, they fill the woods with humming. Although the information is fascinating, the accompanying tale is forced. In order to show the passage of time, the little girl grows up, gets married, and has a child of her own—all within two pages. The confusing illustration that accompanies this transition shows scenes in three time periods, seemingly all occurring in the same woods. Except when providing facts about the cicada, the watercolor pictures and the text are sentimental. Papa reminisces about the no-hitter he pitched the year he first saw cicadas. The grown-up Jenny says softly to a cicada on her sleeve, "Oh, I wondered about you . . . and if I'd ever see you again." All in all, the fascinating subject gets bogged down in the story.

Sharon L. Rizzo

SOURCE: A review of *When the Woods Hum,* in *Appraisal: Science Books for Young People,* Vol. 24, No. 4, Autumn, 1991, p. 53.

Joanne Ryder has woven the life cycle of the periodical cicada into a wonderfully touching and informative children's story.

The book follows one life cycle of a seventeen-year cicada group. The appearance of the cicadas is shared by a father and his young daughter. The father explains the various developmental stages of the cicada as they occur.

By the end of the book, the reader has discovered that not only has he or she read a great story, but has also learned an enormous amount about the life of periodical cicadas.

An interesting feature of this narrative is the parallel drawn between each generation of cicadas and each generation of the family. The father first heard and saw the cicadas when he was a young boy. With the next appearance of cicadas, he has a young daughter with whom to share the experience. At the end of another seventeen years, the daughter brings her son to see the emergence of the cicadas and the creation of a new cicada generation. This parallel helps young readers grasp how much time is actually represented by seventeen years as each cicada generation birth roughly corresponds to each new generation in their own families.

Whether used as a resource or for pleasure reading, this book is a wonderful addition to any young reader's library.

THE BEAR ON THE MOON (1991)

Kirkus Reviews

SOURCE: A review of *The Bear on the Moon,* in *Kirkus Reviews,* Vol. LIX, No. 13, July 1, 1991, p. 860.

The author of several books about children who experience being animals in the wild takes an even more imaginative approach to the bears' world with a polar bears' creation myth: In the beginning, the bears live in the sea. Just one bear is curious enough to try to plumb its depths and to wonder about the moon. One night she climbs the Northern Lights; once on the moon, she throws down rock and ice until just a sliver of moon is left—while the bears now have snowy islands where they can rest. As the ice in the sea melts, the moon grows again; but, each time, the bear climbs back to the moon to throw down more.

Ryder develops her pleasing idea with intelligence, in graceful cadences well suited for reading aloud. In a fine picture book debut, [Carol] Lacey (an experienced wildlife illustrator) provides glorious watercolors depicting sea and sky in impressionistic splendor. In action or repose, her bears are beautifully observed—including the rich array of tones in their fur, a more accurate representation than the white monochrome we imagine. Grand story, beguiling bears, lovely book.

Publishers Weekly

SOURCE: A review of *The Bear on the Moon,* in *Publishers Weekly,* Vol. 238, No. 31, July 19, 1991, p. 56.

According to legend, the great white bears at the North Pole once spent all their time swimming in icy waters. Not until one adventurous bear swims to "the place the sea touched the sky" does everything change. All the way to the moon, this bear climbs a stairway of light; there, she starts breaking off pieces of rock and ice and throwing down the chunks, creating land masses in the sea below. This diminishes the size of the moon until it is a sliver and finally disappears altogether. The bear is sad to see the moon gone, but pleased at the many changes in the environment. Although Ryder's story rambles a bit—and might be confusing for readers at the young end of the age range—her fantasy is generally engaging. Lacey's debut picture book art features striking, realistic bears and haunting glimpses of their barren world.

Louise L. Sherman

SOURCE: A review of *The Bear on the Moon,* in *School Library Journal,* Vol. 37, No. 9, September, 1991, p. 240.

An original pourquoi story relating the lunar phases to the polar icecap. In a time when there was only sea at the top of the world, one curious polar bear swims to the edge of the ocean and climbs the northern lights to the moon. She delights in the ice-covered rocky surface and throws some ice down to the bears on Earth. When her efforts take most of the moon away, she returns home. She is disappointed when the icecap she has created shrinks as the moon increases in size. Since that time, she has returned to the moon each month so the bears will have ice to live on. Lacey's beautifully rendered watercolors make this somewhat farfetched story seem believable. The bear climbing the colored lights, looking down from the moon, and cuffing the icy rocks down to Earth is so realistic that young readers will wonder if it is true. Her bears are attractive and sympathetic while still seeming remote and frightening. The almost mystical story will enchant imaginative readers and listeners, but it is long and may bore more down-to-earth children. It will be a good choice for a moonlight story time with other stories pondering the nature of the moon such as Adelaide Holl's *Moon Mouse* (1969) and Tomi Ungerer's *Moon Man* (1967).

📖 *HELLO, TREE!* (1991)

Carolyn Phelan

SOURCE: A review of *Hello, Tree!,* in *Booklist,* Vol. 87, No. 22, August, 1991, p. 2159.

"One day / you will find / a tree / standing tall / in the sun / hiding secrets / in its branches / and feel / that this tree / is special / to you," begins Ryder, who has previously brought listeners to a heightened awareness of nature through books such as *Lizard in the Sun* and *White Bear, Ice Bear.* Not since Udry's *A Tree Is Nice* has a mood picture book so effectively portrayed a child's vision of the tree as playground, shelter, friend, and source of mystery. The poetic text finds the right path between fact and imagination, a path reflected in the handsome, sunlit paintings [by Michael Hays], which balance the tree's monumentality with the children's lively humanity. A quiet, sustaining choice for reading aloud.

Anna DeWind

SOURCE: A review of *Hello, Tree!,* in *School Library Journal,* Vol. 37, No. 8, August, 1991, p. 162.

A tree can be a special friend, offering cool shade, branches to climb, and a solid point of reference in a changing world. Ryder's soothing, meditative text combines with Hays's sun-dappled paintings to create a quiet yet effective celebration of nature. Children of all races playing in and around the tree convey a sense of harmony and balance. While not a story per se, this book is, instead, a testament to pleasures simple, yet profound.

📖 *WINTER WHALE* (1991)

Kirkus Reviews

SOURCE: A review of *Winter Whale,* in *Kirkus Reviews,* Vol. LIX, No. 16, August 15, 1991, pp. 1098-99.

The best yet of Ryder's "Just for a Day" books: "you" are a boy whose imagination takes you from a rainswept beach to being a humpback whale, exulting in the experience of "gliding up and down between . . . sea and sky." Ryder's evocative text dwells on the joy of movement and also considers the pod, a new calf, and its mother, and the whales' mysterious warm-water song. [Michael] Rothman's whitecapped underwater vistas are gorgeous, from rich purple depths to light-drenched apple-green surface. An author's note extends the informational value. A fine celebration of this appealing creature.

Frances E. Millhouser

SOURCE: A review of *Winter Whale,* in *School Library Journal,* Vol. 37, No. 10, October, 1991, p. 112.

In this imaginative series entry, a chunky boy slips into the skin of a humpback whale, just for one rainy day. Through poetic language artfully arranged on double-page, full-color, acrylic illustrations, the world of the whale is explored, as is the feeling of what it might be like to be a large, grand humpback wintering in a warm tropical sea. The story leads from a beach with whale-shaped clouds to vistas of sea, shore, and sky. Living between two worlds—"of sea and sky, of water and air"—the whale thrusts his head up above the waves into a sky while white birds soar overhead with their orange tails streaming. Back under water, a mother humpback and calf swim slowly by, as do golden colored trigger fish, dolphins, and turtles. The distinctive patterns of the humpback sparkle under water as he hangs upside down to sing his special warm-water song while sharks glide by. The illustrations are tactile and touchable—the rain feels wet on the whale's "bumpy chin" as it changes him back into the boy running home to "bright lights and supper."

📖 *DANCERS IN THE GARDEN* (1992)

Kirkus Reviews

SOURCE: A review of *Dancers in the Garden,* in *Kirkus Reviews,* Vol. LX, No. 16, August 15, 1992, p. 1066.

Drawing on her own observations of Allen's hummingbird (*Selasphorus sasin*) in San Francisco and on scholarly sources, Ryder follows a male through a typical day in which he encounters a female and mates (offstage). Formatted as verse, the narrative is graciously cadenced and informative, celebrating the little bird's appearance and behavior. In delicately detailed, gold-bordered art, scientific-illustrator [Judith] Lopez sets this particular hummingbird in Golden Gate Park's lovely Japanese Tea Garden, presenting in precise detail its morning mists, carefully tended specimen plants, and occasional artifacts; best is the jewel-like bird, in myriad poses in flight and at rest. A final note extends the information and suggests how to attract these nectar-loving birds. LC classes this as fiction.

Debra C. Rollins

SOURCE: A review of *Dancers in the Garden*, in *Appraisal: Science Books for Young People*, Vol. 26, Nos. 2/3, Spring/Summer, 1993, pp. 54-5.

Dancers in the Garden, about hummingbirds, lives up to the quality one expects from a Sierra Club imprint. The exquisite, gold-bordered illustrations, drawn from live subjects, are reminiscent of Oriental paintings, but are not lacking in scientific accuracy. The text is also scientifically accurate. A two-page summary on hummingbirds and their habitat supplements the text without intruding on the narrative—a near-poetic tone—of the text. The binding, papers and printing are of high quality. Few scientific books currently in print match this title for overall quality. This is a very worthwhile purchase for any level school's library.

Leonard T. Garigliano

SOURCE: A review of *Dancers in the Garden*, in *Appraisal: Science Books for Young People*, Vol. 26, Nos. 2/3, Spring/Summer, 1993, p. 55.

The text of this book is written in almost poetic form with the dancing movements of hummingbirds as its main theme. The information presented by this literary approach does not always come across clearly. It wasn't obvious that the hummingbird dancing in the brightness and plucking a spider's web was actually eating an insect trapped there. That connection wasn't made until reading the two pages of author's notes at the end of the book. In these pages readers will find some more factual information about hummingbirds. This material may be of more interest to some readers than the body of the book. Combining the two methods of presentation, readers will be entertained and informed. The drawings throughout the text are excellent. A few photographs of hummingbirds, especially of different species, would enhance the book.

Reading this book and showing the illustrations to children 4-6 years of age identified as the target audience would certainly be worthwhile. Older children, and even adults, would become more informed, aware, and appreciative of these delightful birds after reading this book. . . .

▯ *SEA ELF* (1993)

Edith Winter Sperber

SOURCE: A review of *Sea Elf*, in *The Horn Book Guide*, Vol. V, No. 1, July-December, 1993, p. 52.

With well-crafted descriptions of how an otter dives, hunts, eats, rests, and plays, Ryder evokes the feeling of the life of the otter. Helping students imagine what living life as another animal would be like is an interesting and worthwhile concept. [Michael Rothman's] beautiful painted illustrations allow the reader a clear view of what the otter must see beneath and above the surface of the water.

▯ *ONE SMALL FISH* (1993)

Carolyn Phelan

SOURCE: A review of *One Small Fish*, in *Booklist*, Vol. 90, No. 3, October 1, 1993, p. 354.

The girl in the science class here may not be paying attention to the teacher, but at least her daydreams stick to the subject. As she looks around the room, she sees it filled with seawater, with fishes, octopuses, eels, seals, sea horses, jellyfish, and dolphins. "I tuck my legs under my chair and let the sharks slide by. I can almost touch them." Precise lines [by illustrator Carol Schwartz] define the sea creatures with all the realism of the lab tables and chalkboard, while shades of bright colors shape the spaces. Not quite as vivid as the author's *Just for a Day* series, this nonetheless succeeds at displaying its dreamlike quality. Recommended for larger collections.

Childhood Education

SOURCE: A review of *One Small Fish*, in *Childhood Education*, Vol. 70, No. 4, Summer, 1994, p. 248.

Joanne Ryder's fanciful, imaginative story of a slow Friday afternoon in science class is enhanced by the beautiful, colorful illustration of sea creatures and culturally diverse children. The text and art blend beautifully. Starfish, eels, whales and fish swim about freely in a child's wandering mind until the inevitable ring of the dismissal bell. A wonderful book for science class and just plain enjoyment.

▯ *FIRST LADYBUGS; FIRST GRADE VALENTINES; HELLO, FIRST GRADE* (1993)

Publishers Weekly

SOURCE: A review of *Hello, First Grade; First Grade*

Valentines; First Grade Ladybugs, in *Publishers Weekly,* Vol. 240, No. 41, October 11, 1993, p. 88.

In a format strikingly similar to that of Miriam Cohen's first-grade-class stories, Ryder's First Grade Is the Best series features a cluster of sunny children and their amiable teacher, Miss Lee. In the opener, **Hello,** the pupils fall in love with their class pet, a white bunny named Martha, and plan to star it in a schoolwide first-grade spectacular—but just when they are about to perform, Martha is missing (a happy ending, however, is assured). **Ladybugs** has the first graders planting a garden, while **Valentines** alters the standard holiday-tale formula in that the class sends cards for Miss Lee's convalescing neighbor. Animated dialogue and clearly defined story lines will hold readers' attentions. Like the text, the watercolors [by Betsy Lewin] are cheery and energetic, exuding affability. Instructions for a project related to the story are included at the end of each book.

THE GOODBYE WALK (1993)

Annie Ayres

SOURCE: A review of *The Goodbye Walk,* in *Booklist,* Vol. 90, No. 5, November 1, 1993, p. 532.

"It takes time to get to know a special place, time to explore new paths and see new things. And then one day it's time to say good-bye." And it's time to take a last good-bye walk and revisit each of the summer's special landmarks and tuck within your heart the feelings and sights that will become "memories to keep forever and ever." As is typical of the style of this author of numerous children's books, such as **Where Butterflies Grow** (1989), the prose draws forth a poetic vision of a child's involvement and delight in the natural world. Warmly inviting us to share the child's love of a summer place and special good-bye, Ryder's poignant narration is well matched by [Deborah] Haeffle's sun-shadowed summer landscape illustrations of the girl revisiting her special places: a hill where a "thousand berries tinged the bushes black, and you stopped to eat them sun-warmed and sweet," and the "pebbly beach where a cool wind catches you at last" and you "feel summer blowing away." A special, seasonal book reminding the reader or listener that farewells do not need to be sad when one carries away such rich memories.

A HOUSE BY THE SEA (1994)

Patricia Pearl Dole

SOURCE: A review of *A House by the Sea,* in *School Library Journal,* Vol. 40, No. 6, June, 1994, p. 112.

A fanciful, lilting, rhyming story tells of a boy's wish to live in a seaside cottage in close association with rollicking seals; a smiling, crescent moon; a gentle whale; a nurturing octopus; and a dancing crab. The animals play with the boy and his friend (a little girl) and even do their housekeeping chores while the children savor the beach and ocean. Watercolors [by Melissa Sweet] in sunny and cool pastels with minimal, cartoonlike figures are arranged informally in ragged ovals and squares as though bursting through their backgrounds. They show the youngsters, their dog, and the sea creatures cavorting joyfully over golden sands, in jade-green waters, and through the cozy cottage. The wit and charm of the pictures reflect the text to perfection.

MY FATHER'S HANDS (1994)

Publishers Weekly

SOURCE: A review of *My Father's Hands,* in *Publishers Weekly,* Vol. 241, No. 27, July 4, 1994, p. 62.

In this loving tribute, a girl watches her father as he tends a garden—as well as its wiggling, sliding, bumbling and graceful creatures. He opens his cupped, earth-encrusted hands to reveal a "pink circle of worm," a beetle "shining in gold armor" and a praying mantis "so light, so bold, so strange." The father wordlessly conveys his enthusiasm to his daughter, who narrates: "I bend closer, knowing that nothing within my father's hands will harm me." The crisp clarity of Ryder's prose balances her warm effusion (as the mantis is returned to his bush, father and daughter "watch him / till he melts / green in the greenness"). [Mark] Graham's oil paintings, scumbled beneath a dewy veil of early summer light, perfectly match the intimacy of Ryder's text.

Kirkus Reviews

SOURCE: A review of *My Father's Hands,* in *Kirkus Reviews,* Vol. LXII, No. 14, July 15, 1994, p. 994.

A poet who has frequently celebrated nature in her picture books evokes a child's relationship with her father and the gentle example he sets her by his own relationship with the natural world. The lyrical narrative focuses on the father's hands as he works in the garden: As they lift, the hands are strong; as they dig, they are covered with earth, without apology; always, they are capable. When they reach for something interesting—a "pink circle of worm," a snail, a mantis—"I bend closer, / knowing that / nothing within / my father's hands / will harm me." Wide-eyed, a little hesitant in Graham's lush, romantic paintings, the little girl takes the mantis in her hands to gaze in wonder at a being "so bold, so strange" and wonders what it thinks of her; when it scampers across her shoulder before they let it go free, she grins with delight. Just so it should be, with trust passed from generation to generation. Lovely.

Additional coverage of Ryder's life and career is contained in the following sources published by Gale Research: *Contemporary Authors,* Vol. 133; *Major Authors and Illustrators for Children and Young Adults*; and *Something about the Author,* Vols. 34, 65.

R. L. Stine

1943-

(Full name Robert Lawrence Stine; also writes as Jovial Bob Stine, Eric Affabee, and Zachary Blue) American author of fiction and nonfiction.

Major works include *How to Be Funny: An Extremely Silly Guidebook* (as Jovial Bob Stine, 1978), *Blind Date* (1986), *Twisted* (1987), *The New Girl* (1989), *Halloween Night* (1993).

INTRODUCTION

A popular and prolific author of thriller novels for young adults and humorous nonfiction for children, Stine once jokingly referred to himself as the "Jekyll and Hyde of children's publishing." To preadolescent readers, he is "Jovial Bob," the author of numerous "how to" and joke books. Teen audiences, however, recognize Stine for his tales of supernatural horror, several of which are published in the "Fear Street" and "Goosebump" series which he directs to high schoolers and middle graders respectively. These latter works—among the biggest best-sellers in young adult fiction—have made the author a rather reluctant celebrity. Part of the reason for the success of Stine's novels is considered to be his characters: appealing, resourceful teens around whom the stories center. His youthful protagonists battle with phantoms, murderers, and supernatural forces—often with little or no help from the adults around them. Critical response to Stine's blend of horror and mystery has been mixed: while many commentators have noted the formulaic and undemanding in his books, most reviewers agree that the author has a unique ability to capture the fears, foibles and motivations of teenagers, and have commended him for his creation of realistic and engaging dialogue. Reviewing *The Sleepwalker* (1991), one of Stine's "Fear Street" novels, Alice Cronin has written that Stine "writes a good story," adding, "Teens will love the action; librarians will love the lure for slower and nonreaders." In her review of *Silent Night* (1991), Sylvia E. Mitchell admits, "If all series books were this good, I'd begin to drop my prejudices against them."

Biographical Information

Born in Columbus, Ohio, Stine began his career as a junior high school teacher of social studies. An interest in publishing eventually led the author to New York City and a job with Scholastic, Inc. Stine spent sixteen years at Scholastic, working on four magazines, including two—*Bananas* and *Maniac*—that he created. While working on *Bananas,* Stine accepted an offer from a children's book editor to write a humorous work for younger readers. This effort, entitled *How to Be Funny: An Extremely Silly*

Guidebook, is the first of many juvenile titles he has written under the pseudonym "Jovial Bob Stine." After losing his position with Scholastic during a corporate reorganization, Stine was encouraged by one of his colleagues to write a horror novel aimed at the fast-growing teen market; the result was the best-selling *Blind Date.* Since the publication of that book, Stine has become—along with writers like Christopher Pike and Richie Tankerlsey Cusick—one of the most successful authors of young adult fiction with this audience.

Major Works

Stine's work as "Jovial Bob" ranges from the nonsensical to the funny-but-helpful. *How to Be Funny: An Extremely Silly Guidebook* functions as a joke book in how-to disguise, describing among other things the "10-Step Bumbling Classroom Entrance" and "How to be Funny with Soup." *The Pigs' Book of World Records* (1980) is a pig-centered spoof on the *Guinness Book of World Records.* Of a more informative nature is Stine's *Everything You Need to Survive* collection (1983). Reviewing these works, many commentators have commended Stine's ability to address serious topics of interest to children and their parents—such as sibling relations, dating, and homework—without losing his sense of humor and engaging style. Lee Bock maintains that the *Everything You Need to Survive* books comprise a "well-balanced and well-paced collection of the ridiculous and the useful."

Stine's thrillers, praised for their fast-paced action and inventive plots, characteristically feature normal teens who suddenly find their lives in danger, occasionally from supernatural forces; nearly every book features a murder, sometimes of the protagonist. In *Twisted,* for example, a sorority pledge loses her mind when she finds herself at the center of a bizarre set of deaths, while the hero of *Blind Date* discovers that memory loss can be a very deadly thing. Stine's "Fear Street" series also offers mystery and mayhem, these tales describing a variety of bizarre happenings in the lives of several students at fictitious Shadyside High. "Fear Street" titles such as *The New Girl,* in which a boy falls in love with a young woman who may be a ghost, or *The First Evil* (1992), which follows a deadly supernatural force as it stalks a cheerleading squad, are especially popular with young adults due to their "cliff-hanger" chapter endings. This formula has not fared as well with critics, however, many of whom feel that Stine sacrifices characterization in order to maintain a hair-raising pace. Despite this concern, commentators credit the author with truly understanding his audience, noting that the short chapters and suspenseful endings encourage adolescents with short attention spans to continue reading. "Stine has exciting ideas," writes Samantha Hunt. "It takes a certain talent to convey them as he does."

Awards

Stine has received several child-selected awards for his fiction.

GENERAL COMMENTARY

Paul Gray

SOURCE: "Carnage: An Open Book," in *Time,* New York, Vol. 142, No. 5, August 2, 1993, p. 54.

When the era of network TV violence advisories dawns in September, some such scene will play itself out in millions of U.S. households. Warned that an upcoming program contains material unsuitable for young people, parents order their children away from the set and then brace themselves for whines and grumbling. Oddly, the exiles disappear without complaint and go off to their rooms . . . to read books. Sis, 13, picks up her copy of R. L. Stine's *The Babysitter III:* "His expression was blank, as blank as death. And with a quick, simple motion, he grabbed the baby's head with one hand, twisted it, and pulled it

off." Across the hall, Junior, 11, turns the pages of Christopher Pike's *Monster:* "Mary pointed her shotgun at Kathy's face and pulled the trigger. The blast caught Kathy in the forehead and took off the top of her skull, plastering a good portion of her brains over the railings of the nearby staircase."

Downstairs, Mom and Dad are snoring in front of a flickering car chase.

Books like *The Babysitter III* or *Monster*—and there are suddenly a remarkable number of books very much like them—do not reach such underage readers by subterfuge or stealth. Adolescents now constitute a booming niche market for the peddling of published gore and violence. "Teens' interests go in cycles," says Patricia MacDonald, editorial director of Archway Paperbacks, an imprint of Pocket Books and a major player in the teen-horror field. "In the '70s it was problem novels, the disease of the week. Then it was romance novels, soap operas like *Sweet Valley High* and *Sweet Dreams.* In the '90s it's the thrillers." Hardly a blip on publishers' sales charts a few years ago, such thrillers claimed three of the top four spots on the *Publishers Weekly* poll of the best-selling children's paperbacks in 1992.

Like all genre fiction—gothics, romances, police procedurals—teen tinglers follow a fairly consistent set of formulas. The heroes or heroines are invariably adolescents whose lives fall mysteriously into jeopardy; adults are either the source of the menace or remote, almost inanimate objects. The dialogue comes laced with teenspeak—*gnarly, totally awesome*—and the plot steamrolls over lesser details like setting and characterization. Chapters are short and end in suspense, luring readers with short attention spans to forge onward. The level of violence ranges from the implied to the horrific, and the bloodier bits are sometimes mitigated by context: it was all a dream, the demonic villain got what was coming to him, etc. Explicit sex is largely forbidden.

Still, these hair-raising books are being tailored for and energetically hawked to children. Is that frightening? The two most successful writers of teen thrillers, understandably, think not. Says Christopher Pike, 37, who stumbled into his calling in 1985 and now has 8 million copies of his books in print: "They want to be scared or they would not pick up the book and read it. The kids have fair warning and know it's all good fun."

R. L. Stine, 49, who turns out a thriller a month and has 7.5 million copies of his 27-part *Fear Street* series in print, agrees that such books mean no harm. "Part of the appeal is that they're safe scares. You're home in your room and reading. The books are not half as scary as the real world." At the same time, Stine also implies that the real world needs embellishment; his challenge, he says, is "to find new cheap thrills" for his young readers. "I mean disgusting, gross things to put in the book that they'll like: the cat is boiled in the spaghetti, a girl pours honey over a boy and sets ants on him. They like the gross stuff." Surely his young readers have some taboos? Furry animals? "The pets are dead meat," Stine replies. "If the kid has a pet, he's going to find it dead on the floor."

Such calculated shock tactics seem qualitatively different from the methods of *Alice's Adventures in Wonderland, Treasure Island* or even the horror stories of Edgar Allan Poe. Classical children's literature is full of overt and implicit terrors because some gifted authors could remember and portray a child's view, those feelings of awe, uncertainty and fear inspired by the world outside. Fright requires no invention; conquering it through language does.

Some educators believe teenagers' reading these lurid thrillers, as opposed to playing Nintendo or watching *Beavis and Butt-head* on MTV, is a good thing. Viviane Lampach, a librarian at a Bronx high school in New York City, notes that her young patrons check out new paperback novels in this genre and never return them: "You hope to wean them from horror to something deeper and more meaningful." Roderick McGillis, a professor of English at the University of Calgary and author of a book on children's literature, takes a darker view: "What disturbs me is that we're developing in our culture, in our cities, a kind of siege mentality. A lot of these books reinforce this, make it sort of normal to think that the world is a place in which violence can erupt at any moment."

Maybe the youngsters will move upward in their tastes, through Stephen King and V. C. Andrews to Hemingway, Joyce and Shakespeare. Or maybe they will boil the cat in the spaghetti.

TITLE COMMENTARY

📖 *HOW TO BE FUNNY: AN EXTREMELY SILLY GUIDEBOOK* (1978)

Publishers Weekly

SOURCE: A review of *How to Be Funny: An Extremely Silly Guidebook,* in *Publishers Weekly,* Vol. 214, No. 2, July 10, 1978, p. 136.

Called "the funniest kids' book since *101 Ways to Boil Spinach Neatly,*" the Stine-Nicklaus collaboration is. Cartoon illustrations [by Carol Nicklaus] reflect this how-to's mad suggestions on getting laughs at home, in school, anywhere. But the expert provides warnings: "Rule Number One for Getting Big Laughs With Soup: Keep it simple." Dexter doesn't. Sneaking a rabbit into his bowl, he cries, "Look, ma! There's a hare in my soup!" The poor bunny wreaks havoc; Dexter spends the evening practicing "How To Be Funny All By Yourself In Your Room." Harrison Babble does better with the ping-pong ball he daubs a circle on and plops into his soup, to make "cream of eyeball." Readers adopting Stine's tips might not thank

him when their gags court mayhem but they'll love laughing with him.

Kirkus Reviews

SOURCE: A review of *How to Be Funny: An Extremely Silly Guidebook,* in *Kirkus Reviews,* Vol. XLVI, No. 14, July 15, 1978, p. 753.

A joke book disguised as a how-to book, with a stand-up comic's quick delivery and casual digressions. Stine has readers warm up by matching, completing, and unscrambling one-liners and riddles; then he proceeds with instructions for knocking 'em dead at school, at the dinner table ("If your family doesn't own a table-cloth demand that they buy one. You will never get laughs with placemats no matter how hard you try"), at parties, and "when you're in big trouble." Like any proper text this has review questions at the ends of chapters ("What are the two funniest things you can do with spinach in a crowded lunchroom?"), exemplary and cautionary case histories, lots of rules ("Placing strange objects in your soup almost always gets laughs. Attempting to wear your soup is usually less successful"; "If you must tell elephant or grape jokes, never tell less than thirty at a time"), ploys to be avoided at all costs (buttering your napkin, laughing when you drink so the milk pours out your nose), and an annotated bibliography (authors have names like O. B. Serious). Guess what? It's funny.

Hara L. Seltzer

SOURCE: A review of *How to Be Funny: An Extremely Silly Guidebook,* in *School Library Journal,* Vol. 26, No. 3, November, 1979, p. 82.

Jovial Bob can tell you "How To Be Funny with Soup" (don't suck it through your socks), "The 10-Step Bumbling Classroom Entrance," pencil sharpening laughs to drive the teacher to frenzy, how to tell a joke, how to be funny when you're in big trouble. His bibliography includes *How To Be Funny with Melon Balls* and Bonnie Lassie's *Pie Throwing in Shakespeare's England* (Pants Press, 1976). While Jovial Bob isn't exactly on par with Woody Allen (or a Woody for juveniles), there may be bon mot here to gladden nine to 12 year olds.

📖 *THE PIGS' BOOK OF WORLD RECORDS* (1980)

Patt Parsells Kent

SOURCE: A review of *The Pig's Book of World Records,* in *Children's Book Review Service,* Vol. 8, No. 9, April, 1980, p. 90.

Every joke you've ever wanted in the *Guinness Book of World Records,* but were afraid to ask for is here, pig style. This hilarious mock on the familiar record book has such side-splitting entries as "World's Skinniest Pig." Along with world records there is a pig joke book, a pig *Joy of Cooking* book, and a pig's *Book of Lists.* All are very funny if you've read the originals and even funnier if you haven't. A bizarre and pleasant change in children's fun reading.

Publishers Weekly

SOURCE: A review of *Pig's Book of World Records,* in *Publishers Weekly,* Vol. 217, No. 16, April 25, 1980, p. 80.

Although the Stine-Lippman collaboration is dedicated in part to Miss Piggy, the famous Muppet may bridle at some remarks but will love this gloriously ridiculous spoof, as will everyone else. [Peter] Lippman's cartoons, in piggy-pink and black, rank with the gifted artist's best. As for Stine, his absurdities grow faster and funnier from the contents page on. Besides the pigs' book of world records, we find a collection of the world's worst pig jokes, *The Joy of Swill! A Cookbook* and *The Pigs' Book of Lists.* The world's shortest pig, Bo Bee, has to jump *up* to wallow in mud. The best-educated pig, Bertrand Snuffle, eats only college diplomas. In the lists section, pig parents enter their most common complaints: "Why can't you stay dirty?" "Why do you keep your room so neat?"

Peter Andrews

SOURCE: "Juvenile Wit," in *The New York Times Book Review,* April 27, 1980, p. 62.

If Mr. Aylward tickles the reader's funnybone with a feather duster [in *You're Dumber in the Summer*], Jovial Bob Stine trusses him in a straitjacket and works him over with a pig's bladder. Indeed, his raucous effort, ***The Pig's Book of World Records*** is constituted entirely of 94 pages of pig jokes; funny pig jokes and loathsome pig jokes, cartoons about pigs and poems about pigs. There is a delicious satire on summer-camp swimming rules about how pigs should only wallow in the mud on the buddy system, and a selection of recipes for pig foods ranging from an entree made entirely of corn cobs to a dessert the principal ingredient of which is a very old box of Jell-O. If Leon Edel had turned his encyclopedic mind to the arcane study of porcine waggery, he could not have come up with a more far-ranging compendium. I loved it.

Betsy Hearne

SOURCE: A review of *The Pigs' Book of World Records,* in *Booklist,* Vol. 76, No. 17, May 1, 1980, p. 1299.

This has the glorious double asset of appealing to children's love of record books in the Guinness vein as well as to their "humor of disgust" that peaks between third and fifth grades but seems plentifully active before and after. The word "garbage," for instance, is bound to elicit disgusted gales of laughter, and here are *records* about

garbage eating (funny records), recipes for garbage (ranging from even funnier to moderately disgusting), rules for wallowing (funniest), jokes, lists, and interruptions (all ludicrous). A Timeline of Pig History is appended. This is highly recommended on the basis of being totally unnecessary, which will ensure the interest of reluctant readers and the enthusiasm of natural browsers. With spontaneous pen-and-ink drawings liberally doused in pig-pink, it will pass through any classroom faster than a hog eating slops.

📖 THE SICK OF BEING SICK BOOK (with Jane Stine, 1980)

Kirkus Reviews

SOURCE: A review of *The Sick of Being Sick Book,* in *Kirkus Reviews,* Vol. XLVIII, No. 13, July 1, 1980, p. 840.

"We know that when you're sick, you're just not interested in building a replica of your uncle out of toothpicks"—and, knowing this, the Stines offer their "20 Things You Can Do With Tissues" for reading and rejecting only. The time-killers they do include (code messages; tongue twisters) are mostly designed to drive your friends and visitors nuts. To keep from going nuts yourself, there are a guide to surviving daytime TV, tips on interpreting visitors remarks, and advice on looking properly sick so you'll get the sympathy that's coming to you. The recipes, variations on tea and toast, are relatively straight; the P.Q. (Patients' Quotient) test less so. All in all, it's more fun than a toothpick kit.

Anne McKeithen-Boes

SOURCE: A review of *The Sick of Being Sick Book,* in *School Library Journal,* Vol. 26, No. 10, August, 1980, p. 71.

Stine's advice for getting sympathy while ill is: put on pajamas, look sick and say, "Could you please lift up that tissue for me?" or "Could we turn off the TV? I think I'd better rest my eyes." Headings include "A Guide to Visitors," "Sick Kids' Hall of Fame," and "The 10 Most Popular Medicines of the Middle Ages" ("1. Tree bark 2. Dry tree bark 3. Very dry tree park. . . ."). That such silliness could continue at book length is too much for even hard-core MAD readers. A stack of comics would be funnier and cheaper.

📖 DYNAMITE'S FUNNY BOOK OF THE SAD FACTS OF LIFE (1980)

Hara L. Seltzer

SOURCE: A review of *Dynamite's Funny Book of Sad Facts of Life,* in *School Library Journal,* Vol. 28, No. 1, September, 1981, p. 126.

Jovial Bob's latest, a Dynamite paperback, contains a lot of truth but not much humor. The disappointments with birthday parties and presents, the pitfalls of vacations, sad confrontations with parents, siblings, haircuts, gym classes, tests and the weather are grist for Bob's mill this time around. Drawings [by Jared Lee] are amusing color cartoons, but we get only one or two laughs from the text. This is another sad fact of life.

THE COOL KIDS' GUIDE TO SUMMER CAMP (with Jane Stine, 1981)

Kirkus Reviews

SOURCE: A review of *The Cool Kids' Guide to Summer Camp,* in *Kirkus Reviews,* Vol. XLIX, No. 7, April 1, 1981, p. 436.

Prepare to deal with The Old-Timer, the Prince, the Homesick Kid, the Expert, the Prankster, and, among counselors, the Neatness fanatic (she'll take away points if your mosquito bites aren't lined up) and the Drill Sergeant. The wildlife is not very wild, old horses and gnats being the most common forms, and the only bears near camps are invisible. The real camp sports are food-gobbling, hiding, bragging, towel-snapping, and other such competitive activities. Such minimally funny advice is packaged here along with an update on "what you missed today on daytime TV," "a complete letter-writing guide" listing "every phrase you'll ever need," and a more-or-less serious list of extra stuff to take (an almanac, felt markers, extra socks all the same color, something wild and crazy) as well as what *not* to take-jigsaw puzzles, candy bars (they'll melt), etc. The jokes perhaps qualify as camp humor, a concept comparable to that of military music. A typical joke is "Did you ever wonder what happens to the left-over papier-mache from Arts and Crafts? Try the mess hall hot cereal in the morning and you'll wonder no more!" To a non-camper, it's forced and flat.

Patricia Manning

SOURCE: A review of *The Cool Kids' Guide to Summer Camp,* in *School Library Journal,* Vol. 28, No. 3, November, 1981, p. 98.

Beware of books with "cool" titles. If you're cool, you're cool. If you're not, a how-to book won't chill you one degree. This is a typical "cool" book, ostensibly for kids about going to camp, but really more for older people who have already been there and like to reminisce. Forced humor and fatigued jokes about food and crafts, interspersed with a few genuine nuggets of advice (bring magic markers, don't bring jigsaw puzzles).

GNASTY GNOMES (1981)

Patricia Manning

SOURCE: A review of *Gnasty Gnomes,* in *School Library Journal,* Vol. 28, No. 1, September, 1981, pp. 130-31.

These gnomes have nothing in common with the robust, apple-cheeked bunch in Huygen's *Gnomes* (Abrams, 1977). They would be right at home with Roald Dahl's *Twits* (Knopf, 1980), and indeed could give lessons in Nasty to those despicable characters. **Gnasty Gnomes** have no redeeming social values. They revel in filth, do bad deeds every day and play such happy games as "Deflating Baby Brother." If rottenness is your cuppa, you'll love this. If not, stand clear. Jovial Bob pulls few punches.

DON'T STAND IN THE SOUP: THE WORLD'S FUNNIEST GUIDE TO MANNERS (1982)

Michelle Quinones

SOURCE: A review of *Don't Stand in the Soup: The World's Funniest Guide to Manners,* in *School Library Journal,* Vol. 28, No. 10, August, 1982, pp. 122-23.

Jovial Bob Stine returns with useless advice for young readers on contemporary manners and points of etiquette, ranging from the history of handshakes (or footshakes, whichever you prefer) to proper fork usage (or lack of it). The letter format provides for unlimited silliness and sarcasm through readers' ridiculous questions and Jovial Bob's even more obnoxious replies, but eventually wears thin as the continual absurdity becomes monotonous. More subdued than the new MAD putdown of table manners and eating, *Get Stuffed with MAD,* Jovial Bob still occasionally comes across with appropriately jovial jabs that hit right on the mark.

BORED WITH BEING BORED!: HOW TO BEAT THE BOREDOM BLAHS (with Jane Stine, 1982)

Terry Dunnahoo

SOURCE: A review of *Bored with Being Bored!: How to Beat the Boredom Blahs,* in *West Coast Review of Books,* Vol. 8, No. 6, November-December, 1982, p. 68.

A boring kind of waiting is waiting for the toast to pop out of the toaster when you've forgotten to plug it in. You know it's going to be a boring Saturday when all the cartoons on TV are about grammar. How boring is your family? What are the great moments in school boredom? Why do doctors and dentists always have fish tanks in their waiting rooms? The book gives no real answer to these questions. But kid's won't care. They'll be too busy laughing. And when it's time to stop laughing and go to sleep, they can read the most boring story ever written. "Once upon a time there lived a lonely prince in a lonely gray castle in a gray kingdom on the banks of a gray river. . . ."

Janice M. Alberghene

SOURCE: A review of *Bored with Being Bored!: How to Beat the Boredom Blahs,* in *School Library Journal,* Vol. 29, No. 5, January, 1983, p. 79.

This is supposed to be a light-hearted romp through the following causes of boredom: home, relatives, car trips, school, waiting and insomnia. Thoughtful children and their parents will find some of the targets questionable, especially when they see the authors' fondness for comic clichés. Old jokes can sound new to young ears; the humor's vintage is not the problem. Offensiveness is. Feminists will not enjoy the roster of repressed old maids which includes "Miss Darnia Socks," "Miss Lauren Order," and "Miss Penny Feryerthawts." Parents may wonder why siblings are always enemies. Readers sensitive to the problems of the disabled will be distressed to see "Hard-of-hearing Aunt Millie wants to have a long chat" played for a laugh. In short, rather than appeal to a child's sense of humor, the Stines' book appeals to the need to feel superior to other people or situations. Jerry Zimmerman has illustrated the book with simplified versions of the cartoon characters appearing in *Mad Magazine*—slapstick supersedes humor. Too often, the same is true for the text.

📖 *FIRST DATES* (with Jane Stine, 1983)

Terry Dunnahoo

SOURCE: A review of *First Dates,* in *West Coast Review of Books,* Vol. 9, No. 6, November-December, 1983, p. 68.

"Dates are not always like in the movies unless the movies you go to are horror shows. And first dates are usually creep shows for just about everyone." This is one of the observations in this book of helpful hints and way-out humor. There's a helpful chapter on etiquette that says it's okay for a girl to ask a boy for a date, and a silly chapter on how to practice how to ask for a date. There's a good chapter about non-dates that includes holding ice cream Olympics, and a silly chapter on how to say no when asked for a date. "I'm sorry, I've already made plans to stay home and watch TV that night." Kids will love it.

📖 *EVERYTHING YOU NEED TO SURVIVE: BROTHERS AND SISTERS; EVERYTHING YOU NEED TO SURVIVE: FIRST DATES; EVERYTHING YOU NEED TO SURVIVE: HOMEWORK; EVERYTHING YOU NEED TO SURVIVE: MONEY PROBLEMS* (with Jane Stine, 1983)

Lee Bock

SOURCE: A review of *Everything You Need to Survive: Brothers and Sisters* and others, in *School Library Journal,* Vol. 30, No. 7, March, 1984, p. 166.

Children (like the rest of us) love a good laugh. When those giggles can be woven in and out of information children want, the results can be very effective. Enter the Super Survival Kits on four pressing subjects for young adolescents: money, dating, homework and siblings. Each book is fun to read but, more than that, each is a well-balanced and well-paced collection of the ridiculous and the useful. Where else, for example, could you find "Eighteen Creative Suggestions for Wasting Time" ("Have you polished the *insides* of your shoes recently?") preceding a chapter on hard-core "Test Taking Tips"? Or a serious discussion on whether or not girls should call boys (yes) near a chapter about things *not* to say on a date ("You're not half as boring as you used to be"). Included in the books, also, is a liberal selection of jokes and humorous drawings [by Sal Murdocca], tasty recipes easy enough for beginning cooks and a good deal of basic information. These books provide a fun-coated roster of ways to survive some of the unfunny challenges of youth and should be popular.

James R. Bowman

SOURCE: "The Stines' Super Survival Kit," in *The Book Report,* Vol. 2, No. 5, March-April, 1984, p. 47.

Stine at work.

If you were to ask an average junior high student what bugged him most, his reply would probably include one of these: homework, money, dating, or brothers or sisters. The many books on these topics for this age group are usually serious, well thought-out volumes. These books usually just sit on the library shelf. The Stines hope to put an end to that with these four funny and helpful paperbacks.

Each book deals with a specific problem. The one on dating provides advice on places to go, conversation, clothes, etiquette and things to do. The homework guide gives pointers on improving study habits, organizing time, and studying for tests. If money is your problem, then you'll want to read how to save, spend, and make money. Finally the timeless problem of brothers and sisters suggests ways to keep them busy, what to do in case of an emergency, and how to just keep them from driving you crazy. The big difference that these books offer is fun. Along with sound advice and great suggestions comes the crazy Stine humor. And it is funny.

Each serious chapter is separated by one of jokes, riddles, crazy facts, games, and funny fill-ins. This is the aspect of the book which will get the kids to read the more serious sections. I found the humor to be entertaining and humorous unlike many of the riddle books available today. I was even able to use a few jokes myself. The books are written to help kids survive not to tell them *how* to survive.

THE GOLDEN SWORD OF DRAGONWALK (1983)

Kevin Kenny

SOURCE: A review of *Golden Sword of Dragonwalk,* in *Voice of Youth Advocates,* Vol. 7, No. 2, June, 1984, p. 94.

Sorcerers, dragons, sword-wielding trees, and battles with unspeakable evil await the reader in **Golden Sword of Dragonwalk.** The book pits the reader and Stacey (a seven-year-old who you must care for) against an enchanted world found in a secret passage in Grandma's house. As usual, the action moves along crisply, there's a healthy dose of humor, the writing is simple but reasonably literate, and nothing is taken too seriously.

While not to be confused with serious young adult literature, **Golden Sword of Dragonwalk** should be useful with less able or reluctant readers. Better readers and genuine fans of adventure and fantasy would be better rewarded by Tolkien (*Trilogy of the Rings*), C. S. Lewis (*Chronicles of Narnia* series), Susan Cooper (*The Dark Is Rising*), or Lloyd Alexander (*The Book of Three* or *The Black Cauldron*). This is a genre where young readers need not settle for second-rate.

CHALLENGE OF THE WOLF KNIGHT (1985)

Susan H. Harper

SOURCE: "Wizards and Warriors in Wondrous Array," in *Fantasy Review,* Vol. 8, No. 10, October, 1985, p. 28.

The latest entrants in the Wizards and Warriors series [Stine's **Challenge of the Wolf Knight** and Lynn Beach's *Conquest of the Time Master*] (which is obviously pitched to share in the popularity of Dungeons and Dragons) are, like their predecessors, books that will attract junior high age readers and the older readers known as reluctant readers. A bit different from most of this genre, these books allow some real chance in their choice—paths are selected by tossing a coin or by the day of the week, skills are selected in patterns designed by the reader, and the outcome of the adventure depends upon the choice.

The prose is no match for the novelty, however, and characterization is nonexistent. The style leans heavily upon short sentences beginning with *you.* As a librarian, I find it hard to recommend this sort of book. However, as the parent of two boys ages 11 and 14, I can say that these kept my boys entertained for two hot August days and were the start of some imagining adventures for several more. Clearly, the format is a success.

Chris Zuiderhof

SOURCE: A review of *Challenge of the Wolf Knight,* in *Voice of Youth Advocates,* Vol. 8, No. 5, February, 1986, p. 400.

You, as the wizard or the warrior must find the terrible Wolf Knight before the royal visitors arrive in your kingdom. You can take the Book of Weapons which has a complete arsenal for you to use or the Book of Spells which will make you a master of magic. You had better use the books wisely so that you can kill and destroy the Killer, Wolf Knight. For anyone who likes choose-your-own-adventure-ending roles, as I do, this is great!

JAMES BOND IN WIN, PLACE, OR DIE (1985)

Caroline Ajel

SOURCE: A review of *James Bond in Win, Place, or Die,* in *Voice of Youth Advocates,* Vol. 8, No. 5, February, 1986, p. 388.

In **Win, Place, or Die** agent 007 is searching for missing agent 009. His arch enemy, Max Zorin, is implanting microchips in both horses and people to make them stronger. Settings include the ski slopes of Russia, a race track, and Zorin's underground chamber.

Win, Place, or Die fails because the endings are generally very dull and the characters unrealistic. This book would only appeal to people with special interests in the "Find Your Fate" series. Real fans of James Bond should stick to the Ian Fleming books.

📖 *BLIND DATE* (1986)

Publishers Weekly

SOURCE: A review of *Blind Date,* in *Publishers Weekly,* Vol. 230, No. 8, August 22, 1986, p. 102.

When Kerry accidentally breaks the star quarterback's leg during football practice, it seems like the whole school is against him. The quarterback's girlfriend, Sharon, starts threatening Kerry, and he gets mysterious phone calls that he assumes are from her. He also gets calls from a girl named Mandy; he's never met her, but she wants to date him. On their first date, Kerry ends up at a house where people he's never seen know him—and hate him. The other, horrible phone calls keep coming. His brother Donald, a mental patient, also calls Kerry; his words also carry a threat. Then in a gruesome climax, Mandy takes Kerry to a secluded cabin, ties him up and starts breaking his bones with a mallet. Donald saves Kerry, who suddenly remembers that he was the driver in a car accident that killed a girl; Mandy believes she is the girl's sister, avenging her death. Though the plot is convoluted and some details are stomach-churning, Stine moves the story along, handling the red herrings with finesse.

Kliatt Young Adult Paperback Book Guide

SOURCE: A review of *Blind Date,* in *Kliatt Young Adult Paperback Book Guide,* Vol. XX, No. 6, September, 1986, p. 18.

The suspense and pace of this YA thriller remind me of Jay Bennett's novels—and readers who like those should enjoy this as well. In it, a high school student, Kerry, is trying to lead a normal life even though his older brother has disappeared and Kerry cannot remember anything about a tragic accident that occurred a year before. Don't expect *Ordinary People* here; the author is more interested in scaring the reader than in revealing any psychological truths. Kerry starts getting phone calls, some that scare him and some that tempt him—i.e., the blind date. It is not difficult to race through the book, which should be considered as entertainment only—for boys and girls alike.

Stephanie Zvirin

SOURCE: A review of *Blind Date,* in *Booklist,* Vol. 83, No. 2, September 15, 1986, p. 121.

Kerry has no reason to connect a call from a sexy-voiced girl introducing herself as his blind date to the harassment he is receiving from his classmates, even though the timing is suspicious. In fact, with his memory concerning the whereabouts of his brother still a blank and his relationship with his father difficult at best, the call and follow-up meeting with Amanda give him a real lift—that is, until he discovers his blind date is a thoroughly demented young woman who literally intends to break every bone in his body. Not for the squeamish and riddled with contrivances, the story is well paced and has a TV-ish flair that is likely to appeal to teens. A gr. 4-5 reading level makes this suitable also as high/low material.

Judie Porter

SOURCE: A review of *Blind Date,* in *School Library Journal,* Vol. 33, No. 3, November, 1986, pp. 108-09.

Kerry has a memory lapse. He has shut out some horror in his life, and no one will tell him what has happened. (It's been a year, and miraculously, no one has slipped, and he hasn't been all that curious, either). Then things start happening. He accidently breaks the star quarterback's leg; he is kicked off the football team, and his schoolmates hate him and beat him up. A mysterious girl suddenly calls for a date, and he is lured into her trap by her sexy voice. The subject of his brother, Donald, keeps creeping up, and finally Kerry learns that Donald is not dead, he's in a mental hospital, or he was until he escaped. Kerry's best friend Josh is a prize—full of wit and personality. It's nice to have Josh around because the rest of the people weave in and out of a complicated and not too believable storyline in a rather superficial way. The writing flows well enough to keep readers' attention, regardless of the fact that once the book is finished, they will surely say something like, "Now, come on, that couldn't happen." So it couldn't happen. So what? It's mindless entertainment.

Mary I. Purucker

SOURCE: A review of *Blind Date,* in *Voice of Youth Advocates,* Vol. 10, No. 1, April, 1987, pp. 33-4.

Kerry's teammates blame him when Sal goes into a coma after his leg is broken in a scrimmage. The coach ousts him from the team even though he believes Kerry's not at fault, and even though Kerry's brother was a big star, and even though Kerry . . . is still trying to remember and recover from something that happened a year ago at about the same time that his older brother, Donald, disappeared. His policeman dad . . . knows but won't tell. Then, on the night of the accident, this girl he's never met, Mandy, telephones him and flirts, and he arranges a blind date, but when he gets to where he *thinks* she lives, it's like a haunted house with this crazy old couple who act really strange. Then his teammates beat him up, his car is vandalized and Mandy's kisses draw blood. Everything just gets more complicated and confused when the long absent Donald phones home. The unsophisticated will like this for its dark twists and turns, but mystery buffs will recognize the hoary and convoluted had-I-but-known style and move on to Dick Francis, Mary Stewart, et al.

TWISTED (1987)

Publishers Weekly

SOURCE: A review of Twisted, in Publishers Weekly, Vol. 231, No. 27, July 10, 1987, p. 71.

The author of both **Blind Date** and this book seems to have a peculiar view of women. Here they are mostly shrill, insecure types, who go along with a sorority prank and rob a store. But they end up with a corpse—the owner of the store drops dead during the crime. Then there's Leila and Abby, who both love (for no good reason) a lazy, shiftless boy. *He* (the only male in the book) prevents Abby from killing Leila; Abby has a "split personality," and when the prank is over, she's carried off, babbling, by paramedics in white coats. Of course, no one is really dead; even the murders were a joke. And Leila, who was as shrill as everyone else, suddenly becomes a sympathetic character. For shock value, this book adds up to a lot of cheap tricks.

Rosemary Moran

SOURCE: A review of Twisted, in Voice of Youth Advocates, Vol. 10, No. 5, December, 1987, p. 238.

Abby has been invited to pledge Tri Gammas, the sorority on campus. At the pledges' first meeting, Andrea, sorority president and pledge captain, tells the group that to be initiated they will have to commit a crime. She sets them up to rob a small antique store in a nearby town, but in the course of the robbery, the shop owner has an apparent heart attack and dies. With some girls believing the death is a hoax and others urging a trip to the local police, the pledges are stranded in a big gloomy isolated house with no phone, no transportation, no electricity, an approaching storm, and, with the discovery of Andrea's bloody body, no leader. Abby, stressed to her limit, retreats, and her "twin" sister Gabriella who until now existed only in Abby's mirror, takes over. Soon Andrea and the shopkeeper appear, alive and unharmed, to explain that the whole scenario was staged as a "test of courage." Abby/Gabriella is taken away in an ambulance, leaving the other pledges to bear the impact of the events. . . .

Stine's plot could have made a story that would cause teens to consider the consequences of succumbing to peer pressure. By populating the novel with stereotyped undeveloped characters and by not taking full advantage of the opportunities presented by the plot, Stine has produced what appears to be a summary of a movie script or an outline for a more detailed novel to come later.

English Journal

SOURCE: A review of Twisted, in English Journal, Vol. 77, No. 3, March, 1988, p. 86.

Abby is willing to become part of a weekend robbery in order to be accepted into Tri Gamma sorority. No one knows that her alter ego, evil Gabriella, has decided to accompany her in order to punish another pledge, who took away Abby's boyfriend a year earlier. What starts out as a hoax almost ends in murder. This story should appeal to high-school girls since the characters are college-age. The book is well-written although shifts in point of view and narrator may at first confuse unskilled readers. The "whole truth" emerges only in the last chapters, making this a thrilling story.

THE PROTECTORS: THE PETROVA TWIST (as Zachary Blue, 1987)

Cathryn A. Camper

SOURCE: A review of The Protectors: The Petrova Twist, in School Library Journal, Vol. 34, No. 4, December, 1987, p. 83.

Five kids are, unbeknownst to them, culled by the U.S. government from high schools all across the United States to form a team called the PROTECTORS. Lu is a karate expert, J. W. is a rich kid, Riana has a photographic memory, Mickey is a whiz at theatrics, and Matt is an electronics genius. The kids have been chosen by CENTRAL to help the Soviet superstar gymnast Elena Petrova defect to the U.S. The trouble is, neither Elena nor the guys down at CENTRAL can seem to make up their minds as to where their political loyalties lie. It turns out in both situations to be a case of mistaken identity: Elena is confused with her twin sister, a Soviet loyalist, and the so-called CENTRAL agents are really from the evil organization CONQUEST. In the end, all resolve to work together as a team in what appears to be a series of upcoming books. Stereotypes and poor characterization add nothing to this ephemeral plot, and name dropping (Reeboks shoes and Michael J. Fox) only makes the book more expendable. Skip this one; unfortunately, there's more creativity on Saturday morning TV.

PORK AND BEANS: PLAY DATE (1989)

Kirkus Reviews

SOURCE: A review of Pork and Beans: Play Date, in Kirkus Reviews, Vol. LVII, No. 10, May 15, 1989, p. 771.

An ironic tale of quarrelsome playmates. Billy (a blue goat) comes to play with Pork and Beans (pigs, pink and orange). They argue about who is whose best friend; they play a variety of games, in each of which one of the three is unkindly left out; they complain to Mrs. Pig, who repeatedly responds, "Play another game." But although they have the sort of apparently miserable afternoon that any parent would be delighted to have end, when Mrs. Goat comes for Billy they all weep: "We are having too much fun!"

This is the sort of wry view of a common situation that should make children enjoy taking an honest look at themselves. The elegantly simple, color-splashed drawings [by Jose Aruego and Ariane Dewey] contribute splendidly to the humor. Simple vocabulary and much repetition make this valuable as an easy reader as well as a picture-book.

Jeanne Marie Clancy

SOURCE: A review of *Pork and Beans: Play Date,* in *School Library Journal,* Vol. 35, No. 12, August, 1989, pp. 132-33.

As siblings will, Pork and Beans, two piglets, launch into a heated bicker battle when Mrs. Pig announces that their friend Billy, a goat, is coming for a play date. After all, it's important to know who is whose best friend, and when Billy announces that his choice is Henry (who never appears) that argument is resolved. Arguments continue, though, as each game chosen by the trio victimizes one of the players. In Bad Cold, Pork and Beans sneeze all over Billy, while, in Bump Tag, Billy and Pork repeatedly knock Beans down. As each game in turn reduces one of the participants to tears, Mrs. Pig intervenes, simply telling them to "Play another game." When Billy's mother arrives on the scene, the three simultaneously burst into tears because, "We are having too much fun!" Anyone intimate with the ways of children knows that childhood events often start off on the wrong foot; unfortunately, this play date never gets onto the right one. The unrelenting meanness of the play is unsettling, and the ironic conclusion will be lost on preschoolers who are not generally known for their ability to step back and view their own foibles. Aruego and Dewey's distinctive illustrations do little to relieve the tensions of the situation. While the spontaneity of their line-and-wash paintings successfully captures the active nature of the play, color and motion hardly diffuse the unpleasantries. Every spread, save two, features at least one frowning, scowling, or crying character. Creative though Pork, Beans, and Billy might be, their inability to socialize is more sad than funny.

THE NEW GIRL (1989)

Publishers Weekly

SOURCE: A review of *The New Girl,* in *Publishers Weekly,* Vol. 235, No. 23, June 9, 1989, pp. 68-70.

In the first of the Fear Street series, Corey falls in love with Anna, the new girl at school. The only problem is that he can't tell if she's real—most of his friends have never seen her on campus, and she's not listed in the school's files. When he calls her family's home they are strange and evasive. In desperation, Corey goes to Anna's house—located on infamous Fear Street—and there a man tells Corey that Anna is dead. But a few nights later, Anna calls him and asks him to meet her. Anna's passionate kisses convince Corey that his love object is alive and kicking. The rest of this novel follows the same tedious pattern: each of Corey's torrid encounters with Anna is accompanied by several supposedly eerie incidents. Some-

thing strange *is* going on, but it is unlikely that readers will have the interest or stamina to stay with the mystery until it is resolved. Stine fans will have to hope that the rest of the Fear Street series proves a lot more fearsome than this tame offering.

Molly Kinney

SOURCE: A review of *The New Girl,* in *School Library Journal,* Vol. 35, No. 12, August, 1989, p. 154.

A new entry in the "Fear Street" series—that street where unexplained, terrifying events occur for no particular reason, to anyone brave enough to venture down its sidewalks. When Cory Brooks, high school gym star, meets Anna Corwin, the hauntingly beautiful girl who has just moved to Fear Street, he becomes preoccupied with her. With the help of good friends, particularly the girl next door, Cory unravels the puzzle of Anna's mysterious life. The result is a fast-moving tale that includes obsession, strange events, and the ultimate triumph of good over evil. The book moves along from start to finish, conveying an uneasiness that will keep readers going. Cory and his friends are typical teens, and their conversation and action are believable. The sense of something always about to happen and the cliff-hanging endings to the chapters will make this a good booktalking candidate. The vocabulary is simple, the premise interesting, and the plot compelling, making this book one for reluctant readers, as well as a useful addition for teens who like the "creep" genre.

Fran Lantz

SOURCE: A review of *The New Girl,* in *Kliatt Young Adult Paperback Book Guide,* Vol. XXIII, No. 6, September, 1989, p. 16.

This first novel in a new horror series tells the story of high school student Cory Brooks and his obsession with a new classmate named Anna. Anna is a pale and ghostly creature who drifts in and out of Cory's life, destroying his ability to excel on the gymnastics team. When he tries to learn more about her, her brother tells him, "Anna is dead." Now it's up to Cory to find out the truth—is Anna a ghost?

This is a clever, entertaining novel that starts as a horror story and ends as a scary mystery. The author uses simple sentences and short paragraphs, making this a good book for high school kids reading at an upper elementary school level.

Sue Tait and Christy Tyson

SOURCE: A review of *The New Girl,* in *Emergency Librarian,* Vol. 17, No. 4, March-April, 1990, p. 61.

Probably teenagers the world over love to be scared by a mixture of reality and fantasy, all enjoyed of course in the safety of one's own world, and within the pages of a book that can be closed at will. Such a mixture is dished out in R. L. Stine's new paperback, *The new girl.* Stine is popular with kids locally, but since I don't like to be scared and don't need to push the books, I'd never read any until now. Here is the plot: Cory Brooks was an outstanding gymnast, an untroubled guy who seemed to have it all until he saw the new girl for the first time. She was pale and eerily beautiful, she seemed to be afraid of something, she needed him and she lived on Fear Street. Or did she? He'd been told that she was dead, he could find no school records for her and she was so pale that he almost believed that she was a ghost. He wanted to help her, but didn't know how until the night that he was called to Fear Street. Cory told himself that he wouldn't believe any of the strange stories he had heard about the street, but then he found out for himself.

Stine plays on our fears of the unknown and unexpected, on our fears of the dark. He does not write many confrontational scenes in which he sets up scary situations that crash and bang; rather he sets up scenes in which our imaginations work overtime. Reassuringly, the story ends in the light, with Cory beginning a romantic liaison with a very real young woman who has been his friend for years. Shadows have been vanquished, for the present.

Ryan Tuley

SOURCE: A review of *The New Girl,* in *English Journal,* Vol. 79, No. 5, September, 1990, p. 95.

Four out of five students surveyed in the eighth-grade learning-disabled class I observe recommend *The New Girl* by R. L. Stine for those students who read books. I suspect the fifth student did not read it at all. The story kept these kids enraptured throughout, a feat unheard of with these kids. Why do they find it special?

The story is a continuation of Stine's "Fear Street" series. It follows the budding romance of Cory and Lisa, friends since birth. Cory is an aspiring gymnast; Lisa is his enraptured next door neighbor. But along the way to romance, Cory sees Anna, the new girl in school, across the busy lunchroom. She disappears into the crowd before he can talk to her. Cory is so smitten with this mysterious girl that his gymnastics and schoolwork suffer. Meanwhile, Lisa decides to pursue Cory, even though she knows he is falling in love with Anna. When Cory learns the reason behind Anna's mysterious background, it leaves all hope of romance between Cory and Anna in shambles: Anna is dead, and the girl posing as her is the twin sister who killed her. It is a strange ending which caught the students as well as myself, if truth be known, off guard.

While I was reading the story, I was impressed with the detail Stine put into the book. I must admit, I enjoyed the book so much I went out and read all the books by Stine available at the junior-high library. Unfortunately, only four of his more than seventy books for teens were available. Unfortunate for my budding young readers.

THE OVERNIGHT (1989)

Nancy Cleckner

SOURCE: A review of *The Overnight,* in *Booklist,* Vol. 86, No. 8, December 15, 1989, p. 827.

When the high school Outdoors Club's overnight campout to Fear Island is temporarily canceled, Della O'Connor and five others decide to follow through with the exciting adventure, unchaperoned. The fun suddenly turns scary and chilling when Della chances upon a dark, ominous stranger in the heavily forested woods and, in a struggle to get away, accidentally pushes him into a deep ravine, killing him. Vowing to remain silent, the teens decide to cover the body with dried leaves. Later they receive anonymous notes claiming someone saw what Della did, and they are forced to return to the island to recover some evidence. The second overnight proves to be even more suspenseful and dangerous, taking on a final twist of life-threatening proportions. Part of the Fear Street series, this is a thriller that will keep readers on the edge of their chairs.

PHONE CALLS (1990)

Publishers Weekly

SOURCE: A review of *Phone Calls,* in *Publishers Weekly,* Vol. 237, No. 23, June 8, 1990, p. 56.

Stine's latest work is an all-dialogue piece centered around a succession of telephone calls among a group of high school students. The story begins when Diane encourages her best friend Julie to pursue basketball star Mick Wilson. The reluctant Julie acquiesces, but ultimately winds up feeling humiliated, and blames Diane for what she believes was a cruel prank. To retaliate, Julie lures Toby, Diane's stepbrother, into a plan guaranteed to embarrass Diane. When it succeeds, an enraged Diane plots revenge. Based on an innocent misunderstanding, this good-natured fun provides perfect entertainment for its intended audience. The narrative features slick, contemporary dialogue and a rapid-fire tempo—ingredients sure to entice even the most reluctant reader. Stine's popularity with young people is well deserved.

Barbara J. McKee

SOURCE: A review of *Phone Calls,* in *Kliatt Young Adult Paperback Book Guide,* Vol. XXIV, No. 6, September, 1990, p. 16.

Sophomore Julie Reynolds and Diane Clark, her best friend, get mad at each other when Diane convinces Julie that a certain athlete really likes her. When Julie finds that the guy doesn't know she exists, she decides to play a practical joke on Diane. On and on it goes, with extra added confusion, from Toby (Diane's stepbrother) to Ramar (an exchange student staying with the jock). Hilarious and witty—a great read-aloud for younger teens.

Alice Cronin

SOURCE: A review of *Phone Calls,* in *School Library Journal,* Vol. 36, No. 10, October, 1990, p. 145.

A delightfully funny comedy of errors, based on a series of phone calls among a small group of teenagers. Diane calls her best friend, Julie, to tell her that Mick likes her and that she should try to attract his attention. Miscommunication is the plot device, so Julie ends up telephoning the wrong Mick—superjock Mick Wilson, who isn't interested in her at all. Each chapter begins as one of the characters telephones another. Occasionally it will be difficult for readers to distinguish one character's dialogue from another. However, the story is well constructed, and readers will enjoy the excellent character development (even the parents are funny). All's well that ends well . . . Julie gets Toby, and teens get an excellent read.

Kathy Elmore

SOURCE: A review of *Phone Calls,* in *Voice of Youth Advocates,* Vol. 13, No. 4, October, 1990, p. 220.

Diane convinces her best friend Julie that Mick likes her, so Julie throws herself at Mick only to find out he's not the least bit interested. Thinking Diane has played a cruel joke on her, Julie plots revenge with the help of Diane's brother Toby. It's one trick after another until all the misunderstandings are cleared up and everyone is paired off happily in the end.

The unique aspect of this book is that it's written entirely in telephone conversations. The chapter headings tell who is calling whom; their conversation follows word for word. The result is a story made up of all dialogue with short sentences and short chapters that often end abruptly with the phone being slammed down. Perhaps the author's intent was to attract reluctant readers, but I found it difficult to keep track of the characters. Since teenagers spend a great deal of time on the phone, maybe this style of writing will appeal to them. Reading *Phone Calls* is a lot like listening in on a party line; it may be entertaining for a while but then you get tired and hang up!

📖 *THE WRONG NUMBER* (1990)

Alice Cronin

SOURCE: A review of *The Wrong Number,* in *School Library Journal,* Vol. 36, No. 6, June, 1990, p. 126.

Jade and Deena find typical adolescent amusement in harmless crank calls until Deena's half-brother, Chuck, joining them, overhears a murder being committed. The three teenagers' bravado in seeking out the crime scene leads them into grave danger. This is a good thriller-type mystery in the style of Edith Maxwell's *Just Dial a Number* (Archway, 1988), but is limited by the stilted dialogue of the adult characters and an unconvincing, overwrought portrayal of the killer. The dominant theme, which

Cover from one of Stine's most popular early works.

could have been excellent, is undermined by inappropriate melodramatic scenes. However, high-traffic murder-mystery sections in young adult departments would not be downgraded by adding this title.

📖 *HOW I BROKE UP WITH ERNIE* (1990)

Linda Callaghan

SOURCE: A review of *How I Broke Up with Ernie,* in *Booklist,* Vol. 86, No. 21, July, 1990, p. 2098.

Even though her brothers, parents, and friends love Ernie, Amy is irritated by his smile, his laugh, even the clothes he wears. She wants to date Colin, but no one believes she is serious about breaking up with Ernie—not even Ernie. Amy tells him it's over, but Ernie shows up for dinner as usual; on her first date with Colin, Ernie comes along; and when Colin swims too far from shore, Ernie saves his life. Stine's embroidery on the old adage "familiarity breeds contempt" is deftly threaded with humor and subtle strands of irony. As readers watch Amy sighing over dippy Colin, they will laugh in recognition and be pleased when she comes to her senses about Ernie.

Alice Cronin

SOURCE: A review of *How I Broke Up with Ernie,* in *School Library Journal,* Vol. 36, No. 11, November, 1990, p. 142.

Amy wants to break up with her boyfriend, Ernie, but nobody can understand why—her family loves him, her friends all think they are the perfect couple and that Ernie is a great guy. Amy dates Colin, but Ernie keeps hanging around, and even becomes Colin's friend. Thus flows the well-developed, highly amusing plot of this book, which is one of the most delightful and insightful teenage romances written in years. Highly recommended, for despite its bubbly style, this book will guide readers into learning a lot about emotions.

THE SLEEPWALKER (1990)

Alice Cronin

SOURCE: A review of *The Sleepwalker,* in *School Library Journal,* Vol. 36, No. 9, September, 1990, p. 258.

This well-written, believable book will appeal to thriller fans because of its good characterizations and horror elements that are never out of bounds. A summer job as companion to weird old Mrs. Cottler (who lives on Fear Street) becomes upsetting to Mayra, and she begins to sleepwalk at night after having nightmares. The job really becomes frightening when Mayra's best friend is mistaken for her and is nearly killed in an automobile accident. Although the real villain and his machinations are rather superimposed, Stine writes a good story. Teens will love the action; librarians will love the lure for slower and nonreaders.

Penny Blubaugh

SOURCE: A review of *The Sleepwalker,* in *Voice of Youth Advocates,* Vol. 13, No. 6, February, 1991, p. 368.

When Mayra gets a job on Fear Street as a companion to an elderly woman, she isn't really very worried. She's almost convinced that all the stories she's heard are due to people's imaginations. But she is concerned when she learns that her mother, a nurse, had Mrs. Cottler as a patient, and that Mrs. Cottler always believed that Mayra's mother was trying to kill her. Her first day on the job puts her fears aside. Mrs. Cottler seems very nice, Mayra's new boyfriend is coming home from vacation soon, and the summer ahead looks perfect.

When Mayra first begins sleepwalking, her mother assumes she's upset about her father's desertion. But Mayra's walks get longer and longer, and she eventually wakes on Fear Street on the edge of the lake behind Mrs. Cottler's house. On her next trip, she goes straight into the lake and nearly drowns.

Mayra is now convinced that Mrs. Cottler is a witch who's put a spell on her to get back at her mother. But the bad one turns out to be her new and beloved boyfriend who has hypnotized her to make her forget the hit-and-run accident he caused when he stole a car. Mayra's life is saved by the old boyfriend who still loves her. Easy to read with a moderate amount of excitement, Stine's book will be appealing to people reading Richie Tankersley Cusick and Christopher Pike as well as other books in the *Fear Street* series.

CURTAINS (1990)

Publishers Weekly

SOURCE: A review of *Curtains,* in *Publishers Weekly,* Vol. 237, No. 39, September 28, 1990, p. 104.

Rena, a Michelle Pfeiffer look-alike, is attending a theatrical summer camp with a friend, boy-crazy Julie. When Rena effortlessly wins the leading role in the play *Curtains,* she also provokes the wrath of Hedy, the camp diva, who was sure she had the part sewn up. Julie openly resents Rena's easy popularity with male campers Chris and George. When a series of cruel and bizarre pranks is directed against Rena—a slashed swan in her bed, her wardrobe destroyed—the finger of guilt seems to point at either Julie or Hedy. Leading the unsuspecting reader along various paths, Stine handily arranges an abrupt turn that leads to an unforeseeable ending. The story has a strong yet vulnerable heroine in Rena, and contains just enough gore to sate horror fans. Although **Curtains** will never be mistaken for serious literature, it is sure to engross Stine's considerable following.

Rita M. Fontinha

SOURCE: A review of *Curtains,* in *Kliatt Young Adult Paperback Book Guide,* Vol. XXV, No. 1, January, 1991, p. 14.

A lot goes on here: a murdered swan, a stabbed actor, mysterious tapping on the window, a suicide attempt, a drowning. Just an everyday week at Bax's acting camp! Everyone wants to be in the play "Curtains," but how far will they go? Rena surprises them all as the lead—but someone wants to scare her off. Is it her jealous roommate Julie? Or her stage rival Hedy? Maybe it's even Bax himself. A swift conclusion neatly ties all the loose ends. Though short on description and plot and long on dialogue, a good read for Stine fans. Too transparent and simple for the above-average high school reader.

BEACH PARTY (1990)

Alice Cronin

SOURCE: A review of *Beach Party,* in *School Library Journal,* Vol. 37, No. 1, January, 1991, p. 97.

Many teenage novels that could be good are not because the main characters have no redeeming value, or are not the least bit interesting. **Beach Party,** unfortunately, falls into that category; thus, when the main characters are murdered or their lives are threatened, most readers won't care. Stine is a good writer of many young adult novels, but this particular offering can be passed over without a thought.

Lisa Sampley

SOURCE: A review of *Beach Party,* in *Voice of Youth Advocates,* Vol. 13, No. 6, February, 1991, p. 368.

Karen is really excited about seeing Ann-Marie again. Best friends in grade school, their friendship continued through high school even though Ann-Marie had moved to New York with her family. Now she is in California to visit Karen, and they are going to have *fun!* Karen has conveniently arranged for them to spend the weekend with her father on the very weekend that her father happens to be out of town. Venice, the beach, and the apartment are all theirs, at least for the weekend.

While strolling along the beach, Ann-Marie and Karen run into some trouble with a group of guys. That's when they meet Jerry. Karen is intrigued by Jerry—he's open and friendly, but mysterious, too. He's not like her old boyfriend Mike, who followed her to Venice and wants another chance. Karen and Jerry start spending time together despite the fact that he already has a girlfriend, Renee. Ann-Marie starts acting strangely, and then the accidents begin, at first with seemingly innocent notes telling Karen to stay away from Jerry, then they escalate until Karen finds herself in danger at the Beach Party.

Beach Party is another addition to the suspense/horror genre that is popular with teens. The book is an exciting, fast-paced, page turner. I couldn't wait to find out if I had correctly guessed the culprit (I hadn't). A good addition to meet the suspense demand.

Mike Peters

SOURCE: A review of *Beach Party,* in *The School Librarian,* Vol. 39, No. 4, November, 1991, pp. 151-52.

Frightened girls alone at night, threatening notes and telephone calls, shadowy figures moving through the darkness—such is the stuff of these fictional teenage nightmares. And unwillingly caught up in the strange disappearances and deaths of their young affluent WASP characters is the heroine, who just manages to avoid becoming a victim and eventually succeeds in solving the dreadful mystery. At the end, needless to say, a safe dawn breaks. The source of the mystery is always human. The novels toy with the supernatural for effect—the eerie barbarism of the Rimrocks in [Carol Ellis'] *My secret admirer,* for example; but the real terror is psychological. Continually playing on the question of who is responsible for the crimes which intrude into the summer fun, the narratives make almost everyone, except the heroine, a suspect, allowing adolescent readers to question the moral sanity of the seemingly most sane. Nothing can be taken on trust, for even 'perfect' Justin in [Richie Tankersley Cusick's] *The lifeguard,* whom Kelsey never doubts, turns out to be a murderer. The demands of the plot in the least successful books do produce implausible motivation and paper-thin characterisation. Jenny in *My secret admirer* would have had to suffer from a temporary bout of blinding stupidity to have been taken in by the love notes that lure her into danger; and the revelation of the true criminal in the same book causes us hardly a *frisson* of pleasurable shock, because we have hardly noticed his existence. On the other hand, the portraits of Jerry and Renee in **Beach party** subtly register their disturbing instability, preparing us for the final revelations; and the use of diary extracts in [Diane Hoh's] *Funhouse,* giving an insight into the mind of Guy Joe, makes for a rich narrative pattern. At their best then, these novels work extremely effectively. They provide girls with active female leading characters, and they provide all adolescent readers, caught between the desire for independence and the fear of its reality, with a chance to experience vicariously anxiety and fear in a teenage world where adults have been consigned to the margins. Most important of all, the stories offer the pleasures of consistently gripping suspense.

HALLOWEEN PARTY (1990)

Penny Blubaugh

SOURCE: A review of *Halloween Party,* in *Voice of Youth Advocates,* Vol. 13, No. 6, February, 1991, p. 368.

Terry doesn't really understand why he and his girlfriend Niki have received the black-bordered invitations to Justine's Halloween party. Justine is new at school and has been very aloof to everyone. Now, with seven others, Terry and Niki are pleased to be asked to an all-night party that seems to be a perfect way to spend Halloween.

Justine says that she's invited the people at school that she'd most like to know, but upon closer inspection, the privileged few decide that she's split the list into jocks and wimps. Terry falls on the wimp side while his ex-best friend Alex is a jock. Niki, deaf since second grade and an excellent lip reader, broke up with Alex and has been going with Terry for the last few months. She's the only one who thinks the jocks/wimps idea is stupid and she refuses to go along with the gags and petty, nasty tricks that both groups pull on each other as the party looms closer.

Once at Justine's, the party goes into high gear. A series of "surprises" planted by Justine and her uncle scare and amaze the guests. Everyone is having a shivery time until Alex discovers Les in a closet, very dead.

Suddenly Justine's party takes a sinister turn. She locks her guests in a dining room with grates on the window.

She explains that the only reason she's invited them is that at least one of their parents was involved in a fatal accident that claimed the lives of her parents over 25 years ago (Justine is in her 30s, posing as a high school student). And she sets the huge mansion on fire, planning to burn them as her parents burned so many years before.

Niki is the only one with enough control to save them, and with the help of Justine's uncle she gets them out just in time.

This is a spooky story with enough small shivers to make it interesting. *Fear Street* is a popular series and with the other titles in the horror genre should do well at most libraries.

THE BOYFRIEND (1990)

Miriam Temsky

SOURCE: A review of *The Boyfriend*, in *Voice of Youth Advocates*, Vol. 14, No. 2, June, 1991, p. 114.

Sixteen year old Joanna lives in a small town, probably not far from Fear Street. She is experiencing an unaccustomed cruel streak resulting from her parents' divorce. This causes her to mistreat her boyfriend Dex, and culminates in her leaving him for dead after a failed practical joke. In turn, he "comes back from the dead" to pay her back for her selfishness.

The Boyfriend contains many of the elements readers expect from a Stine novel—a scary story about a single-parent, white, suburban family with one teenaged child engaged in a series of incidents which foster tricks, paranoia, and a certain level of evil. As in other Stine books, the setting is dark, and the events are appropriately creepy and gory. Although the heroine is not a very likable girl, and the same hokey plot twist is used twice—two differences from other Stine novels—there is no question that many readers will request and enjoy this book.

SKI WEEKEND (1991)

[*The following excerpt is from an advance review of* Ski Weekend.]

Publishers Weekly

SOURCE: A review of *Fear Street: Ski Weekend*, in *Publishers Weekly*, Vol. 233, No. 49, December 7, 1990, p. 83.

Driving back from a ski weekend, Ariel, Shannon and Doug have offered their new friend Red a ride home. When a blizzard makes the roads nearly impassable, Red leads the teens to a farmhouse where they can spend the night. Unfortunately, their shelter is not the safe haven it appears: its residents have their own plans for Ariel and her friends. Though filled with action, this addition to the Fear Street series lacks urgency and dramatic tension. The characters are minimally defined and the contrived plot barely manages to hold together a surfeit of bland cliffhangers.

THE SECRET BEDROOM (1991)

Linda Callaghan

SOURCE: A review of *The Secret Bedroom*, in *Booklist*, Vol. 88, No. 2, September 15, 1991, p. 171.

Lea feels ill at ease adjusting to a new high school, trying to make new friends, and moving to a strange house with a boarded up attic room. Intrigued enough to investigate, she encounters the ghost of Catherine, a girl near Lea's age. Sympathizing with Catherine's loneliness, Lea allows the spirit to enter her body and feel alive again. Given this opportunity, Catherine possesses Lea and causes the death of a spiteful girl in Lea's class. After the tragedy, Lea's parents think she's in shock and don't believe her tale of the ghost. Stine maximizes the suspense and tension in a satisfying tale that will appeal to horror tale devotees.

Doris Losey

SOURCE: A review of *The Secret Bedroom*, in *Voice of Youth Advocates*, Vol. 15, No. 2, June, 1992, p. 102.

Lea Carson hates the house on Fear Street from the moment she and her parents move in. Although her parents assure her that the noises she hears are typical for an old house, Lea is convinced that she hears a girl whispering "Let me out" and that she hears footsteps overhead in the attic. Investigating, Lea discovers a secret room in the attic inhabited by a ghost named Catherine, who was murdered over 100 years ago and who desperately wants to return to the "real" world through Lea's body. Helpless to prevent Catherine's possession of her body, Lea soon regrets her actions as Catherine/Lea causes the death of Lea's rival, Marci. Of course, Catherine wants to permanently occupy Lea's body and the ensuing battle of wits is exciting and scary.

Young people will enjoy this entry in the popular horror series which reads quickly and has a plausible storyline. Recommended for all collections.

THE SNOWMAN (1991)

Joe Peacock

SOURCE: A review of *The Snowman*, in *Voice of Youth Advocates*, Vol. 14, No. 5, December, 1991, p. 319.

Heather Dixon has lived with her aunt and uncle since her parents' deaths when she was three. She hates her uncle, often fantasizes about killing him, and really would like him dead. She is dating a guy named Ben, but when she first sees "Snowman" she can't stop looking at him. Eventually, Heather and Snowman start going out. But when Heather does Snowman a favor and he returns it by killing her uncle, Heather's nightmare begins. This is a great book. I suggest it for anyone who reads (and likes) general fiction.

📖 *THE BABY-SITTER II* (1991)

Joyce Yen

SOURCE: A review of *The Babysitter II*, in *Voice of Youth Advocates,* Vol. 15, No. 1, April, 1992, p. 36.

Jenny thought the nightmare was finally over, but it is beginning again. The last babysitting job she had nearly killed her. It turned out that the person who had been responsible for the series of attacks on baby sitters was Mr. Hagen, her employer. At the end of *The Baby-sitter,* when he tried to kill Jenny, Mr. Hagen fell over the edge of a quarry to his death.

Jenny feels responsible for Mr. Hagen's death even though he was the one trying to kill her. Now she is reliving the nightmare and seeing a psychiatrist to help her overcome her traumatic experience. She decides to take another babysitting job, hoping that this new job will also help her deal with the past.

This time she is babysitting Eli Wexner, a ten year old genius who also happens to be a monster. One Friday night at the Wexner's, the phone rings. When Jenny answers it, she hears that all-too-familiar voice: "Hi, Babes. I'm back," Jenny's wild imagination takes off, and she is convinced that Mr. Hagen has returned from the dead. The nightmare has returned.

The Baby-sitter II is a fast-paced novel that whizzes the reader from scene to scene. However, the story is very choppy. This 166 page novel contains 24 chapters with only four having ten or more pages. Many of the scenes, particularly the ones where Jenny is having nightmares, contain short sentences. This detail does create an apprehensive mood, but is used too much. All three aspects combine to create a rough literary style.

Stine does succeed in weaving Jenny's nightmares into the story. It is easy to mistake fantasy for reality. Jenny's emotions during her nightmares are so real that it is easy to forget they are nightmares until Stine brings the reader back to reality. Aside from the choppiness, *The Baby-sitter II* is a fun novel. Readers will enjoy experiencing Jenny's nightmares and trying to discover who is haunting her.

📖 *THE GIRLFRIEND* (1991)

Joyce Hamilton

SOURCE: A review of *The Girlfriend,* in *Voice of Youth Advocates,* Vol. 15, No. 1, April, 1992, p. 36.

Seniors Scotty and Lora have been a couple since sixth grade. He is the star football quarterback and Homecoming King, and she is a cheerleader and the Homecoming Queen. They both do well in school and plan to attend Princeton University in the fall. Scotty's mother has raised Scotty and his younger brother alone, but Lora's family is wealthy and likes to be generous with Scotty. What could go wrong? Well, plenty does.

Lora is gone for a week, vacationing in Paris with her parents. After the football game Scotty plans to go right home instead of attending the school dance alone. However, in the school parking lot he discovers a girl trying to fix a flat tire on her bicycle, and gives her a lift home. Scotty and the girl, Shannon, have only one date before Lora gets home, but Shannon considers Scotty her boyfriend and threatens trouble if he doesn't continue dating her. Scotty's life becomes a nightmare as he tries to convince Shannon he doesn't care for her and keep Shannon's identity from Lora. Shannon does succeed in frightening Scotty by killing his pet and setting his car on fire, but of course, everything turns out fine in the end and Scotty and Lora live "happily ever after"!

This is a *Sweet Valley High*-type story with a bit of mystery thrown in. Although the characters are one dimensional, the readers will like Scotty and Lora, and hate Shannon. The end is predictable but there is enough action and suspense to keep the reader's attention. The book will be a hit with the younger teens. Buy multiple copies.

📖 *SILENT NIGHT* (1991)

Sylvia C. Mitchell

SOURCE: A review of *Silent Night,* in *Voice of Youth Advocates,* Vol. 15, No. 1, April, 1992, pp. 36-7.

Bitchy and witchy, Reva has almost anything money can buy because her dad owns the town's biggest store. After one mind game too many, someone seems to be giving her a dose of her own medicine. Unfortunately, it is impossible to guess who because practically everyone has a good reason to do her in. The real story that makes the reader care involves Pam, Reva's same-age, impoverished cousin. Pam is caught up in a plot to rob Reva's father's store—a plot that backfires.

Reva isn't very believable, but she is fun to hate and a necessary counterpoint for this somewhat frightful murder mystery, a *Fear Street Super Chiller.* If all series books were this good, I'd begin to drop my librarian's prejudices against them.

📖 *THE FIRE GAME* (1991)

Mary Jane Santos

SOURCE: A review of *The Fire Game,* in *Voice of Youth Advocates,* Vol. 15, No. 2, June, 1992, p. 102.

Don't play with matches! Every mother in the world has given this admonition to her children. But, maybe Gabe's mother forgot to tell him, or maybe he just likes playing with fire. When you're playing with fire, however, someone is bound to get burned.

Best friends Jill Franks, Andrea Hubbard, and newcomer Diane Hamilton are enjoying each other and their junior year of high school. While none of the girls has a steady boyfriend, Max Bogner and Nick Malone are part of their group, adding their weird sense of humor and fun-loving attitudes to those of the girls. Then Diane's longtime friend Gabe ("short for Gabriel, like the angel—but Gabe is more of a devil") moves to Shadyside, and he introduces the five teens to The Fire Game.

The dangerous games begin when Gabe dares Max to start a fire in a trash can at school. Max accepts the dare, and after starting a fire in the restroom, the school is closed and the six friends enjoy their self-arranged holiday. Only Diane, with an irrational fear of fire, seems to realize the danger of their games, but none of the group understands or heeds Diane's fearful pleas to stop playing with fire. Only after one of the fires kills a homeless man does Jill realize the danger. But who is setting the fires? And who can Jill trust to help her end this foolish "fire game"?

The Fire Game, a new addition to the *Fear Street series*, twists and turns through a mystery with six possible and plausible suspects. Even with its predictable red herrings and page-turning chapter endings, *The Fire Game* will satisfy fans of the series. Mother was right—don't play with matches!

📖 *LIGHTS OUT* (1991)

Mary Jane Santos

SOURCE: A review of *Lights Out,* in *Voice of Youth Advocates,* Vol. 15, No. 2, June, 1992, p. 102.

"Here I am at Camp Nightwing, just as I promised. The other counselors are already here . . . Everything looks cool so far. Don't worry about a thing, Chief. I'll make them pay. Everyone one of them. Before I'm through, everyone will be calling it 'Camp Nightmare.'"

When Holly Flynn's favorite uncle asks her to help him out by being a counselor at Camp Nightwing, his summer camp, Holly, fearful of all creepy crawlies, reluctantly agrees. Camp Nightwing is in financial trouble, and Holly is anxious to help in any way she can to try to save her uncle's camp. But from the very first day that Holly arrives at camp, strange and frightening acts of vandalism begin happening. And after each, a red feather is left behind—the signature of the culprit.

Holly tries to warn her uncle that someone is sabotaging his camp, but he is too busy to listen to her or to take her seriously. When one of the counselors is found dead, the police label the death a terrible accident; but after finding a red feather at the scene, Holly's intuition compels her to find the person responsible. But with one counselor already dead, has Holly bitten off more than she can chew?

Lights Out follows the formula of other novels in the *Fear Street* series, with cliffhanging chapter endings and red herrings along the way. Fans of the series will enjoy this story, although the dialogue and actions of the teenage characters are somewhat contrived.

📖 *THE KNIFE* (1992)

Stephen M. Richmond

SOURCE: A review of *The Knife,* in *Voice of Youth Advocates,* Vol. 15, No. 2, June, 1992, p. 115.

Part of an on-going series set in and around the woefully wicked Fear Street, this new title, like its weird sisters, will be much sought by the teens. Laurie is spending her summer working as a volunteer at the Shadyside Hospital. After discovering the corpse of a particularly nasty nurse with a surgical knife in its throat in the new wing construction at the hospital, Laurie's curiosity, spurned by some considerable righteousness, involves her in much mayhem and dirty deeds. Our heroine, of course, prevails and gets the guy, too.

This wonderful series is not Proust or Joyce nor does it pretend to be. The books are engrossing reads. Author Stine provided me with a couple oral-manicuring hours and will certainly enthrall the future fans of Stephen King and Clive Barker.

📖 *THE PROM QUEEN* (1992)

June M. Cocklin

SOURCE: A review of *The Prom Queen,* in *Voice of Youth Advocates,* Vol. 15, No. 3, August, 1992, p. 180.

Rachael, Dawn, Simone, Elana, and Lizzy are Prom Queen nominees in Shadyside. However, there is one small problem—the nominees are being murdered.

Stine is an excellent storyteller of horror tales. The way he uses dialogue makes it hard for the reader to be passive. Before long the reader's heart is pounding right along with the action of the story. Stine makes the reader care what is going to happen to the character. When he describes a cold, dark, rainy night, and the reader thinks the character has just run over a body, the reader feels the emotional chaos that would be generated in a situation like this.

The protagonist—Lizzy—is an intelligent, caring person who knows right from wrong, and is not willing to become a victim. The relationship among the girls is filled with competition, betrayal, and a fatal attraction that almost kills them all.

The action in this book is fast paced enough to keep a reluctant reader reading. The more experienced reader will enjoy the plot and the character development.

📖 *GOODNIGHT KISS* (1992)

Mary Arnold

SOURCE: A review of *Goodnight Kiss,* in *Voice of Youth Advocates,* Vol. 15, No. 5, December, 1992, p. 296.

It's a typical summer at the beach for Shadyside teens April, her boyfriend Matt, and Matt's slightly nerdy friend, Todd. But there are dark shadows on the sun this summer—a plague of bats that Matt slowly realizes are a supernatural threat for his two friends. Can it be that the two newcomers, Jessica and Gabri, are more than glamorous and mysterious—can they be deadly? Can Matt uncover their secret before one of them wins the wager that will make Todd, or April, or both, one of the army of Eternal Ones?

The plot consists of the ups and downs of the teen vampires as they undermine one another's attempts to make a human fall in love with them before they feed. It's a fairly typical *Fear Street* entry that manages to hit most of the vampire lore and cliches (bats, garlic, sunlight) without many original twists. It mildly flirts with the sexual imagery of vampirism while maintaining the attitude of unconcern for human victims except as food or the source of amusement for a pair of superficial, self-centered creatures. There have been many recent vampire stories for teens (*Silver Kiss* by Annette Klause, *Vampires* edited by Jane Yolen) that provide depth and characterization for these eternally interesting creatures, but for avid *Fear Street* fans, this will probably prove an adequate fix.

📖 *CHEERLEADERS: THE FIRST EVIL* (1992)

Kevin J. Kenny

SOURCE: A review of *Cheerleaders: The First Evil,* in *Voice of Youth Advocates,* Vol. 15, No. 6, February, 1993, p. 360.

Newly arrived in Shadyside, 17 year old Bobbi Corcoran and her year-younger sister, Corky, hope that their all-state cheerleading skills will ensure places on the squad and ease them into the mainstream at Shadyside High. While the girls' talents quickly land them spots among the cheerleaders, an opening game bus crash at the cemetery on Fear Street leaves squad captain Jennifer Daly paralyzed and the girls stunned. Unfortunately, the inexplicable accident is only a precursor to progressively more bizarre and grimmer occurrences, murder, and, ultimately, a grieving sister's struggle with evil personified.

This is a relentlessly inane effort that manages to be both ineffective and offensive. A vapid premise yields a predictably plodding plot and Stine's cheerleaders, including

his protagonists, seldom rise above the worst-case stereotypes which come to mind. Corky is envious of Bobbi's full figure. Kimmy envies both Corcoran girls and their ". . . lively green eyes, creamy, pale skin, and high cheekbones like models." All the girls admire Jennifer, who just happens to look like Julia Roberts. It continues ad nauseum. On the evolutionary ladder of YA literature, place this one step above the pick-a-plots.

Regrettably, slick cover art, simplicity of style, and a pandering plot will conspire to make Stine's work at least a modest success among less discriminating, less able, or those simply seeking to avoid challenge. For the less insipid, Lois Duncan's *Daughter's of Eve* or just about anything from Stephen King would be a quantum leap forward.

📖 *CHEERLEADERS: THE SECOND EVIL* (1992)

Sherri F. Ginsberg

SOURCE: A review of *Cheerleaders: the Second Evil,* in *Kliatt Young Adult Paperback Book Guide,* Vol. 27, No. 1, January, 1993, p. 13.

Slip into Stine's world, where you suspend belief and reality and the bizarre becomes normal. Corky Corcoran has recently lost her sister in a surreal ritual and cannot focus on her present situation. She is obsessed with her sister's grave and visits it frequently, swearing that her sister rises from the grave. Corky's life has become overfilled with sadness and it takes persistent encouragement from her cheerleader friends to get Corky back on the squad and leading a normal life again.

Events transpire which are frightening and weird simultaneously. A stranger is seen dancing on the graves, a young man is following Corky, and her friend Debbie becomes interested in the occult. A pervasive evil spirit is lurking. Corky cannot get rid of the terrifying screaming in her head, a noise only she can hear. More students wind up dead. Just when we think there is a end to all the evil, a note appears and Stine will write another book. This one is wonderfully eerie and a perfect escape from an overload of school work.

Caroline S. McKinney

SOURCE: A review of *Cheerleaders: The Second Evil,* in *Voice of Youth Advocates,* Vol. 15, No. 6, February, 1993, p. 360.

The second in the *Cheerleader* series continues the battle of Corky Corcoran and the Shadyside High cheerleaders against an evil force that has already taken the lives of several friends and relatives. Corky lost her sister in a mysterious accident, and she finds that she is unable to accept the loss. During a visit to her sister's grave she is pursued by a stranger, and she sees visions of corpses arising from graves. During cheerleading practice she hears screams, and in the biology lab a skeleton hand tries to strangle her. Finally, her boyfriend is killed and his hand is severed by a saw. Corky and her friends decide to solve the mystery of the evil power. They confront Sarah Beth Plummer, the relative of Sarah Fear, who was supposed to be cursed. Before the story ends, Corky has taken a fall during cheerleading practice, broken her arm, and realized that Sarah Beth Plummer is in some way responsible for the evil. At home, as Corky prepares to take a bath, one of her friends attempts to attack her. Corky fights and is able to force the evil spirit out of her friend, but the last pages tell us that the evil is not gone. Corky receives a letter which says, "It Can't Be Drowned." Therefore, the reader needs to read the next in the series, *The Third Evil.*

Young teens who like horror series books such as *The Power* series by Jesse Harris or Caroline Cooney's *Trilogy* will find this story creates the usual suspense, with chapter endings having events which lead the reader right into the next one. However, these formula stories are very predictable and require very little thought on the part of the reader.

📖 CHEERLEADERS: THE THIRD EVIL (1992)

Patrick S. Jones

SOURCE: A review of *Cheerleaders: the Third Evil,* in *Kliatt Young Adult Paperback Book Guide,* Vol. 27, No. 1, January, 1993, p. 13.

The Stine scare machine cranks out another winner! All of his best writing stunts are here: cliff-hanging chapters, gross-outs involving the creepy and crawly, red herring gross-outs like the old fake-severed-head-in-the-bed trick, and that particular Stine genius that makes dialogue seem believable even when the conversation is patently absurd. This is the third volume in his new *Cheerleader* subseries and it really cooks. The "evil spirit" in Kimmy's body from the last book returns to wreak more havoc as the Shadyside High cheerleading squad spends time at cheerleading camp. There the girls from Shadyside meet up with a cheerleader so good she's bad, plus a Ms. Perfect in their own ranks. There is plenty of cheerleading lingo mixed in with the deadly pranks. The body count here is pretty low for a Stine book and the ending is a bit of a cheat, but that is probably because he can't keep killing off these characters if more *Cheerleader* books are planned. With the certain, and deserved, success of this title, the fourth evil will certainly be unleashed soon.

Deborah Earl

SOURCE: A review of *Cheerleaders: The Third Evil,* in *Voice of Youth Advocates,* Vol. 16, No. 2, June, 1993, pp. 105-06.

Corky, one of six Shadyside High cheerleaders, has had a horrible life lately. At the beginning of the school year, she and her sister Bobbi had been the most talented cheerleaders on the squad. But that was before an ancient evil spirit inhabited two of the cheerleaders: first Jennifer, then Kimmy. The spirit was responsible for the deaths of Bobbi, Jennifer, and Corky's boyfriend, Chip. Now Corky is trying to put her life back together and prepare for cheerleader's camp, but strange things are beginning to happen again. Has the evil spirit returned? And if it has, will it be necessary for Corky to die to finally stop it?

📖 THE BEST FRIEND (1992)

Sherri F. Ginsberg

SOURCE: A review of *The Best Friend,* in *Kliatt Young Adult Paperback Book Guide,* Vol. 27, No. 2, March, 1993, p. 10.

Becka has been living a normal teenage life; school, friends, unsavory boyfriends, fighting with parents. All is okay until Honey Perkins bursts into her room and claims Becka was her best friend in 4th grade and then proceeds to recall all those special moments that they spent together. Becka is incredulous over this unexpected visitor and is frantically searching her memory for a recollection of this person.

Honey Perkins is your worst nightmare, the most obnoxious parasite you could imagine. She steals Becka's favorite possessions and has the audacity to claim Becka gave them to her willingly. Honey imitates Becka and ingratiates herself with Becka's parents, and they naturally think Becka is overreacting to Honey's friendliness. Honey's cloying manner is driving Becka insane.

This is not one of Stine's best. It is a detour from his usually frightening, unconventional genre. The events are a little too predictable and nothing truly bizarre occurs. For diehard Stine fans only.

Barbara Jo McKee

SOURCE: A review of *The Best Friend,* in *Voice of Youth Advocates,* Vol. 16, No. 1, April, 1993, p. 47.

Becka Norwood's life is that of a typical teenager: a boyfriend she is breaking up with, two girlfriends, and a set of overprotective parents. Suddenly a girl named Honey appears and seems to think she was once Becka's best friend in fourth grade and has decided to resume that role. As she mirrors Becka physically as well as follows her everywhere, Becka feels she is going crazy. Accidents begin to happen to everyone Becka is close to and Honey wraps her closer in her web. As Becka moves toward the breaking point, a final accident makes her, Honey's best friend forever. Scary and engrossing, this page turner is another winner for Stine.

Russ Merrin

SOURCE: A review of *The Best Friend,* in *Magpies,* Vol. 8, No. 4, September, 1993, p. 32.

Becka Norwood is a friendly, well-adjusted teenager living a normal lifestyle until she is abruptly confronted by her childhood "best friend" Honey Perkins. Whereas Becka can barely remember her, and cares nothing about her. Honey is obsessed with becoming Becka's best friend, and works toward destroying Becka's former lifestyle to create the fantasy of her own new life with Becka. When genuine friends begin to have unexplained "accidents" Becka begins to suspect Honey's duplicity, but is confused by her apparently sincere denials.

R. L. Stine knows most of the strategies to keep readers turning pages. With this latest paperback, he successfully pursues the formula once again. Chapters are short and the chapter endings are teasing enough to lead the reader onwards. The plot is familiar. An obsessive "friend" creates a stifling, destructive relationship and thereby psychologically bludgeons the new found partner into a state of exhausted submission. It is obvious to the reader that Honey is extremely disturbed. However, not surprisingly, nobody takes Becka—or her feelings—seriously. Although characterisation is credible enough, the motivation and responses of the characters themselves seem contrived. If they reacted normally, the story would stop dead in its tracks.

As the cliche goes, the plot of this novel reads like a B-grade movie—or movie serial—but that won't stop upper primary and lower secondary readers from enjoying it. The teen romance is chaste but believable.

BEACH HOUSE (1992)

June Muldner

SOURCE: A review of *Beach House,* in *Voice of Youth Advocates,* Vol. 16, No. 1, April, 1993, p. 47.

When four teenagers in the summer of 1956 play a prank on a new kid at the beach, he responds with murder, and is not caught. Thirty-plus years later, on the same beach, a similar chain of events begins to unfold. The two incidents are related, and connected by the presence of an abandoned beach house with a mysterious secret, a closet built on a time warp that allows travelers to move back and forth between the present and 1956. If you buy the premise, this is a fast, albeit very light read, sure to be a hit for those long summer afternoons (on the beach?).

HIT AND RUN (1992)

Merlyn Miller

SOURCE: A review of *Hit and Run,* in *Voice of Youth Advocates,* Vol. 16, No. 1, April, 1993, p. 30.

Stine's latest thriller is about four teens who accidentally hit a man one night while practicing for their driver's test. When they realize the man is dead, their fear is heightened by the fact they were driving without licenses in a car they had no permission to borrow. They choose to leave the dead man at the side of the road and keep the event a secret. Acting natural, however, becomes impossible when they begin to receive messages from the dead man, messages that promise revenge. The threats become reality when one of the foursome becomes a hit and run victim and is hospitalized. In the end it is revealed the man the four thought they killed was dead before they hit him and that it was all a very elaborate practical joke by one "friend" against the other three.

Thrillers are a popular genre but this one is disappointing. The book has great promise at first with a story that starts out in the real world with a real situation. Eddie Katz nicknamed Scaredy Katz is a teen the reader can sympathize with because he is the victim of some very cruel practical jokes by other teens who profess to be his "Friends." The weirdness creeps in gradually but too predictably to make the story work. It lacks suspense because it is so transparent right from the beginning that it is Eddie who has plotted this morbid revenge on his friends using a corpse from the morgue.

Pick up *The Stalker* by Joan Lowery Nixon or *Spellbound* by Christopher Pike. Don't buy this one.

A. R. Williams

SOURCE: A review of *Hit and Run,* in *The Junior Bookshelf,* Vol. 57, No. 4, August, 1993, p. 159.

Eddie Katz is a teenager who readily falls for any kind of practical joke aimed at ridiculing him and exposing him to humiliation. The worm turns. Eddie organizes an elaborate practical joke of his own showing neither fear nor favour towards his erstwhile 'friends'. Some of the consequences are anything but comical and one or two very serious indeed. His friends are baffled as the author intensifies the mystery behind minatory messages and motor mayhem and unexplained absences. The girl, Cassie, works it out after suspecting her two companions in turn. Sound plotting here although Mr. Stine is not naïve enough to think this is enough. Characters and domestic relationships are stimulating as well and the rancour which the earlier foolery engenders is justifiably established. Not really very nice, but crafted—yes. In view of ongoing publicity and concern over the effects of bullying and persecution perhaps it is a timely reminder that even in fun people *can* be pushed too far?

BROKEN HEARTS (1993)

Julie A. Woods

SOURCE: A review of *Broken Hearts,* in *Kliatt Young*

Adult Paperback Book Guide, Vol. 27, No. 2, March, 1993, p. 10.

Valentine's Day is for killers—not for lovers—in Stine's new Fear Street super chiller. Someone in town is driven to madness when lovely Rachael McClain is seriously injured in an unfortunate horseback riding accident. People in Rachael's life begin receiving chilling, threatening Valentine's messages and blood red—not rose red—is the color of the day. A compelling mystery which offers an effective portrayal of teen rivalries.

Mary Jane Santos

SOURCE: A review of *Broken Hearts,* in *Voice of Youth Advocates,* Vol. 16, No. 2, June, 1993, p. 105.

"Violets are blue / Roses are red. / On Valentine's Day / Josie will be dead." So reads the Valentine that Josie McClain receives in the mail. But who would want to kill Josie? And why?

Broken Hearts follows the author's popular and successful formula for suspense. Fear Street residents Rachel and Josie (sixteen-year-old twins) and their little sister Erica have their lives completely changed when Rachel suffers irreversible brain damage as the result of an accident when all three plus Josie's best friend Melissa are horseback riding. No one is really to blame for the accident and Josie, Erica, and Melissa try to continue their lives.

But resentment among the three girls grows as Erica feels she is always left home alone to care for Rachel and that Josie takes no responsibility at all. What should have been an exciting year in Erica's life, her freshman year in high school, is turning into a disaster because she can't participate in any activities. Josie, on the other hand, is popular and busy, almost too busy, as she avoids her twin sister whenever possible. The relationship between Josie and Melissa is very strained because Melissa feels that Josie secretly blames her for Rachel's accident. And then Josie begins to receive threatening Valentines.

The list of suspects (and the anti-Josie club) grows to include Luke, Rachel's boyfriend, who has remained totally devoted to Rachel and resents Josie's attitude toward her sister; Steve, who thinks the threats are merely a sick joke (could he be sending them to get Josie's attention?); Dave, Melissa's boyfriend, who was dumped by Josie; and Jenkman, who has a crush on the ignoring Josie.

Then Josie's body is discovered on Valentine's Day. Erica, too upset to attend Josie's funeral, is stabbed in the side during the funeral, and Dave is arrested for the crimes. He is sent away to a psychiatric hospital, and Erica and Melissa try to put everything behind them.

And then, in February, one year later, Melissa receives a Valentine: "Roses are red, Violets are blue, On Valentine's Day You'll be dead too." With Dave locked securely away, who could be threatening Melissa? And why?

Using his successful technique of cliffhanger chapter endings and plenty of red herrings, Stine has created another suspenseful novel that his fans will devour. With a sufficiently spooky cover, expect a lot of demand for this one.

THE HITCHHIKER (1993)

Judy Druse

SOURCE: "Terror Hitches a Ride," in *Voice of Youth Advocates,* Vol. 16, No. 1, April, 1993, p. 20.

If you like to read suspense with twists, turns, and surprises, try *The Hitchhiker* by R. L. Stine.

"Don't pick up hitchhikers. It can be dangerous. You never know what kind of a crazy person you might offer a ride." You have probably heard similar warnings from your parents. Picking up hitchhikers is one of those activities parents warn teenagers against that they probably do anyway, at least once. What could happen, right? You might even meet a great-looking guy.

Driving back to Cleveland, Ohio, after spring break in Fort Lauderdale, Florida, Christina Jenkins and Terri Martin pick up a hitchhiker, seventeen-year-old James Dark. James is powerfully built for seventeen, muscular, with big shoulders and a broad, football player neck. He has short blond hair, buzzed close to the sides, a handsome face, serious, seldom smiling, and olive-green eyes. Before long, Christina and Terri learn that James also has a violent temper, one that often, and quickly, flies out of control. In fact, as they travel across Florida with James, they come to realize that everything about him is frightening. His size, his attitude, and, especially, his temper. James's presence means bad luck and trouble—and even death.

Sherri Forgash Ginsberg

SOURCE: A review of *The Hitchhiker,* in *Kliatt Young Adult Paperback Book Guide,* Vol. 27, No. 3, May, 1993, p. 11.

Terri and Christina are driving home after a fun-in-the-sun vacation. While still in Florida they decide to pick up a really cute hitchhiker, James, who is getting out of Key West by using his thumb. He has many problems he wants to leave behind and he really does not care where he is going as long as it is North. The two females have secrets of their own. Is the hitchhiker dangerous or is he in danger?

Stine is masterful at twists and turns in this escapist thriller fiction. It's the perfect combination of teenagers with sinister secrets and grown-up problems that seem insurmountable but strengthen them in their courage to survive. It would not be a bit surprising if this book became a movie.

THE BETRAYAL; THE SECRET (1993)

Patrick S. Jones

SOURCE: A review of *The Betrayal,* in *Kliatt Young Adult Paperback Book Guide,* Vol. 27, No. 6, November, 1993, p. 11.

The folks at Archway don't miss a trick. Not content to sell just monthly *Fear Street* books and the occasional "Super Chillers," Archway and Stine have found another way to make the cash register ring. Like the earlier *Cheerleaders* sub-series, Stine interrupts his normally scheduled programming for a historical mini-series. [*The Betrayal*] is the first (at least one more is promised) in a series that serves as a prequel to the current *Fear Street* books. Although the book "begins" in 1900, it flashes back, in what should come as no big surprise, to 1692 in Salem, Massachusetts. It's the usual Stine magic: Chapter One ends with a character who "feels strong hands grab her from behind" and the scream of "The Evil One!" The rest of the book concerns feuding families (the Fiers and the Goodes), witchcraft, and the usual plot twists and turns. It will be interesting to see how readers react to the heavy supernatural/witch plot elements. It will also be interesting to see how Stine and other writers in this genre react to the article in the August 2, 1993 *Time* magazine which took teen thrillers to task. The larger question is will teachers accept this for their "read a historical fiction assignment" instead of *Witch of Blackbird Pond?*

Margaret Mary Ptacek

SOURCE: A review of *Secret,* in *Voice of Youth Advocates,* Vol. 17, No. 1, April, 1994, p. 41.

Stine has created a new trilogy known as *The Fear Street Saga.* The first two volumes are **The Betrayal** (1) and **The Secret** (2). The story begins in Massachusetts in 1692. A poor farmer's daughter named Susannah Goode has fallen in love with Edward Fier, the son of the town magistrate and the wealthiest man in town. Edward wants to marry Susannah, but his father has arranged a marriage for Edward with the daughter of a wealthy merchant. To prevent his son from marrying Susannah, Benjamin Fier declares that Susannah and her mother are witches. Her father William Goode begs Benjamin's brother Matthew to reason with Benjamin and release his family. Matthew agrees to do so for a price. William gives Matthew all of his savings, but his family is burned at the stake anyway. William curses the Fiers and plans to destroy them. The trilogy plays the theme of revenge back and forth through both families' history. Susannah and her mother were both innocent of witchcraft but William Goode secretly practiced it. Matthew and Benjamin Fier also delved in witchcraft.

Stine is extremely popular with middle school and junior high students. They are always asking for his books. I'm sure that this trilogy will be popular also. . . . These will sell easily and may be the only books reluctant readers will read.

THE CHEATER (1993)

Kristina Lindsay

SOURCE: A review of *The Cheater,* in *Magpies,* Vol. 8, No. 5, November, 1993, p. 35.

Yet another title from R. L. Stine in his Fear Street series. **The Cheater** is based on an affluent American high school senior Carter Phillips, who finds herself a victim of blackmail by a fellow student. Carter is under enormous parental pressure to attend Princeton and needs to do well in her math achievement exam. She allows Adam Messner, a young man from the wrong side of the tracks, to take the test for her in exchange for one date. Of course Adam takes full advantage of the situation and things start to go horribly wrong for Carter.

A very average thriller for teenagers but with R. L. Stine's appeal it will be likely to attract a large readership.

HALLOWEEN NIGHT (1993)

Marlyene E. Schwartz

SOURCE: A review of *Halloween Night,* in *Kliatt Young Adult Paperback Book Guide,* Vol. 28, No. 1, January, 1994, p. 13.

This is an interesting addition to the work of the popular horror writer. Again, Stine has written about ordinary teenagers in terrifying situations. A cousin whose parents are divorcing, an annoying younger brother, understanding friends, and Halloween are the ingredients in this horror story written for young people. This will be very popular with the middle school set.

SUNBURN (1993)

Mary Lee Tiernan

SOURCE: A review of *Sunburn,* in *Voice of Youth Advocates,* Vol. 16, No. 6, February, 1994, pp. 386-87.

As usual in books by Stine, teens are placed in a situation without any authoritative adult figure. In this case, Claudia, Joy, and Sophie travel to Marla's remote seaside mansion for a reunion. Hours after their arrival, Claudia awakens to find herself buried in the sand, her face badly sunburned, with the rising tide splashing in her face. Rescued by a mysterious young man, she finds her friends who apologize for the "accident" of leaving her alone on the beach. Shortly thereafter, more accidents happen, and Claudia, Joy, and Sophie wonder if the real intention behind their invitations is an attempt by Marla to avenge the death of her sister Alison. Alison died the summer before while at camp, and as the terror grows, Claudia admits to herself that they were not quite as innocent as her memory wants her to believe. Eventually, they discover Marla's body, and "Marla" turns out to be Alison who had survived her fall into a chasm and returned to punish the girls for leaving her alone in a dangerous situation. The book is pure plot, but very suspenseful and a "quick" read. The kids will love it.

📖 *THE BABY-SITTER III* (1993)

Dorothy M. Broderick

SOURCE: A review of *The Babysitter III,* in *Voice of Youth Advocates,* Vol. 17, No. 1, April, 1994, pp. 40-1.

Jenny Jeffers is haunted by her close encounter with Mr. Hagen (first met in **Babysitter**), the deranged killer of babysitters in revenge for the death of his child. Mr. Hagen is dead, but for Jenny he appears in busy shopping malls, in her dreams, and every shadow hides his presence. In the hope of improving her mental health she is sent off to spend the summer vacation with her cousin Debra, a self-centered teen who flits from boyfriends the way a bee flits between flowers. The change of scenery does not help. Not only do the nightmares not go away, but soon Debra is receiving telephone calls at her babysitting job: *"I'm alive. I'm back. Company's coming, Babes."* Debra's terror is only slightly less than Jenny's.

Stine ends each chapter with a "cliffhanger" pitch that makes it impossible to not turn the page. The only problem this may pose is that if someone picks it up first, the suspense of reading the two earlier volumes will be lost, making it a series that should be read in order of publication. Stine is very good at what he does and his many readers will devour this one.

📖 *THE DARE* (1994)

Samantha Hunt

SOURCE: A review of *Fear Street: The Dare,* in *Voice of Youth Advocates,* Vol. 17, No. 1, April, 1994, p. 41.

Johanna Wise figures the neighbors would describe her as a quiet, mousy girl. Not at all the kind of person they'd expect to be a murderer. In the latest addition [to] Stine's perennially popular *Fear Street* series, a poor, unpopular teen allows herself to be manipulated by the rich in-crowd to gain acceptance. The rich kids feel they're being singled out for unfair treatment by a teacher; why, he won't even let Dennis Arthur make up his history midterm when he comes back from his vacation in the Bahamas! Doesn't Mr. Northwood realize that a failing grade could cost Dennis his place on the track team, his assured state all-star spot, his chance at the Olympics? It makes Dennis want to kill him, and when Johanna agrees that someone should, she suddenly finds herself the object of Dennis's romantic interest. Soon she's willing to do *anything* for him.

Stine has exciting ideas, and it takes a certain talent to convey them as well as he does depending almost entirely on dialogue, and the occasional three to five sentence descriptive paragraph. Reading his books is a lot like eating potato chips; you can go through one right after the other. (Rather like certain romance and mystery series, beloved by adults of my acquaintance, the individual volumes of which are pretty much interchangeable.) We aren't talking about classic literature here, but they're great for a case of the adolescent series munchies. And, if any of your YAs mention that they particularly liked this one, quick, hand 'em a copy of Lois Duncan's *Killing Mr. Griffin.* YA does not live by potato chips alone.

Additional coverage of Stine's life and career is contained in the following sources published by Gale Research: *Contemporary Authors New Revision Series,* Vol. 22; and *Something about the Author,* Vols. 31, 76.

Rosemary Sutcliff

1920-1992

English author of fiction, nonfiction, and picture books; reteller.

Major works include *The Eagle of the Ninth* (1954), *Warrior Scarlet* (1958), *The Lantern Bearers* (1959), *The Mark of the Horse Lord* (1965), *Blood Feud* (1976), *The Road to Camlann: The Death of King Arthur* (1981), *The Shining Company* (1990).

Major works about the author include *Rosemary Sutcliff* (1962) by Margaret Meek and *Blue Remembered Hills: A Recollection* (1983) by Rosemary Sutcliff.

INTRODUCTION

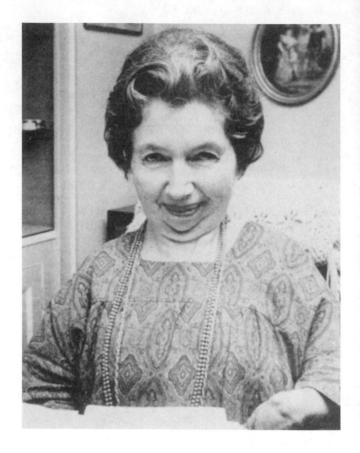

Generally regarded as the foremost contemporary writer of historical fiction for young people, Sutcliff is credited with shaping the direction of the genre and setting its literary standards. The prolific author of works for readers from the early grades through high school, she is best known for the demanding yet exciting tales she directs to a young adult audience. Taken as a whole, these books chronicle the story of Britain, representing its history from the Bronze Age through the Roman Occupation and Norman Conquest. Many of Sutcliff's works center on the struggle between the native Celts and invading Saxons, and several of her most prominent books feature Roman protagonists who become loyal to their adopted land. In rendering her nationalistic chronicles, which stress the continuity of history, Sutcliff uses both her imagination and extensive research to describe the making of a people. Acknowledged for addressing archetypal themes not often considered by writers of historical fiction for the young—for example, the battle between light and dark, the importance of freedom, the value of friendship and loyalty, courage and the nature of heroism, the futility of war, and the need for spiritual fulfillment—Sutcliff underscores her works with the belief that both civilization and humanity are worth saving, even in the face of extreme danger. Against the backdrop of epic events and large themes, she describes the individual rites of passage of her protagonists, young men who are often disabled, orphaned, or outcast. These characters rise above the tensions and transitions of their times as well as personal rejection as they face arduous tests of their fidelity, valor, and honor. Ultimately, the boys define themselves through their choices, overcoming physical or emotional limitations to establish themselves as important members of their communities.

Calling herself an author "of the minstrel kind," Sutcliff is celebrated as a storyteller of the highest order. She is considered a genius for recreating history with particular insight and empathy, bringing time and place to life as if she were an eyewitness. Marcus Crouch writes: "[Sutcliff] feels the past through her nerves. No other writer for children of any age or country gives so vivid an impression of just how it felt to live in Britain after the departure of the Legions or under the weight of the conquering Normans." Neil Philip notes that "Sutcliff involves the reader in the past—not just for the duration of the book, but for ever." Praised for her understanding of both ancient peoples and children with disabilities, Sutcliff is lauded for humanizing history for young readers by concentrating on feelings as well as facts. She is often commended for the authenticity, intelligence, and depth of her books as well as for her realistic depiction of battle scenes and familiarity with both military tactics and religious ceremonies. Although her works include violence, Sutcliff is acknowledged for not sensationalizing the bloody encounters and deaths she depicts, and her stories are often noted for their warmth as well as for reflecting the author's eye for beauty and her sense of humor. "A born writer," according to Frank Eyre, Sutcliff is often commended as a literary stylist. Her prose, which reflects a vivid use of simile and metaphor, is considered detailed, powerful, eloquent, and appropriate to her subjects. Refusing, in her words, to "rob children of the beckoning splendor of words they do not yet understand," Sutcliff uses a rich palette of language in her books, a factor considered essential to the pictorial quality of her writing. In addition, she created her own style of dialogue, "avoiding," as she says, "Gadzookery and modern colloquialism" in favor of a moderately archaic, refined version of present-day speech which retains the flavor of the original sources.

Sutcliff is often acknowledged for creating exemplary introductions to history for her audience, works that involve their readers emotionally while presenting both historical perspectives and important virtues. Writing her books to make heroic readers out of the young, she is considered "the least didactic of authors" by Margery Fisher, and Eileen Colwell adds that after reading Sutcliff's books, "children will remember their own shining hours with a sharpened perception of joy and beauty." While recognizing the weighty themes and elaborate language of her exacting books, most critics maintain that Sutcliff's fiction enthralls young readers through rousing battle scenes, compelling trials of physical and moral courage, and passionate friendships and romances. Although occasional reviewers note that her works are too complex for preteen and young adult readers and focus on strong male protagonists at the expense of female characters, most commentators insist that Sutcliff found an original voice, at once modulated and profound, to tell stories that transcend limitations of history and period, addressing timeless themes in a compelling manner. "To read Rosemary Sutcliff," writes Margaret Meek, "is to discover what reading is good for," and Ann Evans adds that "Rosemary Sutcliff's name will be remembered and revered long after others have been forgotten."

Biographical Information

Born in Surrey, Sutcliff contracted Still's Disease, a debilitating rheumatoid arthritis, at the age of two. An only child, she was isolated from other children for long periods of time due to her illness, often staying in hospitals and nursing homes and suffering painful treatments. Sutcliff credits her mother, Nessie, as the major youthful influence on her writing. Nessie entertained her daughter by reading aloud, concentrating on books that she herself enjoyed, such as Edward Bulwer-Lytton's *The Last Days of Pompeii*, the works of Charles Dickens, and the myths and legends of Greece and Rome as well as those from Celtic and Norse sources. She also read from children's literature by such authors as Beatrix Potter, A. A. Milne, Kenneth Grahame, Hans Christian Andersen, and Robert Louis Stevenson. The works of Rudyard Kipling were special favorites, most significantly *Puck of Pook's Hill*, "whose three magnificent stories of Roman Britain," Sutcliff later wrote, "were the beginning of my own passion for the subject and resulted in the fulness of time in *The Eagle of the Ninth*." Sutcliff's father George, an officer in the Royal Navy, was sent abroad for extended periods during her childhood, regaling her with tales of exotic places when he returned. His absence led Sutcliff and her mother to stay with relatives in the South Downs, where she began to develop her love for the country. On one visit, she discovered a farm with the remains of a Norman gatehouse, of which she said, "I loved with a firsthand love that was all my own."

At the age of five, Sutcliff began working with chalks and found that she had definite artistic talent. In her first school, an establishment for the children of servicemen, she learned to read from the fairy tales of the Brothers Grimm, recited Macaulay's *Lays of Ancient Rome*, and began, as she wrote, "to fight the non-handicapped world on equal terms." Alternating between school and the hospital, she had an experience at twelve that would greatly influence her writing: made a nurse's favorite after recovering from an operation, she was snubbed by the other children in her ward. "I have not forgotten," she wrote, "what it feels like to be the stranger whom the pack turns on." Sutcliff went to Bideford School of Art at fourteen; after finishing her course, she became a professional painter of miniatures. Although she was quite successful and was a member of the Royal Society of Miniature Painters, she felt cramped by working on such a small scale and turned her creative energies to writing. She submitted a collection of Celtic and Saxon legends based on those her mother had told her to the Oxford University Press, who asked her to write a book for them about Robin Hood; this collection, *The Chronicles of Robin Hood* (1950), became Sutcliff's first published work. Her next three titles—*The Queen Elizabeth Story* (1950), *The Armourer's House* (1951), and *Brother Dusty-Feet* (1952)—are acknowledged as transitional works: stories for younger children set in the Tudor Period, they are considered more sentimental and less vigorous in style than her later books, but are noted for the keen sense of period and affection for the English countryside that are among Sutcliff's hallmarks.

Major Works

With the publication of *Simon* (1953), Sutcliff's reputation began to solidify. A departure from her works set in the Tudor period, the story is set in the English Civil War and revolves around two friends who fight on opposite sides; it was praised for its representation of the Puritan viewpoint as well as the Cavalier, an aspect few writers had considered before Sutcliff. Her next novel, *The Eagle of the Ninth*, is usually considered her first mature work. Prompted by Sutcliff's invention of a character to keep her company before a serious operation, the story focuses on the young centurion Marcus Aquila, who risks his life to find his father and the lost standard of the missing Ninth Legion, for which his father is First Cohort. Through his quest, Marcus, whose military career has been destroyed by a leg wound, learns to accept both his lameness and the fact that he is unable to redeem his father's legion. Using the device of a dolphin signet ring to link her characters, Sutcliff continues the tale of Marcus Aquila and his descendants in *The Silver Branch* (1957) and *The Lantern Bearers*. The latter work, a Carnegie Medal winner, is set at the beginning of the Dark Ages, when the last of the Romans were leaving Britain. A small band of Roman Britons under Ambrosius, the son of Constantine, become lantern bearers, attempting to carry the light of civilization into an uncertain future. Sutcliff published her novels about the Aquila family in an omnibus volume, *Three Legions* (1980); twenty years after the publication of *The Eagle of the Ninth*, she wrote *Frontier Wolf* (1980), the final volume in the story of the Aquilas. Set in the fourth century, the novel describes how Alexios, a centurion court-martialed for making a wrong decision, proves himself as the commander of the Frontier Wolves, a band of native British warriors. *Warrior Scarlet* is one of Sutcliff's most popular works: recreating the lives of Bronze Age tribesmen on the Sussex Downs, the story outlines how Drem, a boy with a crippled arm, conquers his fears and wins the coveted Warrior Scarlet, a cloth woven by his tribe when a young man kills his first wolf. Several critics cite *The Mark of the Horse Lord* as Sutcliff's masterpiece. Phaedrus, a gladiator who agrees to impersonate the Lord of the Gaelic Horse People, ultimately embraces the role to the point of sacrificing his life for his tribe; the stark, tragic ending of the book exemplifies Sutcliff's conviction that all elements of a story should be told.

Next to her stories about Roman Britain, Sutcliff is perhaps best known as the creator of a trilogy based on Arthurian legends: *The Light Behind the Forest: The Quest for the Holy Grail* (1979), *The Sword and the Circle: King Arthur and the Knights of the Round Table* (1981), and *The Road to Camlann: The Death of King Arthur*. In these works, Sutcliff outlines the story of the brotherhood of knights from its conception through the passing of Arthur; Mary Sachar notes, "Not since Tennyson has there been such a worthy, deeply moving retelling of the Arthurian tales." Sutcliff is also the author of well-received retellings of the stories of such figures as Beowulf, Finn MacCool, and Tristan and Iseult. With *Black Ships Before Troy: The Story of the Iliad* (1993), she is lauded for retelling Homer with the same vision and sensitivity she brings to her Arthurian books; Jan Mark notes, "If ever a book was unputdownable, . . . it is this one." Sutcliff wrote several works based directly on historical figures and events: for example, *We Lived in Drumfyvie* (1975) uses eight hundred years of Scottish history as its background, while *Song for a Dark Queen* (1978) is a portrait of Boudicca, the queen of the Iceni, who led her tribe in a British revolt against Roman power in 60 A.D. In addition, Sutcliff wrote several informational books on English history for young adults as well as stories of the past for middle graders and, at the end of her career, two picture book fantasies for younger children. She is also the author of a play, a screenplay, and historical fiction for adults; in addition, she wrote *Blue Remembered Hills*, a memoir of her life from birth through her early thirties.

Awards

Sutcliff received the Carnegie Medal for *The Lantern Bearers* in 1959 and a highly commended distinction for this same award for *Tristan and Iseult* in 1971. Four of her books were given a commended listing for the Carnegie: *The Eagle of the Ninth* in 1954, *The Shield Ring* in 1956, *The Silver Branch* in 1957, and *Warrior Scarlet* in 1958; the latter was also placed on the International Board on Books for Young People (IBBY) Honour List in 1960. *The Witch's Brat* won the Lewis Carroll Shelf Award in 1971. *Tristan and Iseult* won the *Boston Globe-Horn Book* Award in 1972 and both *Blood Feud* and *The Road to Camlann* were chosen as *Boston Globe-Horn Book* honor books, in 1977 and 1983 respectively. Sutcliff received the Other Award for *Song for a Dark Queen* in 1978, and *The Mark of the Horse Lord* won the Phoenix Award in 1985. She was presented with the Hans Christian Andersen Medal in 1974 for her body of work, and was made an Officer, Order of the British Empire, in 1975 and a Fellow, Royal Society of Literature, in 1982.

AUTHOR'S COMMENTARY

Rosemary Sutcliff

SOURCE: "History Is People," in *Children and Literature: Views and Reviews,* edited by Virginia Haviland, Scott, Foresman and Company, 1973, pp. 305-12.

All writers with an interest in their work that goes beyond the bread-and-butter level, are aware of some kind of aim, something that they feel they are doing or trying to do. And this I think is, or at any rate should be, especially true of writers for the young. You, reading this, have formed your reading tastes, or had them formed for you; you have also done your growing up (well, most of it; I suppose one never quite finishes until the day one dies) and become the sort of people, more or less, that you are going to be for the rest of your lives, allowing for the natural differences between, say, eighteen and eighty. At any rate, in writing for you, nobody has to feel responsibility for helping to form you, or your tastes. But the reading child is liable to absorb ideas from books which may remain with him for the rest of his life, and even play some part in determining the kind of person that he is going to become. Along with most of my fellow writers, I *am* aware of the responsibilities of my job; and I do try to put over to the child reading any book of mine some kind of ethic, a set of values beyond the colour-television-two-cars-in-the-garage variety. I keep well clear of the treasure-hunt theme (with its under-tones of something for nothing) which in one form or another does seem to rather dog children's literature; I try to show the reader that doing the right/kind/brave/honest thing doesn't have to result in any concrete reward (help an eccentric old lady across the road and she will send you to ballet school), and that this doesn't matter; the reward lies in having *done* the right/kind/brave/honest thing, in having kept faith with one's own integrity—and probably in being given a more difficult thing to do next time.

Another responsibility of the writer for children which I

try my best to fulfil is simply to supply them with words. This may sound trivial and obvious. But the words are man's means, not only of communicating, but of giving shape and manageability to his own thoughts and ideas. I have heard really tragic stories of children and young people failing in all-important exams or in interviews for jobs, not for any lack of intelligence, knowing perfectly well the answers to questions put to them, knowing what they wanted to say, but simply lacking the vocabulary with which to communicate in plain English. Since children learn their English from story books for pleasure as well as from lesson books in school, this is an appalling indictment of their reading matter, and one which we who write books for them must do something about. America has of late years begun the scientific production of books with graded vocabularies, two hundred words, four hundred words and so on. You match the size of vocabulary to the age of the child and it all sounds perfectly splendid. But this is to rob children of the beckoning splendour of words they do not yet understand (It matters remarkably little to a child that he does not understand a particular word; it's the flavour that counts) and possibly of all curiosity as to words later. This is the eighth Deadly Sin, and I don't care how scientific it is!

My kind of book, the historical novel, is sometimes looked on as being an easy retreat from the complications and restrictions inherent in writing a modern story for the young. This is unfair! It is true that one has greater freedom in some ways. In Roman Britain or Norman England a boy of fourteen or fifteen can play a man's part, which is unlikely in the modern world; and the writer can make use of situations which would be far-fetched or even impossible in the present day; and there's a kind of safety barrier which makes it possible to deal with harsher realities than most children can take in their stride, if one were writing of people and events in their own world as they know it. The safety barrier is, I think, becoming less important, both to children themselves and to parents, teachers and librarians; but I don't believe that I could make my hero kill himself, as I did in *The Mark of the Horse Lord,* in a modern story set in everyday England. (One might get away with it in a story set in a far-off and very "different" place, say New Guinea, but this would merely be to substitute distance of place and culture for distance of time, as a safety barrier.)

This is all true, but greater freedom is not in itself a bad thing; and there are plenty of extra problems to set against it, beside the obvious ones of research and historical accuracy. There is the ever-present danger of spilling over into cloak-and-dagger. There is the necessity to keep the people from being engulfed in the trimmings. (This can happen very easily, especially if the garnered results of the writer's research have not been properly digested before being used—nothing is worse for a historical story than undigested fragments of historical background!) There is the problem of making the people as real and individual as their modern counterparts, while at the same time not turning them into modern men and women in fancy dress. There is the problem, too, of the spoken word. Victorian writers, and even those of a somewhat later

date, had no difficulty. They saw nothing ludicrous in "Alas! fair youth, it grieves me to see thee in this plight. Would that I had the power to strike these fetters from thy tender limbs." Josephine Tey, whose death I shall never cease to lament, called this "Writing forsoothly." A slightly different variant is known in the trade as "Gadzookery." Nowadays this is out of fashion; and some writers go to the other extreme and make the people of Classical Greece or Mediaeval England speak modern colloquial English. This is perhaps nearer to the truth of the spirit, since the people in question would have spoken the modern colloquial tongue of their place and time. But, personally, I find it destroys the atmosphere when a young Norman Knight says to his Squire, "Shut ip, Dickie, you're getting too big for your boots." Myself, I try for a middle course, avoiding both Gadzookery and modern colloquialism; a frankly "made up" form that has the right sound to it, as Kipling did also. I try to catch the rhythm of a tongue, the tune that it plays on the ear, Welsh or Gaelic as opposed to Anglo-Saxon, the sensible workmanlike language which one feels the Latin of the ordinary Roman citizen would have translated into. It is extraordinary what can be done by the changing or transposing of a single word, or using a perfectly usual one in a slightly unusual way: "I beg your pardon" changed into "I ask your pardon." . . . But I would emphasize that this is not done by any set rule of thumb; I simply play it by ear as I go along.

I seem to have written the word "people" a great many times; and this I think must be because I feel so strongly that history *is* People—and people not so very unlike ourselves. This is a favourite thumping-tub of mine, and I now propose to thump it for a while.

The way people act is conditioned by the social custom of their day and age—even the way they think and feel with what one might call their outer layers. To take a very simple and obvious example: The men of the first Elizabethan age (and, Heaven knows, they were a tough enough lot!) cried easily and without shame in public. The rising generation of this second Elizabethan age are returning to much the same feeling, that one's emotions are not for hiding; but the men of my generation, my father's and grandfather's, were so conditioned in their extreme youth to the idea that men simply *didn't,* that by the time they were fifteen or sixteen they *couldn't,* even in private, except for such things as the death of a wife or child. But that's not to say that they feel, or felt, any less about the things they would have cried about, four hundred years ago.

I know there are two schools of thought about whether or not human nature actually changes, some maintaining that it does, some—me amongst them—that it doesn't. I believe most strongly that People Don't Change, that under the changing surface patterns of behaviour, the fundamental qualities and emotions and relationships remain the same.—Very much the qualities and emotions and relationships, incidentally, that one finds in Westerns; which is one reason why I like Westerns, and why most of the people in my own books would be perfectly at home in Laramie, while I would have no hesitation in sending The Virginian north of Hadrian's Wall to recover the Eagle of a lost Legion.

But even the surface patterns don't alter perhaps so much as one tends to think; and it is possible, sometimes, through a letter or a line of ancient poetry or some small object held in the hand, to catch glimpses of people separated from us by two hundred or two thousand years, so like ourselves that for the moment it is almost frightening because for that moment it makes nonsense of time.

About ten years ago, on a Hellenic cruise, I visited the museum at Heraklion, and spent a happy afternoon among the treasures excavated from the Palace of Knossos: octopus and dolphin jars, inlaid weapons, jewellery of intensely yellow gold, ivory bull-dancers in mid-leap. In the corner of one room was a case of little ornaments and children's toys; amongst them a tiny pottery tree with five or six branches, each ending in a fat little bird. It was painted in stripes, pale and pretty as an old-fashioned peppermint stick, the most completely charming thing. My first feeling on seeing it was a small sharp shock of delight, and my first thought, "*How* I should have loved to have that when *I* was a little girl!" It wasn't until the moment after, that I remembered that the little girl who must have loved it, and felt that same shock of delight on first seeing it, had been dead for three thousand years or so.

Then Homer has that lovely bit in the *Iliad,* just before Hector goes out from beleaguered Troy on the final sally that ends in his death. He is saying goodbye to his wife and baby son, and

> . . . as he spoke, Hector held out his arms for his boy, but the boy shrank back into the nurse's bosom, crying and scared at the sight of his father, for he was afraid of the gleaming metal and the horsehair crest when he saw that dreadful thing nodding from the top of the helmet. Father and mother laughed aloud, and Hector took off the helmet and set it down on the ground, shining and flashing. Then he kissed his son and dandled him in his hands and prayed aloud to Heaven. . . .

How many infants since Homer's day must have been terrified by the sight of father in an over-splendid hat? . . .

It is important to me, all this, because History *is People* and I try to teach history. The man's eye view of history, not the God's eye view. It is because history books must of necessity take the God's eye view, that they can so often and so easily become dull; that, and because they so often break it up into set, static pictures, each, as it were, separately framed (often by the reigns of succeeding monarchs), instead of treating it as a living and continuous process, of which we are a part, and of which our descendants (supposing that we haven't blown the world up) will be a part also. I feel it to be enormously important that the young should be given this sense of continuity, that they should be given the feeling of their roots behind them. To know and really understand something of where one came from helps one to understand and cope better with where one is now—and where one is

going to. And as we today are standing too near our own particular stretch of history to be able to make out the pattern and "see how the story ends," so I feel that history can best be brought to life for children through people in the like situation with regard to their own stretch of history, people standing too close to see the pattern, and who, like us, "don't know how the story ends." That's my justification for being a historical novelist and not a historian. But they must be people with whom the children can identify through the fundamental sameness—like calling to like under the changing surfaces.

Some years ago, I was struck by a *Sunday Times* article putting forward the theory that the ability to write for children is the result of an unlived pocket of childhood left over in the writer. I think this is very probably true,—it was certainly true of Rudyard Kipling and Beatrix Potter, and it is certainly true of me. But I think also that it draws heavily on a feeling for the primitive and fundamental things of life. The young have this feeling very strongly. It is why myths and legends, certainly not meant for children, have been taken over by them. It is one of the reasons why children like Westerns; and why—as I said before—I like them too. Legends and Westerns and my sort of historical novel are all alike in dealing in the big basic themes, comradeship between men, loyalty and treachery and divided loyalty, love and hate, the sense of property, revenge for slain kinsfolk; and of course the age-old struggle between good and evil. As I say, the instinct for this is strong in children; in most adults it has been pushed down, sometimes only a little way, sometimes almost entirely, into the subconscious; but it is always *there,* forming a common ground on which children's books can appeal to adult readers. Which is why it is not only unnecessary, but wrong, to write down for children; instead, the child should be drawn out and up. This is why books can play such a great part in a child's development, enlarging him and giving him a broader and deeper awareness—and why we who write for children carry such terrible responsibility on our shoulders.

So—I have said what I wanted to say. I hope it makes sense to you. It is all true; but in case you think it all sounds too earnest and didactic, I will add one thing more: —that basically, fundamentally, and at the beginning of all things, I merely find, or am found by, a story which I want to tell, which seems to me worth telling, and above all, which I want to *hear;* and tell it to the very best of my ability. All the rest, if I'm lucky, is added unto me in the course of the telling.

GENERAL COMMENTARY

Christina Duff-Stewart

SOURCE: "Scarlet on the Loom," in *The Junior Bookshelf,* Vol. 23, No. 5, November, 1959, pp. 253-62.

"Anyone can make history," said Oscar Wilde, "only a great man can write it." Almost anyone can produce a readable adventure story with an historical background, but only a great writer can sit at the loom of history and weave the warp of fact and the woof of creative imagination into a finished cloth which has all the colours of life. Such a writer weaves scarlet on the loom; such a writer is Rosemary Sutcliff.

In a review of her latest book, *Warrior Scarlet,* one writer voiced a thought that many who have followed Miss Sutcliff's progress with interest and delight must have pondered: "It is one of the mysteries of the creative spirit that a slight and elegant stylist should have become, quite suddenly, a writer of genius. . . ."

What are the criteria for good historical fiction and how and where does Miss Sutcliff's work illustrate them? The general principles for good fiction apply in the development of plot and character—the story should be a good one regardless of period; the historical background should be accurate but it should not crowd out the story (a tendency which mars the work of many another good historical novelist); there should be a perfect fusion of story and period, a fusion which can only be made by a writer whose mind is steeped in the past and who has a powerful creative imagination; the language should be evocative of the past yet not archaic (yeas, nays, prithees and forsooths are the hallmarks of what G. M. Trevelyan calls "boilers of the pot")—anachronistic colloquialisms must be avoided, too, for they are bound to recall the reader from the past; and, finally, the good historical story is one which not only tells us a story of the past but also gives us a way of looking at the past which illumines the present. It is only justified when, in the words of H. Butterfield, "It makes history a kind of extension of our personal experience and not merely an addition to the sum of our knowledge."

Miss Sutcliff's first four books for children do not illustrate all these criteria though they all stand well above the average historical novel. "I only started to write in the war, when I was in my teens," she writes, "very romantic." Her first three books, all set in the Tudor period— *The Queen Elizabeth Story* (Perdita achieves her ambition to see Elizabeth I), *The Armourer's House* (Tamsyn leaves Devon for London in the days of Henry VIII), and *Brother Dusty-Feet* (a runaway boy joins a company of players travelling the highways of Tudor England)—show promise in their vivid sense of period and a knowledge and love of the English countryside, though the plots are thin and the style lacks the vigour she was later to develop. . . .

Simon is half-way house in the journey of Miss Sutcliff's progress; not only did she wrench herself from the glories of Tudor England to the bitter and disillusioning period of the Civil War, but she chose, as few writers have done, to represent the Puritan as well as the Cavalier. In fact, though this story concerns two friends who fight on opposite sides during the war, it is really the story of Simon who joins the Parliamentary forces. Though the characters still show too little development and the plot gives way too often to chronicle, this book shows great progress.

The style is more vigorous and there is a fine re-creation not only of the English countryside and country life but of the war itself; the battle scenes of Naseby and Torrington are particularly vivid and realistic. The issues of the conflict could have been dealt with more fully but the "feel" of the period is excellent.

It was in her next book, *The Eagle of the Ninth,* that Miss Sutcliff emerged as an author of great distinction; the "slight and elegant stylist" of those early books had hardly prepared us for this suddenly mature and powerful writer. What happened? "The Eagle," writes Miss Sutcliff, "was written under rather special circumstances; I was faced with the prospect of an operation . . . and feeling horribly lonely . . . and very scared. So I invented Marcus to keep me company; or rather, in an odd way, he came to me ready made, so that it was like writing about someone I knew rather than creating a character; and I have always had the rather special feeling for him, and for the book that built itself up around him, that one does have for a friend who has been with one through a bad patch. I can remember now the lovely feeling, three days after I had the operation, when I was allowed to sit up in bed and have my writing things and get back to him; I'd been feeling so depressed and miserable, and quite suddenly everything was different . . . anyhow that book seemed to be some kind of turning point, to set me off in a rather different direction from the one I had been following before." The author says she made the story from two mysteries brought together—that of the disappearance of the Ninth Legion in 117 A.D., and that of a wingless Roman Eagle discovered, in the early part of this century, during excavations at Silchester. But the story of Marcus is much more than an exciting tale of a Roman boy whose quest is to discover what happened to his father, First Cohort of the ill-fated Ninth, and to recover the lost standard, symbol of the legion's honour. It is the story of a proud, arrogant, ambitious young Centurion who, deprived of his profession by a leg wound which invalids him out of the army, learns to make another life for himself. Through his conquest of pain and fear and disappointment; through his friendships with wise old Uncle Aquila, Esca (a British slave whom he buys and frees) and Cottia (a high-spirited British girl); and through the hazardous quest he makes with Esca, he grows in wisdom and strength, and learns at last to love and understand the alien land he came to as a conqueror. In fact all the characters in this book are seen "in the round," and they develop as the plot develops. By the end of the story, Uncle Aquila, a somewhat cynical recluse, has become more human and likable; Cottia grows from a spoiled little spitfire to a charming young woman; Marcus learns that few issues are really simple and is able to accept his failure to redeem his father's lost legion and, hardest of all, his lameness. It is he who helps Esca to accept the fact of his one-time slavery:

> "Are you going to live all the rest of your life as though you had taken a whipping and could not forget it? Because if you are, I'm sorry for you. You don't like being a freed-man, do you? Well, I don't like being lame. That makes two of us; and the only thing

we can do about it, you and I, is to learn to carry the scars lightly."

The background is authentic, historically and geographically—the life of a Roman fort and its separateness from the British town, hardly touched by Rome, and the wild exciting nature of the country passed through by Marcus and Esca on their journey North, are most vividly conveyed. Miss Sutcliff's mind is really steeped in this period which is one reason why she came into her own as a writer with this book. . . .

The romantic element is still there, but in its best sense; the dialogue is contemporary yet suggestive of its period, the descriptive writing shows a poet's sensitive eye for colour and detail. There is a most imaginative use of metaphor and simile:

> The west was a furnace banked with purple cloud.

> The full green flame of spring was running through the forest and the wild cherry-trees stood like lit candles along the woodland ways.

Once, on their journey, Marcus and Esca are hiding from their enemies in a ruined tower and it seems as if discovery and capture are inevitable:

> Suddenly (Marcus) knew that, despite all outward seeming, it had been worth while. There was a great quietness in him. The last of the mist was blowing clear away as the wind freshened; something that was almost sunshine brushed fleetingly across the old signal tower, and he noticed for the first time that a clump of harebell had taken root in a cranny of the fallen parapet close to him, and, late in flowering because of the place in which it grew, still carried one fragile bell aloft on an arching stem. It swayed as the wind blew over, and regained its place with a tiny defiant toss. It seemed to Marcus that it was the bluest thing he had ever seen.

This is not merely poetic imagery but an authentic experience of the inconsequential things the mind registers in moments of danger—as valid and as memorable as Rossetti's Woodspurge was in a moment of grief.

The Eagle was no flash-in-the-pan: the four books which have followed it maintain similar high standards; more than that, they show an increasing development in maturity and wisdom. The setting of the final part of her next book, *Outcast,* was inspired by the ancient sea defence, still traceable, of the Romney Marsh (not far from the author's present home) which "may well have been built in the first place by such an Engineer Centurion as I have made Beric find there when he comes to the Marsh." Beric, rescued as a baby from the shipwreck of a Roman merchantman, grows up with a British tribe until, when bad times come he, as an alien, is held responsible and cast out. Captured by Greek slavers and sold as a slave in his father's land, he is unjustly accused of robbery, condemned to life-long labour in the galleys, flogged unmercifully for insubordination and flung overboard as dead. But Beric, "not born to be drowned," is washed up on the

Marsh edge and rescued by the Roman Commander of the Rhee Wall, then being built, with whom he eventually finds a home and happiness. This is a stronger, more complicated plot than *Eagle* and Miss Sutcliff handles it skilfully in construction and style. The contrast between the miseries of slavery and the opulence of a Roman society which already shows the seeds of corruption is splendidly conveyed. The descriptive writing—particularly of storms and sky scenes of which there are, suitably enough, many—shows again the sensitive poet's eye of this author:

> The moon . . . sailing out into ragged fjords of clear sky.

The character development is excellent: like Marcus, Beric learns to accept the unjust blows that have been dealt him, to overcome them and make a new life for himself. It is when he is instrumental in saving the sea wall that he is, for the first time, happy; his heart free of bitterness because he has found a "belonging place" at last. It is these deeper undertones which transform an exciting, well-written book into a memorable one.

The Shield Ring, which followed, deals with an entirely different period—the last stand of the remnant Vikings of the Lake District against the armies of William the Conqueror. As the author herself says, there is no record of this in written history, only in old tales and name places, so it is even more to her credit that she weaves again an entirely convincing story as bold and strong as the Viking sagas, yet full of the detail of country life which she conveys so well in all her books. Like *Outcast* this is "strong meat": the fate of the Viking truce messengers to the Normans is particularly grisly. The battle scenes are excellent and as in the two previous books, there is a theme underlying the obvious one of the tale itself—this time it is the boy Bjorn's acceptance of the fate of the undefeated but diminished Vikings; of the doom of an old way of life, and his ability, through maturity, to make a "song of new beginnings."

In *The Silver Branch* Miss Sutcliff returns to Roman Britain at a time when the power of Rome is being weakened by the attacks of barbarians and the struggles for power of rival Emperors. It is, in a way, a sequel to *The Eagle of the Ninth,* and like the latter it is partly re-created history and partly an imaginary solution to mysteries brought to light by excavations. It is the story of Flavius, descendant of Marcus, and his cousin Justin; of how they discover a plot to kill Carausius the Emperor, though unable to forestall it; and how, with the aid of the old Eagle and a band of irregulars they help Constantius to defeat the murderer and usurper Allectus. The strength of the book lies in the increasing power of the author to tell an exciting and convincing tale, in the cohesiveness of the plot and the development of the characters as the plot develops.

In *Warrior Scarlet,* her latest book, the author set herself a harder task than ever before—the re-creation of the life of Bronze Age tribesmen of the Sussex Downs—and she carries it off superbly. The final initiation ceremony for boys of Bronze Age tribes reaching manhood was the killing of a wolf unaided; success meant recognition as a Warrior of the tribe, failure, the humiliation of joining the Half People or Flint People, servants of the tribesmen. This story concerns Drem who, because of his crippled arm, has to face danger, overcome fear and learn acceptance before he wins the coveted Warrior Scarlet. Good plot, authentic background, sensitive descriptive writing, profundity of character drawing, perfect fusion of story and period, a dialogue at once contemporary and suggestive-of-its-period—in fact, all the qualities which mark the good historical story are to be found here. And, as with her other books, there is that extra something, necessary to any first-rate work of imaginative literature which, in the words of Miss L. H. Smith, gives the reader "inspiration and courage and insight for dealing with the present." We may add to these qualities the supreme one of integrity; her books themselves illustrate this and also, "I have often wanted to write an 18th century story," she writes, "and have several times tried, only to find that on each occasion, after about the third chapter, the thing goes completely dead. I could produce, I think, 'cloak and dagger' stuff set in that period, but I can't pierce through to the realities that I always feel in my books—have to feel or I can't write them."

If in another 145 years children's libraries still exist, one hopes that Miss Sutcliff's novels, especially *Eagle of the Ninth, Outcast* and *Warrior Scarlet,* which are her finest, will still be found on the shelves. Like Drem, Rosemary Sutcliff has earned her "Warrior Scarlet"—a lasting place among the ranks of writers of distinction.

Eileen H. Colwell

SOURCE: "Rosemary Sutcliff—Lantern Bearer," in *The Horn Book Magazine,* Vol. XXXVI, No. 3, June, 1960, pp. 200-05.

In Sussex, one of the most beautiful counties in southern England, lie the Downs, those green, undulating hills crossed by tracks centuries old. Here, in a small village not far from the sea, lives Rosemary Sutcliff, the writer of historical stories for children. Her early life was spent in north Devon, the background of her first book, but it is the Downs which are home to her, perhaps because they have seen so much of the history which is such a great part of her life. As she sits writing, her eyes can rest on green English lawns and trees, and in the centre of her bungalow is a tiny courtyard, full of bright flowers, which only lacks a household god to seem Roman!

Talking with Rosemary Sutcliff one realises again the qualities one has come to expect in her books—a keen intelligence, a lively interest in the many facets of life, an eye for beauty, a sense of humour, courage, and a shrewd perception of character. Writing does not come easily to her for she has the artist's desire for perfection. Each book costs her months of research—but that she loves and finds fascinating—and many more months of writing and rewriting the four drafts she usually feels she must make. Each descriptive phrase is as evocative as she can make it, every detail of her historical background is carefully verified.

Although she has written adult books, Miss Sutcliff prefers to write for children because of their responsiveness. She credits them with intelligence and the power of appreciation, and refuses to oversimplify her material and vocabulary. Her own interest in history was aroused by the historical stories her mother read to her at an early age, when ill health compelled her to spend many hours in bed. It may be that this rather shut-in childhood led her to look outwards into the wide landscape of history, and later to write historical stories herself. She realises the responsibility of the writer of this kind of story, for the attitude of children towards history and historical events may be formed forever by what they read in childhood. More than a meticulous accuracy of fact is needed if the reader is to receive a true and balanced picture of the chosen period. Few children have strong feeling for history or any conception of its continuity, for to most of them it is a difficult subject, full of names and dates, strange backgrounds and inexplicable customs. Fortunate are the young people whose introduction to history is through the medium of stories by such a writer as Rosemary Sutcliff.

Miss Sutcliff's first book for children, *The Queen Elizabeth Story,* was written in 1950, and since then she has had ten others published. These include two more set in the Tudor period, one in the Bronze Age, one in Norman times, one in the Civil Wars, and four in Roman Britain, the period which has captured her imagination most.

To read these books in the order in which they were written is an illuminating experience. From a writer of pleasant stories with an historical flavour for younger children, Rosemary Sutcliff has developed into a mature artist whose books can be read with interest by adults as well as children. Undoubtedly she has a genius for the re-creation of an historical period. She has learned to restrain her early overenthusiasm, which at times was dangerously near to sentimentality, and to tone down the lushness of her descriptive passages. There is much fine writing in her books, but it is disciplined now in the service of her story. Her style has become vigorous, direct, and mature.

For children, one of Miss Sutcliff's chief recommendations is her ability as a storyteller. Win a child's interest in a story and it matters little that its events took place a thousand years ago. Her choice of period is felicitous, for she seems to have a flair for forgotten or little-known facets of history in which her imagination can have full play and she plunges into a story so that interest is captured from the first sentence. *The Shield Ring* begins, for example:

> The thing happened with the appalling swiftness of a hawk swooping out of a quiet sky, on a day in late spring, when Frytha was not quite five.

At once we are in the midst of the tragedy of a child's loss of parents and home. Endings are equally satisfactory, for we are left to imagine what might have "happened next." Marcus in *The Eagle of the Ninth* thinks how:

> A new life, a new beginning, had warmed out of the grey ash for himself and Esca, and Cottia; perhaps for other people too; even for an unknown downland valley that one day would be a farm.

Of the hours of careful research that must precede these apparently effortless stories we can have little conception. So well does Rosemary Sutcliff absorb her material that she can imagine nothing, it seems, that is out of keeping with her period. Every aspect of those far-off times has been realised in her imagination, with the result that we are in the hero's environment itself, seeing, feeling and hearing as he does. Just as when we learn a language we are taught to think in it, so Miss Sutcliff thinks in terms of her chosen period. It is not surprising, therefore, that her similes are so apt: "It was a day like a trumpet blast," "The village seethed like a pan of warming yeast," "Frost as keen and deadly as the blade of a dagger." There is no period jargon, no archaic or obscure expression, to slow down the story and puzzle the child. This skillful and apparently simple re-creation of a time outside our experience is one of her greatest gifts.

It is perhaps in her reconstruction of religious rites and ceremonies that Rosemary Sutcliff shows her imaginative understanding of her characters and her period most strikingly, for she never dismisses what seem to be savage customs as barbarous and without significance. As a result we are given fascinating pictures of an unfamiliar way of life and find them strangely impressive. In *Eagle of the Ninth* Marcus sees the Feast of the New Spears and, Roman as he is, is moved to kneel in awe. He realises that "the mysterious unforgettable figure of nightmare beauty" is indeed a godlike figure to these people.

In *Warrior Scarlet,* a new king is chosen in the Bronze Age and, as he stands by his father's funeral pyre, half seen in the mist over the Downs, the people swear the solemn and moving oath of loyalty of these ancient folk:

> If we break faith with you, may the green earth gape and swallow us. May the grey sea burst loose and overwhelm us; may the sky of stars fall and crush us out of life forever.

In the same book, when Drem came at last to his initiation into manhood, he gazed into the compelling eyes of Midir the priest and saw there a face that was not Midir's. He was aware of a "shining and unbearable glory, a power that seemed to beat about him in fiery waves; and he knew in a moment of terror and ecstasy that he was looking into the face of the Sun Lord himself. . . ." This power of imaginative insight into the hearts and minds of ancient peoples adds depth to Miss Sutcliff's books and lifts them above the rut of competent historical stories.

What a memorable gallery of characters she has created, from Perdita Pettle, aged eight, the gentle little heroine of *The Queen Elizabeth Story,* to Beric, embittered outcast.

Perhaps her male characters are more strongly drawn, but we cannot dismiss the study of Tamsyn, the lonely little girl who "didn't belong" in *The Armourer's House,* or Blai, the despised slave in *Warrior Scarlet,* with her pitiful belief that her father will come to rescue her. Rosemary Sutcliff's understanding of children, particularly those with some handicap, is sincere and intuitive, all the more perhaps because she knew pain and illness as a child herself. We remember Frytha in her desolate bewilderment, when she knew only that "the world had fallen to pieces and that it was very cold among the ruins." Of how many refugee children during the centuries could this have been said! Drem's experience, when he realised that his trailing useless arm would shut him out from many things that other boys could do, must be that of countless children. With each of Rosemary Sutcliff's books her ability to draw her characters "in the round" has strengthened, until in her latest book, *The Lantern Bearers,* she has given us Aquila who, a man "lost in a great bitterness," comes through a spiritual experience to a "quiet place."

Many of Rosemary Sutcliff's readers are boys, a tribute to the vitality of her writing. Perhaps it is partly because she has described fights and battles so vividly, much as she dislikes them personally! She is not afraid to introduce pain and cruelty into her stories when the period requires it in the interest of historical truth. In *Outcast* the harrowing descriptions of Beric's life as a galley slave shock and move us. Yet, although her stories are set in bloodthirsty times, she has avoided the excessive violence and savagery considered necessary by some historical writers. Many characters in her books die a violent death, as they must, but because she does not dwell on the manner of their death, the young reader is not haunted by it. All children know that there must be death and pain and sorrow, but the sensitive and skillful artist can deal with these things in a way that helps boys and girls to accept them.

In all these books the underlying values are the right ones, an essential quality in books for children. Reading *The Shield Ring,* we realise that no price is too great to pay for freedom and that the bravest man is he who knows he is afraid and yet faces danger. In *Simon* we are shown the futility of war, which divides friend from friend and destroys so much that is good in life. Family life is portrayed as the natural thing and friendship is often Miss Sutcliff's theme. Loyalty, courage, tolerance of other men's opinions and rights, man's basic need to recognise some greater power than himself—all these are part of her stories.

Rosemary Sutcliff's feeling for "place" is strong and, as we read, we feel the misty rain of the Lake District, taste the salty tang of the wind over the marshes and see the wide expanse of the Downs. She can convey the atmosphere of a place or moment most vividly and impressively. To stand with Aquila in the fort when the last Roman soldiers have left Britain, is to be conscious of utter desolation. Running with Drem in the darkness, we feel and share the elemental "Fear that walked the forest, the Terror of the Soul"; battling through the great storm with Beric we are wildly exhilarated as the "great swinging seas fling in blow after blow." How evocative are her descriptive phrases! Hers is the heightened perception of the artist, for she was trained as one and, indeed, achieved some eminence as a painter of miniatures before she began to write seriously. Her trained observation has been invaluable to her and a pleasure to her readers. She sees smoke rising in curls and eddies "like fern-fronds made of jewel-blue air." Dawn comes in "the smell of the little knife-edged wind that shivered and sang through the hairy grasses." A dog has "wallflower brown eyes," and, as a wild swan takes flight, its shadow flies beneath it "like a dark echo along the ground." Note, too, the poet as well as the artist in the songs and verses scattered through her books, most of them her own.

All of us, even children, have had "shining days" in our lives. There are many such preserved in the pages of Rosemary Sutcliff's books. Drem's ecstasy when he holds his puppy, Whitethroat, in his arms and knows that he has earned it fairly and for ever; Aquila with his sister Flavia and their blind father, looking over the Downs, for what was to be the last time, as the twilight comes "lapping up the valley like a quiet tide." Surely Justinius and Flavius in *The Silver Branch* must have remembered all their lives the night they dined with their Emperor: "Outside, the beat of the wind and the far-down boom of the sea, and within, the scent of the burning logs, the steady radiance of the lamps." The magic feeling of Christmas is in *The Armourer's House* for us all as Piers, looking out over snow-bright London on Christmas Eve, whispers: "Lights, and stars, and snow, and people in their houses, all holding their breath and waiting." Children reading will remember their own shining hours with a sharpened perception of joy and beauty.

Rosemary Sutcliff is recognised as one of the two outstanding authors of historical stories for children in England today, and through the medium of her inspired storytelling children can glimpse the pattern of history and man's perpetual struggle to fulfill his true purpose in life. Authors who can bring history to life for young people with such distinction could well claim, in Miss Sutcliff's own words: "We are the Lantern Bearers. . . . [It is] for us to carry what light we can forward into the darkness and the wind."

Margaret Meek

SOURCE: "The Central Theme," in *Rosemary Sutcliff*, Henry Z. Walck, Incorporated, 1962, pp. 51-65.

The pace-makers in any art form are those who dispel our preconceptions about the form itself. Compared with them are books written for children by hundreds of painstaking and conscientious craftsmen who apply the formulae which have proved efficient. Many succeed in infusing much new life into well-worn skeletons. But the outstanding books dare to step outside the conventions which decree whether a story is too 'involved' or 'difficult' for the

young and provide them with a distinctive imaginative viewpoint from which they see themselves afresh. Adults demand this as a matter of course. Lately it has been clear that older children do the same. . . .

Rosemary Sutcliff can not only revivify the twilight period between the age of Imperial Rome and the coming of Christianity, but also create heroes whose standards of values reflect her readers' awareness of the conflict between private conduct and public excellence in a way that extends beyond the limits of formula fiction. In . . . *The Shield Ring, Warrior Scarlet* and *Knight's Fee,* written in between the Roman stories, Miss Sutcliff tackles the most pressing problem of all: how does one win one's place in the world of men? What are the conditions of acceptance? To a writer like Miss Sutcliff, whose circumstances as a child cut her off from much that other children could take for granted, this question had a special significance.

[Several books] highlight three specific 'traces' of importance to an understanding of her work and her personality. They concern the permanence of landscape, which is the Kipling tradition; the settling in England of races or peoples who learn to live together so that their original identity is blended in a new nationality, and the *rite de passage* from youth to manhood, which is, I feel, the central theme.

All three traces are present in *The Shield Ring,* the story about Norsemen who withstood the entry of King William's Norman troops into the Lake District at the making of the Domesday Book. The tribal valour and clan loyalty of the Norsemen formed a 'shield ring' and the Normans were lured up a specially made road that led to nowhere and slaughtered in ambush. From a study of place names and local legend, the author has recreated Lakeland as it was in Jarl Buthar's day, not only as a scholar, but as an artist whose eye can select the details, which, combined with intensity of narration, bring alive the fells, lakes and rock ledges as the tale unfolds, especially in the high and empty places:

> The fellside dropped away from her with a rush and a falcon swoop that almost took her breath away. Far, far below her lay the green ribbon of Rannardale with its thread of a brook winding between steep woods of birch and hazel, down to the Crumbeck Water. Down there at the head of the Dale she could make out the ancient steading of that Ragna who had given his name to the place in the early days of the Northmen's coming, part roofless now, and long since sunk to be a shepherd's boothe, and the little pattern of old fields, once deserted, that had come into their own again since the Jarl made his Shield Ring in Butharsdale.

It is difficult for critics to believe that Miss Sutcliff has never visited the Lakes.

The landscape in *Warrior Scarlet* is the Sussex Downs, those same hills that Kipling found so full of historical significance. *Warrior Scarlet* is set in the Bronze Age, the age of the heroic Golden People. But long before their time an unknown ancient warrior slept under the Hill of Gathering, the Bramble Hill of *Knight's Fee,* which deals with the Sussex Downs when Senlac fight was a living memory. The Little Dark People who lived there before the Golden People came are still there in the Conqueror's day in the shepherd and the wise woman. So the earth remains. This spell of continuity, Miss Sutcliff's best legacy from Kipling, is woven long and wide in a way that Kipling no more than hinted at. The plots of Miss Sutcliff's three stories are bound fast to the soil. The Norsemen know that they will gradually blend with the people round about; the Normans learn that they must settle disputes in accordance with customs now long established. This feeling for the continuing survival of the land is the true historical sense of Miss Sutcliff's novels. Where other novelists for children have portrayed this sense of continuity they have been involved in the chronicle aspects of their material, the unwinding of a tale of successive generations, as in a novel like *The Land the Ravens Found,* by Naomi Mitchison, so that although we could retrace the steps of the families which moved from Caithness to Iceland, so vivid and exact are the details, we miss the mounting tension of *The Shield Ring* which concentrates on a single climax. In it there is the deep brooding fear of being hunted that haunts each episode, a feeling that only by supreme efforts, by surpassing themselves, will the Norsemen survive. The countryside takes on the significance of a human character, especially at night or in time of battle. It is never simply a setting.

The Shield Ring begins with Frytha, driven from her home as a child when the Normans set fire to it and carried into Lakeland by a faithful shepherd. But the central conflict concerns Bjorn, the orphan who grows up to be a warrior and a harper. Frytha alone knows the question with which Bjorn torments himself. What would he do if he were captured and tortured by the enemy? Would he tell them what they wanted to know? Would he break under torture and become like the mazelin, the half-creature whom they found in the hills? To prove himself, Bjorn knows when the time comes that he must go as a minstrel into the Norman camp to bring back details of their strength. The only way to rid himself of his fear and to be a man is to face what he dreads. The taunt of cowardice which has hung over him since childhood cannot be gainsaid in any other way. The climax of the book comes when Bjorn gives proof of his courage—at a price—before the final battle begins.

A reviewer remarked that Miss Sutcliff 'will always put down her harp for a battle'. . . . [It] was not so in the early books, but after *The Eagle of the Ninth* she has made contact with the mainsprings of feeling in her adolescent readers. It is important for them that Bjorn should not fail, for they share his secret fears about the testing day, his driving need to be found worthy. It is a theme common to other books, but in few others is the author so identified with the hero in the day of trial. For all that crises come to the young in other guises nowadays, the conflict is no less. Miss Sutcliff's resolution is, fear is to be faced, not fled from, lest manhood and self-respect be lost for ever.

In *Knight's Fee,* Randal, the dog-boy of Arundel Castle, is won by a Norman minstrel in a chess game and handed over to Sir Everard d'Aiguillon to be a valet and companion for his grandson, Bevis. Randal has been ill-treated all his childhood and learns the mutuality of friendship with difficulty, although he has the faithfulness of the hounds he loves because they have been his brothers. Randal proves himself, becomes Bevis's squire and fights with him at Tenchebrai, another exciting battle climax. There had never been any possibility of knighthood for Randal as he had neither money nor land with which to furnish his helm. Bevis, dying on the battlefield, gives Randal his accolade, and he gains his manor by keeping faith with the minstrel who first won him from the Lord of Arundel.

The theme is again that of Marcus and Esca, set this time in the uneasy beginning of the Norman period. The allegiances of vassal and lord and the knightly code are seen to involve more than the exacted duties of the feudal system. Indeed, the classroom details of manorial holdings are transformed into real situations so that one scarcely notices the didacticism. Randal's chief difficulty is not lack of status but his inability to believe that people will use him well, which makes him feel that he is always on the edge of his group, not wholly accepted if not quite an outcast. This gives *Knight's Fee* a certain tragic grimness. Not that it lacks gaiety; there is a most spirited heroine. But the emphasis is on the loneliness of the knightly vigil, and here, as in no earlier book, the ideal companion, the sworn brother, dies, so that the central figure emerges into full stature alone. Randal's loneliness is a vigil of another kind; it consists of keeping faith with the minstrel, with the villainous knight who coveted the manor, and above all with the manor itself when Bevis is dead.

This book breaks new ground in dealing with the Norman period and the problem of resolving the differences of those who have to live side by side in England. Miss Sutcliff has no preference for Norman or Saxon; she cares for the land and its people. *Knight's Fee* is a book of sound workmanship. Although it lacks the driving intensity of *The Lantern Bearers* and *Warrior Scarlet,* it has a new detachment, as if the author were watching her own skill at work with a certain confidence.

It is well for a critic to confess a preference. *Warrior Scarlet* has been kept until last because I am persuaded that it shows Rosemary Sutcliff's art at its best and combines the qualities of the other tales with a controlled intensity of writing which produces a work of great power and authenticity. Also, I feel that in this book author and reader are most truly identified. For the reader the theme is the one which most concerns the adolescent, that of becoming adult. For the writer the problem is to vivify a period beyond written record, to write a book about the heroic age as compelling as legend itself.

Because we no longer have any recognizable ceremony of initiation, adolescents begin to demand recognition as adults as soon as they can adopt adult roles. Society complicates matters by allowing them to drive a car, enlist in the army, marry, vote, all at different ages, and the certainty of having gained adult status seems elusive. They are also expected to act responsibly before they are given responsibility. In *Warrior Scarlet* the reader sees the problem in clear outline against the background of a heroic age where the demands of the tribe are unequivocal: after a wolf is slain in single combat, the boy hunts with the Men's Side. What if he fails? He is no longer of the Golden People. He is an outcast and keeps sheep with the Little Dark People whom the golden warriors once dispossessed of their lands and to whom tribal privileges no longer extend.

In *Warrior Scarlet* Rosemary Sutcliff has widened her range to cover the hinterland of history and realized, with the clarity we have come to expect, every aspect of the people of the Bronze Age, from hunting spears and cooking pots to king-making and burial customs, from childhood to old age. The book is coloured throughout with sunset bronze. The chief episodes are at dusk: the arrival of the smith with the first iron dagger, the hound fight in the glow of the night fire at the king-making, the final wolf-slaying in the red winter twilight.

> And so, while the flame of the sunset blazed and sank behind the Hill of Gathering, as though the sacred fires blazed there as they did at Beltane, and the faint smell of frost and dead leaves stole up from the forest to mingle with the sharp, blue reek of wood smoke and horse droppings, the bronze-smith brought forth his treasures, laying them first before the Chieftain, then passing them among the eager hands of tribesmen: beautifully shaped axeheads, spear blades all of bronze, neck rings and arm rings of shining bronze and silver and copper, ornaments for a pony's harness, and a sword with studs of red coral on the unguarded hilt. There was little bargaining as yet, men looked at the things they wanted, making no comment; and in a little they would go home and think about it, and see what they had to give in exchange, and come back in the morning maybe with a length of cloth or a couple of fine beaver skins or a lathe-turned beechen bowl.

The important episodes are linked with the scarlet cloth that is woven for a boy who becomes a man after his wolf-slaying, and the story is of Drem, whose right arm is withered and for whom the world changed on the day when he came home without being seen and heard his Grandfather ask:

> 'Is it likely, think you, that the young one will win his way into the Men's Side with a spear arm he cannot use?'

Thereafter everything seems to urge home the fact that he will never be a man; his brother's hint that he will never wield a bow, an overturned bowl of stew. Drem, lashing himself into a fury of anger 'as a shield against fear', rushes into the woods where he is found by Talore, the great one-armed hunter to whom he confides his secret fear. Talore says that on the day he is presented to the tribe after his wolf-slaying he will stand with him. More

From The Eagle of the Ninth, *written by Rosemary Sutcliff. Illustrated by C. Walter Hodges.*

than that, he lets Drem have Whitethroat, one of the best of his wolfhound cubs, in return for his first kill with a throw-spear.

From then on Drem concentrates with ferocious intensity on the trial to come. He fights for, and wins, his place in the Boys' House and gains the friendship of the chieftain's son. He fights in single combat at the king-making and proves himself worthy before his time. In fact, he tries too hard, is too intensely self-absorbed, and despite his preparation and skill he misses his wolf and seems to be for ever excluded from the tribe. He must go to Doli and the sheep. With pain and anguish he learns the deep simple wisdom of the shepherds, humility, self-knowledge and patience which are the only cure for *hubris,* and his pent-up anger gradually abates. The climax comes when Drem saves Doli and a ewe from the wolves and meets his own wolf again, this time to kill him and to win his Warrior Scarlet.

No summary of the plot can do justice to the power and sweep of this tale and the depth of the relationships portrayed. Doli and the shepherd kind are as heroic after their fashion as the chieftain's spearbearers, and the virtues they teach are courage, tenacity, care for simple things and patience. Drem learns with difficulty. He does not realize that Blai, the pale girl left behind at his hearth, is an outcast too. He does not see that she championed him and expected nothing in return, and he rejects her fellowship when he most needs it because she has seen him humiliated when he gave vent to his temper on the sheep and was rude to the shepherds. He cannot believe that Votrix, his blood brother, shared his panic and shame, so he is surly with him. The restrained dialogue in the scene when they meet after Drem's disgrace is masterly. Only gradually Drem learns not to take revenge on the world for the arm he cannot use, until at the last he proves himself, as do the other maimed heroes, by forgetting himself.

Drem's coming to manhood is more than his growing skill to conquer his disability. He sees the power and beauty of the swan he killed.

> Desolation as piercing as the moment of vision had been stabbed through him. How could a little spear that he had thrown almost without knowing it, blot out in an instant all the power and the swiftness and the shining?

He learns to see sheep as a shepherd sees them and to put his own concerns aside while looking after them. He comes to realize that although his world had been 'a harsh one in which the pack turned on the weakest hound, in which little mercy was asked or given', the real achievement is to face the fear, to carry the disability, to save one's life by risking it entirely.

Miss Sutcliff shows again her great artistry in dealing with the menace of dark rituals. The making of New Spears, a ritual scene which first appeared in *The Eagle of the Ninth,* is built into a thrilling climax of darkness and light. The threat of the little grey dagger that flashes in the firelight, and the fear of the wolves gathering for the kill are memorable passages:

> Nearer and nearer, circling warily, came the grey leader, squirming and slinking low-bellied over the snow. In the last moment it seemed to Drem that he had known this wolf before; and the wolf had known him. The wicked grin, the welcome in the savage yellow eyes belonged to a before-time as well as to now. But then it had been the wolf who waited for the meeting. Now it was Drem!

In this book there is also a certain heroic-comic relief in the Ajax-figure of Drem's grandfather, more rounded than Marcus' unapproachable uncle. He has the stubborn peevishness of the very old, and is an exasperating character, scarcely lovable, but instantly recognizable by the young.

> The grandfather was scowling at all of them under his thick grey-gold brows. "I am old, and it is not good for my belly that I do not have what I wish. What I wish is to be left in peace to enjoy myself, on this, the night that the youngest son of my youngest son becomes a man. The fire will burn for a long while yet, Woman, I shall remain here as long as I choose. . . ."

Few of us who are concerned with the young can get as near to their inner lives as a writer can. The author is the ideal companion, Talore the great hunter, the wise one who understands. In this book, Miss Sutcliff makes her experience of the fire of trial clear to the reader, who recognizes its authenticity from its complete lack of sentimental self-regard. To win through to the desired place in the tribe, to be accepted as adult, as artist, one must fulfil the demands of the task in hand and forget oneself. Only thus does one develop integrity. This is as true for the author wrestling with his material as for the adolescent facing the future. In *Warrior Scarlet* they are fully and symbolically identified with each other.

Outside the scope of this essay are Miss Sutcliff's two adult novels, *Lady in Waiting* and *The Rider of the White Horse,* which must be judged in another place. In *Houses and History* published in 1960 Miss Sutcliff brings her skill as a novelist to bear on some of the intimate dramas of history in their settings. She catches fire where the details are such as she would have chosen for her own stories, but on the whole she seems straitened and too much at the mercy of her commission. Her admirers will recognize her response to the material, and she is entirely at home with the houses and their inhabitants, but there is an uneasy in-between-ness about this book, a kind of precocious worldliness from which the novels are entirely free, and, it must be admitted, a relapse in style.

'A labour of delight' is how Miss Sutcliff describes her writing of the monograph on Rudyard Kipling. . . . It has her childhood pleasure in this author in it, and despite all that has been written about Kipling, this short study succeeds in presenting a point of view as original as it is distinctive. Reviewers were quick to notice that it is 'a miniature in prose'. It has also the vision of the creative artist who prefers the selection of memorable details to a more academic judgment. Kipling has continuing popularity with children, and in this little book Miss Sutcliff shows that she is on the child's side. It is a significant tribute, and full of delight which seems as spontaneous now as it doubtless was when the little girl first heard the stories which were to inspire her own.

Despite all the abundance of children's books nowadays, there is still a need to tell the great tales again. To the Bodley Head library of heroic retellings Rosemary Sutcliff has contributed *Beowulf.* Here one can see how her visualizing power bodies forth the story as a sea drama. The heroes are seafarers, the threat is from the sea cave, the firedrake's hoard is under the Whale's Ness. The heroic outlines stand out as the result of economy in the telling which, despite omissions, gives a faithful account of the original. More important, the legend becomes immediately accessible to the young as a rousing tale of courage and magnanimity. In returning to one of the favourite tales of her childhood, Rosemary Sutcliff shares her delight in *Beowulf* with the next generation. Those who have read her other books will recognize her distinctive style. Here is the fight with the dragon:

Fire was in his wings and a blasting flame leapt from his eyes. With wings spread, he half-flew, half-sprang at Beowulf, who stood firm to meet him and swung up his sword for a mighty blow. The bright blade flashed down, wounding the monster in the head: but though the skin gaped and the stinking blood sprang forth, the bones of the skull turned the blow so that the wound was not mortal. Bellowing, the creature crouched back, then sprang again, and Beowulf was wrapped from head to heel in a great cloud of fire. The iron rings of his mail seared him to the bone and the great shield of smith's work glowed red-hot as he strove to guard his face and bring up his blade for another blow.

C. Duff Stewart

SOURCE: "More Songs Tomorrow," in *The Junior Bookshelf,* Vol. 28, No. 5, November, 1964, pp. 279-84.

One of the qualities necessary to a good work of historical fiction is the quality of illumination. In Rosemary Sutcliff's trilogy *The Lantern Bearers, Sword at Sunset* and *Dawn Wind* we have a superb example of that best of all historical fiction in which the past illumines the present.

When the last of the Roman Auxiliaries is recalled to Rome leaving Britain to face the menace of the Saxon invasion alone, one of their number, the 18 year-old Aquila, goes "wilful missing" and returns to his downland home, where his family have lived for generations, because his loyalty to Britain is stronger than his loyalty to Rome. But his home is destroyed by a band of Saxon invaders, his father killed, his sister abducted and he himself taken to Juteland as a thrall. Three bitter years later he returns with his Saxon masters who have decided to leave their famine-struck settlement for the rich farmlands of Britain. In Hengest's camp he finds his sister Flavia, married to a Saxon "savage" to whom she has borne a son, and his cup of bitterness is full when she will not escape with him. He joins the Roman British leader Ambrosius who is fighting against the usurper-king Vortigern and his Saxon allies. The rest of the book deals not only with their constant warfare against the encroachments of Hengest and Horsa, but with the struggle of Aquila to forget his bitterness and regain the ability to love. He is helped by his friendships with Ambrosius, Brother Ninnias, Eugenus the Physician, his British wife Ness and their son Flavian; and as he grows in maturity and wisdom he even learns to accept the fact that the great victory of Ambrosius over Hengest, in which he himself has played so valiant a part is not the end of the Saxons, that there may be only darkness and defeat ahead:—

"I sometimes think that we stand at sunset," Eugenus said after a pause. "It may be that the night will close over us in the end, but I believe that morning will come again. Morning always grows again out of the darkness, though maybe not for the people who saw the sun go down. We are the Lantern Bearers, my friend; for us to keep something burning, to carry what light we can forward into the darkness and the wind."

Aquila was silent a moment; and then he said an odd thing. "I wonder if they will remember us at all, those people on the other side of the darkness."

Eugenus was looking back towards the main colonnade, where a knot of young warriors, Flavian among them, had parted a little, and the light of a nearby lantern fell full on the mouse fair head of the tall man who stood in their midst, flushed and laughing, with a great hound against his knee. "You and I and all our kind they will forget utterly, though they live and die in our debt," he said. "Ambrosius they will remember a little; but *he* is the kind that men make songs about to sing for a thousand years."

He is, of course, Artos, and this leads us to her latest book, *Sword at Sunset,* which opens three days later. Ambrosius has been crowned High King but, though the Saxons are broken in the South, everywhere else they are pressing in. Artos the Bear, bastard son of Ambrosius' brother Utha, whom we met as a boy and young man in *The Lantern Bearers,* has the idea of building up his own free-lance heavy cavalry so that they may move to wherever the need is greatest to fight off Saxon, Scot or Pict in the north, east and west, whilst Ambrosius holds the south. Artos tells his own story: this is the first time this author has written in the first person. . . .

[*Sword at Sunset*] is an amazing recreation from "fragments of known facts . . . likelihoods . . . deductions . . . and guesswork," the kind of man the historical Arthur may have been, and although it is a more slowly-moving plot than her other books, and perhaps a little overwritten, she has told the story with such imaginative power that one is convinced that this is how it *must* indeed have been. I do not know another writer whose power of empathy with an historical period is so strong. She has always shown an uncanny understanding of the superstitions and magics of early peoples, exemplified here by the chapter "Lammas Torches." As always, she makes the countryside in all seasons live for us, and her use of metaphor and simile is outstandingly vivid:—

There was a pause, a sense of rising tension, as when the wine in a slowly tilted cup comes to the rim and rises above it and hangs there an instant before it spills over . . .

The characterisation is excellent: Artos himself in particular is a wonderfully rounded character: half Roman, half Celtic, he belongs to both worlds and thus is able to draw under his banner the many different tribes whose way of life was almost untouched by Roman influence; a born leader who loves the companionship of his men and dreads the loneliness of being set apart on "that unbearable peak above the snow-line" but accepts it as his destiny when Ambrosius dies, for the sake of the dream of a free Britain. When the dream, close to fulfilment, is shattered by the product of his own unconscious sin and the unwilling treachery of the two people he loves most, he knows that, nevertheless, it was all worth while; . . . *"If tomorrow we go down into the Dark at least we will have seen the sunset."* He knows that his successor will not be able to hold back the Saxons for long, but something will remain: *"there will be more songs tomorrow though it is not we who shall sing them."*

The third book of the trilogy, **Dawn Wind,** opens nearly 100 years later on the battlefield of Aquae Sulis in which the West Saxons under Ceawlin have finally destroyed the power of the Princes of Britain. A Roman-British boy, Owain, descendant of Flavian who appeared in **Sword at Sunset,** is the lone survivor of that battle. After several years as thrall to a Saxon farmer he is freed for services rendered, but nevertheless remains with the Saxon family for one loyal reason after another. He sees the meeting of Aethelbert and Augustine at Canterbury before he finally feels free to go, knowing that, as J. R. Green puts it in *The Making of England,* ". . . the coming of the Christian Church heralds the return of the civilisation, arts and letters which had fled before the sword of the English conquerors." It is not the dawn—but the wind which heralds the dawn.

Here we have another exciting plot, interesting characters and good writing. She has shaded down her fine writing without losing that marvellous ability to recreate a landscape in all its weathers and seasons. The opening scene alone is a masterpiece of dramatic stage-setting. All through the book we hear the wind in various weathers: it may be "a little wet wind soughing through the moorland grass and heather" or "a gentle wind blowing puffs of white cloud across a harebell sky," the gusting wind of an autumn rainstorm or "a warm west wind with a faint taste of salt in it and the humming of the sea"—but it is always naturally there, never forced in to underline the theme of the story. It is cunningly put together and as sure historically as anything can ever be.

Not only does this trilogy tell a wonderful and exciting story and illuminate the past with that blinding revelation which only great art gives, but it illumines the present for the young people of our age who move, like Aquila, Artos and Owain, in encroaching darkness—the darkness of materialism, the decline of moral standards and the menace of the Bomb. If they share with Aquila the bitterness of loss, they will share, too, his acceptance of the fact that those who care for the good things are the "Lantern Bearers" and that this is enough *in itself.* If they share with Artos that last glorious stand against the Barbarian flood, they will share, too, his conviction that civilisation is worth fighting for, even in the face of total annihilation. If they share with Owain the end of his world, they will share, too, in the dawn that he lives to see approaching. They, and we, have to believe that if the fight is for Right "something will remain" even when Right is overcome by Might—that "there *will* be more songs tomorrow . . . though it is not *we* who shall sing them."

It is her amazing ability to take an early period of history and make it not only beat with life, but connect it with the further past and present future—to make it a part of the whole tapestry of history, which sets this writer far above her fellows. Many of her readers will have noticed the little ways in which she underlines the continuity of history: the dolphin ring belongs successively to Marcus

(**Eagle of the 9th**), Flavius (**Silver Branch**), Aquila (**The Lantern Bearers**), Flavian (**Sword at Sunset**) and Bjorn (**Shield Ring**); and Drem's left-handed axehead in **Warrior Scarlet** is found by a downland shepherd in Norman times and shown to Randal in **Knight's Fee.**

Writing about Kipling's historical stories in her monograph of her favourite writer, Miss Sutcliff pointed out that children tend to grow up seeing history as a series of small static pictures belonging to Then not Now, and that the Puck books with their linking of past and present in one area of England "must help them to feel it as a living and continuous process of which they themselves are a part, must help them to be at least a little aware of their own times in better perspective than they might otherwise have done . . . The child who has never (read Kipling) has missed something that he will not get from any other writer."

I think that the children and young people who have not read Rosemary Sutcliff's books have "missed something that they will not get from any other writer." As the poet Archibald McLeish recently wrote: "To face the truth of the passing away of the world and make a song of it, make beauty of it, is not to solve the riddle of our mortal lives, but perhaps to accomplish something more."

Joan V. Marder

SOURCE: "The Historical Novels of Rosemary Sutcliff," in *The Use of English,* Vol. 20, No. 1, Autumn, 1968, pp. 10-13.

' . . . A stimulus to the imaginative and critical faculties and an education in human sympathies.' These are the qualities which Professor Helen Cam finds in the best historical novels for adults; the qualities which adults seek in the books they choose to place before children; and the qualities which are to be found in the historical stories of Rosemary Sutcliff. Much has already been written about her work, and her books have set a standard by which contemporary historical novels for children are judged. Her books are praised for the quality of historical imagination which they reveal, for the language in which they are written, and for their excellence as novels. They are not, in the main, easy books, and the children who enjoy them are those with considerable reading ability and enthusiasm for books, but, to these children, they give a deep and lasting enjoyment.

Miss Sutcliff's first book, a re-telling of the Robin Hood legends, and the three which followed, are written for younger children and, while they give pleasure, they do not suggest the range and power of the later books. Signs of this developing potential came with the publication of **Simon** in 1953, a story with a Civil War setting, whose hero fights for the Parliamentary cause. Teachers welcome this book as a counter-weight to the over-romantic view of the war seen from the Royalist camp which is commonly propounded in historical novels; but to the child reading the book, it is very much more than a *'roman à thèse',* it is a story about timeless and enduring problems.

Simon, the name character, has to resolve the rival claims of friendship and loyalty to a cause, to grow up and to move from the protection of his family to an adult life with public responsibilities. This blending of historical setting and timeless problems is the mark of all Rosemary Sutcliff's later work, and one of the main reasons for its popularity with children. Professor Kenneth Charlton suggests that 'the primary urge of children to read any book is for the gratification of their emotional needs, a satisfaction based largely on their being able to identify with one or the other of the characters of the book'. This possibility of identification, this externalisation of the preoccupations of young people growing up in a troubled and dangerous world makes a very direct appeal, ensuring that the books are relevant to their readers, not mere escapist literature.

In the year after *Simon* appeared, *Eagle of the Ninth* was published, and marked the beginning of a sequence of novels which explore many aspects of Roman Britain from the full flush of Roman power until long after the legions had departed, and Rome was only a memory and a hope in the hearts of a few men—a civilisation, a way of life, 'the last brave glimmer of a lantern very far behind'. In each of the novels, the hero has his personal conflict, his particular quest. Aquila in *The Lantern Bearers,* has to overcome the bitterness left by the destruction of all he held dear in his youth and to learn the importance of personal relationships and the value of family love. Owain in *Dawn Wind,* keeps his ideal of Roman civilisation before him through all his years as a Saxon thrall and he, too, discovers the importance of his obligations to his fellow-men. Phaedrus, in *The Mark of the Horse Lord,* wins his freedom in the arena and, with Roman fortitude, gives his life for the safety of the tribe which had made him their lord. These and other heroes, express the adolescent's need to work out a code of behaviour, to discover his public loyalties, and to establish his personal integrity.

Beside the Romano-British sequence, there are three novels which explore similar personal problems in different historical settings. These are: *The Shield Ring,* a story of the Norse community in Lakeland which maintained its freedom and way of life for a generation after the Norman Conquest; *Knight's Fee,* set in Norman Sussex; and *Warrior Scarlet,* set in Bronze Age Sussex. Perhaps even more strongly than in the Romano-British novels, the reader is aware of the theme of quest, of overcoming handicap, of the adolescent's urgent need to play his part in the life around him. Drem, in *Warrior Scarlet,* has the handicap of a crippled right arm. Society's demands are uncomplicated and uncompromising. To take his part in the life of the tribe, he must kill his wolf in ritual battle and be able to take his place in the warrior band; if he cannot fulfil these demands, then he must be banished to live with the conquered Neolithic people, the shepherds and servants of the tribe. Randal, in *Knight's Fee,* is physically whole but spiritually crippled—abandoned as a baby, he has learned to keep alive by lying and stealing—and he has to learn a more ordered way of life. For both Drem and Randal, the major problem is to conquer their handicap, to learn not to allow resentment to colour their relations with their fellows, and to give and accept friendship.

To the history teacher, Rosemary Sutcliff's novels are a valuable teaching aid. The novelist's imagination illuminates and brings to life periods and ways of life that are remote and difficult to understand. Norman land-tenure is a complex study, but the rights and duties of knight-service are the very stuff of the plot of *Knight's Fee,* as is the Romanisation of Britain in such books as *The Silver Branch, The Lantern Bearers,* and *Dawn Wind.* We are today cushioned from the elements, but Rosemary Sutcliff can make us feel the famine that lurked at winter's end, the threat of wolves making each winter night dangerous. We can feel the narrow boundaries, the constriction of the tribal world, or the stretching of the known world under the Roman Empire. The impression of space, of the difficulties of journeying from one settlement to another, and the time consumed in doing so, come with a shock of surprise to the child of today's world of easy transport; to one growing up in this overcrowded island.

In recent years, we have come to demand, as a matter of course, that historical novels should be free from anachronisms; but teachers who wish to make use of such books need a more positive quality than mere absence of error. In Rosemary Sutcliff's work, they should find this positive contribution. A study of local history, an investigation of the tangible remains of the past, are both ways in which history can be invested with a feeling of reality for children, but the good historical novel also has a part to play. Historians can follow a closely reasoned argument and can emerge with a coherent picture, but this is asking for a mature judgement and an already awakened feeling for history. For children, the novelist's imagination, transmuting the minutae of daily life and the political arguments of long ago, can strike the spark which may lead to further investigation and understanding.

'An education in human sympathies'—these novels certainly provide this. We may, in carping mood, wish that some things were different—the male characters are much more memorable than the women in the books (but, on the whole, men did take most of the adventures for themselves), and the books are of a complexity which puts them out of the reach of many children. This is an ungrateful complaint, for no book can be all things to all men, and we should be glad of books which will extend and, at the same time, delight our more intelligent children.

May Hill Arbuthnot

SOURCE: "Realism for Adolescents: *The Lantern Bearers,*" in *Children's Reading in the Home,* Scott, Foresman and Company, 1969, p. 188.

[The] greatest living writer of historical fiction for youth, on either side of the Atlantic, [is] Rosemary Sutcliff. . . . [Each of her books] is built around a noble theme. Her heroes live and die for principles they held dearer than life, and which we still value. As one of her biographers points out, the conflict in her powerful stories is always between "the light and the dark." The light is all that is good and precious in life, and the dark is what threatens its destruction and return to barbarism. In *The Lantern Bearers,* a man sums up their defeats and their hopes, "We are the Lantern Bearers, my friend; for us to keep something burning, to carry what light we can forward into the darkness and the wind." Her heroes value courage and loyalty above all virtues; and a home hearth, children, and enough land for crops and a few animals are precious things that belong to the light and must not be destroyed. The beauty of that little island, England, haunts all the invaders and turns Romans into loyal Britons, loving and working for their "dear bought land." These books are no preachments but action stories about great-hearted men as real to young readers as heroes of today.

Frank Eyre

SOURCE: "Historical Stories," in *British Children's Books in the Twentieth Century,* revised edition, Longman Books, 1979, pp. 107-14.

In the last twenty years there has been a strong revival of interest in historical stories. Although there were many writers of 'historical novels for children' in the first half of the century, most of them were nearer to adventure stories than history and all were marred by an excess of a false type of dialogue that came to be known as 'gadzookery'. Their plots, too, were absurdly artificial, dragging in (and too often distorting) historical events by the scruffs of their necks, as it were, in order to include them, rather than incorporating them naturally and logically in the development of plot and character. As a result historical stories fell into disrepute, being regarded as a largely false form. What was needed was a writer of calibre to give them a new image.

In the first half of the century the only writer to attempt this was Geoffrey Trease. . . . To him, undoubtedly, must go the credit for setting a new style towards a more conscientious, properly researched story of the past that concerned itself as much with the social events of its time, and their effects on the people who lived in them, as with excitement and action. . . .

The first, and still the most outstanding of this new kind of historical writer for children was Rosemary Sutcliff. She has since been at least matched, in maturity and in her depth of knowledge of her chosen periods by other writers, and it is no longer as rare as it was when she first began writing to find warmth and sympathy, good dialogue and fine plots in historical stories for children. But she still stands head and shoulders above most of them. It is not easy to convey the power of her books. It is due to many things—passionate convictions convincingly communicated; a strong sense of history (real history, not just Kings and Queens, Knights in Armour and Battles) and a fine, compelling style—but most of all to the fact that she

is a born writer. This is the thing she needed to do, and she does it supremely well. It is difficult for me to write objectively of her work, for I read her first books in manuscript and still remember the pleasure with which we all read *The Queen Elizabeth Story* when it arrived on my desk, unexpectedly, at a time when she was supposed to be working on another commission. No one could have had any idea then of the books to come, for that is a simple tale, however charmingly told, but we all experienced that unmistakable feeling that one gets when one recognises the birth of a real writer. How rarely that happens!

Margaret Meek, in her Bodley Head monograph on Rosemary Sutcliff's work, has given an account of her development that could hardly be bettered, and the best of her books are so well known that it would be pointless to attempt to analyse them here. The great ones, from *The Eagle of the Ninth* onwards, all give the reader an extraordinary sense of involvement, of being personally concerned with a deeply felt series of events and emotions that is being projected from inside rather than written about from the outside. The sequence of books about Roman Britain, in particular, *The Eagle of the Ninth, The Silver Branch* and *The Lantern Bearers,* paint an astonishingly vivid picture of the Britain of that time, which must have taught countless thousands of children more about history than all the textbooks—and is likely to continue doing so.

Fred Inglis

SOURCE: "History Absolves Nobody—Ritual and Romance," in *The Promise of Happiness: Value and Meaning in Children's Fiction,* Cambridge University Press, 1981, pp. 213-31.

Rosemary Sutcliff reconstructs from Rudyard Kipling's Roman Britain—the tales of Parnesius in *Puck of Pook's Hill* and *Rewards and Fairies*—a parallel structure of regimental loyalty, strong nationalism, honour and duty as the bonds which hold individuals upright in institutions, military courage and colour. Over all she sings a sweet lament for a sun-soaked and lovely landscape, especially on its most Wordsworthian moors, downs, dales and fells. . . . The fine evocation of Sussex in *Puck* can remain unforced because it is directly experienced. Rosemary Sutcliff has to recreate a landscape which, except for odd corners of the National Parks (hence her reliance on heather), is now irretrievably altered, busy with people, and often horrible to look at. Her very deep feeling for the English landscape is given its shape and meaning by Gerard Manley Hopkins and the Scholar Gypsy.

The trouble is that it takes exceptional finesse to prevent such reconstruction becoming vulgar. The appearance in innumerable homes of the farmhouse kitchen as reproduced by Habitat and Guild shops testifies to the longing Rosemary Sutcliff expresses with such plangency. For what are her novels seeking to do? They seek to create in children their author's love for a landscape no longer there.

But not just a landscape; natural beauty in her novels is presented as a frame whose order, tranquillity, cultivation, and culture are metaphors for an analogous order in social and personal life. It is a metaphor with a long pedigree. Landscapes, however, can be deceptive. Sometimes a landscape seems to be less a setting for the life of its inhabitants than a curtain behind which their struggles, achievements, and accidents take place. The tricky part of Rosemary Sutcliff's ambition, as it is of the other children's writers who work to create a picture of history as reasonably continuous with the present, is to avoid her landscape-as-setting becoming another tourist attraction. To move through the curtain is to make the landmarks personal and biographical, as well as picturesque.

She is much too intelligent not to know this. But she writes on the swell of a tide of feeling larger than any one writer; the tide carries her away from writing real history, into the unreal tempests and enchanted islands of romance. Much, of course, may happen on those seas, shores, and grey rocks, which is every bit as real as history—as Prospero, Caliban and Miranda show us. The strong, regressive pull of some, at least, of Rosemary Sutcliff's novels is towards stable institutions and memberships which command a loyalty fixed by ceremony and fealty, deepened by a sweeping iambic prose. The weakness is not that she writes of these things at all, for one duty of a writer is to count the costs of change, to criticize the present values by their own best standard *and* by the standard of those they have displaced. Thus, the gains won this century for human freedom, individual dignity and sincerity, must be judged by the writer against the loss of dread, awe, mystery, which gave gravity and meaning to the grimness of old authority. Too often, Rosemary Sutcliff sounds as though she speaks for the Tolkien formation by simply lamenting the age of chivalry and its demise. In Kipling, and much more in Conrad, the gains to life provided by the immovable structures of Mercantile Marine, Roman Legion, and Indian Army regiment, are clear: they enforce the idea of a job well done, they create the central concept of duty, they permit friendship. By the time Rosemary Sutcliff wrote her Roman sequence, *The Eagle of the Ninth* (1954), *The Silver Branch* (1956), *The Lantern Bearers* (1959), *Dawn Wind* (1963), and *The Mark of the Horse Lord* (1965), the work of maintaining nuclear tankers and political regimes in the bauxite islands of the West Indies and aboriginal Queensland was too boring and too destructive to justify the lives of good men. As a result, her novels, insofar as they commend Kipling's and Conrad's morality, are just romancing. As such, they are fetching, often touching; a child might become rapt and bewitched by them. But if so, it would be a spell bound by an irrevocable past.

This is not all there is to say of these novels, by any means. . . . [Miss Sutcliff] embodies another, more active moral strain in the genteel politics of her genesis. As she works away at the historical experience which absorbs her—the colonizing of Britain during and after the fall of Rome—she outlines a new and shadowy figure in the wide spaces of the heath. This figure—Owain in *Dawn Wind,* or the freed gladiator-guerrilla leader in *The Mark*

of the Horse Lord—breaks clear of the institutions which lie in ruins about him and endures shocking hardship in his own name. In her stately, slightly rigid prose, the novelist sets her heroes and heroines stubbornly to resist the cruelties of empires and ideologies. They will live through, if only just, the advent of both the Saxons and St Augustine. . . .

[Her] message is—to speak crudely—that the individual spirit will survive the loss of nation, family, tribe, or regiment. . . . Rosemary Sutcliff sets herself a large task: to catch something of the movements of empire and history in the thick, unbending prose of the bestseller romance, with its black and white conventions, Maydays and waste lands, perilous chapels, cups and quests, lothely ladies and grene men. As things are, she is more likely to catch teacher-readers than children.

Sheila A. Egoff

SOURCE: "Historical Fiction: *Outcast* and *The Eagle of the Ninth,*" in *Thursday's Child: Trends and Patterns in Contemporary Children's Literature,* American Library Association, 1981, pp. 163-64.

A virtually perfect mesh of history and fiction can be found in the writing of Rosemary Sutcliff. She seems to work from no recipe for mixing fact and imagination and thus, like fantasy, which it also resembles in its magic qualities, her writing defies neat categorization. Still, what cannot be defined can be observed. Thus what one perceives is that Sutcliff begins with a very well stored mind and an affinity for a given period in the distant past that she sets forth as if it were something she herself had once experienced, richly remembers, and recounts—much as some ordinary person talks about the memories of childhood or a trip. Sutcliff easily, unobtrusively, and naturally seems able to supply just the right detail at just the right time to make both setting and plot utterly convincing. Her persuasion is so compelling that readers are imperceptibly led back into the past with such subtlety they feel they are living side by side with her characters.

A good example of Sutcliff's special skill is *Outcast* (1955). In this book her hero, Beric, experiences two civilizations—the primitive, "closed" tribal life of the small, dark people who live beyond the Roman Wall and the luxury and majesty of Rome with its class society, gladiatorial arenas, and galley ships. There are in Sutcliff's works no vague, untrustworthy generalizations but neither are there pedantic, pointless details. A case in point: Beric's time as a galley slave is far more briefly described than the similar passage in Lew Wallace's *Ben Hur,* but Sutcliff's description is at least as accurate historically and far more memorable.

With her first major novel, *The Eagle of the Ninth* (1954), Sutcliff brought a new dimension into historical fiction for children, indeed into children's literature. As she does with Beric, who is in search of his identity and who yearns for love and security, she gives all her characters universal, human problems while making them vital and recognizable in their own time. And with all this she also tells a great story.

This emphasis on character is not entirely new, of course. It is certainly evident as far back as Esther Forbes's *Johnny Tremain* (1943), wherein Johnny, although involved with Paul Revere, also has to come to terms with himself and, doing so, grows up in the process. But nowadays, thanks partly to Sutcliff's influence, such emphasis is the rule rather than the exception and the attention to character is greater than ever. Such recent writers as Hester Burton, Barbara Willard, and Katherine Paterson appear to *begin* with young people in crisis, ordinary young people who are caught in the net of history and whose lives are altered by its forces.

Neil Philip

SOURCE: "Romance, sentiment, adventure," in *The Times Educational Supplement,* No. 3425, February 19, 1982, p. 23.

Like many children's writers [Rosemary Sutcliff] was seriously ill as a child; she was crippled by arthritis. This fact is important because it provided her with a major theme in her fiction: the need to find strength through weakness. And it has left her imagination free to work on a broad sweep, while her experience has emphasized the intimate, the personal, the individual.

She trained as a miniature painter, and in 1940 exhibited at the Royal Academy a miniature with the patriotic title "The Spirit of England". The title could serve as a description of her work; but the patriotism is no blind or objectionable jingoism, but a fierce love comparable to Edward Thomas's. When he was asked during the First World War what he was fighting for, he crumbled a handful of earth and let it fall: "Literally, for this!" Like Kipling—to whom she owes a great debt which she has herself frequently and gracefully acknowledged—Rosemary Sutcliff manages to combine conservatism and radicalism in an unsettling and fertile mixture. Her female characters, though fiery, are generally little more than cyphers, yet she has won the "progressive" Other Award for her novel about Boudicca, *Song for a Dark Queen.*

Most importantly for today's audience, she cherishes cultural diversity even while she stresses continuity. And while she upholds such unfashionable virtues as duty, courage, integrity, she has in her treatment of the theme of male comradeship provided the most sensitive and sustained representation of male homosexual feeling in children's literature.

The main body of her work, the sequence of major novels ranging from the Bronze Age *Warrior Scarlet,* through the great Roman trilogy (published in one volume as *Three Legions*) to the eleventh century *Knight's Fee,* is a magnificent achievement. To call the books historical novels is to limit them disgracefully; the very phrase implies a

deadness, a worthiness of which she has never been guilty, and a distancing which is the opposite of her intention. She does not bring "history" to the reader, but involves the reader in the past—not just for the duration of a book, but for ever. She can animate the past, bring it to life inside the reader in a most personal and lasting way.

This ability is a magical one, and there perhaps lies the key to her success. She is not essentially a novelist but a storyteller. She has the oral storyteller's instinctive grasp of pace, slowing her action till the reader is aware of every breath her characters take, then triumphantly whirling into battle, enmeshing the reader in confusion which seems to pass too quickly for the eye to take it in, yet never losing her grip on her material. And she has a bardic attitude to language. She re-uses phrases which appeal to her, sometimes several times in a book; in her descriptions of downland and health she can become intoxicated with detail, as if the very thought of the open air exults her. Her "one plot; a boy growing up and finding himself" has done her and her readers proud.

Margery Fisher

SOURCE: "Who is the Enemy?" in *The Bright Face of Danger,* The Horn Book, Inc., 1986, pp. 345-77.

Sober, exploratory, moralistic—any of these adjectives might be applied to the stories of past wars offered currently to the young and exemplifying the sense of responsibility fostered in writers by the prolonged scrutiny of psychologists and social theorists of the moral and emotional development of children. The immediate and the distant past have become subject to re-examination in the light of today's attitudes both to war and to young people. Yet there are universal, transhistorical values which can still enliven the old-style adventure story and ensure that it does still exist as an undidactic literary form. As Fred Inglis has suggested, 'it makes sense to speak of courage, candour, trustworthiness, and truth as meaning something in all historical circumstances—in the Trojan ditch, outside Harfleur, at Bloemfontein, or on the picket lines'.

Nobody has spoken out more strongly for these values than Rosemary Sutcliff in novels offering many examples of man as warrior. Although none of her books comes nearer to our times than the late seventeenth century, her approach to the facts of war and destruction in the past has an emotional honesty and force and an underlying philosophy of race and nationalism which offer something like advice to young readers of today if they are responsive enough to her words. The least didactic of authors, she places in the context of war the virtues of courage and loyalty, demonstrated through the fortunes of a young hero or heroes. Rosemary Sutcliff's books are historical adventures as much as they are historical novels, to the extent that she is not seeking to reinterpret received history but to show the effects of past conflict on certain individuals. The great historical personages do not play central parts in her stories. She gives herself freedom to imagine private people caught up in major battles, conspiracies or mass movements in plausible circumstances. While she does not announce any particular attitude to war, as Henty and Captain Johns felt obliged to do, certain points of view are filtered through these chosen main characters—chosen to represent the views of their family, race or period but also to show how these views could change, and for what reasons.

The trumpets and banners of war are present in her books alongside the onrush of fear, the treachery, the wounds and the deaths. Loyalty in arms is demonstrated most clearly in the long linked sequence of books set in Roman Britain (*The Eagle of the Ninth, The Silver Branch, Frontier Wolf, The Lantern Bearers* and *Dawn Wind*) where service to the Eagle of a regiment is the supreme obligation. This loyalty is no cold matter of expediency and duty to the young men who serve in the legions, but a strong binding force, a symbol of the strength of the disparate races that make up the Roman army. . . .

The overriding theme of these stories of Roman Britain . . . is the idea of reconcilement, the picture of an island people created from warring elements, and united over the years by intermarriage and the gradual interrelating of cultures. The sequence of books which starts with the enterprise in which young Marcus Aquila sets out to find the truth of his father's disappearance ends with the growing up of a Viking boy in the Lake District whose link with Rome had come through his father's Welsh forebears. Celtic Britons, Romans, Saxons, Norsemen and Normans fight in turns for supremacy in Britain and each wave of invasion is absorbed into an island nation. The Aquila father and son and their descendants are linked in the stories by a ring of flawed emerald shaped like a dolphin which is preserved in the family (though with many accidental losses and recoveries): the family survives but it survives by taking into itself individuals not of Roman stock.

The enemy of today becomes the ally of the future and this is Rosemary Sutcliff's answer to that question 'Who is the enemy?' which is forced upon the writer tackling the problem of war. The sense of continuity transcends the pattern of invasion and conquest. When Aquila, a young Decurion, deserts the legion when it is recalled to Rome because he feels a stronger tie with the province of Britain, he is enslaved by Jutish invaders; in their country he reads the Odyssey to Bruni, renowned warrior now weak in old age, to whom he has been presented as a gift by Bruni's swaggering grandson. The past lives—in this and in many other episodes we are made aware of this, as we are made aware of the patterns held in the future. . . .

Change is constructive in the context of the slow amalgamation of antagonistic races in Britain. Destructive change as it affects places provides one of the ways in which Rosemary Sutcliff examines the dark side of war, the inglorious opposite to the virtues of loyalty and comradeship in arms. The individual eye operates here, as everywhere in the books. Aquila, torn between his duty to his legion and the pull of the Roman province where he has been born and brought up, is very sensitive to the state of the coastal fort of Rutupiae now being abandoned to the barbarians. Description, as always in Rosemary Sutcliff's stories, is organic and personal; this is not the author's overview of the fortress of the great Pharos but the view of a disturbed, desperate young soldier:

> The vast plinth, long as an eighty-oared galley and three times the height of a man, rose like an island in the empty space, and from it the great central tower sprang up, crested with its iron beacon brazier against the sky. A few shreds of marble facings, a few cracked marble columns upholding the roof of the covered ways for the fuel-carts, remained of the proud days, the days when it had stood shining in wrought bronze and worked marble here at the gateway to Britain, for a triumphal memorial to Rome's conquest of the province. But they had used most of the broken marble for rubble when they built the great walls to keep the Saxons out. The tower rose up bare and starkly grey as a rock, with the seagulls rising and falling about it, the evening light on their wings. The light was beginning to fade; soon the beacon would be lit, and the night after it would be lit, and the night after that, and then there would be no more Rutupiae Light.

In an equally tense mood the boy Owain, orphaned in a Saxon raid, approaches Viroconium, once a thriving Roman city and now abandoned by its few inhabitants and sacked by the enemy. . . .

Owain is still a boy and there is a touch of juvenile delight in housekeeping as he and the waif Regina, banded together against loneliness and fear, set about finding food, fire and shelter; but there is nothing trivial in their plight or their brave resourcefulness against danger and death. When Rosemary Sutcliff uses young heroes, or leads children towards manhood when they will take up a hero's role, she never allows a suggestion of historical charade to dilute the strong emotional content of her stories. Her children are recognisably young but their actions presage their future. They are on trial, apprentices to maturity, and in them courage is no less apparent than the courage of the young legionaries who are her more frequent heroes; merely, it is shown on a different level of experience and action.

There are many reasons why Rosemary Sutcliff's novels could be called, in the widest sense, educational, but as far as young readers are concerned, there is more value in the honest, firm emotional ebb and flow in them than in the interpretation of particular periods of history in which Britain became an island nation. Most of all they can learn from her celebration of certain moods and stages of development in young manhood—a reckless risking of physical forces and a rejoicing in physical prowess; an ardent sexual comradeship in arms; the pride of service to an accepted cause; the half-realised tug of one's native land; a flexibility due to curiosity about other places and other experiences; family ties and affections; the mixture of nervous fury and apprehension in battle; the blow to pride in thralldom; the unexpected tenderness of a relationship with a woman; the bleak despair of enforced loss; the perplexed pain of conflicting loyalties. All this and much more, to open the minds and spirits of the young to worlds larger and more challenging than their own and yet worlds of emotion to which in their own way they too may have to travel. And in presenting her tales of warriors long ago, balancing the nobility and the sordidness of war, she is reaching back to legends—of Beowulf, of Arthur, of Charlemagne—and so, ultimately, to those myths of conduct and creation where story begins.

Michele Landsberg

SOURCE: "Adventure, The Great Game: *Warrior Scarlet*," in *Reading for the Love of It: Best Books for Young Readers,* Prentice Hall Press, 1986, pp. 142-44.

More strictly historical than Garfield, whose Dickensian London seems to float in some mirthful mist of nontime, is the prolific Rosemary Sutcliff. She is unparalleled in her mastery of the form: In each of her novels, particularly those of Saxon and Roman Britain, she brings alive a complete and spacious world, richly and startlingly detailed, in which the reader can move about, observe, sense, and participate in another time and place. Her power lies not only in making us intimate with the daily life of a Bronze Age boy or a Roman centurion, but in letting us see the world through their eyes.

In *Warrior Scarlet,* one of her most emotionally vivid works, the boy Drem must win his place among the warriors of his age group. But he has a paralyzed right arm, which makes it impossible for him to hold simultaneously the traditional weapons of his people, a bronze shield and a dagger.

Sutcliff's prose is lyrical, plangent, almost dangerously romantic, but she certainly makes us see and sense the rolling downs and black night forests of primeval Britain. The landscape is always lit by flaring sunsets or cool gray dawns; when hunters return from the marshes to the huts in the blue summer dusk "a stain of light came to meet them thick and golden like honey trickling from a tipped jar"; there are the flickering illuminations of mutton-fat lanterns, torches, Beltane fires, and shafts of dusty sunlight when the turf roof is rolled back.

It is a complete sensory world, populated by the hardworking shepherds, (the Little Dark People who are the more ancient conquered tribe of the place); by wandering Irish bronzesmiths; by priests who orchestrate the exotically detailed, hypnotic secret rites of initiation; by chieftains and kings. They command our total belief because we see their grip on Drem. We are never taken outside his knowledge of this world and his acceptance of its ways. All the more dreadful and desolating when Drem fails his ritual wolf slaying and becomes an outcast. Without his rigid role of warrior, without his prescribed place in the tribe, he is nothing. "A boy who failed in his Wolf Slaying and did not die was dead to the Tribe. It was the custom." Drem is exiled and must go to live with the despised shepherds on the hill. And his redemption, at last, is also true to the ethos of the tribe; only by stoic

endurance and individual heroism does he regain his identity, now enriched by a deeper, gentler resignation learned from his work with the shepherds.

In the portrait of Drem, there is a forcefulness of empathy that is almost unbearable. When my own son, a precocious reader, read *Warrior Scarlet* at the age of five, I found him in anguished tears over the opened book. "I can't go on," he explained between gasping sobs. "Drem has failed his wolf slaying." I had to hold him on my lap to comfort him and read the next chapter aloud before he could bear to go on by himself.

Perhaps he already sensed how different he was and would be from his peers, set aside and "outcast" not only by his giftedness but also by a lateral lisp which, with his sunny and outgoing character, he seemed outwardly to ignore. Three years later, when he undertook on his own to work with a speech therapist, he concentrated with such ferocious self-discipline that his speech defect, commonly held to be almost incurable, was totally overcome within three weeks.

I was astonished and moved, both by his dedication and his triumph, achieved so independently. I asked him (as parents so often ask unanswerable questions) how he had found the will and the courage to tackle his problem and to overcome it. "I remembered Drem," he said after a soul-searching pause. "He was handicapped like me."

No one who knew this intelligent, strong, athletic child, so unfailingly funny and generous, could have guessed that in the secret prison of his heart he felt that he was crippled. Whenever I speak to audiences of teachers and librarians, many of them devoted to the practice of "bibliotherapy"—prescribing "problem novels" to children with matching problems—I tell them this story. I ask them if they would have thought of prescribing *Warrior Scarlet* to a five-year-old boy with a lateral lisp.

The whole force and mystery of literature is that it speaks to us privately, one mind reaching to another, its "therapeutic" power dependent not on mean-spirited calculations of problems and how to solve them, but on the depth of the author's intuition and the strength of her literary imagination and skill. Hundreds of contemporary novelists for children have tackled this theme of the young boy's agonized desperation to prove his virility and to be accepted as worthy by his "warrior clan." It is a solitary trial, apparently, as ancient as prehistory. That Sutcliff's Bronze Age version could reach so unpredictably into a boy's life, and profoundly change it, is both a testament to the strength of Sutcliff's writing and a brisk rebuttal to the reductive and presumptuous tinkerings of bibliotherapy.

A defender of teenage mass-market novels once accused me of being "against pimples and lust." But a novel's contentious or problematic subject is almost beside the point; what matters is the depth of its treatment, and it is through the author's language that we can most clearly see whether an artist or a mechanic is at work.

In *Warrior Scarlet,* Sutcliff developed a movingly evocative language to create her Bronze Age world. Every image, drawn from the vegetation and animal life surrounding the tribe, deepens the sensory hold the novel exerts on the reader. She makes particularly good use of starkly simple dialogue ("Na, this time there will be no coming back"), as well as a peculiar trick in using the gerund that somehow evokes the primitive mentality: their last hunting, a hard waiting, a long-drawn hushing of wind across open snow.

This elegaic tone is particularly effective in *The Lantern Bearers,* Sutcliff's novel about the departure of the last Roman Legions from Britain. The Jutes and Angles raid, pillage, and loot in their pouncing forays down from the North; already they have begun to make alliances with British warlords and to settle on conquered farms along the coast. Britain teeters on the edge of the Dark Ages. We see the coming chaos through the eyes of the British-born centurion Aquila, who deserts his departing legion because at the last moment he realizes that Britain, not Rome, is his true home. Here the language is crisper, more Latinate, and the repeated images of beacons and failing lights strongly suggest the struggle to "hold back the dark."

Although she never steps outside Aquila's perception that Rome is synonymous with civilization and that the "sea wolves" are barbarians, Sutcliff allows us to see, out of the corner of our eye, how the Saxons, Picts, and Romans have already begun their long, fertile intertwining. She is able to imagine each of these cultures from within, fully and cohesively. Her world view is capacious enough that there are antagonists but no villains.

John Rowe Townsend

SOURCE: "Britons and their past," in *Written for Children: An Outline of English-Language Children's Literature,* third revised edition, J. B. Lippincott, 1987, pp. 195-98.

In Britain, since the end of the Second World War, one name has stood out above the rest: that of Rosemary Sutcliff. Her major books have combined compelling narrative power with the exploration of important and absorbing themes. She began her writing career in the early 1950s with some rather guileless books for younger children, but found her true voice with *The Eagle of the Ninth* (1954), in which a young Roman centurion, invalided out of the army, sets off into wild northern Britain on a mission to find out what happened to his father's lost legion. This was the first book of a sequence, set in Roman Britain, which continued with *The Silver Branch* (1957) and *The Lantern Bearers* (1959).

The last of these, in which a young Roman officer decides to stay on in Britain after the legions have gone, is crucial. The Romans who remain are struggling to carry what light they can into the dark ages that will follow. In *Dawn Wind* (1961), we are in the darkness; the hero Owain

is a boy whose family have been killed in the Saxon invasions and who becomes a Saxon thrall. But the book ends on a note of hope when Einon Hen the Welsh statesman speaks to Owain not only of 'the last gleam of a lantern far behind' but also of 'the hope of other light as far ahead'. He looks to a new union of Saxons and Britons: 'it is not the dawn as yet, Owain, but I think the dawn wind stirring'.

These four books are themselves part of a larger sequence, extended over a considerable body of work, whose subject is the making of Britain. It goes back in time to the Bronze Age in *Warrior Scarlet* (1958) and forward to *The Shield Ring* (1956), in which Norseman meets Norman, and *Knight's Fee* (1960), where the Norman Conquest is over and Normans too are beginning to lose themselves in a common identity. And Miss Sutcliff moves sideways, as it were, from Roman Britain in *The Mark of the Horse Lord* (1965), in which Phaedrus the gladiator first impersonates, then becomes identified with, the leader of the Gaelic 'horse people'. Peoples mix, conquerers are absorbed, and all along, timeless and patient, from *Warrior Scarlet* through to *Knight's Fee* two thousand years later, are the Little Dark People, who endure and survive.

This sequence seems to me still to constitute the basic structure of Miss Sutcliff's work, though from time to time she has added to it or filled it out. Among her later books, I particularly admire *Sun Horse, Moon Horse* (1977), which offers an explanation of the white horse carved into the hillside at Uffington in Berkshire, and which has a hero who is artist as well as chieftain and, ultimately, sacrifice. And *Frontier Wolf* (1980) showed its author still in vigorous possession of the powers that went into *The Eagle of the Ninth* a quarter-century earlier. Alexios Flavius Aquila, kin to the Marcus Flavius Aquila of *The Eagle,* is sent in disgrace to command a rough irregular unit of frontier scouts, recruited from among the tribesmen in northern Britain.

> Looking along the lines, Alexios saw men, long and rangy for the most part, clad in greasy and weatherworn leather tunics and cross-gartered breeks, even their iron-bound caps three parts hidden under the snarling head of the wolfskin cloak each man wore pulled forward over it . . . They stood easily, feet a little apart, and looked back at him out of hard-bitten wind-burned faces, rogues' faces, some of them, cautious or reckless, cunning or blank, all of them careful to give nothing away. But in them all, binding them together, something that was different from the oneness of other army units. Maybe it was the oneness of the wolf pack. Alexios did not know.

Alexios has to win the confidence of this unpromising mob, and eventually to lead them in a long, fierce, fighting retreat, at the end of which the ragged remnants are declaring that if he cared to set up as Emperor they'd be right behind him.

Rosemary Sutcliff's view of early British history was formed some years ago, and would be disputed by many modern historians—a thought that does not worry me, since different interpretations can all contain their own truth, and in any case she is less an analyst of the past than a writer who brings it to pulsing life. Women are not generally important in her books—unsurprisingly, since the fierce physical action she describes with such power was a masculine rather than a feminine field. An exception is *Song for a Dark Queen* (1978), which tells the story of Boudicca, queen of the Iceni in eastern England, who led a revolt against the Romans and was defeated.

Miss Sutcliff's heroes have mostly been cast in a traditional mould: brave, intensely honourable, full of officer-like qualities even when they are not actually officers. But such heroes are no longer automatically required in historical novels for the young. There has long been a growing tendency to replace them with heroes (or heroines) of humbler social status and with a greater share of ordinary human fears and weaknesses.

Margaret Meek

SOURCE: "Of the Minstrel Kind," in *Books for Keeps,* No. 54, September, 1990, pp. 28-9.

The details of Rosemary's early years and her amazing resourcefulness in the face of crippling pain are given with no trace of self pity in her autobiographical narrative, *Blue Remembered Hills.* There's also a revealing paragraph in the collection of stories which she edited with Monica Dickens, *Is Anyone There?,* where she says: 'I had a lonely childhood and growing-up time. My parents loved me and I loved them, but I could never talk to them about the problems and fears and aching hopes inside me that I had most need to talk about to someone. And there was no one else.' Writers cannot be convivial people in work time; their chosen craft is a solitary one. But to be cut off in childhood from the society of the school playground, where the gossipy tales are told, is a particular deprivation. Rosemary Sutcliff could never have been a chatty novelist. Yet her experience of being read to throughout her childhood by a sympathetic adult bears out everything that has been researched or said about reading stories to children. If you want to understand where Rosemary Sutcliff, as a novelist, 'comes from', read *The Jungle Books, Kim* and *The Just So Stories,* preferably aloud.

This year Rosemary Sutcliff is seventy. Her latest novel, *The Shining Company,* appeared in June. For me it's a vintage volume, the work of a writer who has a distinctive view of her readers, a view which many may not know that they can have of themselves. To read Rosemary Sutcliff is to discover what reading is good for. So this anniversary and this accomplishment make me ask what might be the contemporary appeal or, more simply, the enduring attraction of the historical novels for the young. After all, much has clearly changed in children's books and reading since television became their more immediate storyteller, and novelists, now more matey and informal, adopted a more elliptical vernacular prose, in which the readers' ease is more visible than the challenge to read.

But, given her isolation, Rosemary Sutcliff needs her readers. Like her characters they people her world, so she devises means of coming close to them and drawing them into the worlds she makes out of the dark places in history. Sometimes the trick is a first-person narrative: 'I am—I was—Prosper, second son to Gerontius, lord of three cantrefs between Nant Ffrancon and the sea.' Or there's a dedication, 'For all four houses of Hilsea Modern Girls' School, Portsmouth (my school) who adopted me like a battleship or a regimental goat.' The first page swings the characters into action in a situation as clear as a television image. The names of the people and places set the rules of belonging; the relations between the sexes are formally arrayed; the battles are long and fierce. Readers who are unaccustomed to the building up of suspense in poised sentences may need a helping hand. Again, the best way into a Sutcliff narrative, a kind of initiation, is to hear it read aloud. Then you know what the author means when she says she tells her tales 'from the inside'.

Thinking of readers, I remember, with gratitude and some pain, a class of girls in a London secondary school in the early seventies. The parents of most of them had come from the Caribbean; I guess their own children are now in school. Then they were the first of their kind to speak out their awareness of the complications we now call 'multicultural'. They were reading with their gifted teacher, Joan Goody, *The Eagle of the Ninth.* On this particular day they ignored the dashing young Roman hero, recovering from a battle wound in his uncle's house in Bath, and concentrated on the girl next door, Cottia, a Briton. Cottia's uncle and aunt were taking her to the games, and in their hankering after Roman ways had tried to insist that she wear Roman clothes and speak Latin. Cottia protested, and so did the readers, on her behalf. I've never heard a more spirited discussion than that one, when those girls spoke indirectly of their nearest concerns in arguing on behalf of Cottia, who existed only in a book.

The sharing of storytelling that writers do with readers is the dialogue of imagination. Rosemary Sutcliff lives, grows and acts and suffers *in* her stories. The worlds created in her imagination have had to stand in for the world of much everyday actuality. From her therefore we can learn what the imagination does, and how it allows us all to explore what's possible, the realm of *virtual* experience. In Rosemary Sutcliff's world, heroes, heroines and readers alike walk a head taller than usual, as heroic warriors, to confront, like Drem in *Warrior Scarlet,* fearsome events as rites of passage and thus discover what is worth striving for. Readers have to expect to be spellbound in the tradition of storytelling that's much older than reading and writing, when before the days of written records bards and minstrels were entrusted with the memory of a tribe. Rosemary Sutcliff is in this tradition; she says of herself that she's 'of the minstrel kind'. This in itself sets her apart from some of the more, apparently, throwaway casualness of some contemporary writing. In these days, when we've learned to look closely at the *constructed-*

ness of narratives, she will still say that she knows when a story is 'in' her and 'waiting to be told'.

The rest, she insists, is sheer hard work: research, planning the shape and the details of themes rather than plots. But the tale is there, entire, from the beginning. Part of her gift to her readers' reading is that the same care is visible in the little books of single episodes (*A Circlet of Oak Leaves; Eagle's Egg; The Truce of the Games*) which can be read by or read to younger readers with the same spellbinding effect of what is still, for me, her most remarkable achievement, *The Lantern Bearers.* The chapter in which Aquila, the proud Roman soldier, decides to stay in Britain when the legions sail away, and light the fire in the lighthouse is as memorable as anything in a history lesson, and probably more lasting. Although heroism has been an unpopular virtue for some time, we've seen its value for the young in newsreels just lately.

Now think of historical novels, both as a genre and as a particular way of looking at our way of living and our place in history. We're born into our society at a particular time. Society changes; we contribute to the change and are changed by it. The same is true of the way we learn our language; of what it lets us take for granted and how it helps us discover what's new and strange. Historians try to understand these processes in the light of what they admit as evidence. Novelists breathe life into what they take to be the past, recent or long gone, because all novels are about time. Both historians and novelists have different ways of using the past to explain ourselves to ourselves, now.

Rosemary Sutcliff's skill is in recreating spots of time when change is both dramatic and threatening. How, one wonders, do deadly enemies learn to live together? What happens to those who stand in the way of invaders? What of the disgraced centurion (the hero of *Frontier Wolf,* which will spellbind most classes even on difficult days) who has to win back a lost reputation (the equivalent of the worst foul or missed penalty) on the miserable outposts of a crumbling empire, realising that the power he represents will soon be gone for ever? For all their intense singularity and, all right, their kinship with later forms of colonialism, these are abiding, recurrent issues. What, after all, will Europe be like in fifty years' time? Do we care enough to ask? What will our grandchildren think of us if we bring on the dark destruction of the ozone layer? Sometimes we help the young to confront these problems directly. At others we encourage them to understand how our forebears dealt with comparable if not similar ones. At all times there are common and shared as well as individual views of what is the light, what is the dark.

Most of Rosemary Sutcliff's novels have this opposition as their main theme. In a self-deprecating way she likens it to the struggle between the baddies and goodies in cowboy Western sagas. In fact, her stories have more in common with the Earthsea trilogy of Ursula LeGuin, who says we tell stories to keep ourselves from disappearing into our surroundings. The darkest tales of all are *Song*

for a Dark Queen and the most recent one, *The Shining Company.* In the first of this pair Boudicca, a rare heroine in the Sutcliff canon, is bound to avenge the sacrilegious treatment she suffered at the hands of the Romans who have no understanding of her as Queen of a matrilinear tribe. She leads her people in a savage and merciless Holy War which she cannot but lose. The legend is already sketched in the understanding of her readers; the author's task here is to revive it. It's interesting, and significant that this, the women's book, is sterner, more merciless than any of the others. It calls out the dark places in all of us.

The Shining Company is a tragedy, difficult to follow for the uninitiated because there's not the space, the breathing through the descriptions as in *The Lantern Bearers* or even in *Frontier Wolf.* There's one great battle, as good as all the rest, but if the reader does not catch the note of doom early, the end seems unfair. The facts on which the original legend of the Companions rests are scarce, but there is a seventh-century epic which celebrates them: it begins 'This is the Gododdin, Aneirin sang it.' Three hundred horsemen, trained together by ordeal and bonded by the Great Oath, met in the king's seat which is now Edinburgh. The king sent them out to defeat a Saxon war host at Catterick Bridge, but failed to ensure the backup of the rest of the clans. The Company was cut to pieces, their shining and their glory gone in all but the song of the bard who returned to tell the tale. Here he is helped by the young shieldbearer, Prosper, who, in the seventieth year of his creator, stands for all his like in these exceptional books to which children deserve entry.

If I say that reading *The Shining Company* feels like watching the events of Tiananmen Square you'll think I'm spellbound by legend. But I'm sure that the stories of that recent event are already in the making. I also know that those who care for the company children keep when they read will see the relation between the events of now and the stories Rosemary Sutcliff writes to make heroic readers. The conflict of the light and the dark is the stuff of legends of all ages. Those of the minstrel kind still make pictures, songs and tales out of words while there are those who look, listen and read.

Julian Atterton

SOURCE: "Warrior Queen: Rosemary and Time," in *Books for Your Children,* Vol. 26, No. 1, Spring, 1991, p. 18.

I think I first joined the Roman legions in the weekly adventures in one of my comics of a centurion named *Heros the Spartan.* Then my father told me the tale of Agricola and Boudicca, and of the old signal station that had been discovered on the cliff I could see from my bedroom window, and I was hooked. I read everything I could lay my hands on, and one day in Saltburn library I found *The Eagle of the Ninth.* I read it in a state of rapture, convinced it had been written just for me.

I've been reading Rosemary Sutcliff ever since, and I

think of her now with amazed admiration and with gratitude for so many fine tales. She has written some of the best adventure stories that I have ever read. She has taken me on a ride through time from the Bronze Age to the 18th century—always in the company of characters so shrewdly and warmly drawn that I have cried for them at the end. I sometimes sit down with one of her books with the intention of working out how she does it, but it is never any use: the power of her story-telling simply blows me away.

Her novels are the work of a realist. She values courage, and her characters need it, for they are all fighting in one way or another for a place and purpose in a hard world. There are dangers to be confronted, cruel choices to be made, thresholds of experience to be irrevocably crossed. Rosemary Sutcliff's novels are the first I ever read in which the hero grows up.

Yet in her strings of re-tellings from Celtic legend, such as *The Hound of Ulster* and *Tristan and Iseult,* realism gives way to the luminous magic of the imagination. Two of her largest projects have been explorations of the Arthurian Legend. The first was *Sword at Sunset,* in which she stripped away the French romance to get down to the Celtic roots and an utterly credible 6th century war-leader and his brotherhood of companions. The second was the trilogy of *The Sword and the Circle,* where she took every inch of the full-blown 15th century tradition and wove it into a tapestry of the highest medieval romance.

Rosemary Sutcliff.

Sword at Sunset is my favourite of all her books. I read it when I was eleven in a paperback that said it was for over-fourteens, which was nonsense, and I cannot for the life of me understand why this book has been out of print for so many years. So has *The Flowers of Adonis,* her telling of the life of Alkibiades, the golden chancer of Athens. Both these books are set in an adult world with adult passions, but I read them young and they helped me in the bewildering and painful years of adolescence. Let's hope Hodder & Stoughton re-publish them, for they are all *young adult* fiction could and should be.

TITLE COMMENTARY

📖 *THE QUEEN ELIZABETH STORY* (1950)

The Junior Bookshelf

SOURCE: A review of *The Queen Elizabeth Story,* in *The Junior Bookshelf,* Vol. 14, No. 3, July, 1950, p. 114.

Perdita, daughter of the Rector of Broomhill, in Devon, loved stories and her favourite was about the accession of the young Queen Elizabeth. So when rumour said that the Queen intended to visit Devon and Perdita's friends the 'Pharisees' offered her a wish, it is not surprising that she wished to see the Queen 'near enough to touch her.' But unfortunately the royal visit was timed at the gooseberry season and poor Perdita was ill in bed when she should have been presenting flowers to the Queen's Grace.

But with the aid of her loyal friend Adam, Perdita at last achieved her desire and more than she had dared to hope.

This story is for little girls who still believe in fairies and magic but there is much in it to attract some who have passed beyond this stage. The visit to the fair and to old Bideford, the description of Brendon Hall and the Ball, and the pictures of the quiet home life at the Rectory and of Perdita's simple amusements help to create a sense of period sufficient for young readers. The writing has considerable charm. It is simple and unaffected and displays an aptness in choice of epithet, a feeling for detail and a freshness appropriate to the scene. Only in Aunt Phoebe's story is there a somewhat false ring.

New York Herald Tribune Book Review

SOURCE: A review of *The Queen Elizabeth Story,* in *New York Herald Tribune Book Review,* August 20, 1950, p. 8.

Probably American children under twelve, today, first hear of "Gloriana" as legend, perhaps first in a nonsense rhyme by Laura Richards, or in the tale of Raleigh and his cloak. So, too, in Elizabeth's own time, a little girl first met her in a story, and wove a dream about her; but the child's dream could come true.

This new writer has poured into her book about young Perdita a wealth of Elizabethan background. The setting, a village in Devon; the family of the rector, the life of young Adam of the manor house, all are described with the leving care of an enthusiast. Perdita sees the fairies, off and on, then called "Pharisees." There is no exciting plot beyond Perdita's growing friendship with the imaginative Adam, and the long-awaited coming of the Queen. Her arrival and her personality live up to every one's dreams.

For all that it moves slowly and has so many details, this is an absorbing and enchanting book. It re-creates a period through a child's eyes, and leaves her with two Queen Elizabeth stories, her mother's and her own. It belongs on the shelf beside *Master Skylark*.

THE CHRONICLES OF ROBIN HOOD (1950)

The Junior Bookshelf

SOURCE: A review of *The Chronicles of Robin Hood,* in *The Junior Bookshelf,* Vol. 15, No. 1, January, 1951, p. 16.

Some tales are perennially fresh. There is about them a kind of innocency and an uncomplicated vigour which seem to belong to the youth of a people, and if in their origins there is no truth to historic events so much the worse for history! The *Iliad* and the *Odyssey* are in this class; so is the Arthurian cycle and on a lower level, perhaps, the *Lytell Geste of Robyn Hoode.* The learned have argued the matter out to their own dusty content, and consigned Robin to the limbo of discarded folklore. They have made him everything from a wood-spirit to a medieval wish-fulfilment, the answer to feudal tyranny. He survives this kind of treatment as triumphantly as ever he faced the Sheriff of Nottingham, and in the pages of this most recent version of his career, he confounds the wrongdoer and supports the weak with as much verve as ever. His familiar companions are with him, his arrows fly still preternaturally straight, and Sherwood is there again to give him shelter. The famous adventures are retold by Miss Sutcliff in limpid, happy prose, free from false medievalisms, and with a right feeling of urgency where needed.

John Lansingh Bennett

SOURCE: A review of *The Chronicles of Robin Hood,* in *Best Sellers,* Vol. 38, No. 12, March, 1979, p. 410.

[*The following excerpt is from a review of the 1978 reprinting of* The Chronicles of Robin Hood.]

Ms. Sutcliff's **Robin Hood** is, quite simply, a noble tale well wrought. It is an excellent literary work. This is its

glory and its bane. *The Chronicles of Robin Hood* is not a work of children's literature. It is accessible to few young adults—the archaic diction and vocabulary put it beyond the reach of all but the most well schooled. This will not stop me, however, from endeavoring to share it with my children when the time is ripe; for the book is too good for them to miss.

I suggest that you read this book yourself and, should you find yourself carrying it around in your heart as I have, you will find a proper time to share it with another, possibly younger. Such a reader once wrote Rosemary Sutcliff a fan letter which she recalled in an interview: "Dear Miss Sutcliff, I enjoy your books very much, and I hope that when you are dead you will go on writing books and I can go on reading them." I share that hope.

THE ARMOURER'S HOUSE (1951)

Eleanor Graham

SOURCE: A review of *The Armourer's House,* in *The Junior Bookshelf,* Vol. 15, No. 4, October, 1951, p. 180.

The publishers must be proud of this book. The production is excellent and the story worthy of all the care put in to it.

The armourer's house was in London in the days of Henry VIII and thither came Tamsyn, a little Devonshire girl, to live with her Uncle's family though she had left her heart behind her among the ships at home. She was a stranger in the house and she saw the life of London with brighter eyes on that account. The story is told in a free and easy colloquial style which, without straining the reader's attention by the use of stereotyped period jargon, keeps the most lively, vivid pictures dancing across the pages so that the ordinary everyday lives of people like the armourer's family appear as clear and credible and satisfying as any tale of the present day which a child can check for verity against her own personal experiences. There is suspense too, well balanced and sustained, in the fortunes of Tamsyn, her problems, hopes and fears, all coming to a head in a glorious climax of Christmas festivities, happy issues out of many small afflictions and a perfect happy ending. The story is, indeed, genuinely moving and most children, once fairly started on it, will rush on to the end and close the book with a long sigh of contentment which is the greatest tribute an author can receive.

The Times Literary Supplement

SOURCE: "Before Elizabeth," in *The Times Literary Supplement,* No. 2599, November 23, 1951, p. v.

Miss Sutcliff has already over-prettified history, and the habit here seems stronger. She is really best in fairy-tale, as in the tale of Tam Lin, included in this volume. Otherwise she merely creates a pageant, with very modern children peering out of elaborate fancy dress. Her lack of reality is evident even in nonhistorical matters; mint blooms at Easter, children are losing first teeth at 10 or 11, and the family goes "down the river" from Blackfriars to Chelsea. The story has much the same themes as her previous *Queen Elizabeth Story*—the wonder of the new ships, the beauty of the seasons, the older boy being a chivalrous gentleman to the young girl. There is little plot; it is mainly a chronicle of the year's festivals, full of purple patches varied with conversation such as "You'll have to shout awful loud" and "It might be him." Nevertheless it is a book that girls at least will read with pleasure.

BROTHER DUSTY-FEET (1952)

The Junior Bookshelf

SOURCE: A review of *Brother Dusty-Feet,* in *The Junior Bookshelf,* Vol. 16, No. 4, November, 1952, pp. 227-28.

This is the third of Rosemary Sutcliff's stories about children in Tudor England, and it is as attractively produced as usual. This time the central character is a boy; Hugh is an orphan of nearly eleven, and runs away from his unkind aunt to find a friend of his father's at Oxford, taking with him his big dog and a pot of periwinkle flowers from the garden of his old home. Before long he falls in with a little band of strolling players, and attracted by their friendliness, particularly that of Jonathan, who plays "the devil in scarlet tights," he joins the Company to travel with them along the dusty roads of South and West England and to act in their mumming and miracle plays in village, market town and Cathedral city. Adventures befall them, they meet queer characters of high and low degree, Jonathan regales them with tales and old legends, and all goes well until, as the result of a chance meeting, Hugh finds he must choose between this life of wandering excitement and a new life of belonging to a family and continuing his education. . . .

Miss Sutcliff's books are a good introduction for the younger reader to the historical novel. Enjoyable though her books always are, however, one cannot leave them without wishing that her attitude to children and animals were less sentimental, and that she would use greater restraint in her prettily descriptive passages. It has been interesting to read, alongside *Brother Dusty-Feet,* Rhoda Power's *Redcap Runs Away,* a story with a similar theme. This has not the touch of fantasy which may attract the younger child to Miss Sutcliff's book, but is more carefully written.

The School Librarian and School Library Review

SOURCE: A review of *Brother Dusty-Feet,* in *The School Librarian and School Library Review,* Vol. 6, No. 6, December, 1953, p. 428.

Rosemary Sutcliff has already made herself known as a successful writer for children with her two books of Tu-

dor England, *The Armourer's House* and *Queen Elizabeth Story.* In *Brother Dusty-feet,* she tells of the life of a band of strolling players at this time and how they struggled for an existence by travelling from town to town putting on their plays, sometimes with success and sometimes without.

Hugh, an orphan of ten years of age, runs away with his dog, Argos, from his aunt who ill-treats them both, and by chance joins this band of players. He is ambitious to reach Oxford and, like his father, become a servitor to some great scholar and so acquire learning himself. He has a hard life with the players with many adventures, but finally achieves his ambition.

In spite of the hardships, these strolling players are a happy band and are of a friendly and kindly nature. Hugh is an exceptionally likeable youngster and his character is well-drawn. Miss Sutcliff has portrayed the period well, although I do not feel the crudeness of life at that age sufficiently brought out. The author has, too, an unfortunate way of "talking down" to her readers and of giving explanations which should be unnecessary if the atmosphere of the age had been more firmly created. She is, however, a good story-teller and the book is an excellent introduction to the period for children a little younger than the average historical-story reader.

SIMON (1953)

Eleanor Graham

SOURCE: A review of *Simon,* in *The Junior Bookshelf,* Vol. 17, No. 4, October, 1953, pp. 207-08.

Miss Sutcliff is a good storyteller. She draws her characters with a persuasive pen and with considerable imaginative insight. She reconstructs scenes admirably. Yet, a graph of my interest as I read through this long book would have shown marked fluctuations as enthusiasm waxed and waned. I suspect that the book was written over-hastily, before the mass of material which had been accumulated for it had dropped into its proper perspective, and I felt that cutting and trimming would have strengthened both the picture and the grip of the story. Perhaps second thoughts might also have defined the religious scene to better purpose.

Having said so much, let me proceed to praise Simon as a gallant hero, and Corporal Zeal-for-the-Lord Relf as an outstanding figure on a lesser scale. Simon, indeed, was three dimensional, coming right out of the paper to you, a whole person. There are poignant pictures of the English countryside torn by a war in which both sides were Englishmen, often from the same village, perhaps even out of the same house, and though there is a certain amount of reference to the Cavaliers as the lordly ones, it has to be understood that this was no class war. Both sides came from all ranks of society. All were desperately and earnestly convinced of the rightness of their beliefs. I have often hoped that someone would write a story of the Civil

War which would cut right through the familiar conventional pictures of "Cavalier" and "Roundhead", and clarifying the issues with honest appraisal but, good story as this is, it does not do just that.

New York Herald Tribune Book Review

SOURCE: A review of *Simon,* in *New York Herald Tribune Book Review,* May 16, 1954, p. 21.

We know in America three previous stories by this popular English writer. Of the four, we like best, possibly, **Brother Dusty Feet,** with its strolling players and its background for later understanding of the drama of Tudor times. The same sort of vivid background for later reading is offered this year in Rhoda Power's *Redcap Runs Away,* about minstrels and players of an earlier time. These books are the more impressive because their authors haven't yet been affected, as ours have, with the "need" for short books and easy reading.

Simon is the longest and best written of Miss Sutcliff's books, appealing more to readers over twelve. It pictures England of the Civil War in 1640, focusing on the campaign in Devon and the west country, showing how a teen-age boy came to take his share in the fighting, and what happened to his friendship for his neighbor and friend who fought with the Royalists. The battles, the journeys, the narrow escapes, are done with vigorous realism. The setting, always vivid with this writer, is most memorable here, for this is country she knows well. There is romance, for the older girls who like "costume" stories, but chiefly it is for those boys who love old battles with youth as hero whether or not the war is one they have met already in history.

THE EAGLE OF THE NINTH (1954)

The Junior Bookshelf

SOURCE: A review of *The Eagle of the Ninth,* in *The Junior Bookshelf,* Vol. 18, No. 5, November, 1954, pp. 250-51.

The Ninth Legion (Hispania), after suffering heavy losses in the revolt of the Iceni under Boadicea, came eventually by an unexplained disaster, about 60 years later, somewhere in the north. The legion, if any of it survived, was never reconstituted; probably it was not only crushingly defeated, but also disgraced. At any rate the cause of its disappearance has never been satisfactorily explained.

On the basis of this genuine historical mystery Rosemary Sutcliff has written a tale which is of exceptional quality. Marcus Flavius Aquila, Commander of an auxiliary cohort to the Second Legion, is seriously wounded in a sudden rising of tribesmen, and made unfit for further service. This part of the story moves with power and conviction and sets the pace for the rest of the tale, which concerns Marcus's rescue from bitter despondency, in the

prospect of trying to regain the lost eagle of the Ninth, which rumour has reported as a trophy somewhere far in Caledonia. The Ninth had been his father's legion and the eagle his father's charge. How the quest is accomplished and how the eagle is brought home is a thrilling and beautifully planned story, absorbing in its re-creation of a long-vanished Britain. It is the finest historical novel I have read for a very long time.

Lavinia R. Davis

SOURCE: "In Ancient Britain," in *The New York Times Book Review,* January 9, 1955, p. 24.

When the young centurion Marcus Aquila took over his first command in a frontier garrison in ancient Britain his heart was set on a long and glorious military career. He was also determined to find out about his father who had been lost ten years earlier when the Ninth Legion had mysteriously vanished on its way to quell a rebellion in North Britain. A crippling wound in his first battle put an early end to Marcus' military career. How he achieved his second ambition, even to restoring the Eagle, the bronze standard of the lost Ninth, and clearing his father's name, makes an exceptionally fine historical novel.

The two main characters, Marcus and his former slave, a Briton named Esca, are well drawn. Their adventures, whether in battle, on the lonely hills, or in the forbidden temple where the Eagle was finally found, are invariably exciting and credible. The details of life in a Roman garrison and in the more primitive camps of the ancient Britons sound like eyewitness reports.

OUTCAST (1955)

The Junior Bookshelf

SOURCE: A review of *Outcast,* in *The Junior Bookshelf,* Vol. 19, No. 4, October, 1955, pp. 239-40.

Miss Sutcliff seems to go from strength to strength, and this stirring reconstruction of four hard years in the life of a tough young Roman-Briton shows her scholarship sound as ever, with the facts slipping easily into place with no suggestion of text-book flavour, her eye for colour and feeling for places clear as ever without the occasional spilling-over of emotion found in some of her earlier work. Beric, a Roman baby cast up by the sea, is cast out by the clan of Britons who foster him until he is sixteen, kidnapped by Greek slavers before he can gain acceptance as a Roman, sold into a Roman family, escapes and is sent to the galleys for his most gruelling experience, and loses all hope and faith in man. In the final chapters he is slowly rehabilitated by Justinius, a Roman engineer draining the British marshes, and the last page finds him capable of considering the Legion, secure now that he has a place of his own behind him.

Although his life has been one long struggle in often

desperate conditions, Miss Sutcliff avoids the extreme savagery of Henry Treece's historical books, nor does her picture seem less authentic. We still have displaced people and slave-labourers and undoubtedly those earlier ages also had people who saw the human being behind the outcast and the slave. Nor are all exploiters of slavery necessarily sadists—more often they are people like ourselves accepting a convention; an understanding of the slave's emotions rather than a description of the master's cruelty is the best preventative against further acceptance.

This story ranges wide and shows many unfamiliar and stimulating aspects of the Roman Empire; the characters stand out as living people—dowdy, kindly little Lady Lucilla, Justinius, and a host of minor characters—at ease in their setting. Both boys and girls with an interest in the past (and some who think they have none) should find this a book very much to their taste.

W. Gaye

SOURCE: A review of *Outcast,* in *The School Librarian and School Library Review,* Vol. 8, No. 1, March, 1956, pp. 69-70.

A shipwrecked roman baby boy is rescued and reared by a simple Anglo-Saxon peasant family. When, however, famine and trouble come to the village community, he is driven out into exile. He is kidnapped and sent as a slave to Greece and then to Rome, where he suffers cruelty and degradation. His loyalty to a fellow slave leads him into further trouble and finally he is shipped as a convict slave aboard a vessel bound for Britain. Brutality kills his fellow slave and only friend and revolt on his part brings him severe punishment from his Roman masters. He is thrown overboard for dead and is washed ashore on the Romney Marshes, where once more he is rescued and adopted, this time by a Roman General. He soon joins the Centurions and becomes a happy Roman youth.

The story, as we expect from this well known children's author, is very well written, but it is not convincing. After such brutality at the hands of the Romans, this sensitive boy forgives too easily and quickly. The descriptions of the handling of the slaves are unnecessarily highly coloured.

THE SHIELD RING (1956)

The Junior Bookshelf

SOURCE: A review of *The Shield Ring,* in *The Junior Bookshelf,* Vol. 20, No. 4, October, 1956, pp. 218-19.

Nearly twenty years ago, an obscure Lakeland writer, Mr. Nicholas Size, wrote a brief pamphlet about the Vikings in the secret valley of Buttermere. Here, in a hidden fastness, the Scandinavian settlers held out against the armoured strength of the Normans, unconquered, independent, owing allegiance to no man, least of all to a Norman king.

Dr. Johnson's aphorism "No good story is ever wholly true" is quoted on the title page; that, perhaps, is the right attitude in which to read the pamphlet. That the Vikings lived in the valley is certain from the proof of place names. But the recent conclusions of the English Place Names Society's researches offer little conclusive confirmation for Mr. Size's curiously suggestive theories.

They are, however, such stuff as juvenile fiction is made on. In 1946, Joyce Reason's *The Secret Fortress* used the story for a popular and vigorously written children's book; now Rosemary Sutcliff has moulded the same events into a plausible and exciting narrative.

The traditional elements are here, shaped into reality by the truth of fiction; the sudden devastating sweep of the Helm Wind which caused havoc among the Norman troops at Rydal; the mutilation of Ari Knudson, sent to Red William with terms of peace; the locating of the main Viking camp at Fell Foot, in Langdale; the construction of a decoy road which tricked the Normans into the valley of Rannerdale, where they were butchered by the hidden Vikings.

The story is, in fact, the kind of semi-history which asks to be dressed in the full regalia of fiction. Rosemary Sutcliff has used her very considerable powers as a writer to this end. The plot is ready made, but she gives us so much more—a confident excursion into eleventh century Viking life as a background for passions and hatred which end in futile bloodshed and decay, convincing characters swayed by the age-old demands of pride, courage, loyalty.

Told with spirit, skill and intelligent handling of history, this book, like Shakespeare's treatment of Holinshed and North, transforms and breathes life into the human beings of a bygone age.

New York Herald Tribune Book Review

SOURCE: A review of *The Shield Ring,* in *New York Herald Tribune Book Review,* May 12, 1957, p. 8.

A deeply stirring historical tale, one like *The Shield Ring,* is rare. The characters are forceful, sympathetic and interesting. There is a startlingly vivid picture of life in hut and Great Hall in a Viking settlement or *steading* among the northern hills and lakes of England in the eleventh century while the Normans harass its borders. The leader, the Jarl himself, boasts that "he has held the Fells free of Norman kind these twenty years or more" yet "our Shield Ring, our last stronghold, is not the barrier fells and the totter-moss between but something in the hearts of men." He speaks truly for this is a saga of courage; the courage of the three great chieftains, "the golden Jarl himself and Grey Wolf and Aiken whom men called the Beloved, with his odd gentleness and the sheen of a tempered blade about him," the courage of the boy Bjorn haunted by the fear that he might betray the secrets of the dale were he captured and tortured by the Normans, yet forcing himself to go spying among them as a harper; and the courage of his friend, the indomitable Frytha, a girl orphaned at five by Norman pillagers, who dares to spy and fight by his side.

No boy should miss the glorious "last battle," a triumph of strategy planned by the Jarl, with Normans trapped on a "road to nowhere." We see it first as an eagle might, looking down on it from a peak, then we share the bloody hand-to-hand combat under the Raven banner until the great dog Garm howls beside the fallen warriors. Splendid as was the *Eagle of the Ninth,* this is finer.

THE SILVER BRANCH (1957)

The Junior Bookshelf

SOURCE: A review of *The Silver Branch,* in *The Junior Bookshelf,* Vol. 21, No. 5, November, 1957, pp. 272-73.

It is the essence of reading Miss Sutcliff that one should be made to feel, on turning over the last page of her most recent novel, a kind of quiet impatience which has no hint of doubt in it, about the arrival of the next. No doubt, that is, that it will transport one for the time, by the evocative sensitiveness for the past, into the inner crises of dead lives and situations so as to vitalise them to a reality which is almost frightening. How great an art this is indeed, to be found more rarely even among those who write for children than elsewhere; and how much needed here, because children apprehend so largely through their imaginations!

There should, however, be at this point one comment on this splendid book which is in no way adverse criticism. The tale is in a sense a sequel to *The Eagle of the Ninth,* in which that Eagle, again recovered, regains a lost and forfeited glory by leading a desperate band of men, broken by the triumph of Allectus, the murderer of Carausius, that powerful, self-made Emperor of Britain, back to the Caesar Constantius, by whom the shattered Roman peace was restored. The scene is sombre; the struggle, we know, will go on; outside the still comfortable world of Rome the barbarians gather more thickly, and in the end, Britain will founder to disaster.

"We must tell the rest how the wind blows, and get some sleep while we can," says Flavius in almost the last words of the tale.

But the fact is that for once Miss Sutcliff, so magisterial in her control, seems to have got herself deeply involved in her background, and her subsidiary figures, her actual historical ones, have taken on looming proportions; they are stepping, whether she will have it or not, out of the background and overshadowing her own creations. The tale's true hero is Carausius, the real theme not a high adventure but the delusion of a brief gleam of hope in a dying world, and its central problem one of loyalties whose stern demands are perhaps outside the range of a child's

book. But it may be that that is how Miss Sutcliff intended it anyway.

This is not to say that the book is not magnificent for its ostensible purpose. It is perhaps the measure of a greater stature that it should make one think so seriously of then—and now!

New York Herald Tribune Book Review

SOURCE: A review of *The Silver Branch,* in *New York Herald Tribune Book Review,* May 11, 1958, p. 4.

From the "blustery autumn day" when the young doctor, Justin, disembarked from a galley in the harbor of Rutupiae (Richborough) to begin his service in Britain until the moment two years later when he and his friend Flavius Aquila (a descendant of that Marcus who went to search for "the eagle of the ninth") were hailed by a victorious Emperor for their superb work as "underground" agents, the reader of *The Silver Branch* shares the lives of these young daredevils of the fourth century and becomes as familiar as they with the district between the Thames and Southampton harbor as it was in Roman days. Roman Britain is even more completely realized here than in Miss Sutcliff's *The Eagle of the Ninth.* The plot is swift and compelling, rising to a fine climax in the wild scene of battle and flame in the basilica of Calleva (Silchester), in which the "lost" eagle again plays a part. The characters are interesting and varied, especially the daring heroes, the Emperor Carausius who hoped to steer clear of a knife in his back until Britain became strong enough to stand alone, perceptive and resourceful Aunt Honoria, and Cullen, the slave of the "silver branch." . . . This is a living, exciting story which is also good collateral reading, showing research influenced by historical imagination.

WARRIOR SCARLET (1958)

Margery Fisher

SOURCE: "Drem," in *Who's Who in Children's Books: A Treasury of the Familiar Characters of Childhood,* Holt, Rinehart and Winston, 1975, pp. 95-6.

Drem belongs to a tribe living on the South Downs during the Bronze Age. One day he overhears his grandfather and mother talking and realizes that, because of his withered arm, they do not expect him to be able to win the right to be called warrior, when the time comes, by killing a wolf single-handed. Shocked and miserable, he runs from the village and is found in the forest by Talore the Hunter, who has himself learned to do without the hand he lost in battle. With Talore's encouragement Drem returns home and in due time serves the term of initiation with the rest, but through an unlucky accident he fails to kill his wolf and is forced to live and work with the shepherds, the Little Dark People conquered by the tribesmen. Learning their craft and absorbing some of their ancient wisdom, Drem comes to terms with his loneliness, the loss of his home and of his close friend Vortrix, the condition that marks him out from his fellows. Finally, in defending an old shepherd from the wolf pack, he faces and kills the huge brute that had escaped him in his first trial, and wins the scarlet robe of a warrior.

This direct, rich story, with its constant echoes of Kipling, has a theme which may be readily translated into the language and circumstances of any individual and any period and yet it is expressed through vivid and memorable historical details which establish Drem strongly and clearly in a particular time and a particular place. This is a story of growth, of fierce personal pride disciplined and controlled by loss and frustration, of the triumph of will over weakness, of determination over defeat. Cast in the form of a physical struggle, seen in terms of a world of almost three thousand years ago, the story has emotional overtones far beyond historical exposition.

THE LANTERN BEARERS (1959)

The Christian Science Monitor

SOURCE: A review of *The Lantern Bearers,* in *The Christian Science Monitor,* November 5, 1959, p. 6B.

[In **The Lantern Bearers,** Rosemary Sutcliff] amply shows her skill in the dramatic uses of the past. It is the distant past in this case, when the Saxons were invading Britain, and individuals like Miss Sutcliff's leading characters were doubtless being caught in the cross-currents. A brother and sister are placed on opposite sides of the struggle. The sister has a child who grows into a warrior, fighting the brother's army. Emotions become mature if not always persuasive. The ins and outs of the serviceable plot are less important than the period atmosphere and detail caught in prose that gleams and glowers at the appropriate places, with no more gore than necessary to suggest the harshness of the times.

Elizabeth Hodges

SOURCE: "Lights for the Dark Ages," in *The New York Times Book Review,* November 8, 1959, p. 64.

After four hundred years, the last of the Roman Auxiliaries were leaving Britain. With their departure the great harbor light at Rutupiae went out, symbolizing the approach of the Dark Ages and the invasion of the Saxon hordes. But a small band of Roman-Britons under Ambrosius, son of Constantine, became lantern bearers, carrying the light of civilization into the onrushing darkness. One of Ambrosius' band was Aquila, who, as the legions left, made his way to his father's home, a deserter from the soldiers life that he had always known. "He found that he belonged to Britain, to the things that Rome-in-Britain stands for; not to Rome. He thought once that

they were the same thing; but they're not."

From this moment on, Aquila's lot is one of tragedy and bitterness. His home is sacked, his blind father killed, his sister carried off, and he himself made a Jutish thrall. Escaping from his captors, he joins Ambrosius' companions; and by losing himself in a noble cause he finally gains peace of soul and a purpose in life.

Besides illuminating a twilight period of English history, Rosemary Sutcliff has written a story full of exciting adventure and human conflict. Her polished style, along with her gift for story-telling and characterization, makes this an outstanding historical novel for young people with sufficient background to appreciate it.

KNIGHT'S FEE (1960)

The Junior Bookshelf

SOURCE: A review of *Knight's Fee,* in *The Junior Bookshelf,* Vol. 24, No. 5, November, 1960, pp. 308-09.

In her last two books Rosemary Sutcliff has been taken to task for not writing for children—as if anyone but the hack does any such thing. In **Knight's Fee** she has written an heroic, wise, occasionally moving story whose action, setting and psychology are within the grasp of normally intelligent children of twelve. It is in her best vein; one almost wishes the Carnegie Medal could have been saved up for this.

The scene this time is Sussex after the Conquest. In some Manors the Lord is coming to terms with his Saxon people, in others the old hatreds are fed by arrogance and brutality. Into this world, from which the strong hand of the Conqueror has been withdrawn, leaving Rufus and Robert of Normandy to squabble over his heritage like dogs, is born Randal, orphan son of a Breton soldier and a Saxon lady, now a dog-boy in Arundel Castle. Chance, almost plausibly, takes him to the service of the Lord of Dean, an enlightened knight who looks to the emergence of the English from the partnership of Norman and Saxon. Under his guidance Randal comes to the field of Tenchebrai, to knighthood, and to a bitter-sweet entry into his inheritance.

This is a very good story, swift in action, honest, coloured by the author's rich humanity. The characters are finely drawn, if lacking a little in colour; the writing is flexible and sensitive and, at last, free of those purple patches which have been a serious blemish on almost all Miss Sutcliff's previous work. Whether she is fair to bring Dr. Murray's "Dying God-King" theories, however convincing, into a book for children, is open to doubt. Her use of the Old Faith is, in terms of drama, most effective. All in all, this is Rosemary Sutcliff at her best, which is to say that the book will stand comparison with all but a small handful of the best historical stories of the past. Her debt to Kipling is implicit in every page, but this is not pastiche. She writes like Kipling because she shares his vision of the past and his love of Sussex soil.

The Times Literary Supplement

SOURCE: A review of *Knight's Fee,* in *The Times Literary Supplement,* November 25, 1960, p. xv.

Rosemary Sutcliff is a master of the concrete detail which brings home to us that our ancestors, though men like ourselves, lived in very different conditions. In *Knight's Fee,* which tells how a poor dog-boy rose by faithful service to knighthood under King Henry I, we are shown the discomfort of Arundel Castle during a gale: the window-shutters closed against the rain, no light but smoking torches, the whistling draught on the floor which must be endured or the smoke will not get through the roof-lantern. There is hot competition for the few windowless cubbyholes in the thickness of the donjon wall; even gentlemen may be driven to sleep in rows on the floor of the hall. Everyone lives in a crowd all the time.

The reader is told what people ate and at what times, as well as what they wore. The characters are not deeply explored, but the sketches of chivalrous knights and turbulent barons are adequate for the purpose of an exciting story.

In fact this would be a perfect introduction to the Middle Ages, from which older children might learn all they need of its daily life, if one great medieval preoccupation had not been completely omitted. We are told almost nothing about religion or the Church. Miss Sutcliff states that bloodthirsty old Montgomery has chosen to leave the world and make his soul in the abbey he founded at Shrewsbury; because that is history and she is always faithful to her sources. But she does not draw a world in which that sort of thing is likely to happen. Instead, evil friars (a century before St. Francis) incite the populace to lynch witches, a habit of the Renaissance rather than the Middle Ages. Her hero keeps vigil in a chapel before his knighting, a ceremony which he takes very seriously; peasants grumble about tithes; a clerk teaches the gentry their letters. But no one has a friend or relation in religion, though at that time the clergy made up such a large proportion of the population.

Miss Sutcliff does not suggest that her Saxons and Normans were agnostics; she supposes that most of them practised a pagan fertility cult. On the last page she writes flatly: "William Rufus belonged to the Old Faith", as though it were a fact universally admitted by historians. But the clerks who knew William Rufus personally wrote him down a wicked Christian or perhaps an atheist. Thus to state as a fact the fancies of modern anthropologists is to incur the danger of misleading untutored minds, even in a work of fiction.

BEOWULF (1961)

The Junior Bookshelf

SOURCE: A review of *Beowulf,* in *The Junior Bookshelf,* Vol. 25, No. 6, December, 1961, pp. 354-55.

Like others of the Bodley Head "Hero Tales," this is not a new translation but a free version which uses the original text merely as the starting point of an independent artistic enterprise. There is no point, therefore, in comparing Rosemary Sutcliff's **Beowulf** with Ian Serraillier's or any other which holds faithfully to the Anglo-Saxon text.

Miss Sutcliff has had a tough assignment for, poetry apart, **Beowulf** is really rather a nasty story redeemed by physical courage. She does the battle scenes well, as one might expect, but what she has wisely chosen to emphasise is the social life of these primitive kingdoms with its courtesy and its blend of boasting and modesty. Whether she has been equally wise in adopting such an elevated style is to be questioned. Certainly the dialogue should be formal and courtly, but Miss Sutcliff has laid it on a bit in her narrative. She has strong meat enough in the bare facts without trying to make our flesh creep.

Charles Keeping's magnificent illustrations have just that blend of bravura and homeliness which the words lack.

Margery Fisher

SOURCE: A review of *Beowulf,* in *Growing Point,* Vol. 7, No. 9, April, 1969, p. 1308.

Following the order of events in the epic, the author colours her version with her imaginative response to ancient times. Her rhythmical prose brings out the dark aspect of Beowulf's battle with the monster and his descent into the mere, makes us attentive to the heroic courtesy of kings and gives dignity to the description of Beowulf's death.

DAWN WIND (1961)

The Times Literary Supplement

SOURCE: "To the North Where the Vikings Sailed," in *The Times Literary Supplement,* December 1, 1961, p. ix.

[In] terms of its own art [*Dawn Wind*] is a better historical novel than most written for adults. It has substance and depth, it raises questions in the reader's mind about humanity and himself, and it conveys its period. That is, it conveys delicately and powerfully into the reader's mind those aspects of one particular period of stress and change which Rosemary Sutcliff has chosen to illustrate in set narrative. Even so, it is essentially a novel written for older children rather than for adults, with much tactful simplification of character, motive and event.

Properly, its hero and heroine are children when the novel starts with the shattering defeat of the Britons by Ceawlin's Saxons at Aquae Sulis. When it ends, twelve years later, they are man and woman. The boy Owain and his dog are the sole survivors of the British defeat; he befriends a tattered stray, Regina, then loses her and becomes a serf in a Saxon household; later he wins his freedom and shares in the defeat of Ceawlin by a confederacy of Saxon and Cymry. Slowly he finds and accepts his place in a changing society, and hears with the coming of Augustine and his priests a dawn wind stirring which will blow the future clean for all the peoples of this island. And happily he finds his Regina again, and marries her.

Dawn Wind is a beautifully sustained story, exciting, evocative of many moods, and in its final effect deeply moving. It is hard to see how this kind of book can be done better.

Rosemary Weber

SOURCE: "A Second Look: Dawn Wind," in *The Horn Book Magazine,* Vol. LV, No. 3, June, 1979, pp. 335-36.

Rosemary Sutcliff's novels of Roman and Saxon Britain have been highly praised and commended by critics. Her ability to describe other times and cultures is unparalleled today by writers of historical fiction—English or American. Perhaps it is her genius at bringing time and place to life that often makes her characters seem less memorable than her scenes and themes. But one of her novels, set at the time of the great final Saxon conquest over the Britons at Aquae Sulis—today's Bath—provides an exception. *Dawn Wind* introduces the reader to Owain, a lone human survivor of the battle, and to Regina, an orphaned waif.

We first encounter Owain as he regains consciousness after having been wounded in battle and follow him as he finds the bodies of his brother and his father. He lovingly claims his father's emerald ring, which goes back to the days of the first Roman legions in Britain. Although the ring plays a small, albeit vital, part in the story, it serves to link *Dawn Wind* with several other stories by Sutcliff whose settings predate this novel.

As Owain leaves the battlefield, he is alarmed by a shadowy, slinking shape, which he discovers to be one of the young war hounds, another survivor of the massacre. Owain determines to go north with Dog to the British hosting place, Viroconium, hoping to join other Britons. But fever and weakness overtake him at a small hillside steading, and Priscilla and Priscus, a childless couple, nurse him back to health. While Owain is grateful for their care and their offer of a son's place at their hearth, he feels compelled to press on to Viroconium; but he finds it a deserted ruin with only one inhabitant, the girl Regina. Owain, Regina, and Dog band together for survival; and when Saxon cattle raiders make their refuge unsafe at the end of the winter, they flee toward the coast, hoping to take ship for Gaul.

Exposure to the spring storms during the journey makes Regina fall gravely ill. To ensure care for her, Owain sells himself as a slave to a Saxon farmer and follows his new master Beornwulf many miles south. Before leaving Regina, however, he carefully buries his father's ring. Owain proves himself trustworthy, and six years later he earns his freedom by rescuing Beornwulf from a shipwreck. He chooses to fight with the Saxon border kingdoms and the Britons of Wales against the West Saxon king whose army killed his father. When Beornwulf is mortally wounded, Owain promises to oversee his homestead for four more years, until his only son and heir is fifteen. At the end of the fourth year, Owain stays yet one year more, this time to protect one of Beornwulf's daughters from being forced into marriage.

Owain is present at Cantiisburg (Canterbury), where the High King has called a council, when Augustine and his fellow monks arrive to bring Christianity to Britain. Finally free of his obligations, he makes his way north to find Regina, of whom he has had no word for eleven years. He reaches the farm where he had left her, but she is gone. Gone also is his father's ring, and in its place he finds some strands of her black hair. Eventually, he finds her waiting for him in Viroconium. The two set out together for the hill farm of Priscilla and Priscus to make a new life. The young people have hope for the future and a feeling that the dawn wind, which precedes the dawn, is rising: The Saxons and the Britons have declared a truce, and Christianity—teaching love rather than hate—has a toe hold on British soil. The dark is doomed; the light must dawn.

While incident and accident abound, the story is fully centered upon Owain. Events are described from his point of view, and his feelings are explored in depth. It is impossible not to empathize with his helplessness in the face of Regina's illness, with his loneliness during his days as a Saxon thrall—especially after the death of Dog—and with his inability to betray those who trust him. The strength of the bond between Owain and Regina attests to an unspoken love that is deep and strong and self-sacrificing. The point of the story is not lost upon children. I still remember the sixth-grade boy who discussed it with me and asked, "Do you think he really would do all that, just for a girl?"

Rosemary Sutcliff wrote a book filled with ideals that are as enduring today as they were in Owain's time: loyalty, love, and hope. Reading it, we gain confidence in their eternality in the life of humankind.

SWORD AT SUNSET (1963)

Robert Payne

SOURCE: "Britain's Warrior-King," in *The New York Times Book Review,* May 26, 1963, p. 26.

I suspect that the validity of historical fiction has very little to do with history and a great deal to do with the author's affection and understanding of the characters he creates. So in *I, Claudius* it is not the detailed exposition of the Roman background that remains in the memory but Robert Graves's passionate affection for an unruly, cantankerous and stammering emperor largely invented out of the whole cloth. In the best historical novels, history goes out of the window and love remains.

So it is in Rosemary Sutcliff's new novel *Sword at Sunset*—which is only theoretically concerned with King Arthur. As history, it is unconvincing. Miss Sutcliff's king has almost nothing to do with the familiar Arthur of folklore. She has reinvented him, given him a character of her own choosing and placed him outside the accepted legends altogether—in a closed world where nothing happens except at the dictates of her imagination. In this way—though the first-person narrator she presents is more mysterious than ever—he is somehow more credible than his legends.

This is not the Arthur of the history-books—the figure that scholars have puzzled over in the sparse chronicles of his time. At another level, he is not the central figure of Malory's *Morte d'Arthur,* or the more conventional hero of Tennyson's *Idylls of the King.* This time, he is a living presence who moves in a brilliantly lit and fantastic landscape only remotely connected with ancient England. And why not? The author, we feel sure, has studied all the sources—and then, it would seem, discarded them. What remains is an expression of the purest affection for the Arthur of her heart.

The tale she tells is an odd one indeed: as rich and sumptuous as the world described in the *Mabinogion,* as gay and menacing as *The Tale of Genji.* Many strands compose the story, including strands that derive from 19th-century fiction, so that when Arthur discovers Guinevere in the arms of Bedwyr, he speaks in the tones of Turgenev's Lavretsky in *A Nest of Gentle Folk,* gently and mournfully chiding her. Yet he is always in character. He wanders across France to buy horses in Narbonne. He is seduced by his sister. He fights battle after battle against the marauding Picts and the even more murderous Saxons (who destroy entire villages for the pleasure of destruction). Though he is depicted as a man of culture, he is most at home among the Dark People, the aboriginal inhabitants of England, who practice cannibalism and weave spells and provide a shadowy background to the brightness of Arthur, Artos the Bear.

Guinevere goes into her nunnery; Arthur is crowned in a circle of seven swords; the Saxons go down to defeat at Badon Hill, and the smoke rises over the burned-out villages—it is the smoke one remembers most vividly as it clouds the landscape and suddenly vanishes to reveal Arthur in his anguish or Guinevere at her love-making, and then there is smoke again, and the passing of armies.

Rosemary Sutcliff is a spellbinder. While we read, we believe everything she says. She has hammered out a style that rises and falls like the waves of the sea—colorful and admirably suited for the set pieces like the battles and the astonishingly successful coronation scene. She says of one of her characters that it was never any use to clamor for songs or sagas from him. "When he chose, he would give it of his own free will, harping the bird off the tree, and when he did not choose, nothing on the earth could force him." She harps the bird off the tree all the time.

The Times Literary Supplement

SOURCE: "Idylls of the King," in *The Times Literary Supplement,* No. 3200, June 28, 1963, p. 473.

For her new novel Miss Sutcliff has chosen possibly the most ambitious and difficult subject open to the historical novelist of these islands. For the sword is Arthur's, the sunset that of Arthur's Britain. Story-tellers of talent and sometimes of genius have been creating and re-creating Arthur for a thousand years, till it is now a question whether there is one Arthur or a hundred. One or many, he is a tissue of contradictions: primitive and civilized, savage and gracious, simple and sophisticated, furious and faineant, historical, unhistorical, folk-hero, *dux bellorum,* king and emperor, cavalry commander and ruler of the world.

Miss Sutcliff has given us a good story, swift, various, and at all times exciting. The convention throughout is heroic, in language and diction, and in the presentation of action and states of mind. At her best Miss Sutcliff is simple and powerful, but her narrative method involves her in a general over-simplification. Arthur, Artos the Bear, unfolds his own story: the tapestry is rich of surface but lacks depth. Its chief figure is brave and warlike, by nature merciful, by circumstance often ruthless. Above all he is patriotic. His notions are unambiguous: Roman Britain is the warm bright sun; Saxon England the horrid night which must extinguish it. He fights to win battles, but knows he cannot win the war. He is clear as to the part Fate has allotted him; in terms of the heroic ideal he has no choice save to go on fighting with his picked troop of heavy cavalry till some day, somewhere, his enemies, as fated as himself, will make an end of him. So he grows old in his country's service and in a series of battles ringing Britain from its south-western shore to north of the Wall proves himself a source of legend as well as an honest soldier doing his duty. . . .

Sword at Sunset has been constructed with loving care and close attention to detail which is factually or imaginatively authentic. Battles, hunts, the vicissitudes of peoples and the alternating seasons of the year are skilfully presented. Miss Sutcliff has a sure hand with heroism and pathos. But her novel falls short of tragedy and epic alike. It does not fully rise to its great subject. Perhaps this is saying no more than that Arthur is unlikely in the nature of things to be revealed and apprehended within the covers of a book whose strength is its narrative flow and its weakness a failure to show character in depth.

📖 *THE HOUND OF ULSTER* (1963)

The Junior Bookshelf

SOURCE: A review of *The Hound of Ulster,* in *The Junior Bookshelf,* Vol. 27, No. 3, July, 1963, pp. 161-62.

Here we have the legends of Cuchulain the Irish hero, brought together for children in a consecutive narrative. Hitherto, children may well have met only a few of these ancient stories.

Because they are Celtic in origin, the tales are a blend of magic and the everyday, of gods and heroes, of deeds so stupendous that they have no foundation in reality. Cuchulain links these stories together by his epic personality and superhuman qualities.

The stories are inevitably somewhat similar in theme—forays into enemy country, great battles in which magic or the gods decide the outcome rather than strategy or courage, duels between rival champions.

As one would expect, this powerful writer with her trained historical imagination, has given life and rich colour to these stories. They move with a swing and verve that carries the reader on from exploit to exploit. The heroes have personality as well as courage and strength and they live by a code of behaviour and loyalty.

Violence is inevitable in this turbulent and legendary world. Human life matters little and there is no mercy for the vanquished. In the main this is "just a story" to the child and he will not be disturbed by it. At times, however, the author's strong imagination runs away with her, so that occasions such as Cuchulain's battle frenzies become horrific because of the vivid detail.

A useful addition to the story-teller's bookshelf.

Padraic Colum

SOURCE: A review of *The Hound of Ulster,* in *The New York Times Book Review,* May 3, 1964, p. 26.

Ever since Standish O'Grady published his bardic history of Ireland in the nineties, story-tellers and poets have been exalting Cuchulain: James Stephens in prose versions of the sagas, W. B. Yeats in his verse plays. And this hero, out of a world where heroes have divinities for parents, has been an influence on modern Irish history.

In the school, by means of which Padraic Pearse, the moving figure in the 1916 insurrection, planned to put the heroic element into education, there was a fresco of Cuchulain as a boy taking arms, with his declaration, "I care not if my life have only the span of a day and a night if my deed be remembered by the men of Ireland."

Cuchulain's story is the grand episode of the epic tale of pagan Ireland, and, like a good deal of Irish romance, has much of supernatural and irrational in it. Here is the hero who is to die young, the one who defends his uncle's kingdom against the forces of the whole of Ireland, who has to meet a well-loved friend in single combat, who unwittingly slays his son and whose love story is charming in a way that is rare in ancient romance.

Rosemary Sutcliff, who has finely presented the Anglo-Saxon Beowulf, makes a stirring narrative out of Cuchulain's career. Here and there she misses a trick. The ancient storytellers had to make Cuchulain undefeatable. His victorious returns become monotonous as Miss Sutcliff relates them. There is one episode that would have provided relief: his courtship of Emer, a sophisticated damsel, who could be occult as well as charmingly coquettish. It would have been a relief from the raids and the slaughters. At the end, however, not the sternness but the pathos that was in the life of Cuchulain is brought out. She has sensitively presented the superman who is also gentle, loving and chivalrous.

📖 *THE MARK OF THE HORSE LORD* (1965)

William Mayne

SOURCE: "Behind the Wall," in *New Statesman,* Vol. LXIX, No. 1785, May 28, 1965, p. 854.

Bond is not far from my mind, but that's my injection, not the author's. Licence to kill is in the first chapter: the hero, Phaedrus, is a gladiator, and fights to order *à outrance* with a colleague and friend, winning his discharge. Then he meets his M, who briefs him for an assignment, very cunning. The plan involves impersonation, one so unlikely to succeed that I suspect its use as a fictional device. The impersonation is a cardinal joint, a hinge of the story (it has a number of hinges), and it leaves me making allowances for the ingenuity of it. The machining is beautifully done, and the tolerances are very fine. But it is an artifice.

The power in the story, the thing that moves the hinges, is the seven-year cycle of the primitive matriarchal system: a new husband-king for the eternal queen. The system has worked in Caledonia, but kings obtain in Ireland, and in the new wave of invaders from there. The relationship of tribe to *tanist* is made clear to me, who had before thought it a theoretical conceit. In that same cold wind, king (or is it joker?) replaces queen. In that spilt blood the divine right of kings is hard to distinguish from the divine wrong of kings. Brand X and the brand Excalibur are alike unable to leach out, bleach out, the blood. I hope we'll have more of Miss Sutcliff's speculations of kingship, though Phaedrus is, I fear, no more on the heroic scale than 007 is. They are both canny roughnecks. I do not think the last lines of the story make the hero into a Hero, because, somehow, the lines of fate have been surgically stretched. Still, what are plots? But the guinea stamp.

The Junior Bookshelf

SOURCE: A review of *The Mark of the Horse Lord,* in *The Junior Bookshelf,* Vol. 29, No. 3, June, 1965, pp. 159-60.

The debt which children's literature owes to Miss Sutcliff has yet to be assessed. Certainly the real literature for children will be substantially more in her debt after the distribution of [*The Mark of the Horse Lord*]. It has a certain Ruritanian flavour, though it is anything but Ruritanian in period; but the "drafting" of the emancipated Gladiator, Phaedrus, to impersonate the lost Midir, heir to the kingdom of Dalriada, has inescapably Ruritanian consequences, and his expedient marriage to Murna, the Royal Woman, carries the parallel with Rassendyll still further. On all counts it is a story of bloody events which are in no way glamourised any more than they are sensationalised, and the end is perhaps to youthful tastes an unhappy one. When Phaedrus, captive of the Roman garrison, is offered his freedom at the price of selling his adopted people into slavery, he has but one way out and makes a good "Roman" end. Miss Sutcliff's gift for writing matter-of-factly yet vividly about barbarous times is nowhere better illustrated, and her treatment of the situation between Phaedrus and his Queen is a lesson in tact which ought to be widely copied. Her Dalriads and Caledones may be more popularly known as Picts and Scots but her nomenclature in this connection, as in others, makes no difference to the fact that *The Mark of the Horse Lord* is a thundering good story by a complete artist.

Margery Fisher

SOURCE: A review of *The Mark of the Horse Lord,* in *Growing Point,* Vol. 4, No. 8, March, 1966, p. 664.

The Mark of the Horse Lord is vintage Sutcliff—full of movement and excitement, with a strong well-planned story. Here in Roman Britain a gladiator, Phaedrus, has been freed as a reward for his prowess. He is out of a job—but not for long, for strangers in a tavern notice his strong resemblance to Midir, hereditary prince of the Dalriads, supposed dead but in fact blinded and exiled by his enemy, the Royal Woman who rules the west coast of Scotland. Phaedrus becomes a pawn in a complex tribal war in which he discovers new loyalties and ambitions and, like so many of Rosemary Sutcliff's heroes, finds death the only way in which he can help those for whom

hail, the two hosts rolled together, seeming at the last instant to gather themselves like two great animals, then spring for each other's throats.

A few moments later, without ever taking his eyes from the reeling press below, Aquila said to the man beside him, 'Now! Sound me the charge!' And the dull roar of battle and the storm cock's shining song were drowned in the ringing *tran-ta-ran* of the cavalry trumpet. Falcon flung up his head and neighed, adding his defiance to the defiance of the trumpet, not needing his rider's urging heel in his flank as he broke from a stand into a canter, from a canter into a full flying gallop. Aquila heard behind him the hoof-thunder of the cavalry wing sweeping down the hillside into the teeth of the westerly gale. He was yelling the war cry, 'Constantine! Constantine!' And he heard it caught up in a great rushing wave of sound. Guitolinus's cavalry wheeled about to meet them, and as they thundered down upon each other, Aquila's sight was full of a wild wave of up-tossed horses' heads, the dazzle of the stormy sunlight on shield-rim and sword-blade, a nearing wall of faces with staring eyes and open, yelling mouths. He caught the glint of gilded bronze and the emerald flash of a wind-torn silken cloak where Guitolinus rode among his men. Then they rolled together with a shock that seemed as though it must shake the very roots of the fortress hill.

Guitolinus's cavalry crumpled and gave ground, then gathered

From The Lantern Bearers, *written by Rosemary Sutcliff. Illustrated by Charles Keeping.*

he has accepted responsibility. Behind the familiar theme of loyalty and duty lies a tremendous, urgent story of violent fighting and tentative affections, of personal friendship, of travel in distant parts of Dalriada and Caledonia. It is very much Sutcliff country and whether she is describing Romans, Picts or Scots, legionary fighting or primitive poisoning, she is sure with detail and vivid in the pictures she draws, evoking from the reader the response which only a writer of her calibre can expect. Perhaps Roman Britain was not exactly like this but she, like her master Kipling, can persuade us that it was.

HEROES AND HISTORY (1965)

The Junior Bookshelf

SOURCE: A review of *Heroes and History,* in *The Junior Bookshelf,* Vol. 29, No. 5, October, 1965, p. 299.

At first one feels a kind of dismay that a writer of Miss Sutcliff's creative capacity should be forced into any kind of mould, but the feeling is soon dispelled as the book gathers way. Perhaps, in fact, there is no-one better suited to this particular task than this author. She has shown so clearly, time and again, how well she understands the mystique of the hero and the world's recurrent need for a hero-figure on whom to dwell and conjecture. Her own choice of Caractacus, Arthur, Alfred, Hereward, Llewellin, Robin Hood, Wallace, the Bruce, Glyndwr and Montrose demonstrates her instinct. Nor is she content to take some middle way between legend and fact; she relates both and discusses each in terms of the other, a method especially effective with the more shadowy figures of, for instance, Arthur, Hereward, or Robin Hood. She is at times exceptionally informative and much of the text is a necessary corrective to nursery romancing and sundry re-tellings in a white-washing mood. There is no nonsense about "goodies" and "baddies" in these portraits, though recent opinion might balk at the rather abrupt dismissal of King John as "wicked and uncouth." Pedants of style might object to the frequent use of "roaring" as both adjective and verb though it is apt enough in each context. Surprisingly, there are some misprints.

Miss Sutcliff suggests that the particular "hero-light" she has in mind faded with the dawning of the Modern world on Bosworth field. One hopes she may revise this opinion, or at least develop her hint of another type of hero into a fresh anthology of "larger than life" heroes up to and beyond Lawrence of Arabia.

The Times Literary Supplement

SOURCE: "Famous Men," in *The Times Literary Supplement,* No. 3328, December 9, 1965, p. 1144.

The legendary heroes of British history make a good romantic theme. Significantly, with the possible exception of Alfred, they are all representatives of lost causes. Caractacus, Hereward, Llewellin, Wallace, Bruce and Owen Glyndwr were all fighting losing battles for national independence. Arthur and Robin Hood are identified with a lost way of life. They all embody the romantic idea, which is given full rein by Miss Sutcliff. Hereward is "a man in his full strong prime, a man like a west wind, a thundercloud and a burst of sunshine rolled into one". She talks of "bands of kindred spirits", her characters are always "from home". These are clichés of the romantic imagination, and it may be this which has led Miss Sutcliff to perpetuate the attractive, but historically untenable, idea that after the death of Richard III "the Modern World started next day with Henry VII". Romantic imagination cannot, however, explain the curious spelling of Hampden, of ship-money fame, as Hampton, nor the introduction of the English Prayer Book into Scotland ten years early. Miss Sutcliff is always fluent and readable, but her search for "the man behind the legend" does not show her at her best.

THE HIGH DEEDS OF FINN MAC COOL (1967)

Margery Fisher

SOURCE: A review of *The High Deeds of Finn Mac Cool,* in *Growing Point,* Vol. 6, No. 2, July, 1967, p. 943.

Rosemary Sutcliff should be everyone's choice for a re-telling of high deeds of ancient heroes, for she commands a rich prose that gives the full value of dignity and weight to the Irish legends; and the rhythms of her sentences, loose, flowing, full of movement, constantly shifting their emphasis, are those of the traditional story-teller in whose memory the Southern Irish lands, animals, clouds and heroes have a permanent life. Central in the book is the tale of the breaking of the Fianna by the unhallowed love of Dearmid and Grania. Beside the pathos of this familiar tale there is the active account of the finding of Finn's hounds Bran and Skalawn, and, in quite another mood, the story of Finn's half-fairy son Oisin and his sojourn in the Land of Youth for love of Niamh of the Golden Hair. The re-telling here is worthy to be read as an interesting analogue to Masefield's unforgettable poem *Ossian,* and the whole book proves Rosemary Sutcliff's right to a place in the long hierarchy of bards, known and unknown.

THE CHIEF'S DAUGHTER (1967)

J. S. Jenkins

SOURCE: A review of *The Chief's Daughter,* in *Children's Book News,* London, Vol. 3, No. 1, January-February, 1968, p. 21.

Rosemary Sutcliff has never impoverished her rich and rhythmic prose to meet young readers at their own linguistic level. Her assumption that they are able to absorb more than they can explain partially accounts for her success with older children. *The Chief's Daughter* is a welcome addition to an admirable series of books simple enough for six- to nine-year-olds to enjoy reading. In it, a Welsh chieftain's daughter saves a young Irish prisoner from being sacrificed to the Black Mother Goddess and is herself saved unwittingly by him. Some Antelope readers might at first be puzzled by the byres and bothies and, in hesitating over words and sentences, miss the splendid sweep of the whole. Twenty minutes spent reading this story aloud would be time well spent, for few children, I think, will remain unresponsive to this dramatic tale so effectively told.

The Junior Bookshelf

SOURCE: A review of *The Chief's Daughter*, in *The Junior Bookshelf*, Vol. 32, No. 2, April, 1968, p. 106.

This is a little gem by one of our finest historical writers for children, but it is a story of a harsh period in history, and the drama involved will demand a great deal of the reader of the usual age range associated with the "Antelope" series. It is always good to stimulate the child's imagination, and enlarge the young reader's vocabulary in the way that this story does so splendidly, but this is not a story for children who are only beginning to enjoy reading to themselves.

A CIRCLET OF OAK LEAVES (1968)

G. V. Barton

SOURCE: A review of *A Circlet of Oak Leaves*, in *Children's Book News*, London, Vol. 4, No. 1, January-February, 1969, p. 31.

Antelope books, intended for the six-to-nine age group, have a deservedly high reputation for quality of story and good simple writing. . . .

A Circlet of Oak Leaves was originally published as a short story in *Winter's Tales for Children I*. Aracos, now a horse breeder in the hills of Roman Britain, in a rash change of identity in battle long ago earned for a comrade the accolade of a gilt circlet of oak leaves. Now, years later, the circlet finally reaches its rightful owner. This is a superb short story, but I feel that its approach is too mature and its style too complex to be contained within the bounds of this particular series. Also knowledge of Roman Britain is definitely needed, and the meaning of various technical terms will have to be explained to even an intelligent nine-year-old, as there is no glossary.

The Junior Bookshelf

SOURCE: A review of *A Circlet of Oak Leaves*, in *The Junior Bookshelf*, Vol. 33, No. 2, April, 1969, pp. 110-11.

How could a combination of Rosemary Sutcliff and [illustrator] Victor Ambrus be anything but a great success, both give of their best and unlike some authors and artists do not believe that because a book is in a series of "easy" books for younger readers it is inferior, rather the opposite.

The award of a circlet of oak leaves is the Roman equivalent of the Victoria Cross. This excellent book tells how Aracos, the horse breeder, earns himself the right to possess the circlet ten years after the battle where it was won. It is a deeply emotional tale, full of the dourness of the north that Rosemary Sutcliff captures so well. The vigorous illustrations match the text to perfection. . . .

Aracos the hero is a sympathetic figure, so too is Felix, the standard bearer whose place he takes in the fearful battle, full of warmth and humanity as he repays the faith that Aracos had in him.

THE FLOWERS OF ADONIS (1969)

Margery Fisher

SOURCE: A review of *The Flowers of Adonis*, in *Growing Point*, Vol. 8, No. 5, November, 1969, p. 1430.

Alkibiades stands firm in the centre of this novel like a great statue, but the author has moved behind the historical figure, though she admits that he is an enigma who 'casts a glamour that comes clean down the centuries, a dazzle of personal magnetism that makes it hard to see the man behind.' A novel in simple narrative form might well have sagged under the weight of the material she uses but her plan is architecturally brilliant. The story moves forward section by section with a number of narrators, each with his or her personal view of the hero and each taking shape for the reader because of this view as well as because of the particular circumstances of the involvement. The narrators stand for types in the classical world and some (perhaps the whore Timandra and Endius the Spartan) remain types for all their expressed feelings; but there are others—notably Timotheus, the man-in-the-street of Athens, and the loyal, bibulous sailor Antiochus, who stretch the book with the vigour of personality.

Rosemary Sutcliff offers her own interpretation of certain events (especially the collapse of the Athenian Fleet in the East) which neither Alkibiades's contemporaries nor later historians have fully explained. Otherwise she takes the events of history as her skeleton, filling it out with a novelist's episodes but doing no violence to fact. The hero she presents is in the Romantic rather than the Classical tradition; tragedy is touched with melancholy and action is pervaded with richness of feeling. There is tremendous power in the book, power in the descriptions of naval battles and street crowds, in the evocation of the rites of Adonis, in the recurrent images and transitions of atmosphere and mood; and she offers more generously than ever before those effortless small details which spell out the authenticity of her impressive fiction.

W. G. Rogers

SOURCE: A review of *The Flowers of Adonis*, in *The New York Times Book Review*, February 15, 1970, p. 46.

If in your childhood you were treated to the simplified versions of Greek history and legend that captivated most of us, you have carried through the years a picture of Alcibiades (c. 450-404 B.C.) as the Judas of Athens. It was an all-dark picture. Granted, he scored some military and diplomatic victories—but the emphasis was on his blasphemous behavior, his corruption of youth and his betrayal of his country.

When you stop to think (as Rosemary Sutcliff has stopped to think well and long in this novel), you are forced to acknowledge redeeming features in this melodramatic, oversize, godlike figure. He was handsome, fearless, master of the weapons of war as well as of tactics and strategy, and an incomparable orator. He could talk his way or fight his way to victory. Half the time, he was a spectacular success at both.

The balanced mixture of good and bad given us here makes for high-level readability. Miss Sutcliff, by-passing the excesses of the unbridled Alcibiades's youth—he had a dubious relationship with Socrates—begins her story with his departure as one of three commanders to lay siege to Syracuse. Athens, like Alcibiades, was boundlessly ambitious. One goal was hegemony from Asia Minor to Sicily and beyond—as big a bite for Athens as would be the stretch from the Elbe River to Southeast Asia for the United States.

It destroyed Athens in the mad course of the Peloponnesian War—victories alternating with disasters on land and sea, betrayals, surrenders, torture, chicanery in statesmen and shyster politicians. Alcibiades betrays friendly Athenians in Sicily and deserts to Sparta; he betrays Sparta and deserts to Athens. He intrigues; he plunges once again into the thick of the fight—on the battlements, or on the prow of a trireme.

The question always is, was Alcibiades savagely put upon by jealous and vindictive peers, or did his unconscionable behavior drive them to impose sanctions? Which came first, their injustice or his treachery? Miss Sutcliff sympathizes with her hero. A front page in her book quotes from *Cyrano de Bergerac,* and it is most apt thus to imply a comparison between the two egoists and swashbucklers—though the Greek was no romantic lover. In the long run, she stresses Alcibiades's abiding love for the city which, though he saved it and destroyed it, though it condemned him to exile and death, raised him up and provided the base from which he climbed to honor, glory and notoriety.

The story is told by a team of narrators, a bit awkward, but you quickly accept the device. There is an abundance of colorful detail. There are two heartsick women. And whether or not you approve, you wind up an enthusiastic partisan of the indomitable warrior and commander who never says die—yet dies.

THE WITCH'S BRAT (1970)

The Times Literary Supplement

SOURCE: "Conflict and Conscience," in *The Times Literary Supplement,* No. 3583, October 30, 1970, pp. 1264-65.

A hunch-backed, crooked-legged orphan, [Lovel] lives with his grandmother, a skilled herbalist and wise-woman. The countryfolk come to her for healing and advice, but they half fear her as a witch, and when her death leaves Lovel unprotected, they lose little time in stoning him from the village. Ill and starving, he is eventually given refuge in a monastery, where he is allowed to stay on as a general dogsbody when he is well again. The knowledge of herbs he has learnt from his grandmother and his natural inclinations gradually lead to his attachment to the physic garden and later to the infirmary. There he might have been content to stay for the rest of his days had not the outside world called to him in the person of Rahere, the one-time King's jester, who seeks his help in the hospital he is building.

At St. Bartholomew's, Lovel has the opportunity to fulfil all that his innate desires and former training have been leading up to, but, as one of the monks says: "For an Infirmarer there are two ways. One is to bleed a little of your own life away with every sick soul who passes through your hands. The other is to do all that may be done for the sick, but to stand well back while doing it." Much as he longs for the first way, Lovel is troubled to find that . . . he is doing all he can but standing back.

Through Nick, a boy crippled like himself, he finds his salvation, for unlike his own, Nick's leg is crooked as a result of an accident, and Lovel is confident he can straighten it. Over several months of physiotherapy—or perhaps osteopathy—he succeeds in doing so. As he watches Nick go away to his work with hardly a limp, Lovel suddenly feels very tired, and realizes that "he must have bled quite a lot of his own life away with Nick", and that in curing him he has also cured himself.

This is a slight book compared with many of Rosemary Sutcliffs . . . , but it is far from being a trifle. The author takes it as seriously as she does all her work, and there is the same understanding of people and the same care for truth that informs the best of it. Lovel's life may be a quiet one and his story lacking in excitement, but the unusual theme does not fail to hold the reader's interest, for Lovel is a sympathetic figure and more real than Rahere himself.

M. Crouch

SOURCE: A review of *The Witch's Brat,* in *The Junior Bookshelf,* Vol. 35, No. 1, February, 1971, p. 72.

It is, by my reckoning, five years since Rosemary Sutcliff last gave us an historical novel for the young, and in this new one, instead of continuing in the vein begun in **The Lantern Bearers,** she harks back to an earlier manner, to the period of **Knight's Fee** and to the scale of her first books.

I wonder if she would have written this book if Kipling, whom as we all know she reverences, had not written the last story in *Rewards and Fairies.* The sad fool, Rahere, who dominates that incomparable story haunts the imagination, and in ***The Witch's Brat*** Miss Sutcliff sets out to explore the mystery of a king's clown who became something like a saint. She shows something of his gaiety and his bitterness, the driving resolution which created a priory and a great hospital amid the mud and muddle of Smithfield and the wisdom and humility which competed with his deep melancholy.

But this is the story not of Rahere but of the crippled boy whom he befriends and turns into a healer. In Norman England the "breakers" are in control, the "makers" like Rahere come a poor second, and the "menders" like Lovel trail behind, tired, suffering but quiet and free. Lovel has a place in Miss Sutcliff's gallery of "originals", although not a very distinguished one. One has the feeling that the book is not finished, that the material calls for a wider canvas, that this is indeed the sketch for an altogether bigger story. Did time run out? For inspiration surely was not lacking.

TRISTAN AND ISEULT (1971)

C. S. Hannabuss

SOURCE: A review of *Tristan and Iseult,* in *Children's Book Review,* Vol. I, No. 3, June, 1971, p. 97.

'And Tristan said, "I love you. Though it is likely to be the death of both of us, I love you, Iseult". . . . So Tristan put his arms round her and held her fiercely close, and she clung to him so that they were together as a honeysuckle clinging to a hazel tree. But when the night was over, they sailed with the morning tide'. The author has dispensed with the love potion of tradition of Gottfried von Strassburg and the many other tellers of this famous tale of love, and has most movingly portrayed the lovers falling ineluctably in love and Tristan's sacrifice of Duty to Love. This has involved at the same time an idealization of Iseult's character (partly based on fine omission, e.g. of Iseult's use of her maid for the nuptial night with King Mark) and a greater degree of realistic characterization, as when she repents her fatal impetuosity. The ideal fusion of spiritual and sensual their love represents is persistently contrasted with the omnipresent danger of being found out—as Andret, Mark's jealous nephew, spies, the author writes with sympathetic fatalism: 'And the love between Tristan and Iseult would not let them be . . . until at last, whether they would or no, they came together again. And all the while Andret watched'.

Another feature the author has interestingly modified is the figure of King Mark of Cornwall, to whom Iseult is unfaithful. He, like Arthur at the adultery of Guinevere with Lancelot, is filled with anguish rather than rage: his patience becomes exhausted and he chokes as he decides to execute the lovers—'I will make an end'—as if he is consigning his own affections to death. To change the black villain into this sad king hurt so deeply by what Destiny leads his closest friends to be, is to sophisticate the moral issues delicately. It also furnishes another and

unexpected side to this poem to the poignant pessimism and nobility of love. Tristan has his fairytale qualities extended—his battlelust and his victory over the fire-drake seem aspects of youth as he gazes across the sea from Brittany, dissatisfied at the emptiness of his marriage with the other Iseult, Iseult of the White Hands. The triviality of the issue which leads to Tristan's fatal wound, and the arrival of Iseult too late are the final, sardonic comments in this tale of love re-told with such control of sentiment and such verbal beauty.

Kirkus Reviews

SOURCE: A review of *Tristan and Iseult,* in *Kirkus Reviews,* Vol. XXXIX, No. 18, September 15, 1971, pp. 1015-16.

In presenting stories from the past, Rosemary Sutcliff has an unusual capacity for retaining the flavor of the original while discarding antiquated syntax and inconsequential detail. Here, however, although her technique is sound, the power of her story is diminished by a strange (and self-confessed) alteration of the traditional texts. In all other versions Tristan and Iseult are lovers doomed after drinking a magic potion intended for Iseult and her husband Mark; Miss Sutcliff considers this "artificial" and prefers a love springing from natural sources. What follows is a triangle similar to Arthur-Guinevere-Lancelot, dramatic in its own way but not as distinctive as the original. The story is filled with adventure and adversity—a firedrake killed, intrigue at court, a death sentence and escape, the separation of the lovers. Tristan marries another Iseult, remains loving and then breaks with his real love, but they are reunited in death. With all the vagaries of the romance and the conventions of the code it has a strong appeal, but it's not the real thing.

THE TRUCE OF THE GAMES (1971)

Margery Fisher

SOURCE: A review of *The Truce of the Games,* in *Growing Point,* Vol. 10, No. 3, September, 1971, p. 1777.

In the early stage of reading a child may well be caught by a story about the past if it is of a domestic and documentary kind. Such a child does not, at this stage, want or even need to accumulate historical fact so much as to make acquaintance with the feel of a period, so that in his mind a chart may be forming on which he can, as it were, mark the places he has been to—Elizabethan London perhaps or an American frontier a century ago or, as here, classical Greece.

Rosemary Sutcliff's short book, ***The truce of the Games,*** is extremely simple in plan. Two boys, almost due for military service, meet at the Olympics. Amyntas is Athenian: the criss-cross scars on Leon's back bear witness to a Spartan upbringing. Their countries are at war—but even war gives way to the four-yearly Games. The friendly rivals soon realise they are the strongest contestants in the 400 Yards for boys; the race is run and the result is in a sense an open one. Neither boy speaks of the implications of this isolated month in their lives until their leave-taking, when Leon puts into words what has been in their minds—"The Gods be with you, Amyntas, and grant that we never meet again."

The situation is treated briefly and seriously. The author trusts even young readers to follow and sympathise with the confusion in the mind of Amyntas, experiencing for the first time the realities of national rivalry. It is a situation that in itself speaks of ancient Greece, as does every sentence of Rosemary Sutcliff's economical writing. Here is one among many passages that illustrate her unerring skill in placing significant details and words:

> The water was widening between ship and shore: the Bo'sun struck up the rowing time on his flute, and the rowers bent to their oars, sending the *Paralos* through the water towards the harbour mouth. Soon the crowd on shore was only a shingle of dark and coloured and white along the waterfront. But far off beyond the roofs of the warehouses and the covered docks, a flake of light showed where high over Athens the sunlight flashed back from the upraised spearblade of the great Athene of the Citadel, four miles away.

But documentation goes deeper than organic description. All through this simply stated anecdote runs the idea of greatness, expressed in images as well as actualities, suggesting indirectly what Greek myths and Greek culture really give us. In the passage quoted above the reader, like Amyntas, feels the sheer awesome presiding height of the Athene; of the last day of the Games the boy remembers most clearly "looking up out of the torchlight, and seeing, high and remote above it all, the winged tripods on the roof of the great Temple, outlined against the light of a moon two days past the full." When he takes a bronze bull to offer to Olympian Zeus he is awed and dwarfed by the huge statue in the temple; "all the known landmarks of the world of men were left behind," he feels, "in the face of such immensity." It is the measure of this book and of all Rosemary Sutcliff's work that so much comes through her words which is not explicitly stated.

Judith Aldridge

SOURCE: A review of *The Truce of the Games*, in *Children's Book Review*, Vol. I, No. 5, October, 1971, pp. 163-64.

This is Rosemary Sutcliff's third book in the Antelope series, which aims to offer short, single-plot stories for seven- to nine-year-olds. Of necessity, then, this story of the friendship of two boys, one Spartan, one Athenian, who meet at the Olympic Games, lacks the depth and range of the author's full-length novels. It has many of their qualities, however. The writing is easy and colourful, though more succinct and limited in vocabulary than usual, the main characters are convincing, the setting presented with loving and accurate detail.

Some of these details, and allusions to stories and customs of the time may well baffle young readers (unless they are fortunate enough to have a knowledgeable adult to hand, or this book is offered alongside a school project on the Greeks). This apart, the book provides a well-structured tale and challenging, though not difficult reading for many seven- to nine-year-olds.

HEATHER, OAK, AND OLIVE: THREE STORIES (1972)

Dorothy Crowder

SOURCE: A review of *Heather, Oak, and Olive: Three Stories*, in *Library Journal*, Vol. 97, No. 12, June 15, 1972, p. 2240.

In these three stories, Sutcliff does her usual splendid job of bringing the world of antiquity to life. In the first tale, **"The Chief's Daughter,"** heather represents pre-Roman Wales. At great personal risk 10-year-old Nessan saves an Irish captive lad from being sacrificed to the Black Mother, the goddess whose wrath has apparently dried up the water supply. In **"A Circlet of Oak Leaves,"** oak stands for the story of an army medic and a young cavalry officer in Roman Britain; while in **"A Crown of Wild Olive,"** the olive is symbolic of the running of the Double Stade in the Olympic Games and the friendship and rivalry between two boys entered in the race. In each of the latter two stories, a major conflict is presented: whether to conceal the truth about winning the highest award for bravery in battle, the circlet of oak leaves; whether the best runner is the one who wins the race or the one held back by an injury. The brevity and clarity of each of these selections make them suitable for readers younger than the usual Sutcliff fans and they can be enjoyed as well for their own excellence.

THE CAPRICORN BRACELET (1973)

The Times Literary Supplement

SOURCE: "Nasty and Brutish," in *The Times Literary Supplement*, No. 3734, September 28, 1973, p. 1112.

The Capricorn Bracelet is a group of six short stories, based on BBC scripts for a series on Roman Scotland. Each story is set in a different time during the Roman occupation, somewhere on or beyond Hadrian's wall; the link between them is that each concerns the owner of an army bracelet, a kind of distinguished service medal, handed down the generations of frontier fighters.

The qualities that make Rosemary Sutcliff deservedly one of our most admired writers for the young are fitfully in evidence here—the sheer solidity she can give to a remote time and place with a detail here and there, a turn of phrase, a flash of feeling. But the book does not really rise above its semi-educational origin. The link between the tales is very fragile; the life of the outpost soldier which all the heroes lead is the true connexion, the gradual replacement of highly disciplined men who have seen Rome by wild frontier wolves, whose home is a frontier tribe, the true subject. If the true subject were Miss Sutcliff's usual one—the need for courage, the soul-on-the-anvil theme, then her stories would not need the background notes here appended to each one. This is a vivid history lesson, but one must regretfully hope that nobody new to Miss Sutcliff's work stumbles on this book first; or that if they do, they skip introduction and notes, and read the stories for themselves.

Margery Fisher

SOURCE: A review of *The Capricorn Bracelet,* in *Growing Point,* Vol. 12, No. 6, December, 1973, p. 2284.

Rosemary Sutcliff makes a point that seems still more valid for today in **The Capricorn bracelet,** a set of linked stories which in no way mitigate the horrors of war. The first episode, in which a lad survives the sacking of London by Boudicca and her hordes, is as powerful as anything she has written, and the ensuing stories are braced with details of changing strategies of war through four centuries—for example, a night-raid on the mounts stabled under the Wall and a pincer-movement against Saxon marauders in which ships of the Roman Navy play a part. In each story, too, the discipline of Rome is evident, though the pattern changes. The frontier scouts operating beyond the Wall in the fourth century have left formal drill far behind but their feeling of solidarity with the Empire is as strong as it was when the legions first came to Britain; it is as strong even in the soldiers conscripted to follow Maximus in his bid for the Imperial crown, when Rome's power is visibly fading. But the theme of these stories is neither loyalty nor strategy, but integration. Lucius, the boy who flees from burning London, is pure-born Roman, but the bracelet he wins later in his life for exceptional service as a legionary is bequeathed to descendants who through intermarriage with British women are slowly becoming a mixed race. These stirring tales have been expanded from scripts written for Radio Scotland and the settings of all but the first one take us on to or north of the Border. For the first Lucius, the Legion was the only home he had: his descendants prepare to live as natives in Caledonia. The point is salutary and is integral to a strong, active, imaginative picture of the past, to which Charles Keeping has added black and white illustrations that stress the active rather than the morbid side of war.

📖 *THE CHANGELING* (1974)

G. Bott

SOURCE: A review of *The Changeling,* in *The Junior Bookshelf,* Vol. 39, No. 1, February, 1975, p. 52.

The son of Murna and Conan, clan chieftain of the Epidii, is snatched away and a child of the Dark People substituted. This changeling can bring only evil, for the Dark Folk are feared; but Conan rears the boy, Tethra, in spite of black days and tribal discontent. Tethra senses the hostility and slips away to join his own people.

Separation is not easy, and he sees Conan gored by a stag. He persuades his mother to give him the Healing Magic; conscious of his own danger, he saves his father's life.

A tale of conflicting loyalties, it coheres with all the magic of a fine story-teller's art. The plot is uncomplicated, hackneyed almost, but Rosemary Sutcliff's direct, rhythmic prose and her impeccable feeling for the atmosphere of time and place ensure that this tale for the under-nines has merit to match its tensions.

David Rees

SOURCE: A review of *The Changeling,* in *The Times Literary Supplement,* No. 3813, April 4, 1975, p. 372.

Tethra is brought up by the Golden People, but when he reaches adolescence he is filled with a longing to find out about his real parents, and returns to his own tribe. However, there is no easy answer to his problems; even though he is reunited with his mother, he is torn by a sense of loyalty to his adoptive family. When his adoptive father is badly wounded by a stag Tethra returns to the Golden People to help cure him. The background of empty hills and bleak moorland is beautifully evoked, and though its surface seems exceedingly simple, the story involves complex problems of relationships between parents and children.

📖 *WE LIVED IN DRUMFYVIE* (with Margaret Lyford-Pike, 1975)

Margery Fisher

SOURCE: A review of *We Lived in Drumfyvie,* in *Growing Point,* Vol. 14, No. 3, September, 1975, p. 2682.

One of the happiest and most vivid fact/fiction combinations of recent months, **We lived in Drumfyvie,** suitably celebrates the 800 years of Scottish burghs at the moment when they are being merged into wider administrative units. The fictional history of Drumfyvie begins in 1137 when David I confers on the town the status of Burgh and puts it under the authority of one Red Duncan, whose oppressive rule ends, according to old Effie's prophecy, when he is killed in an accident caused by his own goshawk. Under his successor, Sir Donald Maitland, the burgh grows and prospers, through trade and wise local government. Plague hits it in the fifteenth century and a young apothecary's assistant proves his worth; in the sixteenth century a merchant builds a fine house with glazed windows, and an old woman dies after being swum for a witch. Major events and minor changes affect Drumfyvie through the centuries and we last see it in 1897 when a pageant of its history is devised for Queen Victoria's Diamond Jubilee. The book benefits from the links—of family, circumstance or context—which Rosemary Sutcliff has always used to such purpose in her stories, while the book has a direct, positive quality which perhaps derives from its connection with radio broadcasting. Books like this, with their informative aspect tactfully and subtly incorporated in an envelope of fiction, should be for children from ten or so a pleasant and stimulating way to meet some of the economic changes and national events of the past as they must have seemed to ordinary folk.

Gordon Parsons

SOURCE: A review of *We Lived in Drumfyvie,* in *The School Librarian,* Vol. 23, No. 4, December, 1975, p. 341.

What a pleasure to welcome the return of Rosemary Sutcliff to the world of children's writing. There is no indication given here of the respective roles of the co-authors, but the deeply satisfying sense of real people living in history must owe much to her consummate skill.

The map of this book is simple and effective. The imaginary Royal Burgh of Drumfyvie provides a backcloth for seven hundred years of Scottish history. Each chapter is told in the first person by a character from a period of the town's history, ranging from the steward to the first sheriff, the ruthless Duncan the Red, through Jamie the town herd who becomes involved with the famous Black Douglas, and Hugh and Johnnie in the days of the Covenanters, to the minister of St Ninian's Kirk at the time of Victoria's Diamond Jubilee.

Here is a formula for revealing all aspects of social and political history in compelling short stories. The reader is made vividly aware of the parallel and contradictory movements within Drumfyvie society towards ever greater social stratification and social interdependence.

Very strongly recommended.

BLOOD FEUD (1977)

Jill Paton Walsh

SOURCE: "Go East, Young Man," in *The Times Literary Supplement,* No. 3900, December 10, 1976, p. 1545.

[*The following excerpt is from an advance review of* Blood Feud.]

It is always very difficult to review new books by established and accomplished writers. "More of the same" and "what we have come to expect from this writer" are cool praise, however emphatically accompanied by adjectives of enthusiasm. And it is now a long time since there was a new major piece of writing from Rosemary Sutcliff. *Blood Feud* will be eagerly welcomed by admirers of her long and distinguished body of work.

Is *Blood Feud* then more of the same? In some ways, yes. We find ourselves once more with a hero suspended between worlds in transition—half Celtic, half English, Viking slave and Byzantine soldier, he is swept up on that epic movement of the Viking expansion eastwards, so fascinatingly unfamiliar to most of us. We find ourselves also in a moral world where courage and loyalty count overwhelmingly, and men are ruled by a ferocious code—blood binds them as brothers or as enemies. Once again we are brought through darkness to a faint dawn; the hero is suspended between duty to kill and duty to heal, and finds himself defined by the choice he makes.

Rosemary Sutcliff's mastery of her chosen vein of writing is complete, beyond praise. The evocation with a few vivid, always concrete strokes of remote scenes, of battles, journeys, camps, is superb. She can catch the manly tones of voices uttering tough or grand or commonplace sentiments in a language which never seems outré, and never sounds the false contemporaneity which is the bane of so much historical writing. The tale moves swiftly across a crowded and believable world. And this book is as finely crafted as anything Rosemary Sutcliff has done.

And yet this is not quite more of the same. Rosemary Sutcliff's central subject in the past has been "The Matter of Britain," the welding of those manifold strands which made our country; Jestyn of this book is not part of that—he is almost literally a spin-off, thrown violently on a long path that leads him for ever away from home. And though Jestyn never really feels at one with the duty to kill that the old code lays upon him, the inner drama is faintly drawn compared with the sweeping grandeur of the outward one.

And if a little of the zest has gone, and if this is not the Sutcliff novel one would recommend above all the rest, it is still an admirable book, and a splendid read, and we can never have enough work of this quality.

Margery Fisher

SOURCE: A review of *Blood Feud,* in *Growing Point,* Vol. 15, No. 8, March, 1977, pp. 3064-65.

Rosemary Sutcliff is never obvious in her interpretation of old causes lost and won. As Charles Keeping's strong jacket-design shows, *Blood Feud* is in fact what the book is about, the obligation for vengeance not for gain but so that the shades of the dead may rest in peace. Jestyn Englishman, taken from the Dublin slave-market by a Viking warrior, late in the tenth century, and elevated to be his blood-brother, gradually comes to understand what blood-feud implies to a Jute whose father has accidentally killed a neighbour and who has been murdered in revenge by the sons; the English lad willingly accepts his part in the feud as he and Thormod follow the Herulf brothers down the great rivers by way of Kiev to the city the Vikings know as Miklagard. But though his responsibility deepens after Thormod has been killed, the book does not in fact end with honour satisfied. On the contrary, when

Jestyn's chance comes to kill the remaining brother Anders, he does not take it, but fulfils his obligation instead as dresser to a Greek physician, by nursing the sick Norseman till he dies naturally and not by violence.

This reconciliation makes a firm ending to the story of a long journey (starting in Jestyn's Devon home and going East by way of Jutland and the Baltic) which is dominated and directed by Thormod's feud. Relatively short, concentrated, enriched with pictorial detail, the book has an emotional force which relates it, for me, to Rosemary Sutcliff's best work and especially with *Eagle of the Ninth*. Everything in the book—battle scenes, the discovery of love in various forms, weather and landscape, religious polemic—is reflected through Jestyn, the waif whose life is ruled by accident. . . . The first-person reminiscence distances old tragedies and conflicts, as Jestyn, now a physician, sends his thoughts back over the years. It is a narrative method well suited to this richly personal chronicle.

G. Bott

SOURCE: A review of *Blood Feud,* in *The Junior Bookshelf,* Vol. 41, No. 4, August, 1977, p. 242.

Rosemary Sutcliff explores violence with marked restraint: the Emperor Basil's blinding of a whole captured Bulgarian army is merely referred to in passing, for example, and even the bloodiest of encounters are treated with controlled restraint, though the reader is left in no doubt of their ferocity. Jestyn grows in stature as hc faces the challenge of a death feud that is not of his own making; there is a humanity about him that matches his loyalty and the quiet ending of a boisterous military career is fully appropriate. The historical background has patently been researched in depth and is presented with conviction—a story that once again trumpets loud and clear the talents of the one and only Rosemary Sutcliff.

📖 *SHIFTING SANDS* (1977)

Ros Franey

SOURCE: "Village Violence," in *The Times Literary Supplement,* No. 3931, July 15, 1977, p. 865.

[An advancing sand dune] swamped an Orkney community three or four thousand years ago. From the sparse evidence of the ruined village Rosemary Sutcliff constructs scenes from the lives of the villagers before the disaster. The central character is Blue Feather, a little girl who lives in one of the stone cave-like houses close to the sea. She is picked by Long Axe, the cruel and feckless village chief, to be his third woman when she is old enough—a fate she dreads as it approaches because of her love for young Singing Dog. Singing Dog challenges Long Axe's authority over the death of a wild sow, so when word arrives that the dune is shifting towards the village Long Axe chooses Singing Dog as a human sacrifice. Fortu-nately, the dune swamps the village before he can complete the ritual. Long Axe dies and the villagers leave their smothered houses for safer territory. An otherwise gripping story is marred by irritating language—"the Red" (for blood); "Life Thing" (heart/instinct). This gives the unintended impression that the characters are really rather primitive and stupid, and one wishes they might have been allowed to communicate naturally since nothing is known of their language.

Margery Fisher

SOURCE: A review of *Shifting Sands,* in *Growing Point,* Vol. 16, No. 5, November, 1977, p. 3201.

Rosemary Sutcliff is always able to take her readers with her to distant lands and times, for her intuition and feeling for the past have a compelling warmth about them. In *Shifting Sands* she has moved back to prehistoric times to offer a conjecture about the fate of Skara Brae in Orkney, buried in sand for centuries and excavated in our own time. She presents The People, ruled by Long Axe, a tyrant chief who is also priest of the community and whose power turns towards twelve-year-old Blue Feather. Though her father dare not refuse to promise the child as one of the chief's wives, she herself determines to escape with Singing Dog, her comrade and contemporary. The final confrontation of tyrant and boy takes place in a storm so fierce that the dunes move over the stone settlement in a scene dramatic, alarming and superbly described in terms of weather and setting as well as of character. Told in a rhythmic, almost poetic prose, this fragment of archaeology in personal form should go far to suggest to children of the present how life might have been lived in a primitive world.

📖 *SUN HORSE, MOON HORSE* (1977)

Sarah Hayes

SOURCE: "The Breath of Life," in *The Times Literary Supplement,* No. 3949, December 2, 1977, p. 1415.

Rosemary Sutcliff has always enjoyed the idea of the outsider, of the odd one who is isolated by fate to perform some special act. Though it has become almost a formula now, the magic lingers on—even in her new novel which verges on self-parody.

Lubrin Dhu is the small dark son of an Iron Age chieftain who dies defending the clan against a tribe retreating before the Roman menace. Lubrin frees his clan by creating for his captors a vast horse image on the side of the chalk hills, knowing as he does so that only his death will breathe true life into the horse.

All the Sutcliff hallmarks are here: the sonorous descriptions, the perfect evocation of an alien culture, the stilted quasi-primitive dialogue (with its unique use of the soothing phrase "na-na"). And, at about a third of the length of the earlier novels, this spare tale could easily be taken for a faint copy. But it is not. Though it lacks detail and human warmth, it conveys instead the mystery of ancient civilizations: the bleak unadorned style and story suit an age that remains dark and impenetrable to this day. The plot is a simple one, but the use of contrasting images of horses, shadows, birds, and cold winds give it a complex patterning that is the verbal equivalent of early Celtic jewelry.

M. Crouch

SOURCE: A review of *Sun Horse, Moon Horse,* in *The Junior Bookshelf,* Vol. 42, No. 1, February, 1978, pp. 50-1.

By a regrettable chance I have missed Miss Sutcliff's recent work, and it comes as a particular delight to discover that her powers are still at their peak. *Sun Horse, Moon Horse* is a shorter book than, for example, *The Mark of the Horse Lord,* which to some extent it resembles, but it is not a minor work. She is dealing here with some fundamental questions and not shirking the issues.

We are in the Iron Age. A tribe has migrated from East Anglia to the Berkshire downs and has built its dun on a crest of the chalk hills. The old ways are changing a little and the tribe has largely settled below the hill, leaving the strong place itself for, in the main, ceremonial occasions. They are Horse People—I wish that Miss Sutcliff were more sparing of capital letters—rearing and training their herds in the traditional way. Lubrin Dhu, the chief's youngest son, is bound by the traditions, but he has inherited an artist's eye from the Old People with which his family's strain has become blended. When war comes Lubrin is left behind, and so he escapes the slaughter of his tribe and finds himself a slave chief working for alien masters. For them he makes, at a price, one last work of art.

Miss Sutcliff gives a most convincing picture of everyday life in a community in Britain a century or so before the coming of the Romans. Her explanation of the origin of the Berkshire White Horse is equally convincing, for she shows not only why it was made but why, of all the hill figures of the chalk country, it is both the oldest and the most modern in style. Miss Sutcliff still writes with an uncomfortably intense style, as if she wants every other word printed in italics. Her historic instinct, her ability to evoke the smell of the hill grass and the stink of hot blood, her understanding of the motives of her characters, these are as strong as ever, which is to say that they put her books in a class apart from that of her most distinguished contemporaries.

Jill Paton Walsh

SOURCE: A review of *Sun Horse, Moon Horse,* in *The Christian Science Monitor,* May 3, 1978, p. B2.

Sutcliff country is austere and ennobling; her characters are dwarfed by a sense of their historical and mythical significance. But as always, the story is fast-moving and brilliantly vivid, and Lubrin Dhu is a likable hero. He learns how to project a huge picture onto a hillside by holding up an elm leaf before his face; it blocks out the view of his father's hall, and that's a good image of Miss Sutcliff's art, for her simple, almost stark, narratives cast huge symbolic shadows in the mind.

Roderick McGillis

SOURCE: A review of *Sun Horse, Moon Horse,* in *The World of Children's Books,* Vol. III, No. 2, Fall, 1978, pp. 59-60.

The creation of the horse whose stationary gallop dominates England's Berkshire Downs motivates the latest of Rosemary Sutcliff's historical romances. The result is a book written "as a bird sings," familiar in tone and style to earlier Sutcliff novels but filled with the magic of the White Horse of Uffington, its "movement and power and beauty." The horse, as the title suggests, carries the burden of meaning: it is spiritual and material, light and dark, dream and reality, beginning and ending, life and death. The horse reminds us of a people, but it also completes an individual. Sutcliff gives the horse mythic stature with her familiar style of understated significance. Our first glimpse of the white mare immortalized on the Berkshire skyline is through the eyes of Lubrin Dhu, youngest son of Tigernann the Chieftain of the Horse People (Iceni):

> For an instant the mare seemed made of white fire, and the fire of her burned into the inmost self of the Chieftain's youngest son as a brand burns into the hide of a yearling colt, leaving a mark which is never quite lost.

The White Horse represents the energy and nobility of a hardy people, but more profoundly it represents the dream of Lubrin Dhu. And it is here that Sutcliff exerts her power. Her books have rarely appealed to me, but the story of Lubrin Dhu is an exception. The simplicity and compressed emotion work! Quite simply, the story of Lubrin is the story of an artist who saves his people. . . .

In order to gain freedom for his people Lubrin undertakes to fashion a huge white horse on the most prominent loop of the Downs. His creation is his sacrifice. The artist gives himself for his people, and in this action he accepts isolation, death, and the responsibility for the people who have failed to comprehend him. But he also accepts the challenge of self fulfillment, of completing a fleeting pattern. In completing the great White Horse, "Lubrin knew that he had come as near to catching the wholeness of the dream, as near to making it a perfect thing as it is given to mortal man to do . . ."

In her paper "History is People," Rosemary Sutcliff comments that her characters "would be perfectly at home in Laramie" and her point is good. What impresses in her work is the unspoken meaning, the understanding through charged silences such as occur between Lubrin and his enemy Cradoc. These are characters pressed to the limit, yet characters always cool, under control. White man and Indian respecting and seeking out each other do not differ significantly from the silent manoeuvering of Cradoc and Lubrin after the battle. And the battle comes as swiftly, as inevitably, and as brutally as it does in the Western: "So the fighting came." "The wheels of the chariot were juicy-red, and a severed human head hung by its own blood-stained hair knotted to the chariot bow." *Sun Horse, Moon Horse* is Sutcliff at her best: evocative, pithy, simple, and emotional. (Although one could wish she had dropped the "own" from the "bloodstained hair.") History becomes myth; the legend of the White Horse has become truth and so Rosemary Sutcliff has printed the legend.

📖 SONG FOR A DARK QUEEN (1978)

Pauline Clarke

SOURCE: "The Power Behind the Throne," in *The Times Literary Supplement,* No. 3979, July 7, 1978, p. 766.

Rosemary Sutcliff has given us a rounded, convincing and (very properly) rather frightening portrait of Boudicca, queen of the Iceni, who led the tribes to the sack of Roman Colchester, St Alban's and London. In the lyrical, loving, and doomladen tale of Cadwan the harper, she grows from a brave defiant infant to a proud unwilling bride, a happy mother and a vengeful widow, her private self always contrasted with her public, queenly role. Round her stand the equally lively figures of Prasutagus the king, her husband, and those two nameless daughters, here called Essylt and Nessan, whose rape by Roman soldiers, and their mother's flogging, set fire to the revolt.

The Roman point of view, and the Legions' movements in meeting the rebellion, are recounted by young Agricola on his first service, in a letter to his mother in aptly civilized tones which contrast well with Cadwan's: this fictitious letter the author deftly disposes of by letting it become too war-stained to be sent. Agricola, later to be the wisest of Roman governors in Britain, is quick to see the nature of the procurator whose foolishly brutal treatment has brought matters to a head, and who saves his own skin by taking boat to Gaul.

All Rosemary Sutcliff's well-known skills are here: the lovely descriptions of the seasons in a subtly prehistoric East Anglian scene (though I missed an actual sense of the slopes of Venta Icenorum, with the river looped below it): the brilliant evocation of atmosphere, whether happy, foreboding, or sinister (as in the sacred grove, where the atrocious sacrifices detailed by the historian Dio Cassius are more subtly dealt with by this author): the assured narrative power in handling crowded and dramatic scenes, which pile up as this superbly exciting, albeit bloodthirsty story rises to its tragic climax in the battle: the sense of contrast between the "civilized" and the "barbarian", in their own and each other's estimation: the masterly telescoping of the passing years, the skilful

indications of the underlying reasons for the uprising. With her usual confidence she describes Celtic ritual and the worship of the mother goddess: the choosing of the royal bridegroom, the marriage, the funerals, the corn dancing. Her sympathies are totally engaged, so that, despite her refusal to minimize any of the savageries of the British, the reader's are too.

In basing her treatment on the theory that the Iceni were a matriarchy she has surely added great force to Boudicca's thirst to avenge her dishonoured queenship and royal daughters: and there may be a Pictish parallel. But all that Tacitus says is: "In Britain there is no rule of distinction to exclude the female line from the throne or the command of armies".

John Lansingh Bennett

SOURCE: A review of *Song for a Dark Queen,* in *Best Sellers,* Vol. 39, No. 5, August, 1979, pp. 230-31.

In describing the progress of the Roman conquest of Britain, the *Encyclopaedia Britannica* notes that the subjugation was "accompanied by a full share of those disasters which vigorous barbarians always inflict on civilized invaders." *Song for a Dark Queen* is the fascinating story of one such "disaster": the courageous uprising of the tribal peoples of East Anglia in A. D. 60 under the generalship of Boudicca (known to us, if at all, by her Romanized name "Boadicea"), the dark queen of the title. The story is essentially an elegy, beautifully told, of the ignition of the spark of hope for freedom from Roman rule, the valiant effort to fan this spark into flame, and the subsequent extinction of this hope. Told by Cadwan, harper to the queen of the Iceni, the narrative is his attempt to produce the song of glory and fame he had promised Boudicca when she was younger. . . .

The editor Maxwell Perkins used to give writers a copy of *War and Peace* as both an inspiration and an indication of what can be done with prose by a consummate artist. *Song for a Dark Queen* is so well written that it may serve the same dual purposes for the reader with an attentive ear. The language is somewhat difficult and will put off young adults who are less than proficient readers.

Roni Natov

SOURCE: A review of *Song for a Dark Queen,* in *Archeology,* Vol. 33, No. 5, September/October, 1980, pp. 63-4.

Song for a Dark Queen is the story of Boudicca, queen of the Iceni, and her revolt against Roman power in Britain in A.D. 60, a fascinating adventure tale for adolescents, particularly those who like military strategy and battle scenes. To introduce readers to this story, Sutcliff includes a map of Britain, a preface which offers brief but incisive background material, and a glossary of relevant terms. In this version, Sutcliff creates a character of rebellious strength and iron will. In tracing the personal and political history of Boudicca, *Song for a Dark Queen* emerges as a subtle and psychologically astute study of this powerful woman. . . .

[The royal harper and narrator] Cadwan's narrative is his final song to the queen, and the portrait is an intimate one because he is confidant to Boudicca and her family. Most appealing is the poetic language, the vivid imagery and strong rhythmic prose; Cadwan speaks in litanies and metaphors which reveal the world view of the Iceni. Their cultural life is seen in the objects described—the Bride Cup, jewelry, shields, swords—and in the moments chosen for his song. Their rituals, which comprise some of the greatest scenes in the book, dramatize the spirit of the times and bring the reader close to the emotional center of the story.

Cadwan himself is placid, gentle, a dreamer and a poet. As acute observer and recorder of things, he wonders about change or questioning tradition, about what would happen to any man, who, having once been chosen, refused his vocation, only to dismiss it as "a foolish thought. The sun does not take a whim to rise in the west. The pattern of things is the pattern of things." But Boudicca, headstrong and brilliant, thrives on such challenges. Perhaps her relationship to tradition—what she defends, particularly the matriarchal structure of her tribe and the freedom of her people, and what she rebels against—is what is most complex about this story and what generates the most exciting scenes. For example, Boudicca's ritual acceptance at 13 of a husband, and her resistance to the consummation of her marriage, is poignant and reverberates in Cadwan's echo, "She is too young—too young—too young . . . They should have given her more time."

Prasutagus, her husband, drawn with fine, vivid strokes, is a striking contrast to Boudicca, and the relationship between them is subtly presented. Some of the most moving moments of this story record the growth of their love into a real and mutual passion. The domestic story line, including the birth and development of Boudicca's two daughters, dominates the first half of the book.

The second part of the story, the fierce loyalty of Boudicca to her people and her uncompromising determination to maintain their freedom, is more difficult. The story continues to be compelling, and develops the essential theme of the matriarchy. It describes how Boudicca and the other women hide weapons which the men were forced to surrender, and become a strong part of the training force, and how the queen awakens from a period of deep mourning after Prasutagus' death to take vengeance against the Roman soldiers for their inhuman treatment of her and her people. One drawback may be the inclusion of another point of view, somewhere midway in the story. We suddenly read, interspersed with Cadwan's narrative, letters from Gneus Julius Agricola, the personal aide-de-camp of the Roman governor. The letters, addressed to his mother, offer pertinent information and are occasionally moving, but are not well integrated in the book.

The other difficulty with the book, and this might be a matter of personal taste, is that the scenes of rape and slaughter are so gruesome. But Sutcliff's description of the queen after she slaughters many Roman women in a sacrifice to the All Mother at Harvest, is appropriately chilling. The story of Boudicca ends in military defeat and suicide. If it is a brutal one, this novel's end is, after all, historically determined.

Sutcliff is a fine novelist, a vintage writer of historical tales for young adults, and in this respect *Song for a Dark Queen* is no exception. And it is remarkable to explore for once the legendary personality of a brilliant *woman* warrior. The story of Boudicca, her challenge to tradition and devotion to freedom, will strike a resonant chord in adolescents.

📖 THE LIGHT BEYOND THE FOREST: THE QUEST FOR THE HOLY GRAIL (1979)

M. Crouch

SOURCE: A review of *The Light Beyond the Forest,* in *The Junior Bookshelf,* Vol. 43, No. 4, August, 1979, pp. 227-28.

Rosemary Sutcliff stays close to Malory in these versions of the Holy Grail stories, being content to smooth edges and ease corners rather than to 'interpret'. She keeps in the Malory period too, and so does her illustrator, Shirley Felts, in her sensitive and evocative chapter-headings. Not even Miss Sutcliff can make anything but an insufferable prig of Galahad, but Lancelot comes through clearly as a vulnerable anti-hero and there are a number of other neat sketches, notably the maiden Anchoret whose nobility and purity are so inadequately rewarded.

It always seems somewhat of a misuse of Miss Sutcliff's unique talents to devote them, and her precious physical energy, to a retelling. She can invent so splendidly. However, she brings to the old and admittedly bewildering tale her characteristic nobility of style and nobility of soul, and we must be grateful.

Shirley Toulson

SOURCE: "Arthurian Courtly Dance," in *The Times Educational Supplement,* No. 3311, November 23, 1979, p. 34.

The Arthurian stories centred on the adventures that befell Sir Galahad and his companions in their search for the cup of the Last Supper are among the most mysterious and the least familiar of the tales of the Round Table. In retelling them for younger readers, Rosemary Sutcliff never oversimplifies their spiritual meaning, or fudges the allegory of the wounded King Pelles and the Wasteland around the Grail Castle that forms his kingdom; of the mysterious ships which sail to their destinations at the bidding of unseen and un-named forces; of the encounters in ruined chapels; or of the brief glimpses of the Grail, which encourages the knights on their quest. In more literary terms she skilfully blends the medieval tradition in which these stories were first set down, with the Romano-British world from which they originated.

In her retelling she weaves these threads together as intricately as the steps of an elaborate dance in which various recurrent motifs are rhythmically repeated; and the language in which she writes partakes of the same courtly quality. She demands a sophisticated attention, (although the actual words of her narration are simple enough) and the reader who is prepared to give it will probably want to go beyond this book. For this reason it is a pity that she does not give any bibliography of her obviously extensive researches; or at least indicate some of the actual places in Britain that are associated with the Grail legends.

Kirkus Reviews

SOURCE: A review of *The Light Beyond the Forest: The Quest for the Holy Grail*, in *Kirkus Reviews*, Vol. XLVIII, No. 17, September 1, 1980, p. 1168.

A straight, almost solemn retelling of the quest for the Grail: from the coming of Galahad and the knights' rushing off—"knowing well enough where the Grail was lodged," but knowing too that "they must cast themselves on fate, welcoming whichever way it took them"—to Galahad's successfully "coming into the heart of the mystery, where it is not possible for a mortal man to come, and yet remain mortal." Without a hint of divergent sensibility, Sutcliff takes us into a legendary climate where voices sound forth with guidance and direction, strange knights are slain for sport in chance encounters, false ladies pursue the pure young men with evil snares, a perfect maiden sacrifices herself for an unknown lady, Lancelot suffers searing agony in his struggle to choose between God and Guinevere, and the unquestioned supremity of the spiritual mission endows all the headlong adventure with nobility. Inevitably, Lancelot's struggle is the most moving; without the actual miracle of the embodied sacrament of Communion, Galahad remains paler and more strictly allegorical than ever. Before stumbling on a parody, reinterpretation, or contemporary reworking, young people should have some acquaintance with the material and viewpoint as set down by Malory. Sutcliff provides this with grace and an air of wholehearted feeling, for readers who might shy away from a more inclusive volume of Arthurian legends. (Her introduction asks us to remember as well the story's Celtic roots, but their spirit is less evident here.) Librarians should also remember, though, that equally readable but stronger versions exist in such staples as Keith Baines' rendition of Malory's *Le Morte D'Arthur*.

📖 *FRONTIER WOLF* (1980)

Elaine Moss

SOURCE: "Outposts of the Empire," in *The Times Literary Supplement*, No. 4051, November 21, 1980, p. 1323.

[What] is impressive about *Frontier Wolf* is not the story

itself, nor the gradual winning through of Alexios from disgrace to honour. It is Rosemary Sutcliff's extraordinary capacity for recreating a visual and emotional picture, many-textured, of the life of a Roman garrison on the Antonine Wall as the Empire crumbled. She has the writer's equivalent of a musician's "absolute pitch"; her certainty enables her to use language that fore-echoes the future (the Votadini speak with a recognizable Celtic lilt), and to engender situations and characters that carry with them an authenticity and complexity that defy the conventional textbook image of Roman times. . . .

One of the loveliest passages in this vivid book describes the emergence from the loch at dawn of the new chief of the Votadini after his ritual ordination:

> A magnificent deerskin mantle lifted and swung out behind him on the water, and the torchlight caught the great necklace of twisted gold and raw yellow amber about his neck. He was coming up out of the shallows now, wet and shining and flame-golden. . . . The drops of loch water scattered from him like sparks as he came up through the alder trees. He was the Chief, back from beyond the sunset, and the weariness of the journey was upon him. . . . Alexios, standing within an arm's length of him, watched him come, taller, surely, than he had been, unless that was only that his head was held so high.

Whether Rosemary Sutcliff is describing a ceremony such as this, a rudimentary game of polo (played on ponies, with a calf's head as "bull" and spears as sticks), the birth of a baby, the suckling of a kitten, dawn, sunset, hill, valley, sea or stream her prose is palpably alive. It draws us into the vortex of ancient experience from which we emerge, at the end of the story, as from a lambent dream.

M. Crouch

SOURCE: A review of *Frontier Wolf*, in *The Junior Bookshelf*, Vol. 45, No. 1, February, 1981, p. 32.

In 1954 Rosemary Sutcliff's art came to full maturity with *The Eagle of the Ninth*. Now twenty-seven years later and in a very different world of children's books she returns to the mood of that incomparable book and to a later phase in the story of the Romans in Britain.

We are two centuries on. A descendant of Marcus Flavius Aquila has, through the favour of an uncle who is Governor of Northern Britain, gained rapid promotion with the legions. Too rapid. Faced with a crisis among the barbarians in the wilds of the Danube he makes the wrong decision. For most young officers this would have been the end of a career if not of life. Uncle turns up trumps again, and Alexios Flavius Aquila is court-martialled and promoted to command a gang of ruffians who hold an outpost fort on the Firth of Forth. Slowly and painfully Alexios comes to terms with his tough Frontier Wolves, earning their respect and compromising with them in the acceptance of some kind of discipline. He also finds a friend among the local tribes. Then an inspection visit from a martinet from Headquarters combines with the rising of the tribesmen, and Alexios leads his Wolves in a fighting retreat to the Wall.

Jacket illustration from Blood Feud, *written by Rosemary Sutcliff. Illustrated by Michael Eagle.*

Miss Sutcliff has lost none of her magic. She can still take the reader into the heat of battle, hearing the clash of arms and smelling the hot blood. She writes with more restraint now and, although this is a long book, it has fewer of the purple passages which sometimes disfigured her earlier work. She has been called an 'intuitive' historian, and this is still true, but there is plenty of evidence here that the story has been researched in depth. But Miss Sutcliff, of all historical novelists, goes beyond research. The 'feel' of the period is something not to be gained from documents or archaeological specimens, and this she gives us generously. This convincing picture of the past, growing out of a magnificent and action-filled story, is enough to confirm once and for all our debt to this outstanding writer. It would perhaps be carping to add that her characters do not engage our sympathies with the same strength.

Margaret Meek

SOURCE: A review of *Frontier Wolf,* in *The School Librarian,* Vol. 29, No. 2, June, 1981, p. 155.

A quarter of a century separates this new book from *The*

eagle of the ninth. Miss Sutcliff's readers are now the children of those who first went with the Roman legions beyond the wall. Here again is that faithful comradeship of antagonists; the long trail, the confrontations in battle, all in the debateable lands at the edge of the Empire where loyalties are forged and tried. The magic works again, as only this author knows how to make it. Look at the spaces in her dialogue—what is not said. See how the movements of crowds are set against personal encounters. The cumulative effect of heroic respect grows from the entirely localised action within a notion of empire. We may find it an older tradition of writing, but in this kind of book our children can see the archetypal conflict of loyalties in great depth.

Hazel Rochman

SOURCE: A review of *Frontier Wolf,* in *School Library Journal,* Vol. 28, No. 1, September, 1981, p. 142.

An exciting story of action and warfare set in 4th-Century Roman Britain, this is also about a young man's personal struggle for identity and acceptance. . . . As always, Sutcliff has the power to make us care for strongly individualized characters while unobtrusively creating the authentic historical background. The language is poetic in word and rhythm, evoking the desolation of the gray, sullen hills, the stormy darkness, "the wind-haunted stillness of the winter night." The stark physical setting is also Alexios' symbolic wilderness and his place of trial and privation and of his long journey to find himself.

📖 ***THE SWORD AND THE CIRCLE: KING ARTHUR AND THE KNIGHTS OF THE ROUND TABLE* (1981)**

Ann Evans

SOURCE: "The Real Thing," in *The Times Literary Supplement,* No. 4069, March 27, 1981, p. 341.

Very occasionally, the opening sentence of a book works a small miracle on the reader. It is as if a shutter sprang open momentarily, to reveal the essence and truth of the entire book within a single visionary second. There is nothing obviously spectacular about the first sentence of ***The Sword and the Circle*** but the magic is there and with it the certainty that riches lie ahead.

Many followers of Rosemary Sutcliff must have waited and hoped for her to bring her own particular distinction to a retelling of the legends of King Arthur and the Knights of the Round Table. There are other available versions, of course, some of them admirable, and she herself has already entered the field briefly—in 1971 with ***Tristan and Iseult*** and in 1979 with ***The Light Beyond the Forest,*** but ***The Sword and the Circle*** stands far above any collection known to me, and should be seized on by anybody providing books for children upwards of ten years old.

With her usual scrupulous regard for authenticity, Rosemary Sutcliff has rooted the stories deep in history—in the Dark Ages of Britain, when behind a dense tangle of folklore, myth and legend there may well have existed the Roman-British war leader known to us today as King Arthur. The stories about him are so manifold that selection is the first problem. Predictably, Rosemary Sutcliff's choice is unerring; though she draws on a variety of sources for her material (some much earlier than Malory) and though links between stories are sometimes tenuous, yet one emerges as from a single totally involving piece of theatre.

For some, Rosemary Sutcliff's writing may perhaps be over-rich (though much less so than twenty years ago). It has the stately measure of seventeenth-century English prose, the sharp pathos of an old ballad and an echo of Homer in its beautifully tuned imagery, and yet it can be as homely and unpretentious as an old kitchen table. This way of writing has evolved over the years into a style unmistakably her own—so much so that it could be said to be too pervasive, like an over-heavy perfume, masking the individuality of each separate book. For most readers, I suspect, it provides the perfect vehicle for each of the stories she has to tell, and if in this collection the roman-

tic influence of Malory is strong, Rosemary Sutcliff rises above it, a minstrel in her own right.

Of her many gifts as a writer for all ages, perhaps two are especially to be valued: the first, that of involving the reader with a character at a human and emotional level while still preserving the historical perspective; the second, that of gauging the pace of a book to such perfection. The tension is never allowed to slacken and yet there is time to laugh at a pompous ass of a knight being unhorsed backwards, time to ponder the sad truth that even in the Dark Ages a man could be torn apart because he loved his best friend's wife. It is for qualities like these that Rosemary Sutcliff's name will be remembered and revered long after others have been forgotten.

Marcus Crouch

SOURCE: A review of *The Sword and the Circle: King Arthur and the Knights of the Round Table,* in *The School Librarian,* Vol. 29, No. 2, June, 1981, pp. 155, 157.

This is an example of Rosemary Sutcliff's 'high style', which used to dominate her fiction but which more recently has been reserved for these retellings of epic, legend and romance. For myself, I would trade them all for another ***Lantern bearers*** or the other Arthurian novels in which, without benefit of Malory or the French medieval romancers, she puts the Romano-British warlord in his own dark age.

Nevertheless, ***The sword and the circle*** is an impressive and welcome achievement. By associating and linking a number of disparate sources, Miss Sutcliff achieves a remarkable continuity, enabling us to follow the fortunes of Arthur from his conception to the high summer of the Round Table. The last chapter presages the coming of the Grail (which this author has already chronicled in ***The light beyond the forest***) and the final breaking-up of the brotherhood.

In addition to the mainstream stories Miss Sutcliff includes a number of independent episodes—Gawain and the Green Knight, Tristan and Iseult, Geraint and Enid (from the Mabinogion) among them—so that her book becomes, apart from its high intrinsic merits, a useful companion to Malory. And if her style is a shade full-flavoured for some adult palates, many young readers, meeting these great tales for the first time, will find them suitably larger than life.

Zena Sutherland

SOURCE: A review of *The Sword and the Circle: King Arthur and the Knights of the Round Table,* in *Bulletin of the Center for Children's Books,* Vol. 35, No. 5, January, 1982, p. 96.

Using Middle English poems and ballads, the Mabinogion, Geoffrey of Monmouth, and Godfrey of Strasburg for her source material in addition to the *Morte d'Arthur* by Thomas Malory, Sutcliff has put together the parts of the Arthurian legend so smoothly that they form a glowing, brilliant whole—like a stained glass window in which the total effect is much greater than the impact of each jewel-rich part. The language is flowing and courtly without the use of obsolete words and phrases, the men and women of the court are drawn on a grand scale and yet made mortal and vulnerable, and the book is so imbued with high magic and chivalric code that the dear, familiar heroes and their old, familiar deeds have a fresh dramatic appeal.

Kirkus Reviews

SOURCE: A review of *The Sword and the Circle: King Arthur and the Knights of the Round Table,* in *Kirkus Reviews,* Vol. L, No. 3, February 1, 1982, p. 141.

Once more, as in *The Light Beyond the Forest* (1980) whose events follow these, Sutcliff immerses herself and her readers in the sensibility of the medieval legend. It's a world where unproved heroes ride about inquiring "Good fellow, is there any place near here where adventure is to be had for the asking?" and where a knight of the Round Table is likely in his wanderings to come upon four others gathered under an oak tree. Women, except for Queen Guinevere who stands apart, are cast as damsels in distress or subtle and treacherous enchantresses; honor is worth more than life; and, more so than in *The Light Beyond the Forest* with its transforming religious superstructure, the primitive Celtic heritage asserts itself through the thin cloak of chivalry. Sutcliff tells us that her version has "followed Malory in the main" but borrowed also from other (specified) earlier sources. The narrative, which takes us from "The Coming of Arthur" (with some mythological-historical background before that) to "The Coming of Percival" shortly before the grail quest featured in *The Light Beyond the Forest,* includes a very early, alternative version of Tristan and Iseult, a more familiar one of Sir Gawain and the Green Knight, and other Arthurian knightings and romances from Malory. As before, Sutcliff tells them straight, with apparently unswerving and heartfelt conviction.

Mary Sucher

SOURCE: A review of *The Sword and the Circle: King Arthur and the Knights of the Round Table,* in *The ALAN Review,* Vol. 9, No. 3, Spring, 1982, p. 29.

There is great dignity and beauty in this retelling (mainly following Malory) of the legends. The beautiful word pictures seem full of magic and enchantment as they tell of Arthur's coming and the formation of the Round Table. The author's stately prose as she recounts noble adventures, jousts, and quests is worthy of these age-old tales: Sir Lancelot's coming and his encounter with Elaine; Sir Gawain and the Green Knight; his brother, the Kitchen Knight, later known as Gareth; Gaheris and Linnet;

Tristan and Iseult; Geraint and Enid; Gawain and the Loathely Lady; and, in conclusion, the coming of Percival. It was as though Percival were the herald Merlin had foretold, for in less than a year the Mystery of the Holy Grail would come to Camelot—the theme of the author's *Light Beyond The Forest.* The heroism of Arthur, who was undoubtedly a real Roman-British war leader, has left us something of beauty, mystery, and magic in our heritage. Not since Tennyson has there been such a worthy, deeply moving retelling of the Arthurian tales.

📖 *EAGLE'S EGG* (1981)

Jenny Oldfield

SOURCE: "Another Log on the Fire," in *The Times Educational Supplement,* No. 3390, June 12, 1981, p. 27.

Rosemary Sutcliff's Roman romance sits ill at ease. Her old storyteller might almost vent her own frustration with his opening: "All right, then, if it's a story you're wanting, throw another log on the fire." It's a grandfather talking across two generations, covering years while others dwell on seconds, including political thoughts on slavery, not shirking the blood of battle: "smashed chariots and dead horses, and dead men among the blood-sodden heather." Such assurance, compassion and beautiful texture. Rosemary Sutcliff can make us all fall in love with Cordaella by the turn of two or three phrases. One wonders about misuse of talent; how much the format restricts and reduces. The plot is weak where descriptions are strong, and the marching, fighting section may lack immediate interest for a nine year old. Has she wasted her breath? Ah well, throw another log on the fire.

Margery Fisher

SOURCE: A review of *Eagle's Egg,* in *Growing Point,* Vol. 20, No. 2, July, 1981, pp. 3922-23.

A junior officer in the Ninth Legion earns promotion and the means to marry by a neat trick which defuses an awkward situation caused by a long, dismally slow and nerve-wracking campaign in Caledonia; practical and amusing, young Quintus's unusual use of the hard-boiled egg he had no time to eat is not entirely appreciated by his superior but it has saved the dignity, and more, of the Eagle. Rosemary Sutcliff shows in this short book her talent for evoking the military talents of Rome and the dark dangers of the Northern province, in a prose accessible to readers in the middle years (say, nine upwards) but with no lack of the warmth and richness of her longer novels.

M. Crouch

SOURCE: A review of *Eagle's Egg,* in *The Junior Bookshelf,* Vol. 45, No. 6, December, 1981, p. 248.

Even at her slightest—and this story has the inevitable

limitations of the 'Antelope' format—Miss Sutcliff never foregoes her historical integrity. This is a kind of mini-Eagle of the Ninth, which follows the fortunes of her favourite Legion as it moves North to attempt the conquest of Caledonia. Quintus, Standard-Bearer, has fallen in love with a British girl, but Rome does not permit the marriage of low-ranking soldiers, and Quintus will have to wait until he becomes a centurion—but will Cordala wait so long? Quintus does well enough in the campaign, but it is not against the enemy that he shows what he is made of. Quick wit and a sense of humour bring Quintus his century and his girl.

Of course Miss Sutcliff needs space to spread her wings in, but she moves not too uncomfortably within the confines of the 'Antelope'. How good that the very young reader, or the reluctant reader, should look into the past through such eyes and for ever think of history as fine story-telling.

THE ROAD TO CAMLANN: THE DEATH OF KING ARTHUR (1981)

Neil Philip

SOURCE: "Completing the Circle," in *The Times Educational Supplement,* No. 3408, October 23, 1981, p. 30.

If there is one story with which every child growing up in Britain should be familiar, it is the story of King Arthur. There is no shortage of retelling, but most of them are hack rewritings which debase their source material. Even the best attempts—such as Roger Lancelyn Green's *King Arthur and His Knights of the Round Table*—seem to lack the vital spark which animates the early sources, and which received its classic expression in the prose writings of Sir Thomas Malory.

Rosemary Sutcliff's version, told in three books, *The Sword and the Circle, The Light Beyond the Forest* and *The Road to Camlann,* is now complete, and stands with Green's book as a valiant attempt to bring the often tragic, violent and sensual tales within the compass of children's understanding without cutting the heart from them. While story and language stay close to Malory, the shaping spirit is recognisably that of the author of *The Eagle of the Ninth, The Mark of the Horse Lord* and that splendid novel of an historicised Arthur, *Sword at Sunset.*

The Road to Camlann is the best of the three volumes, perhaps because its interwoven stories all tend to the same end. The theme of the book is the destruction of the fellowship of the Round Table through the machinations of Arthur's incestuous bastard Mordred. The stories centre on Lancelot: his threefold rescue of Guinevere and his bitter wars with Arthur and Gawain. To children his betrayal of his best friend out of passion can seem mere treachery, and his slaying of Gareth and Gaheris "unarmed and unwares" unforgivable. Rosemary Sutcliff, by conveying so skilfully "the grete curtesy that was in Sir Launcelot more than in only other man", blocks such a

damaging response. Lancelot is a rounded, convincing character; "poor fulish" Guinevere remains more shadowy.

The element in the Arthurian stories which has above all kept them fresh and eternally applicable is the way in which they measure abstract concepts of sin, truth and loyalty against the realities of human appetites and affections. When Lancelot performs his miracle and cures Sir Urry, the momentary unification of desire and achievement only stresses the usual gap between the two. Malory tells us, "Than kynge Arthur and all the kynges and knyghtes kneled downe and gave thankynges and lovynge unto God and unto Hys Blyssed Modir. And ever Sir Launcelote wepte, as he had bene a chylde that had bene beatyn!" Rosemary Sutcliff keeps that line, and keeps faith with its implications.

M. Crouch

SOURCE: A review of *The Road to Camlann,* in *The Junior Bookshelf,* Vol. 45, No. 6, December, 1981, p. 251.

In this, the most familiar of all the Arthurian stories, there is not much room for individual interpretation, and Miss Sutcliff stays close to Malory, even to the use of actual speeches and phrases at climactic moments where modern words, even those as resounding as this writer's, might have struck the wrong note. Miss Sutcliff captures the profound sadness of the story and the hopelessness of its preordained doom. She writes with conscious nobility of style, as befits the material, using the techniques of the chronicler rather than the novelist, although she shows her characteristic understanding in dealing with the motives of Lancelot and Arthur. Here, young readers and their parents may be assured, is the best of a great and lasting story matched with the best of one of this age's great writers. Those who, later in life, move on to Malory will discover that the spirit of the Arthurian legends has been conveyed without falsification, and that the transition to the fifteenth-century original can be made with no effort.

Miss Sutcliff has added to the great debt which we all owe her for much grandeur of imagination and splendour of writing.

Margery Fisher

SOURCE: A review of *The Road to Camlann,* in *Growing Point,* Vol. 20, No. 6, March, 1982, p. 4032.

The Road to Camlann completes the trilogy in which Rosemary Sutcliff described the young unknown Arthur and the quest for the Grail, with a compact yet rich and resonant account of Mordred's treachery, Lancelot's love for Guinevere and the last battle. . . . Rosemary Sutcliff has assumed a bardic style, rhythmic and full of poetic archaism and reflecting in some ways the manner of medieval poetry. From this source, perhaps, come the delicate natural touches that refresh a tale of intrigue and cruelty—the flowers that herald spring, the dark forest reaches: but the author uses nature for something more than decoration. The last battle at Dover in which Mordred and Arthur strike their last blows is full of the harshness of winter, used almost as a symbol. . . .

Battles and single combat are described strongly but in formal tones, and in formal terms, too, Rosemary Sutcliff outlines the love between Lancelot and the Queen in its latter years, bringing tension to her tale with a felt contrast between their passion and the courtly restraints in which it has to be expressed. The destructive element in this love is recognised as one cause of the final dispersal of Arthur's knights and, with equal importance, the incestuous parentage of Mordred, a parentage which caused his jealousy and led him to undermine Arthur's power and peace of mind. This romantic interpretation of historical chronicle and fifteenth century narrative is finely done in its grave, pictorial style.

Neil Philip

SOURCE: A review of *The Road to Camlann,* in *British Book News,* Children's Supplement, Spring, 1982, p. 9.

This is a marvellous story, the great story of the British Isles, and Rosemary Sutcliff handles it well. She is obliged to soften outlines to suit a young audience, but she makes no damaging compromises. She keeps very close to Malory, with echoes of other writers; sometimes, as in Sir Ector's elegy over Lancelot's body, she barely changes Malory's wording. This is all to the good: originality, in the sense of free invention, is not what is wanted here. What is wanted, and provided, is linguistic sensitivity; a style which dispenses with archaism but not with *gravitas;* the ability to thread a number of stories into one grand, inevitable pattern; the skill to make the characters fashion their doom, not simply be swept into it. This seems to me the best of the three books: more coherent than *The Sword and the Circle,* and clearer than *The Light Beyond the Forest.* The trilogy as a whole immediately takes its place beside Roger Lancelyn Green's *King Arthur and His Knights of the Round Table* as one of the few attempts to simplify the matter of Britain which do not merely trivialize it.

Donald K. Fry

SOURCE: A review of *The Road to Camlann: The Death of King Arthur,* in *School Library Journal,* Vol. 29, No. 5, January, 1983, p. 88.

This book completes Rosemary Sutcliff's Arthurian trilogy, begun with *The Light Beyond the Forest* and *The Sword and the Circle.* Here Sutcliff describes the events from the coming of Mordred to the death of Lancelot. The title refers to The Last Battle, in which Arthur and his civilization perish. Sutcliff writes with her usual economy and rich prose, with a touch of archaic diction in the speeches. Her earlier volumes succeeded brilliantly in capturing the notion of an invisible transcendent world behind events, curiously missing in this conclusion. I find her Arthur a little pale, but her Mordred rises to new heights of vileness. Other than Malory, I can think of no better introduction to the whole sweep of Arthurian stories and values.

BLUE REMEMBERED HILLS: A RECOLLECTION (1983)

M. Crouch

SOURCE: A review of *Blue Remembered Hills,* in *The Junior Bookshelf,* Vol. 47, No. 2, April, 1983, pp. 65-6.

What are the major landmarks in post-war children's literature? One of them, surely, is the emergence of Rosemary Sutcliff, from its tentative beginnings in 1950 with *The Queen Elizabeth Story* to its full flowering four years later in *The Eagle of the Ninth.* Of all this there is only the brief statement, in the last pages, of the acceptance of her first novel in *Blue Remembered Hills.* Her 'Recollection', as she styles it, is concerned with the impressions and experiences which made Miss Sutcliff the writer and the person she is. Her book is of absorbing interest, whether or not the reader is interested in children's books, for it describes in great detail and with devastating honesty how one woman of unique talent and enormous character grew into maturity.

In her book Miss Sutcliff has achieved total recall. There is no sense, as one sometimes finds in the autobiographies of lesser people, of the adult mind tailoring facts to fit later conceptions. She remembers all and puts it all down with beautiful candour: the Service childhood, disturbed by frequent postings of her Naval father, struggles with a strong-minded mother, first love and last love, above all continual suffering following a savage attack of juvenile arthritis. Although Miss Sutcliff was a 'late developer' as a writer as well as a reader, in these experiences are the raw materials of her art. She remembers her childhood friends and acquaintances as a writer does, with a keen awareness of physical shape and personal idiosyncracy. Out of her physical handicap come Marcus, in *The Eagle of the Ninth,* and Drem, in *Warrior Scarlet,* both of whom succeed by coming to terms with their disabilities; conversely, from the same source comes her outstanding skill in the portrayal of violent physical action.

It would be a mistake to use this book as an excuse for literary detection, pursuing clues to the origin of future books. It is best read for its own sake, as a sensitive and sincere self-revelation of a woman who would surely have been remarkable, whatever had been her calling. It contains some of Miss Sutcliff's finest writing, not the 'Fine' writing of some of her earlier novels but refined, economical and eloquent descriptions of things seen and felt. Of this kind are the recollections of Sheppey Marshes and the impressions of the great winter of 1947 in Devon when, her perceptions sharpened by love, she watched the effects of frozen fog on a magical landscape. She has written nothing better than these few pages.

This book is a triumph. In whatever quarter of Heaven Miss Sutcliff's formidable mother has found lodging she is, no doubt about it, having a 'wonderful time being humble!'

Margaret Meek

SOURCE: A review of *Blue Remembered Hills: A Recollection,* in *The School Librarian,* Vol. 31, No. 3, September, 1983, pp. 285-86.

All narrative begins as autobiography, the story we tell ourselves about ourselves. The curiosity that exists about the childhood of those who write for children stems from the same root as our own remembrance of our young days and is, in the end, the unpublished half of the fiction of childhood. Rosemary Sutcliff is a natural object of wonder. At an early age she contracted a kind of arthritis that restricted her growth and movement, so that she became, in yesterday's terms, handicapped. Her interrupted schooling created difficulties for her in learning to read. She developed the compensatory yet easily wounded sensibilities that normal intelligence and refined imagination bring to children with special needs. In this account of her early years the reader can see around inside the restrictions and celebrate the triumph of overcoming them, not as a fear of determination alone, but as a kind of overseeing that, in the author's terms, locks seeing into people and objects. For instance, she transforms tea and toast in a seaside boarding house into an event, and writes about her parents with subtlety and clarity as well as love and ambivalence.

There are many memorable passages, not least about nights in hospital, but absolutely no self-pity. The powerful emotions are laid bare in a way that makes a better case for 'special needs' than many I have read in education reports. The writing has the directness that characterises the famous books which are only on the horizon when this record ends. It is the author's story, and a powerful one with a formidable central character.

Kirkus Reviews

SOURCE: A review of *Blue Remembered Hills,* in *Kirkus Reviews,* Vol. LII, No. 8, April 15, 1984, p. 411.

With the same no-nonsense vigor that is the hallmark of her historical novels for children, Sutcliff recalls her first 25 years—making only the most matter-of-fact references to her permanent crippling by Still's Disease, a rare form of juvenile arthritis. Born in 1920 in Surrey, Rosemary was forever shifting from place to place as a child: her quiet father was a naval officer, stationed in the Mediterranean ("To this day the name 'Malta' means bells to me"), then dockyards at Sheerness and Chatham. Her

mother was Spartan, volatile, doting, difficult: "She was wonderful, no mother could have been more wonderful. But ever after, she demanded that I should not forget, nor cease to be grateful, nor hold an opinion different from her own, nor even, as I grew older, feel the need for any companionship but hers." Sutcliff remembers: sojourns with edgy relatives; beloved playmate Giles, imprisoned (like Rosemary at times) in his "spinal carriage," but peripatetic in his one hour of free exercise each day; terrible loneliness when isolated at home; useful stints at ordinary schools ("no child, I believe, should go to a special school who can possibly cope and be coped with in a normal one"); and grim/cheerful times at children's hospitals—where Rosemary was "the stranger whom the pack turns on." (Class-conflict was more primal than the shared experience of being handicapped.) Later came art school, with training—and technical success—as a portrait miniaturist. But "I could not cope with harsh realities in paint." So Rosemary, a late-reader who discovered book-ecstasy in L. M. Montgomery's *Emily of New Moon,* developed "the itch to write"—an itch that was seriously deepened by her odd 1940s love (wondrous, hurtful) for ex-RAF man Rupert, who was interested in a *ménage à trois* . . . with a non-handicapped woman as the third party. Brief but rich, frank but never sloppy: a crisp little gem for Sutcliff fans and connoisseurs of childhood-memoirs.

BONNIE DUNDEE (1983)

Margery Fisher

SOURCE: A review of *Bonnie Dundee,* in *Growing Point,* Vol. 22, No. 3, September, 1983, pp. 4122-23.

'I have always had the knack of catching a likeness from memory'. The last sentence of *Bonnie Dundee* confirms its plan. It is a portrait in depth painted in words by an old man who, as a lad of fifteen or so, had indeed actually painted a quick, inspired likeness of Claverhouse on the eve of his marriage, while acting temporarily as apprentice to a visiting Dutch artist. If Rosemary Sutcliff had intended to offer a straight reconsideration of history she would have described the deeds of John Graham of Claverhouse, Viscount Dundee, in the third person. Instead, she has used as a mouthpiece a man who can look back to his early and middle years when he served Claverhouse as military leader and saw him in private life as well. What we have, then, is an interpretation, the impressions of one man; and yet, for all the partiality of the narrator, this is no romanticised portrait but one honestly and roundly drawn.

As an orphan brought up among Convenanters, Hugh Herriott had accepted the nickname bandied among them of 'Bloody Claver'se' as denoting a truth. His story, ostensibly written down at the instance of his wife for the sake of posterity, in the years when the memory of the great Colonel had been tarnished, concerns, rather, the man whom the Highlanders dubbed Black John of the Battles. Hugh first saw Claverhouse as a man tall on horseback whose face 'seemed to hover over me as a hawk hovers over some terrified small creature in the grass'. The boy had been captured by Claverhouse's dragoons after Convenanters, including Hugh's cousin Alan, seeking weapons for their resistance to authority, had set fire to a cottage and caused the death of an old woman as well as of their enemies. He escapes by feigning madness, and is sent away as horse-boy to the Covenanting household of Lord Dundonal. Here Claverhouse, courting the laird's grand-daughter, Lady Jean Cochrane, comes into Hugh's life again, and the boy finally takes service with him as his galloper. Through the intrigues and campaigns of the late seventeenth century he observes the man who commands his love and loyalty. He sees him as lover and devoted husband and as a straightforward soldier sickened by the rumour or the sight of treachery; he sees him saddened when James II abdicates and leaves England, alternately hopeful and desperate as he tries to raise an army for the Stuart cause in Scotland, determinedly sharing privation with his troops; he watches him die on the field of Killiecrankie. The facts of the period are here as background to the study of a dominant historical personage.

All the expected skills of Rosemary Sutcliff are present in this new novel. There are fine scenes of action—Hugh's ride from Dundee to Edinburgh when Lady Jean is dangerously ill, the desperate Highland march, the last battle. There are minor characters, some of them slowly and fully realised (in particular, Lady Jean's companion and friend Mary Ruthven, part-gipsy, who becomes Hugh's wife and who contributes to his understanding of Claverhouse) and others more swiftly and sharply sketched. Colour in Rosemary Sutcliff's novels has often come from set pieces like this description of the gipsy Captain Faa:

> A very tall thin man wearing the wrack of a coat that had once been mulberry velvet trimmed on cuffs and pocket-flaps with tarnished silver lace, and a proud if something weather-worn bunch of blue-black heron hackles clasped into his battered bonnet by a brooch like a silver targe. Grey hair hung in thick greasy locks to his shoulders, and out of the mane of it looked a long brown-skinned rogue's face with a great hooked nose that could have belonged to a Roman emperor, and a short stump of a blackened pipe that seemed as much a part of it as his nose did, and a pair of yellow eyes—black and wicked yellow like those of the fish-eagle that the Highlanders call . . . the Bird with the Sunlit Eye.

Like all her books, this one moves forward in a skilful alternation of historical reporting and neatly introduced dialogue, linked by the recurring image and situation of painting and portraiture, the true bent and final career of the narrator. Most important, the book attains unity because of the theme so often used by Rosemary Sutcliff, the theme of loyalty; conflicting duties and alliances, the coat-changing of friends, the intransigeance of Highland soldiers, the aggressive bigotry which blackened the Covenanters' bid for freedom—each in turn throws into bold relief the strong, unswerving loyalty to the house of Stuart borne by the man who moved into popular song as

'Bonnie Dundee'. Truly, the portrait of a hero matching the heroes of legend and, most of all, of a human being.

Geoffrey Trease

SOURCE: A review of *Bonnie Dundee,* in *The Times Literary Supplement,* No. 4200, September 30, 1983, p. 1047.

For all the romantic promise of title and dust jacket this story's opening chapter is as starkly actual as the ugliest news item. A farm-kitchen congregation of Covenanters break off their pious psalm-singing to slip out into the darkness and murder four soldiers for the sake of the carbines they carry. Hugh Herriott, the fifteen-year-old orphan, is a reluctant witness. He never afterwards forgets the dead drummer-boy with the neat round hole in his forehead drilled by a pistol-shot, looking like a macabre third eye. Here is the contemporary relevance which can make historical fiction a valuable elucidation of real life rather than an escape from it.

With Hugh as narrator, Rosemary Sutcliff traces the well-documented career of the man he comes to worship as a hero—the colourful, controversial Claverhouse, Viscount Dundee—right up to his death at Killiecrankie, a splendid battle-piece painted with all her usual power. She faces squarely the now familiar dilemma of the individual caught up in conflicting fanaticisms and incompatible loyalties. Through Claverhouse himself she gives a glimpse of the agonizing predicament of a responsible commander, naturally humane yet unable to combat terrorism save by measures almost as harsh. The action is spread over some years, from the last days of Charles II to the coming of William III and the tension is perhaps too often relaxed, the emotion dissipated, though the historical explanations in the bridging passages are conveyed with such vitality that most young readers will be safely bundled through into the next dramatic episode. Whether the essential deeper understanding emerges—what was it all about, why were people moved to do such things?—is less certain. But it could be argued that, whatever the incredulity of the more speculative modern child, the blind loyalties and hero-worship here depicted may be historically truer to the psychology of the period.

M. Hobbs

SOURCE: A review of *Bonnie Dundee,* in *The Junior Bookshelf,* Vol. 47, No. 6, December, 1983, pp. 263-64.

Rosemary Sutcliff makes a telling parallel between the more violent seventeenth-century Scottish Covenanters and the IRA and Protestant militants of today, in particular how easily fanatical freedom fighters can deny freedom to others, killing as well as dying in God's name. . . . [The] authentic Scottish lilt is skilfully conveyed, and the background most carefully researched. As one expects from Rosemary Sutcliff, the beauty of the setting—lowlands, hills, seasons, colours, wind and scents—permeates the narrative. Hugh's meeting with the Tinkler folk and their leader the swashbuckling Captain Faa, the kin of Darklis, his Lady's waiting woman, introduces something of the same mystery the Britons brought to the Roman novels. The supernatural, in Darklis' vision in a pool and the Washerwoman and the ford who presages defeat in battle, gives a kind of unity and further dimension, and the love-story of Hugh and Darklis also binds it together. But for all these ingredients, and the excellent writing, only Hugh himself really touches the heart and this remains primarily and absorbingly a fine recreation of a lesser-known historical episode.

Margaret Meek

SOURCE: A review of *Bonnie Dundee,* in *The School Librarian,* Vol. 31, No. 4, December, 1983, pp. 382-83.

In the famous books of the sixties, Rosemary Sutcliff lit up obscure corners of history with the clear flame of invention. Her heroines and heroes cut patterns of legendary heroism in tribal warfare or in the rites of passage—as in *Warrior Scarlet.* Now, in a book that shows the same grasp of conflicting loyalties, she tells the story of a Scottish hero, John Graham of Claverhouse, Viscount Dundee, seen through the eyes of a portrait painter who, as a young man, followed the fortunes of this romantic figure. . . .

I've known the story of Bonnie Dundee for as long as I can remember, so I'm tough on retellers who walk in Scott's shadow. But Rosemary Sutcliff's ear is good for dialect and she makes a fair fist at mine. She is still a greater teller of the battle tale which she endows with more real romance than the half-hidden love story. But now she is tied to documented history, so to lighten dark corners she has first to create them, in the character of Darklis, the lady's maid who is of the travellers, or Tinkler folk, in Captain Faa, the hero of this 'left-hand world' of fairy rounds, superstitions and the bitter internecine battles of religious strife. The Scotland of *Bonnie Dundee* is not far away from the trackless heather of *The Eagle of the Ninth.* Rosemary Sutcliff has an artist's eye, and it has never been put to better use than in creating the memorable tale of Hugh Herriot who, like his originator, has 'a knack of catching a likeness' from the metamemory of the imagination.

Kirkus Reviews

SOURCE: A review of *Bonnie Dundee,* in *Kirkus Reviews,* Juvenile Issue, Vol. LII, Nos. 6-9, May 1, 1984, pp. J52-3.

Some readers may find the remote, relatively complex history a bit daunting here—not to mention the Scots dialect. But Sutcliff wisely makes the issues a minor concern, background to more immediate matters of personal loyalty and honor. So, with additional texture from Darklis' part-gypsy heritage and the authentic details on period-

painting, this is rich, tough-minded, warm-hearted historical fiction on the very highest level: an invigorating blend of action, color, and romance.

FLAME-COLOURED TAFFETA (1986)

Neil Philip

SOURCE: "Tomboy," in *The Times Educational Supplement,* No. 3649, June 6, 1986, p. 54.

Flame-Coloured Taffeta is a short novel for younger children, somewhat in the vein of the early books by its author. . ., *The Armourer's House* and *Brother Dusty-Feet.* Its chief character is a 12-year-old girl, Damaris, a typically sparky but sketchy Sutcliff heroine, who is tomboyish without any sense of inner rebellion against the constraints of being a girl.

It is those constraints, however, which prevent this eighteenth-century smuggling yarn making the most dramatic use of its materials. This is not a book of vigorous action in Sutcliff's best mode, nor is it a typical Sutcliff story of the building of character through adversity. Instead it has a gentle, romantic quality, which girls of Damaris's age may well find appealing.

The story, about Damaris and her friend Peter finding an injured man in the woods after a clash between smugglers and excisemen, and nursing him to health in their secret hideaway, is slight. The historical setting is one-dimensional, with a great deal of stage-prop quaint local colour. What saves the book, and reminds us of the great power and authority of Rosemary Sutcliff's writing at its best, is the vivid personal response to locality. The landscape of the Selsey Peninsula is evoked with marvellous economy and skill. Effects of light are recorded and conveyed with meticulous accuracy.

While it falls short of its author's own high standards, this is nevertheless a work with its own sense of movement, its own sense of adventure, its own sense of craft.

Margery Fisher

SOURCE: A review of *Flame-Coloured Taffeta,* in *Growing Point,* Vol. 25, No. 3, September, 1986, p. 4677.

Rosemary Sutcliff for *Flame-Coloured Taffeta* uses the very concrete, direct, open style which made books like *Brother Dusty-Feet* so accessible to children from nine or so. Yet it is a simplicity where every word has its place and where there is much to read between the lines; the layers of past and present and their interdependence are there to be noted by careful readers. . . .

Damaris and her boon companion Peter Ballard, son of the Vicar, have grown up accepting the rights of smugglers; though Damaris's father is not actively engaged in the contraband trade, on nights when horses are needed he prudently leaves his stable doors open. When the two children find a wounded man in the woods they assume he had been in the affray the night before with the revenue officers but it seems that he is not a smuggler, though he bought a passage with their counterparts from France. The date is 1746 and some readers may guess that the romantically styled Tom Wildgoose has something to do with the failed Jacobite rebellion of the previous year. The approach and direction of the story is not political but, rather, it plays on that congenial idea of young sympathies actively engaged for a person rather than for a cause. Damaris and Peter manage to get Tom to Genty the Wise Woman and to keep him hidden in spite of local suspicions. Details of medicinal herbs, housewifery, village hierarchies, weather and landscape have been chosen to blend into a firm, fascinating picture of the past in which the compassion, good sense and resources of the children are properly related to the past but can be readily appreciated in the present. This warm-hearted, concrete and energetic tale could give pleasure to children over a wide range of years from nine or so.

Joanna Motion

SOURCE: "Helping Out," in *The Times Literary Supplement,* No. 4355, September 19, 1986, p. 1042.

The natural world lies close to the surface of [this] novel. Sutcliff writes with her customary illuminating sympathy for the landscape and its creatures.

Out of this comes a strong underlying sense that country ways are good ways—that people who can't tell an oyster-catcher's call from a coaching horn are missing out; and that townies, who leave gates open and go hunting in outlandish yellow coats with lace trimming, are not only out of sympathy with the place but inherently suspect—probably on the side of the Excise, indeed. This is a sunny and gentle novel but Sutcliff is too interesting a writer to suppress the perception that there are grim things under the sun: pistol shots and wax hearts with thorns in them and hangings at Chichester. Without that menace, half the exhilaration of the chase and the rescue would be gone, and Sutcliff is as adept as ever at unrolling a narrative with incidents of high excitement: Damaris, Tom Wildgoose and a half-tamed fox hunted by hounds; a midnight rescue of Tom aided by magic that if not black is distinctly dark; escape through woods on the night of a smugglers' run.

Flame-Coloured Taffeta is a self-contained, good-hearted adventure story where the adventures are better than the slightly flabby excuse provided for them by the fading Jacobite cause—even Tom Wildgoose is lukewarm about the value of his mission. The two central characters, Damaris and Peter, are likeable, capable children evidently destined for a companiable marriage when they grow up, occasionally irradiated, perhaps, by Damaris's yearning imagination. She is a girl who is prepared to sacrifice her cotton underskirts for bandages, though she dreams of a petticoat in flame-coloured taffeta, "which

somehow stood for all the joy and laughter and beauty and shine of the world".

It is not a book that aims at the profundity or the scope of Rosemary Sutcliff's celebrated Roman novels. But it succeeds as an enjoyable, soundly-crafted short novel where no whisker of plot or detail of character is wasted. And the sense of history under the lanes, the past seeped into the landscape, as Damaris looks out to sea from her farm house built of wrecked Armada timbers, will be familiar and satisfying to Sutcliff's many admirers.

Diane Manuel

SOURCE: A review of *Flame-Colored Taffeta,* in *The Christian Science Monitor,* October 3, 1986, p. B5.

One new title this fall has a particularly fine blend of essential ingredients. In ***Flame-Colored Taffeta,*** author Rosemary Sutcliff draws her readers in with vivid imagination, rich language, and compelling storytelling.

Like many Books That Last, it has an uncomplicated, straightforward plot—12-year-old Damaris Crocker and 13-year-old Peter Ballard befriend a mysterious traveler and care for him in their secret forest hideaway.

That's the plot. The story is something else again. Set in the mythical English village of Sormerley Green at the time of Bonnie Prince Charlie's bid for the throne, *Taffeta* is chock full of smugglers and sailors, midnight riders, and crosses chalked on stable doors. Genty Small, the wise woman, dispenses potions and sound advice, while Caleb Henty, the horseman, shivers in his stirrups.

In addition to an impressive array of eccentric characters, author Sutcliff serves up the kind of plum pudding of description and detail that ought to make young readers hunger for more of the same. In the wild countryside, there's the "wild-duck skein of wind-shaped hawthorns" and the "woodwind call of an oystercatcher" in a sky "as blue as a dunnock's egg." In the nearby woods, we see a vixen whose eyes shine "unwinking like two green elf lamps in the gloom," and come upon a cottage "dark and humped like a large sleeping hedgehog."

The only unfortunate note is struck in the last few pages, with an ending that's both too tidy and too abrupt. Still, one hopes that the title of this engaging book won't discourage too many boys, since the questions that are explored here—Where are we going? and What are our obligations to each other?—are the stuff of truly exciting literature.

Ethel L. Heins

SOURCE: A review of *Flame-Colored Taffeta,* in *The Horn Book Magazine,* Vol. LXIII, No. 2, March-April, 1987, pp. 213-14.

Turning from the complexities of her richly textured historical novels, the author adds freshness and skill to the simpler and more direct narrative style of such early books as *Brother Dusty-Feet* and *The Armourer's House*. . . . Unlike much fiction set in the past, the suspenseful story involves its characters less in historical events than in personal interplay; Damaris and Peter are passionately concerned with Tom's survival and safety rather than with his hopeless cause. Rosemary Sutcliff is still a superbly evocative storyteller, conveying a vibrant sense of seasons and of place—specifically a deep feeling for the "sea-haunted land" and for all creatures who live in communion with it. As Damaris hurries away early one morning, surreptitiously taking food to the convalescent Tom, the author notes, "The rain had passed in the night, and there were wet gleams of sunshine lancing through the woods, and the birds singing in the tone of freshly washed surprise that belongs to the first days of springtime."

THE SHINING COMPANY (1990)

Hazel Rochman

SOURCE: A review of *The Shining Company,* in *Booklist,* Vol. 86, No. 20, June 15, 1990, p. 1970.

Far from the docudrama that passes for much historical fiction, this novel of early Britain draws you into a desolate landscape that quivers with flame and shadow, an age-old war story of glory, comradeship, and betrayal. Based on *The Gododdin,* the earliest surviving North British poem, the story is told by young Prosper, who leaves his father's huddled settlement to serve as shield bearer to Prince Gorthyn, one of the 300 Companions summoned by the king. All are young, all younger sons. They spend a year training into a fighting brotherhood and then ride out to meet and hold off the enemy Saxons. But their supporting armies never come. Besieged and encircled, the Companions send back the harper to tell their story; then they make one last night ride, not to break through, but to fight to the death. The war adventure is set within the wilderness of seventh-century Britain, the Roman towns fallen into ruin, roads half lost, hero legends dim. Like a wheeling falcon, Prosper sees his world from the hills, always aware of his connection with forest, valley, wind-feathered sky, and distant sea in an ever-widening circle—a circle that also holds the bonds of friendship. In contrast, when the end comes, the enemy's circle closes in on the warriors, and they die in chaos, "a clotted mass of snarling faces." When his prince is killed, Prosper is still: "I do not think I felt anything, just then," he says. A clear choice for humanizing history lists, this novel is also for those readers everywhere who are stirred by a story dark and fierce and shining.

Christine Behrmann

SOURCE: A review of *The Shining Company,* in *School Library Journal,* Vol. 36, No. 7, July, 1990, p. 90.

Fans of Sutcliff's historical fiction will welcome her re-

turn to the post-Roman British setting of some of her finest novels as she tells a stirring tale based on "The Gododdin," the earliest surviving poem set in Northern Britain. Set in A.D. 600, the story is told by Prosper who, with his bodyservant Conn, joins Prince Gorthyn as a shield-bearer when the prince enlists in a company formed by King Mynyddog of the Gododdin in an effort to unite the British kingdoms against the ever-present Saxon threat. The bulk of the story concerns the forging of men from disparate parts of Britain into a fighting unit, combined in a common cause. The rousing climax comes with their first mission when, sent deep into Saxon territory, they are abandoned by Mynyddog. Prosper, Conn, and Cynan, the lord they serve after Gorthyn's death, are among the survivors, and they return to discover that their betrayal had been planned from the beginning. As the story closes, Cynan and Prosper have turned their backs on Britain to find new lives as soldiers in Byzantium. Sutcliff has called all of her considerable talents into play here, creating strong memorable characters, sweeping action, and a vivid sense of place and time. Her depiction of the final, hopeless charge of the Companions is unforgettable: Prosper's references to the Celtic Wild Hunt ring with haunting truth. Sutcliff remains a mistress of the delineation of the strong bonds that combat and a collective purpose can create among men. Her descriptions of the inevitable violence of war are honest and matter of fact. This is a challenging book, with many names and places that will be unfamiliar to readers not acquainted with early British history, although the map and pronunciation guide should help. Readers willing to surrender to Sutcliff's demanding yet hypnotic language will be drawn into a truly splendid adventure, containing powerful themes of heroism, friendship, loss, betrayal, and sacrifice.

Margery Fisher

SOURCE: A review of *The Shining Company,* in *Growing Point,* Vol. 29, No. 3, September 1990, pp. 5385-86.

When Rosemary Sutcliff uses the first person for a story you may be sure that she intends to present her hero precisely in an historical context but also, by allowing the expressions of feelings as well as facts, to help young readers to understand him in their own terms. So Prosper, son of Gerontius, when at twelve years old he is given Conn, a slave boy of his own age as a body servant, accepts him as the rightful property of a chieftain's son but in helping Conn to tend a festered knee he begins to relate to him as an individual. Though this richly woven tale of war and endurance Prosper's growth into manhood is guided by a strict education in chivalric modes of behaviour but through the years as squire and shield-bearer to Prince Gorthyn he learns also to understand his lord more personally. . . .

The structure of the book depends on time as well as on place and event, never more so than in the open ending, where after the collapse of one particular opposition to the power of the Northmen Prosper and his new lord Cynan ride from Dyn-Edin to the sea to join a merchant ship bound for the east; if they can find service with the Emperor in Byzantium the two men will be helped to put the sombre years of defeat behind them. A large cast of characters—merchant and bard, squires and slaves, the women with their quiet civilising influence on castle and cottage, even the dogs and horses—play their part in a wide-ranging narrative.

For the reader there is also the landscape, seen through historical eyes, more than a mere physical background because of the power of prose to evoke contours of mountain, road and forest and to suggest, through darkness and light, wind and weather, a kind of sympathy with the fortunes of men. The citadel of Dyn-Edin, the empty forts on the Walls, the moorland and forests of Bernicia and Deira, the march of the seasons—every scene directly contributes to the force of the book. Here is part of the account of the siege of Catraeth, a valiant attempt by the Company to capture the Saxon leader Aethelfrith and break the power of the invaders:

> Ahead of us the land was roughly cleared, though overgrown with hazel and alder scrub between broad intake fields that showed faintly green here and there with promises of a threadbare crop. Always the Saxons clear the forest and plant their wheat where the land is not good enough for crops, though it might support black cattle. But the forest would have been better left for timber and hunting. The forsaken town looked from that distance like little more than a kind of grey shingle ridge; save where on the highest ground the remains of the fort crouched like an old hound in the last thickening light of sunset. Of the Royal Village another mile beyond it, there was no sign at all.

Not only can we readily visualise military tactics and marches from this description but we can also think back to a world different from our own but a world whose aims and attitudes may be clearly understood and felt in a story as movingly and strongly told as this one.

Alan McLeod

SOURCE: "A Dagger Forged," in *The Times Literary Supplement,* No. 4578, December 28, 1990, p. 1407.

All but a handful of [Sutcliff's] works have been historical novels for young adults, many of them set in the Britain of the early Dark Ages against the background of the struggle between the native Celts and the invading Saxons that followed the Roman withdrawal. Many feature disabled characters and explore their deep sense of isolation, a subject of special importance to the author who has suffered from Still's Disease, a crippling arthritic condition, since childhood.

The Shining Company is typical in both these respects. It is based on *The Gododdin,* the epic by the bard Aneirin about the disastrous campaign against the Saxon kingdoms of Deira and Bernicia by a fighting force of 300 young noblemen assembled by King Mynyddog. Since Aneirin's poem consists mainly of a series of elegies for the fallen, however, Sutcliff has been forced to imagine the events of the campaign for herself, she has also created Prosper, the teenage son of a chieftain, to tell the story.

Prosper is not himself disabled, but, unloved by his father, who prefers his older brother, he feels an outcast and is quick to make friends with Conn, a lame slave boy who is given to him as a servant. Another close bond is formed with young Prince Gorthyn of Rhyfunnog, who spares a third outcast, a magnificent white stag, during a hunt; and when Gorthyn decides to travel to Mynyddog's capital Dyn Eidin and join his army, Prosper and Conn go with him, the former as a shield-bearer and the latter as a general dogsbody. Their social positions, as well as Conn's lame leg, then lead to the two boys' becoming separated, although they are united once again following the horrific final battle in which most of their comrades perish.

The Shining Company, however, is as much about creation as destruction, as much about art as war. The bard Aneirin, portrayed as a dark-skinned man with yellow eyes, a nose like the beak of a bird of prey, and a white scar on his neck left by a Saxon thrall-ring, figures prominently in the novel, and the eventual composition of his poem becomes the snatching of a kind of victory from a devastating defeat. Equally prominent is a beautiful dagger, brought back from Constantinople by a merchant, which surfaces periodically in the course of the action. When Prosper first sees this object, he begins dreaming of the Golden Horn and the Byzantine Emperor's palace, and is filled with a lust for travel and adventure. Conn, however, is much more fascinated by the merchant's account of the process by which such weapons are made. The crippled young slave goes on to become an accomplished swordsmith during the campaign against the Saxons, and thus not only triumphs over his disability but, since his is a trade which immediately confers freedom on a person, is released from bondage.

Sutcliff's novel has much in common with the well-made dagger it celebrates. Among its many pleasures is a style studded with exotic Celtic words, vivid tableaux of medieval hunts and feasts and exciting battle scenes. There is also a thoughtful examination of some of the pressing issues—from the limits of friendship through the problem of violence to the question of what one should do with one's life—that are likely to confront any sensitive and intelligent adolescent; and the result is a book which is at once lyrical and incisive.

THE MINSTREL AND THE DRAGON PUP (1993)

Lauralyn Persson

SOURCE: A review of *The Minstrel and the Dragon Pup,* in *School Library Journal,* Vol. 39, No. 4, April, 1993, p. 103.

In this elegant picture-book fantasy, a dragon's abandoned

egg is awakened to life by a minstrel's song. The young creature and the solitary young man become true friends, until the dragon pup is abducted by an evil traveling showman. In the end, they are happily reunited, and an ailing prince has been miraculously healed as well. Sutcliff has taken folkloric elements and made them into a tale that seems both timeless and fresh. She claims to know the real truth about dragons, and provides readers with enchanting variations on familiar details. [Illustrator Emma Chichester] Clark's glowing oil pastels truly illuminate the telling. This is a land that seems commonplace yet exotic: there are castles, inns, . . . and palm trees. The dark borders enhance the ceremonial, formal tone. Even the page layouts help express the story's nuances: small intense pictures show the hasty abduction, while a luxurious double-page spread depicts the love between the minstrel and the dragon. All in all, this is a remarkable collaboration that sophisticated readers will take to right away. It may need to be introduced to children who are not used to a graceful pace and literary style, but the effort will certainly be worthwhile, and all youngsters are sure to respond to the book's beauty and emotional power.

Joanne Schott

SOURCE: A review of *The Minstrel and the Dragon Pup,* in *Quill and Quire,* Vol. 59, No. 5, May, 1993, p. 37.

The plot runs in a clear, simple line but the original language and graceful style turn that simplicity into a literary experience and create an atmosphere of a magical time.

Clark's illustrations, with soft outlines and golden light, carry the viewer into that same dreamlike time. Simple at first glance, they reveal unexpected images that keep the reader looking and discovering. Together author and artist have created a satisfying book whose solution, with everything turning out as it should, leaves the reader not just pleased but contented.

Mary M. Burns

SOURCE: A review of *The Minstrel and the Dragon Pup,* in *The Horn Book Magazine,* Vol. LXIX, No. 4, July-August, 1993, p. 455.

It seems fitting that one of the last books written by the late Rosemary Sutcliff should have a minstrel as its principal character. Noted for her historical fiction, she was a modern-day minstrel, celebrating noble deeds and re-creating times when heroes appeared larger than life. But this, her first picture text, is less flamboyant and gentler than her earlier works, more suited to a younger audience as it recounts the story of a wandering balladeer who adopts a gentle dragon pup only to lose it to a covetous, unprincipled showman. How he regains his lost pet and, in the process, restores the king's son to health is a heartwarming tale of virtue rewarded and love triumphant. What makes the story truly distinctive is its ending, for Sutcliff

eschews conventional wisdom and has the minstrel ask only that he and his pet be protected rather than that he be endowed with riches or power. Perhaps this is an echo of Sutcliff's own ambitions, for her works were not written to ensure popularity but rather to satisfy her own passionate interest in specific historical eras and a desire to reflect those times accurately. The formal, serene elegance of the illustrations matches the tone of the text both in composition and color. A lovely story which falls gently on the ear as it delights the eye.

BLACK SHIPS BEFORE TROY: THE STORY OF THE ILIAD (1993)

Kirkus Reviews

SOURCE: A review of *Black Ships Before Troy: The Story of the Iliad,* in *Kirkus Reviews,* Vol. LXI, No. 20, October 15, 1993, pp. 1337-38.

Among the late author's finest books are renditions of the Arthurian legend; to this recreation of *the* classic epic, she brought the same compelling vision and sensitivity to language, history, and heroics. Beginning with Discord's apple, inscribed "To the fairest" (it set off the competition among goddesses that led to Paris's abduction of Helen), she centers on Achilles and Hector while also recounting such significant events as Paris and Menelaus' single combat (inconclusive because Aphrodite meddles, as gods frequently do here), the funeral games honoring Patroclus, the Amazons' death in battle, and Odysseus' devious exploits. Described in vivid, exquisitely cadenced prose, both sides behave with nobility, though Sutcliff's Trojan War also involves atrocity (Hector's body dragged by Achilles' chariot), posturing, loss, and despair. After ten years, the remaining Greeks—with Helen, willingly restored to a husband whose first impulse is to kill her, plus the captive royal Trojan women—set sail for home, leaving Troy in flames; and though Sutcliff has focused on their honor and courage, she ensures that it's the ironic futility of their venture that lingers in the mind. [Illustrator Alan] Lee's subtly muted watercolors, on most spreads, surpass even his fine illustrations for *Merlin Dreams* (1988). Carefully researched, delicately detailed, rich in character and action, they beautifully evoke the setting and heroic ambience. A splendid offering, bringing the ancient tale to new and vibrant life.

Jan Mark

SOURCE: "The Pleasure Principle," in *The Times Educational Supplement,* No. 4037, November 12, 1993, p. 2.

Matthew Arnold listed the four essential qualities to be recognised of Homer by the would-be translator: that he is rapid, plain and direct in thought and its expression, and finally "that he is eminently noble." The responsibility, in turn, of the writer who would re-tell the epic tales of *The Odyssey* and *The Iliad* for children without a betrayal of the poetry and power of the originals is a daunting one.

No children's writer of the present century was better equipped for this task than the great Rosemary Sutcliff who, sadly, died in 1992. *Black Ships Before Troy,* her version of *The Iliad,* was one of her last works. It is a magnificent achievement: scholarly, luminously accessible, the narrative swift and uncluttered, the whole illustrated with a glowing strength and sensitivity by Alan Lee. If ever a book was unputdownable, whether by child or adult, it is this one. To me, it bears the unmistakable mark of a masterpiece of children's literature.

M. Crouch

SOURCE: A review of *Black Ships Before Troy,* in *The Junior Bookshelf,* Vol. 58, No. 1, February, 1994, p. 32.

Rosemary Sutcliff began her career with a retelling from traditional sources. Her *Chronicles of Robin Hood* was important only in marking the arrival of its author, but later retellings, of the Arthurian legends and other medieval stories, were always coloured with her personal passions and sprang from the very heart of her philosophy of history. It is entirely fitting that in her last statements (an *Odyssey* is to follow) she should return to the heroic age and to a faithful, yet thoroughly individual, rendering of the story of Troy. *Black Ships Before Troy* shirks none of the problems of introducing Homer to today's children. All the pointless killing is here, the (by modern standards) dubious morality, the unsporting intervention of the gods; but it has all been digested and reconciled. Above all, the authentic tone has been recreated. The Sutcliff paraphrase is often very literal, as in the moving passage when Hector scares his baby son with his great plumed helmet. For once Sutcliff, who was served by some of the finest illustrators of her day, has to share on equal terms the success of a book. Alan Lee's richly coloured pictures, mostly spread right across the double page, are scholarly, dynamic, adding another dimension to the story. Together author and artist have produced a book which matches the grandeur of its material.

Janet Tayler

SOURCE: A review of *Black Ships Before Troy,* in *The School Librarian,* Vol. 42, No. 2, May, 1994, p. 62.

No one can fail to be impressed by Rosemary Sutcliff's masterful retelling of Homer's *Iliad.* We hear how Helen of the Fair Cheeks 'left her lord, and her babe and her honour' to go with Paris, and how the black ships of Greece put to sea to fetch her back and to seek vengeance upon Troy. The language carries the reader along through the excitement of battle to grief for the dead and honour for the brave. Alan Lee's illustrations befit such a tale of gods and heroes—beautiful water-colours in muted tones on nearly every page. A useful section at the back of the book tells how to pronounce the Greek and Trojan names. It is extremely easy to recommend this book as an excellent introduction to Greek legend for upper primary and lower secondary schoolchildren, as well as for more mature and much older readers.

CHESS-DREAM IN A GARDEN (1993)

Kathryn Jennings

SOURCE: A review of *Chess-Dream in a Garden,* in *Bulletin of the Center for Children's Books,* Vol. 47, No. 3, November, 1993, pp. 102-03.

Sutcliff and [illustrator Ralph] Thompson have collaborated to create a book based on the ancient Lewis chess set, the pieces of which can now be found in both the British and Scottish National Museum. Sutcliff has woven a surrealistic tale of love and battle with the famous chess pieces as the players. The book has a dreamy quality which, combined with the chess-playing, gives it a strong kinship to David Wiesner's *Free Fall;* and as in that book—as in many dream books—sense is often sacrificed for mystery. Surrounding the pieces/players with animals both real and dreamed in a way that's both overelaborate and inconclusive, Sutcliff crowds the conflict with too many motifs, and in the midst of fiction, one feels cheated of a complete introduction to the real chess pieces. On the other hand, Sutcliff's poetic phrases and Thompson's misty watercolors sometimes merge to form a powerful and moody dream fragment, if not a cohesive story.

Lenore Rosenthal

SOURCE: A review of *Chess-Dream in a Garden,* in *Children's Book Review Service,* Vol. 22, No. 3, November, 1993, p. 32.

Based on a set of ancient chess pieces found in a chest on the Isle of Lewis, this is the story of two armies who play out a battle-like chess game. The characters in the illustrations are the chess pieces, done in pastel washed ink sketches. There are elements of fantasy and dream sequences in the brief, italic text, but the humor is adult. Although it looks like a picture book, I can not imagine a child reading it. A teacher might share it with a class as an opening to a discussion about war or medieval times.

Philip Pullman

SOURCE: "Bound to Please," in *The Times Educational Supplement,* No. 4037, November 12, 1993, p. 4.

Chess-Dream in a Garden, by Rosemary Sutcliff and Ralph Thompson, immediately invites comparison with the great exemplar of chess-dreams in gardens, *Through the Looking-Glass.* Furthermore, the story concerns the threat to peace and order posed by illicit love, and thus evokes the medieval legends of Lancelot and Guinevere or Tristan and Iseult. These are big challenges, but the book carries them off. Thompson peoples his lavishly planted garden with figures derived from the Lewis chessmen.

These little beings might not seem promising material for illustration, with their hunched postures and round staring eyes, but Thompson's fluid line and loose expressive colour have found a way of implying movement while retaining the quasi-hieratic stiffness of the figures. Sutcliff's story concerns the invasion of the Red Army as a result of the breach caused by the White Knight's illicit love for the White Queen, and their defeat by the Queen's realisation of her love for the garden itself. This is a striking example of a collaboration in which pictures preceded words; but when the words come from someone like Rosemary Sutcliff, they don't come second.

M. Crouch

SOURCE: A review of *Chess-Dream in a Garden,* in *The Junior Bookshelf,* Vol. 58, No. 1, February, 1994, p. 20.

We have already seen how Rosemary Sutcliff, at the very end of her life, was not only consolidating but extending her reputation. Here is another example. The initial inspiration for this strange story seems to have come from Ralph Thompson through a dream, and this may account for the rare precision of his illustrations. The writer links these visions with a thread of mysterious story which has action and passion but which never quite gives up its meaning. The characters in this dream are chess-men, the wonderful set carved from walrus ivory and discovered on the Isle of Lewis eight centuries after they were created by a master sculptor. Their game is played out in a marvellous garden under the eye of a winged beast, as the White Company and the Red Horde battle for supremacy. A mannered italic script reinforces the other-worldliness of the strange story, and Ralph Thompson's pictures capture each changing mood of the drama. It is all exquisitely done. It is of small importance that the meaning of this tale of violence and guilty love remains elusive to the last. All is in the beauty and the movement of the telling.

David Lewis

SOURCE: A review of *Chess-Dream in a Garden,* in *The School Librarian,* Vol. 42, No. 2, May, 1994, p. 57.

The central characters in this enthralling tale are the twelfth-century Lewis chessmen. The horde of walrus ivory chess pieces, discovered by a crofter on the Isle of Lewis, is now divided between the British Museum in London and the Scottish National Museum in Edinburgh. Rosemary Sutcliff's story appears to be based upon a dream experienced by the book's illustrator, Ralph Thompson, but she has transformed this personal vision into an affecting tale of misplaced love, false accusations, and a life-or-death battle that could have been handed down to us from the Middle Ages.

The white chess pieces comprise a royal court that exists in a state of bliss in a beautiful and magical garden. Sir Alrek, the knight, declares his love for Queen Hrosmunda and is overheard. Chastisement follows and all is apparently made well again, but the coldness that ensues between Hrosmunda and her king, Gudmund, blights the garden, breaches its defences, and lets in the evil red chess pieces. A chess-battle follows in the central court of the garden and the whites eventually triumph, following one or two magical transformations.

Rosemary Sutcliff's story is beautifully written, a condensation of a lifetime's experience of weaving narrative magic, and Ralph Thompson does a wonderful job of animating the squat and immobile figures of the chess pieces, and of bringing the charmed garden to life. I leave it as an open question whether it was an error of judgement to make the virtuous defenders of the garden white and the malign invaders coloured.

Additional coverage of Sutcliff's life and career is contained in the following sources published by Gale Research: *Authors and Artists for Young Adults,* Vol. 10; *Contemporary Authors New Revision Series,* Vol. 37; *Contemporary Literary Criticism,* Vol. 26; *Major Authors and Illustrators for Children and Young Adults*; and *Something about the Author,* Vols. 6, 44, 78.

Eleanora E(laine) Tate

1948-

African American author of fiction and poetry; editor.

Major works include *Just an Overnight Guest* (1980), *The Secret of Gumbo Grove* (1987), *Thank You, Dr. Martin Luther King, Jr.!* (1990), *Front Porch Stories at the One-Room School* (1992), *A Blessing in Disguise* (1995).

INTRODUCTION

Tate is credited with writing appealing realistic fiction for middle graders about African American girls, their families and friends, and growing up. She is best known for her first book for children, *Just an Overnight Guest,* which relates how a nine-year-old girl comes to understand the disorderly preschooler who comes to visit; the story was popularized by a film adaptation in 1983. Tate is praised for effectively combining warm family relationships, especially between fathers and daughters, with significant themes of awareness and identity. She is also esteemed for her insight into pre-teen psychology, her skill in creating memorable, well-developed characterizations, her gift for natural, convincing dialogue, and her ability to lighten serious passages with humor. Although some commentators have noted occasional ramblings and didacticism in her stories, most commend her works for their positive images of black family life, insightful themes embracing black history and culture, and affectionate depiction of small-town life.

Biographical Information

Tate has experienced the settings of her books firsthand: the small town of Canton, Missouri, where she was born, is thinly disguised as Nutbrush, Missouri in *Just an Overnight Guest* and its sequel, *Front Porch Stories at the One-Room School*; the tourist resort Myrtle Beach, South Carolina, where she now lives, is the model for Gumbo Grove, the setting of her trilogy *The Secret of Gumbo Grove, Thank You, Dr. Martin Luther King, Jr.!* and *A Blessing in Disguise.* Raised by her grandmother, Corinne E. Johnson, Tate attended first grade in Canton's one-room schoolhouse in the days of legal segregation. Her class was integrated into the town's white school system the following year. She graduated from Roosevelt High School in Des Moines and received her Bachelor of Arts degree in journalism with a specialty in news editorial from Drake University in 1973. Starting her career as a news reporter and news editor in Des Moines and Jackson, Tennessee, she received a fellowship in children's literature from the Bread Loaf Writers Conference in Middlebury, Vermont, in 1981, shortly after the publication of her first children's title. The following year Tate traveled through West Germany, France, and Italy re-

searching folk and fairy tales. Tate once explained what moved her to write for children: "Part of it . . . stems from my belief that I had a very happy childhood, with a certain richness to it that I want today's children to share. Certainly today's children, many of them, have happy childhoods, and for that I am grateful. I would like to add my voice in print, as well as my emotions, to the thought that children's childhoods can be happy if they can learn that they can do anything they set their minds to, if they try."

Major Works

In her first juvenile work, *Just an Overnight Guest,* Tate writes about nine-year-old Margie Carson and how she feels when her mother invites four-year-old Ethel, a disruptive, abused, and neglected child, to stay overnight. "Ethel Hardisen! I hated that trashy little kid. . . . Some folks said she was half white and other folks said she was half Black. To me she was all bad." Gradually, with the help of her loving father, Margie overcomes her anger and resentment and comes to accept the now permanent guest whom she discovers is actually her cousin. Celia

Morris lauds Tate for capturing "the nuances of small-town life, the warmth of a Black family struggling with a problem, and the volatile emotions of a young child." Discussing both the book and the film version, Tate commented: "The theme is the closeness of a black family that doesn't live in a ghetto in the North or the South. Another theme is father-daughter love. It has been said little black boys need fathers. I believe little black girls need fathers." In her second book, *The Secret of Gumbo Grove,* spunky eleven-year-old Raisin Stackhouse uncovers the town's hidden past in the old segregated cemetery of her church. Despite opposition from both black and white citizens, she ultimately wins a community service award for bringing about an awareness of important local history. Tate has asserted that "*The Secret of Gumbo Grove* is about heritage and being proud of one's heritage, especially Black people's."

Thank You, Dr. Martin Luther King, Jr.! is also set in South Carolina and features fourth-grader Mary Elouise Avery, who yearns to be in the school play about presidents with the rich white girl, Brandy, whom she idolizes. Instead, she is selected as narrator for the new black history skit, even though she hates being reminded of slavery and Dr. Martin Luther King, Jr. Through the visits of two storytellers and a wise grandmother, Mary Elouise finds a new way to see herself and appreciate her heritage. Zena Sutherland notes that in this work "[Tate] doesn't make racial generalizations; one of the strong points of her story is that there is bias in both races, just as there is understanding in both." Her fourth book, *Front Porch Stories at the One-Room School,* a sequel to *Just an Overnight Guest,* relates Margie's father's childhood memories as he takes his daughter along with her cousin Ethel to the old one-room schoolhouse he attended, which proves both entertaining and educational. Tate writes, "Most of the stories that [the father] tells . . . are based on my actual experiences, or on stories I heard and greatly embellished." *A Blessing in Disguise* confronts the issues of drugs and crime in a small community and the relationship of a girl with her not so wise and stable father. Tate has also written poetry, short stories and essays for children that have been published in various collections, including *Children of Longing,* which was edited by young adult novelist Rosa Guy. She has also contributed poetry and fiction to adult collections and periodicals and has published her own volumes of poetry.

Awards

Tate received the Bread Loaf Writers Conference fellowship in 1981. The film adaptation of her *Just an Overnight Guest* was listed among the "Selected Films for Young Adults, 1985" by the Young Adult Committee of the American Library Association. She received a Parents' Choice Gold Seal Award in 1987 for *The Secret of Gumbo Grove,* and has also been honored with awards for her journalism and other writings.

TITLE COMMENTARY

📖 *JUST AN OVERNIGHT GUEST* (1980)

Zena Sutherland

SOURCE: A review of *Just an Overnight Guest,* in *Bulletin of the Center for Children's Books,* Vol. 34, No. 2, October, 1980, p. 42.

The story is told by nine-year-old Margie, who is even more appalled than her older sister when Momma brings a hostile, obstreperous four-year-old to their home. Margie can't stand little Ethel, resents sharing her bed, resents even more sharing her mother's attention, and is sure that when Daddy (driver for a long-distance moving company) gets home, Ethel will be ousted. What she learns is that Ethel is the child of her uncle and a white woman; the latter has decamped. Margie knows that Ethel had no toys, was often locked into her mother's trailer alone for the night, and was physically abused; although she's disappointed when Daddy comes home and seems to share Momma's feeling of responsibility for Ethel, she's learned enough about duty and kindness from her parents to accept the overnight guest who's come to stay. A promising first novel, this gives an effective picture of a loving black family, and it's convincingly and consistently told from Margie's point of view.

Gloria Rohmann

SOURCE: A review of *Just an Overnight Guest,* in *School Library Journal,* Vol. 27, No. 2, October, 1980, p. 151.

Although her beloved Daddy drives a truck and is only home once every few weeks, and her older sister Alberta is growing up and away from the childhood pleasures they share, Margie thinks that her life is just about perfect in the Mississippi River town of Nutbrush until her Mom brings Ethel, "that trashy little . . . half white kid," home "overnight" while the girl's mother is away. The overnight stretches into days and weeks and the secret of Ethel's relationship to Margie's Black family is finally revealed to Margie. The nine-year-old is fiercely jealous of the attention Ethel gets from her parents and resents Ethel's presence in her room. Although her parents are sympathetic to Margie's distress, they don't make the transition very easy for her. Young readers will share Margie's outrage at the intrusion of bratty Ethel and recognize in Margie the adjustments all children must make to growth and change. Contemporary small-town life is evoked with loving detail, and the characterizations are honest and memorable.

Judith Goldberger

SOURCE: A review of *Just an Overnight Guest,* in *Booklist,* Vol. 77, No. 5, November 1, 1980, p. 408.

For nine-year-old Margie Carson things go from bad to

worse when her mother takes in a neglected, half-white four-year-old named Ethel. Ethel is monstrous, not only to Margie but to everyone in their small town. And Ethel, whose white mother keeps calling from St. Louis to postpone her return, seems determined to become a fixture in the Carson household. Jealousy, hatred of the gossip in town, and fear of Ethel's permanent position create tensions nearly unbearable to Margie, who seems regarded by her older sister and mother as just the right person to keep watch over the child. Ethel, who is in fact a cousin, mellows considerably under Margie's mother's warm rule, but it is not until Margie's long-distance truck-driving father comes home that Margie finds sufficient inner resources to cope on a lasting basis. A lengthy book, but filled with solid, realistic detail and convincing manifestations of a family's strengths, trials, and caring.

Celia H. Morris

SOURCE: A review of *Just an Overnight Guest,* in *The Horn Book Magazine,* Vol. LVI, No. 6, December, 1980, pp. 643-44.

Even though Daddy had forbidden it before he left on another trucking job, Momma had taken in that "trashy little kid" Ethel Hardisen, who was half-white and half-Black and known as a troublemaker. Nine-year-old Margie couldn't understand when Momma said it was "'the proper thing to do.'" When the overnight stay lengthened into a two-week sojourn, Margie's tolerance was put to the test. Her boy-crazy older sister Alberta was no help, so it was Margie who had to put up with the behavior of the four-year-old visitor; she wet Margie's bed, broke all her shells, strutted around in Margie's old Sunday school dress, and got all Momma's attention. In a first-person telling Margie vividly describes her feelings of isolation, jealousy, and hatred but also her growing awareness of the tragedy of Ethel's life. When Daddy returned and revealed that her father was their own irresponsible uncle and that the little girl would be staying with them for a long time, Margie reacted swiftly with entirely realistic anger, expressing the fear that now she'd lose her father's affections, too. But her father explained, "A whole lot of things aren't fair. . . . People should do lots of things, like raise their own kids. . . . But some things won't change. People have to change." In her first novel the author captures well the nuances of small-town life, the warmth of a Black family struggling with a problem, and the volatile emotions of a young child.

Beryle Banfield

SOURCE: A review of *Just an Overnight Guest,* in *Interracial Books for Children Bulletin,* Vol. 12, No. 2, 1981, pp. 21-2.

This time around a new Black writer is not a cause to rejoice. It's been many a year since Black people spent time dividing themselves or rating themselves based on gradations of skin color or texture of hair. So a novel set in the present day (even though it takes place in a small southern town) which presents Black characters constantly putting one another down by insulting remarks based on color cannot aid in building self-esteem for Black youngsters and cannot aid in reducing notions of color superiority in white children.

The author introduces a Black mother who doesn't want her daughter dating a boy whose family is on welfare and who says, "I'm not going to allow my children to associate with people who don't want to uplift themselves and their race and lead proper, productive lives!" This subject is then dropped and never resolved or dealt with again in the book. And consider this: the *only* white in the book is described as "white trash"—alcoholic, a child neglecter-abuser, an unmarried mother with a child fathered by a *Black* man. What an interesting message that may give to young readers—that sleeping across the color line is in some way related to being "white trash."

The author throws in a lot of confused messages about color and "proper" behavior. The one message that does come through clearly is that a parent can share love with new children without having less love for the original children. But why this message needs to have all the negative color messages attached remains unclear.

Kirkus Reviews

SOURCE: A review of *Just an Overnight Guest,* in *Kirkus Reviews,* Vol. XLIX, No. 4, February 15, 1981, p. 215.

This takes place about a generation ago, with nine-year-old Margie's respectable and loving black family living quietly in Nutbrush, a small town on the Mississippi River. But Margie's tranquil universe is rudely disturbed when Mama insists on taking in bratty, half-white, four-year-old Ethel while Ethel's trashy white mother makes an overnight trip. The overnight visit is extended; and though Ethel is soon tamed by Margie's charitable schoolteacher mother, it is Margie whose bed gets "peed" on, whose precious shell collection is broken, and whose place in her parents' affection seems threatened by the intruder. By the time Ethel is permanently established in their home, Margie has learned that the child is her cousin and is helped in adjusting to the changes by her understanding father. Readers, for their part, have come to sympathize with Margie and to feel the ambience of her narrow, gossipy community.

THE SECRET OF GUMBO GROVE (1987)

Kirkus Reviews

SOURCE: A review of *The Secret of Gumbo Grove,* in *Kirkus Reviews,* Vol. LV, No. 5, March 1, 1987, p. 380.

The author of *Just an Overnight Guest* tells how the black community at a South Carolina seaside resort comes to value the history represented in the local cemetery where their ancestors are buried.

Raisin, 12, is fascinated with history and disappointed that important local black people aren't mentioned in school. When old Miz Effie ropes her into helping to tidy up the New Africa Cemetery and shares old church records with her, she discovers that there are indeed many interesting tales about the people there, but she meets adamant opposition to her research, both from the community and from her busy, strict parents. Though some of the stories may be heroic, people don't want to be reminded of their tragic history; moreover, they fear a negative response from the white community to the news that the town's founder was black and is buried here. But, beginning with the bullying Big Boy (a girl), more and more people begin to understand that the past is a source of pride. Raisin, whose first oral-history tapes were confiscated as being liable to stir up trouble, receives a community service award as the hero who saved the cemetery and renewed the local sense of identity.

Reminiscent of *The Wheel on the School* in the way a whole community is gradually involved in cooperating in a good cause, Tate's novel skillfully alternates episodes in the primary plot with Raisin's involvement in the con-

temporary town, especially a Miss Ebony contest among the "young, gifted and black"; this source of self-respect also turns out to have roots in the old cemetery. A vividly evoked piece of Americana that should be widely enjoyed.

Betsy Hearne

SOURCE: "Families Shaped by Love, Not Convention," in *The Christian Science Monitor,* May 1, 1987, pp. B3-4.

Although Eleanora Tate has cast her novel in the present, it . . . has roots in the past. ***The Secret of Gumbo Grove*** is an intriguing story about 11-year-old Raisin Stackhouse tracing her black community's history through accounts of those buried in a local South Carolina graveyard. Raisin has a passion for history, even to the point of defying her parents and church authorities who don't want to stir up trouble by dragging out old tales of racial prejudice. But Raisin persists, discovering, with the help of an old neighbor, that one of the state's first senators and richest citizens was a black man. Families, Raisin finds, have deep interlocking connections that can make people both fearful and proud. There's a lot of humor to leaven this message, along with lively dynamics among Raisin's

Jacket illustration from Just an Overnight Guest, *written by Eleanora Tate. Illustrated by Jerry Pinkney.*

friends and sisters, one of whom is competing in a beauty contest. The writing occasionally rambles, but that very quality accounts for some fresh passages of dialogue.

Denise M. Wilms

SOURCE: A review of *The Secret of Gumbo Grove,* in *Booklist,* Vol. 83, No. 18, May 15, 1987, pp. 1450-51.

Raisin Stackhouse is a curious, outspoken, spunky heroine, whose personality is strong enough to deal with the hornet's nest she stirs up when investigating some local history. Her interest is piqued by the elderly Miz Effie Pfluggins, who one day asks Raisin's help in cleaning up a grave in the cemetery near her house. Walking through the graveyard prompts Miz Effie to recall forgotten bits of history, which seem ever more important in light of a movement to forsake this cemetery and begin a new one in another part of town. Raisin gets caught up in Miz Effie's desire to save the cemetery, but other locals aren't, and until Miz Effie's claims about the cemetery are validated by church records, no one takes her seriously. Raisin, of course, is instrumental in bringing the true facts to light and wins a civic award for her efforts. Tate's story, set in a contemporary South Carolina black community, is vigorously and affectionately characterized. Raisin's quest to find out the truth about what happened to Gumbo Grove blacks—some of them her relatives— when slavery and rigid segregation were the order of the day not only spices the story but also imparts well-taken lessons in black history and black pride. One of the stumbling blocks Raisin encounters is an unwillingness on the part of some adults to recall the past, and a few of her friends function as examples of unconcerned and uncaring young black people who fail to appreciate the civil-rights gains made before their time. Tate's story is direct, uncomplicated, and entertaining, but its deliberate probing of some important aspects of black identity will cause readers to stop and think.

Linda M. Classen

SOURCE: A review of *The Secret of Gumbo Grove,* in *Voice of Youth Advocates,* Vol. 10, No. 3, August, 1987, p. 123.

Raisin, a young black girl living in a coastal community in South Carolina, is fascinated by history. She wonders why no one famous or important has ever lived in their town of Gumbo Grove. One day, while helping an elderly citizen with work, she discovers that there is more to local history than she first realized. Through stories told to her by this old woman, she discovers the real roots of the town and why all the citizens, both black and white, are upset to have this information brought into the open. Raisin also learns about segregation in the old days and what it meant to be black in the days before civil rights.

The story line is interesting and characterization is adequate. This does give a feeling for life in a black commu

nity before blacks had rights, which as the book points out, not many young people today can comprehend.

Lisa Firke

SOURCE: A review of *The Secret of Gumbo Grove,* in *Kliatt Young Adult Paperback Book Guide,* Vol. XXIII, No. 3, April, 1989, p. 18.

Raisin Stackhouse is just about the only kid in Gumbo Grove, a coastal resort in South Carolina, who thinks history is important. She likes all history, but hungers for a history of her own black ancestors: "When I asked Miz Gore, my teacher, how come we never studied about anybody Black who did stuff around here, she said nobody Black around here had ever done anything good worth talking about."

However, Raisin's friendship with the elderly church secretary Miss Effie leads her to investigate an abandoned cemetery and read some of the old church records. She discovers that not only did black people from her town do things worth talking about, but that the town itself was founded by a black man. She is surprised to find that her discoveries are disbelieved and suppressed by both black and white people in Gumbo Grove, who would rather forget the painful stories of slaves and Klansmen, even if it means also forgetting stories of community solidarity and personal bravery. But by the novel's conclusion, Raisin is able to make others share her attitude of "lik[ing] to feel good about what people did back in the old days, because it help[s] [us] go ahead and feel good about now."

Raisin's historical interests are realistically balanced with interest in her family, boys, and the local Miss Junior Ebony Contest. The novel is narrated in an appealing vernacular style, including some excellent examples of recorded oral history. *The Secret of Gumbo Grove* is highly recommended, both as pleasure reading and as an excellent supplement to the study of U.S. history. History teachers will, in fact, treasure it as a partial answer to the questions, "How is history relevant?" and "what mysteries remain?"

Pam Spencer

SOURCE: "Winners in Their Own Right," in *School Library Journal,* Vol. 38, No. 3, March, 1992, pp. 163-67.

One of the most engaging characters in recent years is Raisin Stackhouse in *The Secret of Gumbo Grove* by Eleanor Tate. The day Miz Effie asks Raisin to help her clear off the grave of Miz Effie's husband is the day Raisin first hears some of the history of the early black settlers of Gumbo Grove. This history excites her and makes her want to share it with others in her black community.

Unfortunately, some of the "others" don't want to talk about the past, fearing a return to pre-civil rights days.

The characters and events are sketched with a light hand, offering many instances of good-hearted laughter, especially in the scenes of the annual beauty pageant to determine Little Miss Ebony Calvary County, and provide respite from the seriousness of black concerns.

THANK YOU, DR. MARTIN LUTHER KING, JR.! (1990)

Kirkus Reviews

SOURCE: A review of *Thank You, Dr. Martin Luther King, Jr.!* in *Kirkus Reviews,* Vol. LVIII, No. 3, February 1, 1990, p. 186.

Tate returns to the scene of **The Secret of Gumbo Grove,** now with the other side of African-Americans' sometimes reluctant search for pride in their heritage.

In the excellent earlier book, young Raisin's persistence was rewarded by renewed interest in a past symbolized by a neglected but historic cemetery in her Carolina community. Here, fourth-grader Mary Elouise's dissatisfaction with being black has caused her to seek the friendship of Brandy, a snooty, rich, white girl, in preference to her real friends—and even to spurn the black doll her beloved grandmother has given her. The racist assumptions of a white teacher and Mary Elouise's family's casual but constant references to skin color exacerbate her low self-image. Her turnaround is sparked by a black teacher; by a visiting author-storyteller; by the forthright stories of the grandmother; by an incident that finally makes Brandy's underlying contempt clear; and especially by the black-history segment of a school program.

Tate's characters are three-dimensional and believable; their dialogue and interaction are authentic and deftly drawn. But her didactic purpose—although certainly worthy—weighs down a story with only the slightest of plots, making it more a fictionalized essay on the causes and cures of black racism than a novel. Earnest but flawed.

Gerry Larson

SOURCE: A review of *Thank You, Dr. Martin Luther King, Jr.!,* in *School Library Journal,* Vol. 36, No. 3, March, 1990, pp. 220-21.

Fourth grader Mary Elouise Avery struggles with a low self-image in this consciousness-raising story of black pride. When Gumbo Grove Elementary School prepares for its annual Presidents' Month play, Mary Elouise is selected as narrator for the new black history segment. She dislikes the role, as she feels that it emphasizes the difference between her and her Barbiesque classroom idol, Brandy. Her mother scolds her for disposing of black dolls in favor of white dolls, and her perceptive grandmother advises her to "love yourself for who you are." By story's end, her part in the play has given Mary Elouise a better understanding of her heritage. She also has a

new idol, a black storyteller who perceives her angst and challenges her to seek any goal with determination. The message is clear, and the plot is predictable. Except for the condescending naivete of a white teacher, characters offer a positive perspective on black culture. This purposeful novel conveys the challenge of maintaining ethnic pride in a society dominated by whites. Mary Elouise learns about her heritage, herself, and friendship in this first-person narrative. Realistic dialogue and peer conflicts, plus Mary Elouise's insights make this an appropriate choice for young readers.

Denise Wilms

SOURCE: A review of *Thank You, Dr. Martin Luther King, Jr.!* in *Booklist,* Vol. 86, No. 16, April 15, 1990, p. 1636.

Self-worth is the strong message in Tate's story of Mary Elouise, a black girl who is unhappy about who she is. Simply put, Mary Elouise is ashamed to be black—embarrassed about slavery, unhappy over her dark skin, and eager to become best friends with Brandy, a stuck-up, blond classmate. The protagonist's poor image comes from several sources: a pathetically uninformed and insensitive white teacher who patronizes her black students; a hardworking, harried single mother who loves her daughter but unfortunately lashes out at Mary Elouise's shortcomings by denigrating her appearance; and the dismaying ease with which children prey upon each other. In one important scene Mary Elouise and her friends engage in some nasty put-downs of each other's appearance until an angry white teacher demands they stop and have respect for themselves. Mary Elouise's grandmother eventually ferrets out the girl's problem and provides the support and encouragement that start her thinking more positively. Tate tackles a sensitive issue, taking pains to keep characters multidimensional and human. The mother is a sympathetic character despite her flaws, and even Mary Elouise's out-of-touch teacher, who could have been so easily portrayed as mean spirited, acts out of ignorance rather than maliciousness. A companion to **The Secret of Gumbo Grove,** this novel is set in the same community and written with the same energy and uncomplicated style. Clear-eyed and accessible.

Zena Sutherland

SOURCE: A review of *Thank You, Dr. Martin Luther King, Jr.!* in *Bulletin of the Center for Children's Books,* Vol. 43, No. 10, June, 1990, p. 254.

In a sequel to **The Secret of Gumbo Grove** the narrator is nine-year old Mary Elouise, who is black but far from proud of it. In fact, Mary Elouise is embarrassed when her teacher (white, saccharine, tactless) talks glowingly of Dr. King; she is upset when she's chosen class narrator for the Black History segment of Presidents Month. She spends a great deal of time and emotional energy trying to curry favor with a white classmate. Tate doesn't make racial generalizations; one of the strong points of her story is that there is bias in both races, just as there is understanding in both. What weakens her story, less cohesive than that of the first book, is that it is repetitive and slow-paced, as Mary Elouise learns (from her friends, from her mother, and from a black charismatic storyteller) to appreciate her black heritage. The change is convincing, but the style is labored, weakened by such phrases as "He hunched his head . . ." or by such contradictory statements as "She was dark-skinned, too. That made me feel good," and "I don't like real dark skin, not even mine." A good deal of information about black history is introduced via conversation, a device that becomes obtrusive.

FRONT PORCH STORIES AT THE ONE-ROOM SCHOOL (1992)

Kirkus Reviews

SOURCE: A review of *Front Porch Stories at the One-Room School,* in *Kirkus Reviews,* Vol. LX, No. 14, July 15, 1992, p. 926.

Some of the lively characters in *Just an Overnight Guest* return in this celebration of storytelling and small-town life. Matthew J. Cornelius Carson falls into the mood one night, and his daughter Margie and niece Ethel sit entranced for hours, listening to his tales—about the giant shadow that chased Aunt Daisy the time she dared to do wash on Sunday; about laughing and working together at the old one-room Douglass School; about the time Great-Grandpa Wally came back from the grave, or the unforgettable day Eleanor Roosevelt came through town. Linking these incidents into a single, seamless narrative, Tate notes that all of them are based, at least loosely, on her own memories of growing up in Canton, Missouri. Like Margie and Ethel, readers may be moved to find comparable stories in their own lives.

Deborah Abbott

SOURCE: A review of *Front Porch Stories at the One-Room School,* in *Booklist,* Vol. 88, No. 22, August, 1992, p. 2014.

The 11 folksy yarns spun on the front steps of the old, formerly all-black Douglass School on a hot summer's night in fictional Nutbrush, Missouri, offer an entertaining alternative to an evening of television, both in the book and for readers. In lively retellings, a father embellishes high jinks of the past ("The Walnut Wars") as well as memorable community events based in fact (Eleanor Roosevelt's visit in "The President's Wife"). The listeners to his stories are daughter Margie Carson and niece Ethel Hardisen. It is the comfortable tone and style of the father's voice that provide Ethel with the courage to share her own longing for her absent mother—a story in itself. Tate offers warm insights that spark a universal love of stories.

Publishers Weekly

SOURCE: A review of *Front Porch Stories at the One-Room School,* in *Publishers Weekly,* Vol. 239, No. 36, August 10, 1992, p. 71.

A hot summer night in the tiny town of Nutbrush, Mo., proves "duller than dirt" for 12-year-old Maggie Carson—until her father starts to regale her with stories of his childhood. These tales, centered in the one-room schoolhouse for the town's black children, comprise the 10 stories in this collection based on Tate's own childhood. The loosely connected episodes, which range from village ghost stories to an account of a local flood, lack the overall narrative development and the fully fleshed-out characters necessary to support a whole book. Although Tate's evocative language conjures up rural southern life, her book is further flawed by somewhat heavy-handed exposition and stilted dialogue that at times borders on the saccharine. Because of Tate's framing device—readers see Maggie sit on the schoolhouse porch as she listens to her father—the tales lack a certain immediacy. The text also contains an important, but rather pedantically delivered, message about segregation in America.

The Reading Teacher

SOURCE: A review of *Front Porch Stories at the One-Room School,* in *The Reading Teacher,* Vol. 47, No. 5, February, 1994, pp. 404-05.

Eleanora Tate immediately brings the reader into an intimate family gathering in *Front Porch Stories at the One-Room School* as Matthew J. Cornelius Carson tells stories about attending a one-room school and growing up in Nutbrush, Missouri. This collection of stories, sprinkled with pencil drawings by Eric Velasquez, varies from funny to scary and sad, such as when Ethel tells a "once upon a time" story of her momma and how she wishes life could be. This superbly written short chapter book is a perfect read-aloud for children of all ages. The storytelling tradition is kept alive in this heartwarming collection that celebrates family, friendship and childhood.

A BLESSING IN DISGUISE (1995)

Becky Kornman

SOURCE: A review of *A Blessing in Disguise,* in *Voice of Youth Advocates,* Vol. 18, No. 1, April, 1995, p. 28.

Twelve-year-old Zambia Brown is bored with her dull life in Deacon's Neck, SC, with her aunt, uncle and cousin Aretha. She envies her stepsister, Seritta, who lives with her father Snake in Gumbo Grove and works in his nightclub. When Snake announces the opening of a new nightclub in Deacon's Neck, Zambia sees the chance of excitement and attention from her father whom she idolizes. After the nightclub opens, Zambia's uncle's involvement in a community movement to close the club causes friction at home. Zambia does odd jobs for Snake against her uncle's wishes and, in an argument, tells him she is going to live with her father. When she confronts Snake about moving in with him, he only laughs at her and she is forced to make amends with her uncle. However, it is not until Zambia becomes the victim of a drive-by shooting and one of her stepsisters is killed that she comes to terms with the fact that her father is dealing drugs. The book ends with Zambia joining her uncle in a march against drugs and crime and realizing that it is possible to love her father, but hate the things he does.

This novel deals realistically with a small community's battle against drugs and crime and a girl's development of a healthy attitude toward her irresponsible father. . . . This is Tate's third novel in a trilogy of books set in South Carolina.

Additional coverage of Tate's life and career is contained in the following sources published by Gale Research: *Black Writers*, **Vol. 2;** *Contemporary Authors New Revision Series*, **Vols. 25, 43;** *Something about the Author*, **Vol. 38.**

Ian Wallace

1950-

Canadian author and illustrator of picture books.

Major works include *The Sandwich* (with Angela Wood, 1975), *Chin Chiang and the Dragon's Dance* (1984), *The Very Last First Time* (written by Jan Andrews, 1985; reissued as *Eva's Ice Adventure,* 1986), *The Sparrow's Song* (1986), *Morgan the Magnificent* (1987), *The Name of the Tree: A Bantu Folktale* (written by Celia Barker Lottridge, 1989).

INTRODUCTION

The creator of a number of highly regarded picture books for primary graders, Wallace is noted for blending simple stories and spare language with detailed, often intricate illustrations in works that have been deemed warm, humorous, and effectively true-to-life. Celebrating the diversity of his native Canada while relating universal experiences of initiation and growth which all children can understand, Wallace has created stories featuring protagonists who learn of the larger world and their relationship to it, discovering—often with the aid of sympathetic adults—their own inner gifts and strengths in the process. He has been hailed for his direct, understated prose and sensitive treatment of familiar themes, and has been commended for the emotional depth of his characters; however, Wallace's innovative artwork has earned him his greatest acclaim. His illustrations, variously described as "beautiful," "rich," and "shimmering," have been praised by commentators for both reflecting and enhancing the mood of the text that they accompany. Because his subjects have ranged broadly from an urban Chinese celebration to the Ontario countryside of his youth, Wallace varies the style of his illustrations, suiting them to his settings; he is consistent, however, in his dramatic use of contrast, color, size, and perspective, techniques which often reflect the changing emotions of his protagonists. In the relatively short time that he has been creating children's books, Wallace has come to be regarded as one of Canada's most prominent author-illustrators. As Jon C. Stott has observed: "Although Wallace's output is small . . . his status in Canadian children's literature is great."

Biographical Information

Wallace was born in the city of Niagara Falls, Ontario, and grew up spending weekends with his family exploring the nearby Canadian countryside. Enchanted with picture books from an early age, he decided at age thirteen to become an artist—"someone who made dreams real." Shortly after graduating from the Ontario College of Art in 1973, Wallace found a position as a staff writer and illustrator with Kids Can Press, a small publishing company that soon released his first book, *Julie News*

(1974). He later took a position with the Art Gallery of Toronto, frequently taking time off to tour schools on behalf of arts and writers' groups. Since the early 1980s, Wallace has been a freelance writer and artist, working from his home in Toronto while still travelling frequently to share his creations with children. In addition to providing the text and illustrations for his own works, Wallace is the illustrator of books by such authors as Jan Andrews, Tim Wynne-Jones, and the Brothers Grimm.

Major Works

Wallace has stated that his goal in creating children's fiction is to "intrigue, inspire, and touch young readers." To that end, through a combination of thoughtful text and vivid illustration, he has sought to present "characters who struggle, who test limits, and who endure," ultimately coming to a better understanding of themselves and the world of which they are a part. After producing *The Sandwich* and *The Christmas Tree House* (1976), two books which espouse tolerance for others' differences, Wallace spent parts of six years creating the illustrations for what is considered his breakthrough work, *Chin Chiang and the Dragon's Dance,* the story of a young boy who overcomes his fear of failure. Using dramatic perspectives, including a rooftop view of the city, Wallace relates how an elderly woman helps Chin Chiang conquer his stage fright to offer a joyous performance in the New Year's festival. Chin Chiang's gradual gain in self-confidence is paralleled by the increasing hues of red in the illustrations. Creative use of color likewise enhances Wallace's artwork for *The Very Last First Time,* Jan Andrews's story of an Inuit girl's first solo walk to gather mussels underneath the ice on the ocean floor. Contrasting the everyday world of yellows and oranges with the ghostly purples of the sea floor, Wallace endows his illustrations with an emotional aspect that reflects Inuit spiritual beliefs. Earth tones, especially green, come to the fore in *The Sparrow's Song,* a story of emotional growth which tells of a boy who orphans a hatchling and his sister who rescues and raises it, eventually setting it free. Wallace's pointillistic illustrations, in a style reminiscent of French masters Degas and Seurat, supplement the text in creating the romantic feeling of turn-of-the-century Niagara. Warm colors similarly highlight the farm scenes in *Morgan the Magnificent* and are later contrasted with the golden brilliance of the circus. Morgan has a dream: to perform on the high wire like her hero the Amazing Anastasia. Like Chin Chiang, however, she too must overcome fear to finally achieve her goal. Wallace continues to employ inventive illustration techniques in his work, using effective contrasts of light and shadow to highlight the plight of a homeless woman in *Mr. Kneebone's New Digs* (1991).

Awards

Wallace received the International Order of the Daughters of the Empire (IODE) Best Children's Book of the Year award in 1984, the Amelia Francis Howard-Gibbon Illustrator's Award for best book of the year in 1985, and International Board on Books for Young People (IBBY) Honour List recognition for *Chin Chiang and the Dragon's Dance.* He was also honored with the Mr. Christie's Book Award for English Illustration in 1989, the Elizabeth Mrazik-Cleaver Canadian Picture Book Award in 1990, and second runner-up recognition for the Amelia Francis Howard-Gibbon Illustrator's Award that same year, all for *The Name of the Tree.*

AUTHOR'S COMMENTARY

Ian Wallace

SOURCE: "One Author's Tour: Children's Book Festival November 18-25, 1978," in *In Review: Canadian Books for Children,* Vol. 13, No. 2, April, 1979, pp. 11-14.

The night before I left for New Brunswick and Prince Edward Island to help celebrate the 1978 Children's Book Festival I was standing at the corner of Bathurst and Dundas in downtown Toronto. It was a cold wet evening. A wild rain had passed over the city that afternoon.

To my right was a woman approaching seventy, arms folded against her breast, shuffling her boots. The man to my left was about fifty and he wore work boots and a duffle coat.

The woman turned and spoke to us. "You'd think by this time these street cars would be empty. It's all those damn Italians and Portuguese running around this city like a bunch of cockroaches!"

I was stunned. Had I really heard this? But worse still, did she believe what she said? I decided to speak. "Excuse me, but I won't listen to racist talk."

The woman turned and glared at me. "What's the matter with you?" she asked. "You'd better wake up. I should know. I was a teacher."

I hit her again with words out of the dark. "If that's true, then I feel very sorry for the children who were your students." I noticed once again the man to my left. He was shuffling nervously and staring up into the dark November night.

"You're crazy," she yelled and waved her hands in the air. "I don't even want to get on the street car with you!" and walked in front of me as the street car rolled toward us.

"Excuse me, ma'am," interrupted the man. "But we were the ones who discovered this country!"

"Right on," I thought, smiling to myself.

"You're crazy, too," she yelled. "I don't want to get on the street car with you either!" The man smiled at me. No words were spoken as we followed her onto the car.

The incident clearly brought into focus the importance of The Children's Book Festival. If Canadians are to develop a mutual understanding of the diverse cultures in this country then we must begin to expose our children to them. A national program such as The Children's Book Festival can only strengthen this concept.

The incident also made me believe even more strongly in the kind of stories that I want to write for children, that depict people from every cultural group in this country, doing every kind of work regardless of sex or age. It is the responsibility of authors and illustrators to reflect their society whether their books are based in fantasy or in reality. But more important, it is the right of every child in this country to see his/her face reflected in a book.

The Children's Book Festival is also an appropriate opportunity to introduce children personally to the authors of Canadian children's books. I remember as a child taking out books from the Niagara Falls Public Library. At that time, my idea of a book was that it was like a box or a toy except that it had a story inside. It never occurred to me that someone had written or illustrated the story. Yes, there were one or two names on the cover, but they didn't mean anything to me. They were not part of my family or circle of friends—which meant that they didn't exist. The story was real, not the author. The Children's Book Festival shows children that authors are ordinary people; the one thing that sets them apart (besides their age) is the fact that they have written a book.

This is a fascinating concept to a child, as I discovered in my travels in New Brunswick and Prince Edward Island. In every city and town I visited I met children who wrote stories and many who illustrated them too. The arrival of someone who writes and illustrates is therefore even more important to them. They can see the relationship between their stories and a published book and that they are really quite similar.

In the two Festivals in which I have participated I travelled to Boissevain and Morden, Manitoba, Niagara Falls and St. Catharines, Ontario in 1977; Sackville, St. John and Fredericton, New Brunswick and Charlottetown, Summerside and Hunter River, Prince Edward Island in 1978.

I used a program that was developed by Angela Wood and me while working at Kids Can Press, Toronto. The main focus of the readings was our book, *The Sandwich.* The hour long programs began with the introduction of the ingredients of the sandwich, mortedella and provolone. No small feat when you consider the availability of this Italian meat and cheese in such places as Hunter River, Prince Edward Island and Boissevain, Manitoba!

In order to guarantee that children at all readings had a chance to taste this aromatic sandwich I carried a smelly bag of mortedella and provolone onto planes and into cars. I slept in the same room with it nearby, and walked through metal detecting devices at airports as the image of mortedella and provolone appeared on the screen.

Just to see the looks of excitement and wonder as the bag opened and the mortedella and provolone came into the room was worth all the effort. From that moment on we were one. Together we went through the ritual of making sandwiches as noses rebelled and laughter rose to the ceiling. As I read the story I watched their expressions and their body movements closely. Their reactions were the most honest reviews of the book.

Perhaps the most moving moment for me occurred in Boissevain, Manitoba in 1977. I was well into reading *The Sandwich* when I realized that for the first time there was no laughter. The room was still. As I looked out into that room of approximately 70 boys and girls I was met by eyes that were filled with tears. I was stunned and groped for an answer.

A parent later explained their response to me. "You see," she said, "The people of the prairie have never really recovered from the depression. Yes, on the outside we have, but we have never forgotten. We live with the land and so do our children. Through our children we have passed on a respect for what one has and that you do not laugh at someone who wears a strange hat or has a funny sandwich because you are just lucky that you have any at all."

"Has anyone ever been laughed at?" I asked at the end of the story. A strange dance began on the floor. Bodies squirmed awkwardly and some faces turned away. The replies varied as greatly in number as in situation. There were stories of long underwear that fell out of socks, a crazy hat and personal things like a big nose or ears. Every now and then a child would utter the words Coon or Paki. For a moment the room would stop until we began to talk about what it feels like to be laughed at. Everyone began to understand that they were not alone in their hurt and that we have all felt the brunt of someone else's laughter.

Having read the story I then showed them how the book was made. In this stage of the program they could see the similarities and the differences between their stories and a book. I explained the origins of the story and showed them the numerous drafts, the mockup of the book and the illustrations laid out as they appeared on the printed press sheet. I explained the process of making negatives and metal plates and finally the printing and binding of the book.

Each program ended with the reading of *The Christmas Tree House.* Throughout this hour I realized how important it was for an author to read to children. This experience is totally different from writing and illustrating. During the first stages, I work very much in a vacuum for long periods of time. The only people who read what I have written are friends whose opinions I respect. For me, reading to children completes the process and is the most important part of writing, next to the initial idea for a story. My feelings of excitement as a new story unfolds on paper are matched only by the smiles and giggles, the scratching and wide eyes of a group of children. There is a time between the completion of a book and when the reviews start coming in, that I lose all feelings whatsoever for the book I have worked on. My books have been given back to me by reading them to children.

I am constantly delighted by their questions about the origins of a story, the intricacies of book production and distribution, and information about my life.

"No, I am not married . . . yet." I tell an inquisitive girl who giggles at my response.

"How old is Don Valley Rose?" asks a young boy. "Seventy." He thinks for a moment and then answers. "Oh, over the hill!"

Their questions about my life are equally as important as the stories I read or showing them how a book is made. It makes me real in their eyes and gives them a clearer insight into the life of an author.

In St. John, 25 children submitted recipes to the library

for The Sandwich contest. I was elected sole judge. My job was to pick the best sandwich after having tasted all 25 of them. A gastronomic feat!

May I suggest to you the bittersweet taste of a mustard and honey sandwich or the five decker special of bananas, white sugar and cabbage. If you don't fancy either of these then perhaps you would savour the winner of the group, The Cheese Dream with Cocoanut and Molasses by Laurie Henry.

As you can see The Children's Book Festival is many things. It is a roomful of children, stories, laughter and giggles. It's scratching arm pits and the child who doesn't care that you see him picking his nose. It's their desire to touch you and tell you a joke. "Did you hear the one about . . . ?" It's relating. It's sharing a part of yourself and your experiences and taking the time to be with children. A wonderful and exciting experience not just for an author but for a librarian, a teacher and more importantly a parent.

Ian Wallace

SOURCE: "When Fort Nelson's Kids Won Ian Wallace," in *Quill and Quire,* Vol. 51, No. 2, February, 1985, p. 8.

As far back as I can recall I have been fascinated by kaleidoscopes—their tumbling, stained-glass colours shifting and changing before my eyes. In sunlight and even moonlight I have delighted in staring down those darkened tubes, recalling the colours and the patterns that I had seen, long after that first initial viewing.

Today I can still recall those colours and patterns, and for me kaleidoscopes have become synonymous with memories. These, too, I can recall on desire, reliving the cherished, humorous, and sometimes painful experiences of my life. Here then is my latest kaleidoscope, gathered on my recent trip to Fort Nelson, B.C. during the Children's Book Festival 1984.

This remote northern village of 4,800 people, situated at Mile 1 of the Alaska Highway, was the winner of the Children's Book Festival's first Win-an-Author-or-Illustrator Contest sponsored by the Secretary of State through the Department of Multiculturalism and administered by The Children's Book Centre in Toronto.

In her submission to the contest, Gerri Young, chairperson of the Fort Nelson Public Library and assistant librarian of school libraries, wrote: "A visit from an author/ illustrator from Toronto, a cultural milieu as different from Fort Nelson as Asia, would enrich our children as a whole. How often have we wondered if they really knew what we were talking about? The children here are not deprived, but they are isolated, and this week could be a festive week and help to draw Fort Nelson's diverse groups closer together. . . . In a small town where the differences are so readily obvious, it is more constructive to show

how we are similar in basic needs and desires. . . . Each person likes to think that they are special, and I am sure that Mr. Wallace could draw them out, and draw for them, and increase their awareness of Canadian cultures."

Turn the kaleidoscope handle, and the first pattern tumbles into focus . . .

Enormous black birds, "Yukon turkeys," scurrying across the snow-packed ground in their never-ending quest for food. "Any scrap will do," Gerri Young told me as we drove into Fort Nelson from the airport. "Even things that move."

Their Herculean size alarmed me, as I imagined one of these birds, a type of raven, clutching a child tightly in its talons and carrying it far off into the frozen muskeg. What would the film *The Birds* have looked like if Hitchcock had seen these creatures? My imagination soared ominously.

Turn the handle . . .

Daylight. My official welcome to Fort Nelson comes with the rendition of the soon-to-be-classic tune, The Welcome Ian Wallace Song, sung by the students of G. W. Carlson Elementary School. As that delightful ditty soared about the library, I plucked out the phrase, "you're artistic, realistic", reassuring myself that what they really said was in fact "artistic," not "autistic."

Now it was my turn on centre stage. I sat tall in my author-illustrator's chair to perform before a succession of classes from kindergarten to grade 12 over the next five days. With words, actions ("Hey, he doesn't even look at the book!"), and pictures, I brought to life two of my books, **The Sandwich** and **Chin Chiang and the Dragon's Dance.** The age range of the audiences would have unnerved even the most seasoned children's author. Actually, my first exposure to high-school students was a pleasant one. I found them to be keen and articulate—quite intrigued by the process of writing and illustrating, their questions exhibiting a maturity far beyond their years: "What do you think about violence in children's books? How do you get the water-colours to lay on top of one another without turning to mud?"

Turn the handle . . .

At the end of my first day I was drawing a portrait of one of the students, Kyle, for an enraptured group of classmates, when a teacher burst into the library and pulled me down the hall.

"You have to see this," she said animatedly. "Once you have, you'll never forget it. It occurs so infrequently in the North."

The school door opened onto a world turned pink by the setting sun—pink as far as the eye could see. The tall spruce trees heavily laden with pink snow lifted majestically out of their frozen blanket, once white, now pink.

The astonishing sight lasted only a few short minutes, then disappeared with the fading mid-November sun.

Turn the handle . . .

On a visit to a grade 5 class I took the students on my six-year journey to discover the "right" words and "those" pictures that make up my latest picture-book, *Chin Chiang and the Dragon's Dance.* Slowly, systematically, we moved through the rough typewritten drafts that stand five inches high and weigh 12 pounds. We moved through the panoply of thumb-nail drawings, character studies, larger roughs, and final roughs, until we reached our journey's end: the finished original drawings and the completed book. All the while, I was conscious that something unique happens in this classroom. A large paper tree growing up from the back of the room spread its branches out across the ceiling above my head. Attached to each branch were countless leaves, each one representing a book that had been read by those students since September. "This is an extraordinary class," I whispered to myself.

Turn the handle . . .

After my indoctrination to cross-country skiing by some grade 7 students, one of my young teachers reported to his parents, "He skis better than someone from Brazil!"

Turn the handle . . .

During my trip along the Alaska Highway from Fort Nelson to Toad River, we spotted two caribou, 24 stone sheep, and eight moose—one quite dead, hit by a truck and now lying in the dump just outside the village of Toad River.

"Perhaps we could stand it up," said Bob Halmer (he and his wife Barb Halmer were my guides), "and I'll take a picture of you sitting on top." I resisted the temptation.

Turn the handle . . .

"These dogs run at 19 m.p.h. full tilt, 13 m.p.h. when they're just coasting," said Eddie Streeper, world champion dog sledder with whom I travelled over the muskeg on the back of a sled pulled by a team of 12 dogs. Odd-looking creatures, really, nothing like I had imagined, with long, spindly legs that appeared too fragile to run for up

From Chin Chiang and the Dragon's Dance, *written and illustrated by Ian Wallace.*

to two hours at a stretch when in training. Sergeant Preston of the Yukon retreated even further to the outer reaches of my mind.

Turn the handle . . .

A festive dragon, *à la* **Chin Chiang and the Dragon's Dance,** made of 30 decorated cardboard boxes strung together with crêpe paper, was brought to life, writhing and kicking, by 30 young students, much to my delight and that of the student body of R. L. Angus Elementary School. (Each student was positioned under the box that he or she had created.) With every step, leap, twist, and curl of the dragon's tail, the students-dancers breathed life into that mythic creature, bestowing prosperity and good fortune on the coming year.

Turn the handle . . .

"Vincenzo eats stinky meat" became the cry of the day when the students of Pat McKenzie's grade 2 class at R. L. Angus school performed their touching, humorous, and finely acted play *The Sandwich,* based on my book by the same name. My paternal instincts overwhelming me, I felt like a proud father being presented his newborn child for the very first time.

Turn the handle . . .

Friday morning, Chalo School, the Slave Indian Reserve. After a story-telling session, we adjourned outdoors where the 22 students, their two teachers, and I were to toboggan down a steep, slippery hill. Meanwhile, up at the top Adolphus Cabot-Blanc had made a log fire on which we were to cook bannock.

Suddenly, I was speeding down that hill, alone, on my flying saucer. Then as I was climbing up the hill for my third flight, a tiny hand slipped into mine.

"Mr Wallace, can I walk with you?" asked my new friend Wilma who, like the other native children, had shied away when we first met.

"Of course you can. I'd like that very much."

"Can I ride down with you, too?" she asked gleefully at the top.

"That would be great fun! Let's go!"

My trips with Wilma down that treacherous slope lasted only until the other students realized what Wilma had accomplished. And suddenly, I was swamped with kids all wanting to slide with me. (Fortunately, I am tall and there is quite a bit of me to cling to.) All 22 of us sped down the hill, en masse, laughing deliciously as we smashed apart at the bottom.

Turn the handle . . .

Another gift from the people of Fort Nelson. A pair of finely crafted Slave Indian moccasins, embroidered with beaded flowers and trimmed with beaver fur.

Turn the handle . . .

"When you hear the call of the North/Listen for the echo/ You will hear Fort Nelson," inscribed Fort Nelson native John Kudelke in my gift book, *The Fort Nelson Story,* written by Gerri Young.

My kaleidoscope is complete. Its colours and patterns are firmly etched in my mind, waiting for the next time that I hear the call of the North.

This trip was not a one-sided adventure with me arriving as some great educator who comes to the North to impart knowledge. It was a mutually beneficial and satisfying visit during which the people of the Fort Nelson region and I worked, laughed, played, ate, drank, and worshipped together. We learned something about one another, and this experience has given us a deeper understanding of the lives we lead and brought us all closer together.

Ian Wallace

SOURCE: "The Emotional Link," in *The New Advocate,* Vol. 2, No. 2, Spring, 1989, pp. 75-82.

I affectionately refer to the winter of 1985 as the season I walked underneath the ice with a young Inuit girl named Eva Padlyat.

Eva arrived on my doorstep unceremoniously one afternoon during the previous summer in the form of a manuscript written by an Ottawa teacher, Jan Andrews. Clipped to the covering page was a note from my Canadian editor, Patsy Aldana, which simply stated, "Ian, I thought you might be interested in illustrating this story."

Little did I realize when I turned to read what was then a 250-line draft of a rite of passage tale that this story would take me on an adventure few people could have ever imagined. Eva Padlyat's miraculous circular journey would make extraordinary demands on my skills and plunge my art in directions even I had never anticipated.

My exposure to this race of people who live in a harsh northern landscape had been only through books and images that flashed across my television screen. My contact with Eva would teach me a deep abiding respect for our neighbors in the Land of the Purple Twilight. Long before I realized on a conscious level how powerful a spell this tale had cast over me, the story's hooks had caught me under the ribs and reeled me in. *Very Last First Time* captured my imagination, my heart, my soul and sent my spirit soaring.

With eager anticipation I read the opening paragraph of the manuscript:

Eva Padlyat lived in a village in Ungava Bay in

Northern Canada. She was Inuit and for as long as she could remember she had walked with her mother on the bottom of the sea. It was something the people of her village did in winter when they wanted mussels to eat. Today something very special was going to happen. Today for the very first time in Eva's life she would walk on the bottom of the sea—alone.

My mind shuddered to a halt. Claustrophobic feelings engulfed me. I could barely comprehend what I had just read. Still my eyes retraced the line. "Today for the very first time in Eva's life she would walk on the bottom of the sea—alone."

At that moment I realized I had to illustrate this story. What distinguished it from other manuscripts I had received? The first paragraph had done what all good stories should do. It filled me with questions and made me eager to take the journey. Where would Eva Padlyat lead me on her quest for mussels? What would we discover underneath the ice when we arrived in that dark shadowy world? How does one physically walk on the ocean floor? How would Eva be changed by this experience?

A few paragraphs into that initial reading, I made the incredible journey with Eva as she walked on the bottom of the sea. My knees trembled, my heart beat rapidly. My creative journey had already begun.

For those of you who are unfamiliar with Eva's story, let me share the secret with you now. Listen to Jan Andrew's carefully chosen words.

> Down by the shore they met some friends and stopped for a quick greeting. They had come at the right time. The tide was out, pulling the sea water from the shore so there was room for them to climb down underneath the ice and walk about on the seabed.

Almost unbelievable. Incomprehensible. A place on earth existed where the tide goes out far enough to allow people to walk about on the ocean floor. Not only that, the ice remains suspended overhead, creating an under-ice world. The gaping cavity where water once was fills in with air. In reality, the tide in Ungava Bay is one of the highest tides in the world. And, at the age of 12, Inuit children who live in Sugluk, Ungava Bay, take this rite-of-passage walk alone under the winter ice to become adults.

Very Last First Time is a story dependent on its unique setting and, therefore, is one of my strongest portrayals of the Canadian landscape. It is also distinguishable as Canadian by the painting style, especially the color palette, which owes an enormous debt to the historic Canadian painters who have interpreted our landscape—Maurice Cullen, J. W. Morrice, Cornelius Kreighoff, and the Group of Seven.

For me, however, there is a more important **place** where the story belongs, not a setting per se but a place where an emotional link is made from the story to the reader. An elusive creature not found on a map, this emotional link almost never presents itself quickly but rather appears only after delving beneath the story's skin to its heart.

The emotional link is at the core of all book-making. Without it, the reader is left with an accumulation of words and a series of images. In the world of the picture book, the fundamental task of the author, and on occasion to a greater degree the illustrator, is to develop an emotional link between the book's characters and the reader, drawing out the reader's response not in a manipulative way but through a natural evolution. The author's and illustrator's touches must be so sure yet so devilishly light—working in consort with one another—that the reader does not notice their deliberate development.

A larger percentage of authors understand the emotional component in text than illustrators understand the effects of illustration. Far too often artistic techniques and visual gimmicks take precedence over thought and careful consideration of the appropriate means and media to evoke a story's sensibilities. This situation may have developed for a variety of reasons. First, the problem lies in art education where technique (form) is often more important than the intellectual and emotional communication (content) with the viewer. Second, one can argue from a broader perspective that we live in a society that views an artist as someone who can draw or paint, but not think or feel. Hence no demands are made on an illustrator other than to provide a beautiful and pleasing image. This fact is most disturbing; it implicitly points out that the reader is not attuned to "reading" anything other than the written word. On the other hand, our society accepts without question the fact that a writer arranges words to communicate a point of view, an idea, a story.

Lovers of children's literature are well aware of "the beautiful book"—the book resplendent with illustrations, so overwhelming with its singular beauty that we stand in awe of its technical brilliance. The text quite frequently becomes a minor character in the bid for the limelight. Fortunately, time, with its ability to yellow edges, affords the reader the chance to study, reflect, and analyze. This reader will ultimately realize that "the emperor has no clothes." The flash appeal of form over content will vaporize under closer scrutiny. An emotional link has never been established, and the reader has been cheated out of an enriching experience. Readers have been subjected to many illustrated books to which they have enormous difficulty relating to on any level of understanding other than simple visual pleasure. The lack of an emotional link lies at the root of the problem.

To discover the emotional link of a story, the illustrator must understand all levels on which the story functions: intellectual, physical, psychological, and spiritual. This link is then made by a variety of means: appropriate media, color, changing perspectives, shape of the illustrations, shape of the book, style of type, white space around the type and each of the drawings, and the position of each character in relation to one another. Nothing must be left to chance.

In creating *Chin Chiang and the Dragon's Dance,* I employed color as the emotional barometer of the text. This color barometer conveyed to the reader the emotional link of the story, Chin Chiang's vulnerability and his lack of self-confidence. In addition, it permitted the reader to feel Chin Chiang's conflict change as the story progressed and his confidence grew.

This device was set within a format whose formal tone was dictated by the culture and elicited by the text, the design of the book, the dragon motif found in the border of each illustration, and the fine black ink line drawings. The color unfolds from the opening of the story to its conclusion and evolves over the course of the day, from the soft earth tones during the post-dawn hours, progressing to stronger ones as night falls over the city. As the emotional conflict builds in Chin Chiang, the color becomes more vivid, reaching its dramatic peak at the climax of the story when Chin Chiang and Pu Yee dance triumphantly through the gates of harmony under a brilliant red sky.

This emotional barometer is reinforced by the changing perspectives. At two key points, readers find themselves perched far above the protagonist, which amplifies Chin Chiang's vulnerability and increases the power of the dragon and the reader. In the spiral staircase drawing, Chin Chiang is portrayed as running away from his family and his responsibilities, but he is in fact running straight along the back of the dragon, step by step, scale by scale.

Each of my books has demanded a different style of illustration. The intricate detail of *Chin Chiang and the Dragon's Dance* was inappropriate for *Very Last First Time.* The two cultures were completely different in character, history, and landscape. Thus, the style of illustration had to change to capture the different people and their story. From my perspective, the drawings for *Very Last First Time* had to conjure up distinct images that were truly Northern Canadian, hence the strong influence of our historical painters.

Very Last First Time presented a classic structure in children's literature of two worlds; therefore, I employed two dominant colors to reflect the distinct yet inseparable worlds entered by Eva Padlyat. The above-ground world is light, thus yellow (also the light from her candle), and the under-ice world is dark, thus purple. (Remember that the Inuit refer to the land in which they live as the Land of Purple Twilight.) This concept is recognized by the reader upon picking up the book. The world of light is captured within a squarish shape of the cover and contrasted sharply with the rectangular, claustrophobic world of dark, seen in the end papers.

A fascinating incident took place during the creation of the illustrations for *Very Last First Time.* I had been invited to visit a third grade class in Scarborough, Ontario. The teacher asked me to bring along my current project. I took the first nine images, including the illustration where Eva entered the under-ice world alone for the first time. I held that particular illustration up in front of those 32 students and said, "Hidden here is a wolf, a bear, and a seal sea monster." Sixty-four eyes focused on the haunting image before them. As they hunted for the three under-ice images, another far more intriguing and critical discovery took place.

Barely able to contain their excitement, five or six students called out, "And Eva's mother, too!" I uttered a quite audible giggle that betrayed my adult disbelief and said, "I beg your pardon." Again they exclaimed, "Eva's mother is there . . . look . . . and she's talking to the ice."

Giving them the benefit of the doubt, I handed a student in the first row the illustration in question and asked her to hold it up for me to see. Those students were right. On the extreme right side of the illustration, staring out at me was the spirit image of Eva's mother, and she was definitely talking to the ice.

Let me explain. When I draw and paint, my illustrations lie on a drafting table in front of me. What I had painted in the extreme top right corner of that illustration was a pool of water with rocks scattered about the pool and a wall of ice swooping down from the ice ceiling overhead to join the rocks at the far side of the pool.

When you look at the illustration from a distance of five feet or more, however, the three-dimensional pool flattens out to form a two-dimensional image of Eva's mother's face. The rocks in the water form her eyes and nose. The wall of ice behind takes the form of her hooded parka. Directly in front of the pool of water was a triangular shaped piece of ice that, when also viewed from the same distance, took on the shape of a spirit bird.

Without thinking I asked, "How did you know that the image was Eva's mother?" My young charges looked at me incredulously and announced, "Your mother is always with you." They thought me quite silly not to have known that. How could I be more than four times their age and not know that my mother would still be with me! And Eva's mother would be with her, too, they realized, if not physically then spiritually. My illustrations had created an emotional link between Eva's life and the lives of these children.

Research is essential during the process of creating books like *Chin Chiang and the Dragon's Dance* and *Very Last First Time.* Throughout the period of discovery in Eva's story, the significance of the spirit world to the everyday life of the Inuit came clearly into focus. I would have been shirking my responsibility as an illustrator, a storyteller in pictures, if I had overlooked this integral aspect of Inuit life.

At the end of my initial reading of *Very Last First Time,* the one line that haunted me above all others was, "Eva raised her candle high and there appeared in the shadows a wolf, a bear and a seal sea monster." After three months of research I accepted the significance of the spirit world to the Inuit and noted implicitly that these images had to be painted into the under-ice world. Only after lengthy

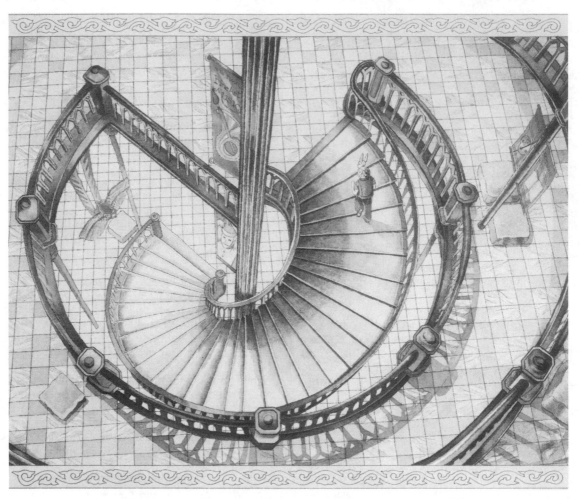

From Chin Chiang and the Dragon's Dance, *written and illustrated by Ian Wallace.*

soul searching did I realize further that these three images had to be painted as if they had been painted by Eva Padlyat. She was the Inuit child, not me. And my perception of what a wolf, a bear, and a seal sea monster would look like would have been entirely different from Eva's vision of these spirit images.

To ensure Eva's vision, I hurried off to the reference library of the Art Gallery of Ontario where my research of Inuit drawings showed me the fine points of Inuit art. Artists of the Eastern Arctic draw and paint in a unique style when compared with the artists of the Western Arctic.

It was not a fluke that Eva's mother appeared in the rock pool. For the previous seven months I had been immersed in the relevance of the spirit world to the Inuit. It seems quite natural, then, that at some point my subconscious would take over and incorporate spirit images into the illustrations, in much the same way that when an Inuit sculptor sits down to carve a piece of bone or stone the sculptor waits for the spirit to emerge. The sculptor does not begin to carve before the spirit presents itself.

Those 32 third grade students had been able to see the

spirit images that I had painted without conscious awareness. Their recognition and easy acceptance of the spirit world made me keenly aware of the vast gulf that often separates the state of childhood and the state of adulthood. Their acceptance of Eva's spirit world knew no borders. It was not a perception reserved for Canadian children. The under-ice spirits were not seen by boys exclusive of girls, nor did it fall to one race to the exclusion of any other.

This humbling experience set off a flashing light of logic. Of course, the spirit world so integral to the lives of our Inuit and native peoples could be housed in all of the illustrations of the under-ice world Eva entered. These images would be hidden in the rocks and in the ice formations, reflective mirrors of her own reality. Out of the mouths of babes!

As much as Eva's story could not have unfolded in any other physical landscape, it owes an enormous debt to the spiritual landscape that it had to follow.

In the fall of 1986 I had the privilege and pleasure of traveling to the North West Territories to celebrate Children's Book Festival Week in Canada. On this journey, my itinerary took me to Inuit communities north of the Arctic Circle and to Dene communities in the southern portion of the Territories. At the close of the reading to the students, teachers, and families in the tiny community of Lac La Marte, the Chief of the Band introduced himself to me. His words that follow are to the best of my recollection.

> I read *Very Last First Time* two weeks ago. I told myself then that I had to come today to meet you because I couldn't believe that you were white even though your name sounded so. But you are! I wanted to thank you for understanding the spirit world of the Dene and Inuit. So few white people treat our spirit world with the respect you gave it.

No higher compliment could have been paid me from any other place or from any more distinguished voice. All the critical glowing reviews in the world, even if stacked to the point where they touched the sun, would never equal the humility and inner satisfaction I experienced at that moment.

In my work as an author I do not sit down to write stories, nor do I consciously choose stories to illustrate because they will be distinguished as being multicultural or Canadian or whatever flag one chooses to wave over them. I write or illustrate stories because first and foremost they are stories that will intrigue, inspire, and touch young readers. The characters who inhabit these tales are people who have earned my sympathy and are ones with whom I can empathize on a personal level. They are universal characters with universal emotions and universal experiences. They are characters whom I respect for their dignity of spirit and purpose in life, characters who struggle, who test limits, and who endure. Most important, they are characters who through the story go through some kind of change.

At the end of a good story, a reader comes away with the confidence that the protagonist has been touched inwardly by the experience, that the protagonist will never be the same and will treasure the memory. It is my hope that the reader of my books will never be the same either.

I firmly believe that an author's and an illustrator's foremost responsibility is not to themselves or to each other, not to the country of their birth, not to their editor or publisher, not even to the reader at home or across the border (although I do believe that the reader stands next in line). Our primary responsibility is to the story. This responsibility demands and deserves our best work, conceived after careful thought, born out of scrupulous research, and realized in words and pictures fundamental to the story. Finding the emotional link is the key, and its discovery will make the search a journey worth taking for both the creator and the reader.

GENERAL COMMENTARY

Jon C. Stott

SOURCE: "Profile: Ian Wallace," in *Language Arts,* Vol. 66, No. 4, April, 1989, pp. 443-49.

Palmerston Boulevard, the home of Canadian author-illustrator Ian Wallace, is only a block away from Toronto's busy, bustling College Street. But after I'd stepped off the street car, passed through the massive granite gateposts at the head of the street, and begun my walk down the shady, tree-lined boulevard, I felt as though I'd entered a new and special world—one that was quieter, simpler, and more natural. And a few minutes later, sitting on Ian Wallace's shady, second-story back veranda, sipping deliciously chilled, fresh squeezed orange juice, talking about art, literature, and human nature, I knew I'd entered a special world. It was the world of an artist and storyteller whose creativity has, for the last decade, been shared with thousands of children and adults in Canada and the United States, and around the world.

We talked about Wallace's childhood years in Niagara Falls, Ontario. Born in 1950, he grew up in a family which loved telling stories and reading books aloud to each other. "I remember my brothers and I piling into our parents' bed to hear them read *The Wind in the Willows* to us. It was our favorite book." He also loved to draw and paint. But when he moved to Toronto in 1967 to attend the Ontario College of Art, he had no thoughts of combining his youthful interests to become a children's author. Graphic art and the challenges and possible rewards of commercial art beckoned.

In 1974, the year after Wallace's graduation, a conversation at the Beverly Tavern, a meeting place of Toronto art students, renewed his interest in children's stories. A year earlier, Ann Powell, Esther Fine, Patti Stren, and Carol Pasternak had started Kids Can Press. Carol invited Ian to become a writer/illustrator for the summer. "It was a very exciting time for children's books in Canada," he remembers. "The Dennis Lee books had just come out and a lot of people were beginning to ask for a vigorous, imaginative national literature for kids."

Wallace's training at art school stood him in good stead. "A few inspired instructors taught me how to think visually," he remembers. "They made me realize that all creative activity begins in the head and the heart, not in the hand as I had naively imagined. These artists taught me how to see a project conceptually, recognizing it as a complete and total work unto itself. The next step involved choosing media to bring about the visual execution. This was a crucial decision whether to use paint or film or clay or wood. And not to rely on one media because one saw oneself as 'a painter,' 'a film maker,' 'a sculptor.' First and foremost we were artists." As admirers of Ian Wallace's books know, they're not only beautiful and engaging, they're very carefully planned and structured. Reading one of them is a total experience.

In his time with Kids Can, Wallace produced three books, *Julie News* (1974); *The Sandwich* (1975), illustrated by fellow art student Angela Wood; and *The Christmas Tree House* (1976). Faced with limited budgets, he could not use a full spectrum of colors. However, he used the restrictions to advantage. In *The Christmas Tree House,* for example, the greypencil illustrations suggest the wintry settings and create a luminous quality which reflects the warmth of new friendship the children experience.

Not only do these books present heart-warming incidents in the lives of children, but also they anticipate the themes of Ian Wallace's major books of the 1980s: individuals' discoveries of their inner worths and strengths, and their growing awareness of their relationships with their communities. Julie, a newspaper carrier, joins with her neighbors in an unsuccessful attempt to stop developers from expropriating their homes. Vincenzo Ferrante must eat his lunch at school for the first time. Embarrassed when his classmates laugh at his smelly mortadella and provolone sandwich, he is told by his father, "You are who you are and you have nothing to be ashamed of." Soon he gains the acceptance of his friends. In *The Christmas Tree House,* Nick and his new friend Gloria discover that Don Valley Rose, the feared local eccentric, is a kindly and wise old lady.

After *The Christmas Tree House,* Ian Wallace did not publish another book for eight years. "I filled reams of paper with ideas and rough drafts of stories. But it was really a time of self-examination and self-discovery. I had a great deal of time to consider the nature of the art and skill of painting and writing for children. It was like the retreat period described by the psychologist Carl Jung, a period of drawing inward. I had to find my way to a threshold which needed to be crossed before I could begin publishing again."

Perhaps Wallace discovered that threshold one day while he was sitting at the information desk of the Art Gallery of Ontario, where he worked at the time. "I heard drums beating and, when I went to the door, I saw a dragon's dance in progress. Before I knew it, I'd joined the crowd following the dragon, and I began to feel the importance of ritual traditions in a culture."

That moment marked the conception of *Chin Chiang and the Dragon's Dance.* But the story didn't appear for another six years. In 1980, Wallace travelled to New York with a version of 'Chin Chiang' that had been worked on for two years and was titled *The Night of the Dragon and the Day of the Hare.* "I had five water colours for the story. Margaret McElderry, one of the foremost children's book editors in the world, examined the manuscript and paintings and wrote a warm letter that explained the exciting and intriguing aspects of my written and visual work. More importantly she outlined for the first time in my professional career how and why the story was structurally faulty and where thematically it lost focus. My task for completing the book was only half realized." With the help of McElderry and Canadian editor-publisher Patsy Aldana, he learned about the importance of the illustra-

tions and how they had to carry what he refers to as "an emotional wallop." "That's what's so good about Maurice Sendak, Chris Van Allsburg, and Warwick Hutton," he notes, referring to three artists whose children's books he greatly admires.

One of the methods of creating an emotional wallop in *Chin Chiang* was to use different colors to depict the hero's changing emotions. "I started with softer colors, browns and greens. As the excitement grew, I introduced more red, reaching the climax as the red dragon moved through the ceremonial gate against a Chinese red sky."

And the rest, as they say, is history. *Chin Chiang and the Dragon's Dance,* the story of a Chinese Canadian boy who must face his inner fears and feelings of inadequacy before he can make his first performance in his community's most important ritual, appeared in 1984. The Canadian Association of Children's Librarians named it the top picture book of the year. It was published in Canada, the United States, and Europe, has received high critical acclaim, and has become a favorite of thousands of children. In 1986, it was named an IBBY Honor Book.

During the course of our conversation, we moved into Ian's studio, where he showed me the original paintings for *Very Last First Time.* They are even brighter and more breathtaking than the printed versions.

When he began to illustrate *Very Last First Time* (1985), Wallace faced new challenges. The story of a modern Inuit girl's first trip under the sea ice to gather mussels, it was written by another author, Jan Andrews, and it was about a culture vastly different from that of prospective readers. "I had to be true to Jan's words, which really thrilled me; but I wanted to give added emotional dimensions. And I needed to understand Eva, the heroine, as a contemporary Inuit and as the heir of a centuries old spiritual tradition."

To depict this culture, he used water colors, as he had for *Chin Chiang,* but he altered the style. In the earlier book, he had used pen and ink outlining to give a crispness to the paintings and had placed a formal, scrolled border above and below each one. "The formal tone of the text and illustrations stemmed from the inherently formal culture and society the book was interpreting. In *Very Last First Time,* I needed a style that was much looser and freer to reflect accurately Inuit society." The pen-and-ink lines are gone and the viewer is conscious of larger, less intricate blocks of color.

"I realized as I read Jan's text that the story wasn't just about Eva Padlyat picking mussels alone for the first time. It was a very important and really dangerous journey of initiation. She was entering a new area of experience. There were two worlds, one of light and one of dark, which had to be contrasted sharply in both their treatment of color and in the design and shape of the spaces. The above-ice world is yellow, and that below is purple. I also changed the size and shape of the pictures." Readers of the book will notice that the pictures of Eva before and after her descent take up only one side of the page. When she is below the ice, the double spreads give a claustrophobic feeling, as if the ice overhead were pressing down.

In his research, Wallace learned about the deeply religious nature of the traditional Inuit people. They lived in a world filled with spirit beings, good and evil, who often held the power of life and death. As she climbs through the hole in the ice, Eva enters their world. The shapes seen in the rocks and shadows represent them; she faces these spirits and understands their importance in her life.

In *The Sparrow's Song* (1986), Ian Wallace turns the clock back three times: to the Niagara Falls of his childhood, to the early twentieth century, and to the era before the coming of the Europeans. While in his teens, he'd taken care of an orphaned sparrow. "I was awed by the strength of that fragile bird; but I was embarrassed when my mother kept telling people about it years later. She kept the story alive, and I dedicated the book to her." But when he came to tell the story of the relationship between a brother, a sister, and a helpless fledgling, he chose the period of the turn of the century, when Niagara Falls was a place surrounded by nature instead of tourist establishments. And in his illustrations, he made visual references to the Onondaga beliefs of the sacred, spiritual quality of the Niagara Gorge.

The Sparrow's Song is about kindness, forgiveness, and the physical and spiritual healing powers of nature. After Charles has thoughtlessly killed the mother bird, his sister cares for the baby and comes to understand that she must teach it to fly so that it can become independent. She and her brother mature in the story, growing in knowledge of each other and the world in which they live. To express his themes, Wallace again carefully chose the appropriate visual effects. The dominant color is green, representing the natural and supernatural powers of the Niagara Gorge. "When I had the children enter the Gorge, I removed the white borders and bled the illustrations to the edge of the page. I wanted the reader to experience their coming into contact with those powers." The overall shape of the book is different from *Chin Chiang* and *Very Last First Time.* Those were horizontal; this is vertical, suggesting the descent into the Gorge that the children make. Incidentally, the six illustrations of the gorge, if strung together would make up a 360 degree view of Niagara Falls at the turn of the century.

The children in *The Sparrow's Song* travel downwards; the heroine of *Morgan the Magnificent* (1987) travels upwards—to a highwire far above the sawdust floor of a circus. Ian Wallace had long wanted to write a circus story, and he'd made a research trip to the Circus World Museum in Baraboo, Wisconsin. "But I still didn't have a central character. One day, after I'd finished an exhausting five-week reading tour, talking to over ten thousand children, I was supposed to go to dinner with a Vancouver librarian. The last thing I wanted to do was see more children, and I wasn't very happy when she arrived at my hotel door with her daughter. But in ten minutes, the girl had me captivated. She told about how

she'd been on the 'Scream Machine,' the roller coaster at Expo '86, three times. I'd found my heroine."

Morgan the Magnificent is another "very last first time" story. The heroine worships the Amazing Anastasia, the highwire artist, and walks along the ridge pole and high beams of her father's barn every chance she can. When the circus comes to town, she goes alone to the grounds, sneaks into Anastasia's hut and dons the star's costume. Entering the big top, she climbs to the highwire where she begins her walk. Panic seizes and she is talked back to safety by Anastasia.

"*Morgan* presented new visual challenges," Wallace notes. "I wanted to integrate text and illustration, just the way the old circus posters did, and I wanted to capture the feeling of an old-time circus parade. When I was in Baraboo, I was fascinated with the gilt figures on the sides of the circus wagons. The angel in the corner of each of my pictures is based on these carvings, and I tried to make the illustrations like the paintings on the wagons."

The angel is much more than a decoration; she's a guardian spirit watching over Morgan, caring deeply but allowing the girl to learn and grow on her own. "Morgan is a girl living alone with her father; but there's a female spirit caring for her, and she's given guidance by a woman, Anastasia. I hope children will read the pictures of the angel and interpret her thoughts and emotions."

The illustrations, like those of the earlier books, use watercolor and pen and ink, and add another medium, pencil crayon, "to create texture," Wallace says. What the attentive viewer will notice is that the pen-and-ink lines become less dominant as Morgan enters the dream-like world of the big top. When she again has her feet on the ground and returns home with her father, the lines reappear.

As my visit drew to a close, Ian discussed his latest project, illustrating *Architect of the Moon,* a story by Toronto writer Tim Wynne-Jones, author of the award-winning children's books *Zoom Away* and *Zoom at Sea,* and talked about one of his greatest joys, visiting schools across Canada to share his art and experiences with young readers.

"After I've finished writing and/or illustrating a book there's a period of time that for me is similar to mourning. The book, 'my child,' with its story and pictures has left home for the printer. All the physical evidence of the completed work is missing. And I lose the book. But when the book is published, a very intriguing occurrence unfolds through my contact with children. In reading after reading they give the book back to me. They breathe life anew into those words, those pictures, but more importantly those characters. The evidence is in their eyes, in the way they sit with their ears perked, and in their body movement." One time while showing the paintings of *Very Last First Time* to a group of grade three students, one of the children pointed out to Ian the presence of Eva's mother watching over her in the under-ice world.

"I must have put it there subconsciously; I'd never noticed it before. What a wonderful gift for the child to present to me."

Our conversation over, I leave and walk along the shaded sidewalk toward College Street and the busy, everyday world of Toronto. But as I do, I carry with me a gift, memories of my visit to the special world of Ian Wallace. It's a world of beauty and sensitivity, a world filled not only with finely crafted words and exquisitely executed illustrations, but also with an understanding of and empathy with young people whose hopes and fears he has expressed in books which are his gift to them—a gift which is also an invitation for them to enter into a world of the imagination which is both Ian Wallace's and that of every sensitive young reader.

Ulrike Walker

SOURCE: "A Matter of Thresholds," in *Canadian Children's Literature,* No. 60, 1990, pp. 108-16.

Although children's books should provide a sense of sanctuary and security, it is equally important that they also offer encounters with what [author Tim] Wynne-Jones calls "Thresholds": those risk-filled but unavoidable passages from one state of being to another. The importance of learning to step through "Thresholds into discovery" is acknowledged, not only in the picture books containing Wynne-Jones' texts, but in most of the books included in this review. Although all of these works are extraordinarily good, the best of them are distinguished by an eloquent evocation of the courage and determination with which the child confronts and steps through his or her individual threshold. The excellence of these books lies in their capacity to do justice, by means of both picture and word, to the profundity and complexity of the child's experience. . . .

Architect of the moon, . . . written by Wynne-Jones, owes much to Ian Wallace's fine illustrations. It is a subtle work which like all picture books must be thoroughly *looked at* before one can appreciate what it has to offer. A story about young David Finebloom, a "brave block builder" who rescues the disappearing moon by rebuilding it with his toy blocks, this work is also about thresholds. In particular, it deals with boundaries which threaten to become stifling enclosures. Wynne-Jones tells of leaving architecture school because "to be an architect was to put up walls, to disconnect spaces one from the other, to remove the possibility of getting from here to there." In *Architect of the moon,* Wynne-Jones and Wallace allow us to get "from here to there" despite the walls, enclosures and rigid geometric shapes which abound in this book. Here the ordered world is invaded by something extraordinary: a message from the moon. In Wallace's illustration, the message ("HELP! I'M FALLING APART. YOURS, THE MOON.") appears in the form of illuminated letters thrust through a window blown open by a gust of wind. Suddenly, a threshold appears: an opening in the enclosed box that is David's room. David,

grasping this opportunity, packs his blocks and launches himself into space. From this point, Wallace's illustrations superbly render the impossible possible. His glowing, pastel images create a playground in space where shape, space and size become entirely malleable. Depending on the perspective of the drawing, shapes and figures can be huge or tiny, near or far. In such a place, David, a little boy with his little toys, has the power to rebuild something as monumental as the moon, even if the job he does is "a little rough in places." David must return to his ordered world, eerily portrayed by Wallace as a desolate landscape where David's blocks become identical but ominously separate square houses. Yet, we are also left with a final, hopeful image. Although it is enclosed within a window frame, David's magical work, a fully rounded moon, glows vividly in the night sky. Without denying the frighteningly empty and restricting omnipresence of a certain kind of "normality," Wynne-Jones and Wallace create a threshold to a "there" not defined by barriers. Moreover, it is a "there" that the child has taken a hand in creating. As in the Zoom books, [by Wynne-Jones], what is offered is an essential opening: something that does not enclose but encourages the child to take a decisive step towards change.

Very last first time, written by Jan Andrews and illustrated by Ian Wallace, beautifully expresses this business of passing from one state of being to another. As the wonderfully paradoxical title suggests, this is a work about an experience which is both an end and a beginning. Eva Padlyat, an Inuit girl, goes under the frozen sea to collect mussels, a traditional activity in her village. However, this time, "for the very first time in her life Eva would walk on the bottom of the sea alone." Here the "vast northern tundra" is the threatening setting for transition. Andrews describes the landscape as desolate and snowbound, but Wallace counters this whiteness with the colour of his images. In these literally brilliant pictures, the "frozen tundra" is imbued with a shimmering richness of light and colour. Visually, Wallace adds an element of vivid life to the dangerous, death-like undertones of Eva's solitary walk.

After dropping through a hole she and her mother have cut into the ice, Eva sees, in the light of her candle, a shadowy sea floor haunted by spirit shapes. Quickly filling her mussel pan, Eva explores this mysterious underworld but goes "too far." Her candles burn "to nothing," and she is left to find her way through complete darkness—with the added threat of an encroaching tide. Wallace's illustration of Eva's solitary moment of terror shares the formidable symbolism of the tunnel in [Wynne-Jone's] *Zoom away.* Here, again, is a dark, vaginal passage spiked with fearful, tooth-like shapes. But, like Zoom, Eva finds a light and locates the opening in the ice where she dances happily in the light of the moon. This moment is accompanied by an inspired illustration. Watched by the spirit shapes, Eva is transformed by the moonlight into an ecstatic, iridescent creature in the throes of metamorphosis. When her mother pulls her out of the ice, Eva announces: "That was my very *last* first time—for walking alone at the bottom of the sea." This transformation is confirmed when we see Eva for the last time, eating a plate of mussels, her head surrounded by a halo of northern lights. She has earned both the light and the meal, symbolic of her new-found self-knowledge and self-sufficiency; for she has harvested both at the cost of a profound and fearful experience. *Very last first time* is, quite simply, a superb and moving picture book. It is a mystery to me that there is no gold medal on its cover. There should be.

Morgan the magnificent, written and illustrated by Ian Wallace, is, like *Very last first time,* an excellent, meticulously designed picture book. Morgan, a young girl who lives on her father's farm, dreams of becoming a "daring highwire artist" like the "Amazing Anastasia" whom she idolizes. Wallace's half-title, illustrated with appropriately circus-like flamboyance, introduces us to Morgan. Enclosed in a cameo image, Morgan, barefoot and dressed in overalls, balances on a picket fence. Around her, Wallace has arrayed the gilt emblems of her dream world. Particularly important is the ambiguous female figure who appears as a twin image on either side of Morgan. This full-breasted, winged figure (like Anastasia, an emblem of Morgan's dream self) appears in the left-hand corner of each illustration, reacting to and sympathizing with Morgan's experiences. With her wings and ripe breasts, this complex symbol embodies both innocence and maturity, fantasy and reality: states which Morgan, herself, must come to terms with.

Each morning, Morgan practises balancing on the roof of the barn. On her "one hundred and sixty-sixth walk," Morgan's father catches her at it and forbids her to continue. In Wallace's illustration, the father, holding a threatening pitchfork, stands in the doorway of the barn while Morgan pleads before him, her arms outstretched like the wings of her female emblem. Visually, Wallace suggests that, although the father's reaction may stem from an understandable fear for Morgan's safety, he is denying her access to an essential threshold. Morgan, though, is determined to prove herself. She goes to the circus grounds, enters Anastasia's tent, puts on Anastasia's cos-

tume and "a pair of fine leather shoes." Seeing herself in a mirror as a "beautiful high wire artist," Morgan decides to perform in place of Anastasia. At first all goes well; but Morgan is not used to the thin wire and begins to lose her balance. Wallace's illustration of this moment is the star act of his own book. In it he captures, not only the vertigo and terror of Morgan's experience, but also its poignancy. Dressed in Anastasia's grown-up costume, with her little girl's undershirt peeping out at the bustline, Morgan is revealed as a child uncertainly and fearfully poised on the edge of adulthood. Luckily, Anastasia herself arrives to help Morgan. Regaining confidence, Morgan finishes her walk along the high wire to the other platform where Anastasia waits with open arms. Morgan has completed her dangerous crossing. The last picture we see of her leaves us in little doubt that she has crossed a threshold. Surrounded by the same emblems Wallace uses on the half-title page, we see Morgan doing a handstand in front of the departing circus wagons while (as the text tells us) her father applauds loudly. Here the secure "reality" of the father's farm world is happily mingled with Morgan's own dream world. As evidence of this transformation, Morgan is no longer the barefoot child she was at the beginning of the story. Proudly displayed in her significantly topsy-turvy pose are the fine leather shoes she has taken such risks to earn.

Ronald A. Jobe and Wendy K. Sutton

SOURCE: "Beyond Munsch: Canadian Literature for Children and Young People," in *The Reading Teacher,* Vol. 45, No. 8, April, 1992, pp. 634-41.

A major award winner in illustrations for children, Ian Wallace has an international reputation, gained in part through his diversity of artistic media and styles. Ever since his *Chin Chiang and the Dragon's Dance* burst onto the children's book scene, Wallace's work has continued to delight children and adults. *Chin Chiang and the Dragon's Dance* explodes with a cacophony of sound and a crescendoing intensity of brilliant colours, resplen-

From Very Last First Time, *written by Jan Andrews. Illustrated by Ian Wallace.*

dent with exquisite details of Westcoast Chinese culture. Author-illustrator Wallace tells the story of how a young boy overcomes his lack of confidence to successfully take his place at the end of the dragon's tail in the New Year's Day celebrations. This book was made possible, in part, by the first collaboration between the editors of Ground-wood and Margaret K. McElderry Books.

In *Very Last First Time,* written by Jan Andrews, Wallace moves away from the formalized designs he used to represent Chinese culture. Instead, he uses a freer, more expressionistic style, rich with subliminal suggestions of Inuit animal spirits. This book intrigues young readers with the idea of searching for mussels under the arctic ice at low tide and captivates them as they experience one girl's fear of the incoming tide and the threat of the spirits.

In *The Name of the Tree,* Wallace's beautifully executed illustrations of the animals and land of the African plains are achieved through his skillful use of pencil drawings, unusual perspectives, and muted, delicate colours. In this Bantu folktale, retold by Celia Lottridge, the animals are forced by drought and starvation to cross the arid plains in search of the lion who alone knows the name of the tree that can provide them with the food they so desperately require. . . . Ian Wallace has added another to his already impressive corpus of books with *Mr. Kneebone's New Digs.* Disgusted with their present digs, April Moth and her dog, Mr. Kneebone, go in search of a more friendly, affordable place to live. Masterfully designed, the beautiful illustrations envelope the text, subtly complementing the optimism of the spirited duo. Rich in language and imagery, the text begs to be read aloud to a primary-grade audience.

TITLE COMMENTARY

📖 *THE SANDWICH* (with Angela Wood, 1975)

Michele Landsberg

SOURCE: "The Quest for Identity: *The Sandwich,*" in *Reading for the Love of It: Best Books for Young Readers,* Prentice Hall Press, 1987, pp. 103-04.

[It is] an added pleasure [for children] to see their own identity mirrored and confirmed in an engagingly warm and humorous story. Ian Wallace's *The Sandwich* is important for [this] reason. Vincenzo Ferrante, who is in grade two at a downtown Toronto school, tastes the mingled bitterness and triumph of an archetypal Canadian schoolchild experience. His peanut butter-loving friends are at first revolted by Vincenzo's "stinky" mortadella and provolone lunch sandwiches; later (though not, to my mind, entirely convincingly) they seem to accept the idea of *chacun à son gout.* Vincenzo wins by sticking to his guns and not trying to imitate his non-Italian friends.

Joan McGrath

SOURCE: "Making Friends," in *CM: A Reviewing Journal of Canadian Materials for Young People,* Vol. XIX, No. 3, May, 1991, pp. 153-54, 156.

It is quite possible to feel the same friendship and to recognize the same sense of kinship and responsiveness to characters one has learned to care for through the printed word as to those met in the flesh. Once a child has shared, for example, the perils of Liza and Jullily in their escape to freedom or Vincenzo's difficulties with his "stinky meat" sandwich, the beginnings of a friendship have begun to take shape. . . .

Vincenzo Ferrantes is humiliated when the other children at his school mock his "stinky meat" lunch and hold their noses when he takes out his mortadella and provolone sandwich, rather than the *correct* tasteless peanut butter and jam on white bread that everyone else has to eat. His understanding papa offers to make him the "proper" lunch, if that is what he really wants, but suggests that it would be better to be proud of what he is, and to let the world know it. When eventually Vincent shares his smelly lunch with the other kids, they discover what they have been missing. Just because it isn't what you have been accustomed to, doesn't mean it isn't GOOD, like *The Sandwich.*

📖 *THE CHRISTMAS TREE HOUSE* (1976)

Virginia Van Vliet

SOURCE: A review of *The Christmas Tree House,* in *In Review: Canadian Books for Children,* Vol. 11, No. 4, Autumn, 1977, p. 63.

Don Valley Rose is a strange gray haired old woman who roams the streets of Toronto's Cabbagetown carrying her possessions in a shopping bag. Local children believe she eats stew made from stray cats, turns people to ice by her touch, conjures up thunder and lightning storms at will and carries all kinds of awful things in her bag.

Two children who believe these stories are Nick and Gloria. Playing near the Riverdale Zoo one December day, they find a tree house which they decide to decorate with a Christmas tree and ornaments. However, just as the children are sitting down to celebrate their creation with shortbread cookies and baklava, Don Valley Rose's safari-hatted head suddenly appears through the trap door of the tree house. Nick is certain Rose will "zapp them dead," but instead she turns out to be a gentle woman and the original builder of the tree house, designed so that she could watch the world go by. Rose even produces a star of prisms from her bag to top the children's tree and Nick realizes "there weren't any tricks in her shopping bag at all."

New Christmas stories are always welcome and this one will be a pleasant addition to any collection. Ian Wallace's soft pencil drawings with their vaguely surrealistic style perfectly capture the mood of the text and of a Canadian winter. While the story does present several important social lessons, these are an integral enough part of the plot that they do not appear as mere didactic moralizing. Kids Can Press and Ian Wallace again maintain the standard set in the author's earlier work *The Sandwich.*

Barbara J. Graham

SOURCE: "Travelling toward Christmas with Canadian Authors," in *Canadian Children's Literature,* No. 14, 1979, pp. 46-50.

Ian Wallace's *Christmas Tree House* is a simple charming story reminiscent of his earlier effort, *The Sandwich.* Nick, who lives in Cabbagetown with his parents and grandparents, is different from other eight-year-olds because on Saturdays he goes out looking for adventure rather than playing with friends or going to horror movies. One day close to Christmas, while looking at the animals at Riverdale zoo, he meets Gloria, a spunky nine-year-old, and has a pleasant scare when Don Valley Rose, a peculiar old lady, who is the subject of many a spooky story, comes into view. Gloria and Nick discover a tree house and decide to have their own Christmas party the day before Christmas. Don Valley Rose interrupts their plans and provides a surprise for two children who learn not to judge by appearances. Young readers will enjoy this quiet adventure of two inner city children. Nick's Macedonian background adds an ethnic interest and the many Toronto references will be enjoyable for those who know the city, but will not detract for those who do not. Wallace's black and white illustrations with their two page spreads are evocative and well-related to the text. The portrait of Don Valley Rose with her soft understanding eyes is particularly effective. The wish-fulfillment aspects of the story will be satisfying to the younger reader while the danger is just to tantalize but not scare.

CHIN CHIANG AND THE DRAGON'S DANCE (1984)

Ian Wallace

SOURCE: "And for the Illustrator . . . ," in *Canadian Library Journal,* Vol. 42, No. 5, October, 1985, pp. 304-05.

Seven years ago when I began the long process of creating *Chin Chiang and the Dragon's Dance,* my objective was threefold: to put down on paper a story that would be fleshed out by drawings bearing the same depth and integrity as the text; to create a universal character in Chin Chiang to whom children of all ages and races could relate and to portray a race of people with dignity and respect.

I reasoned that, if Lady Luck was on my side, this story would be published in the not too distant future. Did I have a lot to learn!

The journey to be published had humble, yet earnest, beginnings that took me out of my studio in Toronto to New York City, Vancouver, and London, England, and to several major cities across Canada. Along the way I was privileged to meet two people who would play an invaluable role in my creative life, [editors Patsy] Aldana and [Margaret] McElderry. Their dedication to producing quality books for young people is legendary in the publishing industry. With their guidance, *Chin Chiang and the Dragon's Dance* ultimately became the book it is. I could not have accomplished this task on my own, and in accepting this award, I share it equally with them.

To this project they brought their keen ears for language, their astute eyes for illustration, and the critical faculty that allowed me, the creator, to draw out of myself the emotional substance, the visual drama and the sense of myth that this book demanded.

I have learned much from these two editors and from the experience of creating *Chin Chiang and the Dragon's Dance,* knowledge that I will carry into future projects and into my personal life.

Daily, as I sit at my drafting table, I am frequently reminded of the words of the esteemed author Katherine Paterson, who had this to say about writing. "We writers are not a breed apart, a privileged aristocracy doling out gifts for less fortunate mortals. But rather that we are like the majority of the human race, day labourers. And if we marvel at the artist who has written a good book, we must marvel more at those people whose lives are works of art . . . However hard work good writing may be, it is easier than good living."

Those inspirational words give me courage to struggle. They keep my nose to the grindstone, my head out of the clouds, and my fingers at my typewriter or clutching a paintbrush, where they must be as a day labourer.

Day labourer—those two words bring a flood of images to mind, and since I am a purveyor of tales I will share one with you now.

My childhood was spent growing up in a city of extreme contrasts, Niagara Falls, Ont. The only grandparents I knew as a boy came from my mother's side of the family: my father's parents having died from poverty and overwork long before my brothers and I made our respective appearances in the Wallace clan.

Grandma and Grandpa, as we affectionately referred to them, lived in a small town on the West Coast known in British Columbia for the advanced age of its citizens, which rivalled the incline and age of its hills. Money was not readily available to them to make a yearly journey across Canada; however, when they did travel east, their arrival brought the sound of their singing voices, which lifted up into the attic of our house. Their voices were not merely capable of carrying a tune, but grew out of a long tradition ingrained deep in the rolling hills surrounding their birthplace, the Forest of Dean, Gloucestershire, England. My grandfather's talent had descended from the same lineage that had produced the acclaimed opera star John Charles Thomas, who was his first cousin.

For my brothers and me, an even greater thrill was to hear the stories of their childhoods. Huddled at their feet, we sat with eager anticipation to hear those two Saxon voices telling stories of a time long ago and of a land far away. We were transported out of our bodies. Yet each time we were reintroduced to those tales, that became our first lessons in history and gave us a sense of from where we had come, my grandparents told them with such freshness, conviction and humour that we felt we were hearing them for the first time.

Here now is my favourite story to the best of my recollection. In the 12th year of my grandfather's life, he left school for the last time to enter the mines that had been dug deep in the rolling hills surrounding his home. Being a small boy for his age, he was given the task of crawling along the narrowest openings in the rock face where older and much larger miners could never have entered.

For the first time his lungs filled with a cold, dank air that clogged his nostrils until the day he died and that caused his fingers to turn in on themselves with arthritis decades later.

At the end of his first day on the job, my grandfather's hands were soaked with blood from skin that had been torn, scraped and bruised from chipping away at that rock.

A seasoned miner recognized his pain. "You know what you do with them, laddie?," he asked with a voice that told my grandfather he already knew the answer.

"No," my grandfather replied.

Without hesitation the miner said, "You piss on them."

Believing implicitly in what the miner had told him, and yet with reluctance, my grandfather pissed on his hands.

As children, my brothers and I always burst into loud peals of laughter at this juncture in the story that soon ushered in a cauterizing sensation that spread like a brush fire down our spines.

The bleeding ceased after the stinging had ended. The skin healed and my grandfather's hands toughened, allowing him to return to that blackness to confront that rock face for many years.

I tell you this story because it is part of my family heritage, and because it has stayed close to my soul all these years. Most assuredly it has given me the confidence to search the darkened tunnels that authors and illustrators must enter in their never-ending pursuit of excellence. It is a quest in which we strive to discover "those words" and "those pictures," those nuggets of precious metal that illuminate human truths.

This award will help me search those darkened tunnels just a little further and a little longer. Once again, I thank you most sincerely for honouring *Chin Chiang and the Dragon's Dance.*

Kirkus Reviews

SOURCE: A review of *Chin Chiang and the Dragon's Dance,* in *Kirkus Reviews,* Juvenile Issue, Vol. LII, Nos. 1-5, March 1, 1984, p. J-11.

Since a picture book may indeed be perused for its unusual and interesting pictures, to the virtual disregard of a weak text, this curiously amorphous amalgam of cultural expansion and psychological breakthrough might find quite a number of takers. The situation is hackneyed, the prose stilted, the storytelling finesse almost nil. "From the time Chin Chiang stood only as high as his grandfather's knees, he had dreamed of dancing the dragon's dance. Now the first day of the Year of the Dragon had arrived and his dream was to come true. . . . But instead of being excited, Chin Chiang was so scared he wanted to melt into his shoes. He knew he could never dance well enough to make Grandfather proud of him." How Chin Chiang overcomes his fear, with the aid of a woman who had thought herself too old to dance, constitutes the plot. The amorphousness comes from neither being told that the people are Chinese nor having any idea where this big city is. (An adult can recognize that it's not in China proper.) But the minutely detailed, shimmering watercolors, old-fashioned Chinese in mode and often surreal in manner (skewed perspectives, vacant space), do draw the eye—and enable the story to be "read," from painting to painting, without in fact reading beyond that opening paragraph. Just the brilliant dragon on the jacket, with Chin Chiang holding its tail, will catch passersby.

Kate M. Flanagan

SOURCE: A review of *Chin Chiang and the Dragon's Dance,* in *The Horn Book Magazine,* Vol. LX, No. 2, April, 1984, pp. 190-91.

It was the first day of the Year of the Dragon, and Chin Chiang's dream of dancing the dragon's dance with his grandfather was about to come true. "But instead of being excited, Chin Chiang was so scared he wanted to melt into his shoes." While his family and neighbors decorated their homes and shops for the celebration, Chin Chiang fled, ending up on the roof of the city's public library. There he met a cleaning lady, Pu Yee, who told him that she had danced the dragon's dance when she was young. The boy decided to teach the old woman his steps so that she could take his place in the dance, but in doing so he regained his confidence. He and Pu Yee rushed hand-in-hand to the marketplace, arriving just in time for the beginning of the dance. Although he stumbled at first, as the dance went on, his "feet moved more surely, his steps grew firmer and his leaps more daring." The straightforward story is illustrated by full-page watercolor paintings that capture the beauty and detail of the colorful costumes and decorations as well as the festive spirit of the celebration. Particularly lovely are the views of the city from atop the library, with the sun setting into the ocean and purple clouds streaming behind jumbles of highrise buildings.

Karen Stang Hanley

SOURCE: A review of *Chin Chiang and the Dragon's Dance,* in *Booklist,* Vol. 80, No. 15, April 1, 1984, p. 1122.

Chin Chiang has always longed to perform the dragon's dance but now, on the day of the New Year's festival, he is consumed with stage fright. He is supposed to dance with the dragon's tail while his grandfather leads the way inside its magnificent head, but Chin Chiang runs away from their last practice session and finds a quiet refuge on the rooftop of the public library building. There he is joined by an older woman who is eagerly anticipating the New Year's parade: in her youth, she says, she danced the dragon's dance. This gives Chin Chiang the bright idea that she could dance in his place, but when they arrive at the parade Chin Chiang has no choice but to dance after all, which he does with mounting enthusiasm and daring. Beauteous, glowing watercolor paintings provide an exquisite framework for this rather mild tale, which is weakened by its wordy narrative and undeveloped characterizations. However, the contemporary Chinatown setting and exuberant festival atmosphere are established with a profusion of well-realized detail, and Wallace is particularly successful at avoiding stereotypes in his portrayals of Oriental characters.

Carolyn Noah

SOURCE: A review of *Chin Chiang and the Dragon's Dance,* in *School Library Journal,* Vol. 30, No. 9, May, 1984, p. 74.

Chin Chiang has always dreamed of dancing the dragon's dance, but now that his time has come, he is terrified. Failure to make his grandfather proud would be unbearable, Chin Chiang is sure. On the first day of the Year of the Dragon, the young boy runs away, wearing on his head a mask-like rabbit lantern. Encountering Pu Yee, a woman who feels her dancing days are over, Chin Chiang encourages her and sparks himself as well. Wallace's watercolors, in full palette, effectively capture the panic of Chin Chiang as the dance draws near, especially through use of angle and perspective. In an extraordinary view of the rabbit-boy ascending the spiral steps of the library, children will see him as small as he must himself feel. Throughout, the colors are vibrant, capturing the texture of a contemporary Chinese New Year. However, many scenes which suggest animation are peopled with figures whose lines remain oddly static. Chin Chiang's story is moving, his relationships with Pu Yee and grandfather are reinforcing and his Chinese community is well depict-

ed by small details in prose and picture. The total impact of . . . *Dragon's Dance* is compelling and vivid. It will be enjoyed by independent readers and deeply appreciated in social studies classrooms.

Frieda Wishinsky

SOURCE: A review of *Chin Chiang and the Dragon's Dance,* in *Quill and Quire,* Vol. 50, No. 9, September, 1984, pp. 80, 82.

Chin Chiang and the Dragon's Dance is the sweet, gentle tale of a young boy's feelings on the evening he is to dance with his grandfather in celebration of the Chinese New Year. It captures young Chin's pride in his rich heritage and his fear of not measuring up to its expectations.

A lovely relationship is developed between Chin and an old woman named Pu Yee. The two of them bridge the gulf of years and help each other overcome their individual fears—Chin's fear of failure and Pu Yee's fear of old age.

The soft water-colour drawings by the author detail life in a Chinese neighbourhood in Vancouver. There is a sense of a tightly knit community, full of colour and activity. Each drawing is framed by a black-and-white border, which gives it a formality to match the traditional tone of the story.

There is much to observe in every picture: the contrast of a boy in jeans and running shoes surrounded by the symbols of his ancient heritage; the life of a market; and the celebration of a festival. The drawing of Pu Yee and Chin Chiang dancing on the roof of the local library as night descends and pigeons soar, has a dreamy, timeless quality that links past and present.

In short, this is a fine book that leaves the reader with a clearer picture of a strong, vibrant community. It is also the story of a very real little boy.

Mary Ainslie Smith

SOURCE: A review of *Chin Chiang and the Dragon's Dance,* in *Books in Canada,* Vol. 13, No. 10, December, 1984, p. 14.

[***Chin Chiang and the Dragon's Dance***] tells the story of a young boy in Vancouver who has been training with his grandfather to perform the Dragon's Dance in the traditional street parade celebrating Chinese New Year's. His grandfather is the head of the dragon and Chin Chiang is to dance the part of the dragon's tail. But on the day of the dance he has severe stage fright and runs away. A new friend helps him regain his courage and become the best dragon's tail ever. Wallace's illustrations make this book special—colour and pattern fill the pages, and the pictures of the dragon's dance are especially rich and exciting.

From The Sparrow's Song, *written and illustrated by Ian Wallace.*

G. Bott

SOURCE: A review of *Chin Chiang and the Dragon's Dance,* in *The Junior Bookshelf,* Vol. 49, No. 1, February, 1985, p. 18.

A traditional Chinese festival provides Ian Wallace with not only a story but also a subject that calls for rainbow treatment. His illustrations are a riot of greens, reds and blues, with meticulous detail balancing broad sweeps of colour—the silk dragon, paper lanterns, swooping pigeons, firecrackers, the pageantry of the procession.

The story is as simple as the illustrations are flamboyant. Chin Chiang is afraid that his dancing will be inadequate to please the Great Dragon who lives in the clouds above the mountains. Disaster will follow his failure. He meets Pu Yee, a cleaner, and cajoles her into dancing with him. Chin Chiang glows with pride at his grandfather's approbation.

It is to be regretted that the author/illustrator of so delightful a book confuses "practise" and "practice".

Kate Flint

SOURCE: A review of *Chin Chiang and the Dragon's Dance,* in *The Times Literary Supplement,* No. 4278, March 29, 1985, p. 352.

The re-telling of a myth and the re-viewing of the world through the eyes of another culture present similar problems for children's literature. Both demand a union of the strange and unfamiliar with points of reference afforded by a known or clearly told story, or by the assumption of shared emotions or experience. The initial worry of Chin Chiang, in Ian Wallace's ***Chin Chiang and the Dragon's Dance,*** is recognizable enough, the situation far less so. He fears he will fail to fulfil his grandfather's trust in him, will trip and stumble, proving himself unworthy of his dancing role at the tail of the magnificent, silken Dragon. His nervousness gets worse as he realizes his community's superstitious dependence on the ceremonial dance: the cloud-dwelling Great Dragon must be moved in order to fill the fishing nets with plump spotted salmon, and the trees with oranges. Wallace's delicate water-colours record in detail the customs of the Chinese New Year celebrations: the fish and rabbit paper lanterns, the pigeons which sweep over the city with whistles tied to their tail feathers. His own sense of intricate design is strong, for example in the bird's-eye view of the public library's curved staircase and marble tiles; his subtle colouring of the cityscape throws into relief the brilliant spectacle of firecrackers and the swirling, dancing dragon. There is an Oriental formality to the layout, however, which may deter some children. The pictures are neatly bordered, top and bottom; the text, invariably on the right-hand page, is ultimately less alluring than the visual richness opposite.

Francis E. Kazemek and Pat Rigg

SOURCE: "There's More to an Old Person Than Appears," in *Journal of Youth Services in Libraries*, Vol. 1, No. 4, Summer, 1988, pp. 396-405.

Chin Chiang and the Dragon's Dance, like [Laurence Yep's] *Dragonwings,* deals with the importance of dragon mythology for Chinese. The boy Chin Chiang longs to dance the Dragon Dance with his grandfather on the first day of the Year of the Dragon. The only problem is that Chin Chiang is certain that he will not be able to dance well and thus will bring bad luck and embarrassment to this family. With the help of an old woman that he meets, Pu Yee, he is able to practice the Dragon Dance and slowly develop his confidence. The end of the book, which presents Chin Chiang and Pu Yee finishing the dance together, is heartwarming, an affirmation of the importance of the old teaching the young about life, helping children to understand their culture and thus themselves.

📖 *VERY LAST FIRST TIME* (written by Jan Andrews, 1985; reissued as *Eva's Ice Adventure,* 1986)

Bernie Goedhart

SOURCE: "Picture-Books: Some Succeed, Others Better Read than Seen," in *Quill and Quire*, Vol. 51, No. 12, December, 1985, p. 24.

Illustration is the weak point of . . . *Very Last First Time* by Jan Andrews—and, again, it is a celebrated artist's work that somehow falls short of its mark. The text is an intriguing, sometimes riveting, account of a young Inuit girl's first solo venture under the ice when the tide is out. She goes to collect mussels off the seabed, and the reader gets drawn into the suspense of whether this child will get out before the water returns. A good story. But the illustrations by Ian Wallace, with their heavy use of purple, pink, and luminescent green, seem glaring and surreal. The child's face is overly pretty, and the whole tone of the artwork seems to romanticize the North beyond belief. (Wallace's use of colour in *Chin Chiang and the Dragon's Dance* was lauded; in this book it is jarringly annoying.) When the text reads, "Snow lay white as far as the eye could see," our eye is treated to a purplish, pebbly-looking landscape.

Lucy Young Clem

SOURCE: A review of *Very Last First Time,* in *School Library Journal*, Vol. 32, No. 9, May, 1986, p. 67.

This look at Eskimo life today combines the ancient custom of collecting mussels with modern features such as airplanes and snowmobiles. The story is well-developed, with just the right amount of suspense. The watercolor illustrations are somewhat uneven in quality; the colors in the land scenes are rather garish, and some figures are

awkwardly proportioned. The eerie shades of the ocean floor are quite effective, however, and the strange seascapes lend an air of unreality. *Very Last First Time* is an intriguing view of a little-known way of life.

Selma G. Lanes

SOURCE: A review of *Very Last First Time,* in *The New York Times Book Review,* June 15, 1986, p. 38.

This particular winter, Eva is old enough to walk alone on the bottom of the sea. And how old is that? Well, we can only determine this—and other interesting but not absolutely essential facts—by poring over Ian Wallace's rewarding watercolors. Just how much is gleaned from these graphic documents, brimful of closely observed details, depends entirely on each looker's visual acuity and curiosity.

Thus, as Eva and her mother prepare for the adventure, a viewer might note that their kitchen is oil-heated; that at least some Inuits eat cornflakes for breakfast; that they possess electric stoves and stainless steel sinks just like many of us.

Almost never does text mention what eyes can plainly see: sled dogs, snowshoes, or animal pelts stretched taut on drying frames. Eva's village is surely remote, yet there are power lines in view and a two-engine plane overhead. Clearly, this Once-upon-a-time is the present, yet Eva's adventure, like all good tales, is timeless.

At low tide, she and her mother walk out together on the frozen surface of the sea. Skillfully they cut a hole through the thick ice, one big enough to lower a person through. At last, candle in hand, Eva is launched on her solo quest for mussels—at the bottom of the sea. Mr. Wallace's factual pictures now turn magical as they capture a blue-purple submarine wonderland, where ice mirrors reflect candlelit images from other ice mirrors. We share Eva's urge to explore farther than task demands. And, like her, we are ever mindful of passing time, of the absent giant—the sea—sure to return with the shifting tide. When Eva's candle drops, our hearts nearly stop. And when unsure steps finally lead her back to the ice-hole exit, we share her triumphant relief at having completed this exotic rite of passage. Only its unbeckoning title does less than justice to an extraordinary picture-book experience.

Mary Ellen Binder

SOURCE: "The Canadian North," in *Canadian Children's Literature,* No. 45, 1987, pp. 82-6.

The beautiful illustrations by Ian Wallace add a great deal to the enjoyment and understanding of this story. His portraits of the Inuit community are full of realistic details instantly recognizable to anyone who has ever lived in a northern settlement. The stretched animal skins outside the house, the bare light bulbs dangling from the ceiling, the fuel tank attached to the outer wall of each house, the skinny huskies with their backs hunched against the cold wind, the stone inukshuks, the furtrimmed parkas and beautifully embroidered mukluks and the bush planes bringing mail and supplies from the outside world are all familiar parts of the Arctic existence.

Wallace also portrays the profusion of colour to be found in the snowy Arctic landscape, particularly in the spring and fall. The northern skies are full of colour, while the snow is not only white, but many delicate shades of blue, purple and pink as well. Through Wallace's illustrations the reader receives a view of the north, not as a lonely, desolate land, but as a land of beauty and adventure, of an on-going life.

Through Wallace's artistry, the story exists on two levels—as an adventure story about a young Inuit girl collecting mussels under the ice, as a tale set in the spiritual "other world" of traditional Inuit belief. While his illustrations of life above the ice are a detailed realistic depiction of Inuit settlement life, the illustrations showing the world below the ice portray a foreign, mysterious, slightly sinister world of sparkling ice caverns filled with animal shapes and human spirits. His use of blues, purples, and dark greens produces images which are beautiful and ominous at the same time, hinting at an ever present danger even as Eva explores the wonders of the sea bed. In addition to their other-world qualities, however, Wallace's sea bed illustrations include such realistic details as seaweed, starfish, crabs, barnacles and mussels. As the danger to Eva increases with the incoming tide, the reader may wonder whether the shadowy human figures are the spirits of Eva's ancestors watching over her to keep her from harm, or the spirits of previous accident victims ready to welcome her to the underwater world of the dead.

Very last first time contains many elements which will appeal to children: an unusual setting, adventure, suspense, vivid descriptive language, colourful detailed illustrations and the opportunity to learn interesting facts about a uniquely Canadian lifestyle. It is an enjoyable and educational reading experience for young and old alike.

Jon C. Stott and Christine Doyle

SOURCE: A review of *Very Last First Time*, in *Children's literature in education*, Vol. 24, No. 3, September, 1993, pp. 226-28.

Throughout this book, the unexceptional and secure aspects of Eva's life thus far are contrasted with the extraordinary natural world outdoors and, in particular, under the ice. Illustrator Ian Wallace enhances this contrast by means of design and color; oranges and yellows depict the ordinary, secure world of the home, while purple shades come into prominence as the story moves outside the house and then below the ice. Eva will go from her house to the outdoors and back again, being much more fully "home" upon her return.

The first picture of Eva in her kitchen as she prepares to go out is a visual cliché of the conventional: Kellogg's Corn Flakes on the table, pots on the stove, a calendar and "Bless This House" plaque on the wall, and a Michael Jackson poster on the refrigerator. All these commonplace items are shown in shades of orange and yellow. Eva herself, however, is framed in a purple fur collar; this day will not be commonplace for her. The text states that Eva had walked under the ice with her mother "ever since she could remember," but "today something very special was going to happen. Today, for the very first time in her life, Eva would walk on the bottom of the sea alone." As mother and daughter leave the house and walk down to the shore, the separation of colors continues to reinforce the separation of the two worlds. The homes they pass are bathed in yellow and orange, while the land beyond is purple. When Eva goes below the ice, the purple shades follow her as the extraordinary world assumes dominance. Wallace forces the reader to experience this change of atmosphere with Eva; not only are the illustrations now dramatically infused with purple, but they also expand all the way across both pages. The only reminder of the existence she has left behind is the yellow light from the candles Eva carries with her. . . .

Eva understands that she has passed her test and will never again be a child on her own for the first time. She has learned that she can coexist with the Arctic environment but cannot control it; she will be able to enjoy the privileges of her emerging adulthood without forgetting its inherent responsibilities. Again, Wallace's artistry enhances the textual indications. The final picture in the book depicts Eva again at home in her kitchen, eating her mussels. Now a profusion of purple shades merges with the yellow, and the Northern Lights shine through the window behind her. The ordinary and the extraordinary blend to provide a richer environment for Eva.

THE SPARROW'S SONG (1986)

Bessie Condos Egan

SOURCE: A review of *The Sparrow's Song*, in *Quill and Quire*, Vol. 52, No. 8, August, 1986, p. 39.

Ian Wallace's previous stories featured a Chinese boy learning a traditional dance, *Chin Chiang and the Dragon's Dance*, and a young girl in an Inuit village, *Very Last First Time*. With *The Sparrow's Song*, the author-illustrator turns his artistic talents to a setting in the Niagara Falls countryside of the early 1900s. Although the theme is familiar—learning to let go of something you love—Wallace's masterful interpretation yields a picture-book that is visually novel and exciting.

The story, based on an experience in the author's childhood, centres on a brother and sister who assume a parenting role towards a sparrow, only to learn that they must eventually release it. The text and illustrations are harmonious, tracing the children's emotional turmoil as they realize that they must allow the sparrow to fend for itself.

The meticulously detailed water-colour illustrations represent seasonal colours: purple, blue, green, and earth tones. The use of purple is at times reminiscent of Wallace's palette in *Very Last First Time.* The illustrations also exhibit a sense of rhythm, with some images evoking tranquility, as in the far reaches of the creek, and others conveying a lively sense of motion.

Structurally, the book resembles a musical composition with four distinct movements—bird is found and taken home; bird is returned to gorge and taught to fly; bird is released; bird returns home—while the continuity and cohesiveness is provided by the sparrow as it flies through the volume from beginning to end.

The Sparrow's Song stands as a distinguished contribution from a talented artist and sensitive writer.

Mary Ainslie Smith

SOURCE: A review of *The Sparrow's Song,* in *Books in Canada,* Vol. 15, No. 8, November, 1986, pp. 35, 37.

The Sparrow's Song, by Ian Wallace, is another book in which the illustrations have more to say than the accompanying text. The story is simple. A girl, Katie, finds a baby sparrow whose mother has been shot and killed by Katie's brother, Charles. Charles, remorseful, helps her care for it, and when it is big enough, they set it free.

The setting is Niagara Falls in the early 1900s, and it seems to be the magic, life-giving force of the falls, a tradition from native legends, that keeps the baby bird alive and heals the trouble between Katie and Charles. Wallace's watercolours are full of light and soft textures. The children are part of a romantic, idealized countryside of luxuriant, flowering plants, colourful insects and birds, and soft mists and clouds.

There are a few buildings in the landscape, all blending harmoniously with their surroundings, suggesting a perfect balance between man's needs and nature. No power turbines churn up the water in the Niagara Gorge. Only a ring buoy from the *Maid of the Mist,* hanging for some reason on the wall of the children's attic, and a few subtle guard rails at the edge of the cliffs suggest that there could be such a thing as a tourist.

Brenda Watson

SOURCE: A review of *The Sparrow's Song,* in *CM: A Reviewing Journal of Canadian Materials for Young People,* Vol. XV, No. 1, January, 1987, p. 35.

The Sparrow's Song is based on a story told to Wallace by his mother. Katie finds one dead sparrow, the victim of her brother's slingshot, and then another young sparrow close by. Katie takes the baby bird home and nurtures it, not allowing her brother, Charles, to come near. Eventually, Katie takes the bird to a mythical valley, dominated by Niagara Falls, to introduce it to nature. Brother and sister resolve their conflict and become children of the forest, with feathers in their hair and markings on their bodies. When it is time to let the bird go, Charles throws away his slingshot. Summer progresses and the children wonder about the sparrow. One day they hear it outside their window, catch up with it, and hold it briefly before it flies away again. A feeling of well being ends the story.

There are too many themes and conflicts in this story for any one of them to be fully developed and satisfactorily resolved. Theme one involves a wild animal taken in by a child and eventually having to be let go. Theme two concerns a boy growing up and throwing away his plaything when he realizes the harm it can do. Theme three is forgiveness between brother and sister. Wallace tries to create conflict, but it is resolved too easily and with little drama. The tension necessary for a climax does not exist, resulting in a flat story.

This is a true picture book in that text and pictures are both necessary for the story to be understood. The illustrations present more of the events of the summer, the characters of the children, and the importance of the setting than does the text. The pictures are detailed watercolour paintings with a predominance of green, blue, yellow, brown, and purple. These are not particularly warm or exciting colours and account for some of the flatness of the story. The drawings of the landscape and the bird are more pleasing than those of the children. Their faces are angular and surreal at times.

Readers will react differently to this story and its illustrations, but Wallace fans and collectors of Canadian children's literature will want to acquire this title.

Kirkus Reviews

SOURCE: A review of *The Sparrow's Song,* in *Kirkus Reviews,* Vol. LV, No. 8, May 1, 1987, p. 727.

A Canadian winner of the CLA Best Illustrated Book of the Year Award was inspired by an episode in his own childhood, as well as by Native American legends, in writing this tale of death redeemed by life.

Charles had scoffed, "It's only a sparrow," killed by his slingshot, and his sister Katie retorted, "And you're just a little boy." She rescues and nurtures a surviving nestling, only forgiving the penitent Charles when the bird lights on his head with its first fluttering hop. Adorning themselves with wild greenery, the two preside over the bird's further flights till their mother insists that he is ready to go free; but in the fall, the sparrow returns to trill a last good-bye.

This account of events not uncommon in the lives of country children is well told, in direct, unhackneyed prose. Raised in Niagara Falls, Wallace uses an unspoiled, turn-of-the-century view of that glorious landscape to suggest reverence for life in an idyllic world, employing an unusual pointillistic technique and delicately muted tones in watercolor. A quiet, lovely book, with a useful seasonal link.

Publishers Weekly

SOURCE: A review of *The Sparrow's Song*, in *Publishers Weekly*, Vol. 231, No. 21, May 29, 1987, p. 76.

Katie is fishing while Charles is hunting birds with his slingshot. He kills a song sparrow but its young one is protected by Katie. She takes the young sparrow home and nurses it until it's healthy and strong. Throughout the summer a remorseful Charles participates in the caring and eventually throws away his slingshot as Katie frees the young bird. The Canadian illustrator, who created last year's notable *The Very Last First Time*, has written an understated story of responsive children growing up in the magical setting of Niagara Falls. Wallace's figures are bathed in light pointillistic landscapes that reveal the grandeur of nature.

Carole Gerson

SOURCE: "The Sparrow and the Sea," in *Canadian Children's Literature*, Nos. 57-8, 1990, pp. 135-36.

Those who choose their books by their covers will be quickly drawn to these two superbly illustrated stories. The audience for [Richard Thompson's] *Gurgle, bubble, splash,* according to my seven-year-old consultant, is the three-to-six year old set, while *The sparrow's song* appeals to five-to-eight year olds. Very different in conception, the two books nonetheless share the distinction of containing illustrations that are more captivating than the text. . . .

In *The sparrow's song,* text and illustrations interact magically. While this book contains no more words than *Gurgle, bubble, splash,* it invites more sophisticated reading as the pictures develop dimensions of the story not stated explicitly in the text. The plotline is simple: Katie rescues a young sparrow orphaned by the slingshot of her repentant brother, and together the two children raise the bird to maturity and release it in the fall. The early twentieth-century Niagara Falls setting is barely mentioned in the words but forms the essence of the pictures, one of which shows an attic room full of local references: a photo of a honeymoon couple, a painting of the legendary Maid of the Mist, a life-belt from the tourist boat of that name, and a Union Jack hanging from a rafter. Even more engaging are the illustrations of the children's games: as they raise their sparrow near Niagara's "mythic gorge" they identify totally with their bird, painting their faces and tying branches to their arms to mimic wings as they teach it to fly, or attaching feathers to their heads to costume themselves like the insects they catch to feed it. Decoding these pictures with my daughter proved the most involving phase of preparing this review, and I predict that the book will be even more attractive to a child who has visited Niagara Falls and experienced their spell.

MORGAN THE MAGNIFICENT (1987)

Bernie Goedhart

SOURCE: "Morgan, May, Melinda: New Heroines Offer Humour and Fantasy," in *Books for Young People*, Vol. 1, No. 5, October, 1987, p. 24.

Children will . . . identify with Morgan in Ian Wallace's ***Morgan the Magnificent.*** At least, they will understand Morgan's wish to do something brave and daring, and they will commiserate with her when her father stands in her way. But they may have a little trouble believing that she would boldly walk into the middle of a circus performance, scramble up a ladder, and walk out on a high wire. Granted, this is not nearly as ludicrous a plot twist as introducing a roller-skate puppy, but humour is the coating that makes even the most preposterous incidents easy to swallow. *Morgan the Magnificent* doesn't offer humour; it celebrates the glory days of the travelling circus, offers a nostalgic story of a child's learning experience, and seems to take itself quite seriously.

Wallace, the award-winning author-illustrator of ***Chin Chiang and the Dragon's Dance,*** has long been known for his talented use of colour, and this book offers some of his finest work in that regard. The farmyard scenes brim with warmth and light, and the circus scenes convey a golden glow and glittering wonder. But there are occasional jarring elements: an awkward pose of the hand; a head that seems out of proportion; a pair of acrobats who appear to be frozen in mid-air. One illustration offers an aerial perspective of hats being flung into the air close to the high wire: their owners, shown as mere specks below, would have had to hurl those *chapeaux* an unbelievable distance.

Such criticism aside, Wallace has given *Morgan the Magnificent* some rich and detailed trimmings. The title-page shows an intricate, gilded image of angels and trumpets surrounding an oval that frames Morgan walking a picket fence. The image shows up again in the final illustration as decoration on the side of a circus wagon. One of the angels appears throughout the book, illuminating the printed text with an expression that reflects the action in each double-page spread. For example, a worried angel covers her eyes alongside my favourite picture—one that shows Morgan balancing on the top beam under the barn roof. Perspective here is wonderful: an owl in the lower left corner catches one's eye as the line of vision soars to Morgan and the barn roof. It's a fitting conclusion to a determined girl's striving—and to an ambitious book.

Kirkus Reviews

SOURCE: A review of *Morgan the Magnificent*, in *Kirkus Reviews*, Vol. LVI, No. 3, February 1, 1988, p. 208.

When she's told to stop walking the barn's ridgepole, Morgan practices on the loft's highest beams (while a guardian angel—in grisaille, and not mentioned in the text—covers her eyes); when the circus comes to town, Morgan sneaks onto the high wire but wobbles, panics, and has to be rescued by the performer, Anastasia. The crowds cheer, her father blows her a kiss, and Anastasia gives her a pair of performing shoes. There is a suggestion that the circus, which first appears like a golden vision at sunset, is a fantasy; the guardian angel takes on more color during this part of the story, but otherwise there's no pictorial change. Though Wallace's watercolors are detailed and attractive and his heroine sturdily competent, the ambiguity here is more confusing than tantalizing; and the worried angel is not quite enough warning that Morgan's feat is downright dangerous.

Carol McMichael

SOURCE: A review of *Morgan the Magnificent,* in *School Library Journal,* Vol. 34, No. 8, April, 1988, p. 92.

Morgan, a young girl living on a farm with her father,

dreams of the circus, especially the high wire act. Avoiding her chores, she sneaks out at every opportunity to walk across the peak of the barn roof or the highest beam inside the barn. Her lively antics lead her to the circus that has come to town with Amazing Anastasia, the high wire performer. Her adventure culminates on the high wire, which is shakier and thinner than the beams were. Luckily, Morgan is rescued by the Amazing Anastasia to the delight of her father, observing from below. Throughout the story, the full-page watercolor paintings done in rich hues are enriched with details of almost idyllic scenes, giving a sense of warmth and security even in dangerous situations. Animals such as the foxes cocking their heads as they watch Morgan turn cart-wheels also give this sense of peace. As with his other books, Wallace has delivered a sensitive story that will capture the imaginations of children as they see one little girl's dream come true.

Anne Denoon

SOURCE: A review of *Morgan the Magnificent,* in *Books in Canada,* Vol. 17, No. 5, June-July, 1988, p. 37.

Morgan the Magnificent is a recent book by the writer

From The Name of the Tree, *written by Celia Barker Lottridge. Illustrated by Ian Wallace.*

and illustrator Ian Wallace. Like his successful *Chin Chiang and the Dragon's Dance,* it tells of a challenge that must be met in the form of a public performance. In this case, however, the challenge comes from within the young heroine herself, rather than being imposed by cultural or familial expectations. In fact, Morgan's determination to be a high-wire artist is discouraged by her father until the circus sets up near their farm and his daughter's almost somnambulistic fulfilment of her dreams wins him, and us, over. Wallace's complex and allusive illustrations place her performance in a magical space somewhere between daydream and reality and surround them with the nostalgic rococo of the quintessential Big Top. His use of pointillist passages, subdued colours, and striking aerial perspectives recalls the circus paintings of [French painters Edgar] Degas and [Georges] Seurat. At the same time, the author's cinematic approach enhances the drama of Morgan's feat: he zooms in for a close-up as she almost falters, then pulls back to show the full dimensions of her triumph. Meanwhile, in the corner of each page, tiny grisaille caryatids provide a mimed commentary on the action. The book ends with Morgan's satisfied return to what had seemed a humdrum life, treasuring a tribute from her idol and mentor, the Amazing Anastasia.

M. Crouch

SOURCE: A review of *Morgan the Magnificent,* in *The Junior Bookshelf,* Vol. 52, No. 5, October, 1988, pp. 231-32.

Ian Wallace is Canadian. Morgan, in his story, is a tomboyish little girl on a farm. In spite of Father's protests she performs dangerous balancing acts on the farm, on the barn ridge and along rafters. When the circus comes Morgan is away to see how the professionals do it, especially Anastasia the high-wire walker. When the show begins Morgan is carried away by the atmosphere. She has already, most improperly, stolen Anastasia's costume, and now she climbs to the high wire. Half-way across she gets into difficulties, and Anastasia has to rescue her. Morgan escapes punishment. Ian Wallace points the contrasts between the natural colours of the farm and the artifice of the circus. Some of his drawings are highly skilful, but I did not warm to the story or its single-minded heroine.

Catherine Sheldrick Ross

SOURCE: "Boiled Bats and Beans," in *Canadian Literature,* Nos. 122-23, Autumn-Winter, 1989, pp. 246-47.

[Sue Ann Alderson's] *Ida and the Wool Smugglers* and *Morgan the Magnificent* each, in their different ways, look like prize-winners. Both books develop the theme of growing up. Ida and Morgan take on dangerous challenges and succeed, Ida through obedience and calm responsibility, Morgan through defiance and a crazy hubris. . . . *Morgan the Magnificent* also starts out with a farm setting of an earlier time, all realistically depicted in stunning two-page spreads. However, the setting shifts to the

world of romance when Morgan finds a poster announcing the coming of Amazing Anastasia and the Condos Brothers' Circus. The text is spare and dramatic; the pictures do not so much illustrate the text as extend and enrich it.

THE NAME OF THE TREE: A BANTU FOLKTALE (written by Celia Barker Lottridge, 1989)

Michele Landsberg

SOURCE: A review of *The Name of the Tree,* in *Quill and Quire,* Vol. 55, No. 10, October, 1989, p. 13.

By far the most beautiful, rounded, and lovely work of the early crop [of the fall publishing season] is *The Name of the Tree,* a Bantu tale retold by Celia Barker Lottridge and illustrated by Ian Wallace. . . .

[Wallace's] full-page illustrations are magnificent. The beautifully naturalistic and expressive animals move across a pale shimmer of heat-stricken land; sudden shifts of perspective startle the eye into quickened perception of the story's drama and emotion.

It must have been tempting to lavish brilliant colours on this African folk tale. Instead, Wallace has opted for a more restrained and evocative palette and a keen eye for details of the landscape. Less is more: a single stark shadow at an unexpected angle, a close-up of a parched and cracking stretch of earth over which the tortoise bravely plods. We feel the heat, and sense the animals' exhaustion in their languid droop.

In a publishing season in which so many stories seem sloppily chosen and underimagined, Lottridge and Wallace deserve laurels for their care, finesse, and evident joy in language.

Linda Granfield

SOURCE: A review of *The Name of the Tree,* in *Books in Canada,* Vol. 18, No. 9, December, 1989, p. 19.

The Name of the Tree, by Celia Barker Lottridge, is a retelling of a Bantu tale. During a drought the animals must learn the name of a fruitladen tree in order to taste its abundant produce and thus live. This is a story of the wisdom of youth and old age, of perseverance and humility rewarded. . . .

Slow speech mimics the weight of the oppressive heat: Ian Wallace's splendid illustrations symbolically and literally interpret the same measures.

The Name of the Tree is Wallace's best work to date. Symbol has always figured in his illustrations: here the fruit tree is painted as a rich, red, pulsating vein, truly a Tree of Life. Sere desert earth lives as scaly skin, or bone. A gazelle's horns mirror the writhing curls of jungle branches and steamy heat hazes everything until the final storm. Wallace has skilfully matched Lottridge's text: together they've created a perfect picture-book.

Denia Lewis Hester

SOURCE: A review of *The Name of the Tree,* in *School Library Journal,* Vol. 36, No. 3, March, 1990, p. 209.

Instead of the lush, primary colors typical of many illustrations in African tales, Wallace masterfully utilizes muted pinks, grays, and greens that bring to life the cracked, dry land that threatens the animals' very existence. Some of the illustrations are so subdued that they seem to fade off the page, as if bleached by the scorching African sun. The effect is a perfect bone-dry backdrop for this tale.

Barbara Knutson

SOURCE: A review of *The Name of the Tree,* in *The Five Owls,* Vol. IV, No. 5, May-June, 1990, p. 85.

Ian Wallace sets the tone in sun-drenched colored pencil illustrations. Their soft colors and shapes seem to be seen through a haze of dry heat. Shadows stretch and twist across the page, emphasizing the size of the great tree or the arid vastness of the African plains. Unusual viewpoints range from bird's-eye views to the scene at tortoise-level. Though based on realism, the treatment is not heavy-handed. The animals reveal their personalities in playful moments hidden in the pictures, where chimps scratch and rabbits dance. That's from the close-up view where amusing details draw us in. But sit back (to story-hour listener distance) and the hazy shapes and shadows take on a firmness belied by the delicate colors without outline. . . .

The Name of the Tree makes a fine adaptation of this traditional African favorite for North American ears and eyes.

📖 *MR. KNEEBONE'S NEW DIGS* (1991)

Annette Goldsmith

SOURCE: A review of *Mr. Kneebone's New Digs,* in *Quill and Quire,* Vol. 57, No. 11, November, 1991, p. 26.

Feisty grey-haired April Moth and her canine companion, Mr. Kneebone, are fed up with their rat-infested apartment building, so they pack up their belongings in a shopping buggy and set out to find new "digs." Their search follows the traditional three stages of a folktale: the first place has too many cats, the second too-loud music, and the third is just right . . . well, at least there are no rats or loud neighbours. They end up staying in a cave in the park. The final spread shows a happy ending for Mr. Kneebone, who is contentedly sleeping. But April Moth looks small and perhaps worried as night falls and the mysterious trees crowd in behind her.

A picture book about the homeless? The subject is certainly timely, but has been done better, as in Eve Bunting's realistic picture book, *Fly Away Home.* In *Mr. Kneebone's New Digs* there is an uneasy tension between form and content: an urban character like Sweet Daddy Three Times, who says everything three times, seems forced into the folktale mould. It's as if Wallace were combining two styles of story best left separate.

The illustrations are quite lovely, though not up to Wallace's award-winning work in *The Name of the Tree.* The soft colours serve to attenuate the squalour of some scenes. There are clever details to help develop character: April Moth's hat has antennae, and the irritable landlady wears monster slippers. The draughtsmanship is uneven, though—Mr. Kneebone resembles a sheep on the cover illustration, and elsewhere looks positively catlike.

It may be difficult for this book to find the right audience. An optimistic story with a bleak ending, it seems inappropriate for young children, and in the wrong format for older readers. For long-time admirers of Wallace's work, this book is a disappointment.

Theo Hersh

SOURCE: A review of *Mr. Kneebone's New Digs,* in *CM: A Reviewing Journal of Canadian Materials for Young People,* Vol. XX, No. 2, March, 1992, p. 85.

A giant landlady, terrifying cats, rats, flies, and ominous rental signs make it impossible for April Moth and her canine companion Mr. Kneebone to find a place to live. . . .

Ian Wallace has created a magical book about an all-too-real situation for many people. The urban setting offers the marvels of big city life and also the misery. In the distance, huge, grey office towers dwarf the small, colourful shops of April Moth's run-down neighbourhood. While the city is unfriendly, it is not totally hostile or ungiving. Small pleasures—a sweet orange, a prophetic street musician—soften the blows as April Moth unsuccessfully looks for a new home.

The water-colour and ink illustrations are among Wallace's best work. Light and shadow play mysteriously with each other and the reader's imagination. The illustrations spill over the page in a way that suggests there is more than what one sees. It is a complex, unsettling book, full of subtle jokes and riddles, a little sad, and yet, in the character of April Moth, upbeat and optimistic. An unusual book, *Mr. Kneebone's New Digs* is wonderful.

Additional coverage of Wallace's life and career is contained in the following sources published by Gale Research: *Contemporary Authors New Revision Series,* Vol. 38; *Major Authors and Illustrators for Children and Young Adults*; and *Something about the Author,* Vols. 53, 56.

CUMULATIVE INDEXES

How to Use This Index

The main reference

Baum, L(yman) Frank
1856-1919 .... **15**

lists all author entries in this and previous volumes of *Children's Literature Review*.

The cross-references

See also CA 103; 108; DLB 22; JRDA;
MAICYA; MTCW; SATA 18; TCLC 7

list all author entries in the following Gale biographical and literary sources:

AAYA = Authors & Artists for Young Adults
AITN = Authors in the News
BLC = Black Literature Criticism
BW = Black Writers
CA = Contemporary Authors
CAAS = Contemporary Authors Autobiography Series
CABS = Contemporary Authors Bibliographical Series
CANR = Contemporary Authors New Revision Series
CAP = Contemporary Authors Permanent Series
CDALB = Concise Dictionary of American Literary Biography
CLC = Contemporary Literary Criticism
CLR = Children's Literature Review
CMLC = Classical and Medieval Literature Criticism
DA = DISCovering Authors
DC = Drama Criticism
DLB = Dictionary of Literary Biography
DLBD = Dictionary of Literary Biography Documentary Series
DLBY = Dictionary of Literary Biography Yearbook
HW = Hispanic Writers
JRDA = Junior DISCovering Authors
LC = Literature Criticism from 1400 to 1800
MAICYA = Major Authors and Illustrators for Children and Young Adults
MTCW = Major 20th-Century Writers
NCLC = Nineteenth-Century Literature Criticism
PC = Poetry Criticism
SAAS = Something about the Author Autobiography Series
SATA = Something about the Author
SSC = Short Story Criticism
TCLC = Twentieth-Century Literary Criticism
WLC = World Literature Criticism, 1500 to the Present
YABC = Yesterday's Authors of Books for Children

CUMULATIVE INDEX TO AUTHORS

CUMULATIVE INDEX TO NATIONALITIES

Nationality Index

CUMULATIVE INDEX TO TITLES

Title Index

Title Index

Title Index

Title Index

ISBN 0-8103-8951-7